Everyone's
MONEY
BOOK

P9-APV-392

Everyone's
MONEY
BOOK

Jane Bryant Quinn

A DELTA BOOK

Published by
Dell Publishing Co., Inc.
1 Dag Hammarskjold Plaza
New York, New York 10017

Portions of this book first appeared in *Woman's Day*.

Acknowledgments

From "The Ingenuities of Debt" by Robert Frost: From THE POETRY OF ROBERT FROST edited by Edward Connery Lathem. Copyright 1947, © 1969 by Holt, Rinehart & Winston. Copyright © 1975 by Leslie Frost Ballentine. Reprinted by permission of Holt, Rinehart & Winston, Publishers.

From A POCKET FULL OF WRY by Phyllis McGinley: Copyright © 1959 by Phyllis McGinley. All rights reserved. By permission of Hawthorn Books, Inc.

From "Thing That Makes the Wolf Go" by Ogden Nash: Reprinted by permission of Curtis Brown, Ltd. Copyright 1934 by Ogden Nash.

From THE FACE IS FAMILIAR by Ogden Nash: Copyright 1935 by Ogden Nash. By permission of Little, Brown & Co.

From LIFE ON THE MISSISSIPPI by Mark Twain: By permission of Harper & Row, Publishers, Inc.

Copyright © 1978, 1979 by Jane Bryant Quinn

All rights reserved. No part of this book may be reproduced or transmitted in any form or by any means, electronic or mechanical, including photocopying, recording or by any information storage and retrieval system, without the written permission of the Publisher, except where permitted by law.
For information address Delacorte Press, New York, New York.

Delta ® TM 755118, Dell Publishing Co., Inc.

ISBN: 0-440-55725-9

Reprinted by arrangement with Delacorte Press

Printed in the United States of America

First Delta printing—August 1980

For
David, Matthew,
Justin, and Dolly

CONTENTS

CONTENTS

Contents

ACKNOWLEDGMENTS

The manuscript of this book was read for factual accuracy by many people in government agencies, trade associations, consumer groups, and private businesses. In particular I would like to thank the Washington offices of Social Security; the Internal Revenue Service; the Veterans Administration; the Federal Housing Administration; the Office of Education; Medicare; the Office of Interstate Land Sales Registration; and the Savings Bond division of the Treasury. Thanks also to the Insurance Information Institute; the American Council of Life Insurance; the American Bankers Association; the Investment Company Institute; the College Scholarship Service; the many helpful lawyers at the National Consumer Law Center in Boston; and the indefatigable table-makers at the Bowery Savings Bank in New York City.

Thanks, too, to Henry H. Foster Jr., professor of law emeritus, New York University; Robert E. Gibson, National Foundation for Consumer Credit; Joseph M. Lobell of the international accounting firm Coopers & Lybrand; Irving Price, Hudson Michael Realty, Hudson, N.Y.; John Kelly and Robert Peck Jr. of Merrill Lynch, Pierce, Fenner & Smith; Edward A. Fogel of the New York law firm Pryor, Cashman, Sherman & Flynn; Timothy Byrne of T.A. Byrne Chevrolet, Mt. Kisco, N.Y.; Richard R. Almy, International Association of Assessing Officers; Wesley G. McCain of Towneley Capital Management in New York City; Lloyd

S. Kaye, of the pension consulting firm William M. Mercer; Jan Thuerbach, Atlas Van Lines; Elizabeth C. Clemmer, Continental Association of Funeral and Memorial Societies; Kenneth B. Platnick of *The Option Trader;* Bruce R. Bent of The Reserve Fund; Kenneth Harney of the *BNA Housing and Development Reporter;* Billie Ann Lopez; and David C. Quinn, my husband and an attorney in Katonah, N.Y.

These people kindly checked the facts. But they're not to blame for the opinions, which are entirely my own.

PREFACE TO THE PAPERBACK EDITION

Toward the end of 1979 and on through early 1980, the U.S. suffered a surge of inflation such as it had never before known. The paperback edition of this book was then in preparation. We held the presses, in order to take note here of the new laws, savings devices, and interest rates that sprang into being, as the financial community struggled to offer savers and investors some sort of attractive inflation hedge.

Some people believe that the country is now on the verge of a great crash. My view is that we're more likely to experience just one more of our regular recessions, followed by renewed—but inflationary—growth. If a crash should occur, the best investment would be long-term government bonds; the government won't go broke, and will go on paying 1980's high interest rates while everywhere else, interest rates and prices are declining. On the other hand, if we should continue in a high-inflation economy, the best investments are likely to be well-timed purchases of stocks, mutual funds, and gold, and carefully chosen real estate (you can't assume that *everything* will go up). For cash, you'd want short-term bank certificates or money-market mutual funds. You'll find in this book the rules you need for making good investments at the right time.

The losers, in a high-inflation economy, are long-term fixed-dollar investments—bonds, annuities, long-term savings certificates, and life insurance cash values.

But investments are only one part of life, and for most of us a small one. We'll still be buying cars, paying taxes, borrowing money, buying life insurance, choosing houses and apartments, getting divorced, getting our children through college, and planning for retirement, in good times and bad. That's the meat and potatoes of life, and that's what most of this book is about.

FOREWORD

Pay no attention to your critics.
Don't even ignore them.
—ATTRIBUTED TO SAM GOLDWYN

Money decisions are highly individual, guided by what you know, what you want, what you value, and how you think about yourself. To some, money is the ultimate taboo—the only remaining thing that nice girls (and nice boys) don't do. To others, it's an earthwork thrown up against the risks of life. To yet others, it's a gambling chip for the big play.

But whether you're comfortable or uncomfortable with money decisions, cautious or free-spending, you need good information—about the implications of what you're doing (or not doing) and about what your real choices are.

Unfortunately most financial information comes from people with something to sell. When in need we consult stockbrokers, insurance agents, bankers, tax shelter salesmen—each sold on the virtues of his financial product and ready to prove that it's better than anything else. It's hard to get an overall picture of the many and various paths to the same end.

In recent years a number of adult education centers and community colleges have begun offering courses in personal finance—some directed at retirees, some at widows, some at investors, some at young people getting their first taste of budget management. Courses like these can be enormously valuable; if one is available in your community, by all means consider it. But even so, the speakers may be salesmen for one financial product or another. Always take a person's natural bias into consideration when you reflect on his advice.

My book also has a natural bias. I believe strongly that given good information, people are smart enough and sensitive enough to their real interests to make their own decisions—and make them well. Many a salesman wants you to think you're a babe in the woods, dependent on his superior knowledge to steer you right. A babe you may be, if you're just starting out in personal finance, but his "superior knowledge" isn't your best source of aid. Believe that it is, and you'll buy what he wants to sell, not what might be more useful for you to have. If any salesman, no matter how gently, implies that you're wrongheaded or aren't in a position to judge what's best for you, stop everything right there and find someone else to do business with. This is a tough area to deal with, because salesmen generally do know more about the product than you do and are experienced in implying that it will solve all your problems. But there may be better and cheaper ways to achieve the same thing —which is what this book is all about.

The chapters that follow were planned with three goals in mind: to explain the vocabulary of personal finance, to clarify the fundamental concepts, and to show you what the many possibilities are for using your income to make yourself financially comfortable. With this knowledge behind you, you can work *with* the salesmen to get what most serves your needs, rather than simply accepting what they say is best for you.

Some men and women go limp when faced with money decisions; they lapse into a kind of mental passive acceptance. That's great for the salesmen who luck into them but not so great for the people themselves or the families who depend on them. If this book does nothing else, I hope it persuades you that the theory and practice of personal finance are truly not difficult. The high priests of money may speak mumbo jumbo in the temple, and the details of some strategies are indeed obscure. But how things work, and why, can be stated in simple English, understandable to anyone with the slightest degree of interest. You don't even have to know arithmetic (I'm *terrible* at arithmetic).

Knowing something is, of course, only the first step. It's easy to read about money and even understand money, but a lot harder to pick up the telephone and attend to things that need doing. It's easy to set financial goals, but harder to search among the many competing financial instruments to find the ones that actually meet those goals. You must, in other words, be willing to *act*, to take the risk of making changes. Leaving things as they are is also a decision, but an intelligent "non act" comes only after you consider the alternatives and conclude that what you're doing now is right.

If this book does what I want it to, it will help you think *less* about money rather than more. To draw up a good financial plan and set it running clears the mind wonderfully.

There are things you know about money that aren't in this book—perhaps because they're true in your state but not in others, or perhaps because I don't know them. There are things that neither of us know but that you may run across in sorting out your own financial affairs. There are things that have changed since this book went to press. But the underlying principles explained here should pretty much apply to all situations. Using this book as a framework, you should be able to fit new knowledge into the general plan.

A final word: I have not solved the grammatical and stylistic problem that plagues writers today—the lack of a gender-neutral third-person pronoun. It's cumbersome to write "he and she" every time, and foolish to turn sentences on their heads in order to avoid the issue. Therefore I've stuck with the traditional "he" to mean both sexes. Politically I'm a feminist, but professionally I cherish the rhythm of prose. Personally, I wish I could have it both ways.

Jane Bryant Quinn
1979

Chapter One

BEATING THE RECORDS

Filing Cabinet: A place to lose things alphabetically.
ANON.

Many parts of your life you can hold in memory, but not your financial life. Affairs of the purse are always linked with important pieces of paper: records of transactions, promises to pay, proofs of payment. Most of these records are rarely needed and have a way of passing out of mind. But when their time comes, you have to be able to put your hands on them.

Most of us know where our important papers are and can come up with them if pressed. But what if you were struck down by a falling ceiling after reading this paragraph? Would your wife or husband, the executors of your will, or your children be able to find all the records they'd need to settle your affairs? Lawyers who handle estates tell story after story about stumbling across a puzzling piece of paper in a bureau drawer that entitled a widow to some payment she hadn't the faintest idea was due. Many such benefits go unclaimed simply because the clues to their existence are never noticed.

Organizing your records is the first stop toward making sense of your personal finances. Not only does it make things easier for your survivors, it also forces you to notice all the holes in your financial planning, through which an awful lot of money can leak away.

Where to Keep Records

Current records go in a filing cabinet, accordion file, or even a cardboard box. Stationery stores often have inexpensive cardboard filing cabinets; or watch the classifieds in your newspaper to see if you can find a used steel file cabinet. The point is to have a single, convenient place for current records, so they don't get scattered. If that place is hard to reach, or too small to accommodate regular additions, your system is going to fall apart.

Not everything has to be instantly available. Such things as old auto insurance policies, old bank statements, and back tax returns are so rarely needed that there's no sense cluttering up your files with them. Set aside a "dead file" on a closet shelf for this kind of material.

For important records that are difficult or impossible to replace, you need a fireproof strongbox or a bank safe deposit box. In either case, make sure your spouse and executor know where you keep the key.

A Safe Deposit Box

This is a comforting place to keep not only important records but also small valuables (such as jewelry when you're away on vacation). A box doesn't cost very much, and can be had in a size large enough to keep gold bars or even paintings, if that's your pleasure. If you use it for income-producing property, such as bonds or stock certificates, the rental fee is deductible on your income tax.

Boxes are rented annually from banks or savings and loan associations, in your own name or in joint names. When a box is held jointly, each owner is allowed access to the contents. But if one of you dies, the box might be sealed, which could temporarily inconvenience the other; ask a lawyer or banker whether this rule applies in your state. If husband and wife each own property, it's often better to have separate boxes. In case of marital problems, there's then no risk that one can raid the other's property. Note: If you own a box solely in your name, provide for a deputy who can open it if you can't.

Generally, you're given two keys. If one is lost, it can be replaced for a nominal sum. But if you lose both, the replacement charge is considerably higher. Since the bank doesn't keep a copy of your key, it has to break into the box, change the lock, and start you again with two keys.

Unfortunately, nothing in this world is 100 percent secure—not even a vault of safe deposit boxes. Thieves have been known to break in, in which case the bank is not responsible for your losses. Neither is the

Federal Deposit Insurance Corporation, which covers only bank deposits. If you want to be supersafe, put a rider on your homeowner's or renter's insurance policy, covering items of special value.

What to Keep

The following list covers most of the records a family or individual is likely to have. To keep things in order, one person should do all the filing, but take care that the system doesn't get so idiosyncratic that no one else can use it. Everything should be clearly labeled; if a piece of paper doesn't obviously fit into one of the established categories, start a new one.

Your Will

You have one, of course. If not, skip from this paragraph directly to Chapter 27, "Wills and Estate Planning," to see what terrible things will happen to your possessions if you die without one. Then call a lawyer, make a date to have your will drawn, and continue reading!

Many people leave their wills with their lawyers, keeping a copy for their files and perhaps sending another copy to their executor. If you'd rather keep it yourself, store it somewhere safe and accessible. A strongbox is a good place; use a safe deposit box only if you're sure there'll be no trouble getting it out. Some states seal safe deposit boxes when the owner (or one of two joint owners) dies. In that case, you might need a court order to get at the will. Other states seal the box but let the will out; still others permit full access to the box's contents. Ask a bank officer what the law is in your state. Whenever you make a new will, destroy the old one along with all copies.

Personal Papers

Anything you need to prove who you are, how long you've been around, and what you've done should be in a strongbox or safe deposit box. This includes such things as your birth certificate, marriage license, divorce papers, separation agreement, naturalization papers, adoption papers, diplomas, licenses, passport, Social Security card, and armed service records. Before stashing military records away, check with the appropriate branch of the service to make sure its records agree with yours; you don't want a bureaucratic error to cut into any GI benefits you or your family have coming. If your passport has expired, keep it anyway; it facilitates your getting a new one.

Life Insurance

Keep the policy in your current file or strongbox, along with any change-of-beneficiary notices, correspondence with the company, and, if you've transferred ownership of the policy to someone else, proof of that transaction. Or keep it in a safe deposit box. In states where boxes are sealed at death there may be a delay in retrieving the policy, but this is generally not a big inconvenience.

Health, Accident, and Disability Insurance

Keep the policies, plus the information booklet that tells what you're insured for, in your current file or strongbox.

Family Health Records

You'll want any information that might be needed in the future, such as the date and type of shots given, date of operations, and so on.

Homeowner's Insurance

You generally get a new homeowner's policy every year. Hold on to the old policies, as well as the current one. If someone injured in your house a year or two ago should suddenly file a liability claim—and the insurance company questions whether or not you were covered at the time —you'd have your old policy to prove it. Lacking it, your canceled checks for insurance should be proof enough. But the language of insurance policies changes over the years, and it might be important to know precisely what you were insured for at the time of the injury. Keep old policies on a shelf, until your state's statute of limitations runs out. Current policies belong in your file drawer or fireproof strongbox. (The name and number of this and other insurance policies should also be in your bank safe deposit box.) If you've insured any art, jewelry, furs, and so forth, file sales slips showing what you paid for them and any professional appraisals you have of their current value.

Auto Insurance

Although you get a new policy every year or less, keep several years' worth of past policies. As with homeowner's insurance, you want to be able to prove you were covered in case you get into an argument over an old claim. Keep current policies in your file drawer or strongbox and keep old ones on a shelf.

Receipts

There's no point in keeping all the receipts for purchases you make. But some are definitely worth preserving. For example, receipts for major purchases should be attached to your household inventory (see page 9), in case you ever have to prove to a cold-eyed insurance claims adjuster that although you live in modest circumstances, your clothes and furniture were worth a fortune. These same receipts can also help you substantiate an extra-large sales tax deduction on your income taxes. If a particular item is tax-deductible, you'll need a receipt to prove the price. There are other uses: Some stores won't take anything back without a receipt. Some stores get so messed up with their deliveries and billing that you need receipts in self-defense. To be on the safe side, you might toss all current store receipts in a box and sort it out when it overflows.

Medical and Drug Bills

Keep these receipts in a separate file, and keep all of them. You must top a certain percentage of your income before medical bills are deductible on your tax return, so you want to be sure you count everything. Canceled checks are normally enough for you to do your taxes with. But if your return is audited, the revenue agent can demand the bills themselves (to see if you cheated by deducting the veterinarian's bill, or nondrug items bought at a drugstore). If, at the end of the year, you find that you can't take a medical tax deduction, throw everything out. If you do take the deduction, keep the bills with your back tax records.

Monthly Credit Card and Charge Account Statements

Keep these in your current file. They tell you how much you owe, whether your payments have been credited properly, and how much interest you paid last year. This last point is important because the interest is all tax-deductible. Lacking the actual statements, you can estimate interest payments—but be prepared to prove the estimate in case you're audited. Stores will generally send you copies of your past bills, but it may take months to get them. At the end of each year, file these statements away with your back tax records.

Warranties

Warranty cards often have a portion for you to keep and a portion to send to the factory; the latter part asks you a lot of questions, such as where you bought the item and for whom. Those questions are pure market research and have nothing to with warranty protection, so you don't have to fill them in. Some manufacturers make their warranties contingent on your mailing in the card (but even if you forget, they'll generally honor their commitment). Manufacturers want the cards for two reasons: to be able to notify you if the product has a safety problem and has to be recalled, and to be able to solicit you for other purchases (for example, a service contract on an appliance you just bought). Always file your portion of the warranty card, noting on it the date and place of purchase. If the item breaks down, you'll be able to check quickly whether it can still be repaired free and what the manufacturer's precise liability is.

Appliance Manuals

Keep instructions on how to operate appliances and other products, and where they can be repaired.

Debts

Your mortgage agreement, personal-loan statements, and installment purchase agreements should be in your current file. When you've paid a debt off, keep the statement proving it so a creditor can't come back and tell your survivors something more is owed. This is particularly important when you borrow money from an individual. He may put a note about the debt in his safe deposit box, then forget to retrieve it. When he dies, his heirs would ask you for payment, and you'd want to be able to prove immediately that the debt had been satisfied.

Creditors

If anyone owes you money, by all means keep the note in a strongbox or safe deposit box. If it's lost or destroyed, you may not be able to get the debtor to sign another. Also make a memorandum of any money lent without a formal note. Your survivors may or may not be able to collect it, but at least they'll know enough to try. When a debt is repaid, cancel the note immediately so that your heirs won't try to collect on it again.

Closing Statements and Home Improvement Expenses

You need records of all the houses you ever bought and sold, along with proofs of the money you spent improving them. Eventually, you will probably have to pay a capital gains tax on the money you made on your houses over the years (see page 334). But every nickel you ever spent on home improvements will reduce the tax, so make sure you save all the bills. Keep a file for current bills and store all your back records in the strongbox.

Deeds, Titles, Surveys

Full purchase records, proofs of ownership, and specific descriptions of any property you own—including title to your car—should be in your strongbox or safe deposit box. Keep them as long as you own the property, then keep the record of sale.

Rental Properties

Your files should contain complete records of all current income and expenses. Keep the records of previous years on the shelf with your back tax records.

Stocks, Bonds, and Other Securities

It is especially important to keep these in a safe deposit box or fireproof strongbox, since they're not easy to replace. Or you might keep them at a brokerage house registered in the firm's name—convenient if you do a lot of trading and don't want to bother mailing stock certificates back and forth. But this arrangement has some drawbacks. There's sometimes a delay in getting dividend checks (although a good broker should get them out to you the day they're paid). And if the broker's records get messed up, so could your dividend payments. More problems arise if your broker goes broke. Your securities are government-insured for up to $100,000. But there will be a delay in getting them back, and meanwhile the market could be tumbling. No insurance covers any decline in market value while you're waiting for delivery of your securities. Also, the broker's records may be in a shambles, with the result that you're given less stock than you're entitled to. You'd need good records of your own to prove you were shortchanged.

The average investor is far, far better off taking possession of his own securities and keeping them in a safe place. Also, keep complete records of when the securities were bought and sold, at what prices, and what commissions were paid. This has become of utmost importance since the recent passage of new gift and estate tax laws. Starting in 1980, if you leave property to your heirs that has gained in value, they will owe a capital gains tax based on the price *you* paid. If you don't have good records, your heirs may wind up paying a higher tax than they ought.

Current Bank Records

Keep all bank statements, canceled checks, passbooks, and correspondence in your current file.

Back Tax Records and Bank Records

All old check stubs, bank statements, passbooks, confirmation of income received, and all receipts necessary to substantiate your tax deductions should gather dust in a "dead file" on a closet shelf. Normally, the Internal Revenue Service can't audit your returns once three years have passed. But there are many situations in which old records can come in handy. For example, if you want to save taxes by income averaging, you have to go back five years. When you sell a house, you might need old canceled checks for home improvements in order to cut your capital gains tax. After you die, questions may arise in a dispute over estate taxes as to whose funds paid for a certain piece of property. If you keep old records, you might save your estate thousands of dollars.

If you've cheated on your taxes, you'll need old records, too. The government has six years to assess extra tax if they discover that your actual income was more than 25 percent above the income you reported. In cases of fraud or where no returns were filed, there is no statute of limitations; you can be hit for back taxes anytime.

Money Order Receipts

These are the equivalent of canceled checks, and in some cases may be your only proof that payment was made. So keep them in your current file and treat them like bank records.

Employee Benefits

The current file should contain any booklets put out by your company or union explaining all the benefits you get. In your strongbox or safe deposit box keep notes on any pension or profit-sharing money you have coming, along with any other information needed to collect your benefits. If you have a retirement plan for the self-employed, or an Individual Retirement Account, the documents should be in the strongbox along with information on where the assets are invested.

Trust Documents

Keep the originals with your lawyer and copies in your file. If you want the originals in your own possession, keep them in a safe deposit box. Also, make a note of any trust income you receive and what is supposed to become of it at your death.

Gifts

All receipts for deductible charitable gifts belong in your current file, for use at tax time. In your safe deposit box keep records of any substantial gifts you make to other people, not only of cash and property, but also of art, cars, jewels, and so forth. This information may save your heirs some money. For example, when you die, the government may tax all the family jewelry in your estate unless your heirs can prove you made a gift of the jewelry on thus and such a date.

Employment and Education Records

Keep on file all permits, licenses, proficiency certificates, résumés, information on union membership, and names of past employers.

Business at Home

You need a current file of all income and expenses. Also, keep records of what you pay to rent, heat, light, clean, and insure your house, so a percentage can be allocated to your home office as a business expense. Records for past years belong with your back taxes.

Business Diary

If you incur tax-deductible travel and entertainment expenses, you need a diary to substantiate them. Keep track of business miles driven, plane tickets, hotel bills, entertainment, and other expenses. And please, be sure to enter these expenses as you go along. The IRS gets tight-lipped about business diaries compiled the night before an audit (they can use chemical analysis to tell how old the ink is).

Safe Deposit Box Key

Keep this in a convenient drawer, and tell your spouse and executor where it is. In case they forget, include its whereabouts on a master list of where everything is (see below).

Household Inventory

Draw up a list of everything you own, what it cost, and approximately how old it is. And I mean everything, right down to an estimate for bobby pins and cufflinks. Add snapshots of your rooms and sales slips proving the cost of major items. In case of fire or theft this inventory shows the insurance company exactly what you had and makes it easier to recover in full on your loss. Keep the list in a fireproof strongbox or safe deposit box, and update it from time to time.

Cemetery Records

Keep the deed in your strongbox or current file, where it can be found immediately. You might leave with it a list of any final instructions with regard to your funeral, donating organs for transplant, or other personal requests.

Master Sheet of Important Numbers

It's easier to replace lost documents if you have a list of relevant numbers. So record the numbers of your insurance policies, savings bonds, securities, bank accounts, and so forth, and keep the list in your strongbox or safe deposit box. Also keep track of all your charge account and credit card numbers so you can cancel them quickly if you lose your wallet. And as long as you're numbering, you might as well add any others that are important to you, such as your Social Security number and armed forces identification number as well as the Social Security numbers of the people in your immediate family.

Master List of Where Everything Is

Your executor will be eternally grateful if you record the results of your masterful filing system on a single sheet: exactly where everything is and the names and phone numbers of any professionals to consult when settling your affairs. This list should cover your insurance policies and insurance agent; employee benefits and the person in the company who handles them; bank accounts and the particular bankers you deal with; the whereabouts of your safe deposit box, an inventory of its contents, and where you keep the key; your Social Security number; where your will is and who the lawyer was who handled it; where all your personal papers are, your tax and bank records; your securities and the names of your brokers; what properties you own and where the deeds are; your debts and the money owed you; your accountant's name and address —in short, a complete reference sheet to your financial affairs. Keep this list in a loose-leaf notebook, so it's easy to make changes.

Annual Budget and Net Worth Records

You say you don't have any? Ah, but you will. See Chapter 2, "How You Add Up."

Chapter Two

HOW YOU ADD UP

I was glad to be able to answer promptly, and I did. I said I didn't know.

MARK TWAIN

No doubt you're worth less than you'd like. But certainly more than you think. Many people believe they don't own anything much, which is why they never bother making wills. Then, come settlement day, it turns out there's property worth $50,000 or $60,000 to distribute. Inflation is one of the big contributors to your net worth. For example, every dollar your house gains in value will eventually become a real dollar in someone's pocket. Add an insurance policy, a car, and a reasonable amount of worldly goods, and you may even find yourself quite wealthy.

Why Figure What You're Worth?

Keeping estate taxes down is one good reason for adding up the value of what you own. Once you know how much money will likely fall into your estate when you die, you can adjust things to reduce, or even eliminate, the tax. Another reason is to estimate how well your survivors would be able to live on the sum you'd pass on to them (if it's not enough, you'll need more life insurance). Yet another reason is to keep track of whether you're acquiring enough property to support yourself comfortably in retirement. The calculation is also useful in smaller ways—for example,

11

to remind yourself to increase the insurance on your house as its value rises, or to get rid of an investment that isn't doing well.

Finally, the value of your holdings is the truest benchmark of how you've done for yourself financially over the years. What net worth means in nonfinancial terms is *security*—the conversion of earning power into property that can provide for you when your earning years are over.

How to Estimate Net Worth

Basically, you add up everything you own (your assets), subtract everything you owe (your liabilities), and what is left is your net worth. It's the money you'd have if you converted all your property to cash and paid off all your debts. If you owe more than you own, you have a "negative net worth"—which you don't want to sit with very long. Gradually eliminating the deficit should be your first priority.

Over the years you want your net worth to rise, through savings and investment, so you won't be a charity case in your old age. If your net worth slides although earnings go up, something's wrong. Maybe you've taken on too much debt; maybe your investments have turned belly up. Whatever the problem, you'd better give it some attention, because it's unlikely to cure itself.

The first time you look at it, a net worth calculation may seem a little formidable. But if you take it line by line, you'll see that each item is something you probably know already or at least can find out pretty easily. Incidentally, when you figure the market value of the items in the following list, put down *only* what they would bring if they were sold today. If you put $5,000 into a mutual fund last year and it's now worth only $3,000, that's its market value. All the rest is hope.

YOUR NET WORTH

Date _____

Total assets   _____

Total liabilities   _____

Net worth (assets minus liabilities)   _____

WHAT YOU OWN
(Assets)

Date _____

CASH AND CASH EQUIVALENTS	DOLLAR AMOUNT
Cash on hand	_____
Cash in checking accounts	_____
Cash in savings accounts	_____
Life insurance cash value	_____
Savings bonds	_____
Money owed you	_____

PERSONAL PROPERTY	ESTIMATED CURRENT MARKET VALUE
Household furnishings	_____
Special items (car, boat, jewelry, furs, antiques, tools, art, etc.)	_____
Miscellaneous personal property	_____

REAL ESTATE

Your house	_____
Other properties	_____

INVESTMENTS

Stocks	_____
Bonds	_____
Government securities	_____
Mutual funds	_____
Other investments	_____

Equity interest in your own business   _____

Vested interest in pension or profit sharing
(money now owed you, even if you leave
the firm)   _____

Keogh or IRA retirement savings   _____

WHAT YOU OWE
(Liabilities)

Date _____

CURRENT BILLS	DOLLAR AMOUNT
Charge account balances	_____
Credit cards	_____
Utilities	_____
Rent	_____
Insurance premiums	_____
Taxes	_____
Other bills	_____

AMOUNT OWED ON LOANS

Mortgage	_____
Auto loan	_____
Personal loans	_____
Installment loans	_____
Life insurance loans	_____

TAXES DUE   _____

OTHER   _____

Roundup Day

Once a year husband and wife should go over their entire financial situation to see where they stand. This is particularly important for a wife who takes little part in the family finances. If her husband should die, she'd have to handle all these things herself. Just a little preparation could save some terrible mistakes.

It's disquieting to consider that one of you might suddenly die, leaving the other alone. But sooner or later it's going to happen. It's an act of love rather than fear to keep your financial affairs in order and your partner fully briefed. And this doesn't apply just to husbands. If a working wife died leaving her papers in a mess and owning insufficient insurance, it would cause her family just as much trouble as if it had happened to her husband.

Roundup day is what I call this annual accounting. A good time for it is the week between Christmas and New Year, when things tend to be slow and you may already be involved in year-end tax planning. Another time is in the spring, just after you've done your income taxes and have money on your mind. Add up all your assets and liabilities to get a net worth statement. Then, based on what you've learned, set some goals for yourselves the following year. You might decide to reduce current debt by a specific amount, or increase savings, or add to investments. Any of these would increase your net worth. At the end of next year, when you again add up your assets, you'll be much gratified to see the improvement.

You also need a plan for your assets, in case something happens to you. For example, you might advise your family to sell a piece of real estate that you manage because they haven't the skill to handle it. Or suggest that the money you have in the stock market be switched over to bonds. The idea is to figure out how all your property can be marshaled after your death so as to produce maximum income for your survivors. They may not follow your plan, but at least it will help them consider their options.

The last chore on roundup day is to figure out what income the family would have to live on if the breadwinner died, and how it stacks up against their probable expenses (the calculation is shown in the following section). Most likely, they won't have nearly the money they need to live in their present style—which will force the husband (or working wife) to think about buying more insurance and a housewife to consider what her earning power might be. If you're not prepared, the family's living standard could fall drastically.

A lot of people duck thoughts like these because they're just too painful. It's nicer not to know what the problems might be because, after all, they might never come to pass. If they do, maybe you'll be safely dead, and the mess you've left will be someone else's worry. All in all, doing nothing saves you a lot of trouble—but at everyone else's expense.

How to Figure What Your Survivor Would Have to Live On

If the earnings of either spouse contribute a significant amount to the family budget, the death of one means the survivor could be in trouble. It's important that each partner know what he or she would be left with in that eventuality. Fill out the following budget, first on the assumption that the husband dies and then that the wife dies. Make realistic estimates of costs—for example, it's quite possible that a widow might want to move to a smaller house, especially if she has to work. Also, decide how you'd want to handle lump sum payments from life insurance or a pension distribution: buy an annuity? add to savings? use the money for living expenses as long as it lasts? Usually this calculation is a little shocking, because it shows income falling well short of expenses. Chapter 20, "Life Insurance," makes some suggestions as to how to plug the income gap inexpensively.

SURVIVOR'S ANNUAL BUDGET

Date _____

INCOME

Widow(er)'s earnings _____

Social Security _____

Interest from savings _____

Dividends _____

EXPENSES

Taxes _____

Mortgage or rent _____

Utilities _____

Insurance _____

INCOME		EXPENSES	
Rents/royalties	_____	Installment payments	_____
Profits from business	_____	Food	_____
Pension	_____	Clothing	_____
Annuity	_____	Gasoline	_____
Annual sum taken from life insurance proceeds	_____	Medical	_____
Other	_____	Repairs	_____
		Savings	_____
		Entertainment	_____
		Hobbies	_____
		Books	_____
		Furniture	_____
		Gifts	_____
		Vacation	_____
		School or college	_____
		Allowances	_____
		Church or charities	_____
		Walking-around money (carfare, lunch, magazines, etc.)	_____
		Other	_____

Total probable income   _____

Total probable expenses   _____

   Gap   _____

   or

   Excess   _____

GAP TO BE FILLED BY:

Widow(er)'s extra earnings   _____

Additional insurance   _____

Other   _____

So much for background data. But don't think you've gone to all this trouble purely for historical interest. You'll be using this material in several contexts: to plan an intelligent insurance program, to solve your estate tax problems, and to work up a better budget than the one you're using now.

Chapter Three

TRYING
A BUDGET

O money, money, money, I'm not necessarily one of
    those who thinks thee holy,
But I often stop to wonder how thou canst go out so fast
    when thou comest in so slowly.

OGDEN NASH

When you reach into your pocket for the $10 that was there yesterday and find only $1.80, you may suddenly be stricken with the need to keep a budget. It's an affliction that's going around. People who gamely used to muddle through can't make it anymore unless they put numbers into columns and make everything add up.

I'm for it. It's okay to keep only a casual eye on daily expenses if you earn more than you need. But if you spend every nickel, you probably ought to rethink what you're doing. All the little things you buy, week in, week out, may make you feel good at the time. But those very expenditures keep you from getting the big things you want, such as freedom from debt, a comforting savings account, a better quality in the things you buy, a wonderful vacation. Many families are in so far over their heads that without a budget they'll never pull themselves out of the hole. Budgets are possible even in a high-inflation economy. In fact, they become more important than ever.

Emotional Problems

Tempers flare when you don't have enough money to pay for your style of living. Couples get angry and start resenting each other—for not earning enough, for spending too much, for not being clever enough to think of a way out. Being financially pressed is a blow to your self-esteem as well as to your pocketbook; you may feel helpless and guilty and then angry all over again for being unable to buy what you want. Spending too much money hurts personal relationships and diminishes respect. Yet at the same time, emotional stress may be the driving force behind your spending sprees. For many people possessions are a symbol of power, an expression of self-regard, a proof of personal worth, or a substitute for happiness. Starting a budget may mean changing personal attitudes as well as spending choices.

But deciding to be more rational about money is no quick fix. At first it can make things worse. When you write all your expenses down on paper, they may add up to so much more than your income that you'll want to jump out the window. Short of that, couples may start screaming at each other. Knowing *exactly* how bad things are can put you in a funk for days. But it's better to worry before you spend money than afterward, when it's too late. Furthermore, a budget is not as confining as it sounds. It doesn't prohibit splurges. It just demonstrates graphically that for every special purchase you want to make, you have to cut back somewhere else if you hope to avoid going further into debt.

When a family has been consistently overspending, it isn't easy to cut back. Husband and wife may argue bitterly over whether certain expenses are really necessary. Inevitably, there will be some irritating spending overruns. But no matter how difficult, you have to work out a budget you can both *agree on.* If you can't settle it yourselves, go to a nonprofit credit-counseling service for help (see page 135). Unless you both think that the budget is fair, it isn't going to work.

What Are You Spending Your Money On?

Do you really want what you have, let alone more of the same? And if so, do you want it under *any* circumstances? Is a full clothes closet worth hours of overtime or an impoverished bank account?

In their unremitting drive for consumables many Americans have become little more than indentured servants, working long hours for

the benefit of the bank, the finance company, the tailor, the uphol-
sterer, and all the other tradesmen to whom they have committed
pieces of their paychecks. They keep none of their earnings themselves;
everything goes for the profit of others.

Why kill yourself for a new set of living-room furniture? Why fight
with your spouse over department store bills? Why mortgage your
present and compromise your future for a powerboat? There are other
things to acquire—such as a good relationship with the people you love,
personal security, leisure, an empty bill drawer, a flashy savings account, and a way of life reasonably free of money worries. This kind of
peace can descend on most people once they stop struggling against the
limits of their spending power. If you can do this, you'll have learned
a lot about accepting yourself, as well as accepting the standard of living
you can afford. It means finding peace within yourself.

How Detailed a Budget?

Some people get a tremendous kick out of keeping detailed financial
records. Their budgets are a joy to read: column after neat column of
precise numbers, with every penny accounted for every day. But this
approach doesn't work for most people. Unless you've the head for it,
any attempt to be too thorough may preordain a budget to failure.
You're much more likely to follow through on a spending plan if you
establish general categories, then check the bills once a month to see
how you're doing. It doesn't even matter whether everything adds up
right as long as the discrepancies stay small. And always round the
numbers off. It's a nuisance as well as unnecessary to add up small
change.

Budgeting for Objectives

The best way to keep a budget on track is to have a clearly defined goal
in mind. That way you're not budgeting for the good of your soul or
because your mother told you you should, but in order to get something
you want, something you otherwise wouldn't have. You establish an
objective for yourself each year, when the budget is set up. For example, you might decide to reduce outstanding debt, start a savings account, buy more insurance, buy some furniture, take a special vacation,
or invest in a mutual fund. Whatever the goal, it becomes top priority

in your budget. You put money aside for this purpose *first*, before buying anything else. If your spending plan is realistic and you stick to it, at the end of the year you'll have achieved your special goal, and this may encourage you to set a more ambitious goal for the following year.

Say you want to reduce a debt by $700, which means setting aside $60 a month. This sum should come right off the top of earnings, *no matter what*. Treat the money as if it didn't exist—as if you were making $60 less a month—and live on what's left. That may sound impossible, considering all the bills that roll in, but it isn't. If $60 were suddenly cut from your monthly paycheck, you'd muddle through. Unless your income is at the poverty level, it's always possible to save money if you really want to.

Deciding on an annual financial objective is where a net worth statement comes in (see Chapter 2, "How You Add Up"). Just a glance at your assets and liabilities will tell you in hard, cold numbers where your strengths and weaknesses are. In the very course of compiling the statement you probably determined to get rid of some debt, or add to investments, or chart some other long-range change in your financial circumstances. A budget is the tool you use to reach those goals.

What Is Your Real Income?

Most families know approximately what they have to spend after taxes. But for a budget, approximations aren't good enough. Natural optimism tends to inflate your notion of how much cash is available, and you're in the hole before you know it.

The following table will help you zero in on exactly how much you have available for spending. Add up all your income, then deduct the amount taken out of your check for taxes, Social Security payments, and any other payroll deductions. The information will be on your check stub. Self-employed people can estimate based on last year's taxes. If you have income from which taxes are not withheld—such as interest, dividends, or rents—find out what bracket you're paying taxes in and deduct the proper amount. For example, if you have $100 in interest and are in the 25-percent tax bracket, deduct $25 for the tax payment.

After deductions you come to *net spendable income*—which is the exact amount of money on hand for all your expenses. No less, no more.

Drawing the Plan

First, see where the money went last year. Go through your bills and checkbooks and add it all up: so much for groceries, so much for rent, so much for repairs, clothing, entertainment. Put down everything you can isolate and lump the rest together under "unexplained cash." Add in last year's inflation rate. This gives you an idea of what your bills will be this year.

(continued on page 28)

A BETTER BUDGET—INCOME

Husband's earnings $ _____

Wife's earnings _____

Other family members' earnings _____

Interest and dividends _____

Rents from property; royalties _____

Profits from business _____

Pension/annuity/disability _____

Social Security _____

Other income _____

Total income $ _____

Deduct state, federal, and local income taxes (estimate from your paycheck stubs, or on the basis of last year's taxes) $ _____

Deduct Social Security taxes (from your paycheck stubs) _____

Other payroll deductions (insurance, payroll savings, garnishments, etc.) _____

Net spendable income $ _____

A BETTER BUDGET—EXPENSES

FIXED EXPENSES	Annual amount	Monthly amount	Spent in January	Spent in February	Spent in March	Spent in April	Spent in May	Spent in June
This year's special objective								
Mortgage/rent								
Heat								
Light								
Water								
Telephone								
Garbage								
Insurance								
Life								
Health								
Disability								
Auto								
Homeowner's								
Installment payments								
Interest on notes								
Loan repayments								
Reducing back bills								
School/college								
Dues								
Children's allowance								
Child care/household help								

VARIABLE EXPENSES

Food								
Clothing								
Savings								
Doctor								
Dentist								
Drugs								
Gasoline								
Entertainment								
Books/magazines								
Repairs/upkeep								
Car								
House								
Appliances								
Cleaning, personal care								
Church/charities								
Furniture								
Household supplies								
Birthdays/Christmas								
Hobbies								
Vacation								
Liquor								
Walking-around money, cigarettes, etc.								
Other								
TOTAL								

A BETTER BUDGET—EXPENSES (continued)

FIXED EXPENSES

This year's special objective

	Spent in July	Spent in August	Spent in September	Spent in October	Spent in November	Spent in December	Totals
Mortgage/rent							
Heat							
Light							
Water							
Telephone							
Garbage							
Insurance							
Life							
Health							
Disability							
Auto							
Homeowner's							
Installment payments							
Interest on notes							
Loan repayments							
Reducing back bills							
School/college							
Dues							
Children's allowance							
Child care/household help							

VARIABLE EXPENSES

Food										
Clothing										
Savings										
Doctor										
Dentist										
Drugs										
Gasoline										
Entertainment										
Books/magazines										
Repairs/upkeep										
Car										
House										
Appliances										
Cleaning, personal care										
Church/charities										
Furniture										
Household supplies										
Birthdays/Christmas										
Hobbies										
Vacation										
Liquor										
Walking-around money, cigarettes, etc.										
Other										
TOTAL										

Now to the plan itself. Make a list of everything your family spends money on, using as a guide pages 24 to 27. Start with your fixed expenses, such as rent, mortgage, personal and property taxes, insurance, and utilities—bills that are about the same from month to month. Put down how much you spend on each category over the entire year, plus an allowance for inflation.

Then go to variable expenses, such as food, clothing, medical care, and entertainment. You probably know about how much food is costing you every week. Other expenses, such as clothing and routine medical care, are best estimated from last year's spending (plus a percentage for inflation). Again, list what each item costs per year, plus an inflation estimate.

Then add everything up. Don't be discouraged if the total comes out to more than your net spendable income. After all, if you weren't overspending, you wouldn't be wrestling with budgets in the first place. Knowing the exact extent of your financial crimes is the first step toward making amends. If it turns out that you're, say, $1,000 over the mark, pare the various categories by a total of $1,000. Keep working your expenses down until they equal your annual take-home pay. That's the level of spending you must accept in order to avoid going deeper into debt.

For a while, you'll probably have to live without your favorite entertainments. But as your debt comes under control, and your salary rises —maybe after a year or so—you'll find yourself with enough money to live better. At that point you'll have your entertainments back and be financially sound to boot.

Writing the Plan Down

The table on pages 24–27 shows how to set your budget up. It's usually easier to use a large sheet of paper than one of those budget books available at a stationery store because with the paper you can fit all the categories on one page. The column labeled *Annual Amount* shows how much money you expect to spend on each category (including savings) over the entire year; added up, it should equal your total income after taxes. Under *Monthly Amount* list the total you plan to spend (or set aside against future expenditures) each month; this should total your monthly income. The next columns show how much you actually spend. The first time you do a budget you'll find that some of your estimates are off, but don't let that discourage you. Just fine-tune it as you go along. The key to success lies in not letting your monthly expenses rise above your monthly income. Whenever you increase one category, cut somewhere else.

Budgets are best handled on a monthly basis, even though some bills are paid bimonthly, quarterly, or even annually. There's a simple way to plan for infrequent bills: Just take the annual total, divide by twelve, and budget for that amount every month. For example, if you make a $300 annual payment for insurance, your budget should show that you pay $25 a month. The money doesn't actually go out each month; it stays in your bank account. But at the end of the year, when the bill falls due, all the cash is there. You can use the same system for many unpredictable expenses, such as doctor bills. Estimate what you spend in a typical year, divide by twelve, and reserve that amount every month. You then have funds to draw on whenever a doctor or dental bill comes in. (This system isn't designed to cover extraordinary expenses; savings do that. It's just for the predictable things.)

Tip: Take the sums you reserve against future bills out of your checkbook and put them into savings. You'll earn a little interest on them, and you won't be tempted to spend the money on something else.

Ways to Cut Spending

The top-rated, first-class, A-one method for bringing your spending into line with income is this: *Make no new discretionary purchases until you have all the old ones paid for.* The usual rule of thumb is that loans and installment debt (not counting your mortgage) shouldn't amount to more than 15 or 20 percent of income, but to the extent that inflation has driven up the cost of necessities, even this may be too much. Cut costly installment payments back. Buy no new furniture, appliances, clothes, vacations, even dinners out until you have some of the debt off your back. This single step can bring most people back to solvency if they have the will to carry it through.

Other ways to save money are just as tried and true, and just as honored in the breach rather than the observance:

• Pay less interest by buying less on credit.
• Pay off high-interest charge accounts with a lower-interest bank loan.
• Don't buy from door-to-door salesmen; you can usually get better prices and more reliable service somewhere else.
• Rent, don't buy, things you rarely use.
• If you have a corporation, ask an accountant how many of your expenses the corporation can pay for and tax-deduct.

• At the grocery store buy house brands, large economy sizes, and meat-counter specials.
• Control impulse purchases by shopping from a list.
• Plan purchases to coincide with seasonal sales.
• Attend garage sales and school swap-nights.
• Check all bills for errors.
• Stop subscribing to magazines you don't read.
• Don't settle for mediocre things just because they're cheap; chances are you won't wear them or use them.
• Pay attention to quality; you often get more out of more expensive clothes because they last longer.
• Declare a moratorium on buying new cosmetics.
• Drive your car less and keep it longer.
• Turn off lights in empty rooms, and turn off heat in unused rooms.
• Consider whether it would be cheaper to take taxis rather than own a second car.
• Serve punch and hors d'oeuvres at parties rather than drinks and dinner.
• Shop at resale shops, factory outlets, and discount stores, always checking to be sure that the "factory" prices are indeed lower than regular retail tags.
• Pool services like baby-sitting, transportation, and food buying with other families in the neighborhood.
• Grow vegetables.
• Learn to repair cars and appliances.
• Vacation at off-season rates.

There are as many more ideas in this vein as there are people trying to get by.

Special Problems with Weekly Cash Budgeting

When you get a weekly paycheck and immediately convert it into cash, prearranged spending plans often go out the window. Especially if you cash it at a store that has things you'd like to buy. The well-disciplined person can put aside cash for special purposes in jars or envelopes, but it's more common to be broke by next payday. It's better to carry your check right to a bank and put it into a checking account (or arrange for automatic deposit). There's generally a small charge, although some banks offer free checking. But to the extent that paying bills by check gives you more control of your spending, you'll generally wind up ahead.

Special Problems
with Irregular Incomes

If you don't have a regular paycheck, neat monthly budgets sound impossible. Lawyers who live from fee to fee, plant workers relying on overtime, substitute teachers waiting for a call, writers living on publisher's advances plus fees for articles—none of these people can predict their income or when it will come in. Yet they can predict their bills, which arrive with clockwork regularity whether the income is there or not. People in this situation should set up budgets just the way everyone else does, conservatively estimating their probable income for the year. Base your spending plan on the least that can be expected: Whenever a fee comes in, put it in the bank and draw it down in strict accordance with your budget. Resist the temptation to buy something extra if an unexpectedly large check arrives; it might have to last for more months than you think. If, partway through the year, it appears that your earnings will fall short, you'll have to revise your spending plan sharply downward. If there's extra, put it into the bank. During the following year continue on a conservative budget for regular operating expenses, using last year's surplus for such things as a nice vacation or a stock market investment. Always take special purchases out of your accumulated surplus, keeping fixed operating expenses within the limits of whatever minimum earnings you expect that year.

Special Problems
If Taxes Aren't Withheld

People paid by fee, with no tax withholding, are true heroes if they can make it to April 15 without spending any of their tax money. To stay out of trouble, it is essential to put a percentage of every single check aside against future taxes—and not to touch that money, no matter what. It's easy to tell yourself that you'll cover the arrearage with a future fee, but if that fee doesn't materialize, you're up the creek. It helps your self-discipline if you make quarterly estimated tax payments to the government (and generally saves you money, since you pay a penalty if estimated taxes aren't filed). Pretend the money you set aside doesn't exist, as indeed it wouldn't if taxes had been withheld in advance.

Budgets for a Working Couple

I dislike budgets that make a big fuss about "his" versus "her" money and allocate household expenses according to who is more "responsible" for them. Where is it written that the husband should pay the mortgage and the wife the baby-sitter? They both live in the house; they both want their children to have proper care. They are equally responsible for their joint bills. On the other hand, there are some personal obligations that clearly belong to one partner or the other. Here's a good way to handle them:

Each person's check could go into a personal account, from which would be paid the bills that are legally his. If the house is in the wife's name, for example, she should pay the mortgage. If the husband owns insurance policies on the wife's life, he should pay the premiums. This prevents questions from being raised as to who owns what, in case of divorce or an Internal Revenue Service audit of estate-tax returns. Each should also put aside savings *in his or her own name,* for emergencies (see Chapter 5, "Ways to Save Money"). The remainder should be pooled in a joint account for expenses common to both—such as food, entertainment, and the children's education.

Some working couples like to keep their money separate, and if that works for you, fine. But don't be too punctilious about who pays for what. If one spouse gets behind and "borrows" from the other or feels that he's paying too great a share, you're setting the stage for a pointless quarrel.

Budgets for People
Who Live Together

If you live together but aren't married, you can handle your spending the same way married couples do, as suggested in the previous section. Alternatively, you might want to have a greater demarcation between your incomes. It's rarely practical to split expenses fifty-fifty, since women so often earn less than men. If you each put the same number of dollars into the common pot, she would be contributing a greater portion of her income, which would leave her less to set aside for herself. A better approach is for each partner to contribute the same percentage of income for shared expenses, reserving the rest for personal obligations and savings.

Budgeting for a Raise

If you've had trouble saving money, a pay raise gives you a perfect opportunity to start. Keep on living on what you had before, and put the raise into savings. But if you do plan to crank the raise into your standard of living, don't forget to allow for taxes. Some people act as if an extra $15 a week gives them that much more to spend, forgetting that $4 or $5 of the raise goes to the government, and another $1 or so goes to inflation. Because of tax withholding, the first paycheck you get after the raise becomes effective will tell you precisely how much more money you have to spend.

Who Handles the Budget?

Families differ. In some homes the husband likes to handle the bills, and in other homes, the wife. Or they may do it together—she keeping track of the spending plan, for example, while he writes the checks. In any case, you can vastly improve your appreciation of each other's budgeting problems by switching roles every now and then—with the person who normally doesn't shop trying to keep the food budget in line for a week, and the person who normally doesn't write checks attending to the bills to see how fast the bank account becomes depleted.

But whatever your arrangement, the monthly budget should be kept by the person who feels most strongly about it. Neither an appeal to duty nor steady nagging will get a disinterested person to fill in the budget sheets on time or figure out what to do about spending overruns.

Budgeting When You're Unemployed

When a family loses a paycheck, one of the first things to do is add up the bills and see how you're going to manage. You may have unemployment insurance, union benefits, even a second paycheck in the house, but in most cases you're still going to come up short. Generally, people in this position try to fill the gap with savings, then seek loans from other members of the family. Meanwhile, you get farther and farther behind on your bills and more and more worried about hanging on to what you have.

But you can put off the crunch if you have the courage. Creditors are generally willing to ride with someone who faces his situation squarely and has a plan for dealing with it. Before you've seriously depleted your savings, make an effort to cut fixed expenses by asking your creditors to accept lower payments for a few months until you're back on the job. The key to getting their consent is a comprehensive spending plan, showing (1) your income; (2) what you need to put food on the table, send the children to school, and look for work; and (3) what you have left to apply to your debts. Divide this in a reasonable way among your creditors and promise to pay them any shortfalls, plus interest, as soon as you start cashing paychecks again. In many cases they'll accept, which relieves you of the pressure of unpaid bills as well as the need to exhaust your savings right away.

Allowances

Everyone should have an allowance—adults as well as children. Call it "walking-around money," sums you use for personal expenses and for which you don't have to account to anyone else. An allowance teaches children how to live within their means. And it relieves adults on a budget from having to account for every single daily expense. In setting the amount each person should have, start with a minibudget—something that shows what expenses they have to pay out of pocket. Then add a little extra for small impulse purchases, and account for the total as a lump sum on the master budget. If the recipient keeps running out before the next payday, you can help him control his spending itch by paying his allowance twice a week instead of once.

Savings

You'll notice that I've built a savings program into the budget *in addition to* your annual budgetary objective. It's natural that when you first think about expenses, you should think entirely in terms of your standard of living, what you want to own and do. But without a cash reserve the smallest emergency may throw you off, even send you to a lender for credit you can't afford. And beyond savings lie investments, a payment toward your own future security (see Chapter 26, "Investments"). It sounds almost un-American to say this, but everyone really should live on a little less than he makes.

Inflation

As inflation hounds us, budgets go through frequent adjustment, mostly in the form of reductions in the things we'd like in order to pay for the things we need. Entering your expenses monthly shows you immediately where overruns are happening, and by how many dollars you have to cut back in order to stay solvent. But try not to let inflation eliminate your fixed contribution to savings, if that's at all possible. The interest your bank account earns at least partly offsets the erosion inflation makes in your purchasing power.

What If You Just Can't Budget?

If your spending is compulsive or your will as weak as custard pudding; if you're getting by and don't feel a strong need to improve; if you can't stand keeping books or adding up columns of numbers; if you break out in hives when someone suggests that you ought to get organized—then you may find it impossible to budget. But that doesn't mean you have to throw all hope of fiscal comfort out the window. Plenty of automatic savings devices exist for those of us who would never otherwise put anything aside (see page 45). Starting such a program—one that requires absolutely no effort on your part—is the minimum budgeting effort you can make, and might be the one that will serve you best.

Chapter Four

WHERE TO KEEP YOUR MONEY

Gives me some kind of content to remember how painful it is sometimes to keep money, as well as to get it.

SAMUEL PEPYS

The major money storehouses—banks, savings and loan associations, and credit unions—have always differed in the number and variety of financial services offered. But these days they are growing more alike. In fact, within a few years they may be different in name and traditions only, while providing customers with a similar range of choices. As it stands in 1980, however, some institutions are better for savings accounts, whereas others specialize in checking accounts and business loans.

Here is the range of services you can expect to find at one or another of the money storehouses: checking and savings accounts; time deposits; mortgages; loans to students, farmers, and businessmen; loans for home improvements, cars, tax payments, appliances, bill consolidation, or any other personal purpose; estate management; safe deposit boxes; sale and redemption of U.S. savings bonds; money orders, traveler's checks, and credit cards; transfers of money abroad or to other banks around the country; low-cost life insurance (in some states); automatic bill paying; and credit counseling.

Commercial Banks

These are the "everything" banks; they provide checking and savings accounts, write all kinds of loans, and offer just about any service you can imagine a bank's being able to give. Their history is entirely mercantile—that is, they once financed only business, not individual, transactions. Deposits came from corporations and wealthy people, not from working folk. It wasn't until early in the twentieth century that commercial banks really began to go after the deposit-and-loan business of ordinary citizens.

Commercial banks are now the principal institutions providing checking accounts, although savings banks and S&Ls (savings and loan associations) are starting to offer some stiff competition (see Chapter 6, "Checking Accounts"). Which bank you should use should depend on three things: price, convenience, and service.

Price

Wherever possible, look for a free checking account rather than one that levies a service charge. Some free checking accounts have no strings attached, others are conditional on such things as keeping a certain sum in a savings account. Commercial banks pay less interest on savings than do savings banks or S&Ls. But if you can save more on checks than you lose in interest by using the savings account–free checking combination, the deal's worth it. Some banks offer no-strings-attached checking only to certain segments of the community, such as older people, students, and veterans. For more on bank charges, see Chapter 6, "Checking Accounts." In general, small banks charge lower fees than big banks.

Convenience

You'll generally want a bank close to your home or office, or one with many branches around town where you can cash checks. Evening hours are helpful. Some banks have check-cashing machines, operating day and night seven days a week. Or you might want to bank by mail in order to use a distant bank that offers free checking.

Service

By all means use a bank that treats you courteously. Some are brusque to customers, slow to carry out requests, and make a lot of mistakes. To do business with places like that only encourages them.

By law, commercial banks have had to pay a lower interest rate on savings than credit unions, savings banks, and savings and loan associations. However, they offer you a chance to save systematically—by having money transferred automatically from your checking account to savings every month. If that helps you put money away, the lower interest is a trifle. If you're a self-starter on savings, however, it's better to keep your money somewhere else, where it will earn more.

You can get all kinds of loans at commercial banks, including a revolving-charge card and a credit line that lets you overdraw your checking account. It pays to have a good relationship, because when money is tight, banks reserve loans for their own good customers. How do you achieve a good relationship? By finding a bank you like and sticking to it, giving it your lending business and repaying loans on time. (It also helps if you have a big account.)

Savings Banks

These banks got their start early in the nineteenth century in order to serve the ordinary people, who were overlooked by commercial banks. The objectives of their philanthropist founders were to encourage thrift among wage earners, give them a source of loans when they needed it, and provide the community with yet another pool of investment capital. Savings banks had their principal development in the Northeast, where people gathered together in cities. The names of the early banks (many of which persist today) proclaim their allegiance to "emigrants," "seamen," "mechanics," "farmers," or simply "peoples." Other banks go by names like "five cents," "dime," or "dollar," which indicated the small sums they were willing to handle.

Today savings banks are chartered in seventeen states and specialize in home mortgages (although other types of loans are available). They pay higher interest on savings than commercial banks do. In some places they offer checking accounts and thus can make automatic transfers from checking to savings.

Savings and Loan Associations

Originally, S&Ls were known as "building and loan" associations, which sums up how they came into being. Members agreed to pool their savings so that each in turn could borrow enough money to build a house. Beginning in the 1830s, this financing method spread rapidly.

Today, S&Ls are located in all fifty states and do more home mortgage business than all other lenders combined. Like savings banks, they can pay higher interest on savings than commercial banks do, and they too are rapidly dreaming up ways to pay interest on checking-account-type deposits.

Both S&Ls and savings banks offer depositors a wide range of services, and the list is growing. They generally have folders advertising their financial services in the racks where you find deposit and withdrawal slips. Some of the services may be free, such as money orders, traveler's checks, safe deposit boxes, notary services, and even free checking with cooperating banks. In many cases, smaller S&Ls and savings banks have more free services, and lower fees, than larger institutions do.

As the banking laws change and new possibilities for all the money storehouses emerge, you'll find them advertised on the business pages of your local paper or in signs in the bank windows. Remember that, in principle, you should always be looking for the highest possible interest on *all* your deposits, both checking and savings, plus the convenience you need to make bill paying as simple as possible.

Credit Unions

The credit union concept grew out of the cooperative, utopian ideals popular in Europe in the 1840s. Most working people hadn't the assets to qualify for loans from commercial banks, and even if they had, they couldn't afford the high interest rates. So they pooled their money into low-interest credit unions. Good character, rather than net worth, was —and still is—the prime requisite for a loan. Credit unions got going in the United States in the early 1900s, but they didn't really take off until after World War II. Now they're a major competitor for savings wherever people are eligible to join.

Credit unions serve people with some common bond—for example, they may all live in the same town, work for the same employer, or belong to the same church or club. It's intended that members should know each other, so as to reduce the risk of bad loans. In general, credit unions pay a higher interest on savings than you can get at banks or S&Ls, and on the average they charge less for loans. (This, of course, varies among credit unions; in some cases—auto loans, for one—credit unions sometimes charge more than the going rate at local banks. As always, it pays to shop around.) At the end of the year, a well-run credit union often has a surplus to distribute to members—either as a rebate of loan interest or an extra dividend on savings.

If you are eligible for credit-union membership—and a growing number of people are—by all means investigate the advantages. All of them offer a wide variety of consumer and home improvement loans. Many also have interest-paying checking accounts (called "share draft" accounts), high-interest savings certificates, credit cards, mortgages, and a small amount of free life insurance. When a credit union is sponsored by an employer, it can offer the most effective and painless vehicle for savings that I know of—the payroll deduction. You ask the payroll department to take a certain sum from each of your paychecks and deposit it in your credit union account. Since you never see the money, you don't miss it; yet all the time your savings are building steadily.

How Safe Is Your Money?

Almost all banks and savings loans carry federal or state deposit insurance—up to $100,000 for each account. As of this writing, some 70 percent of all credit unions are similarly insured (in two states—Ohio and Utah—for the full amount of your deposits); within a few years, most of the rest will also be covered. All kinds of accounts are covered by deposit insurance—checking, savings, Christmas clubs, trust accounts, time deposits, even bank traveler's checks. If the bank were to fail, every single deposit under your name would be added together; as long as the total wasn't over $100,000, you would get everything back within a few days, or at most a couple of weeks. Massachusetts insures savings accounts in full.

If you share accounts with other people, each account is separately insured up to $100,000. For example, in a single bank you can have an account in your own name, a joint account with a spouse, a trust account for a child with yourself as trustee, and a trust account for the same child with your spouse as trustee—and they each would be insured for $100,-000. Individual Retirement Accounts and Keogh plans are insured for up to $100,000.

If you keep a larger sum in bank deposits, it's prudent to divide it between two separate banks (not just two branches of the same bank) so that every penny would be covered. You might, for example, buy a savings certificate at a different bank from the one that keeps your passbook savings. But as long as your total deposits are under $100,000, there's no need to worry about using two banks.

In parlous times, when even big banks get into trouble, it becomes fashionable to keep cash in a safe deposit box instead of a savings account. There's no point in that. Safe deposit boxes don't pay any interest, and if you want the funds insured, you have to buy the coverage yourself.

So far, no one has ever lost a nickel in a government-insured savings and loan association; at liquidation, there have been enough funds to pay off *all* deposits, even those above the insurance level. Banks have paid off on all insured deposits and more than 90 percent of uninsured deposits. The insurance fund comes from assessments on the banks and S&Ls themselves backed up with a line of credit against the U.S. Treasury. Uninsured deposits are repaid out of money secured from the sale of bank assets. The proceeds are put into a pool and apportioned equally among depositors.

Because so much government insurance is available, it's generally a mistake to keep funds in any institution that doesn't carry it. (Private deposit insurance is no substitute, since the insurance company might fold just when you need it most.)

The only time you might want to consider an uninsured institution is when it's a credit union. Credit union insurance is fairly new, which is why so many of them don't yet carry it. But in the past the industry's own stabilization funds have held losses to a minimum. In a group of credit unions that folded in 1974, each member lost an average of only $31.50. When a credit union has a long and stable financial history and pays a high interest rate, you might want to put part of your money there even though it doesn't carry insurance. (But it's not a good idea to entrust such a credit union with all your funds.) On the other hand, if your credit union is new or small, and uninsured, you should risk only small sums to its savings plan.

What Happens When a Banking Institution Gets into Trouble?

The various government agencies that regulate banks, S&Ls, and credit unions examine them at least once a year and keep a list of those that have a lot of problems. If it looks as if the institution is getting deeper into trouble, they have the power to close it down or merge it with a stronger one. In recent years the big banks that failed have done so on a weekend and opened the following Monday morning under a new name. Depositors didn't lose a penny; in fact, except for a sign on the door stating that the bank was under new management, everything was exactly the same.

If it turns out that the only thing to do is close the bank down, you should receive a check for your insured deposits within five to ten days. Uninsured deposits take longer to clear, but generally no longer than a few weeks (although in some cases you may have to wait many months before the final returns are in). You can generally have access to your safe deposit box within a couple of days, if there's an emergency; otherwise, within a week. You receive the insured amount of any certificates of deposit right away; anything over the insurance limit goes into the pool to be paid out after the bank's assets are liquidated. Interest stops on the day the bank is closed, but no penalty is assessed on savings certificates repaid early. If the bank is managing property for you, it will continue to do so until you find a new manager.

Where to Complain

Banks, S&Ls, and credit unions may be chartered by either the state or federal government. The institution itself is required to tell you which jurisdiction it comes under and where to send complaints. State regulatory bodies will be listed in the telephone book under the state listings; if you can't find a specific listing for a commissioner of banking, mail your complaint to the office of the state treasurer, with carbon copies to the state's department of consumer affairs and whatever consumer protection agencies exist in your city.

To complain about a national bank (a bank with *national* in its name or the initials *N.A.*, for "National Association," after its name), write to Office of Consumer Affairs, Comptroller of the Currency, 490 L'Enfant Plaza East S.W., Washington, D.C. 20219.

To complain about a state-chartered bank that is a member of the Federal Reserve System (most big banks are), write to the Division of Consumer Affairs at the Federal Reserve System, 21st St. and C St., Washington, D.C. 20551, and to the Federal Reserve branch closest to you. Their addresses are on page 833.

If the bank is federally insured, write to the Office of Consumer Affairs, Federal Deposit Insurance Corp., 550 17th St. N.W., Washington, D.C. 20429. As you can see, there may be more than one agency responsible for your bank; when you have a problem, complain to every one of them.

If it's a federally chartered savings and loan (an S&L with *federal* in its name), write to the Office of the Secretary, Federal Home Loan Bank

Board, 1700 G St. N.W., Washington, D.C. 20552, and to the Supervisory Agent of the Federal Home Loan Bank closest to you (addresses on page 834).

State-chartered S&Ls, insured by the Federal Savings and Loan Insurance Corporation should be reported to the state regulatory agency with a copy to the Federal Home Loan Bank Board in Washington, D.C. (address in the paragraph above).

If you're mad at a federally chartered credit union, write to the Office of the Administrator, National Credit Union Administration, 1776 G St. N.W., Washington, D.C. 20456.

If any financial institution has discriminated against you in making (or not making) a mortgage loan on the basis of race or sex, complain to the Assistant Secretary of Equal Opportunity, Department of Housing and Urban Development, 451 Seventh St. S.W., Washington, D.C. 20410. Or telephone toll-free at (800) 424-8590. For complaints of discrimination involving other types of loans, write to the agency that regulates that specific institution.

Chapter Five

WAYS TO
SAVE MONEY

You ought to get yourself $400 or $500 million in
cash. Tuck it away and forget about it. It'll come in
handy sometime for a rainy day.
ATTRIBUTED TO HENRY FORD, SR.

Almost anyone can save if he really wants to, even in an inflation economy. You might think that with all the bills you have, it's impossible to put money aside. But if your salary were suddenly cut by $50 a month, would you go bankrupt? Would you have to move? Probably not. You'd make some small adjustments and muddle through as before. Therefore, if you wanted to, you could *save* $50 a month, or $60, or $75, depending on how much you earn. You could slip it into a savings account and pretend you never saw it. It might be missed at first, but once you got into the rhythm of living on what was left, you'd never notice it. Life wouldn't seem any different, yet you'd be making regular payments into savings.

When you hear people say, "We're too broke to put money aside," all it really means is that they've chosen to live right up to the edge of their incomes, or even over the edge. If you buy a better house, another car, a snowmobile, a vacation every year, movies, dinners out, nice clothes, and then say that you haven't enough money to save for the future, I can only reply that you're having your future now. The problem is not solely in the economic system, or the size of your salary, or even inflation (unless you have a fixed income), but in the way you've arranged your life.

When you spend everything you earn, you are, in a sense, working for other people. All your money goes into the pockets of the grocer, the department store, the bank, the finance company. You have no profits left for yourself.

Starting today, why not stop giving everything away? Follow the old precept and *pay yourself first*. Take something off the top of each paycheck as a reward for your labors and put it away. On a middle-class income you might save 5 percent of everything you earn. For a family making $15,000, that's only $750 a year, or about $15 a week. If that sounds like too much, start with something smaller and build up. You might, for example, save half of any raise, all of a windfall payment (such as a bonus or a tax refund), all of the loose change in your pockets, all dividends and interest.

What's building up is all yours, money you have behind you when you need or want it. Something for emergencies, something for good times, something to invest for even more earnings, something to give you a feeling of independence from everyday money cares. A faithfully kept program of savings and conservative investments can give you more money and a better life than that of your neighbors who spend everything they get. This is probably the oldest financial advice in the world, but there are some things you can't improve on.

Automate Your Savings

You want to get into the habit of putting money aside. It's no good to pay the bills and say you'll save whatever is left over, because there's never anything left over. Or if there is, it happens only occasionally. The idea is to make a regular savings deposit off the top of each paycheck and adjust your spending to what's left.

The easiest way to save is to have it done for you. Any way you can arrange to have money taken out of your paycheck before you can get your hands on it puts you ahead. Here are some of the ways to do it:

Payroll Deductions

Of all the ways I've ever tried to save money, this one works best. You arrange with your employer to take a certain sum out of every paycheck and put it into whatever savings vehicle you designate. If the company has an insured credit union that pays more interest than the bank, that's probably the best place. Or you might have the money put into a bank, or U.S. savings bonds. Not all employers offer payroll deduction plans. If you're lucky enough to have one available, by all means use it.

Automatic Transfers from Checking to Savings

You can arrange with your bank to take a certain sum from your checking account each month and transfer it to your savings account. In most cases, this will mean keeping your savings in a commercial bank where the interest rate is a little lower than at savings banks or S&Ls. But if it helps you save, it's well worth it. (In some states, savings banks can offer checking accounts as well as automatic transfers to savings.) The key to making this work lies in your remembering to enter the transfer in your checkbook each month so that you won't overspend by accident.

Saving by Mail

Keep a stack of bank envelopes in the drawer where you put your current bills. In effect, the envelope is a "bill"—something to be paid every week or every month along with the rent and electric bill. It doesn't matter that the amount is small; the idea is to make it regular: weekly, biweekly, or monthly, depending on the cycle of your paychecks. If you're paid irregularly, set aside a specified percentage of each check. Send off the payment you "owe" your savings account at the same time as you mail the rest of your bills.

Bank "Bills"

Some banks and S&Ls will send you monthly reminders of the sum you owe your savings account, which you can treat as if they were bills. Ask your bank whether they offer this or any other service that will help regularize your savings.

Coupon Clubs

Christmas clubs, Chanukah clubs, and vacation clubs, offered by banks, S&Ls, and credit unions, appeal to people who respond compulsively to coupon books. You agree in advance to make a certain weekly (or monthly) payment over a year's time, and receive a book of coupons specifying that amount. Each week you tear a coupon out and deposit the proper sum. In most cases this is not as profitable a way to save as a regular savings account. Some clubs pay no interest (or dividends) at all. Others pay interest only if you complete the club, and even then not at a compounded rate. You generally can't withdraw the money until the year is up. Only a few banks treat coupon clubs just like regular savings accounts, paying normal rates of interest or dividends and exacting no penalties if the club isn't completed.

Therefore, if coupons help you save, it would be wiser to make your own coupon booklet and use it as a reminder to make weekly payments to a savings account. However, coupon club savings are better than none at all; if this is the only way you can put money aside, by all means do so. At the end of the year put the lump sum into regular savings and start the club all over again.

Company Thrift or Pension Plans

Some companies will match any sums you contribute to an employee thrift or pension plan, up to a certain limit. Every dollar you set aside will be worth, say, $2 in the future. If you have an opportunity like this, by all means take advantage of it. Should you leave the company after just a few years, you'll get your own savings back plus interest; if you've stayed there long enough, you'll be entitled to take the employer's contribution as well.

Individual Pensions

If you're self-employed or not covered by a company pension, you can set up your own tax-sheltered pension plan—either an Individual Retirement Account or a Keogh plan (see Chapter 29, "Retirement Planning"). Money you contribute is worth more than bank savings because you can deduct a specified payment from your income when you figure income taxes. However, these are long-term savings. Pension funds generally aren't available until you're at least fifty-nine and a half years old and so are no substitute for ready money in the bank.

Life Insurance

Many people automate their savings by buying an insurance policy with a savings feature. The premiums go partly for insurance and partly into "cash value," which they think of as a kind of savings account. This is a less attractive way to set money aside for these reasons:

1. Life insurance cash values build up more slowly than the same sums in a savings bank or S&L.
2. If you want to use the money, you have to borrow it from the insurance company at an interest rate of 5 to 8 percent.
3. The only way you can get the money free and clear is by canceling your insurance.
4. If the insured person dies, his beneficiary is paid the face value of the policy, but the "savings account," or cash value, vanishes.

For more on this subject, see Chapter 20, "Life Insurance." Let me say this: If you can't save any other way, it is better to save through an insurance policy than not at all. But it's my belief that with just a little thought and a minimum of effort, you can save outside an insurance policy—by using one of the methods listed above.

How Much Should You Save?

Traditionally the question of how much to save is answered in terms of probable needs. You'll want three months' salary to tide you over joblessness; a lot more if you're saving for a house; less when you're childless than if there are several children to educate; more if you have no inheritance coming. But the trouble with thinking of savings as a fixed dollar amount is that once people have reached their goal, they tend to stop. I think savings should be part of your program right up to the day you retire.

The most systematic way to save is to set aside a specified percentage of your salary, year in, year out. Five percent is a good place to start. A family making $10,000 could save $500 a year, or $10 a week. A family making $20,000 could save at least $1,000 a year, or $20 a week. This can normally be done with only the smallest adjustment in your present style of living. If you take your savings off the top of each paycheck and live on what's left, chances are you won't even know what you cut out in order to save that 5 percent.

The following table shows how much money you'll wind up with if you save various weekly amounts at 5¼ percent, at this writing the most that commercial banks can pay on passbook savings accounts. (S&Ls may pay 5½ percent, credit unions, generally 6 percent. These limits will rise in 1981.) Interest is compounded daily. As your salary increases, you can save a larger portion of your income and still have enough left over for a comfortable life.

HOW FAST SAVINGS BUILD*
(at 5¼ percent interest, compounded daily)

Weekly deposit	After 1 year	After 3 years	After 5 years	After 10 years	After 20 years
$ 5	$ 267.16	$ 845.95	$1,489.54	$ 3,431.69	$ 9,265.67
10	534.32	1,691.89	2,979.08	6,863.37	18,531.35
15	801.48	2,537.84	4,468.62	10,295.06	27,797.02
20	1,068.63	3,383.79	5,958.17	13,726.74	37,062.70
25	1,335.79	4,229.74	7,447.71	17,158.43	46,328.37

*All tables in this chapter were provided by the Bowery Savings Bank, New York, N.Y.

The amounts shown in the preceding table are the minimum you can expect. As your savings grow, you'll want to put part of the money into longer-term savings certificates, which pay more interest. At this writing, the maximum that savings banks and S&Ls can pay on most time deposits under $100,000 that are held a minimum of eight years is 8 percent a year. Exceptions: a six-month certificate, costing $10,000 or more; and a two-and-a-half-year certificate, with minimums in the area of $100 to $500, paying rates that rise and fall with the general level of interest rates. The next table shows how much you stand to gain by shifting savings from your regular passbook account into a six-year, 7¾ percent term account, each account compounded daily:

A $10,000 deposit	Six years later
At 5¼ percent	$13,762.67
At 7¾ percent	16,023.29

A $5,000 deposit	Six years later
At 5¼ percent	$6,881.34
At 7¾ percent	8,011.65

The following table is yet another way of showing what a big difference higher interest rates mean to a savings plan. I've assumed an investment of $50 at the first of every month, in savings paying from 4½ to 8 percent. After twenty years, interest alone accounts for a difference of around $10,500 between the highest-paying and lowest-paying plan.

THE IMPORTANCE OF INTEREST RATES
(assuming a deposit of $50 a month, compounded daily)

Interest rate	After 1 year	After 3 years	After 5 years	After 10 years	After 20 years
4½ %	$615.13	$1,932.88	$3,376.53	$7,618.34	$19,641.57
5	616.84	1,948.41	3,422.06	7,831.35	20,832.93
5¼	617.70	1,956.25	3,445.16	7,940.88	21,463.05
5½	618.55	1,964.11	3,468.42	8,052.13	22,115.27
6	620.28	1,979.99	3,515.63	8,281.10	23,496.83
6½	622.01	1,996.02	3,563.61	8,518.04	24,982.45
7	623.74	2,012.22	3,612.46	8,763.73	26,583.82
7½	625.48	2,028.60	3,662.20	9,018.48	28,310.47
8	627.23	2,045.16	3,712.83	9,282.67	30,173.06

You may also want to make an investment in stocks, bonds, mutual funds, real estate, or your own business. Every nickel you can put into savings and profitable investments will make your life easier and more pleasant as time goes on. If you achieve this by setting aside just 5 percent of your salary, you'll be doing it at minimum cost to your present standard of living.

Reaching a Specific Goal

When you know you'll need a specific sum of money in a certain number of years, you might have to step up your level of savings. The next table tells you how much you have to deposit at the start of each month in order to reach your goal. I've shown the arithmetic for savings goals of up to $10,000, but by using simple addition you can calculate even higher amounts. For example, if you want to save $18,000, add the deposit for $10,000 and the deposit for $8,000; if your goal is $22,000, add two $10,000 deposits plus a $2,000 deposit. For time periods other than the ones I've shown, ask your bank if it will make the calculation for you. And remember that if you can put this money to work at higher rates of interest, you'll be able to reach your savings goal earlier.

A PLAN FOR SAVINGS
(at 5¼ percent interest, compounded daily)

If you want this amount	Save This Amount Monthly					
	For 3 years	For 5 years	For 10 years	For 15 years	For 20 years	For 25 years
$ 1,000	$ 25.56	$ 14.51	$ 6.30	$ 3.62	$ 2.33	$ 1.59
2,000	51.12	29.03	12.59	7.24	4.66	3.18
3,000	76.68	43.54	18.89	10.86	6.99	4.77
4,000	102.24	58.05	25.19	14.48	9.32	6.36
5,000	127.80	72.57	31.48	18.11	11.65	7.95
6,000	153.35	87.08	37.78	21.73	13.98	9.54
7,000	178.91	101.59	44.08	25.35	16.31	11.13
8,000	204.47	116.10	50.37	28.97	18.64	12.72
9,000	230.03	130.62	56.67	32.59	20.97	14.31
10,000	255.59	145.13	62.97	36.21	23.30	15.90

The Joy of Compound Interest

Every time an interest payment is credited to your account, you have more money at work, which of course makes the next interest payment even larger. In other words, interest is paid not only on the sums you deposit, but also on the interest those sums earn. Compounding of interest builds up your savings account much faster than if you took the interest out of your account and spent it. At 5 percent it takes roughly fourteen years for money to double, but only twenty-two years for it to triple, and twenty-seven years for it to quadruple. The higher the interest rate, the faster your savings grow. At 6 percent it takes twelve years for money to double, and at 7 percent only ten years. (You can figure for yourself how long it will take for your money to double, at any interest rate, by using the Rule of 72: Divide the interest rate into 72: the answer gives you roughly the number of years you'll have to wait.)

Say you deposit $50 a month into a bank at 5¼ percent compounded daily. The following table shows you how much interest compounding adds to your savings over the years:

WHAT COMPOUND INTEREST ADDS
(saving $50 a month at 5¼ percent interest, compounded daily)

Year	Your total deposits	Amount of interest paid	Total savings
1	$ 600	$ 17.70	$ 617.70
3	1,800	156.25	1,956.25
5	3,000	445.16	3,445.16
10	6,000	1,940.88	7,940.88
20	12,000	9,463.05	21,463.05

Or say you received a windfall payment of $1,000 and decided to save it all. The next table shows how that single deposit would increase over the years at various rates of interest. As you can see, a difference of just one-quarter of 1 percent adds up to quite a bit of money.

HOW A $1000 DEPOSIT GROWS
(compounded daily)

Interest rate	After 1 year	After 3 years	After 5 years	After 10 years	After 20 years
4½%	$1,046.68	$1,146.68	$1,256.24	$1,578.14	$2,490.54
5	1,052.00	1,164.26	1,288.49	1,660.21	2,756.30
5¼	1,054.67	1,173.14	1,304.93	1,702.83	2,899.63
5½	1,057.35	1,182.10	1,321.57	1,746.54	3,050.42
6	1,062.72	1,200.21	1,355.49	1,837.37	3,375.92
6½	1,068.12	1,218.61	1,390.29	1,932.91	3,736.15
7	1,073.55	1,237.28	1,425.98	2,033.43	4,134.82
7½	1,079.01	1,256.24	1,462.59	2,139.17	4,576.04
8	1,084.49	1,275.49	1,500.14	2,250.41	5,064.33

The interest you earn on your savings account is taxed at ordinary income-tax rates. But it's better to pay the taxes out of your current paycheck than to disturb your savings. Anything taken out of that account reduces the size of your next interest payment.

Getting More from Compound Interest

To say a bank pays $5\frac{1}{4}$ percent interest is to tell only part of the story. You also have to know how *often* that interest is paid. Every time interest is credited to your account, you have more money for the next interest payment to be figured against. So the more often interest is compounded, the more money you'll earn. Interest compounded daily gives a better return than interest compounded quarterly (once every three months); quarterly interest is better than semiannually. Some banks brag that their interest is compounded "continuously," which is even more often than daily, but that's more an advertising gimmick than a substantive advantage, since the difference may amount to less than a penny a year. The next two tables show you how much faster your savings grow with more frequent compounding. I've used an initial deposit of $1,000 and an interest rate of $5\frac{1}{4}$ percent.

Of course, the more money you put into your account, the more interest you get, and the greater the dollars-and-cents reward of more frequent interest compounding.

THE HIGHER RETURNS OF MORE FREQUENT INTEREST COMPOUNDING

(assuming a single $1,000 deposit, at 5¼ percent, this table shows the dollars-and-cents difference between annual interest and more frequent compounding)

Frequency of compounding	You have this much more			
	After 1 year	After 5 years	After 10 years	After 20 years
Continuously	$2.17	$13.38	$34.73	$117.09
Daily	2.17	13.35	34.66	116.87
Quarterly	1.04	6.41	16.60	55.66
Semiannually	.69	4.23	10.95	36.67

WHAT YOU EARN AT VARIOUS RATES OF
INTEREST COMPOUNDING
(assuming a single $1,000 deposit, at 5¼ percent)

Frequency of compounding	After 1 year	After 5 years	After 10 years	After 20 years
Continuously	$1,054.67	$1,304.93	$1,702.83	$2,899.63
Daily	1,054.67	1,304.90	1,702.76	2,899.41
Quarterly	1,053.54	1,297.96	1,684.70	2,838.20
Semiannually	1,053.19	1,295.78	1,679.05	2,819.21
Annually	1,052.50	1,291.55	1,668.10	2,782.54

How to Get the Most Interest for Your Money

Under current banking practices, it is next to impossible to discover which savings institution will pay you the most for your money. You'll be close to the top if you have the highest available annual percentage rate, compounded daily or continuously, from day of deposit to day of withdrawal—but slight deviations in the way various banks do their accounting will make a difference in the actual number of dollars paid. There are more than fifty ways of computing interest now in use in the banking community. Several years ago a study by Kansas State University found that banks offering the same interest rate, and compounding at the same frequency, could vary as much as 171 percent in the amount of interest paid on a sample account.

What's needed is a Truth in Savings Act to parallel the Truth in Lending Act. Congress has had such a bill before it for several years, but at this writing there is no sign that it will be passed anytime soon. The bill would require savings institutions to tell consumers the true annual rate they're getting on their money, and how that rate is applied. It would insist that banks disclose, in lucid language, all the little ways in which interest might be gained or lost. And finally, it would set better disclosure standards for advertising. In another study, Kansas State University found that only 23 percent of savings-institution advertising disclosed the true annual yield on savings, and only 19 percent revealed what portion of your savings actually earns interest.

Since we are without a Truth in Savings Act, here are some guidelines that will get you close to the top interest available:

1. The passbook rate is the easiest thing to check. You're usually throwing money away when you save at a commercial bank at 5 percent rather than a savings bank or savings and loan association at $5\frac{1}{4}$ percent, or a credit union at perhaps 6 or 7 percent. Possible exception: If your savings account entitles you to a free checking account at the commercial bank, you might save more on checks than you lose on interest.

2. The more often interest is compounded, the more money you make. Daily compounding pays more than quarterly, which pays more than semiannually.

3. If the bank you're considering doesn't advertise its savings rate or frequency of compounding, make sure you compare it with other savings institutions in the area. It might well be paying less than the competition.

4. Ask the bank for the *annual percentage yield* (APY) on your savings. The APY is the actual number of dollars per $100 that your money will earn if it is left on deposit for a year. It encompasses not only passbook rates and frequency of compounding but also certain technical details like how many days the bank counts in a year. (Some banks use 360 days, others use 365; for reasons only an actuary would believe, 360 is more favorable.) The APY is the best number to use when comparing one savings institution against another. In general, the higher the APY, the better the deal. For example, below you can see how more frequent compounding increases APY:

$5\frac{1}{4}$ percent, compounded	Annual percentage yield
Daily	5.47%
Quarterly	5.35
Semiannually	5.32
Annually	5.25

5. A key thing to check, which won't be disclosed by comparing APYs, is how much of your money actually earns interest. You might think that every dollar there is hard at work, but that is true only where interest is paid from day of deposit to day of withdrawal. Under other methods of calculation, part of your money won't be earning anything. For example, many banks pay interest only on the *lowest balance* you have in the account. That means that if you started out the quarter with $500, drew the account down to $100, then built it up to $500 again, interest would be paid as if you had kept only $100 in the account for the entire period. Another method unfavorable to a person with an active account is *FIFO* ("first in, first out," which assumes that any money you withdraw comes from your earliest deposits). This tends to deprive you of interest earned on deposits made early in the quarter.

The best accounts pay interest from day of deposit to day of withdrawal (not to be confused with "day of deposit to end of interest period"—a confusing phrase that could mean anything). The next most favorable is generally *LIFO* ("last in, first out," which assumes that any money you withdraw comes from your most recent deposits).

6. Find out on which days your interest payments are credited. Most of the banks that compound interest daily don't credit the money to your account until the end of the quarter. If you close the account in midquarter you lose interest, even though you're supposed to be paid from day of deposit to day of withdrawal. In some cases, a bank won't credit you with any interest at all unless you leave your money on deposit until the end of the quarter.

Techniques like this, which deprive depositors of interest, are unfair. Since the bank has had full use of your money, it should be willing to pay you for it.

If you need money before the end of the quarter but will lose a substantial interest payment on funds withdrawn early, you might take a passbook loan for a few days. You'll generally pay less for the short-term loan than you stand to lose by missing your quarterly interest.

7. Penalties and bonuses can substantially affect your rate of interest. A bank might charge a fee if you make a lot of withdrawals, or offer a bonus for leaving your account untouched. There may be "dead days" at the end of a quarter, when no interest is paid. Some banks have "grace days": Money deposited during the first ten days of the quarter may earn interest as if it had been deposited on the first day; money withdrawn during the last few days of the quarter might be treated as if it had been there until the end of the quarter. (Check whether the grace days are counted in business days or consecutive days.)

8. If the bank makes a minor mistake in crediting interest, and banks do, chances are you'll never know it. You have no way of double-checking the computations unless you know the "periodic payment rate," which is the rate they apply to each interest period. Some banks will disclose this to you and show you how to use it; others won't. The Truth in Savings bill would require disclosure.

When you ask about these details, you may find that not even the employees of the bank, S&L, or credit union have the answers right at their fingertips. But they can get them for you, so insist. Ask particularly for a list of all charges. You'll generally find that savings banks, S&Ls,

and credit unions have fewer charges and more free services than commercial banks.

All the terms and conditions of your savings account *should* be on the form you sign when you open the account, but they rarely are. A handful of states require disclosure, but there's no federal law. Do read whatever material you're given, even if the banker looks busy or assures you he has explained everything. He's paid to bring in business, and you're business; it's his job to answer your questions.

Higher Interest Rates by Mail

If you live in a rural area or small city, your local banks may pay lower interest rates than are available in big-city savings institutions. Because of this, thousands of Americans save by mail, sometimes sending their money many states away. Ask your library to help you find the names of large savings banks or S&Ls in distant cities, then inquire into their interest rates and whether they have a bank-by-mail program. You'll want to keep some of your funds in a local bank for ready cash, but it's smart to send the rest to an institution that gives you more favorable treatment.

What Type of Account?

An *individual account,* solely in your name, is all yours; no one else can make any withdrawals from it. A *joint account* is shared by two (or more) people; you both can make deposits and withdrawals irrespective of the amount each of you contributes. It's perfectly legal for one joint owner to empty the account of every nickel any time he wants, so never put money in a joint account unless you trust your coowner absolutely.

If you are the treasurer of an organization, you can open an account in the group's name with yourself the person authorized to deposit and withdraw funds. (You'll want to have another name on the signature card as well, in case you're not around when the group needs money.) You can also open a special account for another person's funds that are entrusted to your management. Ask the bank to help you make these arrangements.

Separate Savings Accounts for Husbands and Wives

Couples generally pool their funds in the interests of fairness, but that isn't always the most practical thing to do. Here are some good reasons for maintaining separate savings accounts:

1. According to federal law, all money in joint accounts is taxed in the account of the first joint owner to die, except for whatever funds the survivor can prove actually belonged to him (or her). You can often save money on estate taxes by maintaining separate accounts (for details on this, see Chapter 27, "Wills and Estate Planning").

2. If one of you is sued successfully, the court can generally reach only those funds that are in his (or her) name or in joint names. Any money in the name of the spouse is usually safe.

3. In some states joint accounts are frozen at the death of one owner, and it may be many days before the survivor gains access to the money. Your personal account can provide your family with ready funds to tide them over.

4. When wives don't work outside the home and have no funds of their own, they become entirely dependent on the fiscal generosity of their husbands. If, after many years, the marriage breaks up, the woman has absolutely nothing of her own to depend on, after all her years of housewifely labor. Depending on the husband's job and the length of the marriage, she may not even qualify for Social Security. It is only just that a wife be able to set something aside for herself every year. In a lasting marriage this becomes part of an estate plan, since by putting money in the wife's name, the husband may reduce the estate taxes his heirs have to pay. It is also recognition of a wife's important economic services. If the marriage should ever turn sour, personal funds give a previously dependent wife some immediate freedom of movement and decision making. Men labor long to secure their retirement; women should also give some thought to theirs.

Joint Accounts with Brothers, Sisters, Nephews, Friends

People who live together and share expenses may put savings as well as checking accounts into joint names. But remember that if one joint owner should die, those funds might be frozen for a while (ask your bank what the law is in your state). Also, the other joint owner may take money you didn't mean him to have. In my opinion, it's best to keep your money in your own name so that you can be sure it's there when you need it, keep jointly only what's wanted for joint household expenses.

Some people use joint accounts instead of a will. An unmarried woman, for example, may add her brother's name to her savings account to make sure he gets it at her death. But she's exposing herself to a couple of risks. First, if the brother has some financial troubles, he might help himself to money from the account and there's nothing the sister could do about it. Second, if the brother dies first and his estate is large enough to owe taxes, she'll have to prove that all the funds were hers, or else the savings account will be taxed to him. (Some people mistakenly believe that if they put their money into joint names, only one half of it will be taxed when they die. But, except for certain property owned jointly by married people, the entire sum is taxed in the estate of the first owner to die, and again when the second owner dies.)

If your objective is merely to ensure that a certain person gets your savings account at your death, consider leaving it by will rather than through the mechanism of a joint account. (See Chapter 27, "Wills and Estate Planning.")

Savings Accounts for Children

If a child is old enough to write, he can generally open an individual account in his own name. This is a splendid place to put small sums he might receive as gifts.

But larger amounts should be handled differently. Typically, you will open an account in your name *in trust for* the child. You, not the child, control all deposits and withdrawals; you can change the name of the person it is being held in trust for, or even close the account entirely. If you die, the money in the account is included in your estate, but the proceeds are passed on to the child as beneficiary.

Some people open a trust account for a child at birth, starting it off with just $5 or $10 and adding something every birthday. As the child grows older, it pleases him to know he has his own savings account (the small sum in it sounds very large to him). It gives him a start in appreciating the importance of savings.

The account also serves as a reminder to parents to give the child all the money due him. When a young child gets a gift of money on his birthday, it should go right into that bank account (rather than vanish, as it sometimes does, into the general pool of household funds).

For information on putting a large bank account into a child's name, see Chapter 27, "Wills and Estate Planning."

Passbook Savings

The everyday account you start at a bank, S&L, or credit union is known as a *passbook account.* You can normally make deposits or withdrawals whenever you want, but receive the lowest rate of interest paid on savings. The agreement you sign when you open the account may give the bank authority to delay withdrawals for thirty to ninety days, but in practice you can take anything but a very large sum immediately. In fact, if a bank or S&L ever appeared to be getting so short of funds it might have to invoke the waiting period for small amounts, it would immediately be taken over by a government agency. The intent of the regulators is never to let matters go that far.

Traditionally you received a bankbook in which every deposit was listed along with interest paid. But today banks are trying to rid themselves of the paperwork. You might instead receive a monthly statement of deposits and withdrawals. If you do your savings and checking at the same bank, a single statement might give you the status of both accounts.

If you lose your passbook, report it to the bank immediately. They'll put a freeze on your account, in case a forger tries to get at your money. You'll then be issued a new passbook under a new account number.

Paying Bills Through Passbook Savings

Some institutions let you write drafts against your savings account, which are the equivalent of checks. Or they'll write preauthorized checks for you against savings account funds. The beauty of this is that your money earns interest right up until the time the check clears, in contrast to idle money in checking accounts, which earns nothing at all. For details on these combination checking-saving plans, see Chapter 6, "Checking Accounts."

Term Accounts for High Interest

If you're willing to leave some money on deposit for a specified period of time, you'll earn more than the passbook interest rate. These arrangements are variously known as *term accounts, savings certificates,* or *certificates of deposit,* all meaning the same thing.

Some of these accounts are quite flexible: You can add money whenever you want and withdraw after giving a certain amount of notice. The amount of interest you earn on these accounts ultimately depends on how long you keep your money there.

Other types of term accounts are more rigid. You deposit a specified amount and must agree to leave it until the term is up. You can usually withdraw the interest any time you want, but if you let it accumulate in the account, the effects of compound interest will produce a large percentage return. Banks and S&Ls (and some credit unions) offer a variety of term accounts, depending on the competitiveness of the market and the institution's own needs. Here is an example of the interest offered on term accounts in 1980 by the Bowery Savings Bank in New York City:

If you put at least this much money in the bank:	For this time period:	At this rate of interest compounded daily:	You will get an annual percentage rate of:	If all the interest is left to compound in the account, your average annual return will be:
$ 500	3 months	5¾ %	6.00%	6.00%
500	1 year	6½	6.81	6.81
500	2½ years	6¾	7.08	7.47
500	4 years	7½	7.90	8.89
500	6 years	7¾	8.17	10.04
500	8 years	8	8.45	11.42

Recently, banking institutions began offering $10,000 six-month accounts and low-minimum-deposit two-and-a-half-year accounts, whose interest rates rise and fall. In high-interest periods, these certificates pay much more than the rates shown above.

Can You Break a Term Account?

There is a minimum penalty, mandated by law, for breaking a term agreement and taking your money out early. In general, you have to forfeit three to six months' worth of interest on the money you withdraw, although the bank may impose additional penalties. The law makes two exceptions: If the depositor dies and the bank allows the heirs to cash the account in early, no penalty need be levied (although some banks may charge one anyway). Penalties for early withdrawal may also be forgiven if your area is officially designated a "disaster area," because of storm, flood, and so on.

As long as you're willing to pay the penalty, you can generally break into a term account ahead of time. But not always. Whether or not you get your money depends on the policy of the institution as well as the fine print of the agreement you signed. Most S&L contracts let you take the money whenever you want it. Most bank contracts, on the other hand, say you can break the term account only with the consent of the bank. Many banks give consent readily; others do so only in a financial emergency (if you simply wanted the money to buy stocks or Treasury bills, they might not let you have it). A few banks refuse you the money unless your situation is really critical. So before you lock savings up in a term account, ask the bank what its policy is on early withdrawals. If possible, choose an institution that doesn't have a "consent" clause in the contract (which probably means you'll be choosing an S&L).

If a term account is held in joint names, one party could theoretically break the agreement. But in practice, banks and S&Ls generally require both signatures.

Don't Be Afraid of Term Accounts

Some people don't like their money "locked up" in term accounts where they can't get at it. So they keep large sums in low-interest passbook savings.

That's all right if you need your savings for day-to-day living. But if you have a regular income, and much of your savings is essentially long-term in character, it's generally a mistake not to put it to work at the highest possible interest. If you choose carefully the institution where you place the term account, you can get high interest and at the same time feel sure that the money will be available whenever you want.

When Your Term Account Matures

Make sure you tell your bank what you want done with your term account money at maturity. If they don't hear from you, one of several things can happen, depending on state law or the agreement you signed. The money might be (1) held at zero interest until you come to collect it; (2) put into an account paying passbook interest rates; (3) mailed out to you by check; (4) automatically reinvested for the same period of time and at the same interest rate (this could be troublesome if the interest rates available on new certificates were higher than the rate you get through automatic reinvestment); (5) automatically reinvested for the same period of time but at a lower interest rate (in this case, the bank is supposed to give you ample warning).

Make sure you know, before you invest in the term account, which of these things would happen if you forgot the maturity date. If you're absent-minded, you wouldn't want a certificate that automatically renews itself. The maturity date is stamped on the certificate's face. Some banks help you remember the date by sending you a note a few days in advance.

How You Can Lose
Interest Due on Savings

Say you have a savings account that you haven't touched for a long time. The bank, S&L, or credit union will dutifully credit it with interest for a few years. But in most states they'll then stop. If there continues to be no activity in the account, they'll start assessing an annual service charge of around $1. This quickly eliminates something small, such as a $5 share account in a credit union.

Your savings account could conceivably stop earning interest even if you have an active checking account with the same bank. But it usually happens when you are not otherwise a customer. (In some states interest stops only if you neglect to give the bank your current address.)

To be sure of earning interest on your savings, ask the bank what its rules are. You may have to do some business in the account every year —if only to deposit or withdraw $5. You can always return to claim an old account, but you won't be paid any interest for the years it lay dormant.

Another point: Your bank may pay no interest on savings below a certain minimum (as little as $5 or as much as $100), and the minimum can change without notice. So if you keep only a small amount in savings, make sure it's above the level that triggers interest payments.

How You Can Lose Your Savings

If you keep an old bankbook for many years but never make any deposits or withdrawals, don't expect the money to be there when you finally go back to claim it. If savings deposits remain dormant and apparently unowned for a long time, they are seized by the state. This is the *law of escheat*, which makes the state the owner of any property whose owner of record cannot be found. And it's not only savings accounts that can be escheated. So can cash balances in checking accounts (assuming they haven't been eliminated by service charges), property in safe deposit boxes, savings certificates, even property held by the bank in trust.

The number of years the property has to lie dormant runs from a minimum of five years to as many as twenty-five in some states (or for some properties). Furthermore, the bank (or S&L or credit union) has to make every attempt to reach you, through registered letters and a public notice in the newspaper. But if you don't show up, the money is claimed for the state treasury.

Nevertheless, all is not lost. If you show up many years later with proof of ownership in hand, the state will give you the money back (although not with interest).

There's one more way you can lose savings. If you owe the bank money and haven't paid, it can, under the "right of set-off," dip into your funds to satisfy the debt. They will raid any account—individual, joint, or trust—to satisfy either your own loan or any loan you may have cosigned.

Some states put minor limits on which accounts can be dipped into for what. Federal law prohibits banks from seizing money to satisfy a disputed bank card bill. But the general right of set-off applies everywhere. So if you have a bank debt that's in dispute, or because of hardship know you're going to have trouble paying on time, you'd be smart to move your savings to another bank.

When to Use Savings

A savings account isn't a museum where money is kept just to be admired. Sums come out for one purpose or another—for vacations, for new furniture, for a mutual-fund investment, for a nice painting, for whatever special things your family wants. Some of these things you might have been able to buy on the installment plan, without dipping into savings. But because of the installment interest due, you'd wind up paying a lot more for them (which means giving up other spending). Also, you'd be deeper in debt. When you're young, savings will most likely be put toward the big purchases every growing family needs. When you're older, you'll start putting more aside for retirement. But as long as money is going into savings on a regular schedule, you don't have to worry about occasionally taking some out.

When to Stop Saving

When you're young, you have to learn how to put money aside; when you're old, you have to learn how to stop. Many older people live on the edge of poverty because they can't get out of the habit of saving or because they're afraid to spend the money they have so carefully accumulated. Past a certain age, you should quit saving and start spending —dipping into capital at a carefully calculated rate so as to give yourself the decent retirement you've been accumulating money for all those years. You'll find some guidelines on setting up your own annuity in Chapter 29, "Retirement Planning."

Chapter Six

CHECKING ACCOUNTS

If a man is wise, he gets rich, an' if he gets rich, he gets foolish, or his wife does. That's what keeps the money movin' around.

FINLEY PETER DUNNE

No other banking service is undergoing such rapid change as the conventional checking account. Since 1933 checking accounts have—by law—paid depositors no interest. In fact, consumers have been content to pay the bank a service charge just to keep their accounts in order. But in today's strenuous competition for depositors' dollars, commercial bankers have sharply cut—sometimes to zero—the overt cost of a checking account. For their part, savings and loan institutions and savings banks have been making it possible to use interest-bearing savings accounts to pay bills. Federal legislation is sure to hasten these trends. So take this chapter not only as a guide to the kinds of checking-account services currently available, but also as a blueprint of things to come.

Who Needs a Checking Account?

If you'd write only five or six checks a month, a checking account generally isn't worth it. Keep your money in a savings institution that charges little or nothing for money orders and that will automatically pay certain bills for you every month.

But in most places savings institutions have not yet made it convenient to pay a large number of bills through savings accounts (although where this option is available, it's smart to use it—see page 69). Having a checking account is far more efficient than running to the bank for money orders, and eliminates the need for keeping a lot of cash around the house. Checks can be safely sent by mail; they provide an instant draw on your ready money; a canceled check is proof of payment; and check stubs give you a running record of household expenses.

What a Checking Account Costs

You generally pay one of two ways: (1) The bank charges a fee for each check you write (around 10 to 15 cents); or (2) you have to keep a minimum balance of $100 to $500 in the account. In either case, the bank may also levy a service charge of around $1 every month. Where there's no service charge, the bank account may appear free—but it's not, as long as a minimum balance is required. After all, if you didn't have to keep that money in your checking account, it could be in a savings account earning interest.

Big banks usually demand larger minimum balances than small banks do, which generally makes the smaller banks a better buy. But don't accept a minimum-balance account at *any* bank if you can't stay above the minimum. Falling below, even for a day, could cost you a penalty of as much as $4 or $5. Generally speaking, minimum-balance accounts are cheaper for people who write a lot of checks, and 10-cents-a-check accounts are cheaper for people who write very few.

But before you accept any charge at all—even in the form of a minimum balance—look around your town for a bank that offers checking accounts free. In 1976, according to the American Bankers Association, 36 percent of the nation's banks offered free checking to at least one segment of the community—students, older people, servicemen, and so forth. And another 36 percent provided free, no-minimum-balance checking to all comers. Free checking is most likely to exist in the big cities, where lots of banks compete for deposits. (Typically, the smaller banks in big cities offer free checking first.) But some smaller cities have the service as well.

If there's no free checking, you may at least find a bank that levies no service fee, and sets so low a minimum balance that most depositors can meet it easily. For example, the requirement might be only that your account *average* a minimum of $100 over the month. By depositing $500 or $600 at the start of the month and not writing checks on it until a couple of weeks have passed, you'd probably qualify, even if by the end of the month your account reached zero. For most people, this kind of arrangement results in free checking.

Some banks provide free checking if you open a savings account there with a certain minimum balance. Since savings accounts at commercial banks pay less than at savings institutions, you're losing something on interest. However, depending on the number of checks you write, what you lose in interest you might more than gain by not having to pay 10 cents a check. Whether an offer like this is worth it depends on (1) the checking-account options offered at other banks in town, and (2) what you otherwise have to pay to keep a checking account.

Banks generally provide plain checkbooks free; if you want something nicer, you'll have to pay for it. It may also cost something to have your name and address printed on the checks. That's done mainly for the convenience of your creditors, but the imprint sometimes helps get a check cashed in a place where you're not known. It's also useful to buy checks that have already been sequentially numbered in case you forget to do it yourself.

You can cash checks—your own or those given you by other people —at the bank branch where you keep your account. If your bank has several branches, ask for a card that will let you cash checks in any one of them. Where cards aren't issued, get your signature on file in any branch you think you might want to use. Having a signature card saves you from having to get your checks initialed by an officer of a distant branch before you can cash them there.

Ask for a list of all the service charges the bank can impose. Typically, there are fees for maintaining the account, stopping a check, bouncing a check, overdrawing your account, and drawing it below the minimum balance. The bank might also charge for servicing an inactive account or providing duplicate bank statements. Reference to all these fees should be on the back of the form you sign when you open an account, but the bank may not bother to give you a copy unless you request it. Some people think it's not worth reading through all those minor terms and conditions, but I disagree. You'll never know when you've been overcharged if you can't tell what the proper charge should have been.

Package Plans

Some banks offer you a smorgasbord of services for a flat fee of $2 to $4 a month. The package may include a "free" safe deposit box, "free" checking accounts, "free" traveler's checks, and preferential loan rates. But it's not "free" if you're paying a package fee of $12 to $48 a year. If you actually use all those services, the group rate may indeed be cheaper than paying for everything individually. But if the package includes a lot of things you really don't need, the deal is expensive. Furthermore, you may be able to get exactly the same services at a smaller bank for even less than the big bank's package price.

Idle Balances in Checking Accounts

On the average, people keep a balance of $800 or more in their checking accounts. Some of that, of course, will go for current bills and some represents the minimum deposit required by the bank. But all too often, people let extra cash build up in a checking account where it doesn't do them one whit of good. At present, money left in checking accounts earns no interest. So you're losing out on any dollars kept there unnecessarily. Solution: Transfer all idle balances from checking into savings. Or better yet, at the start of each pay period deposit part of your earnings to checking and the rest to savings, withdrawing from savings as necessary to meet special bills. Some banks will let you transfer cash from savings to checking with a simple telephone call. By handling your money this way, you could pick up an extra $200 to $300 a year in interest, and maybe more.

"Checking Accounts" That Earn Interest

The law prevents banks from paying interest on checking accounts. But a number of institutions have dreamed up checking-account substitutes that get around that law.

• In New York, New Jersey, and the six New England states banks and savings and loan associations may offer *negotiable orders of withdrawal,* or *NOW accounts;* in 1981 they'll be available in all states. A withdrawal order is just like a check, except that you write it against a savings account rather than a checking account. Your money earns interest up to the very day the order clears (although the interest rate may be lower than on regular savings accounts). NOW accounts would have spread more rapidly to other states had not the U.S. government called a temporary halt a couple of years ago, fearing their effect on the traditional banking system. But other states have found other ways.
• A growing number of credit unions offer *share draft accounts,* which are similar to NOW accounts. You pay your bills by writing drafts

against a credit union savings account; your money earns interest until the drafts clear.

• Some savings and loan associations will write checks against your savings account and mail them to your creditors free of charge. This service is generally available only for those monthly or quarterly payments that go out on a fixed day and are the same amount each time. S&Ls used to be limited to paying household-related expenses, but now any creditor qualifies. Again, your money earns interest until the checks clear.

• A few commercial banks offer customers a free line of credit against their savings accounts. You write checks against the credit line and cover with your savings when the check is presented for payment. This arrangement may sound elaborate, but in practice it's perfectly simple. And it has the same result as all the other checking-account substitutes: Your money earns interest from the day of deposit until the day the checks clear. (Should you overwrite your savings account, however, there will be a finance charge.) If a local bank offers this service, it will be advertised occasionally in the newspaper.

• Some banks and S&Ls will transfer funds for you from checking to savings in response to telephoned instructions, rather than requiring you to do it in person. This makes it more convenient to keep money in interest-bearing savings and transfer it to a checking account only when necessary to pay bills.

• Commercial banks may transfer funds from savings to checking accounts automatically in order to cover a check that would otherwise bounce. This arrangement is called a "preauthorized automatic transfer," or PAT, account. You could write a check on a zero balance PAT account, knowing that the bank would pay with funds withdrawn from interest-bearing savings. Some banks welcome small PAT accounts; others require large savings balances and charge stiff fees.

• Systems for transferring money electronically are making it even easier for savings institutions to offer convenient payment systems. Some banks and S&Ls have computer terminals in stores, permitting people to pay for their purchases with instant withdrawals from savings accounts. In other places customers can make both deposits and withdrawals at store-based computer terminals. All payments are automatic. You don't have to write a check or negotiable order of withdrawal or even make a telephone call. And your money earns interest right up to the moment the transfer is made.

If any of these arrangements are available in your area, they will often be advertised in the bank window. By all means take advantage of any plan that lets you earn more interest on your money.

Writing Checks

Checks can be drawn on anything. If you're ever really stuck for cash, but have plenty of identification, you might find someone who'll take a check written on a plain piece of paper. Just write "Pay to the order of ————," date it, sign it, write the amount in words as well as numbers, and add the name and address of your bank. There are stories of banks cashing checks written on women's backs and men's underwear (what do you suppose happened to the canceled checks?).

But this kind of emergency rarely happens. Normally you'll be using a book of checks with stubs at the side for recording your transactions. ALWAYS fill in the stub before writing the check, so you won't forget it. When stubs are blank, you don't know how much money you have left and might overdraw your account. If you're giving a check to someone you may not deal with again, include his address on the stub, so you can find him if you have to. Don't forget to date the stub; if something happens to the check, it might be important to know when you wrote it. And always note the check's purpose, in case some tax, legal, or budget questions should arise.

When you fill in the amount of the check, use ink. A check written in pencil is legal but is an open invitation for someone to up the amount. Start writing from the left-hand edge and draw a line through whatever space you don't use. This makes it hard for a forger to alter the amount. If you don't do this and the check is changed, the bank may not accept liability, on the ground that it was your carelessness that permitted the crime. If you change your mind about a check, write "void" across the face before tearing it up and throwing it away. Otherwise, someone might be tempted to paste it back together and cash it. Also write "void" on your check stub, so you won't forget what happened to the check.

If you have to write a check for less than a dollar, here's how to make sure the teller doesn't misinterpret it: Write, say, "75 cents" where the numerals go and circle it; then write on the line beneath "only seventy-five cents." If there's ever a discrepancy between the amount of the check as given in numerals and as written out, the written line is considered the legal one, although the bank is more likely to refuse to pay until the discrepancy is straightened out.

Sign your name exactly as it appears on the card you signed when you opened the account, or the bank might not cash it. If the teller doesn't know you, he should check your signature against the card, to make sure everything is okay.

Don't alter a check once it's written; if you must make a change, tear it up and start over. A bank might cash such a check if you initialed the change, but it shouldn't. If it's that easy, other people could alter it, too.

Never sign a blank check if you can avoid it. The person you give it to may be perfectly honest, but if he loses it, the finder could fill in any amount. And don't make out checks to "cash." Anyone who comes across such a check can endorse it and cash it in. If you need money, make the check out to yourself and don't endorse it until it's time to cash it.

Finally, never lend or borrow checks unless you *cut out* the account number. Some people just black out the numbers and write in their own. But account numbers are printed in magnetic ink; the computer will pick it up right through the ink you used to black it out, and will charge the check against the original owner's account.

How Long Does It Take a Check to Clear?

Checks between major cities and major banks in town can generally clear overnight. If the check is on a distant bank in a small town, it may take up to six days. Big-city banks generally clear more rapidly than country banks. Savings banks and savings and loan associations may take a day or two longer than commercial banks.

Some banks won't credit your account with a check you deposit until it actually clears. Some will credit after a certain number of days, as long as there's enough money in your account to cover the check if it bounces. Paychecks from leading employers in town can generally be cashed immediately.

If you deposit several checks at once, you're normally credited with each check as it clears. But some banks and S&Ls won't credit any of the deposit until every single check on the deposit slip comes through. If your bank follows this practice, you should deposit checks on distant banks separately from those on local banks, so your local checks won't be held up.

On checks deposited to savings accounts, some banks credit interest from day of deposit, others from the day the check clears.

It may take three weeks or more for a bad check to bounce if it was written on a distant bank. That's because the banking system's technology is geared toward putting checks through the system for payment, not toward returning them.

Cash and checks put into an automatic deposit machine should be processed the next day. But if you put the money in on Friday, the cash may not reach your account until the following Tuesday. Keep these payment lags in mind if you ever write a check when you have no funds in the bank, intending to cover the check with a deposit the next day.

Making Deposits

Banks normally send you, free of charge, deposit slips imprinted with your account number. Since they're computer-readable, you can be assured that the deposit will be credited to your account with all possible speed. If you run out, banks also have slips available where the account number can be filled in by hand. In either case, be sure you keep the copy given you by the teller. If something goes wrong, it's your only record that a deposit was made. After you've checked your monthly bank statement and found out that all the deposits have been properly credited, throw the slips away.

Balancing Your Checkbook

This is a punishment visited upon us for our sins. But an inexpensive hand calculator is a great help in the enterprise.

When your monthly bank statement arrives, check it immediately for forgeries (see page 78). Then balance it within the week. By letting it languish you're also letting any errors persist in your checkbook, perhaps to the point where a check will bounce. Some banks print a warning on their statements that they won't be liable for banking errors brought to their attention after thirty days have elapsed, but that's more to scare you into reconciling the balance than anything else. State law governs how long the bank is liable for errors. It could be the short period stated by the bank, but it might also be several years.

The point to balancing a checkbook is to make sure that you and the bank agree on how much money you have left in your account. If all the check stubs are properly filled in, this should be a routine thirty-minute chore. Put all your canceled checks in numerical order and check them off both on the bank statement and the check stubs, making sure the amounts agree. Then compare the bank's record of deposits with your deposit slips. Deduct any service fees shown on the statement from the balance in your checkbook.

Bank statements generally have a form on the back for you to follow when you reconcile your checkbook. Start with the amount of money the bank says you have, deduct any checks you've written that have not yet cleared, and add any new deposits not yet shown on the statement. The final amount should equal the sum you show in your checkbook. Here's a form to follow:

HOW TO RECONCILE YOUR CHECKBOOK

Bank statement balance	_____	Your checkbook balance	_____
Plus new deposits	_____	Minus current bank service charge	_____
Minus checks still outstanding	_____		
Adjusted balance	_____ **equals**	New balance	_____

If you write a lot of checks, you might find it a nuisance to balance the checkbook right up to the present because there are so many outstanding checks. It works just as well if you reconcile the statement as of the date of the last check canceled by the bank.

Keeping Track of a Joint Account

A husband and wife (or any other people living together) usually keep a joint account for paying bills. One or both of them contribute to it, and they both write checks against it. This is much more convenient than having the household checking account in the name of just one person, who may not always be home to sign checks when needed.

But it's sometimes a mess when it comes to keeping the checkbook in balance. With two people taking checks for various purposes, check stubs don't always get filled in, nor do deposits always get recorded. There's no perfect system for avoiding this. But your best bet is to keep the checkbook in a central place, put all deposit slips inside the cover, and initial the stub when you take a blank check (so you'll know whose responsibility it was to record the amount).

If each person wants his own checkbook, here's how to handle it: Make the desk checkbook the master book, and give the husband or wife a secondary checkbook. At the start of the month, deduct a sum from the master book and enter it into the secondary checkbook. Say the amount is $300 and the secondary checkbook is the wife's. She writes checks against that $300 until it's gone, then returns to the master book for a second helping. That way, the husband (who is using the other checkbook) always knows how much money is left for his own checks. Without a system like this, neither of you can be sure whether there's enough in the joint account to cover the check you're currently writing.

Joint Accounts with Brothers, Sisters, Nephews, Friends

Whenever two or more people live together and share expenses, a joint checking account is a great convenience. But there are these drawbacks:

1. The other joint owner has a perfect right to clean out the account and leave.

2. If one joint owner dies, the account might be temporarily sealed (although many states allow the survivor access to at least some of the funds).

3. If estate taxes are owed, the entire sum will be taxed in the estate of the first joint owner to die, except for whatever money the survivor can prove he or she personally contributed to the account.

Because of these problems, it's generally wise to keep the bulk of your money in separate names, and put into the joint account only the amount needed to cover household expenses. If one of you dies, the other should take great care not to add anything further to that account until it's cleared for use.

When a Wife Needs a Personal Checking Account

When a wife has a substantial amount of property of her own, it's a good idea for her to pay the expenses—and collect any income—through her own personal checking account. This makes it perfectly clear to the estate tax collectors that the property is hers and has been maintained with her own money. Were there any doubt, the IRS might try to tax it in her husband's estate.

A woman who works might want to deposit her paycheck in a personal account, use it to pay her own bills, and transfer the rest to a joint account for household expenses. A woman who doesn't work outside the home may need occasional gifts from her husband, paid into her checking account, in order to meet her personal and property expenses.

If she owns only a small amount of property—for example, the insurance policy on her husband's life—the extra checking account generally isn't worth it. However, she should still pay the expenses with her own funds—perhaps with a check drawn on her savings account in a savings and loan. For more on this subject, see Chapter 27, "Wills and Estate Planning."

Endorsing a Check

A check is a useless piece of paper until the person it's made out to signs it on the back, or *endorses* it. Then it becomes as good as money and could be cashed by anyone who happened upon it. For this reason, don't endorse a check made out to you until you're ready to cash it. If you have to send an endorsed check through the mail, put instructions on the back to prevent it from being used for any purpose other than the one you intended. For example, when you mail your paycheck to the bank, write on the back "for deposit only" (in this case, you usually don't even have to sign your name). Or when giving an endorsed check to a particular individual, write "pay to the order of [the individual's name]." When accepting an endorsed check from someone else, ask him to write "pay to the order of [your name]" on the back, so if you should lose it, neither of you will be out the money. If your name is forged to such a check, the bank would have to make good (see "Forgeries," page 78).

An endorsement, incidentally, carries quite a bit of legal meaning that check users rarely think about. By signing a check, you are, in effect, certifying that the check is genuine, that you have valid possession of it, and that you can assign payment of the check to someone else. This is why anyone who transfers a check is usually asked to sign his name to it, even if it means a whole line of signatures down the back. The endorsement is a guarantee that you will pay if the person who originally issued the check defaults. For example, if I were to give you a check and you endorsed it and cashed it at a local store, and I then stopped the check, you would be responsible to the storekeeper for the money. You, however, could collect from me—if you could find me. If I had skipped town, you'd be out of luck. That's why it is unwise to accept or endorse strangers' checks.

When you receive a check, cash it immediately. If something's wrong with it, you'll get a jump on recovering your loss. And it gives the person who issued the check less time to change his mind. Technically, a check may be good for years—but in practice, banks may not cash checks after six months or a year have elapsed unless you can show that the check-writer still means for you to have the money.

Always endorse a check exactly the way it's made out. If your name is spelled wrong, endorse it that way, then endorse it again with the proper spelling.

Bouncing a Check

When you write a check and haven't the funds to cover, a couple of things can happen. Commonly, the check is refused, the person you gave it to is sore, you're embarrassed, and the bank levies a $3 to $10 fee on your account in recompense for their trouble in turning it down. You hustle down to the bank and deposit more money, then tell the person who holds the check to resubmit it for payment.

But not all banks are this stonehearted about overdrawn accounts. If you've done business there for a long time, never bounced a check before, and this check is for only a small amount over what you have in your account, they might go ahead and cover it. You'll still pay a fee for your error, but you're saved the embarrassment. Other banks will telephone you when a rubber check arrives and pay it on your promise to get right down there with some money.

In my opinion, this is the way all banks should behave. Considering the money they make on you, they shouldn't embarrass you because of a small error. When you first open your account, ask for the courtesy of being called in situations like this; if the bank bounces a check anyway, close your account and tell the manager why. There are plenty of other banks willing to call a good customer when he's overdrawn, and those are the ones you should deal with. Small banks, or small branches of big banks, are apt to be more cooperative in this regard than big banks. Of course, you can't expect this courtesy if you're always overdrawn.

Many banks sell an "overdraft" service that automatically triggers a loan if you should happen to overdraw your account. That's fine if you want a line of credit (see Chapter 7, "Where to Borrow Money"), but it's a costly and improper response to a rare bounced check.

Postdating a Check

Sometimes you might want to pay someone as an expression of good intent, even though you haven't the funds on hand. You give him a postdated check—that is, a check dated sometime in the future when you expect to be getting some money. This is generally not a good idea. Even though you tell him the check can't be cashed right away, someone else in his home or office might present it for payment. The teller should notice the date and refuse to accept it. But if he doesn't, the bank will bounce it, levying the usual rubber-check charge. When you point out the error, the fee should be rescinded, but the whole thing becomes an awful nuisance.

Stopping a Check

If you change your mind about a check you've just issued, you can tell the bank not to make payment. The law obliges it to stop payment, provided you've notified it within a reasonable period of time. Should the check accidentally get through, causing you a loss, the bank has to make good.

But it's important that you get the stop-check order filed properly, and within enough time for the bank to act. In most states you can issue the order over the telephone, to be followed up with authorization in writing. But some places accept only written orders. An oral order is generally good for fourteen days and a written one for six months, after which it must be renewed. The fee for stopping a check is around $1 to $5.

There are some situations where a bank doesn't have to make good on a check it neglects to stop. This occurs if it appears that you might profit on the transaction. For example, you might buy some merchandise, pay by check, take the goods home, and then file a stop-payment order. If the bank accidentally lets the check through, it is not required to make good on the payment unless you first take the merchandise back. To collect on a check that should have been stopped but wasn't, you have to prove that, because of the bank's failure to act, you suffered a loss. If you've kept the merchandise, there's generally no loss.

Check Theft

Don't carry your checkbook around with you. It's best to take just one or two checks as needed (and don't keep them in your wallet). All a thief needs is some blank checks and an example of your signature to start pilfering your account. If any of your checks are ever stolen, notify the bank immediately. They'll freeze your account (cashing only the outstanding checks you list for them) and start you out fresh with a new account number. If a forger should write a check on your frozen account and it gets through, the bank is responsible for the payment, not you.

If checks made out to you are being pilfered from your mailbox, try to arrange to have them sent directly to your bank. Many employers will do this with paychecks or pension checks, as will some welfare departments. Social Security and the Veterans Administration will also make payments directly to your bank account.

Forgeries

Check your bank statement just as soon as it comes in, even if you don't have time to balance it right away. If any of the checks are forgeries, call the bank immediately. The bank is generally liable for forgeries cashed on your account up until fourteen days after they've mailed your bank statement. If, by then, you have not told them that someone is playing hob with your signature, you yourself shoulder the loss from any further checks forged by the same person. If you wait for more than a year before telling the bank about the check forgeries, you may not even receive any payment for the first check. (*Note*: You have three years to demand restitution for a forged *endorsement,* as opposed to a forged check.)

You can reduce the possibility of forgery by (1) keeping your checkbook in a safe place—not in your purse, briefcase, or the glove compartment of your car; (2) writing "void" across any rejected checks; (3) ripping voided checks into small pieces before throwing them away, so no one can get samples of your signature and checking-account number out of a wastebasket; (4) leaving no spaces in the check that would tempt someone to change the amount; (5) not sending an endorsed check through the mail, or carrying one around with you, unless the endorsement specifies who can cash it (see "Endorsing a Check," page

75); (6) never signing a blank check; (7) writing your name legibly (an "executive scrawl" is easier to forge than a signature with all the letters clearly formed).

Other Ways to Transfer Money

You should use a *certified check* when the person you're paying wants a guarantee that the check will be good. The bank certifies that you have the money by withdrawing it from your account at the time it gives you the check. A similar instrument, which can be used by people who have no checking accounts, is the *cashier's check;* in this case you give the money to the bank and it draws a check on its own account, made out to the person you plan to pay. You generally pay around 50 cents to $1 for either kind of check. Once you've delivered a certified check or cashier's check to the recipient, it's difficult to stop payment. However, if you change your mind about delivering it, the bank will redeem it.

Banks, savings and loan associations, money order companies, and the post office also issue *money orders,* payable to specific people. When buying a money order, you have to pay the full amount plus a small fee. (At the post office, money orders up to $10 cost 25 cents; to $50, 35 cents; and to $300, 40 cents.) If you ever have to transmit cash in a hurry, you can wire it by Western Union or, if you're a cardholder, by American Express. You pay the clerk the amount you want to send plus a fee, and he'll wire the office at the other end to give the cash to a specified recipient. Western Union will also let you wire money by phone and charge it to your Master Charge card.

Keep the receipts you get for money orders, cashier's checks, and Western Union wires. They're your only proof of payment and should be filed as if they were canceled checks.

The Checkless Society—Do We Really Want It?

Bankers rhapsodize about the checkless society they see ahead, when most transactions will be electronic and instantaneous, wiping out checks and money orders as well as long waits for payment. But before you cheer that great day on, consider what you may have to give up. If most purchases are covered with automatic deductions from your checking or savings account, you'll lose control over which bills you want to pay when. It will be like paying for everything in cash. On the one hand, this imposes a greater discipline on your spending, which is probably a good thing. But on the other, it eliminates the flexibility that any family needs in order to accommodate itself to sudden and unforeseen expenses.

Unless the consumer can get some think-it-over time built into the computer, he will lose his leverage in many transactions. Some examples follow:

1. Automatic payment will make it impossible to get a merchant to replace a shoddy product by the simple and effective method of refusing to pay.

2. It might make it more of a struggle to get a refund, since the person who holds the cash is usually in charge in any bargaining situation.

3. If you've been had by a salesman, you won't be able to stop the payment.

4. An institution might not lend you money unless you give it the right to deduct payment from your checking account any time it's ten days overdue. If mail delays the payment, they might embarrass you by moving in on your checking account—charging, of course, an extra fee for doing so.

Bankers are beginning to realize that they must build some consumer and privacy protection into the system and are experimenting with various approaches. But until they can promise you flexibility in making payments, you'd do well to approach this marvel warily.

Chapter Seven

WHERE TO BORROW MONEY

Let us all be happy and live within our means, even
if we have to borrow money to do it.

ARTEMUS WARD

Everybody does it, whether it's for something big, like a house, or
something small, like a television set. When there's a need and you lack
the cash, you look around for someone willing to make you a loan.

Borrowing money adds a lot to the price of what you buy. For example, take a $600 stereo set. If you pay for it in twelve installments at 18
percent a year, you'll owe around $55 a month, for a final cost of $660.
On the other hand, if you put $55 a month into a 5¼ percent savings
account compounded daily, you'd have to deposit only $586 of your
own money to achieve $600. You pay $74 extra by buying on time
instead of saving up and paying cash. That's $74 just to have the set right
now—$74 that could have been spent on something else.

There's nothing wrong with borrowing money, provided that you can
afford the price. Borrowing gets you things that would otherwise take
years to save for—such as a house, a car, furniture, appliances, and
college tuition. In some cases, borrowing may not increase your cash
outlay: For example, if you've been paying $500 a month in rent, you
might get a home mortgage for the same monthly amount. Being able
to borrow is also a great help in financial emergencies.

But beyond these expensive necessities lie all the little luxuries that
don't necessarily require borrowed money. Here's where you make
basic choices about how you're going to live.

81

If you borrow because you don't have the discipline to save . . . if you borrow because you don't want to wait for a year . . . if you borrow because you can't resist it . . . then you're CHOOSING to give money to the bank or finance company that you could otherwise spend on yourself. It often seems as if borrowing improves your standard of living, because without it you'd own fewer things. But although you do get some luxuries earlier than you otherwise would have had them, borrowing, in the long run, *diminishes* your standard of living, because of all the money you waste on interest payments. If you could save in advance for the things you want rather than buy them on the installment plan, you might increase your purchasing power by 15 percent or more.

Who Has the Lowest Interest Rates?

Most people assume that among any given group of lenders, the interest rate is about the same—so they don't bother to shop around for the best deal. In fact, rates vary widely. You could save yourself two to six percentage points just by walking into the right bank.

The only way to compare interest charges is by looking at the *annual percentage rate* (APR) mandated by the Truth in Lending Act. All lenders are supposed to figure APR the same way, so you can get an honest fix on who charges less for the particular loan you want. Some lenders, however, still talk in terms of the old "add-on" and "discount" methods of computing interest, which make it appear as if you're paying much less for the money than is actually the case. A 6-percent add-on rate, for example, actually comes to 10.9 percent the first year. And 6 percent discounted is really 11.58 percent. If you're quoted a rate that's far below the rates of competing institutions, it's probably a misleading price. Ask the lender whether that's the true annual percentage rate as required by law, and check his response on the truth-in-lending form, which must be filled in for each loan.

Ways to Lower Your Interest Rate

1. Pick the right type of lender. Credit unions often charge less for loans than banks and savings and loan associations do; smaller banks and S&Ls often charge less than their larger cousins (sometimes a lot less); and savings banks and S&Ls have better terms on some loans than do commercial banks. These are not hard and fast rules, but they are true often enough to be worth checking out when you have to borrow money.

2. Discriminate among lenders. Interest rates vary more than most borrowers realize. The rate differential between the most and least expensive bank in your area may be as much as two to six percentage points. So just because Bank A tells you that an auto loan will cost 14 percent, don't assume that Bank B charges the same amount. Furthermore, just because Bank A has the highest auto-loan rate, don't assume that all its loans are similarly expensive. It might have a low rate on vacation loans.

3. Bargain if you can. An interest rate is not graven on stone. If your bank charges more than the bank across the street for the same loan, tell the lending officer that you're taking your business over there. He may decide to lower the rate to keep you as a customer, especially if you're planning on moving both your checking and savings accounts to the other bank.

4. Pay off the loan in as short a period as possible. Low monthly payments are always attractive because it makes the loan seem less of a burden. But the longer it takes to repay, the more money you're giving up in interest. For example, a two-year $3,000 auto loan at 14 percent will cost you a total of $671 in interest. If you stretch the same loan out over four years, you'll pay interest charges of $907.

5. Where you can, offer security for the loan, such as stocks, mutual-fund shares, or anything else you have of value. You can often get a lower rate on a secured loan than on a loan obtained solely on the basis of your signature.

6. Be willing to change your savings and checking accounts to a new bank if that's the price of a lower rate.

7. If you're carrying a lot of revolving charge-account bills at 18 percent, ask your credit union, bank, or S&L about a loan that will clean them all up. Assuming you're a good credit risk, you might be able to get a debt consolidation loan at less than 18 percent.

8. Ask if a larger down payment would qualify you for a lower interest rate (it often does).

Types of Loans

When you have a good, productive reason to borrow, aren't over-burdened with other debt, and are blessed with a steady paycheck, you should be able to get money on the most favorable terms in town. Below are the types of loans available from the various lending institutions. *Note*: You may be able to bargain the interest rate down—something many consumers do not realize, and therefore do not try to do.

Unsecured Personal Loans

This is money granted you on the strength of your credit references, the regularity of your paycheck, the purpose for which the money is intended, your good character, and, in tight money times, whether you're a steady customer of the lender. You don't have to pledge any specific property as security for the loan (although the laws may permit a bank, for example, to seize without notice a savings account or other property from a borrower who defaults). If you don't repay, the lender will move against you according to state law and his rights as outlined in the loan agreement. The most you can borrow on an unsecured loan is a few thousand dollars. The interest rate is toward the *higher* end of the consumer loan range.

Secured Personal Loans

Here you give the lender the right to seize a specific piece of property (called *collateral*) if you don't pay. Typically, loans are secured by such collateral as stocks, bonds, a savings account, or a car; lacking those, you're generally asked to put your house or personal property on the line—something to be avoided if at all possible. The lender holds your savings passbook or stock certificates (so you can't dispose of them), usually releasing the collateral to you gradually as the loan is paid off. Secured loans can generally be larger than unsecured loans; the interest rate may be a little lower, but not always.

Anything that is particularly valuable can be turned into cash in a pinch. You can borrow money against furs, jewelry, paintings, antique furniture, or a coin or stamp collection. A bank may accept some of these items as security, depending on their worth; if not, a small loan company usually will. However, they'll demand custody of things like jewelry and paintings, as a precaution against your selling them to someone else.

Both secured and unsecured loans may be paid off in one of two ways: (1) in regular monthly installments, with a late charge of 5 percent or so assessed for any missed payment; (2) all at once, at the end of the lending period—although the interest will probably have to be paid monthly or quarterly. In the second case the loan may be renewable two or three times, depending on circumstances. But in general, personal loans run for no longer than three or four years. An exception is the loan secured by a savings account: As long as the account is held by the bank, you'll generally be able to keep the loan as long as you want, subject only to making regular interest payments.

Passbook Loans

These loans, secured by your savings account, are worth special mention. Because you borrow at a rate just a few points higher than what your savings earn—perhaps two or three percentage points at savings institutions and five or six percentage points at commercial banks—that low differential is sometimes quoted as your "true" interest rate. That's not so. The money earned on savings is irrelevant to the cost of the loan. One might as well say that since you have a savings account, the "true" cost of an auto loan is the difference between the loan rate and your savings account rate. Passbook loans often have lower interest rates than other types of secured loans—but don't count the interest earned on your savings account in figuring the true interest cost.

Also consider this: If you have savings, why borrow at all? One of the reasons for having a savings account is to make borrowing unnecessary. You're generally better off withdrawing the money you need from savings, and then replacing it on the same schedule as you would have repaid a loan. *Exception:* If your savings account arises from a big one-time payment, such as an inheritance, and you've never been able to add to it on a regular basis, you're probably right to take a passbook loan. It's a mistake to eliminate savings if you *know* you won't replace them. But this is an extravagant way to live. Interest payments made to the bank for unnecessary loans deprive you of funds you could otherwise spend on yourself.

Borrowing Against a Future Payment

Many people have money coming to them that could be converted into cash right now. For example, if you're owed a payment for some work you've completed and have a signed paper to prove it, a bank may lend you money against that paper. If you've referred business to a company and have a commission coming, you may be able to get an advance on it. If you receive regular checks from any reliable source, such as rents or a trust fund, you can generally borrow money by signing your interest in a certain number of those checks over to the lender. Almost any sure source of money in the future can be translated into cash today.

Insurance Policy Loans

You can borrow the cash value in your insurance policy for something between 5 and 8 percent. The amount available will be small in the earlier years of your policy, larger in the later years. There's no pressure on you to repay the loan; you can go on paying 5 or 8 percent for as long as you like. But if you die, the insurance proceeds are reduced by the value of the loan outstanding. In effect, you are paying to use that portion of your future insurance payoff that represents your own savings buildup in the policy. Insurance company loans are often touted as one of the cheapest sources of cash. But if you had saved up this sum in the bank instead of in an insurance policy (which is quite possible—see Chapter 20, "Life Insurance"), you wouldn't have to pay interest to use it at all. To the extent that they deprive you of other and more profitable savings, insurance company cash values are expensive sources of money.

Automobile Loans

These installment loans are usually given for twelve to forty-eight months; in recent years some banks have even extended the term for new cars out to sixty months. The longer the term, the *lower* your monthly payment but the *higher* your total finance charge. The risk with forty-eight- to sixty-month loans is that your car might give out before you finish paying for it—a sticky situation if you have to apply for another car loan.

Banks, savings and loan associations, credit unions, and many car dealers arrange auto loans. Credit unions usually charge the least (although sometimes banks beat them out), and car dealers the most. Some chapters of the American Automobile Association provide members with car financing that is even below bank and credit union rates; call your local AAA and ask about this. In general, interest rates on new-car loans are toward the lower end of the lending range for consumer loans, and on used-car loans toward the higher end. (For more on auto loans, see Chapter 11, "Buying a Car.")

Mortgage Loans

Mortgage rates are lower than other consumer loan rates. But because of the size and term of the loan, it's probably the largest interest payment you'll make in your life. Finance charges more than double the cost of your house. Since rates often vary considerably among all the banks and savings and loan associations in your area, it's well worth shopping around. For the ins and outs of mortgage loans, see Chapter 13, "Buying a House (or Condominium)."

Second Mortgages

Once you've paid up part of a mortgage, you might want to borrow the money again in the form of a second mortgage. If your home has increased in value, you'll generally be able to borrow even more than you paid in. Finance companies and second-mortgage companies offer this type of loan at high interest rates. A growing number of banks offer second mortgages, but even there the rate will be higher than on your first mortgage.

Increasingly, people are turning to second mortgages to finance things like a new car or an addition to the house. Over the long run, this is an expensive way to raise money. Monthly payments are low, but the term of the loan is so long that you pay an enormous amount of interest. For example, if you borrowed $5,000 on a 14 percent second mortgage for ten years, you'd wind up repaying a total of $9,176. Whereas if you had borrowed the same sum, at the same rate, on a three-year home improvement loan, your total cost would be $6,118. In general, second mortgages should be reserved for major and necessary expenditures like college tuition, not short-term pleasures like a vacation. The question to ask yourself before embarking on any kind of long-term financing is, "Do I want this purchase badly enough to still be paying for it in ten years?"

Refinancing Your Mortgage

If interest rates today are higher than when you first took out the mortgage, some banks won't let you borrow more money on your house unless you refinance the entire loan. You have to give up the old, lower-interest contract and accept a new one, in the larger amount you want but at a higher rate. For example, if you have $20,000 remaining on a 7½ percent mortgage and want to borrow $10,000 more, the bank may insist that you take a new $30,000 mortgage at 13 percent.

This is an extremely expensive way to finance a purchase. It may raise your monthly payments by $180 or so, and it will cost you many, many thousands over the life of the loan—much more than a second mortgage would cost. However, there may be instances when refinancing a house can turn a profit for you after taxes (for details, see "Refinancing Your House for Investment Purposes," page 280).

Mobile Home Loans

These are granted by some banks, S&Ls, and credit unions, as well as mobile home dealers and finance companies. Some banks and S&Ls also provide government-backed Federal Housing Administration or Veterans Administration loans, at lower interest rates and longer payment terms than most private lenders offer. In general, mobile home loans are not considered mortgages (although you may get better terms if the financing package includes land). Interest rates vary considerably from lender to lender, so be sure you shop around.

Condominium and Cooperative Apartment Loans

Condominiums generally qualify for mortgage financing because you actually own the apartment. But with a co-op, you own a share in the entire building, which is not as attractive a piece of loan security as a deed. So co-ops generally have to be financed with personal loans, which are more costly than mortgages.

Home Improvement Loans

The best buy is usually a government-backed Federal Housing Administration loan, available through many banks and S&Ls. The maximum terms are $15,000 for fifteen years at 18 percent, although some lenders restrict FHAs to five or seven years and provide less money. Credit unions may charge around 12 to 18 percent. Finance companies are more expensive than banks and S&Ls. Home improvement money is available for projects that add value to your home, such as replacing the roof, adding a room, or doing some expensive landscaping.

Government-insured Student Loans

The student himself can borrow up to $2,500 a year from various lending institutions, at a top interest rate of 7 percent. Only the interest is due while the student is in college, and afterward he has ten years to repay. For details on this and other student loan programs, see Chapter 22, "Paying for College."

Overdraft Checking

This lets you write a check for more than the amount in your checking account. In effect, the bank gives you a line of credit (up to $1,000 or $5,000), which you can tap for a loan anytime you want. There's no charge until you start writing checks against it; then, the charge may be 1 to 1½ percent a month on the unpaid balance (which translates into 12 to 18 percent a year). Some banks will move money into this credit line only in multiples of $50 or $100—so, for example, if you write an overdraft for $102, you might find that you've had to borrow $150 or even $200 to cover. It's better if you can tap the credit line only for the exact amount you want. Some banks charge interest from the first day you borrow the money; others assess a transaction fee of ½ to 1 percent but don't start the clock running on interest payments until the first billing period has passed.

These loans aren't usually repaid automatically with your next bank deposit (although in some cases they might be). You generally get a monthly statement and can repay in installments. You're rarely pressed to eliminate the debt (beyond a minimum monthly payment), since you're often paying around the top rate banks charge on consumer loans. But for that very reason, you'd be smart to get it off your back.

Bank Card Loans

Anyone who holds a bank credit card can generally qualify for one of these loans. There may be an initial fee, followed by 1 to 1½ percent a month (12 to 18 percent a year) on the unpaid balance. Loan maximums usually run between $500 and $1,000, and the money is easy to get. The bank may even enclose handy "checks" in your credit card statement, which you are urged to fill in. You repay on a monthly schedule, but it's smart to clear up this expensive debt as fast as you can.

If you miss a monthly payment on overdraft checking or a bank card loan, a late fee of perhaps 5 percent may be assessed. This is added to the debt, which increases the amount of interest you have to pay in the following months.

Overdraft Checking Versus Bank Card Loans

For cash advances, overdraft checking is often less expensive than bank card loans because the initial fee is smaller (or nonexistent). But with a bank card you don't have to borrow in multiples of $50 or $100. So if the loan you need is of an odd size and your overdraft checking agreement doesn't let you borrow the exact amount, you might be better off with a bank card loan. You have to cost it out to know for sure.

If you charge store purchases to a bank credit card, there is usually no initial fee—just the revolving credit charge of 1½ percent a month. Normally, no interest is due at all when you pay your bill within twenty-five or thirty days. Under these circumstances, if you can pay the bill promptly it's better to use your bank card than overdraft checking, which *will* include a finance charge, even if the bill is paid within the month. But check the rules at your particular bank. Some banks charge monthly fees. Some levy interest right from the first day any purchase is charged. Almost all banks levy interest from the first day if you have a balance already outstanding. This raises the effective price of everything you buy.

Small Personal Bank Loans Versus
Bank Card Loans or Overdraft Checking

Some big banks insist that personal loans under a certain size be put on bank cards or overdraft checking. But if you go to a smaller bank or credit union, chances are you could get that same sum on a personal installment loan, which might well be cheaper.

If you're carrying a lot of debt on your bank cards, department store charge cards, and overdraft checking, consider taking a personal installment loan to pay them all off. The installment loan will probably run you in the area of 12 percent, whereas the other debt might cost 18 percent.

Debt Consolidation Loans

When you're being hounded by a clutch of creditors, you naturally seek a way to get everyone off your back at once. That means a debt consolidation loan—a big loan from one source that will pay off all the pesky smaller loans. If possible, get this money at a bank or credit union. Otherwise, you'll have to turn to a small-loan company, which charges a higher interest rate.

A debt consolidation loan lowers your monthly payments by making a single package of your indebtedness and stretching the payments out over a longer period. But it also vastly increases the total amount of interest you have to pay (reducing your total disposable income). If you're so pressed by your creditors that you're a nervous wreck, it's probably worth your while to borrow money to pay them all off. But once you've done it, avoid the temptation to charge a new round of purchases. That only loads more debt on top of the expensive consolidation loan. Down that road lies financial embarrassment, lawsuits, even bankruptcy. If you have to take a debt consolidation loan, DO NOT charge anything or buy anything on time until your loan is practically eliminated.

Family and Friends

This is usually a free source of money. But if the sum borrowed is a substantial one, you should sign a proper note spelling out repayment terms. For the legal ins and outs of borrowed money among friends, see "How to Protect Yourself When You Lend Money," page 96.

Salary Advances

Some employers will give you an advance on your salary to help you out of a bind. But take care that it doesn't get you into even worse trouble because of a shortage of funds the following month.

Interest Rate Ceilings

The enormous rise in interest rates in 1980 caused many states to change their legal interest-rate ceilings. A 12 percent charge account may soon be a thing of the past.

Where to Borrow

Commercial Banks

These institutions lend money for every purpose imaginable, to anyone they consider creditworthy. Some people are afraid to ask banks for money—a hangover from the time when bankers rejected most personal loans. But the modern banker wants to lend money to individuals; he makes money on you; his bias is *for* you, not against you.

In general, medium-sized and smaller banks charge lower interest rates than big banks, and they may impose fewer fees. In tight money times banks may lend only to their own good customers (or require you to open an account as a condition of getting a loan). For this reason it's useful to do as much business as possible with the same bank. If comparison shopping shows that the bank you're using is more expensive than its neighbors, take your business—checking, savings, and borrowing—elsewhere. If you plan to go to another bank because its lending rates are lower, don't hesitate to tell your present banker about it. He may lower the rate quoted, just to keep your business. Bank charges are negotiable—a fact that consumers rarely realize.

Savings Banks and Savings and Loan Associations

The specialty of these institutions is mortgages and home improvement loans, although money is also available for personal loans and other purposes. The breadth of service available will depend on state law and the preferences of that particular institution. In some cases their rates may be lower than those of commercial banks.

Credit Unions

If you qualify for credit union membership, by all means join. In most cases you can get a lower rate on loans (and a higher rate on savings) than at banks or S&Ls. Typically, credit unions make personal, auto, and home improvement loans, with the maximum depending on the group's size and resources. A few also make mortgage loans. When the credit union serves only the employees of a single company, its rules might require that you repay the loan if you take another job (in fact, your entire last paycheck might have to be applied to the debt). However, if you can't repay it all at once, you'll usually get permission to continue the same monthly payments you were making before. Credit unions often provide free credit life insurance, so if you die, the loan will be paid in full.

Finance Companies

In some places they're called industrial loan companies because they got their start making loans to industrial workers. In some places they're strictly small-loan companies, with a top loan of around $1,000. And in some places their consumer services rival those of banks. Finance companies charge a higher interest rate than banks—sometimes a little higher, sometimes more than double or triple the rate, depending on state law. But they will lend in small amounts, like $100, which banks usually won't, and they often lend to people whose credit standing isn't good enough for a bank loan.

Some people who could qualify for bank credit—or a loan from a credit union or S&L—go to finance companies instead, because they seem less forbidding. If you do this, you may be paying dearly for your timidity. Anyone with a steady job, not too much debt, and a record of paying bills approximately on time should be able to get a bank loan. In fact, the first place to look should be the institution where you keep a checking or savings account. Go to a finance company only if that source of money isn't open to you.

"Executive" Finance Companies

These lenders specialize in mail-order loans to people with minimum incomes of around $20,000 to $25,000. You'll probably have to send in a copy of your latest tax return to prove you qualify. No collateral is required, but the terms can be stiff—around 17 to 36 percent. Depending on the company and your own circumstances, you can borrow a top of $5,000 to $10,000. These firms advertise in the financial pages of leading newspapers, professional magazines, and through the mails. (*Note:* Some professional societies have arranged for members to get mail-order loans at slightly lower rates.)

Life Insurance Companies

You can borrow the cash value in your insurance policy (see "Loans Against Cash Value," page 383). In some areas, insurance companies also make mortgages.

Second-Mortgage Companies

These specialize in second mortgages on your home, at a relatively high interest rate. Finance companies also give second mortgages, but as a rule their rates are even higher.

Stockbrokers

Stockbrokers lend money to their customers, usually at low interest rates. When a bank is charging 18 percent for a personal loan, a broker might give you the money at 10 to 15 percent, depending on how active a customer you are. You borrow against your securities—up to 50 percent of the value of your listed stocks, 70 percent of the value of corporate bonds, and 90 percent of the value of Treasuries. But you must be prepared to repay the loan if the market value of your securities falls below a certain point—otherwise, the broker would sell the stocks.

Special Sources

Depending on your affiliations or line of work, there may be special sources of credit available to you. Farmers, for example, can get loans from production credit cooperatives. Students qualify for low-rate government-backed loans through commercial lenders. A club or trade union may be able to give you some help. If you can't get a favorable loan on your own merits, sometimes your company will intercede with its own bank on your behalf.

Pawnbrokers

If you're desperate for a small sum of money and own something salable, a pawnbroker will lend you 35 or 40 percent of its value (according to his appraisal). The interest rate is high (around 36 percent or more) but not illegal. He keeps the item: if you don't reclaim it within a specified time, he'll put it up for sale. Put an identifying mark on anything that you pawn; then copy the mark (or the serial number of the item) on your pawnticket in full view of the pawnbroker. This protects you against substitution. If you think it's likely that you won't be able to redeem the item, don't pawn it—sell it. You'll get more money that way.

Loan Sharks

They shouldn't even be included in a list of money sources. I mention them only to say never use them, under any circumstances. It's better to go bankrupt than borrow money from a crook who charges illegal interest rates. The lending charge might run over 2,000 percent, but that's not the worst of your problems. If he doesn't get his money, a loan shark might destroy your property, hurt your family, or beat you up. And whereas bankruptcy wipes out your other debts, a loan shark will come after you until he gets paid. Nothing can be so important that it's worth doing business with a criminal lender, no matter how friendly and helpful he seems at first.

Sometimes people in trouble turn to a loan shark without admitting to themselves what they're doing. But anyone with his eyes half open can tell the difference between a state-licensed small-loan operator and a crook. *Never* borrow from a stranger who's running his business out of his hip pocket; *never* borrow from someone who charges an excessive interest rate; *never* borrow from someone who won't give you a copy of the note you signed, or who isn't using a truth-in-lending form; *never* borrow from someone who asks you to sign a contract with some of the spaces left blank. Once you are in the clutches of a loan shark, not even the police will be able to protect you.

Cosigners

If your personal credit rating isn't strong enough to qualify you for a loan, you may need a *cosigner.* This is someone who will put his name on the note along with yours, as a guarantee of payment. Needless to say, the cosigner must have the resources to pay off the loan if you default.

It is often difficult to find a cosigner, because people don't like to go on the line for someone else's debt. In fact, if you yourself are ever asked to cosign, take a long look at the person you're helping, because if for any reason he can't discharge the debt, you're going to be liable for every nickel of it. This is true not only for a bank loan but for an apartment lease or any other obligation you cosign with someone else. If the other person defaults, the lender may not even pursue him for payment; he'll just turn to you. And he won't be interested in any of your problems; he'll just want his money. If you don't pay, you'll be sued.

Some lenders have used cosigners as an instrument of illegal discrimination—for example, requiring a woman or a black man to find a co-signer when a white man in the same circumstances wouldn't need one. Since backers are hard to find, this requirement may effectively deny you credit. If you think a lender is unfairly setting obstacles in your path, see the section on credit discrimination in Chapter 9, "Credit: Your Rights—And What Can Go Wrong."

Credit Insurance

This is an expensive form of life insurance often offered with the loan. For a discussion of the pros and cons see page 103.

Prepayment Penalties and the Rule of 78s:

There is usually a penalty if you repay an installment loan ahead of time, which effectively increases the cost of the money you borrowed. The exact amount of the penalty may be spelled out in your installment contract, or it may be buried under a cryptic reference to the "Rule of 78s." The "rule" is actually a method by which interest payments are figured and has the effect of loading more of your interest payments onto the earlier installments, less onto the later installments.

To be precise, you pay 12/78s of the interest on a one-year loan in the first month, 11/78s the second month, 10/78s the third month, all the way down to 1/78 the last month. Over a one-year period, this adds up to 78/78 or 100 percent of the interest payment. However, if you prepay the one-year loan after only six months—one half of the time contracted for—you will have paid 73 percent of the total interest payments. And you don't get that extra interest back; the bank keeps it. This has the effect of making the loan's actual annual percentage rate higher than the rate stated in your truth-in-lending contract.

This is a perfectly fair way to figure interest as long as you repay the loan in the stated period. During the first month of the loan you have the greatest amount of the bank's money in your possession, and therefore should pay the greatest amount of interest. However, it becomes unfair when you prepay. Suddenly you have given the bank an extra sum of money that it hadn't expected to get, but it doesn't recompense you for this windfall. Because of the complaints of consumer organizations against the Rule of 78s, some banks have begun to figure interest on prepayment according to the *actuarial* method, which means they charge you 1/12 of the interest for each month the loan is outstanding. That way, if you prepay a one-year loan after six months, you will have been charged exactly 50 percent of the interest, which is fair.

Some Tips on Borrowing

1. Interest rates usually vary widely, even in the same town. So check two or three banks and S&Ls (of different sizes) before taking a loan. You might be able to save yourself several percentage points.

2. The shorter the repayment period, the smaller the total finance charge you'll have to pay.

3. The bigger the down payment, the smaller the loan, hence the lower the finance charge. Some lenders even charge lower interest rates to people who put up large down payments.

4. Because of the complexity of interest rate schedules you might be quoted an incorrect rate. It's sometimes worth visiting another branch of your bank, or talking to another loan officer, to make sure you were told the proper interest rate.

5. If the bank's rates are out of line with the competition and you say so, it may lower the rate for you.

The Importance of Being Suspicious

Don't take anybody's word for anything when you apply for a loan. Read the forms and request explanations for anything you don't understand. If you have any special agreements with the lender, make sure they're in writing—or you may very well not have them at all. Some credit agreements put your property and your future into jeopardy if you should have trouble repaying the loan. For specifics on your credit rights, see Chapter 9, "Credit: Your Rights—and What Can Go Wrong."

How to Protect Yourself When You Lend Money

If you lend a large sum of money to a friend, by all means protect yourself against the possibility that he'll go broke or go West. That means getting security for your loan (like a car or a piece of property), and having a lawyer draw up a contract that will protect your rights in case of default. Here are the steps:

1. It does no good to insist on security if you don't also put yourself first in line to collect it. Several creditors might wind up jockeying for the same piece of property, and you could be shut out. You need a "security interest" in the collateral, which is a lien against personal property. The security interest should state the amount you're lending and the interest rate (don't be a Scrooge—you, too, are subject to the usury laws); fully describe the collateral; define what will constitute default on the loan, and spell out your rights to the property. Both you and the borrower should sign this agreement.

2. Then you have to "perfect" the security interest, which in effect means to make it airtight. You do this either by filing it with a state official or by taking possession of the collateral; your lawyer will tell you which. Don't give your friend a cent until this is done. If you do and he eventually defaults, your claim on the collateral may be successfully challenged in court.

3. The agreement should state that he can't use the same collateral to secure another loan. With an installment loan, you'll also want the right to accelerate payments or call the loan entirely. If it appears that he's going to skip out, you can call the loan, put him in default, and claim your collateral. Always go to the trouble of making sure he owns the property he's borrowing against and that there are no prior liens on it. Otherwise, you may find that you have no collateral at all. But no matter how good your agreement, certain preferred creditors—such as the U.S. government—might be able to come in and take theirs off the top.

4. If he pledges real estate, you take a lien on the property under a mortgage agreement, which is similar to a security agreement.

5. If your friend defaults and your papers are in order, you'll be able to sell the collateral and get your money out. But if you lend more than the collateral is worth, you'll have to scrabble with the rest of the creditors to collect the remainder.

6. The fee the lawyer charges to draw up the security agreement is tax-deductible, as are whatever funds you expend to collect the debt. You can't write a bad debt off on your tax return until you've made a reasonable attempt to collect.

Lending money without collateral is friendship indeed. But it is commonly done when the amount is not large. Make sure you at least have his note, spelling out how much is due, at what interest rate, and how and when the loan is to be repaid. If he defaults, you'll have to sue and hope for the best. If you lend the money interest-free, and for an indeterminate length of time, get a signed note that the money is owed and put it in your safe deposit box. Should anything happen to you, that note would be the only evidence that the loan existed.

Loans for a Friend's Business

If your friend needs money for his business, try to help him by guaranteeing his personal note at a bank or finance company rather than giving him cash directly. If he defaults and you have to pay off the loan, you may then get a *business bad-debt deduction,* which is deductible in full on your tax return. If you make the loan personally, you'll have to take a *nonbusiness bad-debt deduction,* which is treated as if it were a short-term capital loss. It's deductible dollar for dollar against capital gains; any excess is deductible against ordinary income up to $3,000 in any one year, with the remainder carried forward into the future.

Loans to a Relative

If you lend money to a relative and he defaults, the Internal Revenue Service may refuse you a bad-debt deduction. Loans among family members are generally assumed to be gifts, unless you can prove otherwise. You should handle any such loan in a businesslike fashion, using a formal loan agreement. It should spell out the amount of the loan, the interest rate (if any), and when and how it is to be repaid. If the relative defaults and you make no genuine effort to collect, the transaction is treated as if it were a gift. But if you try seriously to collect and fail, you may be able to take a nonbusiness bad-debt deduction.

If you know in advance that you'll probably make no effort to collect, try to time the loan in such a way as to protect yourself against gift tax consequences. For example, assume you're lending money to your son to help him buy a house. You could loan him $3,000 at the end of one calendar year (which is the most you could give in a single year, tax free) and another $3,000 at the start of the next year; the whole $6,000 will then pass gift-tax-free if it's never repaid. If more money is needed, you could lend $3,000 a year to his wife. Or you and your spouse could jointly lend your son $6,000 a year, and his spouse another $6,000 a year. Your son (and his wife, if she receives some money) should give you a formal note, promising to repay. But if they don't and the IRS dubs the transaction a gift, all of the money will be tax-sheltered by your annual gift tax exclusions.

Chapter Eight

BUYING ON CREDIT

Getting along with women,
Knocking around with men,
Having more credit than money,
Thus one goes through the world.
JOHANN VON GOETHE

When you tell a merchant to "charge it," he has, in effect, made you a loan. Instead of requiring you to pay cash on the spot, he has financed your purchase. It's just as if he had advanced you money to go shopping with.

If you repay the debt within a month, the store usually doesn't charge any interest. On these terms credit is a marvelous convenience. Some of the advantages:

- You don't have to carry a lot of cash.
- You can buy by telephone.
- The bills you get, and checks you write, give you a continuous record of your spending.
- You can buy something that catches your eye even when you don't have enough money with you.
- With enough credit cards you're covered for all emergencies—whether near or far from home.
- It's often easier to return merchandise charged to your account than something you paid for in cash.

The drawback is that charge accounts eventually tend to cost money. If you can't pay off your debts within a month, the store generally bills

99

you up to 1½ percent a month (18 percent a year) on the unpaid balance. If you add new purchases to an account that isn't paid up, many card issuers charge you interest right from the day you buy the goods (bank cards started this practice; watch for it in your credit agreement). On installment contracts, interest is also paid from the first day.

Whenever you pay interest on credit purchases, you increase the cost of the things you buy. If, instead, you saved for those things in advance, you'd earn 5¼ percent interest on your money at a savings bank or savings and loan, and avoid interest payments of perhaps 18 percent. You could increase your purchasing power by 15 percent or more just by saving up for merchandise rather than buying it on credit. That would solve a lot of your budget problems.

Another disadvantage of credit buying is that it's sometimes too easy, because a plastic charge card doesn't feel like cash. You probably charge many things that you might not have bought if you'd had to pay right then in plain green dollars. That's why spendaholics can't be trusted with a charge account. Having to pay cash for everything is a wonderful way to focus the mind.

Types of Credit

Personal Charge Accounts at Local Stores

Many small stores permit you the convenience of charging, with no charge card needed. They bill by hand every month, and often don't add interest for late payment. (The cost of credit is in the price of the goods instead of on your monthly account.) However, an increasing number of small stores either use national charge cards or add a fee for late payment.

Single-Purpose Credit Cards

These permit you to charge purchases with a single company—a department store, oil company, airline, telephone company, or car rental agency. Some levy no interest on late payments, but most do. Department stores may have two basic types of accounts—one charging no interest but requiring payment at the end of the month; the other a revolving account where you pay installments and owe interest on the unpaid balance. With revolving accounts the monthly payments required may get smaller and smaller as the bill diminishes, which has the effect of stretching out the debt. Instead of going along with this, try to pay as much each month as possible, to keep your interest payments down. Charge cards simplify your transactions with a company, but except for an occasional special purchase it's a mistake to charge more than you can pay for in a single month. The habit of overcharging, then taking five or six months to catch up, wastes a lot of money on interest payments.

Multipurpose Cards

These let you buy an enormous variety of goods and services on the cuff from stores all over the world. They include bank credit cards, usually available free (but often with more credit charges than other cards), and travel-and-entertainment cards, such as American Express, for which you may have to pay an annual fee. Bank card companies usually don't object to slow payers because they make most of their money on the interest they charge. But travel-and-entertainment cards generally require prompt payment. If you get behind, they'll often assess a late charge and may refuse to renew your card when the year is up. (You can, however, arrange to pay for certain big-ticket purchases, such as airline tickets, in monthly installments.)

Installment Contracts

When you buy an expensive item, retailers may require that you sign an installment contract rather than put it on your revolving charge account. You make a down payment in cash and agree to pay the rest in monthly installments, on penalty of having the item repossessed if you default. Often, the retailer sells your installment contract to a finance company, which collects the money.

If you sign one of these agreements, make absolutely certain you can afford the payments. Installment buying gets more consumers into trouble than any other type of purchase (see Chapter 9, "Credit: Your Rights —and What Can Go Wrong"). If you qualify, it's cheaper to get a bank loan to cover your purchase rather than buy it on the installment plan.

If You Haven't Had Credit Before

If you're newly married; if you're a widow or divorcee who never had a credit history in your own name; if you always handled your purchases cash and carry—you might have trouble if you suddenly need a large loan. Smaller loans should be no problem, assuming you're in good financial shape. In fact, some lenders might even risk a large loan. But the skeptics don't know if you can be counted on to repay over the long term. To allay this doubt, it's smart to give yourself a credit history.

To prove yourself creditworthy, lenders sometimes suggest that you take out a small bank loan that you don't really need and prove you're a good credit risk by paying it back on time. Or they might advise that you run up a lot of revolving charge account bills and take a few months to pay them off. But that's bad advice because it wastes money on unnecessary interest payments. Here's how to establish a good credit history at no extra cost:

1. Open a checking account and don't overdraw it. Start a savings account, making small but regular deposits.

2. Open charge accounts at leading stores and pay the bills on time. At first you may have to accept a dollar limit on the amount you can charge, but the ceiling is rarely onerous. Eventually, it will be lifted. If you drive, you might also apply for an oil company charge card.

3. After a period of running your checking account successfully, apply for a checking-account line of credit (if your bank offers it—see page 88). This lets you write a check for more than you have in your account, the difference being an automatic loan. You need never use the credit line, but the fact that the bank granted it will be a favorable item in your credit report.

At this point, assuming you have a steady job, sufficient income, and exhibit other reliable characteristics, you should be a good credit risk without ever having paid a nickel in unnecessary interest charges.

How Many Cards?

Don't own too many credit cards. The more you have, the more you'll use—and the more money you'll spend. If one bank card serves most of the stores where you shop, don't get another one; don't open too many charge accounts; don't switch from cash to credit for buying gasoline. It's too easy to lose track of what you've bought when you aren't putting out cash. The end of the month can come as an awful shock.

If you're overspending, start eliminating cards—one a month if you can't manage it cold turkey—until you've limited so severely the number of places you can charge that you're forced to do most of your business in cash.

Interest Rates

You save a lot of money by knowing the true annual interest rate charged by each of the lenders you do business with. And since the Truth in Lending Act was passed, it's easy to find out. When you apply for credit, a lender must disclose the *annual percentage rate* (APR) he charges, along with all his other fees. All lenders have to figure APR the same way, so you can use that figure to compare costs.

APR tells you that bank loans are cheaper than installment contracts; that Store A charges 18 percent a year for revolving credit, while Store B charges only 12 percent; that the sign in the window reading "6 percent add on" really means 11.08 percent a year. Thanks to APR, you can tell when it costs more to sign an installment contract than finance the purchase with a small loan.

But even at the same APR, one store's charge account might cost you more than another's. On a revolving charge, for example, Store A might figure interest on your balance at the start of the month, while Store B deducts your monthly payment before assessing interest. You'd pay less at Store B. With bank charge cards, you generally pay interest on the average outstanding balance during the month, so if you pay toward the end of the month you're charged more interest than if you pay early. There may also be late fees, minimum fees, and other charges. It's all on the truth-in-lending statement, if you'll just read it.

Credit Insurance

When you take a loan, buy something on the installment plan, or open a revolving charge account in a few stores, you may be offered credit life insurance. This coverage pays off the loan if you die or become disabled. Credit property insurance covers the value of property if, for some reason, it's destroyed before it's paid for. Lenders offer the insurance when they make the loan or finance the sale. Typical vendors are auto and mobile-home dealers, stores that sell furniture and appliances on installment contracts, finance companies, and many banks.

A few lenders, like credit unions and some banks, provide coverage free (or with the price built into the interest rate you pay). But most offer it as a separate purchase.

If you're underinsured, the extra coverage may seem like a good idea —especially for big debts, like a mobile-home loan. Unfortunately, credit insurance is, in most states, grievously overpriced. In the few states that have strict regulation (including Maine, New Hampshire, Vermont, New York, and New Jersey), credit life tends to sell for around 40 to 50 cents per $100 of coverage; in other states it often sells for 65 cents to $1. Insurers even compete to create high-cost policies, because the more the lender can charge, the more income he earns in policy premiums. A study in 1973 financed by the credit and insurance industries concluded that consumers were overcharged some $71 to $90 million a year for credit life, and much more if you add in credit disability. Other studies have shown that some banks and small-loan companies get as much as a third of their net income from credit insurance commissions.

Because credit insurance is so lucrative, creditors do their best to sell it with every transaction, whether you need it or not. Typically they'll imply that it's customary, smart, or perhaps essential to sign up. You hear about it at the last minute, when the papers are being filled in. Since the cost seems low in relation to the amount of the sale, your inclination is to go along. Some people sign for insurance without even realizing it, because the salesman doesn't mention it and they don't bother reading all the papers they're signing.

Do you really need credit insurance? For small loans the answer is generally no, since your survivors could probably handle the bills. Skipping insurance is one way to lower the cost of credit. If you're single with no family to worry about, credit insurance is unnecessary. It's also unnecessary for those who have enough regular life insurance to pay off their debts and leave money for their families.

If you're worried about how your family would repay the debt if you died, it makes a lot more sense to increase your regular life insurance coverage rather than to buy expensive credit life. For the same money you'll probably be able to get more term life insurance than the lender provides in his credit policy.

The one place where credit life makes sense is for the elderly who need extra coverage; rates are more favorable than they could get with regular life insurance. Credit life is also good for those in poor health or who are uninsurable, since there's no health exam. Some companies have a good-health statement, but they're rarely used to challenge coverage unless, perhaps, you bought the insurance when you were terminally ill. Where there are no good-health statements, even the terminally ill can get credit life when they make a big purchase or take a loan—a strategy some people use to leave their survivors with something extra.

One point regarding credit property insurance: Premiums paid for this coverage are often completely wasted. Typically property loss will be covered on your homeowner's or renter's policy, and you usually can't collect twice for the same loss.

If you buy credit insurance, be sure to put a note to that effect with the loan papers, so that if you die your survivors will know the loan was insured. Otherwise they might continue to pay it off. Your family should, in fact, get a small refund of the premium paid, for this reason: In most states credit life is sold for the total amount of the loan *plus* interest. If you die and the loan is repaid in full, interest for the remaining term of the loan is unearned; a refund should be made of the segment of the insurance premium covering that sum. Many lenders, however, don't bother with the refund—yet another abuse of credit insurance. A few states have passed laws permitting insurance only for the outstanding face amount of the loan.

Inflation

I keep emphasizing how much you can save by putting money in the bank and paying cash rather than buying on credit. But what if prices are going up? Aren't you ahead of the game by buying today on credit rather than at a higher cash price tomorrow? For short-term credit, the answer is generally *no*, unless tomorrow's price is really a lot higher.

If the cost of credit is 18 percent on the declining balance of the loan, and you can get 5¼ percent in a bank for your savings, the price of a particular item would have to increase by something more than 12 percent before it's cheaper to buy now and pay in twelve monthly installments. Some items will rise by that amount and more; others won't. Should you anticipate a "mere" 10 percent increase, you're better off saving up the purchase price in the bank. On the other hand, if the price were expected to rise 10 percent and you could pay off in two or three months instead of one year, buying on credit might turn out to be cheaper.

Clearly, "buy now to avoid the price increase" is not a cut-and-dried situation. What to do depends on the dollar amount of the finance charge versus the dollar amount of the price increase on the item you want, and the latter is nothing you can forecast in advance.

Cash Discounts

The Fair Credit Billing Act, which took effect in 1975, allows stores to offer price cuts of up to 5 percent to customers who pay by cash (or check) rather than credit card. This applies not only to goods but also to services, such as restaurants and motels.

In the past, merchants' agreements with credit card companies prohibited discounts for cash. It was feared that, if offered, they would encourage people to use cards less. But the new law frees a merchant to discount if he wants to. Since he has to pay the credit card company somewhere between 2 and 8 percent of each purchase charged, a merchant who's had a lot of charge business can offer customers small price cuts for cash and still come out ahead.

There are some other advantages to the merchant:

• Discounts attract customers.
• He has less paperwork.
• He gets his money right away, instead of having to wait for reimbursement. This gives him an extra few days to earn something on his cash.

He can apply the discount any way he wants to—on some days, but not others; on some products, but not all; at some store locations, but not all. The law requires only that the terms of the discount be posted at the doors and cash registers and that it be available to anyone paying cash.

However, the merchant doesn't have to offer any discount at all if he doesn't want to. And most don't. Here's where a vigilant consumer's group can do a lot of good. If you published a directory of which stores offered cash discounts and which ones didn't, and gave the booklet wide distribution in your community, you'd get a lot more merchants to go along.

Buying on Credit Abroad

Credit card companies have different policies for figuring currency exchange rates when you charge a purchase abroad. Some give you the exchange rate as of the day you made the transaction; others, as of the day they billed your account. Make sure you know what the system is, and keep your receipts to see if they follow it. When currency exchange rates are jumping around, it's easy for mistakes to be made. And it's always a temptation to bill in a way most favorable to the company.

Check All Your Bills

Here are some of the things that can go wrong with charge accounts:

1. You get someone else's bills.

2. An item you return is never credited to your account.

3. A payment isn't credited, and when the store finally finds it, they don't rescind the extra interest charged.

4. You aren't charged for something you bought.

5. You're charged twice for the same purchase.

6. Your bill was mailed out too late to reach you before the clock started running on late charges.

7. The bill was mailed to your old address, and by the time it was forwarded, finance charges were due.

8. The item you ordered arrived broken and hasn't yet been replaced, but the store keeps billing you anyway.

The only way you'll catch errors like these is by keeping all your receipts until the bill comes in and checking your bill carefully.

Some banks send charge-card bills that don't include copies of your receipts, just give a general list of purchases. Sometimes they may not even list the store, just the store's corporate owner. If you get stuck with this kind of billing system, it's more important than ever to keep your receipts, since otherwise you'll have trouble checking the bill for errors. For what to do when you catch a billing error, see Chapter 9, "Credit: Your Rights—and What Can Go Wrong."

If You Lose Your Credit Cards

Keep a list of all your credit cards, their numbers, and the addresses and phone numbers of the stores that issued them. If your wallet is stolen or lost, this list will help you cancel everything in a hurry. Call all the issuers, note the date and time of the phone call, and get the name of the person you speak to; follow up the phone calls with letters.

You are not responsible for anything charged to your card after you've reported its loss. If you don't report it, you may be liable for fraudulent charges of up to $50 on each card. This liability is erased, however, if the card issuer hasn't done the following three things: (1) informed you of your liability; (2) sent you a stamped, addressed envelope in which to report the loss; and (3) personalized the card with your signature, photograph, or fingerprints. If any one of these things has been neglected and a big bill is run up on your stolen credit card, you don't owe a nickel.

How to guard your credit card:

1. Sign it as soon as you get it.
2. Treat it with the same care you give cash.
3. Don't leave it in the glove compartment of your car or any other accessible place.
4. When you give it to a waiter or clerk, make sure you get it back. Dishonest employees are one of the main sources of stolen credit cards.
5. Cut an old card in half before throwing it away.

You can get insurance that will cover the $50 liability you might have on each card; there are also services that will undertake to notify everyone when your cards are stolen. Whether you find these things worth paying for is a matter of personal taste.

Chapter Nine

CREDIT: YOUR RIGHTS— AND WHAT CAN GO WRONG

> There is but one reason why anybody ever asks you to sign an agreement, or any piece of paper: he thinks there might come a time when you wish you had *not* signed it; when you might want to deny what your signature affirms.
>
> ERIC REISFELD

With credit, there's one main thing that can go wrong: You buy something you can't afford. All the other problems—bill collectors, wage garnishment, repossession, court judgments—generally arise from this original error. Consumer pressure is doing much to eliminate unfair credit agreements that give lenders all the rights. But if you can't pay your bills, the fairest contract in the world won't save your property or reputation.

Danger Signs

You should quit buying on credit

• If your debts amount to 15 to 20 percent of your *take-home* pay (not counting your mortgage).
• If you're borrowing to meet the expenses of daily living, such as food and electricity costs.
• If you're borrowing to buy things with a short life span, such as clothes or children's toys. (As a general rule, the item bought should outlast the payment period.)

109

• If you're already so far behind on your bills that you're being dunned for payment.
• If you have no cash reserve.
• If you never can get your revolving charge accounts paid up.
• If you continually have to send your creditors less than is actually due.
• If things get so bad you need a debt consolidation loan.

Down this road lies severe financial embarrassment. You can prevent it by putting away your credit cards and vowing not to touch them until you're out of debt. In fact, if you went to a professional budget counselor, one of the first things he'd do is cut up your credit cards right before your eyes.

How to Go Straight

There's only one way: *Spend a year or so paying off old debts and adding no new ones.* Only then will you be ready to use your income for your own security and pleasure, without cutting a finance company in for 18 percent of it. This means living for a year with approximately what you've got, without adding anything more. It means shutting your eyes for a while to all the new "needs" that keep popping up.

Many people get used to living slightly beyond their means because they've always been bailed out by a rising income. But what if your income held fairly flat for a couple of years while inflation drove up the price of necessities like food and fuel? At that point you'd *have* to reduce debt . . . *and you would.* Which proves you could have done it before hardship struck, at great savings in interest payments. Furthermore, once out of debt, you're better able to cope with inflation. Spendable income rises by the amount of interest you no longer have to fork out.

Credit Abuses

Not all credit problems are the consumer's fault. Some stores delude unsophisticated low-income consumers into thinking that the credit terms are "easy," make no investigation into their ability to pay, charge high interest rates, and repossess at a moment's notice—often without giving the buyer a reasonable chance to defend himself. In other cases consumers may find themselves subject to outrageous harassment while withholding payment during a legitimate dispute with the creditor. Later in this chapter, you'll find a list of illegal debt-collection measures and one-sided installment contract terms that ought to be illegal. I have previously stressed that consumers bring problems on their own heads by buying things they can't afford. But conversely, businesses should not use the simple fact that money is owed to justify unfair or abusive collection practices.

The Truth in Lending Act

This law has ended much of the deception practiced on consumers with regard to how much loans cost. But it won't do you any good if you don't use it to get yourself the lowest rate available. Truth in lending covers most of the commercial borrowing you do, whether it be to buy a house or a car, open a charge account, get a bank credit card, buy an appliance on the installment plan, or borrow cash from a small-loan company. The contract you sign *must*, by law, tell you these things:

• The finance charge. This includes all the dollars you have to spend for the loan itself, and covers not only interest charges but any other costs, such as finder's fees, service fees, the cost of credit life insurance (if it's required), and handling charges. The only exception is mortgages, where the total finance charge need not be expressed in dollar terms. (I think that lenders are afraid it would be too great a shock for you to learn that interest payments over a twenty-five- or thirty-year mortgage will more than double the cost of your house.)
• The annual percentage rate. This is the total finance charge expressed as a percentage. Mortgages are not exempt from this provision. Until the law was passed, lenders used to advertise such rates as 6 percent "add on," or 6 percent "discounted," which tended to give the borrower the illusion he was paying only 6 percent a year for his loan. In fact, because of the way the calculations were made, he was paying a true annual rate of around 11 to 12 percent. Some lenders still tell you "6 percent add on" or even just "6 percent"; that's now illegal, and you should tell them so. When you take a loan, make sure the annual percentage rate shown in the contract agrees with the rate the salesman told you.
• A description of any of your property the lender has a right to seize or repossess if you fail to pay.
• A full and lucid description of any charges that will be assessed for late payment; also, any penalties you might incur by prepaying the loan (see "Prepayment Penalties and the Rule of 78s," page 95).

• On revolving charge accounts—the monthly and annual percentage rate, how the finance charge is figured, when it is applied, the minimum amount you must pay per month, and the late charges.

• Your right of *rescission*—which means your right to change your mind and cancel certain contracts (see page 154).

• Whether there's a balloon payment. Some contracts have low monthly payments until you get to the final installment, which is a big one. These "balloons" can be a shock to unprepared borrowers, sometimes forcing them to take out a new loan. The law now requires that balloons be prominently labeled, along with terms for refinancing that payment in case you don't have enough money.

• The Truth in Lending Act also regulates most advertising for loans. A lender can't lure you by touting just the attractive part of the deal, such as "no money down," and neglect to mention that his interest rate is 25 percent. If he mentions some of the terms, he must mention them all.

If your contract violates any part of the law, you may sue for twice the amount of your finance charge (but no more than $1,000 or less than $100). If you win, the lender has to pick up court costs and your lawyer's fee, but you still have to pay the debt, including the finance charge.

Financially, truth-in-lending suits are rarely worth an individual's while (although you, or a lawyer, may want to pursue the principle at stake). But by all means report any violations to the appropriate enforcement agency (listed on page 832). The agency may be able to straighten out your particular problem. If the lender appears to have made law violation a practice, the government may take him to court.

Your Credit Rating

Most people have a good credit rating. What you mainly need is a steady job with a past history of paying bills approximately on time. Your rating won't be ruined if you occasionally pay bills late, or stretch out a particular bill for longer than you should. You can even go through a period when several department stores are sending you stiff overdue notices, without doing any real damage to your basic creditworthiness. It's not smart to apply for new charge accounts at a time when other bills are overdue. But once you're caught up, you'll generally be back in everyone's good graces.

There are, however, some things that potential lenders won't forget. They don't like it if a bill had to be turned over to a collection agency —and that fact may be carried on your credit report for up to seven years after the bill was paid. They like it even less if you've been sued for money due, an incident that also may follow you for seven years. Many credit bureaus don't immediately erase a slow-pay period from your credit record after you've caught up, so creditors may be reminded for two or three years that you were once six months behind on your bills. Bankruptcies are reported for fourteen years. There are also personal circumstances that creditors don't like; for example, they're leery of a job hopper, or of someone with so few roots he doesn't even have a telephone. But remember this: The only way a lender makes money is by lending it, so he's more apt to let you take on too much debt than too little.

Furthermore, there's no such thing as a hard-and-fast "credit rating." One lender may turn you down, while another welcomes you with open arms. One department store might refuse a divorced woman a charge account because her alimony appears unreliable, while the store across the street is willing to take the risk. A bank might turn down a borrower who already carries a lot of debt, while a finance company might advance him yet another loan (although at a higher interest rate). Even former bankrupts can usually get credit somewhere as long as they put up security for the loan (unsecured loans are harder to come by).

Many lenders use a *credit-scoring* system to assess your general reliability—for example, you get so many "points" for owning a car, so many for a telephone, so many if you've held your present job for more than a year. If you come out with more than a certain number of points, you're considered creditworthy. But again, each lender weights his credit-scoring system a little differently, which might make you acceptable in some places but not in others (see details in the following section).

So if you're turned down by one lender, don't assume you'll be turned down by everyone else, too. Do, however, give careful thought to the reasons for your rejection. If the lender thinks you're already carrying too much debt, you'll do yourself a favor by paying some of it off before trying to open any more charge accounts.

Credit Scoring

Some lenders have built a computerized "model" of the borrower most likely to repay his debts. You're given points for the various circumstances of your life, and if you score high enough, you will be considered for a loan. A weakness of credit scoring, from the lender's point of view, is that it often doesn't screen out the middle-class deadbeat, so some stores have gone back to relying mainly on credit-bureau information about how prompt you are in paying bills. If a credit-scoring system is used, it will look something like this:

Customer Stability

This accounts for more than 25 percent of your credit score. You get points for owning a house or renting the same apartment for many years, having a telephone, and having such assets as a checking account, savings account, and investments. Middle-aged people get more points than younger people. People with just a few dependents get more points than people with many.

Employment Stability

This also is weighed at more than 25 percent of the score. You get points for the number of years you've worked and the length of time you've been on the same job. People in professions considered steady get more points than those whose line of work is characterized by job hopping and sudden unemployment. (See the list on page 115 to find out whether your job works for you or against you. Notice that lawyers are well down on the list, not only because their fees may be erratic but because they're less intimidated than others by the thought that the creditor might sue.)

Credit History

This accounts for less than 25 percent. You get top marks if you have just a few paid-up accounts. A large number of credit cards on a modest income, even if everything is paid up, may lower your score, because you could so easily get overextended. This section also covers how timely you are in paying bills and whether a creditor has ever had to sue you for payment.

Outstanding Debt

This also accounts for less than 25 percent of the score. The size of your income is measured against your obligations in order to see how much money you have to play with. If a large part of your paycheck is already committed, your score will be low.

Credit-scoring systems vary in detail from lender to lender and will be applied differently to different classes of customers. For example, many lenders use a different model for people under thirty, which gives more points for fewer working years and deemphasizes home ownership.

Credit and Your Job

Over the years the credit industry has learned that people in certain lines of work are more likely than others not to pay their debts. In general, the suspect jobs are poorly paid or characterized by frequent unemployment. Also, some lines of work seem to attract people who don't think twice about ducking bills. Conversely, other jobs are associated with a high probability that debts will be paid on time.

The following job ranking is typical of those in general use in the credit industry, although it may vary in detail from lender to lender. Those in the top groups are considered the most likely to repay their bills, and those in the bottom groups, the least. Being low on the list doesn't mean that you can't get a loan, but in order to qualify you'll have to show a high degree of personal stability, such as working in the same job for many years and rarely being behind on your installment payments. Also, you're more likely to need a reliable cosigner.

TOP GROUP: Business executives, teachers, engineers, scientists, accountants.

GROUP 2: Dentists, doctors, factory foremen, draftsmen, office supervisors, female office workers.

GROUP 3: Commercial aviators, civil service workers, clergymen, credit specialists, farm owners, lab and medical technicians, milkmen, journalists, news pressmen, registered nurses, railroad trainmen, male office workers, pharmacists, post office employees.

GROUP 4: Firemen, commissioned military officers, heavy equipment operators, policemen, skilled factory workers, railroad shopmen.

GROUP 5: Bus drivers, union janitors, sales clerks, salesmen, truck drivers, warehousemen, nonregistered nurses.

GROUP 6: Auto mechanics, building tradesmen, contractors, insurance salesmen, nonunion janitors, tenant farmers, lawyers.

GROUP 7: Self-employed businessmen, cooks, bankers, butchers, miners, noncommissioned military officers, gas station personnel, liquor manufacturers and salesmen, painters, retirees, union officials, unskilled factory workers.

GROUP 8: Barbers, beauticians, cab drivers, common laborers, domestics, housewives, longshoremen, musicians, restaurant and hotel employees, amusement park employees, merchant seamen, lower-level military personnel, nurse's aides, oil field workers, students.

BOTTOM GROUP: Farmhands, people on welfare, bartenders. To get a loan from conventional sources a bartender generally has to have an extraordinary history of personal and financial stability.

What a Credit Bureau Knows

A credit bureau does not assign you a credit rating. Its job is merely to collect information about where you have loans and charge accounts, and how timely you are in repaying debt. The credit bureau will also report any judgments that have been filed against you and whether your bills ever had to be turned over to a collection agency for payment. Its files may or may not contain such supplementary information as how many children you have and where you work.

Some agencies investigate your personal life and habits (see "Investigative Reports," page 123), but credit bureaus generally don't. They confine themselves entirely to reporting on your financial transactions.

Credit bureaus get their information from the stores and other lenders you do business with. A computerized bureau gets monthly or quarterly computer tapes from leading stores regarding the status of all their accounts, and that information is fed into the files. If the bureau still uses index cards, entering credit information by hand, it generally lists far fewer of your accounts and may not be as up-to-date on your current payment record. Stores also file information on which accounts have been turned over for collection. (The collection agencies themselves generally do not report unless they're affiliated with the credit bureau.) To check on your legal problems, credit bureaus keep employees stationed at the local courthouses, recording judgments awarded, tax liens, and wage assignments. Some bureaus also report lawsuits, without waiting to see if the case is won or lost.

Whatever personal information is carried in your file—such as where you work, how much money you made on a certain date, and how many children you have—is usually picked up from credit applications you file. In some instances the credit bureau independently verifies it. For example, when a person who hasn't had credit before applies for his first charge account, the store may ask the bureau to double-check with his employer as to whether he indeed works there and what his position is.

A typical computerized credit report will cover the following points: (1) when you opened a particular account; (2) the date of the last sale or payment; (3) the largest amount you've ever owed that particular store, or the top you're allowed to charge; (4) the current amount owed; (5) your account number; (6) the amount that's past due; (7) the terms of any installment loan; (8) the type of loan; (9) the manner of payment. That last item, "manner of payment," means how promptly you pay. A "1" may mean you pay within thirty days; "2" might mean thirty to sixty days, with the code running all the way to "9" for "bankrupt" or "skipped out." Some computer systems also carry your slowest payment; thus, you might show as "1" because of recent on-time habits, but on the next line of the credit report, a "3" might indicate that you were once three payments past due.

The report will also carry such court actions as wage assignments, judgments awarded to creditors, tax liens, bankruptcies, notices that you're not responsible for your spouse's debts, foreclosures, and judgments that have been satisfied. It may include arrests, although there's rarely a follow-up as to whether or not charges were brought. This is a bad practice, and many bureaus are dropping it. They're also gradually dropping the reporting of separation and divorce suits.

If you have an open dispute with one of your creditors, a code explaining your side of the story will also be included (for example, "AA" might mean "merchandise repaired but still doesn't work right"; "AK," "merchandise never received"; "AI," "payments made have not been credited," and so on). If the merchant wants to know more about the dispute, the credit bureau will give him your detailed statement.

What a Credit Bureau Doesn't Know

Most people assume that credit bureaus know all the shabby little secrets of their financial lives. In fact, if you check your report, you'll likely be amazed at how little they know. They rarely have your salary, your position, and the number of children you have—and may not even note your job. The report may cover fewer than half of your charge accounts, loans, or money owed on overdraft checking—simply because those particular stores or banks don't report to the bureau. The record may suggest that you repay faster than is actually the case (this happens because some stores consider payment within sixty days satisfactory and give it the same top rating that other stores reserve for thirty-day payments). Creditors who usually do not report their bad debts or slow payers to credit bureaus include hospitals and doctors, oil companies, the telephone and electric companies, savings banks, savings and loans, and small merchants. Mortgages usually aren't reported, either. In fact, one of the reasons some people may be extended more credit than they can handle is that credit granters often are not aware of how large a debt burden the customer is already carrying.

If it happens that several of your reported accounts have poor records, you might want to offset them with data not shown on your credit history, from stores where you're paid up. If you've recently been denied credit, the bureau will request additional reports from any creditor you mention at no charge (otherwise there's usually a small fee). But of course, there's no guarantee that the creditor will reply.

How to Get Your Credit Record

Anytime you want, you can see your credit record. Ask a store or bank which bureau it uses, or look in the yellow pages of the phone book under "credit-reporting agencies." Some bureaus will mail you a computer printout of your record; others require that you come in to the bureau personally. Some give you a copy of the file; others don't. In any case, you'll be charged $4 or $5 (unless the report has led to your being turned down for credit, in which case they must show you the record free).

Before any information is released, you must fill in a form giving such data as name, address, spouse's name, how long you've lived at your present address, your previous address, birthday, and so on. This verifies that you are indeed the person you say you are. It's not a fail-safe method for keeping credit reports out of unauthorized hands, but it usually works. Some bureaus will automatically send your spouse's credit record if you ask for it; others require his or her express consent. However, reports are always sent to the address of the person reported on, which makes it difficult for a separated or divorced spouse to peek into the other's records.

If you move and expect to need a lot of credit immediately, it may be useful to drop your credit bureau a note, asking it to forward your records to the bureau serving your new town. In most cases, however, this isn't necessary. Your credit record will soon catch up with you. In fact, computerized bureaus can now exchange records between cities in minutes.

Errors in the Record

Aside from the many omissions, which you may or may not want to fill in, your credit record may contain one or two small errors. By all means correct them. But if you otherwise wouldn't bother looking at your credit report, the probability of finding a minor error is rarely worth a special trip. As long as the error doesn't prevent you from getting credit, it's usually not worth bothering about.

A possible error that is worth checking is the confusion of names that can grow out of a divorce. For a while, the ex-wife's transactions will still be reported on the joint account she had with her husband. If a second wife then comes into the picture, the records can get enormously tangled. You may not be turned down for credit on this account. But you'll want no confusion to exist about whose credit history is whose if one of you should ever fall behind on his bills. It's a smart idea to drop a note to your credit bureau, giving your new addresses and that of your "ex," and specifying that from now on those accounts should be reported separately.

If you've ever had a judgment against you, you'll want to watch out for another common error. The credit report may show the judgment but not pick up the fact that the judgment was paid. This often happens because, after paying the money owed, the consumer fails to file a "satisfaction" form at the courthouse (although in some areas, courts require that the creditors file the form for you). You don't actually have to file the form to have your credit report corrected. The bureau will generally be satisfied with canceled checks or other proofs of payment.

If you once had a period of slow pay and now want to apply for an important loan, a trip to the credit bureau is certainly worth your while. You'll want to know whether your current good-pay habits show on all your accounts, and exactly what the nature is of any negative information carried on the record. Assuming you had a good reason for falling behind, such as illness or unemployment, and have since caught up, you can explain the circumstances to the lender in advance. By so doing, you may be able to defang the effect of a below-average credit report. You might also want to check the record if you've had a major dispute with a creditor, to make sure your side of the story shows.

If You're Turned Down for Credit

Lenders are required to tell you why they turned you down for credit. If it had anything to do with information received from a credit bureau, they *must* tell you which bureau and give you the address. You are then entitled to a free look at the record to make sure it's accurate. If you were rejected for reasons other than your credit record—for example, because you didn't get enough points in the lender's scoring system— the credit bureau doesn't have to show you your record at no charge. But many of them will.

When you go into the credit bureau, you may be angry about an error you suspect is in the record or defensive because you didn't realize that things were so bad. Quite possibly, you'll begin the interview in a hostile or unreasonable manner. For this reason, credit bureaus try to hire people of calming temperament, who can declaw the tigers who come in to roar. Do keep in mind that credit bureaus are simply handling data, not passing judgment. If their data is in error, they will be quick to fix it.

Sometimes, the reason for your turndown will not be apparent on your credit record. To you, and perhaps even to the person you talk to at the credit bureau, your credit history may not look all that bad. Each store, however, applies its own yardstick to the data. You'll have to ask the store, not the credit bureau, exactly what was wrong.

When they inspect their records, some people are shocked to see mention of a credit problem they had years ago. Once they pay a bill that, say, had been turned over to a lawyer for collection, they assume the incident will be erased from their record. In fact, it can follow you around for up to seven years.

Here are your specific credit rights, as outlined by the Fair Credit Reporting Act:

• You must be told the name and address of the credit bureau.

• You must be shown all the information the credit bureau has about you (except medical information—see page 476—and information on the sources of investigative material). It's not required that you be given a copy of your file (although many bureaus do so). If there's only one copy, you may not even be allowed to handle it lest you destroy it. But you must be permitted to see it.

• You must be allowed to take anyone with you to help you check your file.

• You must receive this information *free* when you have been denied credit, insurance, or employment (within thirty days of the job interview) based on information from the credit-reporting agency. Otherwise, a reasonable fee can be charged.

• You must be told the names of everyone who received a report on you within the preceding six months, or within the preceding two years if the report was furnished for employment purposes.

• The credit bureau must reinvestigate incomplete or incorrect information (unless the request is frivolous). If the information is incorrect or cannot be verified, the credit bureau must remove it from your file.

• The credit bureau must notify creditors who received your file during the past six months that an error was made. This must be done at no cost to you. Many bureaus will send corrected files to people who inquired about you even longer ago than six months.

• The credit bureau must put your version of a dispute that cannot be resolved into your credit file, and include it in all future reports to would-be creditors. You will continue to be listed as bad-pay on that account, but everyone will see that you haven't paid because, for example, the merchandise arrived broken and wasn't replaced. You're allowed one hundred words to tell your side of the story. The credit bureau will help you frame your case succinctly (but it can't help you resolve the dispute).

• The credit bureau must send your version of the dispute to certain businesses. The bureau may charge a small fee for this service.

• You must be assured that the reporting agency will not give out your file to anyone who does not have a legitimate business need for the information. Credit bureaus are supposed to investigate new business clients to be sure they are entitled to receive credit reports. A government agency that does business with the public can look at them, for example, but not a government agency that is merely seeking information about you.

• You may sue a reporting agency if it willfully or negligently violates the law. If successful in your suit, you can collect damages, attorney's fees, and court costs.

• The credit bureau must report no adverse information about you after seven years have passed (unless you've applied for more than $50,000 in credit or life insurance, or for a job paying more than $20,000). Bankruptcy, however, can be reported for fourteen years.

If you have any complaints about how a credit bureau handled your affairs, write to the Bureau of Consumer Protection, Federal Trade Commission, Pennsylvania Ave. at 6th St. N.W., Washington, D.C. 20580. Also, write to the Associated Credit Bureaus, 6767 Southwest Freeway, Houston, Tex. 77036—a trade association that helps iron out problems between members and the public.

You may have to do some extra work if you find an error in the file and your city has more than one credit bureau. When the error results from information sent by a store or bank, the correction should automatically be sent to all the bureaus the creditor uses. But if it's something the bureau picked up during "verification," it will correct only its own files. If you think that other bureaus may have the same error, you'll have to write to them individually, asking that the record be checked and corrected. When you have a dispute with a store that can't be solved, make sure you file your side of the story with all the bureaus to which that store reports.

How to Restore a Good Credit Rating

It's hard to get a really bad credit rating, but once you have it, it's equally hard to get rid of.

Here are the general steps you'll have to take:

1. Pay off all your bills. If even one store is still pursuing you for money, no one else will want to talk to you.

2. Prove that you can pay off an installment loan. You'll probably have to give collateral, since lenders won't trust your signature alone. Try for something like an auto loan, where the lender can repossess if you fall behind. Finance companies are generally your best bet; they charge higher rates, but are also willing to take customers that banks turn out the door.

3. After a year or more of clean living you should find department stores willing to give you a try. But they'll keep you on a short leash. You'll be allowed to charge only a small amount at first—with larger amounts contingent on good behavior.

4. Banks are generally the hardest to convince. But once everyone else pronounces you worthy, they'll come around.

How rapidly you can restore your rating depends principally on the reason you fell behind in the first place. Lenders understand if your troubles arose from illness, unemployment, or divorce. Once your circumstances change (and your income seems reliable), they'll generally give you a second chance. But if you simply bought more than you could afford and then ducked out, you'll get a fish eye. Lenders particularly resent the middle-class deadbeat who runs up a $200 or $300 bill and has to be wrestled to the mat for payment. Chronic delinquents may not get another charge card for years. The credit manager of one major store says that, in his book, a chronic delinquent is someone who, more than three times, has been at least six months late in paying his bills.

You can't escape a bad credit rating by moving. When you apply for a loan or charge account in a new town, the first thing the credit manager will do is query the credit bureau in the city you're from. Computer-linked bureaus can get your entire credit history in just a few minutes. But eventually, the slate will be wiped clean. In general, credit bureaus aren't allowed to report adverse information about you after seven years have passed (except for bankruptcies, which are carried for fourteen years).

Investigative Reports

When you apply for a life insurance policy, the insurer wants to know more about you than whether you pay your bills on time. It's important to learn if you have a history of drunken driving, whether you've been honest about where you work, and whether sky-diving is your hobby. So they turn to one of the reporting bureaus that specializes in gathering personal information. Investigative reports may also be requested by employers on people they have just interviewed for a job. Typically, the form you sign when you apply for insurance (or a job) will contain a clause giving your permission for an investigation to take place.

The reporting agency will usually try to reach you for a direct interview, but if it can't get you with one or two phone calls, it will give up. Other people likely to be interviewed include people in your household, former employers, and neighbors. Normally, the investigator will talk to only two people (including you, if you were home when he called). If one of them had something bad to say about you—that you drink a lot, for example—the reporting agency normally tries to corroborate that with another witness. However, more people may be contacted if your life and financial affairs are tangled and you've applied for a $1-million insurance policy. The interviewer must always identify himself and his purpose before starting to ask questions, and you should ask to see his identification.

Investigative reports are normally not kept very long because the data gets stale. At one major agency they're junked after thirteen months. If a query comes in about you after your file has been destroyed, the agency starts all over again from scratch. Derogatory information may be rechecked after as little as three months have gone by. Because of the type of information covered, investigative reports usually are not computerized. They're kept on cards or sheets of paper, with entries made by hand.

If you're curious to see what an investigative report on you might contain, walk into the bureau and ask. The question will cost you $4 or $5. You'll be shown the file, but normally you can't have a copy to take home. However, there are two things the reporting agency doesn't have to tell you: (1) the names of the people who gave them the information and (2) the nature of any medical information they may have (although medical information will be released to a doctor you name).

If you've been turned down for a job because of information secured from an investigative report or if you had to pay more than usual for your insurance, you must be told the name and address of the reporting

agency. Your rights to see the records and challenge the facts are outlined on pages 120–121. However, since you aren't shown the medical
information, you can't argue with the agency about it. In that case you'll
have to argue with the doctor. If he thinks that the situation warrants
reconsideration, he'll file an amended report.

Credit Discrimination

It is illegal for anyone to refuse you credit solely on account of color,
religion, sex, age, marital status, national origin, or the fact that you're
on welfare. But it happens. And when it does, it can be hard to prove.
Lenders will tell you that you haven't held your job long enough, that
you have too many debts, or simply that their credit-scoring system
found your application to be substandard. There's no way to be sure you
were discriminated against unless you know of other people in your
circumstances who got loans with no trouble. Another indication might
be that you qualify for credit with similar lenders.

In any case, if you think that your financial circumstances warrant
credit, write to the federal or state agency responsible for investigating
discrimination complaints. Sometimes, just a letter from Washington is
enough to straighten out the matter. But even if it gains you nothing,
your complaint may touch off a full examination of that lender's practices. *I can't emphasize enough that when you think you've been taken
advantage of, complain, complain, complain.* It may not help you
today, but over the long run your letter can make a difference. Federal
and state watchdogs don't know where to start looking for law violations
unless the public tips them off.

By law every institution that grants credit is supposed to display a
poster explaining the antidiscrimination law and telling you where to
complain if you think the law has been violated. If you don't see the
poster, ask about it; not displaying it "prominently" is itself a violation.
The various agencies that investigate complaints, and their addresses,
are listed on pages 832–834.

Special Rules for Women

Under the Equal Credit Opportunity Act, passed in 1975, lenders may
not discriminate on the basis of sex or marital status. Here are the
specific rules:

1. Lenders may not refuse credit solely because of your sex or marital status. If you are denied credit, you may request an explanation, which can be given either orally or in writing. Anyone planning to challenge her rejection should note down an oral explanation and ask the lender to initial it. If he won't, that in itself may be useful as evidence.

2. A lender may not inquire into your childbearing intentions or birth control practices. Furthermore, it is illegal for him to apply any general characteristics of women as a group to you in particular. That means he can't assume that just because you're young and recently married, you'll soon get pregnant and quit work. However, laws don't change people's basic convictions. Young, recently married women should weigh carefully any reason given for refusing them credit or discounting their income, in case it's just a lame excuse.

3. A wife's income may not be unfairly discounted when a couple applies for a loan. However, lenders may make a reasonable judgment as to whether that income is likely to continue, using the same criteria they apply to the husband's income. In their deliberations they may not classify part-time income as inherently unstable.

4. Lenders may not say anything to women—in person or over the telephone—that would discourage them from seeking credit on account of their sex.

5. A married woman may open or maintain a charge account in her own name, her maiden name, or in her maiden name hyphenated with her husband's name.

6. A woman applying for credit in her own name can cite as proof of creditworthiness the credit history of accounts carried in the name of her husband or ex-husband, if she also used them. Conversely, if the joint credit history is bad, she can present reasons why it should not reflect on her personal ability or willingness to pay.

7. You need not reveal that you receive alimony if you are not depending on it to prove creditworthiness. However, where you do rely on it, the lender is entitled to ask questions relating to how dependable your ex-husband is likely to be about making future payments. You may need your ex-husband's permission to have his credit rating examined. If the lender decides that he's a poor risk, that part of your income may legally be discounted.

8. In general, you cannot be asked your marital status when applying for credit based entirely on your own resources. However, the question is legal in the eight community property states (Arizona, California, Idaho, Louisiana, Nevada, New Mexico, Texas, and Washington), because your earnings may be seized for your husband's debts, and in any other state where your husband has an interest in your assets. On many mortgage application forms, the question is required. The purpose

there is to give federal bank examiners data to check in order to see if the lender discriminates. But you don't have to answer the question if you don't want to.

9. A lender may ask about your husband if he will use the account, if he's contractually liable for it, or if you rely in any way on his income to prove your own creditworthiness.

10. When you open a margin account for purposes of trading stock, a broker can ask about your marital situation. He is obliged by law to understand your circumstances in order to make suitable suggestions for investments. However, he may not discriminate against you in opening a margin or commodities trading account.

11. Where marital status is a factor, you must be listed either as married, unmarried, or separated—not as widowed or divorced.

12. You cannot be asked to find a cosigner for a loan if a man in your circumstances would not. However, wives in some states will find that because of state law defining financial responsibilities their husband's signature will still be needed. A husband's signature is also required if a loan is secured with property in which he has an interest, which will include most loans to women in community property states.

13. Just as your husband cannot be required to cosign loans you independently qualify for, you cannot be called on to cosign his loans. For example, when you take out a mortgage, both husband and wife are usually asked to guarantee the debt even if she has no income. The bank may still try to get you to sign. But if you refuse, it cannot reject the loan or tighten its terms. The advantage of not being on the loan is that if your husband defaults, the bank cannot come after you for payments (although it can foreclose the mortgage). You'll probably have to sign something subjecting your interest in the property to the bank's mortgage. But better to lose the house, in circumstances like this, than lose the house *and* have a substantial personal debt as well. Not all bankers realize that the Equal Credit Opportunity Act has this result, so you may have to point it out to them. *Note:* You are legally required to cosign if the loan is granted partly on the strength of your income or you live in a community property state.

14. If you get a divorce and your charge accounts were previously granted solely on the basis of your personal income, the store cannot arbitrarily close or limit your account. However, should you show any evidence of being in financial trouble—such as missing two monthly payments—the store can then require a new application. If your credit cards were based in any way on your ex-husband's income, a store may legally require you to reapply for credit following a divorce, even if you haven't missed any payments. Your account can be closed if your present financial situation does not meet its standards.

15. In the past, most married women had no credit history, since all transactions were kept in their husband's name. But for all charge accounts opened after June 1, 1977, stores must report the credit history in both names if both use the account. If you opened your account before that date, you must specifically notify the store that you want it reported in both names; otherwise, the credit history will still be chalked up entirely to your husband. Where the credit history is good, don't fail to make the change in case you ever have to apply for credit as a widow or divorcee. If your husband's credit rating is bad, however, try to stay away from it and start a credit history of your own.

16. Whenever you apply for credit, you should be given a printed reminder that the antidiscrimination law exists plus information on where to complain if you smell a rat. You'll find the addresses of the agencies that act on complaints on page 832.

However, just because lenders can no longer discriminate, it doesn't mean women are automatically entitled to credit. All the law requires is equal treatment for "creditworthy" women. To be creditworthy you need reliable income or property of your own, besides a good credit history. Here's how the Equal Credit Opportunity Act affects various classes of women:

If you're married, don't have a private income, and don't work outside the home, you will probably still be unable to get a loan or charge account for which you alone are responsible (but why would you want one?). This isn't discrimination; a man without income couldn't get a loan either. When you apply for credit, you will be asked about your husband's income and creditworthiness, and he will be responsible for the bills. You may, however, ask that the charge plate itself be issued in your own name, or even your maiden name. Just make sure that this won't prevent your husband from using the account if you want him to.

If you're married, don't work outside the home, but live in a community property state, your position is a little different. The law provides that half your husband's earnings are yours; therefore, you may be considered creditworthy in your own right even though you don't hold a job. The lender is entitled to investigate your husband's credit history. If it's good enough to qualify him for a charge account, it's good enough for you, too.

If you have a low-paying job, you're in the same boat as the woman who stays home. Your earnings alone won't qualify you for much, if any, credit, so you'll have to depend on your husband's income or a cosigner.

If you're married but have enough income or property to be responsible for yourself (and don't live in a state that gives your husband an interest in your property or restricts your right to it), you can apply for a loan based entirely on your own means. Lenders cannot insist that your husband guarantee the debt or refuse a loan if he will not. Nor can they impose stricter credit terms on you than they would on a man.

If you're single and support yourself, you must be considered for credit on exactly the same basis as a man would be in your circumstances. However, you still may be burdened with the effects of "title discrimination." Lenders' scoring systems for identifying creditworthy borrowers may give extra points to lofty job titles, and women often have less prepossessing titles than men doing the same work. The only way to avoid this is by demanding a decent title from your boss. In the meantime, when you apply for credit, emphasize the continuity and importance of your work, your salary increases, your past credit history, and other positive factors.

If you're newly divorced or widowed, your credit situation is better than it used to be, but it's not secured. If you got your accounts based in any way on your husband's income, stores can require you to reapply for credit in your own right. Should they find you less creditworthy, they can close or limit the accounts. But you are ahead in two respects: You can use the past history of the accounts as proof of your personal reliability, even though they were guaranteed by your husband; and stores can't automatically discount your alimony income (if you rely on it) without considering evidence that it's likely to be paid regularly.

If you were previously granted accounts in your own right, and then are divorced or widowed, stores cannot automatically close your accounts or change their terms. They first must have evidence that you can't pay. Skipping two monthly bills in a row, however, may be considered "evidence." So even if you're going through an emotionally difficult period, don't let the bills stack up. Once lost, a charge account may be hard to get back.

The Equal Credit Opportunity Act grants rights, but it also imposes responsibilities. Married women can no longer be denied the benefits of a good family credit record—but neither can they be sheltered from the effects of a bad one, if the bad one is partly their fault. Credit bureaus will be carrying the credit history in both your names.

To avoid the burden of a bad credit history, you have to be able to show that the burdensome bills were your husband's fault and that you always tried to keep things paid. One way to do this is to have a charge account in your own name (even if your husband is liable for it on the credit agreement), use it for your own purchases, and keep it paid up. You'd also be wise not to cosign any loans your husband takes out.

If you and your husband are both sloppy about paying bills, that fact could return to haunt you should you ever find yourself on your own. The new law, therefore, makes it just as important for you as for your husband to keep your financial house in order.

How to Read a Credit Contract

People rarely read such things as installment contracts and bank loan agreements. To begin with, they're long. Second, the language is often meaningless to a layman (although a growing number of companies are translating their contracts into plain English). And finally, there's not much you can do to alter them. In the face of all this, and with the salesman hovering over your shoulder assuring you that the terms are "standard," it takes a person of strong character to insist on reading all the clauses.

But you should try. Ask the salesman what the contract says, then tell him to feel free to wait on someone else while you read it. Mark anything you don't understand, and ask him to explain. *Here are the most important things to look for:*

1. Double-check to see if the salesman has filled in the terms just as you and he agreed. Some salesmen make optimistic promises that the contract doesn't convey. Verbal assurances mean nothing if they're not down in black and white. If you don't catch them at this point, it will be too late.

2. See if the contract imposes any terms the salesman neglected to mention, such as buying extra items or putting up all your furniture as collateral. If your house is named as security for the loan, you'll have to sign that agreement separately—so make sure that every time you sign your name, you know what it's for. When you put your house on the line, you have a three-day period in which to change your mind (see "The Cooling-Off Period," page 154). If at all possible, don't pledge your house and furniture for minor loans.

3. Check the penalties for late payment. Any unreasonable debt collection procedures will probably be obscured by foggy wording—however, keep alert for the practices mentioned on page 137.

4. Don't leave any blank spaces in the contract or space above your signature. Where there are spaces, draw a line through them—as protection against something being added after you've signed.

5. Make sure all the carbon copies agree. In a bad establishment, the carbons might impose terms that aren't on the original. If there is any discrepancy, you are dealing with dishonest people who will take every advantage of you. Do not under any circumstances do business with them.

6. Also check the terms of the warranty. If a salesman tells you, for example, that a used car is guaranteed for ninety days and you notice that the warranty says thirty days, he may change the warranty to agree with his promise. But if you sign the thirty-day agreement, an oral promise will usually do you no good.

7. If you're signing up for a number of services, have them all separately itemized rather than rolled into a single price. It's harder to overcharge with an itemized bill.

8. Don't do business with anyone who won't give you a copy of the contract.

Bad Provisions in Credit Contracts

When you sign an installment contract or loan agreement, you promise not only to pay a certain sum of money but also to abide by whatever terms the contract contains. Naturally, these contracts are written to favor the lender (unless restricted by a good state consumer credit law). The terms are generally not negotiable; if you need credit, you have no alternative but to sign. Following are some provisions that can get you into trouble (the Federal Trade Commission has proposed a rule eliminating some of these abuses, but at this writing nothing is final):

A Lien Against Personal Property

You agree that if you don't pay, the merchant can seize any valuable property you own and sell it to satisfy the debt. If you don't pay an auto loan, for example, your car may be repossessed *and* your motorcycle and TV set, too.

A Confession of Judgment

You agree that should the lender find you in default, you are indeed guilty and will waive your right to defend yourself. If you miss one payment, the lender could declare the whole loan due and get a judgment against you without your even knowing what's happened. You may have quit paying deliberately because the merchant cheated, but you'll never get a chance to tell your story in court. The collection process will roll ahead without regard for your opinions. You've signed away all your rights.

Waivers of Other Rights

Some states protect consumers by declaring that certain items cannot be sold to satisfy judgments. But lenders, if they can, may include a clause in the contract waiving these rights. By signing, you agree to exempt yourself from the protection of the law.

Wage Assignments

You agree that if you miss a payment, your employer is empowered to deduct the money owed from your paycheck and pay it to the creditor. Like the previous provisions, this happens automatically—without your having a chance to fight the debt in court.

Add-On Clause

With this gimmick a merchant can hold your prior purchases in hostage for your present one. Say you're buying some expensive auto mechanic's tools. You buy one tool on the installment plan, a few weeks later buy another, and two months later buy a third. Each purchase is added to the same contract, so if you miss a payment on the third tool, all three can be repossessed—even though the payments on the other two tools are up to date or even completed. With an add-on contract, nothing is paid until everything is.

Attorney's Fees

You agree that you will pay the lender's legal expenses if he has to repossess or otherwise force collection of the debt. The fees are often exorbitant, and you can't challenge them.

Extra Fees

Many contracts provide for late charges that substantially exceed the advertised loan rate. Furthermore, some lenders add a chain of special fees that increase the cost of taking the loan. Charges directly related to the loan are supposed to be figured into the annual percentage rate, but certain types of fees are not included.

Balloon Payments and Acceleration Clauses

These have a legitimate place in the credit cornucopia, but they can be abused. A balloon is a particularly large payment due as the last installment. It helps keep monthly payments down during the course of the loan, but it requires you to have a lot of money ready at the end. The abuse occurs when borrowers are swayed by the low monthly payments and don't realize the balloon exists.

An acceleration clause says that if you default, the entire amount of the loan falls due. A lender needs this provision so that he can sue for the entire amount, rather than having to go to court separately to collect each payment as it's overdue. But unscrupulous lenders abuse this clause by calling a loan if just one payment is missed.

What If You're Shafted by a Bad Contract?

Normally, once you've signed a contract that deprives you of your defenses, there's nothing you can do about it. But that's not always true. In some cases the abuse is so clear and the one-sidedness of the agreement so apparent that courts have abrogated the terms. So if you're in a bad spot but think justice is on your side, take the contract to a lawyer or Legal Aid and ask if there's anything you can do about it.

"Holder-in-Due-Course"

This doctrine used to be at the head of everyone's list of credit abuses. The Federal Trade Commission substantially corrected it in 1976, although at this writing banks are trying to get exemptions for themselves. Holder-in-due-course works this way: Assume that you buy something on the installment plan and find out it doesn't work or was misrepresented. The seller refuses to do anything about it. Nevertheless, you have to keep on paying because your debt has been sold to a bank or finance company that isn't responsible for whether or not the product worked. They are entitled to their money no matter what. (In fact, they were generally entitled to their money even if they were in cahoots with a dishonest dealer who knowingly sold you something that wouldn't work.)

Now, however, you can generally link your continued payments on an installment contract to whether or not the product (or service) performs as promised. This protection applies to items costing more than $50, when the transaction took place in your home state or within one hundred miles from your home (in other words, you're not covered when you're traveling). The distance limitation does not apply, however, for things bought directly from a card issuer (like Sears, Roebuck) or from mailed ads that urge you to charge your purchase to the card.

The law works this way: If the item breaks, you must do your best to get the merchant to repair or replace it. But if he won't respond, you can write to the finance company saying that you won't pay until it's fixed. The finance company may then lean on the merchant, to get him to handle your complaint.

If the merchant won't handle your complaint and you do, in fact, stop paying, the finance company may still sue you. But it isn't as assured of winning as it was in the past. You can now defend yourself by showing that the product was shoddy and the merchant won't repair or replace it. If the judge agrees with you, he can tear up your installment contract. You may even be able to sue the finance company to get back what you've already paid.

In practice, these cases usually don't go to court. If it's perfectly clear that the sewing machine won't sew or that the correspondence school went out of business before you got all your lessons, it is pointless for finance companies to demand further payment. They'll be happy if they can just hang on to the money they already have. If you want your money back, you'll have to be the one to sue.

In some of the states that previously abolished holder-in-due-course rules, some finance companies found a loophole. They would give you a *personal* loan, which you could use to buy the item you wanted. If the item didn't work, it was then your problem, because the finance company didn't own a credit contract on it; they had simply given you a loan. The FTC rule partly closes this loophole. If a salesman refers you to the lender or has a business relationship with the lender, and the money you borrow is used to buy the salesman's product, the loan will be treated as if it had been an installment contract. The same is true if the seller and the lender have a continuing business relationship. You can refuse to pay if the product doesn't work and isn't repaired or replaced. However, if you make your own arrangements for a loan, you'll have to pay no matter what.

Please note that to be truly effective this FTC rule depends on sound state consumer credit laws. If your state law consistently favors the seller rather than the consumer, making it hard for you to prove your case, you'll have a tougher time getting out of your contract or getting your money back than in a state that's more consumer-minded. For example, you might lose your protection in those few states where the "confession of judgment" clause is still legal. If you sign a contract containing that clause, you give away any right you might have to your day in court. However, in most states the "confession" question can be reopened under certain circumstances, and this FTC rule may help to reopen it.

When You Can't Pay Your Bills

If you're suddenly stricken by illness or unemployment, or if you become overextended, bills pile up rapidly. Typically, you'll pay your rent, mortgage, utilities, telephone, and the most vital installment payments, and juggle the rest. By paying a little here and a little there, you let your creditors know you mean well. If you make no new purchases and gradually work your bills down, you can get away with this for many months. You'll get some stiff letters and perhaps a phone call. But if you tell the caller that you ran into temporary trouble, are working out of it, and will keep on paying as much as you can, he'll usually wait.

But what if it's worse than this? What if you haven't enough to meet your essential payments, let alone incidental department store bills?

At that point, you'll have to take your courage into your hands and confront the situation directly. Some people duck their creditors out of embarrassment or fear. But this is exactly the wrong thing to do. *When debtors clam up, collection efforts grow more severe.* By admitting to your creditors that you're in trouble (they know it, anyway), you usually get a chance to work out a repayment plan you can afford.

Pay a visit to each of your creditors—first the bank, then the finance company, and finally the department stores. Tell them the whole story. If your arrearage is a result of illness or unemployment, tell them so; if it's just plain overspending, tell them that, too. Also tell them what your plan is for getting out of the hole and how long it will take.

Large stores and financial institutions often have credit teams that will help you work out a plan for getting everyone paid. Naturally, they give their own bills priority. You might prefer to decide for yourself how much you can afford to pay everyone each month, and visit the creditors plan in hand. That way, you not only keep control of your budget but also show yourself as a person capable of financial planning —a plus for someone in your situation.

Assuming you've been pretty regular about your payments in the past, the creditor will often (but not always) be willing to accept less while you get yourself straightened out. The bank, for example, might let you pay just the interest on the mortgage for a few months. The finance company and department store may accept lower monthly payments. (The finance company might suggest that you take a debt consolidation loan, but this might make things worse—see page 90.)

It's smart to come to some agreement with your creditors before your account is turned over to a lawyer or collection agency. They are apt to be tougher on you than the original creditor, both psychologically and financially. Much of a collection agent's work, moreover, involves determining an elusive debtor's financial circumstances. Once he finds out why you haven't paid your bills, he'll try to work something out— which you could have done yourself, had you faced the problem earlier.

Creditors won't hang in there forever. If your unemployment persists or you fall behind on the reduced payment schedule, they'll move in on you—suing, repossessing, foreclosing, or shutting off service. But they'll generally work for a surprisingly long time with a good customer who's making a good-faith effort to pay his bills. They do it for several reasons:

1. They'd rather have your money than their merchandise back, and the interest charge on late payments helps recompense them for their patience.
2. It's cheaper to accept payments piecemeal than give the bill to a lawyer or collection agency.
3. They want your business when you're back on your feet again.

All of the above applies to honest businessmen doing an honest day's work. But some merchants make a living by selling people things they can't afford, then repossessing, suing, and selling the item again. They have no interest at all in working with you. If you're caught in the claws of a merchant like this, see a lawyer or Legal Aid.

Credit Counselors

If you find it impossible to work out a payment plan by yourself and haven't the courage to dicker with creditors, ask a credit-counseling service for help. These are nonprofit agencies set up to help people in financial trouble. You're charged little or nothing for the service. The agencies get most of their financial backing from local merchants and bankers whose interest it is that people pay their bills.

Credit counselors offer two levels of service:

1. *General advice on how to set up your budget and live within your income.* This is especially helpful for families that can't agree on what expenditures are "luxuries," or can't figure out how to bring their living costs down. There's almost always a way to cut your cost of living if you really are determined to do it.
2. *Managed programs of debt repayment* for people who are too overextended to make it without help. Here, the counselor looks at your income and expenses and determines how much you need to live on. You give him the rest of your salary, which he allocates among your creditors. Once they know that you're working with a budget counselor, most creditors will accept reduced payments for the year or so it generally takes people to get out of debt.

For the name of the nonprofit counseling agency closest to you, write to the National Foundation for Consumer Credit, 1819 H St. N.W.,

Washington, D.C. 20006. If there's no office in your area, free credit counseling may be available through your union or employer, a Family Service Agency, credit union, or the credit department of your bank or department store.

Don't be embarrassed to ask for help. Credit counselors don't pass judgments on how you got into trouble; they just do their best to help you get out of it.

Beware the Proraters

Some "credit counselors"—called *proraters* or *debt poolers*—are in business for profit. Like nonprofit counselors, they take part of your salary and allocate it each month to your creditors. But instead of the $2 or $3 charged by agencies affiliated with the National Foundation for Consumer Credit, they charge 20 percent or more of your salary for the service! At rates like that, you'll find it even more of a struggle to pay your bills.

Many states have made prorating illegal, with the result that operators gather in more hospitable states and run their businesses by mail. If you get a letter promising a way out of debt if you'll just send the writer part of your paycheck, throw the offer away. Even if you could afford the high rates a debt pooler charges, you couldn't be sure he would in fact use the money you send to pay off creditors, or, if he did, that the creditors would be willing to accept the low monthly payments he imposes on them. Bona fide credit counselors get your creditors' agreement before they embark on a stretched-out repayment plan.

Debt Collection

When you owe money, a creditor is entitled to make strenuous efforts to collect. He can send you stiff letters, telephone you at reasonable hours at home or work, and take whatever legal steps are open to him. But he can't harass you or trumpet your embarrassment to the world.

The 1978 Fair Debt Collection Practices Act governs what collectors can and cannot do. Unfortunately, some collectors ignore the law and get away with it. Debtors are easily victimized—first, because they're too embarrassed at owing money to think of complaining, and second, because they don't realize that debtors have rights.

In the following paragraphs I've listed some of the more common illegal abuses of the debt collection process. If you should be subjected to any one of them, don't be afraid or embarrassed to complain. The job of a consumer protection agency is to keep collectors honest, not to worry about your debts. They won't judge you; they'll be grateful to you. With so many small firms in the field, it's hard to find out who is doing what to whom unless the victims speak up. Remember that a bill collector who harasses you for not paying bills is worse than a bankrupt. He's a lawbreaker. Here are the things you should—no, must—complain about:

• *Complain* if a bill collector calls you late at night, or places a series of phone calls one right after another. However, he is allowed to call you a reasonable number of times, at decent hours, both at home and at the office.

• *Complain* if he threatens to tell your employer and your friends that you're broke and can't pay. He may not tell others about your debt without your express permission. He can't call or write your employer without permission, except to verify employment or find out where you're living.

• *Complain* if he becomes abusive or obscene over the phone or in person.

• *Complain* if the dunning letters sound as if they came from a credit bureau or government agency. The letterhead should not suggest that the company is anything other than a bill collector.

• *Complain* if the notices read like court summonses, or appear to begin proceedings to garnish your salary. Only a lawyer has the authority to pursue legal procedures.

• *Complain* if the collector pretends to be taking a survey and asks about your finances. (If you tell him, he'll immediately pounce on anything you have of value.) Another trick is telling you that you'll win some money if you can answer certain personal finance questions. Yet another is posing as a Social Security officer in search of information to validate your records.

• *Complain* if the collector talks his way into your house by posing as a repairman and then berates you about your bills. Complain if he takes anything from your house. In fact, complain about any lies or unreasonable actions.

• *Complain* if he tries to shame you by publishing your name as a debtor, sends letters with "debt collection service" marked on the envelope in large letters, communicates by open postcard, or parks a car in front of your house with the words *debt collection agency* prominently displayed.

• *Complain* if he tries to collect more than is due.

• *Complain* if he ignores your claim that you don't owe the money. If you challenge the correctness of the debt, in writing, the collector must verify it and show you proof.

• *Complain* if he files suit against you in another city or state, which would force you to travel to contest the debt. It's illegal to sue you in a place where you don't live.

• *Complain* if he goes on calling and writing after you've told him, in writing, to stop, or after he's learned that you've given the case to a lawyer. He may formally inform you, once, of what further legal steps can be taken to collect the money, but can't dun you any more.

One loophole in the law is this: It applies only to independent bill collectors. You can't sue if you're harassed by the creditor himself, or his lawyer. But complain, nevertheless—you may be able to get some help.

Begin your complaint by confronting the collector himself. Tell him that what he's doing is illegal, and if he doesn't quit you'll turn him in. That often stops him cold. Next, complain in writing to the head of the collection agency. Send carbon copies to the Better Business Bureau, the consumer protection agencies in both your city and state (look them up in the Yellow Pages under the city and state listings), and the Federal Trade Commission, Bureau of Consumer Protection, Washington, D.C. 20580. This almost always ends the harassment (but not the legitimate effort to collect).

If abuse persists, complain to the FTC and the consumer agencies directly, giving them all the details on what's been happening to you. They will write to the collector on your behalf. If enough people complain about the same company, the government may bring suit. You, too, have the right to sue. (*But note:* You can't sue a debt collector solely for the purpose of harassing him.)

Don't Let Your Money Be Seized

If you have a loan that's overdue, banks and savings and loan associations can normally seize money from your checking or savings account —without prior notice—to satisfy the debt. It's called the right of set-off and is applicable, with some limitations, in all states. (However, a bank can't seize your money to pay off an overdue bank card loan without getting a court order.)

It is of course important for you to pay your debts. But if unemployment or illness leaves you short of cash, you'll be in even deeper trouble if you let a bank move in on what remains of your savings account. Therefore, consider moving your accounts to another bank where they'll be safe. You can then attempt to negotiate a lower scale of payments with the bank that holds your outstanding loan.

Some banks and S&Ls require as a condition of the loan that you tell them where you keep your other accounts and authorize them to debit those accounts for any monthly payment you might miss. If possible, avoid doing business with those institutions. Otherwise, don't hesitate to move your accounts if unemployment or some other emergency temporarily prevents you from paying. When you're in trouble, you don't want a lender to deprive you, without notice, of money you may need to live on.

What If You're Sued?

Call a lawyer immediately. If you can't afford one, go to Legal Aid. It does no good to ignore legal papers. Once sued, you must be prepared either to fight your creditor or make a deal with him. If you don't show up in court on the appointed day, you will lose by default, which means you won't even be able to raise any defenses against the creditor's claim. Once judgment is entered against you, you'll need a pretty good reason to reopen the case.

Some creditors use illegal methods to deprive consumers of their day in court. These include:

1. *Sewer service:* the papers notifying you to appear in court are never actually given to you (were "thrown down the sewer"). You miss the court date, and the creditor wins a judgment by default. When the sheriff shows up to collect, you protest that you were never notified of the suit, but the creditor falsely swears that he served you with a summons. The authorities often tend to believe the creditor, especially if you are poor or foreign.

2. *Inconvenient venue:* you are sued in a court so far from your home that you can't afford to go there to defend yourself. Again, the creditor wins by default.

If either of these things happen to you, see a lawyer or Legal Aid.

Liens

A lien is a right someone has to have your property sold for payment of a debt. For example, if you don't pay your property taxes, the state can put a *tax lien* on your land for the amount owed. That means they could force a tax sale of your land, although in most cases the state will simply wait until you want to sell the land yourself. The presence of a lien makes it virtually impossible to transfer title, so at that point someone will have to pay the tax. If you build a house, or make alterations, and don't pay the laborers, they can hit you with a *mechanic's lien.* This, too, threatens you with the loss of your property unless you pay up. If someone sues you for a lot of money and wins, he might obtain a *judgment lien* against your property to ensure payment. If he has good reason to think you might try to sell the property before he can win his case, the court might approve an *attachment lien* to hold off the transfer. If you're hit with a lien, and you think you have good reason not to pay, go to a lawyer to find out what your defenses are.

The Repossession Trap

When you've struggled to pay a debt but can't manage any more, repossession might seem almost a relief. Let the auto dealer take back the car and the store the furniture. At least the battle will be over. Except that after repossession you might find yourself sued for even more money than you owed before.

In most states the creditor doesn't have to settle just for his merchandise back. He can charge for any expenses connected with seizing and reselling the repossessed item. If the money he gets from resale isn't enough to cover your debt (it usually isn't), he can come after you for the rest. Here's an example of what might happen:

Say a dealer lent you $3,000 to buy a car and you paid off $1,000 of it. Then you lost your job and couldn't keep up with the payments. Your first move would be to tell the dealer what happened and try to get the payments reduced or suspended for a while. He might go along with you for one or two months. After that, if you still couldn't resume payments, he'd probably repossess the car.

If he resold it at retail, he might get $2,000 for it, which would cancel your debt. But he's more likely to wholesale it to another dealer at much less than its retail value. For argument's sake, let's say he wholesales your car for $900. He can then sue you for the difference between the $2,000 you owed and the $900 he got. On top of that, you'd have to pay court costs and lawyers' fees. So you still have a debt (called a *deficiency judgment*) and don't even have a car to show for it.

A cheating dealer would wholesale the car for a fraction of its fair value, which lets him sue you for an even larger amount. When the wholesaler disposes of the auto, he kicks back part of the price to the dealer.

Rather than have your car repossessed, you might do better selling it yourself. With luck, you'd get a good enough price to pay off the loan; in any case, you'd certainly get more than the wholesale price. Selling is a little tricky, since the dealer retains the right to repossess until the debt is paid. But if you tell him that you want to sell, he'll tell you how to handle it. Do not sell to an unwary buyer and neglect to repay the debt. The dealer will repossess the car, and then the buyer will be suing you, too.

When furniture or appliances are repossessed, their resale value is so small that the deficiency judgment, plus legal fees, may well amount to more than the original debt. One of the credit traps that afflicts the poor in many states is to buy overpriced items from high-pressure salesmen, miss a payment, suffer repossession, then have their wages garnisheed for more than they originally paid. They wind up paying a large sum and don't have anything to show for it.

The consumer movement is pressing to eliminate this inequity. A few states have abolished deficiency judgments—in effect, saying that a creditor can have his goods *or* his money but not both. In a few other states deficiency judgments are not allowed on relatively small debts (under $1,000 or so).

In most states repossession usually occurs without your being notified in advance. A collector will arrive at midnight and drive the car away from your front door. But he is generally prohibited from breaking into your garage, and he can't remove you from the car by force. Neither can he force his way into your home (although he can carry out whatever it is he came for if you admit him voluntarily). If you refuse to admit a collector, it's illegal for him to repossess without a court order.

Before you submit to repossession, visit a Legal Aid office to see what the alternatives may be. Possible defenses against repossession are

1. The car or appliance never worked properly and the dealer wouldn't fix it.
2. The interest rate violated local usury laws.
3. You weren't given notice of repossession as required in your state.

In a few states such basic items as the essential furniture needed to live may be exempt from repossession.

Wage Garnishment

If you don't make payment on a debt, the creditor can ask a court for permission to *garnish your wages.* If so directed, your employer must deduct from your paycheck the money owed and send it directly to the creditor. Other things can be garnisheed—bank accounts, for example —but creditors usually go after wages first. As many paychecks as necessary will be garnisheed until the debt is paid.

The federal government limits the amount that can be seized. Following are the general rules:

1. If your disposable earnings are thirty times the minimum wage or less, you can't be garnisheed. In January, 1979, the minimum wage was at $3.10 an hour, which exempted a weekly paycheck of $93 or less.

2. If your disposable earnings are between $93 and $124, a creditor could garnish only the amount above $93.

3. If your earnings are $124 or more, you could be garnisheed for up to 25 percent of your disposable income (which is essentially your paycheck less deductions for taxes and Social Security).

Some states have stricter limits on garnishments, and a few don't allow wage garnishment at all. But there are exceptions to the limits. The federal government, for example, can grab your entire paycheck for overdue taxes. You can also be garnisheed in full for court-ordered child support payments.

Garnishment starts as a court proceeding. You should be notified of the suit and given a chance to defend yourself. Most debtors, however, don't show up in court—so the creditor wins the suit by default. Ignorance and apathy account for the no-shows, not to mention the fraudulent service of court papers (see "Sewer Service," page 139). If you're ever sued for an unpaid debt, by all means talk to a lawyer before the court date (at Legal Aid, if you can't afford your own). In some cases there's a good reason why you shouldn't pay.

Once the creditor has a judgment against you, you may not hear another thing until your wages are actually garnisheed. The news may come from your employer rather than the creditor; in some cases you may not even know until your paycheck comes up short. Once things get this far, debtors generally find some way to pay off the debt short of garnishment, such as borrowing money from a relative or a friend.

The threat of garnishment is a potent one. Employers resent the paperwork involved in having to see that an employee's debts are paid and think less of him for it. It's illegal for a company to fire you just because you've been garnisheed for a single debt (if this happens, see a lawyer). But two such debts can cost you your job.

Bankruptcy

A number of self-help books on the market call bankruptcy an "easy" way to wipe out your debts and get a fresh start. Its procedures are easy, but emotionally it can take an awful toll. You may also be forced to give up property that's important to you and radically change the way you live.

In some states, bankrupts are allowed to retain more property than in others, so the "easiness" of the procedure depends on where you live. But even if you hang on to most of your property, the word *bankrupt* can remain a blot on your reputation for years, affecting family relationships and perhaps denying you a significant amount of credit when you need it in the future (for example, if you want to start a business). People with reasonable earning power, and a good shot at paying their debts, should make every effort to do so. But if you're hit with some large expenses that could cripple you for years, bankruptcy may be the only sensible course to take.

Are You Responsible for Your Spouse's Debts?
That depends on the situation. Generally not, if they occurred before the marriage, or after the marriage but for purposes unrelated to it—for example, if the wife signed a note in order to start her own business. But you generally are responsible for debts incurred after the marriage and considered "necessaries" of support, or if one spouse made a purchase as "agent" for the other. You're also responsible if you cosigned a note with your spouse.

The Homestead Exemption
In the interest of allowing you a fresh start after bankruptcy, the states make various provisions for securing your home from the demands of creditors. Some are quite generous in the dollar value of the home you're allowed to keep; others aren't. You may find that you're not entitled to this exemption (or the full amount) unless you're the head

of a family. If a man and wife own a home as tenants by the entirety (see page 714), and only one of the couple goes bankrupt, creditors can't seize even an expensive home. That's because this kind of property arrangement confers full ownership of the house on each of the couple; the spouse not declaring bankruptcy cannot have her (or his) property taken away.

Exempt Property

States exempt certain property from bankruptcy in addition to your home. The items and dollar values vary depending on where you live. You might be able to keep the tools of your trade, a small amount of savings and life insurance, personal property below a certain value, clothing, a certain amount of furniture and appliances, your watch, a car, and so on.

Gifts

It is illegal to transfer assets into the name of a spouse or friend in order to protect them from bankruptcy proceedings. If the court finds these transfers, it may cancel them *and* deny you the protection of the bankruptcy laws. In general, any gift transferred within twelve months of filing for bankruptcy may be considered fraudulent, and perhaps earlier gifts as well. If you pay off just one or two creditors within four months of declaring bankruptcy, while ignoring the others, that payment may also be set aside.

What About Nonexempt Property?

Generally you get more money by selling it yourself, before bankruptcy, rather than allowing a forced sale under bankruptcy proceedings. You can also convert property from nonexempt to exempt status. *Note:* Exemptions usually apply only to property that's paid for. If you put up property as collateral for a loan, or are paying for something on the installment plan, creditors can generally repossess it. Homes with a large equity build-up will generally be sold to help satisfy creditors, but where equity is small, the home may not be touched. Nevertheless, your mortgage will remain payable.

Some Debts Are Not Dischargeable

These include alimony, child support, certain taxes, some federal student loans, debts contracted fraudulently (so don't fill out a false financial statement in order to get a loan), debts arising from embezzlement or theft, and debts not listed on your bankruptcy petition, even those you simply forgot to mention.

Cosigners

Declaring bankruptcy means throwing your cosigners to the wolves. Any loans they signed with you they'll have to repay in full.

Do You Need a Lawyer?

Definitely. It's possible to file for bankruptcy by yourself—the fee is $50 and the court clerk will help. But because of your unfamiliarity with the bankruptcy laws, you may not claim all your exemptions or even get all your debts discharged. A lawyer experienced in bankruptcy proceedings will know how to get the homestead exemption and how to take maximum advantage of all the other exemptions allowed by your state. He'll also see that all the debts are listed, so you don't have any hanging over, and protect you from creditors who may be demanding last-minute payments. His fee could be $500 to $700, but normally he'll save you more than that by his expertise alone. Alternatively, you could fill out the papers yourself, then see a lawyer for guidance in getting the job done right. This might cost only $100 to $200, depending on the lawyer. Some people try to do it with the help of a how-to book—again, not recommended unless a lawyer oversees the job.

Your Credit After Bankruptcy

Some places, such as finance companies, may grant credit right away, since they know that you have no overhanging debt and cannot go bankrupt again until six years have passed. But they charge a higher interest rate than other lenders; being forced to use finance companies is itself a penalty of bankruptcy. You'll likely be granted only secured loans—for example, an auto loan—where the property can be repossessed if you don't pay, and no more than one or two loans at a time. Department stores will be reluctant to give you a charge card, although they may sell a particular item on the installment plan. You'll generally have to show a good payment record for some time before a bank or savings and loan association will take a chance on you or a store will grant you an open charge. And even then, the bankruptcy may come back to haunt you if at some point in the future you want a major loan or try to start a business. Bankruptcies can be reported on your credit record for fourteen years.

The Wage-Earner Plan

This little-known section of the Bankruptcy Act protects you from law-suits and repossessions while you toil to pay off your bills. It's for the person who doesn't want the stigma of bankruptcy and thinks he can meet his obligations if he's just given a little time.

How It Works

You file a plan with the court, showing your income and expenses, and setting aside enough money each month to pay off your debts over a given period of time (not to exceed three years). The plan can propose to pay the debts in full, or you can ask for a reduction—for example, to pay only 70 cents, 50 cents, or even 30 cents on the dollar. You can also ask to be relieved of certain contracts, such as a long-term apartment lease, student loans, debts incurred as a result of a fraudulent financial statement, taxes more than three years old, and certain fines and court judgments. The court must determine that you can reasonably be expected to meet the repayment schedule.

It's generally not difficult to get creditors to agree, even to a reduction of debt. They realize that a wage-earner plan is their only hope of getting the money back. If this fails, you'll declare bankruptcy and they'll get nothing.

Once the plan is formally accepted, the court appoints a trustee to receive your weekly or monthly debt repayments and distribute them to creditors. He'll charge a small fee for this service. As long as you're under the wage-earner plan, the court has a good deal of power over your earnings. If you get a raise, for example, you can be ordered to spend it on larger repayments. During the repayment period creditors can't sue you for past debt, repossess anything, or even evict you from your house or apartment (you are not protected, however, for debts incurred after filing the plan). As soon as the plan has been fulfilled, your debts are considered wiped out.

What If You Can't Meet the Payments?

If the reason for nonpayment is illness or unemployment, the court may grant you extra time to cover the debts (or even reduce the amount due). But if you spent the money in other ways, the court may end the wage-earner plan, exposing you to the creditors' collection efforts and probably forcing you into bankruptcy.

Do You Need a Lawyer?

Absolutely. You can file by yourself for just $15; the court clerk will help you fill in the papers. But a lawyer can advise you on what debt reductions to ask for and can negotiate with creditors to get their consent. Setting up a reasonable repayment plan isn't easy, and if it fails, bankruptcy may be the only alternative. *But note:* Many lawyers don't like to bother with these plans. They're tedious to administer and not very remunerative.

Advantages of the Wage-Earner Plan

You are never judged a bankrupt; you've proved willingness to pay, even under straitened circumstances—a plus when you're next able to apply for credit; none of your property has been seized to repay creditors (although some assets might have to be sold).

Disadvantages of the Wage-Earner Plan

You can't call your earnings your own during the three years the plan is in force; you must live extremely frugally, under the continuous eye of the court and trustee, with little chance to improve your standard of living until past debts are paid; if you find the plan too onerous, you may be forced into bankruptcy anyway.

Secret Plans for Paying Debts Without Going Bankrupt

You often see newspaper ads selling this kind of advice. It sounds like something magic and painless, but it is only the wage-earner plan. Talk to a lawyer about it, don't pay $10 or $20 for a useless pamphlet.

Chapter Ten

YOUR RIGHTS IN THE MARKETPLACE— AND HOW TO KEEP THEM

When a fellow says it hain't the money but the principle o' the thing, it's th' money.
FRANK MCKINNEY HUBBARD

There's a lot of law around to protect you from getting rooked. Most merchants obey it. Nevertheless, you've probably had some hassles, even with good stores. At times like that it pays to know exactly what your rights are so you won't accept too little (or demand too much). It's also important to know where to complain if the store won't cooperate.

Truth in Warranties

Failure to make repairs on a warranty has always been one of the leading consumer complaints. Shoppers have often been misled as to how much a warranty covered. But the 1975 Magnuson-Moss Warranty Act set these new standards that warranties must meet:

1. Anything carrying a *full* warranty must be repaired during the warranty period, within a reasonable time and without charge. If it still doesn't work after a reasonable number of attempts at repair, the manufacturer must replace the item or give you a full refund.
2. Anything short of this is a limited warranty, and the word *limited* should appear prominently on the tag. The warranty must state specifi-

cally what parts are covered and for how long a time. All exclusions must be noted. There can be no obfuscating language that conceals how limited the warranty really is.

3. Manufacturers are not obliged to offer warranties at all if they don't want to. Nevertheless, everything they sell is generally subject to the doctrine of *implied warranty.* This guarantees buyers that the product will perform the function for which it is sold. For example, if you bought an alarm clock and the alarm didn't work, the vendor would be obliged to take it back—even if it didn't carry a written warranty.

4. Manufacturers offering written warranties may not use the fine print to avoid responsibility under the implied warranty.

5. If the buyer has to shoulder the expense of shipping the item back to the factory for repairs, this must be disclosed.

6. The tag must give the name and address of the warrantor and list the procedure for getting warranty work done.

7. The law provides for arbitration boards, established by manufacturers, to settle complaints. If one is available to you, that fact should be listed on the tag. So should the steps to take if you want to sue for refusal to perform under the warranty.

8. This law applies only to merchandise manufactured after July 4, 1975, so it doesn't yet cover all the warranties written on used cars.

9. A copy of the written warranty must be available at the store, so you can read it before you buy.

Some Important Exclusions to Watch For in Warranties

1. Vital plastic or glass parts often are not covered. They might not cost much but may be so located that the labor involved in replacing them is large.

2. The product could be warranted for use only at home. A refrigerator installed in your office might have no coverage.

3. The manufacturer may say he won't pay for "consequential damages," which means damages resulting from the failure of the item you bought to work properly. For example, if a defective washing machine overflowed and ruined the floor, the manufacturer wouldn't fix the floor; he'd repair only the machine. Fortunately, manufacturers are having trouble making that unfair provision stick. When consumers take them to court, they're often forced to pay for consequential damages no matter what it says on the warranty. So don't let the disclaimer prevent you from bringing suit if your damages are large.

4. Coverage may be limited to parts only, not labor (which is often the most costly part of a repair).

5. Coverage might take effect only if you mail in a warranty card,

although this is rare. Most of the cards you're asked to mail either are part of the company's market research, are used to compile a list of buyers who might be offered other products, or are used by the manufacturers to find owners of a product that is recalled for safety reasons. Failing to mail those cards normally makes no difference at all to your warranty protection. But check the card carefully in case coverage depends on it.

6. The manufacturer of the total product (such as a mobile home) might not warrant the component parts (such as the built-in refrigerator and stove). Instead, you have to rely on the warranties (if any) offered by the various suppliers.

7. The warranty is usually good only for the original buyer. If you give or sell the item to someone else within the warranty period, it may not be covered.

8. The warranty may be void if an identifying serial number is defaced.

Mail-Order Sales

A Federal Trade Commission rule, effective February 2, 1976, requires mail-order merchants to get the goods to you promptly or risk losing the sale. Here are the rules:

1. Merchandise must be shipped within thirty days of receipt of a properly completed order unless a longer waiting period has been specified in the advertisement. For a cash sale, this means thirty days from the day the company receives your check or money order. If you're buying on credit, it's thirty days from the day the item is charged to your account.

2. If delivery can't be made within the required period, you must be notified of the delay and given an opportunity to cancel the order at no cost. You generally get a postage-paid postcard to return if you want your money back. If the store doesn't hear from you, it is entitled to assume that you're willing to wait another thirty days.

3. If they still can't ship the goods, they have to assume the order has been canceled. It can be kept on the books only if they get your positive consent—in effect, a reorder of the merchandise. If you don't communicate with the company at all, you should receive a refund.

4. Refunds must be mailed within seven days of cancellation. If it was a credit sale, any charges to your account must be removed within one billing cycle.

5. This regulation does not apply to merchandise ordered by telephone. If a company you're unfamiliar with gives you a choice of sending your order by mail or calling a toll-free number, you might consider using the mail so you'll have some protection.

6. Not covered under this regulation are services; services connected with merchandise, such as mail-order photo finishing; magazines and other serial shipments (except for the first order); seeds and growing plants; "negative option sales," such as book and record clubs, where the merchandise is shipped unless you specifically say no; and COD orders. However, even where contract law might seem to bind you to accepting a COD order months after you expected it, you can refuse the item at the door and as a practical matter probably won't hear from the company again.

If you want to cut down on the amount of junk mail that lands in your mail box, write to the Mail Preference Service, Direct Mail/Marketing Association, 6 E. 43rd St., New York, N.Y. 10017. The DM/MA maintains a special list, updated quarterly, of people who do not want to receive consumer mail of *any* type. Periodically, mailers run this list against the names they rent in order to remove all the people who feel that direct mail is a nuisance. About 65 percent of all consumer mail is passed through this service, so it should make a sharp difference in the number of solicitations you receive. The process is all or nothing—you can't asked to be removed from some lists but not others. But if you've ordered from a particular company, it will usually continue to mail to you unless you specifically write and ask it not to. Your name will also remain on charitable, political, and civic lists, which don't use the Mail Preference Service. If you move, the mail will start again unless you resubmit your name.

You can also increase the flow of mail in areas of your interest. The DM/MA will send you a list of twenty-two subjects (including such things as gardening, photography, sewing, electronics, auto accessories, investments, books, and food), inviting you to check those you'd like to hear more about. Mailers in that field will pick up your name from a coded tape.

If the problem is pornographic mail, you'll have to turn to the federal government. The post office keeps a list of people who do not want to receive any sexually oriented mail; you can submit your name and the name of any child in your house under nineteen (ask the local post office for the proper form). Once your name is on the list, mailers have thirty days to get you out of their files. If you continue to get pornographic mail, the sender has broken the law. Write on the envelope your name and the date you received it, slit it open (since no one but you is allowed to open first-class mail sent to your name), and forward it to the U.S.

Postal Service for action. Each adult in the household has to file his own form (and that includes your children nineteen or over). If you move, you'll need a new form. After five years the listing expires—which means you'll have to refile if you once again start receiving pornographic items.

Unordered Merchandise

If anyone sends you unordered merchandise through the mail and follows it up with a bill, you don't have to pay. Nor do you have to return it. A law passed in 1970 says that anything sent to you unsolicited is a gift. You're under no obligation whatsoever to pay. Some charities send out small gifts in hopes you'll feel obligated to return a contribution. There is no need to do so. In fact, it's questionable whether a charity should even be spending contributors' money on gifts.

Billing Errors

The Fair Credit Billing Act, which took effect in 1975, helps protect you from abuse by computer. If you think there's something wrong with a bill you get and ask the store for a correction, it *must* respond to your complaint immediately rather than let the computer wrongly bill you over and over again. The fine for not following the procedures listed below is the first $50 of the bill, even if it turns out that no error was made. It's not clear under the law how you're to claim your $50 forfeit. Best advice: Deduct $50 from your bill and send the store a written explanation for it. If the store keeps trying to collect, complain to the Federal Trade Commission.

"Billing errors" include the usual kind of mistakes that clerks make —such as failing to credit a returned purchase, billing you for the same item twice, or applying the wrong finance charge. It covers certain acts of unfairness, such as billing you for something that arrived broken and hasn't yet been replaced. Also, stores can no longer assess a finance charge when a bill, incorrectly sent to your old address, wasn't forwarded in time for you to meet the payment deadline. As long as the store gets your change of address ten days before the end of the billing period, it's assumed the computer should be able to send your mail to the right house.

If you think there's something wrong with your bill, here are the steps that you and the store or any other credit card issuer (such as a bank or American Express) must follow:

1. Report the error in writing right away, but in any case no later than sixty days after billing. Don't telephone; the law applies only to written notifications. Make sure the letter includes your name, address, credit card number, and all the information the store will need to investigate the complaint, and keep a copy of the letter.

2. The store must acknowledge your letter within thirty days unless it can correct the bill before that time. In any case, it must explain the charge to you within ninety days. During this period you don't have to pay any part of the amount in question. You do, however, have to pay any charges not in dispute.

3. While the error is being investigated, the store can't levy finance charges on the amount in question, or dun you for the money (although it can send the regular statements). Your account can't be closed because of failure to pay, nor can the store report you to the credit bureau as delinquent.

4. If you've authorized a bank to deduct funds automatically from your account to pay your bank card bill, notify it of the error within sixteen days. Payments will then be stopped until the dispute is settled. Should you miss the sixteen-day deadline, the card company is nevertheless obligated to investigate the problem within ninety days and refund any money owed.

5. If it turns out that the store made a mistake, it will correct the bill immediately (or notify the card issuer within seven days). However, if the bill was correct, you have to pay whatever finance and late charges the store or credit card company normally applies.

6. If you don't accept the store's explanation of the charge, you can still refuse to pay. At that point, however, the card issuer is free to begin normal collection procedures against you. It may also report you as delinquent to a credit bureau. But as long as you tell the store you won't pay, and why, within ten days after receiving the explanation, it also has to tell the credit bureau that you believe the money is not owed. The fact that you dispute the charge is then included in your credit record.

The Cooling-Off Period

If you sign any agreement that puts your house up as collateral, you're permitted three days to think the whole thing over. The lender must give you a notice of your "right of rescission," in duplicate, one to be mailed back if you want to cancel the contract and get back any money you put down. If he fails to give you the cancellation form, you can rescind the agreement any time (up to three years). Typically, people give their houses as collateral for second mortgages, home improvement loans, and installment purchases from contractors who ring your doorbell to say that you need such things as siding or a new roof. Think twice before doing so, and then think again; if you can't pay the bill, you could lose your home. The contractor shouldn't start work until the cooling-off period has passed; if he does, you may still be able to rescind. (But watch that he doesn't give you an incorrectly dated contract and cancellation form showing that your waiting period ran out earlier than it really did.) The right of rescission does not apply to first mortgages on a home.

You're also allowed a three-day cooling-off period if you buy goods worth $25 or more (less, in some states) from a door-to-door salesman. Again, you must be given a cancellation form, which you can mail up to three days after the contract was signed. If you change your mind, you get *all* your money back with no penalty subtracted. The refund must be made within ten days, and the seller must bear the cost of returning the goods. If the seller agrees to pick the goods up, but lets twenty days pass without doing so, you can keep or dispose of them. But if you agree to put them in the mail and don't, you remain liable.

The cooling-off period generally does *not* apply to the following transactions:

• Contracts you sign at home after you visit a store where your buying decision was made. (But if you telephone a salesman and ask him to come to your home, the law applies.)

• Contracts signed in the home, when the salesman is there at your request and the situation is an emergency—such as an immediate need for pest control. However, you must have given the salesman a separate statement, noting the emergency and specifically waiving the cooling-off period.

• Sales conducted and consummated entirely by phone.

• In-home repairs initiated by the buyer (although if the repairman then sells you an additional service, the cooling-off period would apply to that transaction).

• Sales of real property, insurance, securities, or commodities.

Some state laws may modify these exemptions slightly.

If any of the laws discussed above are violated, report it to the Bureau of Consumer Protection, Federal Trade Commission, Washington, D.C. 20580.

Swept Away by Sales?

It goes without saying that sales attract the thrifty consumer. But don't be misled by the illusion of a sale. "Bargain basement" prices are sometimes the same as they are upstairs, where the merchandise is less picked over. Merchandise at "warehouse" sales may cost the same as in the store downtown. "Everything must go" means only that the storekeeper wants to sell, not that he's going out of business and must sell. These tactics are not restricted only to disreputable merchants. Good stores may also mislead you as to the extent of the bargain offered.

If you are drawn to a sale, keep your critical faculties on red alert. One store's "sale" price may be more than another store's regular price. The sale items may be deliberately unattractive, which persuades you to spend more in order to get what you really want. Small markdowns may tempt you to buy items with major defects or drawbacks. A big pile of shoes or scarves, all jumbled up, may look like sale merchandise when in fact the items carry the regular price. Three rules for attending sales:

1. Don't buy anything on sale that you wouldn't buy at the regular price. If you settle for something you don't like just because it's on sale, you'll never be happy with it and may decide to replace it sooner than necessary. Better to wait and find something you like.

2. Don't buy things you don't really need. If you otherwise wouldn't have bought the item, the sale has cost you money rather than saved you money.

3. Don't buy something in poor condition. If the dress has a stain on it, you won't want to wear it, even though the stain is inconspicuous. If the table teeters, it will be a continual irritation. Damaged goods give you neither the wear nor the pleasure of things in good condition and hence are rarely worth even their reduced price.

Those Phony List Prices

Many catalogues and discount stores make gaudy comparisons between "manufacturer's suggested retail price" and "our low price." Both prices will be given for each item offered. An electric shaver might "list" at $35, but be available through the catalogue at $28—apparently a saving of $7. Except that manufacturer's list prices are enormously misleading. Most goods are not sold at "list," but at something less. That electric shaver might sell at $30 in your neighborhood, making the catalogue saving only $2 (less, once you pay for shipping). A local discount store might have it at $27, $1 less than the catalogue offers. So when shopping through catalogues or at discount stores, ignore the fictitious "list price." Look only at the price you have to pay and compare it with the price on the same item in other stores.

How to Complain

When something goes wrong with an item you've bought or you think a law has been violated, call the merchant first. Don't get nasty; courtesy generally works. Explain the problem, note the date of your call on the calendar, don't pay for the item (if it was charged), and wait for something to happen. In most cases the store will respond promptly. If it doesn't, call again. Find the supervisor responsible for handling problems like yours and tell him what happened. Follow up with a letter. Keep a copy of this and all subsequent correspondence, in case you have to get tough. If your request is still ignored, here are the next steps:

1. Write to the president of the company (or head of the store), attaching a copy of your previous letter. You now have two complaints —first, that the item needs repair, and second, that your request has been ignored. Don't threaten, wail, or gnash your teeth; the president hasn't done anything to you (yet). Just give him an accurate rundown of the situation and tell him exactly what you want: the item repaired, the item replaced, a credit given, or your money back. Remind him of the Fair Credit Billing Act (page 152) or any other law that applies. Generally, this will solve it.

To find the name of the president, call the company switchboard and ask (also check how to spell his name). Another way of finding the top banana is by getting the *Complaint Directory for Consumers,* published by the credit union magazine *Everybody's Money.* It lists the names, addresses, and phone numbers of the presidents of more than 350 American and Canadian companies that deal with consumer products and services. You'll also find the names and addresses of state and local government agencies that handle consumer complaints; federal regulatory agencies; all the U.S. senators and representatives; private consumer groups; and consumer complaint panels run by various industries. The directory costs $2 from *Everybody's Money,* P.O. Box 431, Madison, Wis. 53701.

2. If the president ignores you, it will obviously take outside pressure to make him accept his responsibilities. Start with the pressure groups in your community. Write to the Better Business Bureau or Chamber of Commerce (their addresses will be in the phone book), stating your problem and the store's failure to respond. Also write to whatever consumer protection agencies serve your area (you'll probably find them in the phone book under your city or county listings). Send copies of these letters to the store's president. These groups should respond by writing to the store in your behalf.

3. If the product you bought was under warranty, the instruction booklet will tell you exactly where to write to get satisfaction (see page 149). Even when there's no warranty, whatever literature came with the product will probably include the manufacturer's address, and he should certainly receive a separate complaint letter. Sometimes, the manufacturer will settle with you even though the retailer won't. Or he may push the retailer into action.

4. Send letters to your state consumer protection agency (in the phone book under the state listings, or call the information operator in the state capital for the phone number), and to any federal agencies empowered to supervise the situation. You'll find a list of useful agencies beginning on page 831. Distant groups may be less effective than local ones in getting your specific complaint handled fast. The federal government doesn't file lawsuits on behalf of individual consumers, but it will write letters and sometimes send inspectors. Forward copies of your letters to state and federal agencies to the president of the store.

It's important to write to the state and federal governments, even though you know they'll take weeks to respond. The only way they discover which companies are breaking a law is by hearing from unhappy consumers. If several complaints come in about the same company, it may form the basis of an important lawsuit. Should the company eventually be ordered to pay damages to everyone hurt, you could even get some money back. It's important to realize that YOU are the first line of enforcement—so always let the government know who isn't obeying its laws.

5. If you were conned by a company that does business by mail, speak to the post office. Your local postmaster has consumer service cards on which to register your complaint. One copy goes to the local postmaster, who tries to solve the problem; another copy goes to the U.S. Postal Service's consumer advocate in Washington. The post office intervenes in about five thousand cases a year between consumers and mail-order companies and will try to get your money back if the company misrepresented itself. In some cases the company may be prosecuted for mail fraud. You can write to the Office of the Consumer Advocate at the U.S. Postal Service, 475 L'Enfant Plaza W., N.W. Washington, D.C. 20260. Also use the consumer service card to complain about problems with mail service, such as lost letters, damaged packages, or rude postal clerks.

6. In many cities a newspaper or radio station may have an "action reporter," whose job it is to follow up on complaint letters received from readers. By all means report your problem. If several people complain to the paper about the same store, it might even lead to a news story. There's nothing like bad publicity to encourage a high-handed shopkeeper to mend his ways.

7. Some industries run their own complaint bureaus, where consumers can bring problems they haven't been able to solve. Such groups exist for manufacturers of cars, major appliances, furniture, TV sets, stereos, and other electronic equipment (you'll find their addresses on page 842). Even where there are no formal complaint panels, most trade associations nowadays make an active effort to see that their members resolve disputes brought to their attention. You can find the address of the trade association representing almost any product or service in the *Encyclopedia of Associations,* available in most libraries.

8. Complaints against professionals are harder to resolve than complaints against purveyors of goods and services. Consumer agencies rarely step into problems between you and your doctor, lawyer, or architect. If you think you're being overcharged, you can always refuse to pay. By all means complain to the grievance board of the local professional association (ask another professional where to find it). As you might expect, these bodies favor their members, but sometimes they'll side with you. Even if you get no specific satisfaction, the very act (or threat) of filing charges may encourage the professional in question to settle. If the problem is a badly botched job, consult a lawyer about a malpractice suit—even if the person you want to sue is himself a lawyer.

What to Put in a Complaint Letter

Always include your name, address, and telephone number; the name, address, and phone number of the store (if the complaint is to a government agency); a precise description of the problem, including date of purchase, dates that complaints were made, and what went wrong; copies of your previous letters, if you have them; copies of pertinent documents, such as the sales slip or your canceled check (never send originals—inexpensive copying machines can usually be found in your post office as well as other places around town); a precise description of the product, including serial number if any; a statement of what action you expect—repair, replacement, a credit to your account, or a refund in cash.

Better Business Bureau Arbitration

Many BBBs run consumer arbitration services that are speedy, free, and don't involve a lot of hassle. When you and a local businessman have a dispute you can't resolve, you can both agree to submit it to arbitration and accept the decision as binding. You receive a list of potential arbitrators along with their biographies; a panel of one to three people is picked who you both agree will be fair. All the arbitrators are citizens of the community—clergymen, teachers, housewives, artisans, lawyers, businessmen—who have undergone special training for this job.

You each tell your story to the panel, which hears the argument and usually renders judgment on the spot. Unlike a small-claims court, BBB arbitration hearings are held whenever it's convenient for you—evenings, weekends, or even holidays. The panel may convene in your home to inspect a shoddy repair job that you've refused to pay for. You can bring witnesses, if you need them, and can even be represented by a lawyer (although most people aren't, and legal precedent has no place in a BBB hearing). If the judgment goes against the businessman and he refuses to pay, the law in most states allows the arbitration decision to be enforced by the court. (In a few states, however, it's not legally binding, which diminishes the effectiveness of arbitration there.) But wherever arbitration is available and enforceable, it's one of the best ways there is to get a dispute speedily resolved.

Lawyer's Letters

What can you do when you think you've been gypped but the money involved isn't worth a full-scale lawsuit? Most people hesitate to see a lawyer because it sounds expensive. But in fact, a lawyer may be able to settle your problem in a matter of days, and at nominal cost. He does it simply by writing a lawyerly letter stating your claim and strongly suggesting that it's time to settle up.

A "lawyer's letter" often has an electrifying effect on the person who gets it. Shopkeepers who have ignored your demands suddenly pick up the telephone, assure the lawyer that it was all a misunderstanding, and settle the claim. True, there are some people so unresponsive that a stiff letter brings no results. But in the vast majority of cases, a settlement occurs. For the letter to work, however, your claim has to have merit. If your demand is unreasonable or contentious, your adversary is likely to say, "Sue me."

For this service the lawyer should charge only a modest fee (perhaps $15 to $40). If the matter gets more complicated than a letter, the cost will rise, but you can drop out any time you want. For a small matter like this, it's best to use a lawyer who knows you—such as the person who did your will or handled the sale of your house. He may be inclined to give you a price break in hopes you'll remember him when you have a more substantial case. He may even do it free.

Small-Claims Court

When you have a problem that doesn't amount to a lot of money, and arbitration isn't available, take it to small-claims court. Court fees are nominal there, and in most areas you don't need a lawyer. You simply tell your story to a judge, who questions you, questions your adversary, and makes a decision he thinks fair. Here's how to handle a claim:

1. Look in the phone book under the city or state listings for the small-claims court. Or get the phone number from your union, Legal Aid, or the local consumer affairs department. In the few jurisdictions where there are no small-claims courts as such, ask which court is used instead. It might be the court of the justice of the peace or the mayor's court.

2. Call up the court clerk and ask him whether they handle cases like yours. Most small-claims courts accept disputes between buyers and sellers, negligence cases (such as auto accident claims), and landlord-tenant disputes (although big cities may have a separate court for this). Typical cases include rent security deposits withheld by landlords, defective products, breaches of warranties, damage done by movers, clothing lost or ruined by dry cleaners, unreturned deposits on goods never delivered, shoddy repairs, unpaid insurance claims, checks the bank failed to stop, and contract disputes with self-improvement schools and reducing salons. There is a ceiling on the amount of damages you can sue for in small-claims. In some states it's as low as $100 or $200, which doesn't make those courts very useful. In other places you can go in for $1,000 or more.

The person or business you sue must live, work, or do business within the court's territory. Out-of-town firms with no local representative generally have to be sued in their own areas. Because of this, many consumers with just complaints against mail-order firms find it too expensive to file charges—certainly a deprivation of their rights.

3. Visit the court in person and ask the clerk what the court's procedures are. He's there to help you get your claim in order. You might, for example, have to find the *legal name* of the firm you're suing rather than use the name on the sales slip (otherwise, the suit might be thrown out). Some (but not enough) courts have bilingual clerks, and some (but not enough) have informative brochures about filing a small claim. It would greatly encourage the use of these courts if they all printed instruction manuals for distribution by consumer groups.

4. Prepare for trial by gathering whatever documentary evidence you have—receipts, canceled checks, written estimates. It helps if you can set the events down in chronological order, checking dates carefully. If you're friendly with a lawyer, ask his (free) advice on how to prepare. If it's convenient, observe a session of the court in action. (Again, a problem: Too many courts operate only during the day, forcing the consumer to lose a day's work—and often a day's pay—to have his case heard.)

If you are charging shoddy workmanship, it helps to have as a witness a disinterested specialist who can testify that the job was botched. If he can't come in person, the court will often accept his written statement. Where possible, bring physical evidence with you, such as the dress the dry cleaner ruined. You are also allowed to subpoena witnesses (which means order their appearance in court). The clerk will tell you how.

5. If your opponent offers to settle out of court, get the terms in writing and file a copy with the court so the agreement can be enforced by law. Don't forget to include your court costs as part of the settlement.

6. Not all small-claims courts are as informal as they should be. Some require lawyers to plead certain cases and insist on proper legal procedures when they do. This defeats the entire purpose of small-claims by forcing consumers to hire lawyers they can't afford.

7. If the person you sue doesn't show up to argue his case, you win by default. But sadly, a victory may be the start of your troubles rather than the end of them. One of the great scandals of consumer law is that even a person who has won his case in court may have great difficulty in forcing the loser to pay up.

Collecting a Judgment

Estimates of how many small-claims judgments go unpaid range from 20 percent in some courts to 50 percent in others, with the collection rate depending on the persistence of the judge and the severity of state law. Sometimes you can't collect because the firm you sued has gone out of business. But it's more likely that the nonpayer is perfectly capable of meeting his obligations. An individual might simply ignore your attempts to collect; a business or landlord might hide behind a lawyer. Whatever the tactic, they hope to make the chase so frustrating and expensive that you'll eventually give up.

Every state has procedures for collecting a small-claims judgment. The court clerk will tell you what they are and exactly how to use them. If the debt is owed by an individual, the simplest way to collect is generally to have his wages garnisheed, which can be done with a court order. When your adversary discovers you're actually willing to go this far, he'll usually come up with the money rather than get his employer involved. Alternatively, you can arrange to have the sheriff seize some of the debtor's property and sell it, but that's a more complicated procedure and often requires the help of a lawyer.

It is much more difficult to collect from a recalcitrant corporation. There are no wages to garnish, so you have to proceed against the company's assets. This will definitely require a lawyer. If the judgment you're owed is a large one, a lawyer will push the case in return for around one third of the recovery. But if you're owed only $200 or $300, it's not worth his while to pursue it very far. Corporations sometimes fight back by miring you in a swamp of expensive legal procedures and exhausting delays in hopes that you'll give up or settle for much less.

People who deliberately thwart legitimate collection efforts may be held in contempt of court and ordered to pay a fine. (They can even be jailed, although the courts rarely push the issue that far.) But unfortunately, many consumers expend all their time, money, and patience before reaching this point.

There is a clear need for improved collection procedures for small claims. In a few states judges can order the merchant or landlord to pay through the court; if he doesn't, he is hauled in for contempt of court. In New York any business that ignores more than three small-claims judgments can be sued for three times the amount of the original judgment, plus lawyer's fees. That is a significant reform and should be adopted in other states.

Swindles

Swindles go on forever because they appeal to our deepest vanity and greed. Unheard-of bargains! Hard jobs made easy! Be more beautiful, desirable, important, intelligent! Get rich quick! When someone makes a pitch like this, alarms should go off in your head. If you sign up, you'll have spent money and gained nothing. Among the more common swindles:

Weight Loss

Belts, vibrators, mattresses, suits, machines—all guaranteed to pare pounds in fourteen days without effort (although the need for a proper diet might be mentioned in the fine print). You know in your heart that the only way to lose weight is by working hard at it.

Home Improvements

Sincere-sounding workmen promise "miracles," then aren't around when the job goes sour. New roofs, siding, driveways, pest control, "energy-saving" windows, water softeners, fire alarms, paint jobs, instant basement and roof sealers, and furnace repairs are among their specialties. The salesman may lie to you about the need for work (by showing you shingles he said fell off your house, or "inspecting" your furnace and pronouncing it dangerous). When he gets the job, he'll apply expensive but phony materials (like a "roofing spray" that looks good long enough for him to get away, but oozes off in the rain). Never buy from a stranger who rings your doorbell, drops an official-sounding reference, claims to have worked for your neighbors or says he's a town inspector, and strongly advises that you undertake expensive repairs. Don't admit a termite, electrical wire, or furnace "inspector," unless you've called him yourself. (If the town wants to send an inspector, let them call and tell you.) If the salesman applies high-pressure tactics, offers "bargain" prices, and gives astounding guarantees, take it on faith that you're about to be gypped. Buy only from an established shop in town, after getting more than one estimate and opinion. You must have a reputable dealer to go back to if the job isn't right.

Insurance Plans

You may read an ad promising large health or life insurance benefits for a ridiculously small amount of money per year. Be assured that low premiums mean small values. Payout may be so hedged with limitations that you or your beneficiary may not collect what you or he expected.

Magazines

The youngster who says he needs only two more sales to win a college scholarship probably uses that line on all his customers. If you buy, make sure you haven't signed up for four years when you only wanted one.

Freezer Food Plans

You buy the food and also get a freezer "free," except that the cost of the freezer is always hidden somewhere in the food prices, and some of the food delivered to you in bulk may be no good. If you want a freezer, get one for itself alone and then decide on the most economical way to stock it.

Earn Money from Home

In your spare time, you can earn "millions" just by selling products to your neighbors or by addressing envelopes at home! Except that the products are so chintzy your neighbors don't buy. And the envelope promoter won't buy your work; he just sends instructions on how you might find an employer who will. Naturally, you had to put up money to buy the products and envelopes, which the promoter assured you would be returned along with a big profit. As you might have expected, he is the only person who'll make any money.

Avoid work-at-home schemes that require you to put cash up front, even if the amount is small. Before you go into any business of your own, even a small one, determine (1) how much time you have to give it; (2) whether the product is well made, competitively priced, and something people would want to buy; (3) whether you have any talent for selling or whatever else the business requires; (4) how many sales you can reasonably expect to make in a month, and what return on investment this represents; (5) whether you really want to be in this business for the long term.

Inventions

You get a letter from an "agent" offering to evaluate your invention for possible commercial development. When you send a $100 evaluation fee, he finds your idea "excellent," then talks you into putting up $2,000 or so to get the marketing underway. No one ever buys.

Get Out of Debt

People with money problems are especially vulnerable to this one. An ad promises that if you'll send your paycheck and a list of debts to a "debt management" service, the manager will get your creditors paid off systematically with no further pain to you. However, he takes 10 percent or more of your money for himself, then pays creditors less than they're owed without even asking whether they'll accept that amount. Furthermore, he may pay late. Result: You incur late charges, the creditors are even madder, some may repossess—and you're out 10 percent of your paycheck (see "Beware the Proraters," page 136).

Another debt gimmick is the "magic, little-known plan" for wiping out all your debts without going bankrupt, which you may be offered for a mere $15 or $25. This is simply the wage-earner plan (Chapter 13 of the Bankruptcy Act—see page 146). In return for respite from your creditors, you have to put your paycheck under court supervision for as long as it takes to pay the creditors off (something the ads never mention).

Chain Referrals

The salesman says that if you agree to have your house roofed or invest in expensive photography equipment, you'll get your money back by persuading eight, or ten, or twelve of your friends to do the same thing. Typically, you won't make the sales, your friends will be mad at you, and you'll have bought a product priced far above its worth.

Encyclopedias

A good one can be interesting to own. But since schools and libraries stock encyclopedias for your children to use, don't feel you've denied them something important by not having one of your own. If a persuasive salesman gets you to sign, remember that you have three days to change your mind (see page 154). If you do buy, you'll probably get a special bonus, but don't imagine that it's really free; all "gifts" are built into the price.

Get Rich Quick

"Secret" formulas for making money (yours for only $8.95 plus tax) work only for the person promoting the scheme. Typically, the "secret" involves buying something else from the author, such as an "expert" newsletter on options, gold, or other complex investments. You'd be smart to cut your loss at $8.95.

Carpets

High-quality wall-to-wall carpeting, at unusually low prices, can lose its quality in transit. The broadloom installed in your house may not be as thick a weave as the one you saw in the store.

Bait and Switch

This classic sales technique is used by respectable merchants as well as crooks, so watch out for it. A good buy is advertised in the papers, but by the time you get there, it's "all sold out" (even if you're the first one in the store). So the salesman has to show you something more expensive. Or the advertised item is there, but the salesman downgrades it as not worth the price (although he just happens to have an excellent buy to show you—costlier, of course, but well worth it!). Sometimes stores won't sell you the advertised product even if you insist on it. If you're baited and switched, *don't buy.* Instead, write a shocked letter to the head of the store, the Better Business Bureau, and the consumer agency in your city.

Dance Studios, Exercise Salons, Judo Lessons

Typically, these sell their services through long-term contracts that sound cheap but actually run into hundreds of dollars. Sign up only if you want the skills and have the time, not because you hope to find true love in the dancing master or self-confidence by flexing your muscles. You usually have to pay for the whole course (or most of it) whether you complete it or not.

Correspondence Courses

Low-grade schools steal hundreds of thousands of dollars every year from people who can't afford to lose it. They imply that their course will guarantee you a good job, when in fact it may be virtually worthless. Skilled-job training needs machines for you to practice on, not just living-room instruction. Nor can expert services like nursing be learned outside the hospital. If the course promises to prepare you for a certain exam, write the exam givers to see if they agree. In general, correspondence schools don't get you what you hope to gain.

Beauty Creams

Preparations said to banish pimples, enlarge breasts, eliminate wrinkles, make teeth white, and give you as dewy a skin and luscious a figure as the woman in the ad, won't.

Hair Growers

Are there still men who believe that a little cream and a stiff massage will restore lost hair? Say to yourself ten times, "Bald is beautiful," and forget it.

Land Sales

I suppose that anyone who buys into a "planned retirement community" or "vacation heaven" sight unseen deserves what he gets. But then, it's sometimes hard to believe that the nice young salesman, with the beautiful brochures and promises, can really be lying to you. Don't ever buy land without actually walking around the property and without inquiring carefully into the existence of such amenities as water and electricity (see page 354).

Charities

Some charities touch your heart with a picture of a homeless waif and list a variety of splendid programs, when in fact most of the money raised goes toward paying the salaries of the money raisers and the cost of the mailing. For information on the financial and ethical reliability of the major national charities (but not religious, fraternal, or political organizations), write to the National Information Bureau, 419 Park Ave. South, New York, N.Y. 10016. NIB sets strict standards for charities and will send you a free list of which ones pass muster. You can get up to three in-depth reports on specific charities, free in the same mailing. The Better Business Bureau also sets standards for charities, although they're not as strict as NIB's. However, they report on a larger list of charitable groups, including even some local charities. The BBB's approved list plus up to three reports on specific charities cost $1 from a local BBB office or the Council of Better Business Bureaus, 1150 17th St. N.W., Washington, D.C. 20036.

You can be pretty sure that much of your donation will be spent on fund raising if the charity sends you a free gift or sponsors a lottery. Also, think twice about giving cash to people who approach you on the street with a canister and a brochure. Some of these volunteers collect strictly for themselves. Nor can you be sure that the money you drop into a charity box by the cash register of a local store finds its way to the charity intact.

Diamonds by Phone

Pitchmen have recently been doing a good job of selling low-quality diamonds over the phone at high-quality prices. They claim there's a guarantee, which is good only if the diamond's plastic box is unopened, so buyers are afraid to open their purchase to have it checked. Often the stones come with fancy certificates from gemological institutes that don't mean a hill of beans. Smart investors never buy diamonds by phone. In fact, it's a mistake to invest in diamonds at all unless you're experienced in telling the good stones from those of poorer quality. It's also important to know the basic facts of the diamond marketplace— for example, that two half-carat stones are worth less than one stone of one carat. Rubies, emeralds, and other precious stones are similarly being retailed by phone by salesmen who promise more than the investment is likely to realize.

Other Phone Frauds

The diamond con isn't the only phone fraud going. Investors have been conned in commodity futures, antique musical instruments, works of art, and other items that turned out to be not worth the price. Businessmen have been conned by sellers of industrial chemicals that turned out to be of poor quality, overpriced fluorescent lights and poor-quality office fixtures. People also collect by phone for phony police and firemen's charities. Best rule: When you get a cold call about a terrific bargain, you can bet your wallet it probably isn't.

Business Frauds

Con men sell fake listings in fake business directories; send bills for unshipped merchandise; send and bill for unordered merchandise, at an exorbitant price; offer low-quality office furniture from fake distress sales. You may be urged to buy an ad in a nonexistent minority publication, under threat that if you don't, you might get into trouble with the Equal Employment Opportunity Commission.

Stolen Goods

Here's another situation where the bilked buyer probably deserves what he gets. Nevertheless, be reminded that someone who furtively offers you a gold watch "cheap" is probably selling a brass watch at triple the price he paid.

Medical Quacks

The elderly may be called on by a sympathetic salesman who chats with them, ascertains their problem, then sells them an expensive drug regimen to cure it. Sadly, some people even become attached to their worthless pills. Any medicine you take should be okayed by a doctor—which is no guarantee of its value, but at least it weeds out the more egregious frauds.

COD Deliveries After Death

A particularly heartless con is the delivery of a COD package (sometimes a Bible) to a widow just after the death of her husband. The thief says her husband ordered it, and the widow, believing him, pays two or three times what the item is really worth. If anyone like this shows up on your doorstep, send him to the person handling your spouse's will or send him away. You are under no obligation whatsoever to pay.

Missing Heirs

You might receive a letter saying that unclaimed money has been located, belonging to the descendants of a person with your last name. By sending $25, the "genealogical firm" will trace your ancestors to see if the money belongs to you. Such a letter will be mailed to hundreds, perhaps thousands, of people at the same time, and the "unclaimed money" could amount to as little as $25. Forget it.

What to Do About Frauds

Report phone fraud across state lines to the Federal Bureau of Investigation (local phone fraud to the police). Report mail fraud to the post office. Inform local consumer agencies and the Better Business Bureau. When you make a complaint, include all the details: your name and address, the name and address of the offending company, the nature of the fraud, and proof that you were taken—for example, a copy of a canceled check. You can also bring suit individually. If there's any hope of success, a lawyer may accept the case for no money up front, one third of the recovery if he wins, nothing if he loses.

Warning: The FBI or U.S. Postal Service generally pursue only those cases significant enough to justify the expense involved. If yours is the only case, you may be discouraged that no action is taken. That's why it's so important to report every case of fraud. The more complaints against a specific operator, the more likely the government will follow through on prosecution.

Second warning: Many people trust work-at-home schemes advertised in newspapers because they think newspapers screen the ads. They generally don't. If you're bilked by such an ad, complain bitterly to the newspaper; maybe it will change its policy.

Chapter Eleven

BUYING
A CAR

The first and great commandment is, don't let them
scare you.

ELMER RICE DAVIS

Many people approach the car-buying process with mistrust, even fear.
They need a car and may see just what they want on the showroom
floor. But as soon as a salesman walks up, they get nervous. Will he lie
or mislead? Will he take advantage of my ignorance? Will he sell me a
lemon? Will he get me to pay more than I really should? Some buyers
love the bargaining process; for them, a good haggle is the sauce of life.
Others are frightened by the need to make and refuse offers. For the
timid bargainer it's particularly intimidating to know that the salesman
knows exactly how low he's willing to go in price, whereas the customer
doesn't. You can't evaluate his statements—is the offer really just $100
over cost?—or tell whether you're paying more than you have to. But
there's a simple way to get your courage up: Find out in advance the
wholesale price of the car you want. Add $200 or $300 for profit, and
figure that any price in that ballpark is a good one. It's as easy as
snapping your fingers to find out a car's wholesale price—for directions,
see the following.

Armchair Pricing

There are more facts available to consumers about automobiles than any other product I can think of. Here are two good sources to consult:

1. Edmund Publications, 515 Hempstead Turnpike, Hempstead, N.Y. 11552. They publish nine books a year on the wholesale prices of cars (including light trucks and vans)—three on new cars, four on used cars, and two on foreign cars. Single copies are available on newsstands or from Edmund at $2.50 each, plus 50 cents postage.

2. Davis Publications, 380 Lexington Ave., New York, N.Y. 10017. Davis publishes Car/Puter's annual *New Car Yearbook* (which describes the cars), three editions of wholesale new-car prices and one used-car price guide. All are $1.75 each, on newsstands or from the publisher.

Both Davis and Edmund also give the wholesale prices of all the options you might choose for each model. By adding them together you can get the true wholesale price of exactly the car you want.

Computer Pricing

If the price guides confuse you or you don't want to bother figuring the cost out yourself, there are two companies that will do it for you. Just fill in one of their forms, specifying the make and model you want, plus all the options; they'll send you a computer printout detailing exactly what the dealer would have to pay for the car at the factory. Car/Puter charges $15 per quote (1603 Bushwick Ave., Brooklyn, N.Y. 11207), and at Computerized Car Costs, it's $5.95 for the first quote and $5 for each additional (Eleven Mile Lahser Station, Southfield, Mich. 48037). Dealers say that these prices are right to the penny.

When you go into an auto showroom, look on the car sticker to see what the freight charge was (for shipping the car to the dealer). Adding this to the wholesale cost tells you what the dealer paid for the car.

Armchair Buying

The computer-pricing services just mentioned are each affiliated with low-markup car-selling operations. All three offer most American cars (except luxury makes) for $125 over dealer's cost. Luxury makes, certain foreign cars, and light trucks go for a little more but often less than your local dealer offers. Car/Puter's United Auto Brokers is by far the largest in the business, and delivers in most cities and areas throughout the country. The Motor Club Auto Buying Service, affiliated with Computerized Car Costs, delivers in twenty-two cities. The addresses for these services are given in the previous section. Some corporations join buying clubs, such as the United Buying Service, to provide discounts for their employees.

These groups work with local auto dealers who agree to accept the low markup in return for the volume of business the affiliation brings. They are just as obliged to do your warranty work and handle other complaints as if you had paid the full sticker price. Other auto dealers may give dire warnings about dealing with auto brokers, suggesting that service will be bad and warranty work nonexistent. But I've talked with a number of people who buy cars this way, who say that's not the case. There are occasional problems—but that can happen with any auto dealer.

If the dealer affiliated with the auto broker is some distance from your house, using the buying service may not be practical. It's a long way to go for warranty work, and although your local dealer is usually required by the company to make warranty repairs even for cars he didn't sell, he might do it slowly and grudgingly.

One warning: Dealers make extra money on their low-markup cars by charging a fee for "dealer preparation," so be sure to figure that into the price. They might also jack up the price for undercoating, waxing, or other special jobs you want done. If the price sounds high, tell them you'll have that work done elsewhere. Another trick is to tell you that the car came with one or two "extras" that will cost you $200 more (see "Dirty Tricks Dealers Play," page 180). In that case refuse the car and complain to the buying service. Most likely, the car will suddenly materialize as ordered. If the dealer treats you rudely or is tough about warranty work, again, complain to the buying service. They generally drop dealers who treat their customers badly.

Ten Thoughts on the Kind of Car to Buy

1. Four-door cars are much easier for people to get in and out of than two-door cars.

2. Safety harnesses that are both comfortable and easy to reach will more likely be used.

3. If you travel a lot and are considering a foreign car, buy from a manufacturer with a large network of dealers and competent mechanics. Otherwise, you might find yourself stuck on the road with no ready help available.

4. The extra cost of large station wagons is worth it only if you often carry a lot of cargo. For occasional haul jobs a roof rack or rented trailer will do just as well.

5. The Environmental Protection Agency checks all models for the number of miles they get per gallon of gas and publishes the list. You'll find it in consumer publications; also, each car has a sticker noting its gas mileage. That won't necessarily be the mileage you get. But by making comparative use of these figures, you'll get a car that's less expensive than others to operate.

6. The honesty and reliability of the auto dealer is usually more important than the make of car you buy, or even the price. You've gained nothing if the shop that gave you the best price does incompetent warranty work. If you know of a particularly good dealer, it's worth buying from him whatever kind of car he sells.

7. Hatchback cars or station wagons that reveal what's in the trunk can be a temptation to thieves.

8. The lowest-priced car of a particular line generally has about the same basic components as the highest-priced. The difference lies in upholstery, trim, and other nonessentials.

9. Sedans generally cost less than hardtops, have more room inside, and are less prone to rattles.

10. If you buy a compact car to save money and improve gas mileage, you're defeating your purpose by loading it up with expensive and power-consuming options.

Options

Manufacturers offer an enormous variety of extras. Any car you buy right off the dealer's floor is probably loaded with them, since they add considerably to his profit. So if options aren't your game, shop for a car well in advance of the time you'll need it. It might be several weeks before the exact car you want can be shipped from the factory.

Two Cars?

Many American families think they can't do without a second car, and for some that's true. But for many others a second car costs far more than the good they get out of it. Look at it this way: A compact car driven as a secondary car costs you around $1,600 a year in depreciation, maintenance, gas and oil, insurance, and other expenses. If you borrow money to buy it, you might pay another $500 a year in interest, bringing your total annual cost to around $2,100. If you eliminated the second car and applied its cost to alternate transportation, you'd have $40 a week to get around with. A wife at home with only an occasional need to drive might find it cheaper to take taxis than own a car. If you both work, you could car-pool together, saving time-consuming errands for Saturdays. It is certainly more convenient to be able to jump into your own car anytime you want, and for many people that comes first. But at least examine your options before deciding. You might well prefer to put that $2,100 a year toward something else.

Choosing a Dealer

Ideally, you want a place that's nearby, run by a person who performs reliable warranty service and who offers fair prices. Ask your friends who maintains their cars; it's often worth it to locate a dealer with a good repair shop, then buy whatever kind of car he happens to sell. Look at his service area. It should be two to three times the size of his showroom, or he's not serious about repairs. It should also be neat and busy, with all the parking spaces taken up by customers' cars, not some old wrecks. Check around for diagnostic equipment, such as an engine oscilloscope, that can take the expensive guesswork out of repairs. You want a shop that the dealer has spent a lot of money to equip properly. If he says you can't look at his repair area "because the insurance policy won't allow it," forget him: He's putting you on. Also don't do business with a dealer who misled you during the selling process. Unethical salesmen usually mean unethical repairmen.

When to Buy

1. You often get a price break in the middle of winter, when traffic is slow and the dealers are eager to move cars. In the past, prices have risen in the spring and tapered off toward the end of summer. But thanks to inflation, manufacturers are now raising car prices several times a year—so you'll probably pay less early in the model year rather than later on. Any leftovers from the old year are discounted after the new models arrive in October.

2. Because of sales contests prices may be a little better at the end of a month. Dealers are willing to give a little in order to sneak in a few more sales before the deadline.

3. If you read in the paper that this or that kind of car is in oversupply, you can be pretty sure of getting a price break if you want to buy one. Friday's *Wall Street Journal* lists the production figures for each model; zero production is often a tipoff to cars in oversupply.

4. From time to time a manufacturer will offer special discounts in order to move his merchandise. These will be announced in newspaper ads or signs in the dealer's showroom.

Estimating the Price

If you've done your homework, you'll walk into the showroom knowing the wholesale price of the car you want and how much you're willing to pay over cost (see page 172). People who don't price in advance can get a fair approximation of wholesale cost of American cars this way: Get the sticker price of the car you want plus all the options (but leave out freight charges, taxes, and any other fees). On a full-sized car the dealer probably paid around 83 percent of that price; on a compact, around 88 percent; and on a luxury car, around 80 percent. These are rough estimates, but they give you some idea of where the bargaining line lies. Dealers like to make at least $300 over cost, although some will take as little as $125 for some cars, and occasionally less. Your price, then, is the dealer's cost, plus whatever markup you accept, plus freight, plus taxes, plus whatever other fees the dealer tacks on. Watch out for the extra fees. The dealer may let you bargain down his markup, then recoup by charging a big car preparation cost or selling you credit life insurance. Consider every nickel you lay out as part of the price of the car, and comparison-shop accordingly.

There's no rule of thumb for figuring the wholesale cost of foreign cars; you'll have to get a price guide. In past years foreign cars were all sold at list price with little or no bargaining. But lately, dealers have been more willing to give a little.

How to Negotiate a Price

There's no single "right" way to haggle. But the following elements will be part of any successful negotiation:

Knowledge

Have a good idea of what the car cost the dealer and how much markup you want to pay. If the salesman offers $600 over cost, you know it's too high. You can counter with $125 over cost, which for this dealership may be too low but not so unrealistically low that the salesman decides you're not serious. By keeping the haggle in the right ballpark, you keep the negotiation alive.

Ammunition

If you have a new-car price guide or a computer printout price for the car you want, take it with you. It shows the salesman you can't be fooled. Lacking this, you should have prices from other dealers, so the salesman knows you're shopping for a "skinny deal." If this is the first showroom you've visited, don't lie about lower offers you've had elsewhere, but let the salesman know you'll be comparing his price with others.

Time

When you need a car immediately, you may not be able to do the comparison shopping that a good haggle requires. Also, you have to buy a car off the showroom floor, which means it may be loaded with more options than you'd otherwise choose. However, remember that the dealer has had to borrow money to purchase all those cars he has on display. If the floor model is approximately what you want, you can probably get it for less than a similar model ordered from Detroit because you're taking it off the dealer's hands.

Good Temper

Most auto salesmen like to haggle. It's their business. But they don't like to be pushed around or treated like crooks. Keep the negotiation friendly, and don't try to win a point by saying (falsely) that you've had an unbelievable offer from the dealer down the street. The salesman knows you're lying, so it won't affect his offer. And it locks you into an unrealistic request because you might feel you'd lose face by backing off. One other point: If you're rude to the salesman, then wind up buying from him, he may be less than thorough about checking out your new car, and the dealership might be grudging about warranty repairs.

An Approach

Don't ask, "What's the price?" Say, "I know what you paid for this car, and I want to pay as little over that as I possibly can. I'm ready to make a deal right away if you give me a good price." Or, "I'm shopping for the best price I can get from a good dealer, and I've visited other showrooms [or am going to]. I'm not just browsing—I definitely mean to buy a car. But I want to know the very best price you can give me." And, "Quote me a total price—taxes, fees, everything. I don't want any extra charges thrown at me after we've agreed to a deal." This last point is important; many a salesman wins you with a low price, then at contract time adds $150 for "dealer preparation," which brings his total price above that of another dealer who charges nothing extra for dealer prep.

When the salesman quotes you his "best price," counter it with something lower. If you're hoping to pay $200 over dealer's cost, start at $125 over and go up.

Don't be afraid to say "I can't afford" a higher price. If he comes down a little, shake your head and say, "still too high." When you increase your offer, ask if he'll throw in floormats, a luggage rack, or some other small item. Keep talking, looking, comparing, thinking aloud until the salesman really holds firm—which at bottom may be somewhere between $200 or $300 over cost. Say, "Is that the best you can do for me? Is that really your lowest offer?" If so, ask if it's a firm price, or if he has to check with the sales manager first. When you have a figure, write it down, thank the salesman, and say you're going to think about it. Even if you've said that you're ready to make a deal, you can still write the price down to think about it overnight.

Savvy

If a dealer offers you a price far lower than you're getting from everyone else, it's probably a "low ball." When you return to his showroom ready to buy, he'll have some excuse for not holding to the original figure. But in the same breath he'll ask what your next lowest bid was, then give you a price $50 or so below it. By doing business with him you'll save yourself $50. But he's put you on notice that he'll cheerfully lie to get what he wants, which could mean you'll have trouble getting warranty work done. It might be better to pay the extra $50 and buy from a dealer who gave you an honest price. In fact, it might be wisest to buy from the nearest good dealer to your home, using the prices you got from the other dealers merely as counters to bargain him down.

A Sense of Priorities

There are generally two points to negotiate: the new-car price and the price the dealer will pay for your old car on a trade-in. Often, dealers will offer you more than the old car is worth, then make up their loss by keeping the new-car price higher than it need be. Since so many customers don't know the wholesale price of the new car, they don't realize they've paid more than necessary. All they see is the "good deal" available on the trade-in, and sign up. You'll get maximum advantage by bargaining hard on the new-car price first. If the dealer then tries to recoup by offering less for the trade-in, you might consider selling your old car privately (see "Pricing the Trade-in," page 191).

Dealer Prep

The once-over a dealer gives your car when it comes from the factory is called dealer preparation. His fee for this service is normally built into the sticker price of the car. But because manufacturers don't allow as much as dealers would like, some of them put a second "prep" sticker on the window, in effect charging you twice. Or a prep fee may be preprinted on the contract, to make you think the charge is standard. Most foreign cars and a few compact and subcompacts don't include dealer prep in the sticker price, so in that case, a small extra fee is legitimate. But otherwise, it's just another way of raising the price.

Dealers can deceive you as to the true price you're paying for a car by quoting $100 less than the competition, then hitting you with a $150 prep charge when you sign the contract. It's for this reason that you should ask the salesman for his total price, including all extra fees. If he quotes you $4,000 and then tries to slip an extra $150 into the contract, refuse to sign. Say, "This price exceeds the final figure you gave me. It's not what we agreed on." Or, "With this prep charge your car is more expensive than that of the other dealer I visited. I told you I'm shopping for price, and you're no longer low bidder." When they see you mean it, the prep charge will vanish.

Other Charges

There are other odds and ends that a dealer might tack onto the final price. Some list an "advertising cost," which is the dealer's share of the manufacturer's national ad campaigns; other dealers merely include it in the general markup. You pay the freight charge for transporting the car from the factory. There are excise taxes and sales taxes (in some states you can deduct the value of the trade-in from the new-car cost and pay sales taxes only on the difference). Generally there's a charge for the initial gas and oil. They may also add such extras as title fees and inspection fees. When you're comparison shopping, figure every one of these fees into the total cost, so you can get a true picture of what each dealer charges. If you finance through a dealer, he also makes money on the finance charge and any credit life or property insurance he sells you.

Dirty Tricks Dealers Play

Car dealers use a variety of "gentle gimmicks"—little tricks of salesmanship intended to speed your buying decision and perhaps add some extras you hadn't originally wanted. There's nothing wrong with using normal acts of persuasion; you expect it from all salesmen. But some dealers go beyond little tricks to dirty tricks. If you even suspect that this might be happening to you, *walk out*—before he gets his hand on your wallet. Here's how a car crook works:

1. When he learns that you're shopping around, he'll give you a deliberately low bid (low ball) to be sure you come back. Then he "discovers" that he made a mistake and ups the bid.

2. He'll give you and your spouse a private room where you can talk the matter over, but the room is bugged. Listening in on your conversation tells him how much you're willing to pay and how to counter your doubts. (This, incidentally, is illegal, but it may be done.)

3. He'll go to contract with an unusually low price, then call three weeks later to say it will take six months to get the car unless you're willing to accept a similar one this weekend for a few hundred dollars more.

4. He'll remove factory-installed options from your car (such as expensive radial tires or a good radio) and replace them with cheaper

ones. As far as you are able, check all the options against the sticker before accepting delivery.

5. He'll make you wait a long time for your car in order to make you impatient. When it comes in, he'll add something extra, such as a vinyl roof or other options. The next step is to call you, tell you the car has finally arrived but with some "extras" you hadn't ordered; you can have it as is for another $200, or reorder and wait several months more. In most cases the customer accepts the costlier car.

6. He'll tell you (falsely) that the truck carrying your car had an accident and you'll have to wait several months for another car—unless you're willing to take a car in stock that's about what you want but just happens to cost a little more.

Your Defense Against Dirty Tricks

It's simple. Walk away from the guy. If the salesman comes back from the manager's office with the bad news that the manager just couldn't approve the low price the two of you just agreed on, *leave*—he's playing you for a sucker. Do the same if you got a "low ball" offer that was upped on some pretense when you returned. Any dealership that lies to you once will lie to you twice.

If you learn that your car "came in" with $200 worth of extras, say, "Gee, that's too bad, but I'll wait for the right car." The right one should materialize pretty quickly. Of course, if you wait until your car is on its last legs before buying a new one, you may be stuck. The dealer knows you can't wait another two months for the "right" car to arrive. Crooked dealers are tough when they know your need is great; even if you earnestly protest that you can't afford the "extras," they'll make believe there's nothing they can do except order you another car. Most customers eventually pay up. To beat a crook, you have to be willing to say no. If you've waited overly long and then get a runaround, you'd do best to demand your down payment back, threatening to complain to the Chamber of Commerce, Better Business Bureau, and anyone else you can think of. You're better off starting fresh with an honest dealer, no matter what the temporary inconvenience, than depending on a dishonest dealer for any warranty work that might come up. One final thing: When you run into a crook, spread the word. The sad fact is that a dishonest dealer can spend a lifetime stealing from people who walk into his showroom, always using his false low prices to bring in new customers. The more people you tell about your experience, the more customers you'll deny him.

Dirty Tricks Customers Play

Not all the graft in car trading is on the dealer's side. Plenty of customers cheat, too. They do it by keeping their mouths shut about what's wrong with the car they're trading in, in hopes of getting a better price than the heap is worth. Some aggressively mask the car's faults—dirty tricks that hurt not only the dealer but the next buyer, who'll probably get stuck with the major repair expenses. Here's how the game is played:

• If the transmission is bad, a dishonest owner will load it up with fluid, which masks the problem for fifty or sixty miles. Since dealers rarely drive the car much more than around the block, this ploy often works.

• Owners rarely admit that their car was in a major accident. Yet in some states it's illegal for a dealer to sell such a car without informing the customer that it was once badly banged up. If an accident occurs between the time of appraisal and actual trade-in, many owners will try to mask it—hammering out dents and having other cosmetic work done. Also, they'll fail to report any new mechanical problems that develop.

• If the car was appraised with new tires on it, some owners will replace them with worn ones before turning the car in. This might be caught if the dealer checks the car carefully against the appraiser's sheet. But if the customer insists the sheet is mistaken, the dealer will sometimes let it go to keep the peace.

• Some people get a mechanic to turn the odometer back in order to make it appear that the car was driven fewer miles than is actually the case. This is illegal, but it is rarely caught. Many dealers themselves turn odometers back, which makes the recorded mileage a poor guide for judging a used car.

• Some people sell cars they still owe money on without revealing the debt. When the bank or finance company stops receiving payment they will repossess, despite the fact that the dealer or other new owner bought in good faith. Similarly, a person might sell a car that has been attached to pay off a judgment. If you ever buy from a private individual, it should always be someone you know, or someone who is known to one of your friends, so if problems like this arise, you can be reasonably sure of finding him again. Always check for a clear title before you buy in a private sale.

If a dealer finds out that he's been cheated, he may come back at you and try to collect. But if the case would be hard to prove, or the financial damage is small, he will absorb it as a business expense. Generally, he'll just wholesale your car to another dealer, who'll sell it with as few repairs as possible to an unsuspecting customer. It's transactions like this, involving dishonesty on the part of both dealer and car owner, that help give the car-selling business such a bad name.

Signing the Contract

Read it closely to make sure you're ordering exactly the car you want. Ask the dealer to include a specified, and reasonable, delivery date (not just an "anticipated date," which isn't binding). Don't leave any spaces blank (lest something be added after you sign). Double-check that it includes *only* the services you want; if you rejected undercoating, make sure it was taken out of the price. The dealer generally reserves the right to raise the price if the manufacturer suddenly raises the price charged to the dealer, but in that case, the contract should permit you to cancel the deal. The contract may also give the dealer the right to reappraise your old car at the actual time of trade-in and adjust the allowance downward, although, again, you should be able to cancel if you don't like the new offer. Don't let any last-minute surprises be put over on you at contract time. If the salesman suddenly comes up with a little cost he overlooked, he's kidding you. That's the moment to say *no,* and be willing to walk out the door to a more honest dealer unless you can get the price that was agreed on.

Getting Financing

For many people buying a car is principally a matter of "how much a month" and "who'll lend me the money." If a dealer offers financing at a monthly payment they can afford, questions of car price and even interest rate go out the window. They sign the dealer's loan agreement on the spot. This is particularly true if an old car has to be turned in before it's all paid for, meaning that the new loan will have to be enough both to close out the old car and finance the new. The more a buyer is pinched for money, the less attention he often pays to making the wisest economic choice.

But even when money is a problem, don't go for the dealer's loan right at the start. Try to arrange financing before you walk into the showroom. A credit union generally (but not always) offers the lowest interest rates, a savings and loan association or bank second, and a finance company or auto dealership third. Some chapters of the American Automobile Association offer low-cost financing to members. Go to the cheapest source first and work up. In some places the rates offered by auto dealers are competitive with some bank rates; in that case you have an overpriced bank. Sometimes you're offered a slightly lower price on the car by financing with a dealer (because he makes something on the loan), but because of the way the bargaining process works, it's hard to tell if this has actually happened. Anyway, paying via the credit agreement what you "saved" in the car price is no bargain. If you must rely on a dealer for financing, don't let that fact interfere with the bargaining process. Negotiate for the best total price you can get, without being lulled by the notion of "only" so much a month.

When you shop for bank or S&L financing, always try more than one place. The spread in interest rates is often large. A big bank downtown might charge 16 percent for a three-year loan, while a smaller bank or one in the suburbs is charging 12 percent. On a $4,000 loan that's a difference of $17 a month. That may not sound like a lot, but over three years it comes to $612—and I can certainly think of things to do with $612 rather than give it to a high-priced bank.

If credit union, bank, or S&L financing isn't available, check the rates offered by a finance company and see if you qualify for a loan. But don't sign up yet. Do your bargaining with the auto dealer, telling him (if he asks) that you're going to finance the car but haven't yet decided where. Once you've fixed on a price, ask what *annual percentage rate* he charges for loans. If his terms are better than what the finance company offers, borrow through the dealer.

In recent years autos have grown so expensive that many people are financing them over four years (or even five) rather than the traditional three. Their object is to keep the monthly payment down, even though it means stretching out the term of the loan. However, the longer the term, the more interest you ultimately have to pay. The following table shows your monthly payment and total cost for a $4,000 auto loan, at various periods of time:

THE HIGH COST OF LONGER TERMS

at 10% interest*			at 12% interest*		
Number of years	Monthly payment	Total cost of borrowing	Number of years	Monthly payment	Total cost of borrowing
1	$351.29	$ 215.48	1	$354.86	$ 258.32
2	184.21	421.04	2	187.76	506.24
3	128.69	632.84	3	132.31	763.16
4	101.07	851.36	4	104.77	1,028.96
5	84.60	1076.00	5	88.40	1,304.00
at 14% interest*			at 16% interest*		
Number of years	Monthly payment	Total cost of borrowing	Number of years	Monthly payment	Total cost of borrowing
1	$358.42	$ 301.04	1	$361.97	$ 343.64
2	191.32	591.68	2	194.89	677.36
3	135.96	894.56	3	139.63	1,026.68
4	108.53	1,209.44	4	112.33	1,391.84
5	92.27	1,563.20	5	96.20	1,772.00
*For a loan of $4,000					

As you can see, the longer you take to repay, the lower your monthly payment—but the more interest you owe over the life of the loan. The cheapest loan is one where you put down as large a down payment as possible and pay off as fast as possible.

Lenders nowadays often urge that you buy insurance to pay off your loan if you die, lose your job, or become too ill to work. You can get it through the auto dealer or the lender—but be aware that it's *overpriced*. For the pros and cons of credit insurance, see page 103. If you need more insurance coverage, it's generally better to buy an inexpensive term policy from a life insurance agent. Credit unions and some banks and S&Ls provide credit insurance free.

Warranties

Repairs done under warranty can be a battlefield between dealer and customer. Some dealers give you no trouble at all: They take the car in and fix it promptly. Others put you off, accept the car in bad grace, take weeks to get around to it, and finally give you a sloppy repair job that doesn't last a month. Dealers don't like warranty work because the automakers don't pay them as much as they'd get if the work were out of warranty—but it's a dealer's obligation to honor a warranty (even if you didn't buy the car from him). If he gives you any guff, complain in writing to the manufacturer (your owner's manual will tell you where to write), but there's no guarantee that the manufacturer will do anything, either. The National Highway Traffic Safety Administration handles warranty problems as well as other complaints against dealers or manufacturers; their toll-free number is (800) 424–9393. Under the new holder-in-due-course law (see page 132), you may even be able to quit making time payments on a car that isn't being properly serviced under the warranty.

Many of the squabbles about what is or is not covered under the warranty have been ended by the Magnuson-Moss Warranty Act (see page 148). When you buy a car, read the brochure that spells out exactly what is covered and for how long a period. Some manufacturers have better warranties than others—something to consider when you are deciding what make to get (you can get copies of the competing warranties from car dealers). Look particularly for exceptions, which the warranty doesn't cover. Typically, the warranty does *not* extend to tires; normal maintenance (such as replacing spark plugs, ignition points, filters, and brake and clutch linings that have suffered normal wear); conditions arising from misuse, negligence, or an accident; and cars that have not been properly maintained. In other words you can't mistreat and neglect your car for eleven months, then take it in for major repairs just before the warranty runs out and expect the dealer to fix it for nothing. At this writing, warranties normally run for twelve months or twelve thousand miles, whichever comes first. Particular parts may be warranted for two years, and the manufacturer of the battery may give you three-year protection. It's all spelled out in the warranty folder, along with directions on what to do if you aren't satisfied with the repairs.

Tips:☐When you take your car in for its last regular servicing before the warranty expires, ask the mechanic to give it a thorough going over, checking all the major components. You might find a badly worn part that should be replaced, which otherwise would give out just after the warranty expired.☐Sometimes dealers make free repairs after the warranty expires, if the problem is serious and should have been caught before, so by all means ask.☐If there's an imperfection in the paint or trim, point it out to the dealer right away. The longer you drive with it, the more likely he is to conclude that it developed because of misuse rather than factory error.☐Warranty work is normally done by the dealer who sold you the car. But if you move away, you can take it to any authorized dealer, who is required to make the repairs at no charge.

The Magnuson-Moss Warranty Act has *not* solved the most persistent problem with auto warranties: namely, how to get a reluctant dealer to perform as promised. The Federal Trade Commission has proposed amendments to the act in order to strengthen consumer protections.

If you buy a lemon, a dealer is required to take it back only if you have a "full" warranty and you've allowed him a reasonable number of chances to make repairs. At this writing, only American Motors offers a full warranty, so the vast majority of car buyers don't have this protection. Under a limited warranty the dealer has a right to tinker with your lemon until you give up and trade it in. State law grants you rights not mentioned in the warranty. By suing under state law, many consumers have in fact won replacement for their lemons. But before you can sue, you generally have to return the car to the dealer and revoke ownership. You'll need another car, and the lawsuit could take years. There is, in other words, little effective help for the consumer who has bought an expensive, ill-functioning car that a dealer can't repair. For a free fact sheet on private legal remedies, write to Public Reference Room 130, Federal Trade Commission, Washington, D.C. 20580.

Secret Warranties

Some models of cars develop problems that aren't serious enough to warrant a public safety recall but that make so many customers mad the company is willing to make good. Instructions go out to dealers to make a certain type of repair at no charge, *if* the owner complains. So anytime something goes wrong with your car that you blame on shoddy manufacture, complain to the dealer. There may be a secret warranty that will take care of it.

What About Gas Mileage Claims?

The Federal Environmental Protection Agency checks how many miles per gallon each model will get. The results are affixed to the car by sticker, and in the case of gas-efficient cars they are widely advertised. But don't expect to get that kind of mileage yourself. The government's tests are done on a machine rather than on the highway, so the cars aren't penalized by wind or road resistance. Also, due to technical peculiarities of the test, a small change in car weight may make the mileage appear to improve more than is actually the case. Nevertheless, the EPA tests do provide a general guide as to which cars get the better mileage.

The Owner's Manual

It's not a piece of great literature, but the owner's manual is certainly one of the most valuable books you'll ever own. Regrettably, some people lose it, throw it out, or never read it; then they get sore when their car doesn't last as long as they think it should. Everything you need to know about operating and maintaining your car, as well as getting complaints resolved, is covered in the owner's manual. It tells you how to operate all the controls efficiently; what the warning lights on the dashboard mean and what to do when they flash; how to handle a car when you're hauling a trailer; how to find out whether a foreign country you plan to drive through has the right gasoline for your car; the proper way to maintain the car, inside and out; which tires to buy and how to rotate them; what might be wrong with the engine if it won't start, or runs badly, under certain conditions; how to make minor repairs; where to complain if you get poor service from the dealer; and specific warnings about what not to do when driving or tinkering with your car. For a novice the owner's manual is the ideal guide to car care; for the experienced driver, it's a reminder about car basics plus a detailed guide to the peculiarities of that particular model. Read it through when the car is new, then keep it to consult as needed.

When to Trade Your Car In

Is there a "right" time to trade in your car? A magic moment when the cost of maintaining an aging auto is so high that it makes economic sense to pack it in and start again? The answer is no. Speaking purely from an economic point of view, it's smarter to drive your car into the ground than trade it in—undertaking whatever repairs are necessary as long as you can hold it together.

But people don't make new-car decisions based entirely on cost. Reliability is equally important, and as a car ages, it becomes more likely to suffer breakdowns. If you drive a lot, especially far from home, it's important that your car get you there and back without throwing a piston on the freeway. When, then, does the average car grow so unreliable that you might not want to keep it as your primary means of transportation?

This question has an approximate answer, gleaned from figures published annually by the U.S. Department of Transportation on the average costs of running a car.

It appears that the average driver should be able to keep his car for around seventy thousand miles (probably around the sixth year). During that time he will likely encounter only *one* period when a lot of big things might go wrong with the car. That's around the forty-five-thousand-mile mark—generally in the fourth year of ownership (but earlier, if you drive a lot). The bills for maintenance and repair build up to a peak in that year and then drop off. They don't increase again until after the car has gone around seventy-five thousand miles, generally in the seventh year.

Many people replace their cars in the fourth year, when the first big thing goes wrong. They imagine that from that point on, the repair bills will just get bigger and bigger. But in fact, once you make that major investment in new parts, the car is pretty much set to run for another two years. In the fifth and sixth year of ownership the repair bills average about the same as they did in the third year.

Whether your car is standard-sized, a compact, or a subcompact, repairs follow the same cycle: taking a jump in the fourth year, falling back, and not rising to new peaks until year seven. If you sell the car in year six, or after it has gone around seventy thousand miles, you'll generally escape the next major round of breakdowns.

Of course, you could repair it again in the seventh year and drive it another thirty thousand miles (as its next owner will). But most people are reluctant to depend on cars of that age as their family's primary means of transportation if they can afford something better. If the car is kept, it will usually be as a second car and driven less.

Conventional wisdom has always held that depreciation is an important factor to consider when you decide on when to trade in your car. You're said to be "losing money" at the point when the cost of car repairs is higher than the depreciation, which generally happens in the fourth year.

In fact, it costs far less to repair the car and keep it than to turn it in for something new. That's because a new car depreciates so much in the first year that it "loses" you far more money than you'd spend repairing the old one.

For example, if you kept a standard-sized car three years, then traded it in, your total cost of transportation after four years—including everything from depreciation on the new car to insurance and gasoline—would be $9,485, according to 1976 government figures. By comparison, if you had your old car repaired, the four-year cost would by only $8,693—leaving you $792 ahead. After six years you would be $1,468 ahead. Savings in depreciation alone, after deducting for repair and maintenance, come to $834 if you drive your car for six years rather than trade it in after three.

Some people don't like to hang on to cars too long because they steadily lose trade-in value. But by focusing on the trade-in, you lose sight of the big picture. Between the third year and the sixth year, a standard-sized 1976 car loses around $1,112 in value. But if you traded it in after three years, depreciation on the new car would have cost you $2,393—which is $1,488 more than you "lost" by holding onto the old one.

Even if you drive your car so many miles that it needs a new engine and a new transmission, the economic arguments are on the side of making the repair and carrying on.

However, if you like to trade your car in often, it's unwise to buy toward the end of the model year. That's when depreciation really does get you. If you buy a 1979 car late in the summer, it becomes officially one year old in just a month or two, when the 1980 models come in. If you trade it in the following year, you'll be charged two years' worth of depreciation for only one year of driving. To come out even, your late-summer price would have to be discounted by at least the second year's depreciation. It's a rare dealer who will give you a price break of that size, on top of the few hundred dollars you expect to cut off the price through standard negotiation.

Preparing Your Car for Trade-in

Give the car a thorough cleaning inside. Since people like to ride in a pleasant environment, the condition of the interior is an important factor in determining the price. Don't leave a lot of clutter on the floor or back shelf. You want the dealer to see it at its best. Dealers sometimes don't clean the outside of their used cars because dust hides many a flaw in the paint. But individuals trying the same trick aren't likely to get a higher price, since the dealer will know what's being done to him.

If the car needs a tune-up, by all means have it done. A motor that sounds rough could make a dealer think that something is seriously wrong. Also, be sure the car has enough water, oil, and transmission and brake fluid. Don't bother spending money on a major repair; it's unlikely to raise the trade-in price enough to make it worth it. If you invest in a paint job, the dealer might suspect you're trying to cover up the signs of a bad accident. Minor repairs, such as fixing a clock, are rarely worth it, although you might want to replace a missing knob for cosmetic effect. If you can, bring the dealer the book that shows how often you've had the car serviced, so he'll know it was well taken care of.

If you hide serious defects that the dealer finds when you deliver the car, he'll adjust your trade-in price downward. Normally, someone will check your car against the initial appraisal sheet in order to make sure you haven't removed good tires or other equipment.

Pricing the Trade-in

It pleases people to get a higher price for their old cars than they had expected. For this reason a dealer may add $100 more to his offer than he thinks the car is worth, just to get your business. He'll then make it back by charging you $100 more (or perhaps $200 or $300 more) for the new car. When you're buying a car, never go by the new-car price or the trade-in price alone. Subtract the trade-in allowance from the dealer's best new-car price. The difference between the two is your price—the only price to use when comparing offers between competing dealers.

Dealers use standard books for pricing trade-ins. Your bank or credit union probably has one of the books if you want to know in advance about how much your car should bring. The offer is based on how old the car is, how many miles it's been driven, and its general condition. If it's a pretty good car, the dealer will overhaul it and resell it himself. Shabby cars are usually wholesaled and wind up on the lot of a used-car dealer. In any case the price the dealer offers you is a wholesale price, generally allowing a profit for him no matter how he disposes of it.

Sell Your Old Car Yourself?

You might be able to get $100 or $150 over the book value of your car by selling it yourself. Of course, you'll have advertising expenses and will have to put some time into the sale. If there's something seriously wrong with the car that you didn't disclose, the buyer might come back to you accompanied by his lawyer. Another problem is timing; the buyer might want the car before your new one arrives. But if these problems are no obstacle, you might want to try for the extra $100. Always get a cash binder from someone who says he wants the car subject to his finding a loan, and specify in writing the number of days he has to find it before you put the car back on the market (two days should be enough). Check the prospective buyer's driver's license, and don't let him take the car on a test drive without you; it may be the last you'll see of it. And unless you know him well, ask him to give you cash or a certified check (this guarantees that the check is good). If he tries to bargain you down to around the same price you'd get from an auto dealer, turn him down and sell to the dealer. Unless there's extra money in it, there's no sense opening yourself to possible complaints from a dissatisfied customer.

BUYING A USED CAR

Because of the high price of new cars many people who used to buy new autos now shop the used-car lots. Cars that are two to three years old are reliable enough to serve as a family's main means of transportation. The repair bills for a used car are higher than on a new one. But the initial cost of the car is so much less that you're well ahead of the game by buying "used" and spending whatever is necessary to put it in top running order.

Because the condition of used cars is so variable, the purchase is far more fraught with suspicion and potential for larceny than it is with a new car. Unless you're a mechanic, you really don't know what's under the hood. You pay your money and keep your fingers crossed. Here are some ways to minimize the risks of buying a beautiful wreck:

Where to Buy

The best cars are generally owned by a new-car dealer who has a used-car business on the side. When customers trade their cars in, he keeps the cream puffs for resale. The older cars and lemons are wholesaled to used-car lots. If you're lucky, you'll get a car that has been maintained right there in the dealer's shop, so the mechanic knows its history. He may even give you the original owner's name, so you can call him to talk about the car's strengths and weaknesses (and whether he's a traveling salesman and used it on the job—usually a sign of a hard-driven car). Used cars sold by new-car dealers aren't cheap, but they should be reliable. If they break down during the warranty period, they can be fixed right there in the dealer's own shop. In general, dealers in middle- and upper-class areas will sell a better quality of used cars than those in lower-class neighborhoods.

Cars sold on used-car lots are more of a mixed bag—some good and some that are rotten inside. As with anything else, you can't expect more than you pay for. A $600 car will give you a lot more trouble, and be laid up more, than a $2,000 car. But if all you want is wheels for local errands, or something for a teen-ager to cut his tinkering teeth on, a $600 car might be just the ticket.

You can also buy privately from an acquaintance or through an ad in the newspaper. Apply the same rules in this buying situation as you would on a used-car lot; never assume that just because a seller's a friend, he will be candid about the car's condition. If someone puts a classified ad in the paper, it's usually an attempt to get more money for the car than a dealer offered—perhaps justified, perhaps not. Only a mechanic can tell you for sure. Private sellers rarely give warranties of any sort. If you think you were fraudulently misled as to the car's condition, you can sue. But no matter who you buy from, if you're inexperienced, take someone with you who knows what he's talking about. That's your best insurance against being taken advantage of.

Warranties

If it isn't in writing, you don't have one. There are many used-car salesmen who will give you all manner of verbal assurances about the wreck you're looking at, but when you come around to collect, it's no dice. The only time to bargain with the dealer is before you've paid your money. Ask him to put his promises in writing, on the warranty or on the contract; if he won't, try another dealer.

In the past, printed warranties have been almost as unreliable as verbal promises. The large type says "thirty-day guarantee," while the small print excepts from coverage most of the car's running parts. (The Magnuson-Moss Warranty Act will eventually eliminate cheating clauses, but since it applies only to items manufactured after July 4, 1975, many used cars still aren't covered.) Dealers usually have several different warranties in their pockets, giving the better terms to the better cars. A cream puff may have a three-month guarantee, during which time the dealer will pay 50 percent of the repair costs if malfunctions arise. A car in poor shape will be sold "as is," with no promise as to how well it will work. (In some states, however, you can get your money back if a car bought "as is" is so broken down you can't move it off the lot.) A typical guarantee is for thirty days or one thousand miles, whichever is first, with 50 percent of the repair costs covered. Major parts, such as the drive train, are usually not included. In many cases the warranty is for parts only, with none of the labor costs covered. Some used-car dealers offer a special warranty on low-mileage cars, covering the major components for twelve months or twelve thousand miles. This raises the price of the car by $80 to $100 or more but gives the buyer some peace of mind.

New-car dealers with good shops are in the best position to honor their used-car warranties. Used-car lots generally have to use an independent repair shop and will probably select on the basis of low price rather than quality of work. But any way you slice it, the normal used-car warranty doesn't reach very far. Your best protection is to make a thorough mechanical check before you buy, rather than rely on a dealer's willingness to fix it if something goes wrong. At this writing, the Federal Trade Commission has just proposed a new disclosure rule to protect used-car buyers.

Odometers

One of the first things people look at in a used car is how many miles it's gone. But don't count on the odometer's being accurate. Mileage is still widely tampered with, despite a law making it a federal offense. If the car shows low mileage, look for points of wear elsewhere that might tend to give the odometer the lie. If the brake pedal is worn (or brand new), or there's heavy wear on the seats, floor mats, steering wheel, and other controls, it means the car has gone a lot of miles (perhaps as part of a fleet). Also, look for the sticker often put on cars by mechanics to show what the mileage was when the oil was last changed; if it's missing, there may be a reason.

It's not easy to prove that an odometer was set back. But if hard evidence comes your way, go to the dealer and demand a price adjustment (better yet, have your lawyer demand it for you). There are stiff penalties for violating the odometer law, and he won't want to be sued. Also, report violators to the Better Business Bureau, your area's consumer protection agency, and the Bureau of Consumer Protection, Federal Trade Commission, Washington, D.C. 20580.

Value

You get more for your money with a car that has few fancy accessories. A spartan $2,000 sedan is a better value than a $2,000 car with air conditioning, electric windows, and a vinyl roof. A newer car is generally a better value than an older one; a sedan is better than a hardtop; and a family car is better than a sporty car (which may have led a hard life). Complex accessories such as electric windows not only add to the price but also guarantee more repair bills in the future.

When you've narrowed your search to a particular model, call the National Highway Traffic Safety Administration in Washington, D.C., to see if they have any information about it. People all over the United States call the NHTSA with complaints about cars, which the information desk may be able to pass along to you. You'll also be told whether that particular car has ever been subject to recall for a safety defect, so you can check to see if the repair work was actually done. The toll-free number of the National Highway Traffic Safety Administration is (800) 424–9393.

Price

There are three ways to judge the fairness of the price you're offered.

1. Check the classified newspaper ads, to get an idea of what similar cars are selling for.

2. Ask your dealer (or bank, or credit union) to show you one of the standard wholesale price guides that dealers use as a basis for pricing (and lenders use as a basis for making loans).

3. Compare prices in one of the used-car price guides published for the public: *Edmund's Used Car Prices,* $2.50 plus 50 cents postage, from Edmund Publications, 515 Hempstead Turnpike, West Hempstead, N.Y. 11552; Car/Puter's *Used Car Prices,* $1.75, from Davis Publications, 380 Lexington Ave., New York, N.Y. 10017. Both publications are also available on some newsstands.

Note: Prices can change suddenly if there are changes in market conditions. For example, after the Arab oil embargo, prices on small used cars rose, whereas those on large gas guzzlers collapsed. A car found to have a safety problem will sell for less because it's a higher risk to drive than other cars. Changes in manufacturing decisions can suddenly change a price; for example, when it was announced that convertibles would be phased out, their price on the used-car market rose (despite the fact that parts for cars no longer in production can be hard to find). Sometimes dealers may offer you a special price because the car was repossessed, but in that case, the car is probably no bargain. Anyone who couldn't afford to make car payments also couldn't afford to keep the car properly maintained. If the car had been in good condition, the dealer would have charged a higher price.

Financing

The interest rate on used-car loans is higher than that for new cars, and the lender generally requires a higher-percentage down payment. If the car is quite old, you may not be able to get a car loan at all. Instead, the lender may insist that you take a personal loan, secured by some other collateral. But always visit more than one lender. The interest rate on car loans varies tremendously from lender to lender (see page 86), and although one might turn you down, another might be glad to have you.

Inspecting a Used Car

Once a car satisfies your layman's eye and driving sense, ask a mechanic to come to the lot to give it the once-over, or arrange for the car to spend an hour in his shop. The $40 or $50 you might spend on the inspection is pennies compared to the value of the advice you'll receive, especially if the mechanic warns you that a car you planned to buy is rotten at the core. Any used-car dealer can arrange the time to have the car checked. If he refuses to do so, don't weaken and buy the car anyway. Tell him politely that although you want the car, you wouldn't dream of buying it without a mechanic's okay; if he persists in his refusal, assume the worst and walk away.

Some tips on inspecting a used car, from the National Highway Traffic Safety Administration:

In the Lot

1. Go in the daytime, when it isn't raining. Rain and the bright lights of a nighttime used-car lot keep you from seeing all that you should. Also, don't shop when you're tired or haven't the time to thoroughly check out every operating part of the car.

2. Carefully check the exterior. You're looking for rust, dents, and evidence that parts of the car have rusted out and been repaired with putty (which will fall out pretty soon) and then painted over. Pay special attention to the bottom of the door and the rear fenders. Look for evidence of a new paint job, which may indicate that the car was in an accident and has things to hide.

3. Look under the car for breaks in the frame, signs that the frame has been welded, and excessive rust. Check the condition of the muffler, tailpipe, and exhaust pipe—if you don't know what those items should look like, shop for your car with someone who does. Check the ground under the car, for signs of oil or transmission-fluid leakage, or fluid leaking from shock absorbers.

4. Unevenly worn tires sometimes indicate mechanical problems. The tip-off tire may be the spare in the trunk. Good, new tires normally go thirty-five to forty thousand miles—so if the tires on the car are badly worn (or brand new), assume at least that much mileage, no matter what the odometer says. Look for signs of brake fluid leaking on the inside of the tires.

5. Check all the windows and window glass. Be sure all the lights are working—headlights, taillights, flashers, backup lights, brake lights, turn signals, running lights on the fenders. If a light is out, there may be something wrong with the wiring.

6. Check the shock absorbers by pushing down on the corners of the car, front and back. If the car bounces up and down several times, the shocks are worn.

7. While standing at a distance, look for evidence that the car has been in an accident. Some telltale signs: ripples in the fender, dents, paint that doesn't match around the edges of the door and trunk. Also from a distance, see if the car is level. If one corner is lower than another, one of the springs may be weak or broken.

8. Be sure the car has a jack that works.

9. Under the hood, look at the belts and hoses, and check the battery to see if it's cracked. Pull out the oil dipstick to see how dirty the oil is. Lubrication stickers on the doorposts or under the hood will tell you how regularly and carefully the previous owner attended to the car's maintenance.

10. Inside the car, badly worn carpeting—or worn upholstery under

the seat covers—may give the lie to a low odometer reading. Be sure
that all the instruments are in working order. If anything at all is wrong,
ask the car dealer to have it repaired—don't take his word that it's just
a little thing you can easily fix yourself. Check the heater, air condi-
tioner, radio, and windshield wipers.

On the Road

A few turns around the block won't tell you whether the car is in good
working order. Plan a several-mile test drive, over smooth and bumpy
roads, up- and downhill, and through heavy traffic.

1. Listen for any unusual sounds or vibrations from the engine,
transmission, rear end, or wheels. They may mean nothing to you, but
everything to your mechanic. Let the engine idle, and listen for sounds
that might indicate bad valves. Unusual odors also mean that something, somewhere, is wrong.

2. Test the brakes, to see if they pull the car in one or another
direction, or if they let you stop smoothly and straight on.

3. Any vibration in the steering may mean front-end trouble. Test
for prompt steering response when going around corners.

4. If the car has manual transmission, push the gearshift through its
various positions to see how the car reacts. Watch for loose gears, grab-
bing, or a rattle in the clutch. With automatic transmission, see if it shifts
smoothly, without hestitation. Don't fool around with a questionable
transmission; repairs can be expensive.

5. Step quickly on the gas, and look in the rearview mirror for smoke
from the exhaust. A lot of white or bluish smoke means that the engine
may be bad, or in need of a major overhaul.

6. How much power does the car have on a hill? Slow response may
indicate that the car needs an expensive valve job.

7. A good long drive warms up the engine, and reveals noises that
the thicker oil in a cold engine often masks. It also shows whether the
car has a tendency to overheat.

If possible, get the name of the previous owner and talk to him about
how the car was used and cared for. Also ask why he traded it in. Don't
conclude that the car is in good shape just because it passed its last state
inspection. Inspectors look at superficial things, such as whether or not
the lights and horn work, not at the soundness of the engine under the
hood. The auto dealer himself may also be the inspector, or may be able
to get stickers from friendly inspectors, even though the car can't pass
legally.

For more help in buying a used car, look for *The Lemon Book* (Center for Auto Safety; Nader, Ditlow and Kinnard; Washington D.C.), due out in the fall of 1980.

MAINTAINING A CAR

Cars last longer and get more miles per gallon if they're properly kept. The owner's manual says how often the oil and other fluids should be changed or checked and at what point various mechanical parts ought to be replaced. In general, the car should go in for a checkup and oil change every six months or seventy-five hundred miles. Take care to use the kind of gasoline and oil specifically recommended for your automobile. If you use leaded gas in a car designed for unleaded, for example, it will foul the sparkplugs and ruin the catalytic converter that controls poisonous exhaust pipe emissions. Anytime something sounds or feels wrong in the way the car drives, take it right in to be corrected. The problem won't go away by itself, and the longer you drive with a malfunction, the more damage it will do.

The possible life of a car can be established during the first five hundred miles when the engine is being broken in. During this time it's important not to drive over fifty-five miles per hour, make jackrabbit stops and starts, drive fast when the engine is cold, and drive for a long time at the same speed. "Break-in" rules will probably be listed in the front of the owner's manual. Ignore them, and you're throwing money away.

You don't have to have normal maintenance done by the dealer who sold you the car, even during the warranty period. But if you choose another shop for this work, keep track of what was done and when, so that if you have to take the car back to the dealer for warranty repairs, he'll know you've been maintaining it properly. When you sell or trade in your car, a complete maintenance and repair history may help you get a better price.

Recalls

Auto manufacturers are supposed to notify you if a defect has been discovered in the car you own. These recalls may be initiated either by the company or by the government; word goes out to the dealers, whose job it is to get in touch with you. Recall notices may also be printed in the newspapers. If your car is recalled, by all means take it in for repairs, which should be free. You may also be reimbursed for previous repairs. *Don't continue to drive with the hazardous condition, even if you've never noticed any difficulty.* A car with a hidden defect is a hazard to everyone on the road. Some dealers are less than conscientious about getting the word to all their customers. You can find out if your car has ever been recalled by calling the toll-free hotline at the National Highway Traffic Safety Administration, (800) 424–9393; or write NHTSA, U.S. Department of Transportation, Washington, D.C. 20590, giving them the car's make, model, and serial number (you'll find the serial number on your automobile registration).

How to Find a Good Mechanic

The best way is to ask your friends whom they use, and try their recommendations until you find one that makes you happy. Many people like to patronize the repair shop of the dealer who sold them the car. He can easily get parts from the manufacturer, is experienced in your make of car, receives all manufacturer's service bulletins, may get briefings about complex repairs, and will sometimes go to bat for you to get a defect corrected after the warranty period has run out. Dealer's shops are also apt to have good diagnostic equipment not found at a small garage. On the other hand, a dealer's nonwarranty repairs are sometimes more expensive, because he's trying to make up for the low rate the manufacturer pays on warranty jobs. Also, dealers use company parts, which may be more expensive than competing brands. Try to compare prices with another shop before committing your car to a dealer for an expensive repair.

Whether the shop belongs to a dealer or an independent, it should meet certain minimum tests. Good shops are busy, so be suspicious of a place where the mechanics are just sitting around and valuable parking space is taken up by old wrecks. Give high points for general neatness, low points for garages in a state of filthy confusion—meticulous, well-organized mechanics normally don't work in the middle of a mess. Look for good diagnostic equipment, which helps the mechanics find an engine problem in a hurry. A list of the specific machines wouldn't mean anything to the average owner, but you can tell a lot just by looking around the shop and seeing how much capital has been invested in such things. If few mechanical aids are in sight, you can assume that a good tune-up will be a lucky guess, whereas a shop with an engine analyzer and oscilloscope is probably serious about repairs. A lot of machines is no guarantee that the mechanics will use them properly, but at least it's an objective standard for making an initial judgment.

The National Institute for Automotive Service Excellence certifies mechanics in eight different repair specialties. Anyone who has passed an NIASE test is at least competent to do the job, although he's not necessarily honest about it. *One warning:* A shop may advertise that it hires NIASE mechanics, but you have to ask to be sure that the person who works on your car is one of the employees who passed the test. Some NIASE mechanics advertise that fact by wearing an approved patch on their work clothes.

Any honest repair shop should be willing to give you a written estimate on a job and not exceed that estimate without your express permission. One point: Don't let the engine be taken apart until the estimate has been approved! If the actual bill often runs over the estimate, you're being "low-balled"; you should take your business elsewhere. Ask for a written guarantee of workmanship and parts for ninety days or four thousand miles—something any good repair shop should be willing to give, since the parts are guaranteed by the supplier. For major transmission work or an engine overhaul, you're due a guarantee of one year or twelve thousand miles (unless the mechanic installs a transmission or engine rebuilt elsewhere, in which case expect the ninety-day/four-thousand-mile guarantee). Get the guarantee in writing—perhaps scrawled across the bill and initialed by the shop owner if he doesn't give guarantee forms. If you've done business there a long time and know them to be reliable, you may not bother with a written guarantee, but don't forget that only a written promise is enforceable.

Mechanics vary enormously in competence, honesty, speed of work, and reliability. It's worth trying several places before settling down. Any expensive job should be taken around for a second opinion before the work is okayed, as estimates may vary by as much as $200 or $300. Once you find a good mechanic, stick with him. If he moves to another garage, move with him.

If you have a dispute with a repair shop, it can be impossible to get satisfaction, since the shop will keep the car until the bill is paid. If the dispute drags on, it may even sell your car to pay the bill. State and local consumer agencies generally lack the power to deal with complaints about auto repairs that didn't solve the problem.

AUTOCAPs

The National Auto Dealers Association has Consumer Action Programs in several cities, providing dispute settlement procedures. Consumers who have warranty or repair problems with member dealers can bring their case and receive a hearing. Decisions are generally enforced against members, but there's no recourse if your problem is with a nonmember dealer. Also, the AUTOCAPs have no authority over manufacturers. As an alternative to an AUTOCAP, try bringing your case to an arbitration board of the Better Business Bureau, if there is one in your city.

Diagnostic Centers

Repair frauds are so prevalent in the business that no one less than an auto expert can ever be sure whether or not his mechanic is stealing from him. In 1972, for example, the Automobile Club of Missouri re-checked more than one thousand cars after they had been repaired by auto mechanics. Nearly 29 percent of the repairs were done poorly or not at all; the average repair bill for the incompetent work was $127. The club ran the test again in 1974, this time finding that nearly 38 percent of the jobs were bad, at an average price of $148. In a test in Huntsville, Alabama, it was found that 24 percent of car repairs were unnecessary.

Your best defense against this kind of treatment is to take your car to a diagnostic center if there happens to be one nearby. These places don't do repairs, they just examine your car to see what repairs need doing. You pay them for their advice, then take the car elsewhere for the needed work. This procedure should remove any conflict of interest the mechanic may have; there's no sense in his lying to you about what work needs doing because he doesn't profit by it. Another possibility—when it appears that repairs will be expensive—is to get a second opinion. Take the car to a garage and offer to pay only for the examination. You may not want to do this because it appears to cost extra money. But if $20 for an opinion can save you $100 in fake repairs, you're way ahead of the game.

Breakdowns on the Road

You are particularly vulnerable to car repair bandits if your car collapses far from home. The best safeguard is prevention: Have the car checked thoroughly before you leave and know what was done, so a highway robber can't talk you into any unnecessary repairs.

Here's how to avoid having your car damaged deliberately at a gas station:

1. Get out of the car when you drive up and watch the attendant while he works. If he starts to crouch down by a tire, suspect that he might puncture it.
2. Watch over his shoulder when he goes under the hood to check the oil.
3. Don't leave your car unattended at the pump (park at the edge of the station when you use the bathroom).

If you suspect car trouble, get off the road right away so you'll have as much time as possible to find a garage. Call the American Automobile Association if you're a member; if you have a citizen's band radio, ask for local recommendations; check the Yellow Pages for a dealer who sells your make of car; or ask the proprietor of one of the local stores who his mechanic is.

What If You've Been Taken?

If you break down on a highway, or in a strange town, and the nearest repair shop overcharges you for the work, you have little choice except to pay. But *always* follow up such an experience with a stiff letter to the local Better Business Bureau and Chamber of Commerce. If the shop was along a major state highway, write to the State Highway Commissioner with your complaint; enough of these might persuade him to replace the offender with someone more honest. If the shop is affiliated with one of the major auto manufacturers or oil companies, write to them. If everyone who got rooked wrote an angry letter about it, more dishonest repair shops might get into trouble. Give the same complaint treatment to any repair shop in your own town that does you wrong.

Tires

Most cars now come equipped with radial tires, which give you the longest wear and best mileage (around forty thousand miles) of all the tires on the market. Belted bias are the next sturdiest (around twenty-five thousand miles), then bias ply (fifteen to twenty thousand miles). In tires, as with everything else, you get what you pay for; an inexpensive tire won't give you the wear that an expensive one will, and you shouldn't expect it. But whatever you get, don't mix tires of various types; it will interfere with the smooth handling and steering of the car. If you buy new tires two at a time, put the two on the same axle.

Pay close attention to what your owner's manual says about which size and type of tire to use; the wrong ones could affect riding comfort as well as speedometer and odometer calibration. The manual also advises you on how high they should be inflated. (Always check the pressure when the tires are cool.) Overinflation or underinflation will wear the tires down faster. You can tell your tires are overinflated if the center is wearing out faster than the sides; with underinflation, the outer edges show heavier wear. Radial tires often look a little underinflated, but don't worry about it; that's the way they're made. As long as the tread wears evenly, they're all right. You might want to increase the pressure by around four pounds for turnpike driving or when carrying or pulling heavy loads, but don't exceed the recommended maximums. Also, remember that outdoor temperature affects tire pressure, so check the pressure as the seasons change.

For the longest possible wear rotate the tires according to the instructions in your owner's manual. The manual also tells you how often to rotate; generally, it's in the area of every six to eight thousand miles.

If the tires wear unevenly even though they're carrying the proper pressure, ask a mechanic to check such things as wheel alignment, springs, and shock absorbers. An oddly worn tire can be a sign of something seriously wrong. Replace a tire when its tread wear indicators (generally, an absence of grooves in a pattern across the tire) begin to show, or if the tread is less than one sixteenth of an inch deep. (Test this with a Lincoln penny. Insert the penny in the treads head first; if the entire head shows, you need new tires.) In most states it's illegal to drive on tires with a tread of less than one sixteenth of an inch. Tires should also be replaced if they have any splits, cuts, or cracks deep enough to expose the fabric. Bulges usually mean internal damage. If you replace just one tire, place it across from the tire that has the least wear, to try to equalize braking traction.

There's a lot of misleading advertising with respect to tires, but you won't be misled by "fantastic bargains" if you just use your common sense. No one gives tires away or sells them below cost. You can trust a bargain if you buy at a reputable place that you feel sure will honor its warranty.

Uniform grading standards have been developed for tires, so you can make informed comparisons. The NHTSA rates each model for tread wear (on a scale of 60 to 200, with the higher-rated tires lasting longer); traction in straight-ahead braking on a wet road (A, B, or C); and temperature resistance during high-speed driving (an A grade withstands heat better than a B or C). The ratings are molded into the tire, and explained with an accompanying tag.

Dealers are supposed to register your name, address, and the identification number of each tire in case a defect is found and it's recalled. This is such a nuisance that many dealers don't bother, but you should ask for it, nevertheless. It might save you a serious accident someday. Report defective tires to the National Highway Traffic Safety Administration, U.S. Department of Transportation, Washington, D.C. 20590.

When you buy tires, ask how much the dealer charges to mount them. If the cost is high, load them into the trunk and have the tires changed at your local service station.

Snow tires are essential in the northern parts of the country, but where the winter brings only light snow, you can usually get by on reasonably new radials. Snow tires are not as safe as regular tires on dry pavement, however, so be sure to remove them early in the spring. You can get snow tires with studs, which make it easier to drive in hard-packed snow. But they decrease traction on ice or clear roads. Studs can also tear up a paved driveway in short order, as well as damage roads.

Retreads

A tire retreaded by a reputable dealer is probably just as safe as a new tire and costs about half as much. But retreads don't have to meet the same range of federal standards that new tires do. There's a dimension test, to make sure they're the right size; a test for resistance to puncture; and a test of whether the tire will come off the rim on a quick turn. But there is no high-speed or performance test, as is required of new tires. So although good manufacturers can generally be expected to do good work, there are insufficient standards to fall back on. For this reason be especially wary of the small retreader who may not even give you a warranty.

When a bald tire is retreaded, soft rubber is wrapped around the tread area of the tire body. The tire is then put into a precision mold

under pressure and high heat, which forms the new tread and bonds
it to the casing. There are several retreading processes but no particular
reason to choose one over the other. The National Tire Dealers and
Retreaders Association tries to police its seven hundred members in
order to ensure that they do good work. Members can display a shield
in their window; if you have a complaint about the quality of the work,
write to NTDRA at 1343 L St. N.W., Washington, D.C. 20005; they're
supposed to straighten things out.

Some retreaders give warranties and some don't, so check before you
buy. A reliable dealer should replace a tire that failed because of poor
workmanship; if there's a puncture, you should get credit for that part
of the tread that is still unused.

If you like, you can have your own tires retreaded, but people rarely
do so. Generally, they turn their old tires in and buy retreads that are
ready to go. Dealers advise that you buy the same brand of retreads for
all four wheels. In most cases you'll be buying bias ply or belted bias
tires, because radials have so far proven difficult to retread. But remember: A retread is only as good as the original tire; if it cost $20 new, don't
expect miracles.

Gas and Oil Additives

Don't waste your money on things to drop in your gas tank to make your
gas last longer. They don't work. There's also no evidence that oil
additives will make your car run better, and in fact car manufacturers
specifically advise against them except for special jobs (like a high-
detergent oil to reduce a sludge buildup). Regular use of additives will
do your engine no good and increase operating costs.

RENTING A CAR

The cost of rental cars varies so widely that it's hard to make a quick
comparison. There are daily rates, weekly rates, weekend rates, mileage charges, gas included or gas extra, and sometimes special discounts.

The only way to compare prices is to estimate how many miles you expect to drive over what period of time, and compute a probable daily rate based on the charge of each rental agency. If you expect to drive a lot of miles, you're probably better off with a deal that includes gas, whereas if it's just a short commute, it might cost less to buy the gas yourself. But there's no way to tell for sure without adding the numbers up. This exercise is well worth doing; you might save yourself $100 or more by choosing the right company.

Local car rental agencies are usually cheaper than the major ones located in airports. But they don't always allow you to drive the car to a distant city and drop it off there. Big-name renters encourage you to believe that smaller companies have rotten cars—and perhaps some of them are indeed older—but you can get a lemon from any company. New-car dealers in the rental business often have excellent cars. You sometimes have to wait a few minutes for a budget car company to deliver your car to the airport, but when you're spending your own money, the wait is worth it. Economy cars cost less than big cars and usually have to be reserved in advance. When you reserve cars in distant cities, it's easiest to use the toll-free lines of the major rental agencies. If you plan to pay cash, you generally have to put all the money up in advance, and you may have to show a credit card besides so the rental agency will know how to reach you if you don't turn the car in when you should.

Insuring a Rented Car

Car rental rates include liability insurance that covers you and anyone authorized by you to drive the car (although drivers under twenty-one are usually prohibited). The size of the policy and a few other details are included in the fine print on the back of the rental agreement. Ask the agent about the coverage and when it does, and doesn't, apply. You may have to inform the agency in advance if there will be drivers other than yourself.

You're generally not responsible for damage to the car from fire or theft, but ask about it. Your liability in case of collision should carry a specific limit—such as $100 or $250; if you like, you can eliminate that by paying a daily charge. If the collision was someone else's fault and the rental agency collects from his insurance company, any money you had to pay to cover the crash should be refunded (again, ask about it).

LEASING A CAR

For individuals, leasing a car is more expensive than buying one. But if you own your own business, consider having the business lease a car for your use, which makes the lease payments tax-deductible (check with your accountant on this).

When you lease, you specify the car you want and the lessor gets it for you. Contracts generally run for two to three years at a set monthly fee. Leases are of two types:

1. *The open-end lease,* the cheapest, makes you responsible for maintenance and depreciation. If the car sells for less than a specified book value at the end of the lease (presumably because you drove it hard), you have to make up the difference; conversely, if it sells for more, you get some or all of the extra dollars. If the used-car market is bad when the lease is up, you generally have the option of extending the lease for one more year. This kind of lease makes sense if you don't expect to put many miles on the car.

2. *The closed-end lease* costs an extra $100 to $150 a year but removes the market risk. You turn the car in at the end of the period, and the lessor absorbs the loss or gain over book value. Typically, you'll have to pay extra if you drive more than a specified number of miles—which could add up to a hefty charge. You might also have to pay for hammering out dents and replacing worn tires. Read the fine print in a closed-end contract with close attention. By the time you add up the potential extra costs, you might decide that the open-end lease is a better bet.

A maintenance option comes with either lease, and costs perhaps $400 to $500 a year. Here, the lessor pays all the upkeep, including insurance, repairs, replacing worn tires, regular servicing, and other expenses. But this is a costly way to lease. You'll generally pay less if you cover these expenses as they occur.

You can insure a leased car with your own company or through the lessor. Compare rates and coverages in order to see which is more favorable.

Chapter Twelve

INSURING
A CAR

Take Care to Sell Your Horse before He Dies. The
Art of Life Is Passing Losses on.

ROBERT FROST

Because all drivers can't be trusted to do the right thing voluntarily, many states make them carry a certain amount of liability insurance. If they smack into someone, damage his property, hurt him, perhaps kill him, there's a guarantee of at least some compensation. At this writing, twenty-two states won't let you drive unless you carry insurance. The rest permit you to drive uninsured until your first accident (or conviction for a moving violation); after that you have to get insurance before your license will be restored. As a practical matter, however, the majority of people even in the latter states protect themselves with insurance before they have an accident.

It is a false economy to buy only the minimum coverage demanded by law, especially as the cost difference between minimum and maximum protection isn't large. Should you cause an accident, damages will be awarded without regard to the size of your insurance policy. If a judgment against you is for $100,000 and you're insured for only $25,000 of it, the other $75,000 comes out of your flesh. You can lose your home, your car, and your savings, and be in hock for payments for years to come. A large insurance policy not only assures compensation to an accident victim, it protects you and your family from the financial consequences of your carelessness (or the carelessness of other drivers in the family).

209

A large amount of liability insurance is recommended both in "fault" states, where the person who caused the accident pays the damages, and in "no-fault" states. In the latter, your own insurance company reimburses your medical claims and loss of wages, even if the other guy caused the accident, but the person at fault can be sued for pain and suffering if your doctor's bills are above a certain level, or if your injuries are serious enough.

Where to Buy Auto Insurance

The most important fact to know is that auto insurance can be relatively cheap at one company and tremendously expensive at another. There's no such thing as a "standard price." Each company prices its policy to match the type of risks it's willing to insure and the amount of money it wants left over for profit and expenses. You could pay as much as 100 percent more than necessary if you inadvertently went to the wrong company.

A handful of state insurance departments publish abbreviated lists of comparative prices to help consumers find one of the less costly insurers. (To see if your state has one, call the local consumer protection agency, or the insurance department in the state capital.) Illinois publishes a comprehensive list—something more states should imitate. Lacking an easy way to price-shop, people usually insure with the first company that comes to their attention. According to a survey sponsored by a leading auto insurer, 73 percent of policyholders considered only one company before buying. Only 8 percent compared the rates of four or more insurers. Blind decisions like that cost consumers untold millions in premium dollars.

If you can't get guidance from the state, turn first to an independent insurance agent. He writes insurance for several companies, which gives you at least a limited rate comparison. Compare the agent's best rate with those offered by other independent agents, and by agents who work exclusively for one insurance company. Also, check mail-order companies (but check with the Better Business Bureau and state insurance department to see if the mail-order company that interests you has been the subject of complaints). This method may not turn up the single cheapest policy in your state for someone in your circumstances but should at least put you near it.

The other thing to consider, besides price, is how honest the company has been about paying claims (see "Getting Your Injury Claims Paid," page 216; "Getting Your Collision Claims Paid," page 217). An insurance agent may be helpful on this point; also, ask your friends about their experience with various companies. Some insurers are quick to raise rates on people who cause accidents, even small ones, but that fact shouldn't necessarily bother a good driver. After all, that's the very attitude that keeps the basic rate low in the first place. If your rates are raised for something that wasn't your fault, shop for another insurance company.

If you've never compared the cost of your present insurance with that of other companies, use the method just outlined to shop around a little. It will speed your search if you ask your friends what they pay for coverage. Should you find a better deal, be sure your new policy is in effect before you cancel the old one. Typically, a new policy can be canceled by the company within the first sixty days for any reason whatsoever, so you might want to keep your old policy alive during that period. Once sixty days have passed, a company generally can't cancel (although in most states it can refuse to renew at the end of the term). Some companies assess a penalty if you cancel midterm, in which case it's better not to make a switch until the old policy is running out.

What Auto Insurance Covers

If you cause an accident, you want your policy to pay the cost of the other person's injuries, damage to his property, legal costs, and whatever "pain and suffering" damages the court may award. In cases where the person is seriously injured or dies, those damages will be large. You also want to be covered for the medical bills of anyone in the car with you; physical damage to your car; car theft; and the chance of being struck by a hit-and-run driver, or a driver who's uninsured. Many policies also offer such extras as emergency towing, renting a substitute car if yours is damaged, and loss of earnings as a result of injuries. Every company's policy is slightly different in detail, but here's how the coverage generally runs:

Liability

This policy pays for the injuries or deaths of other people and damage to their property when you have caused (or, in some states, contributed to) an accident. It protects your home and savings because if you didn't have liability insurance, you might have to give up all you owned to pay a judgment. There are *single-limit* policies, which spell out the maximum amount the insurance company will pay for each accident. If the limit is $300,000, for example, the company will pay any combination of personal injury or property damage that doesn't exceed that amount. This is the most flexible form of coverage. It sometimes costs a little less, but it is often reserved for better risks by those companies that offer it (companies that offer it to everyone generally charge a little more). Alternatively, there is *split-limit,* which sets specific ceilings on each segment of coverage. For example, if your policy is written for $100,-000–$300,000–$50,000 (referred to as 100–300–50), it means the company will pay up to $100,000 for the injuries of one person (including medical bills, loss of earnings, death, and "pain and suffering" awards); up to $300,000 for the injuries of two or more people; and up to $50,000 for property damage. (However, this policy doesn't cover damage done to your own car or property.) Any judgment awarded over the limits of the policy is not paid by the company; it has to come out of your pocket.

Liability also covers the cost of investigating the accident and settling the claim. If the case goes to court, the company provides a lawyer and pays his fee. If the person bringing suit attaches any of your property to ensure payment, the company will generally put up a bond to release the attachment. It often pays any reasonable expenses you may have in getting to court, including loss of wages. Be sure that the coverage includes anyone driving your car with your permission, or any replacement car you may be driving while yours is in the shop for repairs. But the policy won't cover your car if you rent it out or enter it in a race.

HOW MUCH LIABILITY INSURANCE

Many states require that you have a certain minimum amount—perhaps $10,000 for the injuries of a single person, $20,000 for two or more, and $5,000 for property damage (called 10–20–5). In a single-limit policy, the minimum might be $25,000. But given the high cost of serious accidents today, minimum coverage is peanuts. If you have a $25,000 policy and the damages come to $60,000, you are personally liable for the extra $35,000. It can cost you your house, your car, your savings—everything. The more you have to lose, the larger the insurance policy you should carry. The extra money you pay for larger policies may not be very much, as the following tables show. The well-to-do should consider *umbrella insurance* of up to $1 million, to cover a liability judgment over $300,000 (it doesn't cost very much).

But no matter how much liability insurance you personally carry, it won't pay for your own losses if you're hurt in an accident and your state does not have no-fault insurance. You'd have to collect from the other guy's insurance company, and they'll pay no more than the limit of *his* policy. If your damages are $100,000 but he carries only $10,000 per person, $10,000 is what you'll get. You can try to collect the other

BODILY INJURY INSURANCE

Insured amount	Percent increase in cost above the minimum coverage	Sample annual costs
10/20*	—	$120
20/20	26%	151
15/30	23	148
20/40	38	166
25/50	50	180
35/35	52	182
50/100	80	216
100/200	105	246
100/300	114	257

*Up to $10,000 for the injuries of one person, up to $20,000 for the injuries of two or more people.

PROPERTY DAMAGE INSURANCE

Insured amount	Percent increase in cost above the minimum coverage	Sample annual costs
$ 5,000	—	$52
10,000	5%	54
15,000	6	55
25,000	8	56
35,000	10	57
50,000	13	59

$90,000 from him personally, and if you're lucky, he'll have some property he can liquidate. But he probably won't have enough. So although you personally may be responsible enough to insure yourself against any major accidents you might cause, you could be turned into a basket case by someone whose minimum coverage won't pay a fraction of your loss. This is clearly unjust—and is one of the major arguments for no-fault insurance (see page 230).

Medical Payments

This covers "reasonable" medical and funeral expenses for you or anyone riding with you, whether or not the accident was your fault. The typical ceiling on payments per person is $1,000, which means that it's usually used to cover small injuries where there's no lawsuit involved. It applies to anyone driving the car with your permission; you and your family when driving in another car; and you and your family if struck by a car while walking or bicycling. Coverage extends for one to three years from the date of the accident, depending on the policy, and there may be a small death benefit if you or anyone in your family dies of his injuries within ninety days. The car need not run into anything or even be moving for this coverage to apply. If an elderly lady stumbles while getting into your parked car and breaks her hip, her bills will be paid (up to the limits of your policy). Policies vary in comprehensiveness—for example, some pay for eyeglasses or prescription drugs needed as a result of the accident, and some don't. These details can add up to a lot of money, so make a list of what the competing insurers cover before you decide which policy to buy. Some policies double your coverage if you were wearing a seat belt at the time of the accident.

Many policies won't pay benefits that are also covered on your regular health insurance (although they'll fill in for your health insurance deductible and pick up—to the extent of your coverage—bills that exceed the limits of your medical policy). In cases where your regular health insurance offers skimpy benefits, you might want to step up the medical payments segment of your auto coverage from $1,000 to $5,000.

Collision

This pays for the repair of your car if it runs into something or rolls over, even when the accident is your fault. If the car is ruined beyond repair, the insurance company will give you its *cash value,* which is generally the cost of the car less depreciation (although something more may be deducted if it was driven more than the usual number of miles). In theory, this should enable you to replace it with a car of like age and in like condition.

People generally insure new cars, because they're worth a lot of money. Ruining a new car in an accident would be a major loss. Collision coverage is especially important when you buy a car on borrowed money: You want to be able to pay off the loan after a crash rather than spend the next two or three years paying for a car you no longer have. The lender, in fact, will probably insist on collision insurance and may even offer to sell it to you (although you can generally get it cheaper somewhere else). But when your car is old and worth just a few hundred dollars, you might as well cancel the insurance. You wouldn't even be covered in full for a major repair, because the company won't pay any more than the car's cash value.

Collision policies include a *deductible,* which is the amount of the bill you have to pay before the insurance company steps into the picture.

If your deductible is $100 and the repair bill comes to $99, you pay it all; if the repair bill comes to $250, you cover the first $100 and the insurance company pays the remaining $150. One way to lower the cost of your insurance is to increase the size of the deductible, which means that you pay for the relatively small losses but remain insured against a major crash. Your out-of-pocket costs won't be as great as it first appears; all but the first $100 of your unreimbursed casualty losses are deductible on your income-tax return. Typically, collision insurance also includes a small allowance for towing your wrecked car to a garage (although some policies bill this as an extra).

Comprehensive

This covers theft as well as damage to your car from such things as vandalism, fire, projectiles, animals, flood, explosions, and other perils. It might also include towing costs and other incidentals. But it won't pay for normal wear and tear or mechanical breakdowns.

If you get full coverage, comprehensive will cover your losses right from the first dollar. But you can lower the cost by taking a deductible. The company won't pay that part of *any* claim that exceeds the car's cash value (generally, your cost less depreciation), so if your car is old and worth only a few hundred dollars, it may not be worthwhile keeping the insurance. Alternatively, you might want to restrict the coverage only to fire and theft, which is quite inexpensive.

Uninsured Motorist

This important coverage pays whatever damages for bodily injury (and in some states, property damage) you're legally entitled to receive from a driver who carries no insurance, or from a hit-and-run driver. You and your family are covered while in your car, riding a bicycle, or walking along the street; other people driving with you are also covered, as is anyone using your car with your permission. Unfortunately, in most states you can collect no more than the state's minimum liability level, no matter how severe your injuries. In states that allow you to buy a higher level of uninsured motorist coverage, it's smart to do so. Around 15 to 20 percent of drivers are uninsured, many of them the worst risks on the road.

Wage Loss and Substitute Services

Required in no-fault states and generally included in other policies as well, this coverage repays at least part of the income you lose because of injury as well as the cost of services (such as child care) that your injury keeps you from performing.

Getting Your Injury Claims Paid

In no-fault states you submit medical bills and proof of lost earnings to your own insurance company, which should pay them promptly (up to whatever limit the policy provides). The same should be true in "fault" states for claims under a medical payments policy. Any attempt to chivvy you out of the full amount of the damages should be met with an angry holler—to the claims adjuster, your insurance agent, the president of the company, local consumer agencies, and the state insurance department. (If your claim is borderline, however, you may have to pursue it in court.)

The real fight comes in fault states (and no-fault states when major injuries are involved), when the accident was the other guy's fault and the injured party wants to collect. If the other driver was clearly in the wrong, his insurance company may offer to pay you immediately, before a lawyer gets involved. *Don't accept, or sign anything.* You don't yet know how serious your injuries are. That pain in your back may go away, or it may last the rest of your life. If you accept a small settlement and your injuries turn out to be far more serious than you had thought, there's no way of going back to the insurance company for more compensation.

When you've been in an accident you didn't cause, see a lawyer right away. You need a person who handles a lot of accident cases and is experienced in the courtroom (a poor courtroom lawyer might lose a case that should be won). Ask your friends for recommendations, or call the Bar Association's referral service. Tell the lawyer exactly what happened and what evidence you have to prove it, not neglecting anything you might have done to contribute to the accident. He'll be able to tell you how strong your case is and what dollar settlements have been made in similar circumstances. Typically, he'll file suit for more than the price he hopes to get, then sit back and see what the insurance company does.

Meanwhile, the insurance company will be talking with the other driver, asking him the same questions your lawyer is asking you. If it's obviously his fault, the only question is how seriously you have been injured and what the company should pay for it. Your lawyer and the insurance company will haggle back and forth until there's a reasonable offer, which the lawyer will recommend that you take. The haggle takes quite a while, even when the company knows that eventually it must pay. Typically, you'll get more if you can wait until the very eve of the trial (which may be one to three years away). If your financial circumstances compel you to settle early, the company will generally take advantage of that fact by offering less.

You face a much tougher fight if it's unclear who really caused the accident. In some states if you're even one speck at fault, you get nothing at all no matter how serious your injuries. In other states you collect according to your degree of fault. If you were 20 percent responsible for the accident, for example, and the other driver 80 percent at fault, you get 80 percent of the damage award. Degrees of fault are determined by a judge or a jury. In some states your award goes down if you weren't wearing a safety belt.

In cases insurance companies hope to win they'll offer nothing in advance of the trial; where their case is weaker, they'll offer as little as they think they can get away with, with the offers increasing as trial day draws near. Typically, just before the trial gets underway, the judge will ask the attorneys, "Can't we settle this?" At that point, the insurer's offer may go up, your demands may go down, and agreement might be reached. (Sometimes insurers even make an offer on cases they hope to win, just to save the expense of a trial.) If your lawyer likes the offer, he'll recommend that you take it. Or he may recommend against it. You need not take the lawyer's advice. Trials aren't sure things, and you might prefer to settle rather than gamble on getting something more from a jury. If you decide to go to trial, the insurance company could increase its offer at any time during the proceedings; conversely, you could decide to accept a previous offer if it's still available. If you come to terms, the case will be closed.

You pay your lawyer one of two ways: (1) by the hour or day, which costs money whether you win or lose, or (2) on contingency, which means he'll take a stated percentage of whatever you win (perhaps one third) and nothing if you lose. Some accident victims and their lawyers concoct serious injuries in order to press for a high payoff—an unconscionable practice that raises everyone's insurance rates. It's to avoid this tendency to play poker with the system that no-fault insurance was proposed (see page 230).

Getting Your Collision Claims Paid

Some companies are fairer than others in paying claims. Naturally everyone tries to weed out fraud: Paying false or inflated claims will just raise rates for everyone. But there are instances when companies, in order to improve profits, resist claims or send checks for less than the claimant is entitled to, counting on the fact that only the most aggressive will fight for what's owed. But fight by all means—it gets you farther than you might think. You may have extra leverage if you insure your house with the same company, because if you get mad enough, you might move all your insurance business somewhere else. Whenever you think you're being cheated, complain to your insurance agent, the president of the company, your local consumer agency, and the state insurance department. Some tricks of the trade:

Collecting Property Damages from the Other Guy

If the accident was the other guy's fault, you can collect the full repair cost from his insurance company. You should also be able to claim reimbursement for renting a car while yours was being fixed (check this point with the company). But getting payment may involve proving his fault (in other words, a court case), so many people elect to collect from their own companies instead (under their collision coverage). With your own company there's a deductible ($50 or more depending on your policy), but there's no hassle over whose fault it was. Furthermore, your company can turn around and sue the other insurer for the amount paid; if they collect, they should refund all or part of your deductible (ask about it).

The Estimate

Half the battle in the claims business is getting an honest estimate. Good companies ask you to get an estimate from your own mechanic; they'll double-check the damage themselves, and if the estimate seems reasonable, okay the work. But other insurers make their own (low) estimate and refer you to a body shop that will do the work for that price. (In some states it's illegal to make referrals without being asked—in which case they may give you a ceiling price for the job, and leave it to you to find a shop willing to do the work for that amount. If you can't, just ask them for a referral; it will be forthcoming!)

The fact is that many shops willing to take an insurer's low estimate do a poor job of repair. The price is so skimpy they can't give the work the attention it deserves and still make a profit. Furthermore, the insurer may insist on receiving a discount on parts, which squeezes the repair shop's profit margin even more. The sad result is that although your car may come out looking like new, the dents may have been filled with plastic rather than hammered out, some parts may be of poor quality, corners will have been cut wherever possible, and some repairs won't have been done at all. In some cases the insurer guarantees the work, so if problems arise, you can have them fixed at no charge. But it's often hard to prove that an engine problem arose from poor repair rather than from a mechanical problem that developed later. Also, there will be a time limit on the guarantee, so by the time the plastic falls out of the dents, the insurer may no longer be liable. If you've had the repair done at a shop suggested by the insurer, don't sign any release until you've had the work examined by your own mechanic. A few extra dollars spent on inspection could well get you $100 or more in additional repairs you're due. One other point: Don't sign a piece of paper accepting the insurer's estimate as the total payment until you've learned whether that sum will cover a thorough repair. The claims adjuster may try to pressure you into signing by threatening to withdraw his offer, but resist. If you hold out for what you're honestly due, you'll probably get it.

Rather than accept the insurer's estimate, which may be low, get a price from a body shop you trust. If the insurer insists on more than one estimate, fine—but add the price of getting the estimates to your insurance claim. Bargain with the adjuster for enough money to make a safe repair. If he balks, invoke the arbitration clause contained in many policies but seldom used. This allows you to submit your claim for more money to an arbitration panel chosen partly by you and partly by the insurer. You both agree to abide by the decision. One point: If the insurer guarantees repairs, it will do so only for body shops it recommends. But assuming that the guarantee is more talk than substance, you haven't lost anything by going to your own mechanic. Furthermore, your mechanic, if he's reliable, will guarantee his own work.

Betterment

Insurers may reduce your claim by an amount attributed to "betterment." This is the sum by which the insurance company says the repair job will actually improve your car. If a new hood is installed, for example, the company may reduce your claim by the cost difference between a new hood and a used one; the same thing applies to tires and parts. But it's hard to see how an accident so severe that parts had to be replaced has "bettered" your car in any way (unless the car was truly battered to begin with). Decline to accept a betterment charge (except perhaps for new tires) unless you specifically asked for new parts when used ones were available. If the insurer objects, get testimony from a used-car dealer that the new parts haven't improved the market value of your car (whereas the accident has reduced the value), and take your case to arbitration.

When Your Car Is Destroyed or Stolen

If your car is a total loss, the company is supposed to give you enough money to buy a new car of like age and in like condition (less the applicable deductible). It arrives at a price by consulting a used-car retail price guide and adjusting for special factors, such as the equipment you had and how many miles you'd driven. But in some cases, the used-car guide may give a retail price that's below the current market —in which case, get prices from local used-car dealers and present them to the company. In fact, even if the price sounds fair to you, check it out with a dealer so you won't be underpaid (sometimes an insurer tries to get away with quoting a wholesale price). If the price is too low and the adjuster refuses to raise it, make a fuss with your agent and write letters to the company president, the local consumer protection agency, and the state insurance department. Should he still not budge, ask for arbitration. Sometimes insurance companies try to apply used-car price guides to cars that are practically new. Resist this vigorously, again by getting prices on comparable cars from dealers in your area. You are owed the market price of the car you lost and are justified in doing whatever is necessary to collect the money.

Delays

A few companies discourage claimants by giving them the runaround. They might, for example, be slow to examine your car, figure an estimate, answer your correspondence, or send out your check. If, in exasperation, you have the car fixed and send them a bill, they may refuse to pay part of it because the price was never okayed. If six weeks pass without full payment, write the company a stiff letter. If that brings no results, complain loudly to everyone in sight. Many states have passed laws requiring auto insurers to attend to claims within a certain number of days (see the following section). If you've encountered delays, call the state insurance department or local consumer agency to see if the company is in violation of any law.

Fair Settlements Laws

Many states have laws that try to protect you from abuses in claims settlements. These laws require that (1) when a company turns down a claim, it tell you which specific policy provision ruled it out; (2) your claim be acknowledged within ten working days, and questions you have regarding it be answered within seven working days; (3) investigation of the claim begin within fifteen working days after it was received; (4) a settlement be paid, or repairs authorized, within ten days from the time agreement was reached. If you're having trouble collecting on a claim, write to the state insurance department or local consumer protection office to see if the foot-dragging is in violation of law.

Attorneys

The insurer may try to talk you out of hiring a lawyer, warning that if you do, it will take twice as long to settle the claim. He'll also warn that the lawyer will take one third or more of the settlement. Both may be true. But the lawyer may help you win a large damage claim to which you're entitled, whereas the company may be willing to pay only a small amount. Always talk to a lawyer about the merits of the case before signing an insurance settlement.

When You're Sued

Your insurance company defends you. When you're at fault and the injuries are severe, the other person may sue for a huge amount but indicate a willingness to settle for the upper limits of your insurance policy. If the insurer refuses to settle and you lose in court, you may be hit with a tremendous judgment. This might not bother the insurer, because he is liable only up to the policy limits. But you have recourse against an insurer who deals with you in bad faith. If you feel that your company was unreasonable in refusing to accept the settlement, you can sue for the difference between what the policy paid and the size of judgment against you.

Salvage

If you want the remains of your wrecked or stolen car back, the company will make an adjustment on your claim, deducting the sum it thinks the hulk is worth from the money you're owed. If you think the wrecked car was overvalued, get a dealer to make his own valuation and take any dispute to arbitration.

The Good Companies

Good companies don't underestimate repair costs, direct you to shoddy shops, underpay your medical claims, or give you the runaround. They check your car, ask for an estimate from one or more body shops, then authorize the repair in jig time. When you submit the repair bill, they send you a check for the full amount. If your company does anything less, start shopping for another insurer. There's no reason to keep on doing business with places that give you a hard time.

Don't Steal

Some people lend themselves to grubby lawyers who try to turn their bumped heads into brain damage—not because they expect to be able to prove it in court but simply in hopes that the insurance company will pay something to avoid the expense of a lawsuit. Others go along with thieving body shops, presenting inflated damage estimates and splitting the overcharges. This is the stuff that drives insurance rates up and makes insurance adjusters so quick to suspect honest people with honest claims. An accident is a tragedy, a brush with death. I have no patience with people who treat it like a lottery, a chance to win a thousand bucks, by teaming up with a shabby lawyer to fake a claim.

What Sets Your Insurance Rates?

Insurers have a lot of guideposts for spotting drivers likely to have accidents. If you're a member of a statistically risky group, it will—in most states—make no difference that you yourself are careful, steady, and reliable; you'll still get high-risk rates. Personal irresponsibility, however, will push your rates even higher. Here are some of the things that generally affect the premium you pay:

Age

Young men under thirty and young women under twenty-five may pay considerably more than other drivers. The only way that a young, single driver can get a price break is by insuring with the same company that insures his parents. If he's a teen-ager, that may be the only company that will take him at all. He'll get the best price possible by having his parents insure the car under their name, listing him as principal driver. At the other end of the scale, the elderly may get slightly lower rates based on the fact that they drive less and are involved in fewer accidents.

Marital Status

Young married men and women usually pay less than single men of the same age and circumstances. Married adults, whether male or female, generally pay the same rate. Some insurance companies put the widowed or divorced into higher-risk categories, which requires them to pay more.

Sex

Young women pay less than young men because they have fewer accidents. Single women pay less than single men up to about age sixty-five.

Residence

People in the suburbs or the country pay less than city drivers do, and residents of small cities pay less than those of large cities. If you live in a city but garage your car in the suburbs, you should get a lower rate. Sometimes you have to pay more because you live in a certain section of the city where insurers are reluctant to do business.

Occupation

Insurance companies keep lists of "risky" occupations, which differ from company to company and for which they generally have no rational statistical proof. Taxi drivers, bartenders, and cocktail waitresses may be thought of as higher risk, not because they have more accidents but because they make less believable witnesses if the insurance company decides to fight the claim in court. Also, those on the risky list are considered less likely to pay their bills. If you work in a job the insurance company dislikes, you may be unjustly classified as "high risk," or refused coverage altogether.

Driving Record

Safe drivers often get discounts, while those with a couple of speeding tickets or an accident behind them pay extra. Some insurance companies hike your rate or cancel your coverage if you do little more than run a stop sign. Others will ignore a couple of minor violations or even a small accident. Some people don't report minor claims for fear the company will raise their rates, and in fact, if your claim is just a few dollars over the deductible, it's probably not worth it. But an honest company generally won't penalize you for a claim that's not your fault. After all, that's what you bought the insurance for. *Warning:* Anytime you're in an accident where someone was hurt, report it, even if the damage claim is small. If that injury turns into something large and you let the accident pass unreported, the company may not honor your policy. If your company gives you a hard time about minor claims, look for another company. It will be even worse with a major claim.

Inexperienced drivers generally pay higher rates, even if their record is clean. As time goes by and they stay out of accidents, their rates will come down to normal. Drivers whose premiums have risen because of an accident can earn the right to regular rates again by keeping a clean record.

Use

If you car-pool to work, or drive your car less than seventy-five hundred miles a year, you can probably get a lower rate. On the other hand, people with a long daily commute (of fifteen miles or more) or who use their cars mainly for business, have to pay more. You aren't penalized, however, if you use your car on business only every now and then, or drive fifteen miles to work perhaps once a week.

Other Drivers

You may be a safe driver, but if your spouse has had his or her premiums increased, your rate will go up too (insurers assume that spouses will drive each other's cars). You'll also pay more when your teen-agers start driving the family cars.

Type of Car

Large, powerful cars cost more to insure than sedate sedans because they can do so much more damage. Insurance for inexpensive, low-priced cars often costs less. Sports cars may be insured normally if bought for a family, but if owned by a single man and equipped with extra horsepower, the rate will rise.

Merit Rating

A few states (at this writing, Massachusetts, North Carolina, and Hawaii) have banned rates based on such personal characteristics as age and sex. Instead, most drivers within a given geographical area are charged about the same. If they have an accident, their rates go up sharply. The idea is to link insurance rates more closely with actual performance as a driver. In merit-rating states, insurance costs for the good driver who happens to be in a statistically high-risk group (for example, a young man) go down sharply, whereas rates for the average driver rise a little. This is a fairer way to spread insurance risk and is being considered by several other states.

Ways to Cut Insurance Costs

1. Check the rates of other insurance companies, or ask an agent to do it for you. You may be able to get the same or better coverage at a lower rate.

2. If you're eligible, join a group auto plan.

3. Cancel collision insurance on an older car that's paid for. There's not enough value in it to make the policy worthwhile.

4. Cancel comprehensive insurance (for theft and general damage) on an older car. If you want to keep it, eliminate perils such as flood and flying objects, and insure only against fire and theft.

5. Take a larger deductible on collision and comprehensive insurance. This means that you pay for the small repairs yourself but are still insured against a major loss. (Remember that all but the first $100 of unreimbursed losses can be claimed as a casualty loss on your income tax return.)

6. Don't buy a super-high-performance car or load it up with a lot of flashy extras. Insurers will suspect that you mean to speed and charge you more.

7. Insure all your cars with the same company in order to get their volume discount. If one of the cars is rarely driven, say so.

8. Ask about discounts for such things as car pools, a good safety record, low annual mileage, better bumpers, and compact cars. There may also be discounts for good students, students (and adults) who have taken driver education, and people who don't smoke or drink.

9. Tell the insurance company about any changes in circumstances that might lower your rate. For example, a married woman who finds herself single again may pay less because her husband no longer drives her car. A family's premiums fall when a teen-ager leaves home. Rates also fall if you join a car pool or move closer to your place of work, so you no longer have to drive more than fifteen miles a day. It's also grounds for cheaper insurance if you leave a "risky" occupation like bartending and take up another line of work.

10. Insure a car belonging to your young son or daughter in your name, listing him or her as principal driver.

11. One place *not* to save is on the amount of liability coverage you get. The difference between $20,000 worth of protection and $300,000 worth may be only $70 or $80 a year. With today's high costs and high jury awards, top-of-the-line protection is practically a necessity for anyone with substantial assets to protect.

12. Another way not to save is by lying on your insurance application just to get a lower rate. If the lie is found out, the company may refuse to pay part of a claim against you. However, if the insurance agent inadvertently puts down incorrect information without your knowledge, you shouldn't be penalized.

If You're a High Risk

You don't have to be a poor driver to be a high risk. You only have to
be a member of a statistically high-risk group, such as young drivers,
new drivers, or drivers living in neighborhoods that have produced a
lot of losses for the insurers. Your record can be absolutely clean, yet
you'll be charged the same as a driver who's had some accidents.

In good times insurance companies tend to write regular policies for
a fair number of statistically high-risk people with good driving records.
But when profits fall, the higher risks are—in most states—shuffled off
into special insurance pools. Also, if the companies are having trouble
getting higher premiums okayed in a state, they may decide to write
less business there, which also forces more people into the pools.

If your agent can't find you an insurance policy at normal rates but
your driving record is clean, start shopping around. Your own agent
probably deals with no more than five or six of the hundreds of insurers
licensed to do business in your state. It's possible that another agent
might find a company willing to take you on. If that's not possible and
you're forced into a high-risk plan (see the following discussion), try
again next year. Around 50 percent of the people in high-risk plans
don't renew after the first year, presumably because they've found
coverage at a better price. By the end of the third year, 90 percent are
back in the regular market.

Most states have *assigned-risk auto plans,* where people who can't
find insurance at regular rates are assigned in rotation to each of the
insurers doing business in the state. This sometimes makes it difficult for
your agent to get your claim processed because he doesn't normally do
business with the company you're assigned to and doesn't know their
system. Rates in an assigned-risk plan may be around 25 to 50 percent
higher than normal. The amounts of liability coverage available may be
more limited than in the voluntary market. In some cases collision and
medical payments insurance may not be obtainable at all.

Some 70 percent of the drivers in high-risk plans have clean records!
Because of the complaints this generates, a number of states have ex-
plored alternatives. Maryland has a state fund for drivers who can't get
insurance anywhere else; a few states have joint underwriting facilities,
which assign all the high-risk business to certain insurers.

An increasing number of state insurance commissioners are looking
with favor on a system called *reinsurance.* This lets you insure with any
company you want, at its regular rates. If it thinks you're a bad risk, it
will reinsure your policy with a central facility. The losses that this

facility generates are parceled out to all the insurers in the state. This is a fairly new approach to auto insurance, in use only in a handful of states (Massachusetts, North Carolina, South Carolina, New Hampshire). Over time it will probably raise rates slightly to the average driver, in order to offset losses from bad drivers. Estimates of the average increase range from $1 to $10 per policy, depending on state. Good drivers often object to this idea; on the other hand, as things now stand, those good drivers forced into assigned-risk plans (and who make up its majority) have to pay an excessive amount—perhaps several hundred dollars extra—to compensate for the losses of bad drivers. It is the opinion of the Federal Insurance Commission that reinsurance spreads the cost in a fairer manner.

Misleading Policies

High-risk drivers may be a target for low-reliability insurance companies. If the rates you're offered sound unbelievably low compared with other companies you've shopped, you're probably being insured for less than meets the eye. It's all buried somewhere in the contract's fine print, but the contract may be so incomprehensible that you won't find out how limited the coverage really is until you crack up your car and try to collect. If you think you've been rooked, complain to the Better Business Bureau (so they'll have it on record), the local consumer protection agency, and the state insurance department. And note: Some judges have required insurers to pay reasonable claims even though the policy excluded them, on the ground that the terms of the policy were written too murkily to be understood even by a careful reader.

If Your Company Goes Broke

Most states have guaranty funds, supported by all the insurers in the state. If your company goes out of business, the funds will pay claims, refund at least some of your premiums, and guarantee your continued coverage until you can switch your policy over to another company.

If Your Insurance Policy Is Canceled

Almost all insurance companies won't cancel your policy after the first sixty days, unless you don't pay the premiums or your license is revoked. However, any insurer can refuse to renew at the end of a year. If this happens, ask your insurance agent what the problem is in order to see if there's anything you can do about it. Perhaps the company is no longer doing business in your area, in which case it may be an easy matter to change companies. If you're considered too great a risk, ask the company for an explanation. Should its information be erroneous, it may reinstate you. But in cases where the company simply considers you a poor driver, or has decided to stop insuring your type of risk, you'll have to shop for coverage elsewhere. If you can't find any (except in an assigned-risk plan) and you think the situation grievously unfair, ask your insurance agent if the state puts any limitation on a company's right to cancel coverage. And send your complaint to the Better Business Bureau, the local consumer protection agency, and the state insurance department. In the few states where insurers are required to take all comers, you can't be canceled—although your rates can be raised.

What to Do When You Have an Accident

It's not a bad idea to keep this list of rules in the glove compartment, just in case:

1. Attend to whatever injuries there may be; have someone call an ambulance and the police.

2. Move your car to a safer place if necessary to prevent more accidents. (Your insurance probably won't cover damage from crashes caused by leaving your car in the middle of the road.) Warn oncoming drivers away from the wreck.

3. Get the name, address, phone number, license number, vehicle registration number, and insurance company of the other driver, and give him yours. Look at his driver's license to see if there are any restrictions that he wasn't observing (wearing eyeglasses, for example). If the car is registered in someone else's name, get that person's name and address.

4. Get the names and addresses of any witnesses and, if possible, their statement of what happened. This is particularly important if you believe that you were not at fault. If you can't get names or a statement, at least write down their car license numbers. Remember that the witness list can include any passengers who were in your car and saw how the accident happened. Also get the names or badge numbers of the policemen who arrive on the scene.

5. If you think the other driver was drinking, insist that you both take a breath test.

6. Jot down your recollection of how the accident happened, including the speed you were traveling at. Note the weather conditions, any hazardous conditions (such as a stop sign down or a misleading road sign). Describe the area, writing down exactly where you are located. Fresh impressions are usually the most telling ones in court.

7. Don't sign anything. Don't admit guilt or say your insurance will cover everything. Don't say how much insurance you have.

8. Call your insurance agent as soon as practicable, tell him what happened, and summarize all the evidence you have. Don't rely on the other driver's promise to have his insurance pay; he may change his mind. Report even small accidents if someone was injured; the injury could grow worse, and you might lose coverage if you don't report promptly.

9. If you or any of your passengers were injured in any way, see a doctor.

10. Cooperate with the insurance company, filling in all necessary forms and making appearances in court.

11. Don't be willing to settle too soon. It's important to see whether your injuries continue to give you trouble.

12. Report a hit-and-run driver to the police within twenty-four hours. Failure to do so may cancel your insurance coverage.

13. Keep records of all expenses connected with the accident, such as the cost of renting a car until yours is fixed. If the accident was your fault, your company won't reimburse you for such incidental costs, but if it was the other guy's fault, you should be able to collect from his company. Your own company will reimburse you only for medical payments and collision damage, towing, loss of earnings, and other direct expenses if your policy provides for it.

14. See a lawyer about what happened in order to get a handle on your rights and how to figure your damages.

No-Fault Insurance

Under this system (if properly set up), victims of accidents should be compensated more swiftly and justly. Without no-fault, it may take two or three years before an accident case can be heard in court. In the meantime there are medical bills to pay and loss of income to endure. Poorer families often have to settle right away for whatever they can get, which always means less. Richer families, on the other hand, wait out the court fight and eventually win higher judgments. Under no-fault, this inequity is mended by having your own insurance company promptly pay for your medical bills and loss of earnings (up to the limit set by the policy).

Furthermore, good no-fault laws cut the lawyer out of small cases by setting limits on who can sue. If you bumped your head and the doctor bill was $30, your insurance company pays. A lawyer can't carry the case into court and demand further damages for your pain and suffering. This prevents the escalation of small claims, eliminates many unnecessary legal fees, and helps keep insurance premiums down. Some sixteen states have written no-fault laws, some of them better than others. In states where you need around $2,500 worth of injuries before you can sue, the number of auto cases has dropped sharply and the rise in insurance premiums has been contained. However, in states where the threshold is as little as $500, small accidents have a way of escalating into $500 cases—raising the amount of money demanded and continuing to clog the courts with dubious "pain and suffering" claims. Some people point to these latter states as proof that no-fault doesn't work, but it can fairly be said that, there, it hasn't even been tried. When the limits are set at realistic levels, no-fault performs well, ensuring that everyone will get his bills paid swiftly while keeping victims of small accidents from puffing their whiplash injuries into big settlements. It is in the interest of all consumers that true no-fault be allowed to spread. But it will take a big push from the voters to get the legislators (mainly lawyers) to act.

Campers and Trailers

A *trailer* is normally covered under your regular auto insurance, as long as it's properly listed on the policy. Check with your agent to see if physical damage is included and if coverage is in force even when the trailer is detached from the car. *Campers* and *motor homes,* on the other hand, must be covered separately. You need collision and physical damage insurance to protect the value of the vehicle itself, and unin-sured-motorist and liability insurance to pay for injuries. And you need these before you drive the camper out the dealer's door, because your auto coverage for a "newly acquired automobile" means a passenger car, not a recreational vehicle. You might also want personal-effects protection for the camping equipment you carry. Check the medical payments policy carefully; you might have to pay twice as much if people ride in the camper rather than in the cab while you're on the road. Also, check to see what coverage there is when the vehicle is parked or detached from the cab. Policies may include such incidentals as towing costs and expenses for alternate lodging if the camper breaks down while you're on vacation. The scope and cost of camper insur-ance, like auto coverage, varies from company to company, so you'd be wise to have more than one agent checking around for you.

If you rent a camper, it might be covered under your regular auto policy for the duration; ask your agent about it. But the insurance might be in force only if you and your spouse do the driving, not when a teen-age driver or a friend is at the wheel. Also, the insurance might last only for a limited period of time. By all means check these points before taking off on vacation. If additional coverage will be needed, you can usually get it from the dealer, but his policies typically focus more on protecting the vehicle than on defending you against liability claims. Before buying, compare the dealer's insurance with the coverage your own agent can provide. If you borrow a camper or trailer from a friend, you both should ask your agents what the coverage is. If you own a camper or trailer and rent it out to someone, it's likely that your cover-age will not apply.

Motorcycles

Rates are relatively high, with drivers under thirty paying twice the premium older drivers do. The range of coverage is far more limited than that available for cars. For example, it's hard to find medical payments policies for the driver, or any policy covering injuries to a passenger. Physical damage policies may also be unobtainable because it's so easy for a motorcycle to tip over. There are no special rates for good students or safe drivers, as there are with autos, and married people don't get better rates. Where differentials are made according to weight, lighter-weight motorcycles are more costly to insure than heavier ones, since they tend to be involved in more accidents (perhaps because lighter-weight bikes are more apt to be bought by inexperienced operators). Most insurers differentiate according to engine size, measured in cubic centimeters, charging lower relative premiums for bikes with smaller engines. Again—shop around. There's a high-risk pool for motorcycle drivers, just as there is for auto drivers. Finally, be sure you understand all the exclusions in your policy. If you have an accident while racing, for example, your coverage may not apply.

Snowmobiles

There are so many snowmobiling accidents that driving one for recreation can cause your life insurance rates to go up. If you have a lot to lose in a lawsuit, it's worth having maximum coverage, for bodily injury and property damage. For your own protection add physical damage and collision, if the snowmobile is fairly new, and uninsured-motorist coverage. Some other points to look for: (1) liability and medical payments insurance for anyone you may be towing on a toboggan (you don't need medical payments for yourself if you have a good health insurance plan); (2) coverage for all equipment used exclusively with the snowmobile, not just that equipment which is permanently attached; (3) coverage during organized competition or snowmobile rallies (hard to find, but some policies have it); (4) payment for losses that result from breaking through ice; (5) twenty-four-hour coverage (some policies restrict operations to daylight hours); (6) medical payments for people you lend your snowmobile to (you generally lose this coverage if you rent the vehicle out).

Watch for exclusions, such as not paying off if you had the accident on ice or while racing with a friend. Most policies are written on a one-year basis, so you can't cancel them over the summer. Supposedly, the months the snowmobile is laid up are considered when setting rates. Some companies, however, will write a six-month liability policy (with extra coverage for snow days before and after the lay-up dates). The fire-and-theft portion of the policy will be continued year-round.

Insurance While on Vacation

U.S. auto policies generally cover any driving you do in Canada. But all Canadian provinces require that you carry specific proof of financial responsibility. Without it your car could be impounded if you had an accident. It's sufficient to carry a special financial responsibility card, which you can get from your insurance agent. If the provinces you plan to visit require more insurance than you actually carry, your company may treat your policy as if it complied with Canadian minimums. Alternatively, you'll be required to take out extra insurance for the vacation period before being issued your financial responsibility card.

If you're driving in Mexico, you need liability insurance issued by a Mexican company or a company licensed in Mexico. Policies issued by other companies are not recognized by Mexican law: if you had an accident, you might find yourself in jail with your car impounded until you could prove that you're financially able to satisfy all claims. It's important to get the insurance before you enter Mexico—usually through a border-state insurance agent, although your own agent may well be able to help. (If you plan to buy at the border, be sure to check the cost—it's quite expensive.) Some U.S. companies belong to a foreign insurance association and are licensed to write policies for Mexico. But don't confuse these with the "Mexican Tourist" endorsement, good for only fifty or one hundred miles across the border. Tourist endorsements cover you if you hit another American tourist and are sued in the United States, but since they aren't recognized by the Mexican government, they won't help you at all if you hit a Mexican citizen.

If you're planning to drive in any other country, ask your agent to find out how to insure yourself. Or write for information to that country's tourist office.

Chapter Thirteen

BUYING A HOUSE (OR CONDOMINIUM)

The buyer needs a hundred eyes, the seller not one.
GEORGE HERBERT

In these inflationary years the financial advantages of home ownership are quite clear-cut: (1) As earnings rise, your mortgage payments stay steady, which makes them less of a burden over the years. Although home-related costs like fuel and property taxes continue to rise, the vast majority of homeowners find that increased incomes more than cover the added expense. (2) Increases in the value of the property belong to you, not to the landlord. (3) If an older person sells his house and moves to an apartment, the equity value of a lifetime of homeownership gives him a fund he can live on for many years. (4) Interest paid on the mortgage and property taxes are deductible on your income tax form. If you pay about the same per month for a house as for an apartment, the house is actually costing you much less—and is an appreciating asset, besides. (5) Houses are a vehicle for "forced savings," and a splendid investment. (6) Money aside, homeownership provides tremendous emotional satisfactions that renters may not even realize until they buy —a sense of proprietorship, privacy, and the joy of puttering in your own garden.

Even in inflationary times, however, a house is not automatically a good investment. If you work for a company that transfers you often, for example, you may lose money on frequent resales. Families in this position should consider renting instead of buying—leaving the money

234

that would otherwise be the down payment in a bank term account drawing high interest. Money earning 8 percent compounded quarterly will double in nine years, which may be better than you'd do by buying and selling three different houses during that period, especially after closing costs and broker's fees. If you're lucky enough to buy during recessions and sell during recoveries, or move into a spiraling real-estate market, you might come out ahead of the savings account after taxes, but that's hard to predict. Some houses lose value—if the neighborhood declines, unsightly public works go up nearby, or there's no zoning protection against commercial and industrial development.

Can You Afford a House?

Meeting the mortgage payment is only the first step in carrying a house. On top of that you have property taxes, insurance, electricity, water and perhaps sewerage, heat, garbage collection, maintenance, repairs, and —if your job is some distance away—commuting. These expenses will very likely rise regularly. If you've never had the experience of home-owning, talk to a real estate broker about what the monthly costs might be. For any particular house the agent should have a list of all the basic expenses.

The rule of thumb is that a first-time homebuyer probably can't afford a house that costs more than two and a half times his annual income. If you make $16,000 a year, your top price range is in the area of $40,000; at $25,000 a year, your top is around $62,500. That often rules out newly built houses—first timers will find more space and better value in older homes, perhaps in the city rather than the suburbs. After building up some equity, you'll be in a position to buy a new house, if that's what you want.

Families heavily in debt will have to lower their sights—lenders probably won't give you a large enough loan to purchase a house worth two and a half times your annual income. Conversely, if you own a home that has shot up in value, you might sell it and use the proceeds toward a house worth three or four times your annual income. It pays to visit at least two banks or savings and loan associations before going house hunting in order to see how much they'll lend you and whether it's enough for the kind of house you want. *In general, a lender won't let your monthly mortgage payment exceed 20 to 25 percent of your monthly salary. The combination of mortgage payments, taxes, homeowner's insurance, and installment payments on other long-term debts usually can't exceed 33 percent of your salary.*

How To Get Your First Down Payment

Most banks or savings and loan associations will lend you 75 to 80 percent of the purchase price of a house (except in tight-money times, when they may lend less). The remainder is the *down payment,* and must come either from another loan or from your own pocket. How to do it? Here are nine possibilities:

• Save the money, perhaps using one of the automated savings plans suggested on page 45.

• Borrow from your parents. It's common among parents who can afford it to add some money to their children's savings, in order to get them into their first house. If the loan is to be repaid, be sure you give your parents a proper note (see page 98).

• Get a mortgage insured by the Federal Housing Administration, where the down payment is smaller than on conventional mortgages. In rural areas you might qualify for a loan from the Farmers Home Administration. Mortgages insured by the Veterans Administration may require no down payment at all (see page 257).

• Get private mortgage insurance, offered through many banks, savings and loan associations, and mortgage companies. Under this arrangement the lender may give you 90 to 95 percent of the money you need. You pay an annual premium for the insurance (typically, ½ of 1 percent the first year and ¼ of 1 percent thereafter). This guarantees that if you default, the loan will be repaid. After a few years, when the mortgage amount has been reduced to the lender's normal 75 to 80 percent of equity, you can drop the insurance. But you'll usually have to ask that the coverage be terminated; mortgage insurance doesn't stop automatically. Not all lenders participate in private mortgage plans. A real estate agent should be able to tell you who, if anyone, offers it in your area.

• A buyer with a good income might be able to borrow the down payment from a bank or credit union in the form of a personal loan. This is a likely course for a young professional couple, recently out of school, and with no children yet. You may also be able to borrow against assets, such as an insurance policy, a mutual fund, stocks, an interest in a business, a paid-up car. Think of everything you own that's worth money and ask the bank if they'll take it as collateral for a loan.

• Make a deal with the seller to wait for part of his money. For example, say you want to buy a $50,000 home but are $5,000 short. If the seller doesn't need all the money right away, he might be willing to take that $5,000 in installments over three or four years, or as a lump-sum payment four years hence. You'd normally secure the debt by giving the seller a second mortgage on the house; interest would likely be payable at or above the going mortgage interest rate. If you're going to need this kind of financing, tell the real estate broker about it. He's in a good position to single out the sellers most likely to agree.

• When money is tight or there's a building glut, builders sometimes give second mortgages in order to get their new houses sold. Typically, they advance part of the down payment at low interest. When you visit a model home or talk to a builder, ask what kind of financing is available.

• If a house has been on the market for a while, an owner may be willing to rent it to you with an option to buy. Part of the rental payments will then count toward the down payment. In general, the longer a house has remained unsold, the easier it is to make whatever financial arrangements best suit your convenience. (But remember: If the house has problems, and they're not of the sort that can be repaired, you, too, may have trouble reselling it.)

• The smaller the down payment you arrange, the higher your monthly carrying costs will be. By and large, the bigger loans are made only to buyers with steady jobs, good incomes, and improving prospects.

Large Mortgage vs. Small Mortgage

Some families want to put down as much cash as possible when buying a house in order to minimize the mortgage. Others like to borrow as much as possible, saving their cash for other purposes. Assuming you have a choice, which approach is right? Here are the pros and cons:

For a Large Down Payment

• The more you put down, the less interest you pay over the life of the loan. Say you buy a $60,000 home with a 14 percent mortgage for twenty-five years. With $12,000 down, or 20 percent, you would repay $174,556 over the full term. With $6,000 down, or 10 percent, you would repay $195,015, making the smaller down payment $20,459 more expensive. This calculation is immaterial to people who expect to move in just a few years, but important to those who hope to stay in their present homes for a long time.

• A large down payment sometimes results in a lower mortgage rate.

Many banks and savings and loan associations will shave perhaps ¼ to ½ of 1 percent from the rate for those with more cash.

• Many people like the feeling of a smaller debt. This is especially important if you want to own your present house, free and clear, by the time you retire.

Against a Large Down Payment

• Mortgage interest is deductible on your income tax. This gives you a chance to use your cash for other investments and do better, after taxes, than if you had put everything into your house. For example, a high-bracket person might take a larger mortgage at 12 percent and use his remaining funds to buy tax-exempt municipals at 7 percent, thus putting himself ahead. A lower-bracket person might put the extra into a 12 percent corporate bond mutual fund. Because of the size of the mortgage deduction in the early years, he, too, would be ahead. When interest rates rise, your bonds would lose value—but that could be offset by an increase in the value of your house. When interest rates fall, you could make money on both your house and your bonds. In other words, you're looking at investment options and measuring the probabilities of profit and loss.

• If you expect to sell your house after just a few years, a small down payment yields a higher and faster return on investment. Suppose, for example, you bought a house for $50,000 and sold it for $60,000, giving you a $10,000 profit. That $10,000 is a 100 percent gain on an original investment (down payment) of $10,000. But if you had put only $5,000 down, it would represent a 200 percent gain.

• Keeping cash in places other than your home makes you more liquid in case of trouble. For example, if you lose your job, the bank might not grant a second mortgage to give you cash to live on. But other investments could easily be cashed in.

• If you're apt to be transferred by your company, it's important to be able to sell your house quickly in any kind of housing market. When money is tight, it's easier to sell when the buyer can assume your mortgage rather than find one of his own. A larger mortgage is usually easier for buyers to assume, because it means a smaller down payment.

• If you have large obligations such as college tuition coming up, you need money on tap even at the cost of higher mortgage payments.

Should You Prepay a Mortgage?

Yes, if your objective is to enter retirement free and clear of mortgage payments. When retirement income is low, the tax-deductibility of mortgage interest is of little or no value, and high monthly mortgage payments may make it hard to meet other bills. A common way for retirees to prepay their mortgages is to cash in their insurance policies.

Yes, if money burns a hole in your pocket. Prepaying the mortgage can be a way of forced savings.

Yes, if you're a widow left with life insurance proceeds but insufficient income. By using the insurance to eliminate the mortgage, you might be able to live on your earnings without having to give up the house. On the other hand, if you think you'll probably give up the house in any event, keep the insurance proceeds invested elsewhere.

Yes, if you can make an advantageous deal with your bank. People with low-interest mortgages, dating back to the days when they could borrow at 5 and 6 percent, might offer to prepay the amount remaining if the bank will reduce the remaining amount of the loan. These arrangements are privately negotiated; you make an offer and the bank takes it or leaves it. You'll never know what can be done if you don't ask.

No, if prepaying the mortgage means that you have to borrow at higher interest rates for things like a car or appliances.

No, if your objective is to lower your monthly mortgage payments. Generally, prepayment shortens the term of the debt but monthly payments remain the same. However, if you make a substantial prepayment, the bank may be willing to rewrite the mortgage at a lower monthly amount (there may or may not be additional fees involved—it depends on the bank and what you can negotiate).

No, if you can earn more on your money, after taxes, than you'll save by reducing the mortgage debt.

No, if you expect to move within just a few years.

Old House or New House?

The chief advantage of a formerly occupied house is that it costs less than a comparable one that's brand new. In addition, any major structural defects should have shown up by now and been corrected; the landscaping—always a costly item—is done and the trees have grown;

there's often better workmanship and materials than in new houses; and the taxes are apt to be lower than on new houses in the community. The chief disadvantages of an older house are that it may need renovation and repair (which could bring the cost up to that of a new house); it could be more costly to heat; it may not have modern appliances (or even the wiring for them); if you want air conditioning, you might have to use wall units; and upkeep may be more expensive than on a house made of more modern materials.

A new house, on the other hand, has all-new appliances, paint, floors, perhaps even rugs, which make it look perfect when you move in; there are usually no major repairs needed; you often can start right out with a carpet and paint that go with your furniture rather than having to live with clashing colors until you can redecorate; and it may be easier to get a mortgage on a new house than on an old one. But a new house generally costs more than an older house; you have the expense of landscaping; hidden structural defects may cost you a pretty penny; and the work may be shoddier and materials cheaper than in a comparable older house.

When you're house shopping, look at both new and old in order to get a feeling for what your money can buy. The more you look, the surer you'll be about which type of house you'll be happier with.

Which Neighborhood?

If you live in the area, you probably know already which neighborhood will suit you. But if you're heading for a new city, talk to any friends or business connections you may have there to learn the lay of the land. Once there, get a city map, drive through the various residential areas, and visit two or three real estate brokers. Ask everyone you come across —from the motel manager to the waitresses—which neighborhoods they like best. Within a short period of time you'll be able to zero in on two or three likely places to live. Then find a real estate agent you like and get answers to these following questions:

• Of the several communities you're considering, which has the lowest tax rates and which the highest? When were the older houses last reassessed? If many years have gone by without a reassessment, you can be sure the tax rate on an older house will jump fairly soon—perhaps just after you buy. (For information on fighting a high tax assessment, see page 538.)

• Which communities are considered to have the best schools?

(Chances are it won't be the one with the lowest taxes.) When you zero in on a neighborhood or a house, check out the schools your children will attend. Call up the principal and ask if you can come for a visit. Find out how large the classes are, what programs are available, and whether they had to cut the school budget or raise school taxes last year (if a school is in a financial squeeze, it means either that programs will go or property taxes will keep on rising). A walk through the school will tell you whether it's a cheerful or a forbidding place. Also, walk through the neighborhood and ask some of the residents what they think of the schools. If a particular school district is important to you, double-check to be sure the house is within that district.

• What college facilities are available? Your children may want to attend a two-year community college, or you may want to return to school to brush up on skills. Community colleges are far less expensive than private schools.

• What transportation is available? What's the nearest bus or subway stop? If the neighborhood is some distance from your job, try the commute two or three times to see if you can stand it. If you'll need a second car, you're adding $5,000 or more to the cost of buying a house there.

• Where are the community facilities? The parks? The library? The YM/YWCA, the YM/YWHA? The softball field or Little League? The bike paths or hiking trails? The community pool? The public tennis courts or golf course? The theaters? The concert hall? The shopping centers? Where's the nearest police and fire station? Gas station? Hospital? Bank? All-night delicatessen? Where's your church?

• How good is the neighborhood? Hallmarks of a desirable area are a steadily growing demand for homes; expanding businesses and industries, which assure growing incomes for residents; new stores and shopping centers being opened nearby; block or community associations that take pride in keeping up the neighborhood; a neat and cheerful appearance; and a trend for families to move into older houses that have deteriorated, and rehabilitate them. If you're doubtful about the neighborhood, visit it at night and on weekends to see if its character changes. Consult real estate brokers from various neighborhoods. They'll tend to puff the areas where they have listings, but will give you all the poop on a neighborhood where they don't do much business. Take it with a grain of salt, but at least listen to it.

• Are there any differences in maintenance costs from one community to another—for example, is one serviced by a less expensive power company?

• Is there discrimination against blacks? For the black homebuyer this can mean a discouraging round of visits to unattractive houses, with real estate agents who hope you won't buy. Short of bringing a lawsuit, this practice is extremely difficult to get around—although the threat of a lawsuit may persuade the broker to show you something better. For the white homebuyer a "white flight" community carries an increasing risk to property values that you may not realize. Where communities integrate peacefully, letting anyone who can afford the price buy a home, property values are unaffected. But recalcitrant communities are increasingly sued because of exclusionary zoning that keeps apartment houses (or low-rental units) out of the area. More and more courts are rewriting local zoning laws—changing what might have remained a single-family area, had it not practiced racial discrimination, into a neighborhood of mixed homes and apartments. This definitely does lower property values—a long-run risk for any exclusionary community.

• What are the zoning restrictions? If you want to build an apartment over the garage for your mother-in-law, will that be possible? Can you add a wing? If there are open fields in the neighborhood, are they all zoned residential, or could some of them become office buildings or shopping centers? Is it possible to build tracts of houses that will sell at a lower price than yours? Either of those things could depress your own property values. If the real estate agent isn't dead sure about the zoning (and he may not be), visit the town hall and ask there.

Should You Use a Real Estate Broker?

You normally don't pay a broker anything directly for the service he renders in showing you houses and helping to complete the transaction. His commission (around 6 to 7 percent) is paid by the seller and included in the general level of house prices. If you watch the classified ads and find a house "for sale by owner," which means that a real estate broker is not involved, the owner might pass some of his savings in brokerage commissions on to you. But before buying such a house, check the price of comparable places; it's common for owners to overprice their houses.

Because of the small number of houses "for sale by owner," the odds on your finding what you want from that source are small. For most house hunters a real estate broker is essential. He knows most of the houses for sale in the area and can save you a lot of time by weeding out those that would probably be unsuitable. He can give you good estimates of maintenance and carrying costs, provide contacts with local mortgage lenders if you need them, and answer questions about the neighborhood and town. Look for a broker you feel comfortable with and who grasps rapidly just what it is that you're looking for. If you think you're being pushed around or given short shrift, try another broker; there are plenty around.

Your principal obligations to the broker are to be frank about what you can afford, explain as clearly as you can the kind of house you want, and show up (or cancel in advance) when he's made an appointment for you to view a house. During the negotiation to buy a particular house the broker advises you on what price the seller will accept, but always remember that he's working for the seller, who pays his commission. It's the broker's duty to get as good a deal for the seller as possible, within the limits of the buyer's budget.

Some General Buying Tips

• A house that has been on the market for some time, because of some peculiarity, may carry a bargain price tag. You might love the house despite its quirks. But if you ever had to resell, you'd have the same problem getting rid of it that the former owner did. On the other hand, if the only reason it hasn't sold is that it's rundown, you could buy it cheap, fix it up, and make a handsome gain.

• When you buy a tract house from a builder, don't base your decision solely on the model home. That home was built and decorated with special care, as a sales tool. To find out how well the rest of the houses are built, walk around the area and ask the residents what they think, based on a few years of occupancy. Ring doorbells if no one is out on the street. Also ask how the builder-installed rugs, appliances, and heating plant are standing up. If you're a gardener, ask about the soil; often builders scrape up the topsoil for sale elsewhere, leaving residents to make do with subsoil for their gardens and lawns.

• The farther from the center of business and social activity you go, the lower the prices in general and the lower the taxes. However, there are larger commuting costs, and the community services will probably be poorer.

• Foreclosed properties are sometimes lower priced. But the person who couldn't afford to pay his mortgage probably also couldn't afford to keep the place up, so have it inspected carefully.

• When mortgage rates are unusually high, it's sometimes wise to wait a bit before you buy. Eventually rates will fall, saving you some money. Many people argue that it's not worth waiting for lower rates because in the meantime house prices will rise, canceling out your savings. This may be true for new houses, whose prices in recent years have risen even during recessions. But in many markets, the price of older houses generally holds steady or falls a little during recessions, so you won't be risking much by waiting for lower rates. Paying 13 instead of 15 percent on a $40,000 twenty-five-year mortgage will save you $61.20 a month, which may not look like much but adds up to $18,360 over the term of the loan. Even if the house did go up a little in price while you were waiting for mortgage rates to fall, it's unlikely to rise $18,360. But if, at best, mortgage rates are likely to fall only ½ of 1 percent, it's probably not worth waiting to buy. That translates into a saving of $15.47 a month, or only $4,641 over twenty-five years.

• Two people buying a house should both look at it before signing the contract. If a husband buys without the wife's having had a look (as sometimes happens when a family moves to a distant city), she might hate it when she arrives. That could make the house a sore spot between them for years to come. Let the husband do the advance screening if he's on the spot, but then he should bring his wife in. If possible, it's best to look at houses together so you'll both get a feel for what's on the market and how prices run.

• If part of a house's charm is its beautiful garden, don't buy unless you have the time and interest to keep it up.

• Make notes as you go around on what's right and wrong with each house you're interested in, and who the real estate broker is. When you see a lot of houses, they tend to blur in your mind.

• Ask the owner why he's selling. If he doesn't have a good answer, such as "I've been transferred" or "We need something bigger," he may know something about the house he isn't telling.

• If you're seriously interested in the house, ask for copies of the utility bills, the taxes, and the termite inspector's most recent report. Find out how often the taxes have gone up in the past several years. If the taxes haven't gone up, you're probably due.

• Don't fall in love with one aspect of a house—say, its lovely view or large living room—and ignore the unattractive side, such as a kitchen that's a dank hole. Once you've moved in, the inconveniences will loom larger and larger. If you decide to buy despite the dank kitchen, figure the cost of renovation as part of the house price.

• If you have the time to wait, look at houses priced perhaps $10,000 or $15,000 over your price range that have been on the market a year or more, or where death or divorce dictates a quick sale. Offer $15,000 less and see what happens. After ten or fifteen tries, one might work.

• Ask whether any covenants, restrictions, or easements go with the land. Does anyone draw water from your well? Do you owe any lake assessments? Are there timber rights? Are you prevented from adding an apartment over the garage or having a tenant?

• If your parents are going to help you with the down payment, bring them along on some of your house-hunting trips. It's important that they get a feel for the market and a sense of what houses cost today. Otherwise, they may be shocked when they learn that you're buying a small split-level for $80,000.

• Be perfectly frank with the real estate broker about how much money you have to put down and how much you can pay each month. If you're reluctant to disclose financial details, you'll probably start off looking at houses that you can't afford. Then, when you step down to a more realistic level, you'll be disappointed. If you've never owned a house before, the real estate broker will be able to estimate the monthly payments for various types of houses and help you figure out what you can afford to buy.

• Don't go house hunting with pets. And if possible, leave the children at home.

• Don't judge a house by its wallpaper. If the land, layout, style, and price are right, the wallpaper can be changed. Many people let good houses go simply because they're put off by the owner's taste in decorating.

• Don't be afraid to buy the first or second house you see if it's what you're looking for. By the time you've inspected a lot of other houses, that first, perfect house may be gone.

• When you make a deal, ask the present owner for any manuals or service contracts he has on the appliances; the house plans; a plan of any underground wires and pipes, including the septic field, if there is one. Find out how deep any wells are. Get directions on how to operate any gadgetry in the house. If you come from out of town, ask for recommendations on local handymen, such as a plumber, electrician, and carpenter.

• Once you've decided to buy, don't dawdle. Move swiftly to get a lawyer, a termite inspection, an engineering report, and a mortgage. If a week or so goes by with no action, the owner might put the house back on the market. If you get cold feet after making an offer, tell the real estate broker right away. The sooner he knows, the easier it is to undo the deal at no cost to you.

• Licensed real estate brokers belong to the National Association of Realtors and local real estate boards. If you have a complaint against a member—because he has high-pressured you or misrepresented a house—complain to the board. If he misrepresented a house to such an extent that it cost you a lot of money, you may be able to sue.

The Inspection

Always have a house inspected before you buy it, even if it's brand new. Flaws and defects may not be readily apparent, nor can the average buyer tell whether the furnace is hefty enough to heat the house or how much longer the roof will last. An inspector will (1) reveal any serious flaws in the foundation or structure that make the house a bad buy; (2) take note of less serious flaws and give you an estimate of what it will cost to make repairs (with this in hand, you may be able to bargain down the price of the house); (3) give you an estimate of how much longer the roof, furnace, pipes, and so on are going to last; (4) advise you on how to maintain the house so as to avoid further defects.

Have the inspection done by a professional engineer or architect experienced in this line of work, not by a carpenter or contractor who does it on the side. An engineer knows far more about the stresses and strains a house is subject to. You'll find the names of local firms in the Yellow Pages under "Building [or House] Inspection"; or ask the real estate broker or lawyer for the names of several inspectors who are familiar with the neighborhood. *Important note:* An FHA "inspection" is only for purposes of appraisal; it won't tell you anything about possible hidden defects in the house.

A few real estate brokers discourage inspections because they're afraid you'll learn something that will blow the deal. Owners often don't like it either, since the discovery of a serious flaw may mean they'll have to come down in price. But a growing number of brokers strongly recommend it. They want clients to know exactly what they're getting so that if something goes wrong, they won't hold the real estate broker responsible.

You can usually make the seller an offer "subject to the inspection"; if he accepts, he'll take the house off the market. Some sellers, however, leave the house on the market until the inspection is over. This worries some buyers, who are afraid someone else will come along and snap it up. But that's unlikely to happen, considering the time it takes to make a decision on a house, and anyway, inspection firms usually move quickly. You should be able to get a house looked at within two or three days and get a verbal report of its problems on the spot. A complete written report will follow in a few days.

The inspector looks at the foundation, drainage, siding, roof, heating and cooling systems, plumbing, insulation, structural soundness, and septic system. He hunts for obvious signs of termite damage, but for a more thorough check you need a termite expert. It's smart to walk around with the inspector, so you can ask questions about things that bother you. But if you can't be there, he'll handle your questions by telephone. The cost of an inspection is minimal—perhaps $80 to $150. That's next to nothing compared with the size of the investment you are about to make.

The inspection report does not usually cover appliances or such gadgets as sprinkler systems. These items can break if they are used incorrectly, and they have an uncertain life span. By all means check before buying to see what's working and what isn't, but don't look to the inspector for an estimate as to how long they will last. The inspector also can't tell you much about the condition of the soil, since he doesn't take borings. But if his firm specializes in foundations (as some do), he may have an opinion about land conditions around a newly built house and whether the cellar might sink.

You yourself can weed out the houses in the worst condition by using your eyes and your nose when you look them over. Here is what to watch for:

The Basement or Crawl Space

Look for water stains on the walls and floors. If the basement is newly painted, sniff along the walls for moist odors. A sump pump means water, so ask the owner how often and how bad. If in doubt, revisit the house after a heavy rainstorm to see for yourself. Sight along the beams and girders for twists, sags, or columns out of plumb. Sometimes people remove a column to make room for a Ping-Pong table and don't bother shoring up the gap. If this is the case, the floor will sag eventually, even if it hasn't yet.

The Foundation Walls, Inside and Out

Watch for large cracks, a quarter of an inch wide or more. Fine cracks are usually the result of normal settlement, but bigger ones mean trouble.

The Structure

Check for slopes in floors, slanting walls or sagging rooflines, uneven door frames, bad cracks in the plaster, windows out of plumb. In a newly built house a twisted frame may show up only in a small slant here and there, but it means costly repairs over time. Look for watermarks around windows that suggest poor caulking. Watermarks on the ceilings mean a roof problem.

The Roof

A failing roof is easily spotted. You'll see a lot of black on the shingles (especially along the roofline) where the mineral grit has worn off. The life of an asphalt shingle roof is eighteen to twenty years; if the house is about that old, you'll probably have to put a new roof on fairly soon. Slate and tile roofs can last fifty years, depending on weather, before the material underlying them dries out and starts to leak.

The Attic

Here's where the thickness of the insulation shows. If there's three inches or less, your heating and cooling systems won't do the job they should, so you'll probably want to add some more. If you do, be sure there's enough ventilation in the attic to avoid condensation. Houses thirty-five years old or more may have no insulation at all in the walls. A quick test is to stand, in cold weather, in the corner of a room where one wall backs up on another room and the other backs up to the outdoors. Put your hands on both walls. If the wall that backs up to the outdoors is markedly colder, the insulation is poor. This can be repaired by taking off the siding and blowing insulation into the spaces between the studs, but that's an expensive job, and often yields poor results. It's more cost-efficient simply to insulate the attic, caulk all the cracks, and add storm windows. (If a house's heating bills are high, you might not want to buy it at all.)

The Heating System

If the pipes and boilers look old, they are, and may need replacing soon. The average life of a hot-air furnace is twenty years; a cast-iron boiler, forty to fifty years; a steel boiler, fifteen to twenty years. (If you're in doubt as to the age of the house, take the top off the toilet tank. Its date of manufacture is usually inside the top. Assuming that it's original equipment, it will show you the year the house was built.) Also check whether all the rooms actually get heat.

Hot Water

A glass-lined hot water heater lasts eight to ten years. One-bathroom houses need at least a forty-gallon capacity, and you may well want more. For two baths, you need at least fifty or sixty gallons. Ask the engineer who inspects the house whether the heat and hot water systems are adequate to do the job.

Plumbing

Turn on all the faucets to check the pressure, and look for rust in the water. Low pressure or rusty pipes could be costly to fix.

Electricity

The minimum standard service for today's electrically applianced home is about 100 amps, and you may need even more. Again, this is a question to put to the engineer who does the inspection.

Drainage

All grades must slope away from the house, or you're inviting a water problem. If any slopes run toward the foundation, have them fixed right away.

Septic Tank or Cesspool

Check for odors or slicks on the ground surface. Around the trap look for water marks or dried bits of paper—signs of a previous backup.

Your own inspection can root out the obvious bad buys. But don't let it substitute for a final inspection by an engineer before you sign the contract.

The Negotiation

Once you've hit on a house you want, the question is price. You can generally assume that the seller has priced it a little over what he's willing to accept, but you don't know exactly how far down he'll go. The real estate broker knows his bottom limit, however, and also knows your upper limit. Somewhere between those two figures he'll try to put together a deal (making it as favorable to the seller as possible, since the seller pays the commission).

When you make your first offer, it can't be unrealistically low; if it is, the seller won't take you seriously and probably won't budge on his price. So take the broker's advice as to what's in the ballpark. You'll probably have to go higher than your first offer, but try to get something thrown in when you raise the bid—the drapes and curtain rods, perhaps, or refrigerator and washer-dryer. When you've reached your upper limit, make that fact very clear to the real estate broker so he can tell his client that it's that price or nothing. Some sellers are willing to wait for another buyer to get their price; others will accept a lower offer just to get the house off their hands. If your best offer is turned down, start the house-hunting round again. You'll eventually find something you like, and in your price range. It's an error to stick yourself with a house that costs more than you can afford.

Do You Need a Lawyer?

In some states only lawyers are allowed to draw up real estate contracts. In others it can be handled by real estate brokers. The chief advantage to letting an agent do it is that it saves you the legal fee. However, since the real estate broker primarily represents the seller, who pays his commission, your interests won't be getting the attention they would if you had your own lawyer. Furthermore, real estate transactions touch on legal complexities that the real estate broker may not manage well. Among other things, he may not investigate any covenants, restrictions, or easements that go with the land. Nor may he protect you from the risk that the seller may change his mind, or damage the property. In short, *get a lawyer*, even where the law doesn't require you to have one.

Typically, lawyers charge around 1 percent of the sales price. But if you make it clear that you're price shopping, it's quite common for lawyers to charge less. If you don't know a lawyer in the area, the real estate broker can recommend one. *Tip:* It's smart to use a local lawyer. People from other areas, particularly from distant big-city firms, aren't familiar with local customs, which generally makes the negotiation take longer than necessary.

The Contract

When the seller accepts your bid, the real estate broker will usually ask you to put down a small deposit and perhaps sign a *binder*. This indicates the good faith of your offer and your willingness to proceed to contract—on the strength of which the seller will take his house off the market. During the contract negotiation, however, the deal still might fall through—so get the real estate agent's *written* agreement to refund your deposit if you and the seller should be unable to come to terms.

Take care that the binder isn't too specific. If it mentions the property, the seller, and the sales price—and both you and the seller sign it —the binder itself can become the sales contract, and you've lost the chance to negotiate any further protections for yourself. In fact, it's best not to sign a binder. If the seller insists on one, be sure that the language does no more than identify the property; also, it should state specifically that any agreement is subject to your getting a mortgage and negotiating a satisfactory sales contract. A proper binder does not bind you at all in legal terms; it is merely a gesture of good faith.

The *sales contract* is the formal document obligating you to buy the house. Here are some of the protections your lawyer should include:

• You need a full description of the property, backed up by a survey. If there is no survey, have one done. Who pays for it can be part of the price negotiation.

• It's essential that the seller give you a clear title. In many cases this means the ability to obtain title insurance. The seller should list all restrictions on the property, any debts for which the property is security, and state that there are no other claims. Where it is the custom, the deal may be made subject to getting title insurance (see page 263).

• Whatever deposit you put up should be held in escrow until the house is actually transferred to you on settlement date. If, in the meantime, the seller violates the terms of the contract, you can get your money back. The contract should state that the house will be turned over to you in the same condition it's in now, except for normal wear and tear. If it burns down between the time you sign the contract and settlement date, the loss will not be yours.

• The contract must be subject to your getting a mortgage within a specified period of time and, if you wish, at an interest rate no higher than a specified ceiling. If you can't find financing at terms you can afford, the contract will be void and your deposit returned.

• What is being sold with the house? *Fixtures,* which are anything permanently attached to the house, are normally considered part of the price, whereas *furnishings* can be packed up by the seller and moved. But it's not always clear what's a fixture and what's a furnishing. The contract should specifically list what goes with the house—such as appliances, rugs, curtain rods, shades, drapes, awnings, and anything else that appears to have been custom-made for that particular dwelling. Other things may also have been part of the deal, such as furniture or lawn-care equipment. If any fixtures are to be removed—for example, certain garden plants—that, too, should be mentioned.

• Who pays the various transfer costs? The cost of the termite inspection? The price of fixing the furnace if it breaks down between the time the contract is signed and settlement date?

• In many states both husband and wife must sign the contract as sellers, even if the house is owned by only one of them. That's because state law may give the other spouse an interest in the property. You'll want to be sure both of them have conveyed their rights to you.

• The lawyer should investigate any restrictions, covenants, and easements that go with the deed and restrict your use of the property. Often, they're more complicated than it first appeared. You may even want to change your mind about the purchase.

• You need to define the circumstances of a default on the contract, and what happens in that case. Any special agreements between you and the buyer—such as his promise to get a porch fixed—must also be in the contract, or you won't be able to enforce them.

• If the house is being rented, you'll want the tenant out before you give the seller any money. Otherwise, you might have to go to the expense of having the tenant evicted.

• You and the seller should agree to adjust certain costs at the closing. If you take possession May 1 and the town taxes for the first six months are due June 1, the seller should pay the tax for the months he occupied the place. Likewise, if the seller filled the oil tank in March and it's only down one third, you should pay him for the amount of oil you're taking over. Such payments as insurance premiums, water and sewer charges, and utility bills may also be prorated between you.

Getting a Mortgage

In some states they're called *mortgages,* in others, *deeds of trust,* but they amount to the same thing—a pledge of property to ensure that the loan will be repaid. In addition to the mortgage you sign a *bond,* which is a personal promise to pay. If you don't pay, the lender may foreclose, subject to whatever safeguards are written into your state law (see page 281).

When you're ready to buy, the real estate agent may ask if you have arranged for a mortgage, and if not, he may reach in a desk drawer and pull out a mortgage application form. Brokers do a steady business with two or three of the lending institutions in the area. By sending the institution as many clients as possible, they assure themselves of a mortgage source during those periods when money is tight and mortgages hard to get. Brokers also know about any special mortgage deals being offered in town. These arrangements can be extremely helpful to a person who otherwise doesn't have a source of money. But it's worth a little checking on your own before you fill in the form.

Lending institutions vary quite a bit, in mortgage terms and in the fees they charge at closing. It pays to talk to several lenders, to see

where you can get the best deal. Among the things you'll want to ask
are

• "What is your best interest rate if I make a large down payment?"
• "What is the largest loan you will make me?" Some lenders will give
you several thousand dollars more than others, a fact that many borrowers don't realize. You may even be turned down by one lender but
accepted by another.
• "Will you strike out or reduce the *mortgage prepayment penalty*?"
You want to be able to repay the mortgage ahead of time (which would
happen, for example, if you sold the house) without an extra charge.
Federal banks and savings and loan associations are the most likely to
have a life-of-the-contract prepayment penalty, which they'll usually
reduce, if asked.
• "Is the mortgage *assumable*?" (Is it a loan that can be taken over
by another buyer?) That's often a plus at resale, since it saves the buyer
some closing costs. In a tight money market, when loans are hard to
come by, an assumable mortgage may make the difference as to
whether or not your house can be sold.
• "What's the *delinquency charge* if I miss a payment?"
• "Is the mortgage *open-ended*?" If so, you can reborrow money
you've repaid (although probably not at the same interest rate) with a
minimum of extra charges.
• "Do you charge *points*?" This is an up-front charge that adds considerably to your costs—see page 264.
• "How much are your *closing costs*?" Lending institutions vary tremendously in this regard—some charging fees of $75 or $100, and
others, $400 to $600. Some real estate brokers have the attitude that an
extra $600 doesn't mean anything in a $50,000 deal—but it means
exactly $600, which you'd probably be glad to have.

Under the Real Estate Settlement Procedures Act the lender must
furnish you with a list of estimated closing costs (see page 264). But he
doesn't have to do it until you've made formal application for a mortgage, which might cost you a nonrefundable $50 to cover processing
costs. So you can't very well use the RESPA disclosure forms as a basis
for comparing costs among several lenders. Instead, make comparisons
this way:

1. Call any banks or savings and loan associations that you regularly
deal with, to see what mortgage rate they're charging, what the prepayment penalties are, and what they estimate their closing fees will be.
If you can't get the information over the phone, pay them a visit.

2. Get a local attorney who handles a lot of real estate closings and ask him which lenders charge the lowest fees. He knows.

3. Ask the company you work for to recommend you to a lender who will handle your mortgage on favorable terms.

4. Visit the lenders in the area, say you're just moving in and are looking for a place to do your banking business, and say you are also shopping for a mortgage. Ask what their rates and fees are. If a bank is uncooperative, assume it will always be hard to deal with and go somewhere else.

5. Ask the real estate broker if he has a list of the lenders in the area and their closing costs.

I cannot stress enough that your mortgage loan may be far more costly than necessary if you sign up with the first lender you talk to. Since the sales contract usually requires you to get a mortgage fast, it's wise to make mortgage cost comparisons early in the game, while you're still house hunting. Then, when you find a house, you'll know exactly where to go for funds.

The mortgage subjects you to certain terms. You must keep the property in good repair, keep your insurance up, not fall afoul of local building or zoning codes, and not sell off part of your property or remove buildings without the lender's consent. Arrange for your fire insurance yourself rather than through the lender, since you'll generally be able to find it at lower cost.

If the mortgage is granted solely on the basis of the husband's income, and the deed is in his name, the wife does not have to sign the mortgage bond. Under the Equal Credit Opportunity Act she cannot be made liable for his debt. The advantage of not being on the bond is this: If the husband defaults, the bank forecloses, and the house sells for something less than the amount of the outstanding mortgage, the bank cannot come after the wife personally for the additional money. These occasions are rare, but there's no sense assuming a debt if you don't have to. It's a tradition, however, to have the wife's name on the line, and most lenders expect her to sign as a matter of course. On principle, she should resist; in practice, that may be hard to do.

Where the law grants the spouse an interest in the property, she can be required to sign a document giving the bank authority to foreclose if the mortgage isn't paid, but that document should not also make her personally liable for the loan. Unfortunately, it generally does. Your lawyer should be acquainted with this new point of law and keep the wife's name off the bond if at all possible. Of course, if the mortgage is based in part on her income, she must sign.

Assuming a Mortgage

To assume a mortgage means to take over what remains of someone else's mortgage loan. The advantage is that you'll save on closing costs. The disadvantage is that you'll generally have to come up with a larger-than-usual down payment (although if you can't afford it, the seller may let you meet the down payment in installments). Generally speaking, the lender must give his permission before a mortgage can be assumed. Interest rates are usually changed to reflect current rates.

The Importance of Interest Rates

Borrowing from a lender that charges a quarter-point more than the competition may cost you only a few extra dollars a month, which hardly seems a difference worth worrying about. But over the life of the loan, that will add up to many thousands of dollars in interest. The following table gives you an idea of how much you can save over thirty years by getting a lower mortgage rate:

THE HIGH COST OF HIGHER INTEREST RATES

Total Loan*		at 9½%	at 10½%	at 12½%	at 14½%
$25,000	Monthly payment:	$ 207	$ 225	$ 267	$ 306
	Total interest:	49,480	55,834	71,120	85,160
30,000	Monthly payment:	$ 248	$ 269	$ 320	$ 367
	Total interest:	59,377	67,002	85,200	102,120
35,000	Monthly payment:	$ 290	$ 314	$ 374	$ 429
	Total interest:	69,274	78,166	99,640	119,440
40,000	Monthly payment:	$ 372	$ 359	$ 427	$ 490
	Total interest:	94,064	89,333	113,720	136,400
50,000	Monthly payment:	$ 414	$ 449	$ 534	$ 612
	Total interest:	98,961	111,669	142,240	170,320

*For 30 years.

Some lenders offer *variable-rate* or *renegotiable-rate mortgages,* which can rise and fall along with major movements in interest rates. If rates go up, so will your mortgage payments (usually to a ceiling established by law); if they go down, your mortgage payments will fall. When money is extremely tight, it's possible that you might have to accept a variable-rate mortgage or nothing. But given a choice, you're generally better off with fixed rates. If inflation continues, variable-rate mortgage payments have nowhere to go but up, whereas fixed-rate mortgages will stay level. If inflation subsides and interest rates fall, variable-rate mortgage payments would go down. But you would also be able to refinance a fixed-rate mortgage at a lower rate. (There is one attractive feature to certain variable-rate mortgages: They are guaranteed assumable by the next buyer. If you had to sell your house during tight money times, you could be sure the buyer would get a mortgage.)

When you shop for a fixed-rate mortgage, compare the prepayment penalties assessed by the various lenders. Some will let you prepay at any time with no penalty; others assess penalties during the first three to five years; still others will charge a fee if you prepay anytime during the length of the mortgage (a most unfavorable provision). If you have a prepayment penalty, it cuts into the money you can save by refinancing the mortgage at a lower rate. (Some lenders waive the prepayment penalty if, when you sell your house, the buyer comes to them for his mortgage.)

Where the law keeps mortgage rates lower than lenders would like, they make up for it by charging extra *points.* A point is 1 percent of the mortgage, and it's deducted from the loan before you even get it. For example, if you're getting a $30,000 13-percent mortgage, the bank might charge you five points—5 percent, which is $1,500—deducted in advance. So you'll get only $28,500 in proceeds, but will have to repay $30,000. That has the effect of adding around $3/4$ of 1 percent to the bank's yield, raising the effective interest rate to $14\frac{1}{4}$ percent. If you need the full $30,000 to buy the house, you'll have to borrow around $31,500. When you're shopping for interest rates, be sure to ask each lender whether he charges points and if so, how much—because it will make an important difference to your costs. Sometimes the seller will pay part of the cost of the points (by reducing the house price a few hundred dollars). Ask the real estate agent to try to negotiate this for you.

Veterans Administration Mortgages

An eligible veteran, male or female (or the surviving spouse of an eligible veteran who died as the result of military service), may apply for a mortgage backed by the Veterans Administration. Its chief advantage is that you pay less money down. In fact, depending on the lender, there may be no down payment at all. Interest rates on VA loans are occasionally lower, but usually they're the same or even a little higher than on conventional mortgages. All the normal mortgage sources—banks, S&Ls, insurance companies, and mortgage companies—can give VA loans. But because the maximum interest rate may sometimes be lower than that available in the free market, not all of them do. Furthermore, they don't like the paperwork. Your real estate broker can generally tell you who's making VA loans. If you can't find a lender, write to the nearest VA office (or to the Veterans Administration, Washington, D.C. 20420), asking for a list of local lenders who participate in the program. If there are none, the VA may make you a direct loan (although proposed changes may limit direct loans to the handicapped).

A VA loan can be made in any amount (as long as it doesn't exceed the value of the house), but lenders usually put limits on the program. In general, you can afford to buy a medium-priced home with a VA loan but not an expensive one (this, of course, varies according to lender and according to how much cash you can put up yourself). In its direct loan program the VA gives a maximum of $33,000. Mortgage terms run to thirty years.

VA loans are available for buying a house, condominium, or mobile home; refinancing a house; building a house; or for repairing and improving a home. You need a certificate of eligibility, which the lender can help you get. The VA must appraise the property before the loan can go through (which may take many weeks); the mortgage guarantee is based on the appraisal, not on the selling price. Not until the lender has all the paperwork in hand can he approve the loan.

Lenders are not allowed to charge the buyer a loan origination fee of more than one "point" (1 percent of the face amount of the loan). If they want two or three points to make a VA loan worth their while, the extra money has to be paid by the seller. In that case, however, the seller generally adds the fee to the price of the house, so the buyer gets stuck with it in the end.

VA mortgages can be prepaid without penalty. They can also be assumed by the buyer of your home, even if he's not a veteran, without having to get permission from the lender. But you will remain liable if

the buyer defaults, unless both the lender and the VA expressly release
you (always ask to be released). You won't be able to reuse your loan
entitlement for another VA mortgage, however, until the property has
been disposed of and the loan paid off (or unless the buyer was an
eligible veteran who assumed the mortgage under his own VA entitlement).

The VA requires that builders give a one-year warranty on newly
built homes. If you have problems after moving in and the builder won't
make repairs, complain to the VA, which will talk to the builder on your
behalf.

Federal Housing Administration Mortgages

Everyone is eligible for a mortgage insured by the Federal Housing
Administration. Down payments are generally lower than with conventional mortgages. Interest rates may be lower or higher, depending on
the market at the time. Lenders may charge the buyer no more than
a 1 percent service charge on top of the mortgage rate and closing costs.
(If additional "points" are needed to make the loan worth the lender's
while, they must be collected from builder or seller. But as builder or
seller will probably tack the cost of the points onto the house's selling
price, the buyer pays them in the end.) The buyer must also pay a ½
of 1 percent mortgage insurance premium, which helps finance the
FHA program. By contrast, the VA program has no such premium
charge, which is why VA rates are generally lower than those charged
for FHA loans.

The FHA must appraise the house before the mortgage can be
granted; the loan guarantee is based on this appraisal, not on the selling
price. It usually takes many weeks for the FHA paperwork to come
through, which is the reason so many lenders don't like to be bothered
with the program.

The minimum down payment on FHA loans is 3 percent on the first
$25,000 of appraised value and 5 percent on the remainder, but lenders
usually demand more than these government minimums. The top limit
on FHA mortgages is currently $67,500. As with VA mortgages, prepay-
ment penalties may not be assessed. When you sell, the mortgage can
be assumed by the buyer without the lender's permission, but the
lender need not release you from liability if he doesn't want to. Your
lawyer should always try to get your name off the mortgage when it's
assumed, so the bank can't come after you if the buyer defaults. FHA
loans are available for building, buying, or improving a house or condo-

minium, for buying a mobile home, or for refinancing an existing mortgage.

Apply for an FHA loan at a mortgage company, bank, or S&L—your real estate broker can usually tell you who's making them. If you can't find a lender who's participating, ask the local FHA office who's making loans (look the office up in the Yellow Pages, or ask a banker where to find it). Unfortunately, if the nearest lender is some distance from where you live, he's not likely to take you on as a customer—but it doesn't hurt to ask.

There's a one-year warranty on new homes that were appraised for FHA financing before construction began. It runs from the date the first buyer takes title to the house or the date the house is first occupied. If, during the warranty period, defects appear, write to the builder asking him to correct them. If he doesn't, write to the local FHA office and they'll try to pressure him into complying. Usually they're successful.

Lower-income people and people displaced by urban renewal, seeking to buy inexpensive houses, qualify for an FHA mortgage with little or no down payment. Under this special program the maximum mortgage allowed for single-family homes is $31,000 to $42,000, depending on location and family size. Not many lenders grant these loans, so you'll probably have to write to the FHA to find one. (Ask for information on lenders making mortgages under the Section 221[d] [2] program.)

Farmers Home Administration Mortgages

If you live in a rural area, are without decent housing, can't get a mortgage from private sources on terms you may be able to afford, *but* have enough money to make house payments on a reasonable level, you may be able to borrow from the Farmers Home Administration (FmHA). There's no down payment; interest rates are relatively low; and repayment can run as long as thirty-three years. Should your income improve enough to make you acceptable to banks or S&Ls, you're expected to refinance the loan in the private market. Look in the Yellow Pages to see if there is an FmHA office in your area; if not, write for information to the Farmers Home Administration, U.S. Department of Agriculture, Washington, D.C. 20250. Loans are available for buying, building, improving, repairing, or rehabilitating rural homes and for providing adequate water and waste disposal systems.

Graduated Payment Mortgages

Lenders and politicians are casting around for ways to help more people buy today's expensive houses. One idea is to have a graduated payment mortgage—one that costs you less in the early years, when you're making less money, and more in later years when your salary has gone up. The FHA is offering some experimental plans, and private lenders are also studying the field. At first glance, graduated mortgages sound like a good idea, but here are the drawbacks:

1. Over the years they cost more than regular mortgages.

2. If you sell, you have to pay the lender the difference between what you've actually paid on the mortgage and what you would have paid if the monthly payments hadn't started out low. The money comes out of the profit you make on the house (if any), which leaves you less cash to put down on another house. As a result, it becomes harder to trade up to a larger and better home.

3. With a regular mortgage you may feel pinched at first, but over the years the mortgage payments become less burdensome. Every time you get a raise, your house costs less in relation to your overall income and you have more money to spend on other things. But a mortgage whose cost increased over the years would change all this. When you got a raise in salary, part of it would have to go toward higher mortgage payments, leaving you less discretionary money. You would be "house poor" longer.

4. Your mortgage payments would go up even if your salary didn't.

Graduated payment mortgages do help families get houses earlier. But basically, they're just a gimmick for encouraging you to buy something you can't afford.

When You've Bought a New House but Haven't Sold Your Old One

How do you find enough money for the down payment if the old house isn't sold yet? What if you're stuck with two mortgages? To avoid that kind of money squeeze, try these tactics: (1) Negotiate a delayed closing on your new home, to give yourself more time to sell the old one. (2) Ask a bank or savings and loan association for a "bridge loan" to help you meet the down payment while waiting for your old house to be sold. You pay interest every month, but the principal isn't paid until the loan comes due. Presumably the loan will be repaid out of the money you get for your old house. (3) Get money for the down payment by refinancing your old house. You should be able to work it so that only the interest is due for a number of months. However, if you don't find a buyer, that loan will eventually be converted into a regular mortgage, with amortization payments due every month.

Redlining

You've been redlined out of a mortgage loan if the bank's decision to turn you down was based solely on where the house is located, rather than on the house itself or on your own qualities as a borrower. It happens because banks sometimes draw a "red line" around certain neighborhoods on a map, and either refuse to make mortgage loans within the circle or make them only in limited amounts. Residents of a redlined area may also be denied money for home improvements. If no one can get enough money to fix up his house, and if potential buyers can't get mortgages, the neighborhood has nowhere to go but down.

Whites often think redlining is a problem only for black neighborhoods, but in fact, if they live in a city, their section, too, may be in trouble. Lenders start to redline long before an area becomes a bombed-out urban menace. A redlined neighborhood might have solid, comfortable homes built forty years ago, with wide porches and cool shade trees. You'd never know the lenders had written it off until it turned out that you could get only a $15,000 mortgage on a house there, whereas if you bought in the suburbs, you'd qualify for a $30,000 loan.

Laws have recently been passed in some cities and states making redlining illegal; it's also prohibited by federal regulation. In 1976 a federal court judge ruled that redlining on account of race is prohibited by the Civil Rights Act of 1968 (the decision was silent about redlining where race is not involved). If you suspect you're a victim of redlining and want to do something about it, write for information to the National Committee Against Discrimination in Housing, Suite 410, 1425 H St. N.W., Washington, D.C. 20005.

Note: Very recently, a number of urban lenders have begun "positive" redlining programs. They select certain rundown urban neighborhoods and make an effort to help rehabilitate them, by providing mortgage and home-improvement money at attractive interest rates. Most of the funds come from the federal government, but there's local participation, too. Ask a lender or a housing agency if any such money is available in your city.

Housing Discrimination

It is illegal to discriminate in the sale or rental of housing, or in granting mortgage loans, on the basis of race or sex. But as house or apartment hunters know, it's done all the time. You can file your own suit in federal court if you're in a position to do so. Or you can make a complaint to the government. Call the toll-free number (800) 424–8590, or write to the Assistant Secretary for Fair Housing and Equal Opportunity, U.S. Department of Housing and Urban Development, Washington, D.C. 20410. A HUD official should write to the person accused of discrimination, to find out the facts and try to settle the matter. He should also be able to refer you to a local or state Human Rights Commission that may be in a better position than the federal government to bring pressure on the offender. *Always complain if you've been discriminated against.* It may not help you personally, but if enough people complain about the same lender, landlord, or real estate broker, the government eventually may bring suit against him for violating the law.

Mortgage Life Insurance

A smart buy for most families, this kind of insurance guarantees that the mortgage will be paid if the breadwinner dies or becomes too ill to work. Technically, it's called "decreasing term" insurance, because the insurance company's total obligation to you decreases over the years. In the first year of a $30,000 mortgage, for example, the company would owe you $30,000 if the breadwinner died; a few years later it would owe you only $25,000 (because $5,000 of the mortgage has been repaid). When the mortgage is finally paid, the insurance contract terminates. Decreasing term insurance is the most inexpensive form of life insurance there is—in fact, you really can't afford not to have it. Generally speaking, the lowest rates are on non-dividend-paying policies sold by insurance companies; mortgage lenders usually charge more. New York and Massachusetts, however, have competitive savings bank mortgage insurance plans.

If both husband and wife work, you might want to cover a $30,000 mortgage with $20,000 worth of decreasing term on the husband (leaving the wife to pay off $10,000 if he died) and $10,000 worth on the wife (leaving him with $20,000 to pay). Or you might want to buy $20,000 worth on each of you so that either survivor would be left with a debt of only $10,000. Some insurance companies will write a joint contract, paying $30,000 if either of you dies. How much coverage to get depends on the earning power and resources of each spouse.

Should You Buy Title Insurance?

Many areas of the country do without title insurance, and the business of homeowning still manages to stay afloat. This suggests that title insurance might be one of the more forgettable expenses. Where it's available, however, the lender usually requires it to protect his investment. If any claim turns up against the title—as occasionally happens—the insurance company either straightens it out or pays the lender his money back.

But even if you have to buy a *lender's* policy, should you bother with an *owner's* title policy, which protects your own equity in the house? Some homeowners don't. They figure that if a claim arises, it will probably be handled, and settled, under the lender's policy (which is generally the case). On the other hand, in the rare instance where there's a total wipeout, a lender's policy would reimburse him, but you'd be out the amount of your investment. Also, there are a few situations (such as a previously undiscovered easement for utility lines) where your interests may be affected but not those of the lender or where the lender decides not to act—in which case a lender's policy would not be of any help.

In general, buyers in new developments should certainly cover themselves with owner's policies, since title to their piece has not been tested by time. On older houses it's more of an open question. The incidence of title challenges on houses that have been occupied for a number of years is extremely small, so whether or not you should buy title insurance becomes a matter of personal preference. In any case the cost is not large.

On Settlement Day

Inspect the house before you go to the closing, to be sure it's in proper order. Also check to see whether the seller did everything he promised —made repairs, cleaned out the basement, left certain furnishings. If you don't check, then find out after the closing that he didn't do certain things, it's generally too late—you bought the house "as is." The only demands you can make are for guarantees that were included in the contract. Be sure the seller has moved out of the house before you make your final inspection and sign the settlement papers; if he does any damage after you close, there's not usually much you can do. It is unwise to let a seller stay in the house after you've taken formal possession; if he hurts himself there, he may sue. If he can't move by closing date, delay the closing.

You must have all the money needed for the down payment and closing costs on the day of settlement. If your old house has been sold but the closing on it was put off, delay closing on the new house. Alternatively, ask the bank for a short-term loan against the sales contract on the old house so that you'll have the cash you need.

Settlement Costs

Settlement day, or closing day, is when you actually acquire ownership of the house. At that time there are a number of additional costs to meet, which could run you $1,000 to $2,000 or more. Your lawyer (or the real estate broker) should tell you in advance what the fees will come to. In addition, the mortgage lender is required by law to mail you his good-faith estimate of closing costs no later than three days after receiving your mortgage application. The specific types of charges vary from area to area, and transaction to transaction. Local custom (and hard bargaining) dictate which costs are paid by the buyer and which by the seller. Here is a list of the various kinds of closing costs you might have to meet:

LOAN ORIGINATION FEE
Paid to the lender, to cover the administrative costs of processing the loan.

LOAN DISCOUNT, OR "POINTS"
A sum deducted by the lender from the proceeds of the loan. It has the effect of raising the profit the lender makes on the loan and is used to get around interest rate ceilings that lenders think are too low. One

point is 1 percent of the loan. It's usually paid by the buyer, but with close negotiation, you might be able to get the seller to split it with you.

APPRAISAL FEE

Covers the lender's cost for having a fair value set on the property. The maximum you can get on a mortgage is based on the appraised value, not on the amount you've agreed to pay. If you're paying $50,000 for a house the lender thinks worth only $45,000, an 80 percent mortgage will come to only $36,000 (80 percent of $45,000) rather than $40,000 (80 percent of $50,000). You'll have to make up the extra yourself. Ask to see the appraiser's report. If it's low, you might be able to use it to get the price of the house down. If it's higher than you've agreed to pay, you're already starting to build equity in your new house.

CREDIT REPORT FEE

Covers the cost of checking credit bureau reports on how promptly you pay your bills and how heavy your debt load is.

LENDER'S INSPECTION FEE

For inspecting the structural soundness of a house. In general, lenders will inspect only newly constructed houses and houses old enough for questions to be raised about their basic condition.

MORTGAGE INSURANCE APPLICATION FEE

Covers the cost of applying for insurance to protect the lender from loss in case you default.

ASSUMPTION FEE

For clerical costs, plus a fee to the bank, when you assume the seller's mortgage.

INTEREST

Interest due for the fraction of the month between settlement date and the date of your first regular mortgage payment. For example, if you close on April 16 and your first monthly payment covers mortgage costs starting May 1, the lender will want to collect the interest for April 16 to May 1 on settlement date.

PREPAYMENTS

Advance premiums for mortgage insurance and fire, wind damage, and flood insurance. The prepayments may be for a few months or for an entire year.

RESERVES DEPOSITED WITH THE LENDER
Payments toward local property taxes, annual assessments, and perhaps mortgage, fire, and flood insurance. The lender puts these tax and insurance payments into an escrow account, out of which he pays the bills as they fall due. In most states these escrow accounts earn no interest (where interest is required, it is minimal). Some people prefer to make these payments into their own interest-bearing savings account, if the lender allows it, rather than into the escrow account. When the tax and insurance bills fall due, you pay them yourself rather than have the bank do it for you. The amount of interest you pick up, however, is not large. Most homeowners prefer the discipline of having to make property tax and other payments along with their mortgage to ensure that the money will be there when the bills come in.

TITLE INSURANCE
Where it's customary, required by the lender to secure his loan. You may also want to insure your own interest in the property (see page 263). The premium is a one-time charge, good as long as you own the house.

TITLE SEARCH
Covers the cost of examining the records to be sure the title is clear.

SETTLEMENT, OR CLOSING, FEE
Paid to a settlement agent, if one is used in your state, for getting the transaction together.

DOCUMENT PREPARATION; NOTARY FEES
Odds and ends of charges for preparing papers and witnessing signatures. These costs should be included in the overall service, but sometimes they're charged for separately.

BANK'S ATTORNEY'S FEES
Covers the cost to the lender of having its attorney prepare or examine documents. This is an area where charges can vary widely. One bank may let its lawyer charge only $75, while another permits fees of $600 or more.

YOUR ATTORNEY'S FEE
An amount negotiated in advance. Some lawyers bill you, but many others want the check right at closing.

RECORDING AND TRANSFER CHARGES
Local fees and taxes associated with property sales.

SURVEY
Cost of preparing a survey if no reliable one exists. Sometimes the seller can be persuaded to pay for a survey.

PEST INSPECTION
Covers the cost of inspecting for termites and other infestations. If the seller has guaranteed that the house is pest-free and inspection turns them up, you'll want some assurance that the place will be fumigated at the seller's expense. The easiest way to do it is to lower the house price by whatever the extermination will cost.

ADJUSTMENTS
Reimbursments to the seller for any tax, insurance, or maintenance payments he made on the property that extend past the time of closing. For example, you pay for the oil left in the tank and your pro rata share of any property taxes he has paid for the year as a whole. In return, he owes you his pro rata share of any tax payments falling due that include the period he still owned the house.

PERSONAL PROPERTY
Payment for anything you bought from the seller, such as carpets or curtains.

All this adds up to a lot of money—generally over $1,000 and often close to $2,000. And you need it at settlement date, in cash. Since the down payment is likely to wipe out most of your savings, your ability to buy the particular house you want may depend on your finding a lender with low settlement costs. Lenders can't estimate every single fee for casual loan shoppers, but they should at least give you a general estimate of "points," application fees, lawyer's costs, and perhaps a lump sum for incidentals.

The Deed

You generally get a deed in which the seller guarantees that he has done nothing that would cause the title to be defective—for example, that there are no judgments against him that would cause the property to be seized, or if he's selling the property out of an estate, that he has full authority to do so. However, he can't be held responsible for any title problems that arise from prior owners.

A *warranty deed* would guarantee the title free of all defects, from any owner, so isn't normally given. The instrument to avoid is a *quitclaim deed*, where the seller conveys whatever interest he may have in the property, *if any.* He makes no promise that the title is clear. A lawyer would generally refuse to accept a quitclaim deed, since it doesn't convey you a secure piece of property.

After settlement, be sure the deed is recorded. Only then will you have secured your absolute right to the property.

Whose Name on the Deed?

A married couple usually puts the deed in both names, assuming joint ownership. But this is not always the most desirable way to hold property. Check Chapter 27, "Wills and Estate Planning," and talk the matter over with your lawyer before you decide in whose name or names the house should be held.

Warranties on New Homes

The federal warranty law doesn't cover real estate, so if promises aren't met, there's little you can do. But the National Association of Home Builders has a warranty program of its own that so far has proved fairly effective. It's called the *Home Owners Warranty* (or HOW) plan. There's no promise that your builder is a top craftsman or that he won't go broke. But HOW does insure you against major structural defects for ten years and other defects for one or two years.

The key to the effectiveness of a HOW plan is the reliability of the builders who participate. It's administered by state or regional builders' councils; those who offer the warranty agree to abide by certain standards of workmanship. If one of their members goes broke and can't finish a house, members of the HOW council sometimes do the job themselves (although this isn't guaranteed). Here's how the plan works:

• Participating builders pay $2 per $1,000 for the coverage; a $50,000 house, for example, would cost $100 to insure. Condominiums and townhouses can be covered, as well as single-family homes.

• During the first two years the builder agrees to make certain repairs at no cost to the homeowner. The first year of coverage includes workmanship, because that's the year that shakedown problems usually show up. In the second year, however, builders have to answer only for major defects in the mechanical systems (electrical, heating, cooling, and water) or structural problems.

• In years three through ten, financial responsibility shifts to an insurance company, which insures the house against major structural defects. There's a $50 deductible for each claim and a $50 inspection fee. The insurance policy also covers warranted repairs during the first two years if the builder goes bankrupt.

• If there's a dispute about coverage, you complain to the local HOW board and ask for reconciliation hearings. Should no agreement be reached with the builder, you can request a hearing before the American Arbitration Association. This saves a lot of legal hassle. If a decision is brought in your favor and the builder still hangs tough, courts in most states will enforce the AAA order.

One important thing that HOW doesn't cover is completion. If the builder skips town before putting up the moldings or finishing the porch, there's no recompense. But in several of these cases the local HOW council has voluntarily finished the job.

There's another advantage to using a HOW builder: In some areas mortgage interest rates on HOW homes are ¼ of 1 percent below normal because the insurance lowers the lender's risk.

Some states have additional protections available to home buyers. For example, in New York there's a Qualified Builder's Program that bonds your down payment, so if the builder goes bankrupt, you get your money back. Your state home builders' association can tell you if any special protection plans operate in your neighborhood. Get the address of the state association from the National Association of Home Builders, 15th and M Sts. N.W., Washington, D.C. 20005. To find a HOW builder, write to the Home Owners Warranty Corporation at the same address.

Warranties on Older Homes

In some parts of the country you can get a one- or two-year warranty to protect yourself against hidden defects in older homes. At this writing, there are three types of coverage available:

• Certified Homes Corporation, based in Columbia, Maryland, offers one-year warranties through offices in some eighteen states. An engineer makes a thorough inspection of the house, checking out the heating, cooling, and electrical systems, plumbing, roof, walls, ceilings, floors, and basement. You get a report on the condition of these elements. If any of them appears likely to break down within one year, the engineer explains the problem and excludes it from the warranty (the reason for this is that the company protects you only against *unforeseen* expenses, not those you can predict before you buy). Everything else is covered, with a $100 deductible.

Should a warranted component give out, Certified will send a contractor to determine the repair price. You can hire that contractor for the job or use one of your own choosing. The cost of one-year coverage: $100 plus the price of the inspection, which averages $95.

• Soundhome Assurance, based in Newark, New Jersey, is managed by the insurance company Alexander & Alexander. It differs from Certified in that it offers a straight insurance policy rather than a warranty, and as such must submit to strict state insurance regulations. Coverage runs for *two* years. The price, for both inspection and insurance, ranges from $200 for a house costing $35,000 to $430 for houses priced at $50,000 or more.

Like Certified, Soundhome has a $100 deductible and excludes from coverage items that are likely to give out during the insurance period. The condition of everything, however, is pointed out in the inspection report so you're on notice before you buy that certain parts of the house won't last. If an insured item breaks down, Soundhome sends inspectors to check out the problem but does not offer the services of its own contractor.

• American Home Shield, based in Pleasanton, California, operates through thousands of real estate brokers in California, New Jersey, Florida, and Connecticut. The broker attaches the coverage to all his listings, charging the seller $195 for the service. If possible, the seller passes this cost on to the buyer, in the price of the house.

Under this program there's no inspection, so you don't get a full report on the condition of the house. AHS covers appliances (which the other programs don't), plumbing, heating and electrical systems, and hot water heaters, but *not* structural elements—such as roof, ceilings, walls, and floors (which the other programs include, and which cost the most to repair if problems develop).

When the owner lists the house with an AHS broker, the coverage goes right into effect—so if something broke down even before the sale, the *owner* could collect on the policy. Once the house is sold, coverage continues for one year. There's a $20 deductible on each claim, and you have to use AHS contractors for the repair job.

Since there's no inspection, any warranted component that's on the verge of a breakdown is covered. But having no inspection is also a drawback, since you don't get a general report on the basic condition of the house. If you buy under an AHS plan, be sure to get a full engineer's inspection before signing the contract.

Buying a Two-Family House

Many people cut their personal cost of living by buying a two-family house and taking a tenant. The rent helps to carry the mortgage and you get some useful deductions on your income tax. If the neighborhood is well chosen, you also have a good investment. You must, of course, accept the responsibility of being a landlord, including prospecting for reliable tenants, making prompt repairs, and keeping the property as a whole appealing and attractive.

The key to happy landlordship, besides personal care, is getting an honest tenant. Ask him for references—his bank, his employer, his last landlord, some personal references. Call the bank to be sure he has an account there. Ask him how long he's held his present job and approximately how much it pays, then call his employer to confirm the facts. If you can, check with his last landlord to see if he paid his rent on time. If you get a deadbeat, he'll be hard to get rid of and may damage the apartment on his way out.

When you look at two-family houses, pay special attention to the attractiveness of the rental quarters. The nicer they are, the easier they will be to rent and the more you can charge.

Before you take on a house, add up the cost of the mortgage, utilities, maintenance, repairs, advertising, and any other costs. Then figure the rent you're likely to get, and see if you can really afford to carry the place. The level of rents is set by the price of similar apartments in the neighborhood. You'll want a large enough cash reserve so that if you get a deadbeat or have trouble renting you'll have enough money to tide you over for a few months without rental income.

Ask an accountant what's deductible, and keep detailed records of your income and expenses. At tax time, ask an accountant to help you figure depreciation and other deductible items.

Building a House

It usually costs more to build a house than to buy one (unless you build it yourself). But in return for the extra money, you get a unique place, designed especially for your needs, where you've been able to select every doorknob and light fixture. It takes tremendous patience to build, because so much will inevitably go wrong along the way. In the end, however, you'll forget the pains and feel only the special pleasure of moving into an environment designed like a glove to fit the way you live. One warning: The more idiosyncratic a house is, the more difficult it may be to resell. But even unusual houses find their buyers eventually. If you're going to the trouble of building, you might as well put up exactly what you want.

Buying the Land

When you find a piece of property you admire, here are the things to check before you close the deal:

1. What kind of buildings will the zoning laws allow in the area? You don't want commercial buildings as neighbors. Nor do you want to build an expensive house in an area where small tract houses are allowed.

2. What does the lot look like after a heavy rain? If it stays wet, you'll want to take that into consideration when you plan the house. It might be better not to build a basement, but instead put the house on a slab.

3. Is the title clear? Is the survey recent?

4. Is the lot part of a landfill? If so, it might settle, cracking a house's foundations and walls. Discuss the probabilities with both the town engineer and an architect.

5. Find out about water, electricity, sewers, street lights, gas, and other services. If the facilities aren't already there, check with town hall about when development is expected (and who is supposed to pay for it). Don't take the word of the subdivider that "sewers will be in next year," because they might not be. If you have to build a septic system, you'll need a percolation test to be sure the land isn't too wet or heavy to absorb the wastes. If a well is necessary, check with the neighbors on how deep they had to drill to find water. You might even make the contract subject to finding potable water on the site within a specified drilling depth.

6. If the site appears to be a difficult one for building, because of rocks, water, or the slope of the land, ask an architect to look at it with you. Practically any site can be built on, but the extra costs of overcoming disadvantages of terrain may be more than you want to pay.

The Architect

Some people build without an architect. They buy ready-made plans from a magazine, make their own modifications, then take it to a building contractor. If your local ordinances require the signature of an architect on the revised plans, the contractor usually has someone who will look at the drawings and approve them for a nominal fee. Many builders also have standard plans.

However, after looking at the plans in the magazines, you may decide that none of them fits the bill—at which point you'll look around for an architect. For recommendations turn to friends who have built houses, builders you know, acquaintances you may have on the town planning board, and the Yellow Pages. (When you pick a name out of the phone book, ask first if the architect does houses; many of them accept only commercial work.) Make a date to visit two or three architects and discuss your plans.

THINGS TO TALK ABOUT

• What styles does he principally work in? If most of his clients want colonials and Tudors, and you want something modern, don't employ him—even if he has a few modern houses to his credit. Look for an architect who works principally in the style you want.

• Get pictures of his previous work and a tour of two or three places in your price range.

• Tell him your house-building budget to see if it's something he can work with (some architects can't handle relatively inexpensive houses). Discuss his ideas on how to cut costs.

• Ask him his fees. If he's to supervise the work, he'll want a percentage of the overall costs, probably 10 to 12 percent, paid in installments as the work progresses. On the other hand, you may be able to hire him at an hourly rate simply to draw the plans. But be warned: If he doesn't supervise the work, the house may not be constructed with the precision of detail that you expected. The builder is apt to make alternative suggestions that sound sensible in theory but, once built, destroy the integrity of the general design.

• When can he do the job? Is he the architect who will work on your house, or will he assign a subordinate? If someone else will work on it, talk to him to see how you like him.

• Get the names of some of his clients and ask them how competent they think the architect is. Were his cost estimates reliable? Was he easy to work with? Did he understand the constraints of budget? If they built another house, would they use him again?

• Talk to two or three architects to get a range of opinion on your house-building objectives. If one architect tells you your budget is too low, it might be that he only builds expensive houses, but if three architects tell you the same thing, perhaps you can't afford to build. Talking to several people also helps you put everyone's answers in perspective. When you make your final choice, it must be a person you like and feel comfortable with. As the building progresses, the relationship between owner and architect often becomes strained (because of mounting costs, or differences of opinion on details), so it's important to have someone you think you can get along with.

WHAT YOU SHOULD EXPECT AN ARCHITECT TO DO FOR YOU

• Talk with you at great length about how you and your family live, what you like to do, and what your design ideas are. He may ask you to keep a log of everything that's done in a typical day, or make a list of your hobbies and space needs, or clip pictures of rooms that you like out of housing magazines.

• Study the site to determine the best placement for the house, what kind of design limits the topography dictates, and how the building can best harmonize with others in the area.

• Show you rough sketches of his preliminary ideas. They may not look anything like what you had in mind, in which case tell him so. If your taste exceeds your budget, the architect should make that clear. *It's essential that the architect know exactly what you can afford to spend,* so he won't waste time on designs that you can't afford. The rough sketches should go back and forth between you and the architect until you finally have the design exactly the way you want it.

• Execute the final drawings. This is the set of plans that the builder will work from, showing how the house will look from the outside, the floor plan, how the various elements are to be constructed, and what type and quality of building materials are to be used. Once the building gets underway, any changes that you want to make in these plans will be far more expensive than if you made them now.

• Help you select a general contractor (see the following section). You'll want to submit the plans to several responsible builders, then accept the lowest bid. If you're going to be your own general contractor, the architect may help you select the subcontractors, such as electricians, masons, carpenters, plumbers, and so on.

• Periodically inspect the construction work to be sure it's right. The architect protects you against defects and deficiencies; advises on when a job is so poorly done it must be redone; comes in with fast alternative solutions if time pressures prevent a job from being redone; ensures that his specifications are met and designs followed; explains details of his drawings to the contractor. He reviews and approves samples of materials to be used and equipment to be installed. He may even go shopping with you for doorknobs and lighting fixtures. You'll make your progress payments to the contractor only after the architect has certified that the work done so far meets his expectations.

• Handle any changes. Like it or not, changes usually do arise—perhaps because you change your mind about a room; because certain materials aren't available; because the contractor has a good idea on how to change something; or because the architect's drawing contained an error. Have the architect incorporate any change into his plans, and get a price quote from the contractor on the change before authorizing it. You'll need a contingency fund for these surprises. Building a house almost always winds up costing more than you'd planned.

• Make a final inspection, before you give the contractor his last payment. It's wise to have the architect handle all your dealings with the contractor. Because of your inexperience with building methods, you might okay a proposal that the architect thinks is not up to the standard of workmanship he wants.

The Contractor

The architect can generally recommend two or three general contractors. You send them the plans and specifications and get back their bids on the job. Before making your choice, discuss the following with each:

1. What are his ideas on how to cut building costs?
2. Which houses has he built in the neighborhood? What are the names of some of his customers? How long has he been in business?
3. Does he do business through a number of corporations (risky), or will one company stand behind everything he builds?
4. Does he build houses principally in the style you want? A builder of colonial houses won't know a lot about detailing a modern house, and may, contrary to the architect's instructions, finish it off with colonial moldings around the doors and ceilings because that's what looks "right" to him. Conversely, a builder of modern houses may not care a fig about getting an antique look into a colonial-style staircase.
5. How much business does he do? A large builder often can do a job for less than a small one because he buys in large lots. But a large builder may specialize in the most common house styles—colonial or raised ranch—and not have the finesse to handle modern or Tudor.

Talk to his former customers about how good a job he did: Were his subcontractors of high quality? Did he do everything he promised? Was he easy to work with? Did he finish on time? If they built another house, would they use him again? Ask the bank where you plan to get your mortgage whether they know him and if they've had any trouble with houses he's built. See if there are any complaints about him at the Better Business Bureau.

Don't get excited about a contractor who submits an unusually low bid. The only way he can build at a low price and still clear a profit is to use cheap materials, cut corners, and hire subcontractors who do hasty, insufficient work. By all means save money where you can, perhaps by using modern materials that may be lower in cost, but don't scrimp on basic quality. Also, walk away from a builder who makes inflated claims for his work or whose personality irritates you.

When you've chosen a contractor, ask about the insurance he carries to protect the workmen at the site. If anyone is not covered, ask your insurance agent if your homeowner's policy will pay for injuries. If you have problems with your contractor, and he's a member of the National Remodelers Association, you can appeal for help to its Consumer Affairs Division, 50 E. 42nd St., New York, N.Y. 10017, phone (212) 687–5224.

DO YOU NEED A CONTRACTOR?

In theory, you can save perhaps 15 to 20 percent of the house's cost by not hiring a general contractor and doing the job yourself. This means that you manage the work and hire all the subcontractors (mason, plumber, electrician, carpenter, roofer, heating specialist, and so on). I say "in theory," because unless you have had some building experience, you'll make mistakes that will result in your paying more than necessary for some parts of the job. However, if the architect supervises the work, he can help you keep things running along in orderly fashion. Acting as your own general contractor can be a tiring and frustrating experience and will take many hours each day away from your regular work. You'll have to get bids on every detail of the job; ride herd on the artisans to make sure they're doing what they're supposed to; get jobs done in the right order so that one incomplete item won't hold another subcontractor up; keep peace between architect and artisans (they frequently don't get along, which makes it hard to use the architect as supervisor); and insist that an artisan redo anything done incorrectly. Don't take this job on unless you have time, energy, patience, and good advice on how to tell the difference between a good job and a poor one.

Prefab Houses

These can be quite economical to build. You're saved the architect's fee; large segments of the house come prebuilt from the factory, saving local labor costs; and you pay less for high-grade materials used because the manufacturer buys them in large lots. There are many fine companies that offer excellent designs. Check their ads in the home-building magazines, or look in the Yellow Pages under "Buildings—Pre-cut." Typically, you'll buy the outer house—windows, doors, walls, roof—from the manufacturer, who delivers it in pieces to the site. Here, a builder assembles it (sometimes the manufacturer sends his own crew) on a foundation you've already built. Local craftsmen complete the inside. You can turn over the job of completion to a general contractor or serve as your own contractor and hire individual artisans to do the work.

There's another form of "prefabbing," where the factory takes your plans, preconstructs the walls and roof in the plant, then delivers them in sections to the site. You get a carpenter to put it together and finish the interior. This saves money for large tract builders, but individuals will probably find that it's cheaper to build in the conventional fashion.

Inspecting a Newly Built House

If an architect is supervising the construction of your house, that's all the inspection you need. But if the job was turned over to a contractor, or if you bought based on a builder's model home, you need more protection. The inspections done by the town's building inspector merely check compliance with codes, not workmanship. *Best bet*: Hire a professional engineer who specializes in residential building inspection (see page 246). For a small fee he'll inspect the model home before you sign a contract, and advise you whether you need, say, a bigger furnace or hot water heater. As your own home progresses, he'll check to see that it's built according to specifications and will make a final inspection before you take possession. Even if you haven't had the earlier inspections, be sure to do a "final." Once you close on a house, it's next to impossible to get the builder to return to correct defects.

Closing on a Newly Built House

When you buy a house, you buy it "as is," unless provision has been made in the contract for the seller to make certain repairs. If the bricks are falling out of the front porch and the builder promises to fix it, don't sign the sales contract until he does. Otherwise, he may walk away from the house, leaving you to fix it yourself. Unless the sales contract was *subject to* repairing the porch, he has no legal obligation.

If you're buying an unfinished house, you must have a lawyer of your own (not the builder's lawyer) to protect your interests. Typically, he will arrange for part of your money to be paid into an escrow account, pending completion or repair of specified items. If those items are not done by a certain date, you get the escrow money back and can use it to finish the house yourself. Sometimes you find a hidden defect in the house after you move in, such as plasterboard put over a foundation wall bowed in by a careless bulldozer. In that case your only recourse is to sue—and even if you win, the builder may have arranged his finances so as to make it impossible for you to collect.

Homesteading

Several cities have urban homesteading opportunities—some backed by a local agency, others backed by the U.S. Department of Housing and Urban Development. If you can get into the program (demand far exceeds supply of houses), you may wind up with a solid, comfortable house at a fraction of its rehabilitated value.

Under a homesteading program a housing agency acquires a group of repossessed or abandoned homes that are fundamentally sound. A list of needed repairs is drawn up for each one, along with an estimate of what the repairs will cost.

The house is then sold to a qualified buyer for perhaps $1, and the buyer agrees to make the repairs. He gets a rehabilitation loan from a bank or S&L (if private lenders are participating in the program) or else from HUD itself. The buyer can reduce the size of the loan by agreeing to do some of the repair work himself, an arrangement called *sweat equity*.

The size of the rehabilitation loan generally runs around $5,000, although it could be higher. Typically, the buyer doesn't get clear title to the house for one to three years, during which time he must complete the renovation. Call your city's housing agency or the local HUD office (look in the Yellow Pages) to see if there is a local homesteading opportunity.

Second Mortgages

If you need a large sum of money, look to the equity you have in your home as a source of cash. You can reborrow that part of the principal you've already repaid, AND you can borrow against the amount that your house has increased in value in the years since you bought it. When money is tight, mortgage lenders may not grant second mortgages, preferring to save what little money they have for "firsts." But you can usually get it from a finance or second-mortgage company.

Don't take out a second mortgage for short-term purposes, such as paying your bills. Monthly payments will be low because of the long term of the mortgage, but you'll wind up paying an excessive amount of interest. The rule of thumb on borrowing is to keep the term as short as possible. If you must borrow long-term, do it only for long-term investments, such as a college education for your children or starting your own business. Any time you're tempted to take a second mortgage, ask yourself, "Do I want this badly enough to still be paying for it ten years from now?"

The following table shows how the interest charges mount up when you borrow long-term. I've assumed that you have a $20,000 7½-percent mortgage with twenty years to run, and need $10,000 to add a room to your house. You could finance the job in one of four ways—with an FHA-insured home improvement loan (see page 283), a commercial bank home improvement loan, a second mortgage, or by refinancing your house (which means taking out a brand new mortgage for a larger amount; see next page). Here's how the alternatives compare; your actual interest rates may be higher than the table shows, but the conclusions remain the same:

FOUR WAYS TO RAISE $10,000

Type of loan	Monthly loan payment	Regular mortgage payment[a]	Total monthly payment	Total interest paid over the life of the loan
FHA home improvement[b]	$220.99	$159.73	$380.72	$ 3,259.40
Bank home improvement[c]	235.56	159.73	395.29	4,133.60
Second mortgage[d]	152.93	159.73	312.66	8,351.60
Refinancing[e]	237.85	—	237.85	47,290.80[f]

[a]On a $20,000 7½% mortgage.
[b]Five years at 12%.
[c]Five years at 15%.
[d]Ten years at 14%.
[e]$30,000 for 30 years at 9%.
[f]This excludes the amount the homeowner would have paid anyway on his original $20,000 mortgage and hence is the true extra cost of obtaining the new mortgage in order to get an extra $10,000.

Second mortgages cost more than firsts, but the rate varies from lender to lender. A mortgage company might charge in the area of 14 to 16 percent, and a finance company up to 18 percent. You'll get a better deal from a bank or an S&L, but some of them don't write second mortgages at all, and others do so only when money is easy. The term of the loan generally runs from five to ten years, and the amount, to $10,000 (although if your income is large and your credit good, you'll be able to get more).

Each state has its own laws controlling the specifics of second mortgages. Some keep the interest rate ceiling so low, or so sharply limit the amount of the loan, that "seconds" are generally not offered. Other quirks in the law might also keep lenders out of the business. However, there are other ways to reborrow against your house.

Some banks offer *open-ended* first mortgages, which allow you to come back and borrow more once you've paid off part of the principal. Or the bank might give you a new mortgage for a larger amount *(refinancing)*; you have to give up your old mortgage, which might be at a lower rate, but at least you'll get the extra money you need. As you can see by the foregoing table, the penalty for refinancing can be large, so do it only in a real emergency. When you sign up for a "second," you have three days in which to change your mind (see "The Cooling-Off Period," page 154).

Many banks and S&Ls write clauses into their mortgages prohibiting "seconds" without their permission, but this usually isn't a stumbling block to your getting a loan. There are generally no prepayment penalties except those associated with the Rule of 78s, which has the effect of raising the interest rate slightly if you prepay (see page 95). The fees and charges for a second mortgage run in the area of $100.

Refinancing Your House for Investment Purposes

There are situations where it makes sense to give up an older, low-rate mortgage and take out a larger, high-rate one. If it is possible to make more with the money you take out of the house than you pay in mortgage interest, refinancing becomes a road to building a larger net worth. But figure the costs and risks carefully before you do it. You have to have (1) enough income to carry the larger mortgage without worry, in case the investment you choose doesn't work out; (2) the investment savvy to keep your position liquid in case of emergency; and (3) the temperament to live with a highly leveraged situation.

Assuming you take a larger mortgage, you hope to invest the money in such a way that it returns enough after taxes to cover the extra interest cost, also figured after taxes. If bond yields are high, that's the safest way to do it. Or you might put part in bonds and part into a mutual fund with a withdrawal program (withdraw as much as necessary each year to meet the extra mortgage payments, while leaving the rest in the market to appreciate over twenty or twenty-five years). If it all works out, you'll have covered the extra cost of your mortgage and made something besides. Assuming that the stock market will continue to show appreciation over the long term, you might profit handsomely. But don't do it without the advice of a good financial planner. You'll want to have the numbers laid out for you exactly, along with an assessment of the risks. One point: If you lost your job, your banker wouldn't let you refinance your house to raise cash to live on. But if you've done it already, you could liquidate some of your investments and use them to live on between jobs. Viewed this way, refinancing is a conservative response to the risks of life.

When Your Land Is Condemned

The government has the right to grab your property if it's needed for a highway, reservoir, or other public purpose. But you're entitled to a fair market price, and the government's offer is often low. There's a procedure for contesting the price, which the agency that condemned the land will explain to you. You'll need the services of a real estate appraiser to establish the land's true value. *Best bet*: Hire a lawyer to handle the case. When confronted by an obdurate homeowner demanding more, the government is likely to raise its offer. The lawyer's fee is often a percentage of everything he gets *over* the government's original offer.

Foreclosure

Lenders are willing to work with honest debtors who suddenly find themselves in trouble. If you've always paid on time but are now laid low by illness or unemployment, they may let you delay principal payments on your mortgage for up to a year, as long as you can cover interest, taxes, and insurance. But chronic late-payers are called on the carpet pretty quickly.

State foreclosure laws generally favor the lender. In some places proceedings may begin as few as thirty days after a payment was missed. But in practice, banks and S&Ls don't move as fast as the law allows. You may have five months or so to get yourself together and resume payments. Even after foreclosure begins, lenders will generally reinstate the mortgage if it appears that you'll be able to resume payments (unless, of course, you've been in foreclosure two or three times before). Eighteen states have procedures for redeeming a house after default, but since it generally involves paying off the mortgage in full, they're rarely used.

If you hold an FHA mortgage, there's a special escape clause. Rather than allow foreclosure, the FHA might take the mortgage over and work out a payment schedule. But you have to meet the following qualifications:

1. Nonpayment must be due to a temporary problem, such as illness, a layoff, or a death in the family.

2. The mortgage must be on your principal home, not a summer home.

3. You must be able to resume payments within thirty-six months. Once you are notified by the lender that he's going to foreclose, ask your local FHA office for help (the lender will tell you whom to see). There's no similar program for holders of VA mortgages, but the VA does bring pressure on lenders not to foreclose quickly.

When a mortgage is foreclosed, the house is sold at auction, and the lender is usually the only bidder. He bids the amount of the mortgage plus his foreclosure costs; if no one bids higher, he gets the house. Since your house is generally worth more on the open market than the amount of its mortgage, you lose money by permitting a foreclosure sale to occur. So if it ever appears that foreclosure is inevitable, sell the house yourself first. You can then pay off the lender and have a chunk of cash left over, whereas a foreclosure sale would wipe you out.

When you can't pay the mortgage, don't be afraid to tell the bank about it. They're willing to cooperate if you're in trouble, but will foreclose if you aren't paying and they can't get any explanation. Always go to the bank, tell them what's happened, and try to work something out.

Home Improvements

Never hire anyone who comes to your door offering to fix your roof or pave your driveway, no matter what "bargain" price he offers. Maybe he's straight, but more likely he'll do a shoddy job and vanish. If something needs doing to your home, call two or three contractors in your town who have been in business for a while and ask them to bid on the job. You can then choose the lowest bidder, confident that if something goes wrong, you'll at least be able to go back to the contractor and have him repair it.

The least costly way to finance home improvements is through a credit union, if you belong, or with an FHA-insured loan. At this writing, the FHA would insure single-family home improvement loans up to $15,000 for fifteen years, at a maximum of 18 percent interest. However, the banks and S&Ls, where you actually get an FHA loan, often limit the term to five or seven years and may not lend you the maximum amount. Banks and S&Ls also offer uninsured, personal loans for home improvements, but the interest rate is usually higher. You can finance home improvements with second mortgages (see the cost comparison on page 279). The contractor, too, may offer to arrange financing, but his terms are usually higher than a bank or S&L would give.

Keep records of all the money you spend improving your home. When you sell, your capital gain is reduced by the sum of the improvements—which could save you thousands of tax dollars over your lifetime (see "Tax Consequences of Selling," page 334).

When you start a big job, get a contract spelling out exactly what's to be done. Don't give the contractor any more than 10 percent down, and as the job goes along, pay only for work done. Arrange to make the last payment—of 20 to 25 percent—not earlier than thirty days *after* the work is finished, in order to give yourself time to find any defects. The contract should also provide that the final payment won't be due until the job passes inspection by a professional engineer (see page 246). If you have problems with a contractor, and he's a member of the National Remodelers Association, you can appeal for help to its Consumer Affairs Division, 50 E. 42nd St., New York, N.Y. 10017.

If you're adding a room or undertaking a major remodeling, consider hiring an architect. It will cost you an extra 15 percent or so, but you'll get a much better job for it.

CONDOMINIUMS

For the convenience of an apartment, plus the financial and emotional advantages of owning a home, a condominium is the answer. Genevieve Gray, in her excellent book *Condominiums: How to Buy, Sell, and Live in Them,** accurately describes this kind of ownership as a fifty-fifty mix of real estate and politics. You own your own unit, but the "common areas" of a condominium—the halls, streets, elevators, yards, clubhouse, pool, and so on—are generally owned by all the residents; how well they're kept depends on the willingness of everyone to make payments (called *maintenance*) and share in the governance.

A condo where nobody cares, where people have to be dragooned to serve on the board and other committees, will gradually fall into disrepair. Condominiums are no place to be antisocial. You'll enjoy them most if you like your neighbors and want to make a contribution to the community.

You pay for the unit with a conventional mortgage. The common areas are financed and kept up with money raised from monthly maintenance fees (and occasional special assessments). Failure to pay the fee, as well as the mortgage, can result in foreclosure.

Buying Into a New Condo

The riskiest time to buy into a condominium is when it's still mostly a gleam in the developer's eye. He'll have built streets, the first few units, and the recreational facilities to attract early buyers. But from that point on, he expects to build further units with the money he gets from selling the first ones or selling from floor plans. As more people buy, the development expands until finally it reaches its planned size. At least, that's how it's supposed to work.

If the builder skimps, say, on the recreational facilities, he may not get as many buyers as expected. New units are added slowly. Soon he finds that he can't afford to build the big pool shown on the architect's drawings. He finally decides to drop the project and build elsewhere, leaving the residents without the landscaping and facilities originally

---

*A Barnes and Noble paperback. I am indebted to Mrs. Gray's expert research for some of the points of view developed in this section.

promised and with fewer owners than expected to share the expense of the common areas. As a result, the value of the units drops. In some cases builders have walked off the job without paying all the subcontractors, who then hit the surprised owners for the bill.

If you buy before any units are up, your down payment may be used to pave the roads and put in streetlights. Should the builder then go broke, you might not be able to get your money back.

New York, Michigan, and California are three of several states that have laws requiring financial responsibility from builders. In New York, for example, there must be guarantees that the project can be completed as planned. At this writing, a federal law is under consideration. But even where there's protection, don't rely on the law alone. When buying into a new condo:

1. Find out how you get your deposit back if the condo doesn't get past the planning stage, and ask the salesman to show you where it says that in the contract. If your funds are mingled with the builder's funds, your chance of recovery is small. Look for an escrow arrangement, where your funds are segregated until the promises made to you are kept. Never take the salesman's word for anything (no matter how nice he is).

2. Get details on the planned amenities. How big is the pool (big enough to serve all the families expected to live there)? How big are the rooms and halls (are model rooms built to a larger scale than that planned for the units themselves)? Will there be enough parking space? Buy only after you've studied site drawings, floor plans, and elevations. The more attractive the condo, and the closer it is to business and population centers, the easier it will be to attract buyers.

3. Will the builder be living there until the development is finished? If so, that could be a good sign. It means he doesn't plan to duck the early buyers.

4. Salesmen can be expected to underestimate real estate taxes and maintenance fees, so add 15 to 20 percent to the figures they give you. Some sales literature makes the cost look low by deducting a sum for "tax savings" (your mortgage interest and property tax deductions). The figure is accurate only for a specific tax bracket, which may be quite different from yours. Also, it implies that you have to pay less a month than is actually the fact. Ignore the calculation and work only with the actual out-of-pocket costs. Ploys like deducting "tax savings" are a specious way of selling. When you see them, suspect that perhaps the whole deal is likely to be far less attractive than it appears on the surface.

5. If you're good at figures, ask for the proposed budget for the condominium to see if it's reasonable (in fact, ask for it anyway, to make sure they have one). Assuming you haven't the faintest idea whether enough has been allocated to, say, groundskeeping, your best bet is to make comparisons with a condo similar in size to this one. Hunt up a contact at another condo and ask what the maintenance comes to. You may find that costs have been underestimated. Fees at a high rise will be more than at a comparably priced townhouse development.

6. Take all the documents—the budget, the sales contract, the bylaws, the basic condominium agreement—to a lawyer experienced in condo transactions. He knows what to watch out for. If the salesman says it's "policy" not to give you the documents ("someone might steal our good ideas"), walk away from the project. There's something there they don't want your lawyer to see.

7. Make it a point to visit a condominium previously built by this developer, and ask the residents what they think of it. Knock on three or four doors to get several opinions. Or ask for a meeting with one of the board members. What the builder has done before is the best clue to what he'll do again. If he has never built a condo before, think twice before buying in; he's going to make mistakes that could cost you some money.

8. Beware leasing arrangements with the builder. This is perhaps the leading condominium abuse. The builder might sell you the unit but lease you the land it sits on; or he may retain ownership of the pool and clubhouse, and lease it to the owners' association. It seems superficially attractive, because the price may be lower than at a condo where you buy the land. But every year he'll hike the rent drastically, and your sales contract will force you to pay his price. A few states have ruled out this sort of arrangement, but in most places it's perfectly legal. You'd be wise not to buy unless you can get clear title to the land and common areas.

9. Beware situations where the builder takes a long-term, noncancelable management contract to look after the condominium. As with leasing arrangements, fees will go up annually and you'll have to pay them. It's all right to hire the builder on a short-term contract, but you should be able to fire him if he performs poorly or his price is not competitive.

10. When will the unit be ready? The contract should state that if it isn't finished by a specified date, you'll get your money back.

11. Older buyers might try to negotiate a clause that exempts them from paying for future additions to the condominium, which they don't use.

12. Keep a list of things that go wrong after you move in. There should be a one-year warranty on defects. If the builder doesn't correct

the problems, shout, scream, complain to the bank that finances him, the building inspector, city hall, the consumer protection agency, the Better Business Bureau. Write letters to your local paper; do everything possible to bring pressure on him. When you spot defects before buying the unit, don't close until they're fixed; or have your lawyer arrange to put part of the money into escrow, not to be paid unless the builder makes repairs by a certain date. If he doesn't get around to it, you can take the money and make the repairs yourself.

13. To the first owners falls the job of setting up the condominium's governing boards and committees. A responsible builder will help them do it; a careless one walks away and lets them muddle along. If you need help, turn to another condominium nearby, meet with its officers, and find out how things ought to be run. If the board makes mistakes, it could cost the owners a lot of money.

Buying Into an Ongoing Condo

In this case you don't have to buy a pig in a poke. The amenities are up, you know who your neighbors are, they've met the initial problems, and the costs are known. Spend a little time at the condo to see who lives there: Are they people you think you'll feel comfortable with? Attend a condo meeting if one is scheduled around the time you want to buy, to see what the gripes are and how they're handled. Call on three or four residents to see how they like the place and what their chief complaints are. Meet with a member of the board to discuss finances: Are some special assessments planned? Will maintenance fees have to go up?

If the common areas look rundown and ill kept, it's a sign that the condo isn't getting along very well. Perhaps some residents are refusing to pay their maintenance fees, and the board hasn't the nerve to collect. Buying into a place like that is like buying into a declining neighborhood; your property values will likely fall. It's also a sign of trouble if a lot of units are for sale.

Inquire into all the costs: what you have to pay out of pocket as well as your monthly fee. Read the bylaws. If there are rules you can't live with (such as no pets), don't expect to move in and get an exception made for you. Find out whether the owners have clear title to the land and recreational facilities, or whether they're being leased from the builder (who will raise the rents). Get all the documents to your lawyer for him to examine. Expect the association to check you out before the sale goes through.

Buying a Condo on Conversion

Many a landlord, dissatisfied with the profit he's making on his apartment building, converts it into a condominium and sells to the tenants. If the building is sound, the price is often attractive. But if, after buying, you learn that the place needs a new roof, modern wiring, and a new boiler, you'll be horrified at the size of the financial obligation you've taken on.

Don't buy into a conversion condo without having seen an independent engineer's report of the state of the building. In fact, the tenants should get together to pay for the report themselves, so there's no chance of a coverup. You'll need a cost estimate for repairs, as well as a copy of the building's maintenance budget. After conversion the real estate taxes will rise, perhaps substantially, so get an estimate in advance. A few states have laws requiring full disclosure on these and other points, but in most places it's up to the ingenuity of the tenants to keep the landlord honest. You'd do well to hire a lawyer jointly in order to negotiate with the landlord on your behalf. As with any other type of condo, don't accept a long-term noncancelable management contract with the former owner. You want to be able to fire a manager if he charges too much or performs poorly.

Tenants who don't want to buy their apartments must be allowed to stay in the condominium, without harassment, until their leases run out. If you're not a resident of the building, find out how many of the tenants are leaving rather than buying in. A lot of desertions could mean it's not a pleasant place to live. It may also be a sign that the landlord has made only cosmetic repairs, leaving big expenses for the new owners. One more word about older buildings: Unless they have snob appeal or are in splendid shape, their value will probably not appreciate at the rate of a new condo.

Vacation Condos

If you expect to occupy your condo during only one season, buy into a development of like-minded people. If a majority are year-round residents, you might find yourself assessed for a summer swimming pool even though you're never there to use it, or winter snow removal even though you spend winters in the South.

If you hope to help cover the condo's cost by renting it when you're not there, examine the deal with a clear eye and a cold heart. The manager of the building may assure you he can rent your unit for three months, but is that the experience of the other owners? Ask them what rentals they actually get and what they'd recommend to ensure a steady stream of tenants. It often pays to buy a slightly more expensive condo because it will rent more readily than a small unit on the first floor rear. For more on vacation homes, see Chapter 19, "A Second Home."

The Condominium Documents

No piece of advice is more important than this one: Have all the condo documents examined for pitfalls by a lawyer experienced in condominium problems. Don't sign anything until he's explained them to you. He'll need your deed to see exactly what you own (the driveway? the front yard? the front of your townhouse? the plaster on your walls? or just the paint?). Whatever is yours will have to be maintained at your expense. He'll need the *sales contract,* which sometimes runs to hundreds of pages of clauses and commitments. Is the builder selling you the land and recreational facilities, or are you leasing from him at an open-ended cost? Under what circumstances might you lose your down payment? He'll need the *master deed,* or *declaration,* or *charter,* which set the condominium up. This tells you how big the development is expected to be, what the common areas are, when the builder will relinquish control of the owner's association, and what the association can do to you if you don't pay your maintenance fees or assessments. Then there are the *bylaws,* which tell how the association proposes to govern itself. These set out your rights as a member of the group and your responsibilities to the other members. Among other things, you're entitled to a vote on who runs the association; a veto over any major changes; insurance for the common areas; freedom to sell with a minimum of restrictions; and a mechanism for ensuring that the bylaws will be obeyed.

All these documents could be written in plain English for any buyer to understand. But they often aren't. Because of the tiresome legalese, many people don't bother trying to struggle through the clauses (which was the general idea); they just buy and move in. Don't do it. Pay a lawyer to read them for you.

Insurance

The condominium association buys fire and liability insurance for the common areas, paid for out of maintenance fees. Be sure the amount is adequate; if it's too low, your fee will have to rise to cover an increase. The association can also get blanket insurance for the entire structure; it's cheaper than having each owner insure his unit separately and eliminates squabbles between insurers if a fire damages two units. Builders may skip blanket coverage because it makes the maintenance fee higher in comparison with other condominiums. But the owners' association can buy it when they take over the management.

Where there's a blanket policy, you'll still need individual coverage for the contents of your home and for liability if someone hurts himself on your property. Tell your insurance agent exactly what the blanket policy covers, so your own insurance can pick up the missing pieces. Where there's no blanket policy, you'll have to purchase regular home-owner's coverage (see page 314).

Taxes

Taxes and town assessments may not be levied against the condominium as a whole but only against individual units. Therefore, you assume no liability if your neighbor fails to pay his taxes. Each unit also bears its own mortgage, so if your neighbor defaults, it doesn't affect the property you own. The taxes and mortgage interest you pay are deductible on your individual tax return.

The Owners' Association

An interested, awake, imaginative owners' association is what makes a condominium a good place to live. If no one pays any attention to it, maintenance fees won't be paid and the building will run down. In the beginning the association is set up by the builder, with bylaws that permit him to control it. So the first bit of business when the builder withdraws should be to make the association more democratic, with everyone permitted to vote on changes in the bylaws. It's important to get skilled people on the board and the committees; accountants, business people, parliamentarians, lawyers, people with the special knowledge needed to keep the place running efficiently. The owners' association is your town government. Without a good one your property values will erode.

COOPERATIVES

A cooperative apartment gives you the tax advantages of home ownership but is not as favorable a financial arrangement as a condominium. With a cooperative you don't own your unit outright. A corporation owns the entire building; you own shares in the corporation that give you the right to occupy a specific unit. You pay a monthly maintenance fee, out of which the corporation pays the mortgage, the real estate taxes, and the building maintenance. Your proportionate share of taxes and interest can be deducted on your personal tax return.

The big disadvantage is this: If your neighbor defaults on his maintenance fee, all the rest of the residents have to contribute something to make it up. So it's essential that everyone buying in be financially responsible. The board generally won't let a unit be sold until the buyer has been investigated and approved by the other residents. The board also maintains more control than in a condominium over structural changes in anyone's apartment.

Otherwise, cooperatives and condominiums are much alike. You'll want to see the budget and bylaws before buying in, assess the competence of the board of directors, and evaluate the building's financial status. Talk to several of the residents about the building's advantages and disadvantages. Have a lawyer go over all the documents.

Because you're buying shares in a corporation rather than real estate, you can't get mortgage financing. Lenders make personal loans at one or two percentage points over the mortgage rate. The amount financed runs from 50 to 80 percent, depending on circumstances. If your apartment house is converting to a co-op, you can often buy in at a relatively low price. But pay close attention to the engineer's report to see what expenses for repairs and maintenance lie ahead.

Chapter Fourteen

RENTING
AN APARTMENT

A Manual: Training for Landlords
Lesson Two: Rooms
The most important factor here is that you understand that a room is a matter of opinion. It is, after all, your building, and if you choose to designate a given amount of space as a room, then indeed it is a room. Specifying a function of the room is also your responsibility, and tenants need frequently to be reminded of this as they will all too often display a tendency to call one of your rooms a closet. This is, of course, a laughable pretension, since few tenants have even seen a closet.

FRAN LEBOWITZ

There's a lot to be said for apartments. When the faucet leaks, you call the superintendent (free) instead of the plumber ($$$). No one complains if you hate to mow lawns. You can live downtown, if that's your pleasure, where townhouse prices may be out of sight. Your savings go into investments other than a down payment, and there's no need to pour money into upkeep and repairs. Because you don't have to find a buyer, apartments are easier to move out of than houses or condominiums. Renting for a year lets you get the lay of the land when you move to a new town.

On the other hand, there's the landlord. Leases favor him, as do many legal precedents. In a battle with a landlord the tenant may be right, but it could be too costly and frustrating to fight on to victory. Many landlords are splendid fellows, while others take every advantage of their tenants. Before you move in, try to talk with some of the other tenants about their experiences with the landlord and the building, and whether they'd recommend it. If the building is in a city where people are afraid to open their doors to strangers, wait on the street and ask people on the way in or out for a few moments of their time.

What Can You Afford?

The rule of thumb is that housing costs shouldn't exceed 25 percent of your take-home pay. That figure should include everything—rent, utilities, parking, insurance, and any other related fees. Single people can probably afford more, but if you pay more than 30 percent, your living standards start getting squeezed. Rent will likely go up as often as the lease and the law allows, so it's better to have a little leeway in your housing budget than to be right up against the ceiling.

The Hunt

Looking for a place to live is tiring and often discouraging. But keep pounding the streets until you find what you want. The quality of your living space is so important to peace of mind that it's worth the effort to find the right place. A rental agent may be able to save you time by showing you apartments most likely to please; his fee is generally one month's rent. If your heart is set on a certain building, keep calling the management office (or superintendent) to find out about openings. You may have to cross someone's palm with silver to keep yourself at the head of the line.

Try to visit apartments during the active time—evenings or weekends—to hear how quiet the place is. On weekends you'll be able to get a look at some of the neighbors. Open and close all the windows and doors, to see if they stick; turn on all the faucets at once to check water pressure and hot water supply. If the apartment is still occupied, ask the tenant why he's leaving and what the apartment's problems are. Is the landlord cooperative? How fast does he make repairs? Are there cockroaches or mice? Where do you put the garbage and how often is it collected? Does the fireplace really work (smoke stains are a bad sign)? Is there enough heat in the winter? Is there a tenants' organization? If so, call on the head of the group and ask him about the building. If there are doormen or elevator operators, check both the daytime and nighttime staffs to see what they look like. Is the security good? Have there been recent robberies? Below are some items to check as you're walking around the apartment:

Neat personnel
Clean lobby and halls
Guarded lobby

Good lighting
Good locks on doors and windows
No drafts around windows

Screens, storm windows
No water stains on walls, floors, ceilings
No drafts
Clean, working appliances
Exhaust fan in kitchen
Enough electrical outlets
Fireplace, no smoke stains
Telephone jacks
Master TV antenna
Enough daylight
Regular window washing
Repair services
Incinerator/garbage pickups
Adequate heat and air conditioning

Enough hot water
Good water pressure
Windowshades
Soundproofing
Clean walls, floors, ceilings
Fresh paint
Superintendent on premises
Fire alarm, fire escape
Safe stairs
No roaches or mice
Parking
Storage
Laundry facilities
Locked mailboxes
Receiving room for packages
Children's playground

Write down what's wrong with the apartment, to see if the landlord will make repairs. Does it need painting? Does it need a doorknob on the closet? Is there a cracked pane of glass that should be replaced? Will he sand and stain the floors, or is that your expense? Are you or the landlord responsible for maintaining the dishwasher, refrigerator, washing machine? Look for water stains around the windows and on the ceilings; if the landlord won't fix the leaks, you'll have problems when it rains. When you're renting a furnished apartment, see if any of the furniture is broken. Make a list of all repairs the landlord agrees to make and ask him to sign it. Otherwise, you may never hear of them again. Send a list of everything that's wrong with the apartment and the furniture to the landlord (registered mail, return receipt requested) in case, at the end of the lease, he tries to charge you for damage that was there when you moved in.

The Lease

The lease can be a bloody battleground between landlord and tenant. If your landlord is courteous, honest, and concerned, it hardly matters what it says in the fifth clause, part B. If not, that clause might get you evicted. Some landlords are willing to strike out sections of the lease that offend you; others deal on a take-it-or-leave-it basis. Naturally, you will read the lease before signing it and ask about clauses you don't understand. Lease laws vary from city to city, some offering tenants more protection than others. Here are some of the general things to watch for:

The Rent

Is the rent a firm figure, or can the landlord raise it to reflect increased costs, such as higher bills? Are there extra costs for storage, parking, use of a swimming pool? Who pays for utilities? At the end of the lease is there any limit on how much the rent can be raised?

Option to Renew

Some localities require that a tenant be given an option to renew the lease, but in most places the landlord has no obligation to let you stay for another term. You can ask for a renewal option, but don't expect the landlord to commit himself this far in advance as to what the rent will be.

The Condition of the Apartment

You agree to rent the premises as is, unless the landlord has specified certain repairs *in writing*. That's why it's so important to make a list of repairs and get it attached to the lease. Some landlords honor their verbal commitments, but others will promise you anything, then forget it after you've signed. If the landlord has intentionally hidden a serious defect, however, you may be able to walk away from the lease.

Subleasing

You'll want a clause allowing you to sublease in case you have to move before the lease is up. The landlord has to approve the new tenant, however. If the subtenant defaults or damages the apartment, you can try to collect from him—but you remain responsible to the landlord for rent and repairs. For this reason you may prefer to break the lease rather than risk a subtenant.

Breaking the Lease

If you must move and can't sublease, landlords have various procedures for letting you break the lease. The penalty may be that they keep the security deposit and get an extra month's rent, or even two month's rent. Whatever you agree, be sure to get it in writing. Some landlords will tell you one thing over the telephone, then hold you up for an extra month's rent on the eve of departure. If you simply leave and refuse to pay, your rights vary according to local law. Normally, the landlord can't collect rent from you if he has another tenant for the apartment. But if the apartment remains empty for many months, you will likely have to pay.

Repairs

You will normally be expected to repair any damage you did to the apartment, from breaking a window to pounding picture hooks into the walls. However, you shouldn't be charged for reasonable wear and tear, such as scuffing the floors or wearing down the arms of upholstered furniture. Some leases require the tenant to paint before leaving, others don't. The landlord usually deducts the cost of repairs from your security deposit and sends you what's left.

The Security Deposit

Landlords generally collect a month's rent (sometimes two) to hold as security in case you don't pay the rent or repair damage to the property. At the end of the lease you should get your security back, less whatever the landlord decides to deduct to cover damage he says you've done. This deduction is highly arbitrary. Some landlords make a habit of finding just enough damage to justify their holding on to the whole amount. If they do return any money to you, it may take months. Some states have laws to limit abuse. The size of the deposit may be limited, and the landlord may have to return your money within a specified length of time. He may even be required to hold the money in escrow and pay interest.

Tenants often balance the books by refusing to pay the last month's rent, assuming that it will be covered by the security deposit. This is illegal in most states and could lead to an embarrassing eviction the week before your lease runs out. But it's often done.

Many tenants wind up in small-claims courts trying to extract the security deposit from landlords. It helps prove your case if you made a summary of the condition of the apartment when you moved in and sent a copy (registered mail, return receipt requested) to the landlord. But even assuming you win, you may have another struggle getting the landlord to pay.

Improvements to the Apartment

If you make improvements—such as building in some shelves or adding a deadbolt lock to the front door—the lease will probably require that you leave them behind when you move out. Typically, the landlord must okay all improvements, even at your expense, and gets to keep them in the end. If you can remove them with no apparent damage, he may not charge you for his "loss"—but don't count on it. If he doesn't like your improvements, he may insist that you pay to restore the apartment to its original condition.

Additional Tenants

The lease usually prohibits anyone from moving in and sharing the apartment with you, except your immediate family, without the landlord's written consent. If you find a friend to share the rent, the landlord, if he disapproves, can have him evicted. That may not happen, however—it all depends on the situation.

Liability

Leases generally relieve the landlord from any liability to you. But if he behaved negligently, you can often collect in court no matter what the lease says. Ask a lawyer what rights you have beyond the lease.

Access

Leases differ on the amount of access a landlord is given to your apartment. Some limit it sharply, others let him come in any time he wants. If you change the lock, he may be permitted to open your door by force. You should have twenty-four hours' notice before a repairman is sent. You should also have the right to keep prospective tenants from looking at your apartment until the month before the lease is up.

Landlord Obligations

Leases usually require that you keep on paying the rent whether or not the landlord lives up to his part of the bargain. If you held back the rent until a broken window was repaired, it could be grounds for eviction. Some states permit rent withholding under certain circumstances—see page 299.

Rules and Regulations

The lease includes a list of apartment house rules, such as no putting nails in the walls, no playing the piano, no pets. These rules may not be enforced unless the landlord wants to get rid of you, in which case you may suddenly be evicted for something your neighbors are still allowed. This can be grounds for suit, but few tenants have the time or the money to contest the move. Try to have some of the rules removed before signing the lease.

Loss of Rights

You may have to agree that in case of a dispute you waive your right to a jury trial. Where "confession of judgment" clauses are still legal, you may waive your right to any trial at all. You also agree to pay any legal expenses the landlord has in the course of throwing you out. A "waiver of notice" clause means the landlord doesn't even have to tell you in advance that you're going to be evicted—the sheriff can take you by surprise. If these waivers are legal in your state, there's generally not much you can do about them.

Tenant Protection Laws

A number of states and cities have passed laws protecting tenants from some of the abuses mentioned above. The key document is the Uniform Residential Landlord and Tenant Act, adopted in whole or in part by several states. Among its provisions:

—It obliges landlords to provide housing units that are fit to live in, according to local housing codes. Depending on local law, a tenant in an unfit apartment may break the lease, sue for damages, reduce his rent, or make repairs and deduct the cost from his rent.

—It protects tenants from landlord retaliation, if they join a tenants' organization, file a complaint, or report a housing-code violation. Landlords are prohibited from evicting people who complain, increasing their rent, or decreasing their services, for at least a year. In New Jersey —the state with the most advanced tenant laws—landlords even have to renew a complainant's lease, if asked.

—It limits the security deposit a landlord can ask to only one month's rent, and requires its return within two weeks from the day the lease is ended. If the landlord uses any of the deposit to make repairs, he has to itemize the expenses.

—It abolishes a landlord's common-law right to seize a tenant's personal property or lock him out of his apartment.

—It prevents landlords from shutting off utilities.

—It requires that any rules made by landlords be reasonable and uniformly applied. If a rule is generally ignored, a landlord can't suddenly enforce it to get rid of a tenant he doesn't like. Several states have broad "warrant of habitability" laws, which require that an apartment be fit to live in. Superficially, it sounds as if these laws apply only to run-down housing. But many courts have extended them to cover middle-class and luxury housing, too. If you pay a high rent, the landlord is, in effect, "warranting" certain luxuries and can't renege. Cases have been won where tenants complained that their air conditioners didn't work or that the swimming pool leaked. One tenant paying $650 a month in a luxury building won a rent reduction because a leak made his parking spot in the garage unfit to use.

In states without habitability laws, lawyers have successfully used another approach. Buildings fall apart because cities ignore their own housing codes, so suits have been filed to require enforcement. The end result may be that landlords are forced to make repairs, or that tenants get a reduction in rent.

Using Your Local Housing Agency

Your town or city has a housing code and a mechanism for filing complaints. If a landlord has repeatedly ignored your *written* requests for essential repairs and services, visit the housing office and ask if he's in violation of the code. He may well be, in which case the office will help you file a complaint.

An inspector should investigate your charges and file a report of his findings; be sure you get a copy. The landlord (or his representative) will probably have to go to the agency to answer the complaint, and he may eventually be fined. Often the fine isn't large enough to make him mend his ways, but go through the process anyway; should your tenants' group ever want to start a rent strike, you may need proof of a code violation. If you take your case to court, it helps to show that the landlord had indeed ignored a violation.

You'll get more attention from government if you belong to a tenants' organization than if you act alone. Ask your local housing agency or consumer protection agency whether there are any tenants' organizations in your city.

Rent Strikes

In many localities tenants must pay the rent whether or not the landlord lives up to his obligations. But other states provide a mechanism for withholding rent until an apartment or building is brought up to snuff. Tenants who go on individual rent strikes are vulnerable to harassment, but if an entire building bands together, a landlord will usually be forced to act.

Get a lawyer to advise you on proper procedure, so you won't fall afoul of the law. Your rent should go into some form of escrow account to be ready for payment if so ordered by a judge.

You need a list of grievances for use in the negotiation. It should contain the specific problems of each individual apartment as well as those of the building as a whole. Some states don't specifically protect strikers or others exercising their tenants' rights from eviction; a lawyer can help you hold out against harassment from the landlord, but be prepared to fight. If the building is unprofitable, the landlord might react to the strike by abandoning it. In that case conditions will gradually worsen until you finally have to move.

Eviction

States vary in the protection they give tenants from eviction. Some specify only a limited number of grounds, such as nonpayment of rent or breaking a reasonable clause in the lease; others give landlords carte blanche, even to letting them remove (on technical grounds) tenants who file complaints with the housing agency or try to start a tenants' organization. In states with poor laws you may be thrown out with little or no prior notice; strong laws require that you be informed of the violation and given time to correct it before the landlord can act. The landlord generally has to notify you that he's seeking an order of eviction so that you can show up in court to defend yourself. If you don't, and he can show that you've violated the lease, he wins the right to put you out into the street. If you're determined to fight an unfair eviction, you can generally do so, even in states where the law appears to be against you, but it takes time, money, and enormous devotion to principle. It's far easier to stand your ground where you're backed by solid tenant protection laws.

Renting a House

Since there's no superintendent on premises to fix a leaky faucet, you'll have to take care of things like that yourself. The lease should spell out whether you or the landlord has to pay for them. Normally, the tenant pays for minor repairs and the landlord for major ones, although some leases require the tenant to fix everything. If you pay for something that's the landlord's responsibility, how are you reimbursed? By check? Or can you deduct it from the rent?

Be sure the landlord carries adequate insurance on the house; if he doesn't, get it yourself. There have been cases where the tenant was charged with the cost of rebuilding a house after it burned. If there's a dangerous condition on the property, notify the landlord. If he does nothing, you might have to fix it yourself lest you be held responsible for any injuries or damage that result.

If you're renting a house that the owner wants to sell, make it clear what right you have to protect your privacy and your domicile. Can the owner bring prospective buyers through the house? If a buyer is found, can you stay until the lease is up or will you have to move? Don't accept a verbal agreement on this; have the conditions written into the lease.

If you're renting the house in advance of buying it, the lease should state when the sale will take place, at what price, and how much of the rent will be applied toward the down payment. You should have an escape clause in case you can't find a mortgage on terms you can afford. In any lease/buy situation have a lawyer handle the lease and the sales agreement.

Renter's Insurance

You need a tenant's policy, which covers the contents of the home but not its structure. You'll also want liability insurance, in case anyone hurts himself on the premises. Depending on circumstances, the landlord might be responsible for injuries from, say, a broken front step if you told him of the problem and he didn't repair it. On the other hand, you might also be liable for letting the dangerous condition persist. And it certainly isn't the landlord's fault if someone trips over your children's bicycles in the yard. A tenant's policy is like homeowner's coverage, but without provisions for the building itself (for details, see page 313). Buy enough insurance to cover the *cash value* of your belongings (the current retail price, less depreciation), not their replacement price. Most policies won't pay any more than cash value. Some companies, however, do offer replacement cost coverage, at a higher price.

Renting a Summer or Winter Home

When you rent in an unfamiliar area, you'll have to let the real estate agent pick the house. Be as specific as possible about what you'd like, but don't be surprised if it doesn't measure up to expectations. If you find that you simply hate the house, ask the agent to move you into another one. It's done all the time, when there's space available.

Once there, spend a morning looking at other houses, so that if you want to rent again, you'll know exactly what houses are available. Highly desirable houses are often rented a year or more in advance, so it pays to get your bid in early.

When you rent with a group of people or buy a season's share in a ski house, have all the rules laid out in advance. Who collects the rental shares? What happens if someone doesn't pay his share? Is the owner's insurance sufficient? What happens if one of you does some damage? How is food paid for and cooking arranged? Who cleans? Are guests allowed? Is there any limit on your occupancy? Do the other tenants like to live the way you do? Will people pledge to be quiet after certain hours? The more you can get settled in advance, the more pleasant your group tenancy is likely to be.

Chapter Fifteen

MOBILE
HOMES

The great advantage of a hotel is that it's a refuge
from home life.

GEORGE BERNARD SHAW

These have become far less "mobile" and far more "home." You can
buy them up to sixteen feet wide in some states; two long units put
together (called double wides) may provide nearly two thousand square
feet of living space. The cost of the home typically includes rugs, curtains, appliances, even furniture especially designed for smaller rooms.
They're about the cheapest good housing available in America—but
owners face some special problems:

Where to Put it

Never buy a mobile home until you know exactly where you're going
to put it. Most town and county zoning codes discriminate against
mobile homes, so even if you own a piece of land, you may be unable
to use it for this kind of housing. Someone could live in a tumbledown
shack, an eyesore by any standards, but if he tried to replace it with a
mobile home, he'd be violating an ordinance. Mobiles are okay where
there's no zoning (generally, rural areas) or where the zoning codes
don't specifically rule them out. If your county confines mobile homes
to just a few parks, you might consider bringing suit on the ground that,

303

as a homeowner, you're being unreasonably discriminated against. This has worked in a few places. Some mobile home owners' groups have successfully lobbied politicians to have zoning laws changed. In Vermont, for example, mobiles are now treated like any other single-family home. If you want to file a suit, you'd be well advised to seek the advice of a local mobile home owners' organization (see page 310).

If you can't put the unit on land of your own, you'll have to find a mobile home park. A few parks sell land and home as a package, but most of them rent spaces. In many places you can't get into the park unless you buy your unit from the park owner. Where exclusionary zoning limits the number of mobile home parks, a large fee (the *entrance fee*) may be charged to anyone moving in. Parks vary enormously—from plush developments with sidewalks, swimming pools, and clubhouses, to shantytowns strung along major highways. When you shop for a park, it isn't enough just to talk to the dealer and go with him on a conducted tour of the grounds. Although some parks are excellent and filled with satisfied tenants, there can be serious problems with park living. The only way you'll get a handle on them is to talk to park residents without the owner present. Walk around, talk to people on the roads, even knock on doors, and ask how they like their park. You may get an earful!

The Eviction Problem

The most serious drawback to renting space in a mobile home park is the risk of eviction. The landlord owns the property, rarely gives leases, and in most (but not all) states can evict you for whatever reason he chooses. This places a much greater burden on the mobile home owner than it does on the ordinary tenant. The owner has a considerable investment in his home, not to mention the money spent landscaping his lot and installing a driveway. If the landlord tells him to move, he loses his landscaping investment, has the expense of moving the unit, and may well suffer serious damage to it en route. If other parks in the vicinity accept only units sold by the park owners, he may literally be unable to move. An eviction notice thereby forces him to sell his home (usually at a loss) and buy into another park. Because of the homeowner's fear of eviction, the park owner has considerable power over him and may engage in a number of abuses (see the following section).

A few states have passed "just-cause" eviction laws. In Florida, for example, a mobile home owner can't be turned out of the park unless he (1) doesn't pay the rent; (2) is convicted of a crime of the sort that is detrimental to other park residents; (3) violated reasonable park rules; or (4) the park owner wants to convert the land to another use. But even if your state is one of the handful that gives mobile home owners protection from unreasonable eviction, it's no good unless the law is enforced. In many places just-cause eviction laws can be violated with virtual impunity because the state doesn't put enforcement into the hands of the attorney general (many homeowners can't afford the expense of a private lawsuit). So before you decide to become a mobile home owner, find out what the eviction situation is in your state and whether any laws in your favor are enforced. Ask the park residents about it; also seek advice from a local mobile home owners' association.

Other Problems with Parks

Residents are usually hedged in with dozens of park rules—some in their favor, such as noise regulations, others tending to make their lives either more expensive or more difficult. Always get a full list of park rules before you sign up for space; if the landlord won't give them to you, assume that it's a difficult park to live in. Residents may tell you that certain rules, such as pet prohibitions, are not enforced—which makes you feel it's safe to move in even though you keep a cat. But if the landlord decides he doesn't like you, he may use your pet as an excuse to throw you out. Landlords can also change the rules overnight. For example, if you bought into a family park, the landlord might decide to switch it to a place for retirees only and throw you out. Some landlords consult with tenants on rules changes, but most don't.

A list of the most objectionable rules, from the tenant's point of view, follows. On your walking tour of the park ask the residents about them. Even though one or more of these practices may be illegal in your state, don't be surprised to find them going on anyway.

Entrance Fees

Where park space is tight, owners may levy an entrance fee of anywhere between $300 and $1,500. No services are provided; it's simply a payoff for letting you in. Even people who buy used units on resale may have to pay, or else the management won't let the sale go through. The family moving out may also be charged an exit fee.

Sharp Rent Increases

New parks typically charge low rents in order to attract customers. But when space gets tight, rents may suddenly double or triple. Some residents—for example, older people on Social Security—can't afford the hike and have to leave. Since the vast majority of mobile home owners are not protected by leases, the rents may go up more than once a year. You wouldn't expect to escape higher rents that are associated with higher costs. But where exclusionary zoning gives the park owner a monopoly, he may charge rents higher than the open market would allow.

Selling Your Unit

A park owner typically won't let you sell unless the buyer meets his approval, which is reasonable, since he has to collect the rents and is responsible to other tenants for who moves into the neighborhood. But sometimes approval may be unreasonably withheld. Then you'll have to sell to the owner at his price. Some park owners require that you pay them a fee when the unit is sold, even if they didn't act as broker. Or they may insist that they handle the sale.

Products and Services

The park owner may insist that you buy your awnings, skirting, patios, porches, and sheds through him, even though you can get them elsewhere at a lower price. Or he may set "park standards" for these items, which effectively rule out all but one or two dealers. Only certain servicemen may be authorized to do business in the park—and their prices may be high because they have to pay the park owner a percentage of each job. The park owner may also insist that residents buy their gas and oil from him at a premium price.

Unreasonable Rules

A landlord might charge a mobile home owner an extra $5 or $10 a month if he adds a patio or awnings. If the water bill is higher than he'd like, he might ban hoses or order residents to remove their washing machines. Children may be required to show more decorum than can reasonably be expected—creating potential conflict in families and risk of eviction if a teen-ager happens to have an obstreperous year. Rules can be changed suddenly and arbitrarily. The extent of this problem depends very much on the attitude and personality of the park owner.

Checking the Parks

In areas where there are plenty of parks and where the law prevents a park owner from renting only to people who buy units from him, prices may be quite competitive and living conditions excellent.

When you look at a park site, be sure the grading slopes away from the slab so that water won't settle around the house. Look for slabs that are at least four inches thick, level, and without cracks. Larger lots mean more attractive parks and more outdoor living space. If you hope to add a room or a porch in the future, be sure there's enough space. Federal standards require tie-downs on all homes to stabilize them in a severe windstorm, so ask if the park has anchors for the ties. You'll want at least 100-amp service for your electrical needs and 200-volt service for dryers and other major appliances. If you don't have a washer and dryer, see if there's a laundromat in the park. When you're visiting with residents, ask about the water pressure and where they buy their oil and gas. Higher-quality parks require residents to hide the wheels of their homes with skirting, do a certain amount of landscaping, buy carports, and install attractive front steps. Where this much is demanded, you should expect park owners to provide underground utilities (so wires and oil tanks won't be eyesores), paved roads, and such recreational facilities as a pool or a clubhouse.

Which Home to Buy

Mobile homes come in a variety of traditional home styles, including shingled roofs and bay windows. You can get carports, porches, patios, room extenders, or two units put together in a "double-wide" home. Some are even installed on sunken foundations so that they won't be that telltale wheel width above the ground.

Before you buy, talk to other mobile home owners to see what their experience with various makes and models has been. Some models can better withstand two or three moves than others can; some designs have been found to be more convenient. There's just no substitute for personal information from someone who's using his unit the same way you plan to. If possible, inspect a unit that's ten years old to see how well that model stood up. If you're buying a used home, have it checked out for structural soundness (the owner may be trying to palm off something that was severely damaged in a windstorm). Visit the used unit in a rainstorm as well as in good weather to see if there are leaks.

It's important to have a reliable dealer, since he's the person you normally turn to for warranty work on a new unit. There's been a lot of trouble with mobile home warranties in the past—with the buyer bounced back and forth between dealer and manufacturer, neither one of them wanting to do the job. The new Magnuson-Moss Warranty Act requires that the precise extent of your warranty be set down in writing, but it hasn't solved the problem of getting work done promptly. When you're visiting the park, ask the residents about how the dealer treats warranty repairs. Also ask them which dealers have the best reputations. But even with a recommended dealer, don't rely on verbal promises or guarantees; get everything he offers you in writing.

The Price

As with buying any other kind of home, the price of the unit is just the beginning. Initial costs may include the price of moving the unit to the site, building a foundation and driveway, landscaping, tying the unit down if it's in a high-wind area, connecting the water and electricity, and paying the park's entrance fee. If you own your own lot, you'll have to grade the site, lay sewer and water pipes, put in a slab foundation and driveway, and bring in electricity. You'll owe taxes—either a personal property tax or a real estate tax. There's insurance, financing charges, maintenance, and monthly park rental. All the ongoing fees are likely to increase over time—a warning if you're on a fixed income.

You can dicker with the dealer over price. But if you have to buy from him to get into his park and space is tight, you're unlikely to get much, if anything, off. If you have your own furniture and its scale is small enough to look right in a mobile home, you could save yourself some money by asking for a price without furniture (which is normally included as part of the package). You pay extra for things like air conditioning, dishwashers and other appliances, large water heaters, shutters, screens, and storm windows. The park's own rules may add to the price of your home by requiring skirting to hide the wheels, carports, shutters, and other items.

Financing

The dealer usually offers financing, and sometimes it's the best you can do. Local banks and savings and loan associations might prefer to do business through the dealer rather than check each prospect out themselves. But if you can get your own financing, it's usually cheaper. Credit unions are your best bet, followed by savings banks and S&Ls, and then commercial banks.

Unfortunately, mobile homes generally don't qualify for mortgage financing. In some places, where the unit is being placed on a private lot, mortgages are allowed—but in general, you'll have to get a higher-cost, shorter-term consumer loan. Interest rates will probably run three or four percentage points higher than mortgage rates, and the term will likely be no more than ten years.

If you qualify for a loan guaranteed by the Veterans Administration, you can borrow up to $17,500 for fifteen years on either a single-wide or a double-wide unit. No down payment is required by the VA, although the lender usually insists on one. Interest rates are generally a little lower than on conventional loans. The VA will also lend money to buy used units, although the amount of the loan can't exceed the home's appraised value.

The Federal Housing Administration also guarantees loans on more favorable terms than the private market offers. You can borrow up to $18,000 for twelve years on single-wides or $27,000 for fifteen years on double-wides. Also, you can get $6,250 for fifteen years on undeveloped mobile home lots, and $9,375 on developed lots; up to $27,500 for twenty years on single-wide–lot combinations; and $36,500 for twenty years on double-wide–lot combinations. The FHA wants a down payment of at least 5 percent on the first $3,000 of a unit's price tag, and 10 percent on the rest (the lender may require even more). Down payment for a lot is 10 percent; and for a unit-lot combination, 5 percent on the first $10,000 and 10 percent on everything over that. Loans are available on used units only if they were previously financed through the FHA.

In rural areas, farmers and people sixty-two or over may qualify for financing through the Farmers Home Administration. The dealer, your credit union, bank, or S&L will have information on government-backed loans. Just remember that there's nothing mandatory about offering them. If the local lenders don't want to make government-insured loans, they don't have to.

After you decide which home to buy, check the rate of interest the dealer offers compared with what you're able to find for yourself. Don't sign with the dealer until you've done this. If the dealer asks 18 percent on a $10,000 loan for ten years, and your credit union asks only 15 percent, you can save yourself $2,280 in interest. Even if you can get no more than ½ of 1 percent less by getting bank financing, it's worth $360 over ten years.

If dealer financing is your only option, don't inadvertently sign up for extras you don't want. For example, the dealer might quote you a monthly price that includes homeowner's insurance. That sounds fine, since you need the insurance, but you might well be able to get it cheaper—with perhaps a better policy—by buying from an insurance agent instead. The dealer's quote may also include credit life insurance to pay off the loan if you die or become disabled. If credit life is mandatory, its cost must be included in the annual percentage interest rate on the truth-in-lending statement the dealer is required to give you. If it's optional, and you do want to be sure the home is paid for in case of your death, you can get cheaper coverage from an insurance agent.

Depreciation

Unlike regular homes, mobile homes generally depreciate in value. In places where zoning is tight and few mobile homes are available, fairly new units, in good parks, may hold their value or even increase a little in price. But over the years you must expect the value to decline. However, unless the unit is seriously damaged or you let it fall into disrepair, you'll at least get part of your money out on resale—which is more than renters can say.

Safety

Serious safety questions have been raised about older models of mobile homes. Many of them didn't make adequate use of fire-retardant materials or pay enough attention to wiring, furnace ducts, and insulation, with the result that fires have been far more common in mobile homes than in regular housing. Furthermore, windows were often too small to escape through, and there was only one center door, which fire-trapped occupants might not be able to reach. The better manufacturers finally established a voluntary set of safety standards. If you buy an older model on resale, look for an oval tag that says it meets the standards set by the Mobile Homes Manufacturers Association/Trailer

Coach Association. In 1976 the federal government provided for mandatory national standards—the first national building code ever. It requires such things as more insulation, firmer construction, fewer flammable materials, wider hallways, safety glazing in glass doors, engineer-designed tie-downs against the wind, storm windows or insulated glass for homes sold in the North, and other technical improvements. This law superseded conflicting state standards. When you buy a mobile home, look for the label that says it was built in accordance with the standards set by the U.S. Department of Housing and Urban Development.

Maintenance

A mobile home must be set up and maintained properly if it is to last. Improper setup can cause plumbing leaks, warped doors and windows, roof leaks, unaligned panels, and floor squeaks, and throw toilets and appliances out of whack. Getting the home level and keeping it there is the most important thing. Check the setting level every six months to be sure it hasn't slipped slightly. Gas and utility connections should be professionally done, or you're flirting with fires. Reseal the roof regularly; check your owner's manual for when it should be done. Double-wides, in particular, may have problems with leaks along the roofline. If a small leak develops, do a temporary repair job right away before it damages interior panels; then call a professional. But try not to walk on the roof, lest it dent. When you take delivery of a new house, walk around it carefully looking for cracks or openings around the windows or roof. A crack that's small today will enlarge as the house settles, and you'll want to be sure to have it repaired while the warranty is still good. Your owner's manual will give specific information on maintenance, safety, and repairs—be sure to read it and do what it says.

Where to Complain

The owner's manual that came with the house will tell you how to resolve a warranty dispute. But if you're being treated capriciously by a park owner, the only place to turn is the organized tenants' group now found in many parks. There are also state organizations, and the American Mobilehome Association (P.O. Box 710, Golden, Colo. 80401) is welding the state groups together into a national network. Various tenants' associations have won many rights for park residents—long-term leases, more reasonable park rules, reconsideration on evictions. They have also helped lobby state legislators to get more mobile home zoning and more protective laws for owners. In many parks residents are afraid to join an association because if the landlord hears about it, he'll evict them. If that's the case in a park you're considering, maybe you'd better look somewhere else. Before you buy, ask the AMA in Colorado for the name of the tenants' group for your state. They'll give you information on your state laws, what to watch for in the parks, and other valuable tips on mobile home living. If you're unjustly evicted or have other troubles with the landlord, the association will back you if you want to file suit. If you're having problems with a dealer or manufacturer, the tenants' groups may also be of help. The manufacturers themselves run a consumer complaint panel. Write to Consumer Action Bureau, Manufactured Housing Institute, 1745 Jefferson Davis Highway, Suite 511, Arlington, Va. 22202.

Mobile Home Insurance

These policies protect your property against damage and cover you if you're sued. Insurance is available against certain named perils, but for just a few dollars more you can get comprehensive coverage against virtually all types of physical loss. (There are exclusions, however, even in comprehensive policies, so note what they are.)

A new mobile home should be insured for its cost; a used unit, for its cash (or market) value. As your mobile home depreciates over the years, less insurance is necessary, since the policy will never pay more than the home's cash value no matter how much it's insured for. Some policies include furnishings, others insure them separately. In either case, be sure the personal property segment is sufficient. Many mobile home policies cover flooding, but if yours doesn't and you're in a flood area, apply through your agent for federally backed flood insurance. The liability segment of your policy will typically be $25,000 (which means the insurance company will pay any judgments against you up to that amount—see page 318). But with today's large legal settlements you might consider increasing that amount. It may cost you no more than $4 to $6 a year to raise your liability to $50,000 or more. When you move your home, check the trucker's coverage and if it's not enough, get supplemental insurance of your own. In order for your policy to stay in force, your insurance company may require notice before you move.

Chapter Sixteen

HOMEOWNER'S AND TENANT'S INSURANCE

A bad earthquake at once destroys the oldest associations; the world, the very emblem of all that is solid, had moved beneath our feet like a crust over a fluid; one second of time has created in the mind a strange idea of insecurity, which hours of reflection would not have produced.

CHARLES DARWIN

There's one key point to remember in buying and maintaining a homeowner's insurance policy: *The coverage should be for at least 80 percent of the home's current replacement cost.* If it meets that test, your repair bills will be paid in full, up to the limits of the policy. If the house is insured for less, the insurer will pay less than the full amount of the bill (the exact amount depending on the age of the house and the payment formula used).

For example, say you have a $40,000 house (not counting the value of the land) insured for $32,000—which is 80 percent. If a fire did $10,000 worth of damage, your insurance would pay the full $10,000 (less the deductible—usually around $100). However, if the house were insured for only $24,000 (which is just 60 percent of cost), and it was several years old, the insurance company might pay only around $7,500 for the loss (or a little more, depending on circumstances).

If the house burned to the ground, the first policy would pay $32,000 and the second, $24,000. To be protected for your home's full value, you must insure for the total amount.

Replacement cost means the amount it would cost to have the house rebuilt (excluding the price of the land and the foundation). It does *not* mean market value. With a newly built house, the replacement cost may be the same as the market value (not counting land). But an older

313

house may sell for less than its replacement cost. If you've just bought an older house, ask your insurance agent how to figure the replacement cost; he'll probably have some tables that will help. Or ask a builder to make an estimate for you.

As building costs rise, the amount of insurance you maintain should rise, too. Otherwise, the policy will fall below 80 percent of the replacement cost.

When premium costs rise, homeowners may be tempted to save money by taking a larger deductible. A $100 deductible (for each claim, on each building) saves around 10 percent of the premium; a $500 deductible saves 25 percent. With this arrangement, you pay more of the smaller losses yourself but are still covered in case of major damage. Think twice before taking this approach. If you're paying, say, $80 a year for $25,000 worth of homeowner's insurance with a $100 deductible, you can save $25 a year by raising the deductible to $500. But one expensive accident can wipe out the premium savings of sixteen years.

Some insurance policies offer an "inflation guard," which automatically increases your coverage by 1 percent or more every three months. It increases your premium slightly but saves you the trouble of having to remember to revalue your home. The trouble with such guards is that they may not properly reflect the rate at which building costs are rising in your area—which may be faster or slower than the inflation guard allows for. Better than relying on predetermined percentages, you'd be well advised to have the replacement cost checked every year or two.

Types of Policies

You can get separate coverage for fire, wind and miscellaneous hazards, theft, and personal liability (in case someone injures himself on your property). Or you can get a "homeowner's" policy that packages them all together. Homeowner's insurance comes in three types, each progressively more expensive:

• *Basic form* protects your home against fire or lightning, windstorm or hail, explosions, riots, aircraft, vehicles, smoke, vandalism, theft, and broken glass.

• *Broad form* covers all of the above, plus damage from falling objects, weight of snow or ice, building collapse, broken steam or hot water heating systems, heaters, plumbing, frozen pipes, heating or air-conditioning systems or appliances, and injury from faulty electrical wiring. But it won't protect against damage to pavements, fences, patios, or damage to pools from freezing, thawing, or water. And note that although it covers damage from broken steam pipes and so on, it doesn't cover replacing the pipes themselves. Broad form is the most widely sold homeowner's policy.

• *Comprehensive form* includes all conceivable perils, except flood, earthquake, war, nuclear attack, and anything specifically excluded in your policy (be sure to check it).

What's Covered

Any of the policies just mentioned will cover your house (one- or two-family houses, but generally not farmhouses; farmers get a farmowner's policy); your garage; other structures on your property, such as a tool shed or guesthouse—but not any building that you lease to others (except for the garaging of a car) and not any buildings that you use entirely for business.

Each company's policy has different wrinkles, so read yours closely to see what's in it and what's excluded. Some typical provisions: ☐Garages, tool sheds, and other outbuildings are covered up to a limit of 10 percent of the policy's face value; if they're more valuable, you'll have to increase this segment of the coverage. ☐If you leave your home empty for thirty consecutive days before the loss, your protection against vandalism and broken glass may not apply. ☐Damages resulting from the freezing of pipes, heating systems, and air-conditioning systems, occurring while you're away, may not be covered unless you exercised "due diligence" in maintaining the heat or draining the pipes. ☐If you run a business from your home and a disaster causes your business income to stop for a while, the policy won't cover that loss. ☐Renting to someone for an extended period may lead the company to refuse to renew your insurance. ☐If you have to live in a motel and eat in restaurants while your damaged house is being repaired, the insurance will cover those expenses that exceed normal living expenses, up to the limits of your policy. ☐Some policies pay up to 5 percent of coverage for debris removal. ☐Plants and trees are typically covered only to a limit of $250 or $500, and not at all if they were run over by anyone who lives in your house. ☐There's usually no coverage for TV antennas, gutters, fences, or awnings unless your house collapses.

Rates on the fire insurance segment of your policy vary depending on the amount of fireproof materials in your house and the efficiency rating of your local fire department. You may be able to lower your rates by installing sprinklers, alarm systems, or fire extinguishers.

Your insurance costs less if you pay annually rather than quarterly. Some companies offer a discount to people who can prepay three years worth of premiums.

Policies typically exclude water damage, whether by sewer backups, rain, ground water, or flood. But rain damage may be covered if the house was first damaged by wind or hail, which allowed the rain to get in. You're also covered for damage from firemen's hoses. If you need flood insurance, your insurance agent can get it through the government (as long as your community has met the conditions for coverage). You can get earthquake insurance as a rider to your regular policy.

When you have a loss, notify the company immediately. Board up the windows if they're broken or burned out, to protect your property from further damage, sort the damaged goods from the undamaged, and give the company a list of the losses. You'll need proof of loss—a copy of the report you made to the police in case of theft or vandalism; snapshots of damage; perhaps a visit by the company's representative to check the extent of fire loss. A household inventory made before the fire will help stake your claim. If you think the company's appraisal of your property's current value is too low, your policy generally provides for arbitration.

If you live in a high-risk urban area and can't get insurance through a private company, you're eligible for coverage under the federally backed Fair Access to Insurance Requirements (FAIR) plan. An inspector will visit your house or apartment to see if it meets minimal safety standards and is structurally sound. If so, you'll get coverage from an insurance pool; if not, you may still be able to get insurance while you're having the property repaired. People with incomes under $3,000 qualify for federal grants to pay for repairs; others can get low-interest loans. Apply for FAIR plan coverage through your insurance agent. If it's not available in your state, write to the Federal Insurance Administration, U.S. Department of Housing and Urban Development, Washington, D.C. 20410.

Personal Property

Whether your policy is basic, broad, or comprehensive, it includes the same amount of personal property coverage. Typically, your belongings (on premises) are insured for 50 percent of the coverage carried on your house. For example, if your house is insured for $30,000, your personal property coverage will be $15,000. But when your belongings are damaged, you don't normally get the full replacement cost. Instead, the company takes the current retail cost (not what you paid for the item) and reduces it according to how old the item is. For full reimbursement you'd have to buy a "replacement value" rider, not available from all companies. If 50 percent of the house's value isn't enough to cover the depreciated value of your personal property, you can increase this segment of the policy. If you have a tenant's policy, you simply buy whatever amount of personal property insurance is appropriate.

When you take personal property away from your home, it's typically covered for up to 10 percent of your total policy amount on basic and broad form coverage; comprehensive form (and some basic and broad policies) continues the 50 percent coverage. (A few policies cover you 100 percent anywhere in the world.) The property of a houseguest or resident employee (such as a housekeeper) is covered only up to 10 percent, even though on premises.

The theft insurance section has some special wrinkles, depending on company: ☐With basic form you're usually not covered for "mysterious disappearance," when something is missing but you can't prove theft. However, this should be covered under broad or comprehensive form. ☐Policies generally don't insure against losses due to the theft of a check or credit card. If you want this kind of protection, you'll probably have to pay extra. ☐You're covered for property taken from a safe deposit box or storage warehouse. ☐Theft of materials being used to build an addition to your house is not covered. ☐Basic and broad form policies won't pay for a precious stone lost from its setting unless you can prove theft. ☐And they don't generally cover theft from an unattended automobile, boat, or trailer unless you can prove forcible entry.

Many items of personal property aren't covered, or are covered only up to certain limits. Motorbikes, golf carts, pets, aircraft, paintings, sculpture, and business samples are excluded; maximum reimbursement for lost cash, coin collections, and bullion is a meager $100; securities, deeds, stamp collections, jewelry, watches, furs, and gems are insured only to $500 in the aggregate; manuscripts are covered to $1,000, boats to $500 each; some policies put a $1,000 limit on silverware and guns. However, you can boost coverage on any of these items by buying a personal property *floater* in the amount you need. Floaters usually insure against all risks, not just those listed in your homeowner's policy.

More clauses to watch for: ☐You need a specific endorsement for incidental business equipment needed to run a business at home. ☐If you move, personal property is covered for thirty days at the new location. ☐Property lost or damaged while someone else rents your house is not covered. ☐"Consequential losses"—say, a power line blows down on the next block and causes the food in your freezer to spoil—are excluded; but it would be covered if the line blew down on your property. □Property lost in the mail is not insured. □Losses due to a "friendly fire" (one confined to where it's supposed to be) are not covered. For example, if you dropped your watch into the fireplace, you'd be out of luck.

Make an inventory of all your household furnishings, how old they are, and if possible how much you paid for them. You can't imagine how difficult it can be to convince a doubtful claims adjuster that although you live in a modest house, your furniture was worth a fortune. Have any items of special value appraised. Keep the inventory, appraisals, and snapshots of each room in a fire-resistant strongbox or safe deposit box. When you make a significant new purchase, add the sales slip to the file as proof of value. Tell your agent about particularly valuable items or collections; you may need separate policies to cover them.

If you live in a high-crime area, insurance against burglary will probably not be available except through the state or federal government. Your insurance agent will help you apply. Rates and coverage are about comparable with private insurance, but claims won't be paid unless your doors and windows are protected with specified locks. Maximum federal crime insurance coverage is $10,000 on residential property and $15,000 on commercial property, including up to $500 for losses from a locked car trunk, $100 for stolen cash, and $500 for securities. There's no claim limit on jewelry or furs. However, you're subject to a deductible of $50 or 5 percent of the loss, whichever is greater. Crime insurance doesn't pay for items that are inexplicably missing or where theft is only surmised. There must either be proof of forcible entry into your house or apartment, or you must observe the theft.

Liability

This segment of your homeowner's or tenant's policy protects you in case you're sued for property damage (say, a tree in your front yard topples on a neighbor's car) or personal injury (when a visitor breaks an ankle on your front walk, or your daughter beans your neighbor's daughter with a rock). The minimum amount of liability protection is $25,000, but the policy can be written up to whatever level of coverage you need—the amount depending on the value of the assets you have to protect. A wealthy family has more assets that could be seized to pay a judgment than a family of modest means, and so should carry more insurance.

Only unintentional injuries are covered, unless the person who did the damage was under thirteen. State law sometimes holds parents partly responsible for the malicious acts of their older children, in which case insurance will usually have to pay. But unless the injury was caused by a weapon that the child received from the parent, there's a dollar limit on damages—generally in the area of $500 to $2,000.

Liability insurance covers actions by your family and pets, whether on your property or away from home; people under twenty-one who live in your house (older relatives can be covered with a policy rider); the actions of domestic employees while working for you; and the actions of people using your property for nonbusiness purposes. A new trend is for the insurance to cover injuries done by one family member to another. For example, if your child used a rotary mower to pull his brother on a cart, lost control, and cut off the brother's foot, the insurance company might have to pay the damages. Some companies, however, specifically exclude these situations.

The insurer will handle all negotiations for an out-of-court settlement; defend you in court; pay for any bail bonds or interest on judgments you want to contest; and may even reimburse you for any income you lose by leaving work to come to court. But it will pay claims for bodily injury or property damage only up to the limits of your policy —higher amounts come out of your own pocket. If the company refuses to settle a large claim against you for the upper limit of the policy, and the court awards higher damages, you may be able to sue the company for dealing with the claim in bad faith (check with a lawyer about this).

Some points to watch for: ☐Most business activities are excluded from coverage. However, you can get a rider for visitors to a studio or office in your home. ☐You need a rider to cover boats larger than a specified size when off premises. ☐Vehicles licensed to operate on public highways, racing cars, and aircraft aren't included. ☐Any additional property you acquire is covered under the policy, but at renewal the premium may go up. ☐You're covered if liable for the actions of a building contractor and his workers while working on your property. ☐Unattached campers, boats, and trailers are covered, as are unlicensed vehicles such as dune buggies and lawnmowers while on premises.

Bites and other damage done by your dog are fully covered. But if the dog bites more than once, the insurer may cancel your policy. Some companies won't cover German shepherds and Doberman pinschers at all, but don't accept a policy that excludes them. Shop for an insurer that protects you fully. In some states a second bite may be cause for "punitive damages," which is an extra sum you have to pay the injured person as punishment for not keeping a dangerous dog restrained. Depending on state law, the insurer may not have to pay punitive damages, which could cost you a pretty penny. If your dog has bitten someone once already, ask your lawyer and the insurance company exactly what your liability might be if it happens again.

For a little extra you can get medical payments coverage, to pay for the minor doctor and hospital bills of people accidentally injured on your property, or injured by your family or pets away from the property. The basic protection is $500 per person, but it can be increased. It's paid regardless of who's at fault, but only to nonrelated people who are not residents of your home. It covers accidents caused by an employee while working for you and injuries to an employee even though you're required to carry workmen's compensation but didn't. If you have employees, ask your insurance agent what the requirements are in your state for workmen's compensation.

You can also get supplementary coverage for minor physical damage to someone else's property. The basic amount is $250, and this sum can't be increased. Like medical payments insurance, it doesn't depend on proof of legal liability. Rather, it's for situations where you feel morally obligated to pay, whether the other party sues you or not.

If you're well-to-do, you might consider an *umbrella policy*, to insure all liability losses above the limits of your regular insurance policies. These policies generally don't cost very much, and are written for amounts in the area of $1 million.

Chapter Seventeen

SELLING YOUR HOUSE

His name was George F. Babbitt. He was forty-six years old now in April, 1920, and he made nothing in particular, neither butter nor shoes nor poetry, but he was nimble in the calling of selling houses for more than people could afford to pay.

SINCLAIR LEWIS

Most people use real estate brokers, and with good reason: □The broker knows what the house is worth on the current market. □He'll advertise it. □He has a constant flow of customers to whom he shows it. □He can separate the "lookers" from the serious buyers. □If a buyer is found, he can help with the financing, without which the deal might be lost. □For all these services he charges 6 to 7 percent of the selling price (although some brokers are willing to shave their commission, if asked).

The agent you choose will want an *exclusive-right-to-sell contract*, probably lasting a minimum of ninety days. That means that even if you find a buyer yourself, you'll owe the broker his commission. (However, if you know when you call the broker that your neighbor or brother is seriously interested in the house, you can usually have that particular buyer excluded from the right-to-sell agreement.)

Alternatively, you can give him an *exclusive listing*, which means that although you won't sell the house through another broker, you reserve the right to sell it yourself and save the commission. Brokers may put less effort into an exclusive listing—less advertising money and less time—because they suspect that you're hustling to beat them to a buyer. There's another potential disadvantage to this arrangement: Many areas have *multiple-listing services*, which disseminate information on local properties to all subscribing brokers; if your broker can't sell the house right away, perhaps another one, who spots it in the listing service, can. (In that case, the second broker would get a percentage of the commission.) But if he doesn't have an exclusive right to sell, the broker usually won't list your property with the service.

A house can be listed with several brokers at once (although many won't accept this arrangement). Generally speaking, this gets you less attention rather than more because brokers put their best efforts into exclusive listings.

If the house doesn't sell, people tend to blame the broker, but maybe it's something you're doing wrong. You might have insisted on a higher price than the broker thought reasonable, given the current state of the housing market. Or the house might be so untidy that it turns buyers off. By all means ask the broker what the problem is. However, if you find that you don't like the broker or mistrust his efforts, by all means give the house to another agency to sell.

Pricing the House

An active broker will know within a very narrow margin just what price your house will bring. He's dealing in houses constantly, knows what people want, and has a file of what else is on the market at the same time. Follow his recommendation on price. If you try to price it much higher, you could get lucky and find a buyer, but more likely the house will just sit on the market. The longer it doesn't sell, the more likely it is to acquire a reputation as a house that has something wrong with it.

When you first call a broker and say you want to sell, he should come to your house, look it over carefully, and go away without committing himself on price. He'll then compare it with other properties he has and get back to you in a day or two. When he recommends a price, he should be prepared to back it up with evidence as to what other houses similar to yours have recently sold for.

You might want to ask two or three brokers to look the place over, to see if they agree. The temptation is to go with the one who gives you the highest estimate. But before accepting it, take a hard look at the evidence he has to back up his price. If he "high-balls" you just to get the listing, you'll sell for less in the end *and* find yourself stuck with an unethical broker. Look at the supporting data offered by all the brokers, and then use your common sense.

Don't be tempted away from a sensible price because of the gossip of friends. Someone may tell you that you're "giving the house away," but how does he know? Someone else may say that a friend down the street got $10,000 more—but that friend may only have been *asking* $10,000 more and may actually have settled for much less. In pricing your house, follow fact, not rumor.

After the broker has estimated what the house is likely to bring, he'll suggest that you set the price 5 to 10 percent higher. That gives you negotiating room. But be sure the broker knows exactly where your bottom line is, so he won't encourage a buyer to think he can get it for any less. Turn down offers below your line and wait for something reasonable.

Tips on Getting Your House Sold

1. Look for a broker you like and can trust. If you don't have a friend in the business, ask other people in town whom they've used. You're going to have to rely on the broker's word for a lot of things, so it's important to start out with confidence in him.

2. When the broker comes to look at your house, he may suggest certain repairs that would make a difference to salability. If they don't cost too much, do them. Even a fresh coat of paint on the front door can help a lot. When you figure your taxes, add the fix-up costs to your base cost for the house, thus reducing your capital gain (see page 334).

3. Clean the house and keep it clean. Get rid of the heap of smelly rags in the basement, straighten the closets, wash the walls, rake the yard, trim the hedges, polish the brass on the front door. Be sure the beds are always made and the grease scrubbed out of the kitchen sink. Potential buyers are guided as much by their feeling for the house as by the layout itself, and if it's dirty, their feelings will be negative. Anything positive you can do, such as plumping the pillows and putting out flowers, will help. Turn the lights on and the TV off.

4. Put pets out of the house when people come to look. You may know the dog is harmless, but if he growls at a child, the buyers may leave fast. Also keep your children out of the way during the house tour.

5. Don't follow the real estate broker around. Buyers may be afraid to ask negative-sounding questions if the owner is right there. Furthermore, your "salesmanship" may hurt rather than help. You may be outraged because the broker doesn't point out the glories of your automated kitchen, but the broker may know that the client hates to cook and is trying to get her out of the kitchen as fast as possible. Similarly, you may be enormously proud of your large living room, but if the customer likes small rooms, the broker will concentrate on other desirable features while dropping a suggestion as to how the living room might be divided in two. Assume that only the broker knows how to sell to this particular customer.

6. If you cannot resist trying to sell the house yourself, be sure your advertisement contains the same price the broker is offering. If you publicly undercut him, he'll lose all interest in your property.

7. An unusual house may have to be on the market a month or so before it can be properly priced. The broker has to get feedback from the public as to what's wrong with it and how its drawbacks can be corrected.

8. If your house is an antique, it's smart to get it inspected at your own expense. The broker then has the inspection report to show to prospective buyers who may be worrying about repairs.

9. Be ready to show the house at all reasonable hours, and be willing to let the broker go in without you. If your presence is necessary and you're not always at home, you could miss the very person who would make an offer.

Selling Your House Without a Broker

This isn't for everyone. It takes time, research, and good salesmanship. You have to be constantly on tap to answer the phone and show people through the house (including all those who are "just looking"). There are advertising expenses, and you'll have to be ready to help the buyer find a mortgage. But if you can make the sale, you'll have saved yourself the 6-to-7-percent commission. On a $50,000 house, that's a saving of $3,000 to $3,500. Here's how to do it:*

What Price?

Too low a price gives you a fast sale but loses you money you ought to have. Too high a price means no takers. The most common error owners make is to overprice their houses based on gossip about asking prices in the neighborhood, without checking the true selling prices. To find the right price, hire a professional appraiser experienced in residential real estate. You'll find appraisers listed in the Yellow Pages, or ask the mortgage department of your bank or savings and loan association for a recommendation. The fee is not high. Just be sure to get one whose business is mainly in homes rather than commercial properties, and

*For a fuller discussion, look up *For Sale By Owner,* by Louis Gilmore, or *How to Sell (and Buy) Your Home Without a Broker,* by Kenneth S. Gaines.

who is completely familiar with your neighborhood. How to find this out? Ask him.

In a booming real estate market, actual selling prices may be rising faster than appraisers realize. So double-check their work by scouting for-sale houses similar to yours to find the asking price. If someone recently moved into such a house in the neighborhood, perhaps he'll tell you what he paid. Another approach is to call a real estate broker, tell him you plan to try to sell the house yourself, but if you can't, you'll list it with him. Then ask if he'll visit your house and advise you on the price. Some brokers won't bother; others will. Try to get two or three estimates: an unethical broker might advise too high a price (in hopes you'll eventually feel forced to list with him).

Assuming the appraiser gives you a fair market value, you may want to set your asking price 5 to 10 percent higher, to give yourself some negotiating room. Ask the appraiser's advice on this. If you push the price too high, you'll simply drive away buyers.

You'll also want to decide on your minimum price—the line below which you won't negotiate. Typically, this is dictated by the amount of cash you need to make a down payment on your next house. You hope that the proceeds of the sale will be enough to buy the new house, pay the closing costs, and get you moved. If you're going to need $15,000, the minimum price must be at least $15,000 above what you owe on the mortgage plus selling expenses. With luck, you'll realize a considerable profit beyond that minimum.

But remember: It isn't graven on stone that you'll make the profit you want. The price you actually get for the house and how fast it sells depend on such things as economic conditions at the time of sale, what has happened to your neighborhood since you moved in, how well you've kept the house up, whether mortgage money is readily available, and whether your town is growing or declining.

How to Advertise

Call the newspapers you think are most likely to attract your kind of buyer and get their rates for classified ads. You'll want to advertise on days that carry the bulk of the real estate ads—typically, Sundays. An ad with a headline as well as a description will cost more, but it's money well spent to draw attention to your offer. Advertising expenses may run you several hundred dollars before you're through, but remember that you're saving two or three thousand on the real estate commission.

At the top of your ad should be the words "BY OWNER," in big type. That indicates to buyers that since there's no brokerage commission, the price might be a little lower. Below that should be a few big-type words that sum up your house: "Elegant renovated brownstone." "Rambling farmhouse, beautiful views." "Split level, near good schools." "Fine contemporary design." "New colonial, good for children." "Lots of property, good value." Don't exaggerate, but make it sound good.

The next five or six lines should generally describe your house, always including its architectural style and its most attractive features. Don't use a lot of abbreviations; they make the ad hard to read and people often don't understand them. Among the features that might be listed: the amount of land, the attractiveness of the views, the neighborhood, the number of bedrooms and bathrooms, the fireplace, a home office or study, game room, two-car garage, swimming pool, modernized kitchen, large screened porch, the amount of privacy, and whether there's air conditioning. Everything doesn't have to be included—just enough to indicate the house's size and most interesting aspects. For example, mention "two wooded acres," but not a quarter-acre building lot; list "large family room with fireplace," but skip an ordinary living room and dining area which everyone knows the house is bound to have. Use one or two encouraging adjectives, such as "antique," "homey," "spacious," "secluded," "charming," "convenient." Close with the address, the price, and a call for action: "Call us at 223-4567." "Call 223-4567, or visit us Sundays, from 2 to 5 P.M." "Call us now, at 223-4567, for an appointment to see the house."

To get started, look at all the other real estate ads in the paper to see which ones sound like your house and which appeal to you. Use them as models in writing your own ad. Just be sure to include any special features that are yours alone—such as a stream on the property, a view of the woods, a cathedral ceiling, built-in bureaus, an apartment over the garage, beautiful gardens, anything that you think gives your house special appeal.

The newspaper, of course, isn't the only place to advertise. You should have a printed "listing sheet" (see the following section), which can be tacked on community message boards. If your company has an employee newsletter, there's usually a spot for classified ads. You can announce your home's availability (and distribute listing sheets) at any group you belong to—a church group, club, PTA, at the office. Perhaps a local university or employer has a housing office that helps people moving into town; your listing sheet should certainly be there. The objective is to tell as many people as possible that your house is on the market.

Lastly, you need a sign for your front yard—big enough to be seen clearly by passing cars, bright letters on a white background, printed on both sides, and put it at right angles to your house so it can be easily read from either direction. At the top it should say "For Sale by Owner." Below that in letters large enough to be seen from the street: "For Appointment, Call 223-4567." A sign from a professional sign maker doesn't cost a lot and will look more inviting than a homemade sign.

The Listing Sheet

You need a single printed sheet of paper to hand out to prospects that tells them everything they need to know. It should include a good photograph of the house, to help the buyer remember exactly which of the many houses he has seen was yours. Next, put your name, address, phone number, and a capsule description that emphasizes the home's most desirable qualities. List the number of rooms, number of bedrooms, number of baths, and the house's price. Below that give the following information:

The architectural style
Age
Type of construction (brick, frame, etc.)
Size of lot
Square feet of living space
Size of each room
Special features, such as porch, swimming pool, outdoor barbecue, darkroom
Number of fireplaces
Rugs and drapes, if they come with the house
Basement features

Attic features
Size of garage
Type of heating
Air conditioning
Source of water supply
Method of sewage disposal
Brand and age of kitchen and laundry appliances
Special closets
Amount of real estate taxes
Which schools the children would use
Nearby transportation
Nearby shopping centers

Type up all the information and take it—with a good black-and-white photograph of the house—to a printer. Ask him to put the picture at the top and list the rest of the information in double columns. Or type it perfectly yourself, attach the picture at the top (with the white edges trimmed off), and take it to a place that will make copies.

The Cost Sheet

You'll need some additional data for serious prospects—the cost of heat, water, electricity, oil or gas, garbage removal, sewerage, insurance, and any other operating costs. Also, get an estimate of what the monthly principal and interest payments will be on a mortgage suitable to the asking price (ask your bank or savings and loan association).

The objective is to be able to tell the prospective buyer exactly what he'll have to pay a month for your house—including principal, interest, taxes, insurance, electricity, heat, water, and other charges. List principal, interest, and taxes together; that's usually the monthly sum he'll pay to the bank (although banks may include insurance payments, too). Add up what you spend annually on the other items and divide by twelve for an average monthly cost. Or make a list of exactly what you paid for each item, month by month, over the past year. These costs should be shown on a separate sheet for people seriously interested in buying the house.

How to Sell

First impressions mean a lot. When people visit the house, they should walk up a swept walk, past trimmed grass and sheared shrubbery, to a front door with clean windows and without fingerprints or mud stains, ring a doorbell that works, and get a prompt, cheery hello. The buyer's first look, at the house and at you, can be crucial.

Even before he looks at the house, he'll have called on the telephone in answer to your ad. Be cheerful, enthusiastic, welcoming. Tell him your name and ask for his—and when you've got it, use it. You might say, "Let me tell you something about the house," and launch into a prepared little speech about what the house is like, its chief features, how nice the neighborhood is, how convenient. If the prospect has any questions, answer them cheerfully—and always in a positive way. For example, if he asks about a screened-in porch and you haven't got one, you might reply, "There's no screened porch, but we have a large patio with built-in barbecue in the back, and it would be easy to screen that if you'd like." Or, "At the moment we have no porch, but there's a perfect spot for one right off the family room under the shade of a large oak." Invite him to make an appointment to see the house—this is the critical thing. You want him to come and look, not just talk. If he doesn't want to make an appointment, ask for his address so you can send him a listing sheet. The picture of your house might be enough to interest him.

When he arrives at the house, the place should look as warm and homey as you can make it—flowers on the table, pillows plumped up. Put pets outdoors (and children, too, if you can) so you can concentrate on selling in a serious and adult atmosphere. Dress nicely. Turn off the television. Open some windows so there will be a fresh-air smell in the house.

Preplan the house tour so as to cover all its rooms in a logical way, ending up in a comfortable, attractive spot where you can sit down for further conversation. Don't try to hide any of the house's bad features, but don't harp on them either. If the dining area is small, just say, "And here is where we have our family meals." Should the prospect mention that there's no room at the table for guests, you might reply, "When we entertain—and we do a lot—we have a buffet meal. As you can see, keeping down the size of the dining area gives us a much larger living room."

Don't deny the bad features, and never argue with prospects about them. Just try to come up with a positive answer to their objections. If there's no positive answer possible, smile and move on to the next room. One thing to remember is that the prospect who goes through the house complimenting everything, is probably not really interested. The person who raises questions may be seriously considering the house, which is the reason he brings up any difficulties he notices. You'll advance the sale if you can help him resolve those difficulties. During the tour ask about the size of the family and what they like to do. You can then point out why the house will suit their activities.

When the tour is over, say, "Won't you sit down? Perhaps I can answer some of your questions about the neighborhood." If the answer is no, don't push. The prospect has seen enough. It's a waste of your time as well as his to talk further. If he does sit, take the opportunity to describe the area and where the churches, recreation areas, shops, and bus lines are. If the family has children, they'll want to know as much about the schools as you can tell them.

Prospects will want to know why you're moving (is there something about the house that you're not telling?). Never give an answer that knocks the house you're trying to sell. The best response is, "We just love it here, but I've been transferred to another job." If that's not true, you might say, "We need a larger house now that we have three children." If the prospect also has three children, try, "We had an opportunity to buy a house with a swimming pool, which we've always wanted." Sellers who don't like their house and are moving to buy a nicer one might lose the sale if they let it show. Instead, say something like, "This was a good first house for us [if it's also the prospect's first house], but now we need something larger." Or, "This is a nice neighborhood. I'm sorry that our need for a larger house forces us to leave it." Never say you're buying a "better" house, just a "larger" one. Your objective is to make the prospect feel happy, secure, and satisfied with himself. For *him* to be proud of buying the house, *you* must be proud of it, too. For *him* to imagine himself living there happily, it must be clear that *you* lived there happily before him.

But there's a limit to being positive and cheerful. Cross it, and you're suddenly lying and pushy. Don't ever misrepresent anything and don't talk too much. The good features of the house will sell themselves if they meet the buyer's needs. You can't force a house on him that's not right for the way he lives. It will help if you listen carefully to what he says he's looking for, and point out how admirably your house suits those desires. But if he disagrees, it won't help to argue.

Do not expect the buyer to look at your house, fall in love with it, and sign the papers right there. Houses are a big expense and even an interested prospect will want to leave, talk it over with his family, visit again, and perhaps leave again before deciding to buy. Be courteous and helpful but don't show impatience. You can indicate gently that it's time they made up their minds ("Have you any other questions I can help you with?") or remind them that others are looking ("Four o'clock isn't available for a visit because I'm showing another family through for the second time. Could you come at five thirty?"). But if you push, you might scare them off.

It may take weeks or months to sell your house. You may get several nibbles without ever closing a sale. Some sellers will get discouraged and turn to real estate agents (agents may, in fact, solicit your business from time to time). But there's no guarantee that they can sell your house any faster, or for a higher price, than you can yourself.

The Extras

Some of the things in the house, such as the awnings and wall-to-wall rugs, may be included in the price. Others, such as the drapes and curtain rods, you may be willing to sell at a low price. When you show a prospect around, tell him exactly what's included and what additional items can be bought if he'd like them.

The Closing Price

Once someone decides he'd like to buy, the issue narrows down to price. Assume, for the moment, that you got an appraisal on your house of $65,000, and put it on the market for $68,000. That's your "asking price," but never refer to it as such. As far as the prospect is concerned, that price is firm. He knows, of course, that houses rarely sell at their first price and may ask, "What are you willing to take?" At that point, your best reply is, "We haven't seriously thought of a lower price. But if you'd like to make an offer, please do so, and we'll consider it."

If his offer is well below what you're willing to accept—for example, $60,000—tell him you're sorry, but you couldn't possibly let the house go for so little. If he doesn't come up to a more reasonable figure, show him the door. There's no sense talking further with someone who's trying to steal the place. But let's assume that the offer is in the ballpark —for example, $64,000. Tell him you need a day to think it over but that you'd first like his offer in writing. Also say that you'd like a "good-faith" deposit—say $200 or $300—which you'll return if you can't come to terms. Hand him a letter you've prewritten (with blanks where the amount of the deposit is to be filled in), guaranteeing that the check will either be applied to the down payment or sent back. The letter should be prepared by a lawyer (see the following section).

The next day call him with a counteroffer. Say that $64,000 is too low, in view of the value of the house and the money you've put into it, but you are willing to accept $67,000. He may make another offer—perhaps $65,000. Once you're this close, you can probably come to terms. Point out to him that the price started out lower than normal because you didn't have to include a broker's commission. Tell him that $66,000 is absolutely as low as you can go, and that's a firm price. If he wants the house and wasn't looking outside his price range in the first place, he'll probably pay it. But don't be stubborn about retreating another $500 if that's what it takes to do the deal.

Using a Lawyer

Before you start showing your house, visit a lawyer experienced in local real estate closings. Tell him you're selling the house yourself and will need his help in drawing contracts and letters of agreement. (In many cases this isn't an extra expense; you'd need him even if you sold through a real estate broker.) The lawyer will word a letter for people who make a deposit, and prepare a contract when agreement is reached. If you're unsure about your ability to negotiate, he may also be able to help you with that.

Once you've agreed on a price, the lawyer will want the buyer to put down 5 to 10 percent of the price as "earnest money." If he can't get a mortgage, the money will be returned, but you want that cash down to encourage the buyer not to back out of the purchase. Don't make agreements with the buyer about such details as date of purchase without consulting your lawyer. Don't misrepresent anything in the house; it might cause the deal to fall through or leave you liable for repairs. If the buyer wants anything special—for example, making the sale subject to his selling his own house—the lawyer will handle it. It's a temptation to make promises on the spot in order to get the house sold, but you could live to regret them. In the conversation you have with the lawyer before putting your house on the market he'll tell you the danger spots to stay away from.

The Financing

To get your house sold you may have to help the prospective buyer arrange financing. This means sending him to a bank or savings and loan association where he can get a mortgage large enough to buy your house. If he doesn't have a big enough income to get the mortgage needed, you've wasted your time. So at some time during your first discussions, tell him how large a mortgage is generally obtainable, how much down payment will be required, and what the monthly payments will be. Also tell him what minimum income is generally needed to get the loan. Once you've laid out the facts, ask him directly if he can afford to buy. If he hesitates, write him off; or ask him to make a preliminary, qualifying visit to a lender before you draw up the contract.

You get information on financing from neighborhood banks or savings and loan associations. Before you even offer the house for sale, visit two or three lenders to find out their terms (some could be quite a bit different from others). Ask to see a mortgage loan officer, tell him what you're doing, and show him the appraisal on your house. Based on that, he'll be able to tell you about how much money he'd lend a qualified buyer, on what terms, and what the monthly payment would be. Also ask him what terms are available on FHA and VA mortgages (see page 236), and whether the lender offers privately insured loans to buyers with an insufficient down payment (see page 257). The lender should tell you, too, what minimum income is required for the mortgage (although if the borrower turns out to have a lot of debts, a larger income will be required).

Your lawyer can be a help in finding loan sources. Assuming that he handles a lot of local real estate closings (which is the type of lawyer to have), he can tell you which lenders have the best terms, where to get FHA or VA mortgages, and which banks and S&Ls have the lowest closing costs.

Once you've lined up two or three lenders willing to give a mortgage to a qualified buyer, you're ready to offer the house for sale. When you send a potential buyer to a bank, call the mortgage loan officer first, so he'll be expected.

In tight money times it may be difficult to scare up mortgages. In that case it would be better to work with a broker, who is more likely than you to have contacts at the banks and S&Ls. You might also have to give a second mortgage on the house for part of the down payment (see pages 236–237). If that isn't possible, you may not be able to move until money loosens up.

The Real Estate Broker

Early in the game you may be visited by a broker who says he has a buyer for your house. What to do? If he really has one, it will save you time and trouble. But he may simply be trying to get you to sign a listing contract, whereupon he'll proceed normally to show the place to clients. Don't sign the listing contract if it's still your intention to sell your house yourself (if you sign, then make your own sale, you'd still owe the broker a commission). If you wouldn't mind a fast sale, tell the broker you'll give him a contract and pay a commission for the single, named buyer he says he has. Generally that will end it, since he may not have a buyer at all.

Giving a Second Mortgage

If the buyer doesn't have a large enough down payment and you're in a hurry to sell, you might let him make the down payment in installments. Set up the deal as a second mortgage, perhaps payable over two to five years (as you mutually agree) at an interest rate higher than the current mortgage rate. Ask a lawyer to draw the agreement, so you'll be protected in case of default. If the buyer's problem, however, is that the bank won't give him a mortgage of standard size, a second mortgage is unwise; the bank probably thinks that this particular buyer can't afford the payments.

Giving a First Mortgage

In certain circumstances, you might want to give the mortgage yourself. The buyer gives you a down payment, then makes monthly payments to you rather than to a bank or S&L. This can be a good investment for a retired person who is selling his house and moving into an apartment and wants income from his capital. The interest he earns on the mortgage (perhaps 8 to 10 percent) may be higher than what's available in alternate investments.

If properly done, this arrangement can also be a tax shelter, and here's why: When you sell your principal home, receive all the proceeds at once, and don't buy a new house for the same price or greater, you owe a capital gains tax on the profits. But if you take no more than 30 percent of the price as a first installment, your capital gain is stretched out over the life of the mortgage, with only a small tax due every year.

Be sure to work out the mortgage contract with a real estate lawyer to get the tax angles straightened out and to protect yourself against default. Ask the purchaser for a financial statement, and consider carefully whether he can afford the payments.

Should You Let a Buyer Assume Your Mortgage?

With an assumption, the seller takes over what remains of your mortgage rather than getting his own. This saves him closing costs, and can help sell your house in tight-money times. But be warned: If he takes over your loan and defaults, the bank can come after you for payments. To avoid this, have the bank specifically release you from liability for the loan at the time the mortgage is assumed.

Tax Consequences of Selling

When you sell a house for more than you paid for it, you have a capital gain. That gain must be reported currently on your income tax returns. You can, however, put off paying the capital gains tax if the house is your principal residence and you buy another principal residence within eighteen months. Tax deferral is also available if you build a new principal residence within two years. The requirement for tax deferral is that the new residence cost the same or more than the house you sold. Under these circumstances you can sell and buy several houses, reporting the gain each time but continuing to defer the capital gains tax. If, at a later age, you buy a less expensive house, part (or all) of the deferred tax will fall due; if you move into a rental apartment, it will all fall due. (Note that there is no tax-deferral on vacation homes or houses you rent out as business properties; the capital gains tax is due in the year of sale.)

There are two ways to reduce the capital gains tax:

1. Your gain is the difference between what the house cost and what you sold it for, but "cost" doesn't mean only the purchase price. Your true cost includes the following expenses: ☐*Expenses incurred in buying the house.* This includes such things as survey, appraisal, title insurance, lawyer's fees, and closing costs (except for "points" charged on the mortgage, which are deductible in the year they occur). ☐*Expenses incurred in improving the house.* This includes such things as putting on a new roof, adding a room, landscaping, modernizing a kitchen, replacing a furnace, adding air conditioning—anything, in fact, that could be considered a permanent improvement that prolongs the life of the property or increases its value. Keep a file of receipts for all these expenses. Over a lifetime of making property improvements, these costs mount up to enormous sums. *Note:* In most cases, the cost of simple repairs and maintenance are not considered improvements. You can't include such things as patching a hole in the roof, painting a room, or fixing a broken window. □*Expenses incurred in freshening up the house for sale.* Any repairs and maintenance made in the 90 days before the house is sold are considered improvements and treated as part of the cost of your house, as described above. □*Expenses incurred in selling the house.* The main thing here is the brokerage commission, but it also includes the lawyer's fees and any other costs of sale.

Records of these expenses should be kept in a permanent file. When you sell your house, just add these costs to the price you paid and subtract the total from the selling price. The difference is your actual capital gain. Keep the records with the copy of your tax return, in case you're audited. If you have no records of all these costs, you (or your heirs) may be forced to pay a far higher capital gains tax than is actually owed.

2. If you sell a house when you're fifty-five or older, you get a special one-time tax break. There is no capital gains tax at all on the first $100,000 of profit. You can claim this tax exclusion only once—so don't use it to shelter a small gain if you think you may have an even larger gain in the future.

Note: Although you owe a capital gains tax on profits made from your houses, you can't deduct any losses unless the house qualifies as a business property. A vacation home that you rent out may be a business property; you may also be able to convert a principal residence to a business property by renting it out (or offering it for rent) before you sell. Ask an accountant about this possibility if you have a loss on the house, and what effect it will have on your total tax picture.

Installment Sales

An installment sale is a way of stretching out the capital gains tax due on a house. You might use it when selling a vacation home (because the capital gains tax can't be deferred by buying another home, as it can when you sell your principal residence), or when moving into something less expensive—a cheaper house or an apartment.

The requirement for an installment sale is that you receive no more than 30 percent of the selling price of the house in the first year. In that case, you would pay only a pro rata portion of the capital gains tax due, with further tax payments due only as you receive the proceeds of the sale. Since the buyer pays interest on the unpaid balance, an installment sale is a way of earning money on sums that would otherwise be paid to the government. *Warning:* If you receive more than 30 percent of the price in the first year, the entire capital gains tax falls due right away, even though full payment for the house may not be completed for several years. Talk to a lawyer before drawing up an installment sale contract, to be sure you don't inadvertently fall afoul of the rules.

Chapter Eighteen

MOVING

Give me where to stand, and I will move the earth.
ARCHIMEDES

More than anything else, you need a reliable moving company that comes when it says it will, takes good care of your furniture, gives you an honest price, and pays promptly for damage accidentally done. That company does not exist. Interstate movers work through local agents, which may be splendid in one city and careless in another. Last year your neighbor might have gotten a fine job from a particular company, but this year's crew may be less competent. In other words, any company can give you a good job or a dreadful one. The best you can do is play the percentages and keep a close eye on things yourself.

One thing to check are the *performance reports* that interstate movers have to file with the Interstate Commerce Commission, purporting to show how often they overestimated or underestimated a shipment's cost, picked up or delivered late, and damaged goods in transit. Companies are required to give these reports to prospective customers—so by comparing them, you should be able to select the mover with the best record. Unfortunately, these reports may not be reliable. The ICC checked four major companies for accuracy in 1975, the first year reports were required, and found many instances where the data made performance look better than it really was. This situation is supposed to have improved since then. But there is no one at the ICC specifically assigned to confirming performance reports, so only a few audits can be made each year.

Besides comparing performance reports, call any friends who have moved recently and ask how they found their mover. If you're being transferred, try your company's personnel office for help.

But just as important is the attitude shown by the people who come to estimate your job. Ask two or three companies to bid on the work, and compare not only their prices but their manner. Was the estimator courteous? Did he take the time to answer your questions? Was he prompt? Was he thorough in checking your possessions so as not to give you a misleadingly low estimate? Did he give you the pamphlets required by the ICC—particularly the *Summary of Information for Shippers of Household Goods* and *Lost or Damaged Household Goods: Prevention and Recovery*—along with his company's latest performance report? Did he discuss all his company's services? Liability coverage? Probable loading and delivery dates? If he's brusque and doesn't provide the information and services he should, you can presume that the moving crew will be the same.

Local moving companies are not under the jurisdiction of the ICC, although your state probably has laws regulating their actions. Their rates will generally be lower than those of the large companies, hence they're usually better for local moves. Again, get recommendations and judge the attitude of the person who estimates the job. If you run into problems, call your local consumer protection agency to see what state or city laws govern moving companies.

Prices

Local moves are generally based on hourly rates, with an advance estimate of what the entire job will cost. Longer moves are governed by the weight and distance of the shipment. An estimator comes to your house, looks at everything that goes, and gives you a probable price. But the truck will be weighed before and after it's loaded in order to determine the actual charge. Because of this there's no advantage in concealing how much actually has to be moved. It also means that you can't choose a long-distance mover based on the lowest estimate, since any estimated price might well rise at the scales.

Get several bids on your job, because movers' prices do vary. The charges to compare are: • how much per 100 pounds for the given distance; • for boxes, barrels, and cartons to pack your goods in; • for packing and unpacking; • for preparing your appliances for shipment (if the mover provides that service); • for moving unusually heavy items, such as pianos; • for using an elevator or climbing a flight of stairs. Also, ask if you qualify for any seasonal or geographical-area rates. Write these specific charges down and compare them company by company. You might find that the mover who gave you the lowest estimate has the highest item charges—and it's the item charges that have to be paid.

The key to an honest price is an honest weight. A long-distance mover has his truck weighed by a federal weighmaster before loading your goods; the weight should include a full tank of gas, the driver at the wheel, any other goods on board for another customer, and the ropes, padding, and dollies needed to load you up. You can watch this weighing procedure, if you like; just tell the agent and he'll arrange the time. In any event, you'll get a ticket showing the preloading weight. To protect your interests go with the truck after your goods are aboard and watch the second weighing. You should be charged only for the amount of weight added by your household goods. If any of the crew other than the driver are aboard, they're tipping the scales against you. Four men might weigh seven hundred pounds; at a moving charge of $15 per hundred pounds, they'd raise your bill by $105.

Confirm the weights of the truck before and after loading with the weighmaster. Also check the weights on your bill of lading and on the driver's weight certificate, because it's from those numbers that your bill is figured. If in doubt, you can request a reweigh when the shipment arrives. There's no charge for the reweigh *if* the shipment turns out to be more than 120 pounds lighter than the mover claimed, or *if* the final bill exceeds the estimated bill by more than 25 percent. Report any problems to the Consumer Affairs Officer, Interstate Commerce Commission, Washington, D.C. 20423. For problems with local movers, call your state or local consumer agency.

Unless you have specifically arranged for credit, you must be prepared to pay the mover before he unloads your goods. He'll want cash, a certified check, a money order, or a traveler's check—*not* a personal check. To pay with a money order or certified check you'll have to ask the mover for the charges in advance, or get a certified check for 90 percent or so of the estimated charges and carry enough cash to pay the remainder. The law requires that you be prepared to pay the amount of the estimate plus 10 percent, in case the bill is higher than expected. Any additional amounts don't have to be paid for fifteen business days. If you don't have the money owed on arrival, or have only a personal check, your goods will go into storage at your expense.

Ways to Save Money

1. Sell, give away, or throw away everything you're no longer going to need. All that stuff in the attic or garage adds to the moving weight.

2. If a heavy item, such as a stove or refrigerator, is on its last legs, consider selling it and buying a new one after the move.

3. Consider shipping books by parcel post at the low book rate.

4. Check with your gas, oil, electricity, water, and telephone companies to see if you have any refunds coming.

5. Be prepared with pots, silverware, and a hot plate in case the van is late and you have to stay a few days in a motel. It's cheaper to cook in your room than eat three meals a day out.

6. Keep track of expenses for tax deductions. If you're moving to take a new job and expenses aren't paid by the company, you can deduct up to $3,000 for house-hunting expenses, temporary living costs, and fees incurred for buying, selling, or leasing a home. This generally applies to moves of more than fifty miles (for details, see a current guide to tax deductions).

7. Do the packing yourself, rather than turning the job over to the mover (although it's generally better to let movers pack the fragile items).

8. Move between October and May rather than during the peak summer months. Prices should be lower then and shipments more likely to arrive on time. Families don't like to take the children out of school, but look at it this way: A few months in the new school gives the child a start on finding friends for the summer. You may also be able to get a more expeditious move (although not necessarily a cheaper one) toward the middle of the month; the big rush comes at the first of the month, when apartment leases expire.

9. Rent a truck or trailer and do a good part of the moving job yourself.

10. If you're moving to another part of town, send the curtains and rugs out to be cleaned or the furniture to be refinished, and have them returned to your new address.

11. Don't tip the movers. It's illegal in interstate moves and in many states as well.

Packing

You'll save a lot of money by doing most of it yourself—perhaps $200 or $300. The mover remains responsible for breakage, but if you did the packing, he might give you a harder time over a claim. If something does arrive broken, leave the box intact to prove to the mover's inspector that you packed it right. Here are some packing tips:

- Note the contents of each box on the top and sides.
- China and glassware—In cartons with tops; three inches of cushioning material on the bottom; each piece wrapped separately with at least two thicknesses of paper; heaviest and largest items on the bottom; glassware and fragile items on the top; each layer packed from the outside edge in to the center; three inches of cushioning material between each layer; plates, platters, and bowls put on edge, never flat; three inches of cushioning material at the top before the top is sealed.
- Silverware—In a silver chest; or in a carton with each piece wrapped separately in nontarnish tissue paper.
- Mirrors and pictures—Mirrors without backing and certain pictures should be crated by the mover; check the cost.
- Lampshades—Separately wrapped in tissue paper (newspaper makes them dirty); don't force one inside another.
- Appliances—Mover advises on how to disconnect and prepare for shipping; use his crew or call a serviceman, but get it done before moving day; wrap glass refrigerator crispers separately; wrap newspaper around front end of refrigerator shelves so they won't chip the inside of the door.
- Books—Valuable bindings separately wrapped; placed on end in small cartons (not flat or on their sides).
- TV and stereos—Some require service before moving; consult mover.
- Grandfather clocks—Need specialized service; consult clockmaker.
- Rugs—Roll, don't fold; roll small ones inside large ones.
- Clothing—Use mover's cardboard wardrobes for unwrinkled transport.
- Records—Stand them on edge, don't lay them flat.
- Bedding and linens—Light items, such as pillows and quilts, in bureau drawers; but don't overload drawers, since that may cause damage.
- Medicine and toilet articles—Seal tops with clear nail polish; tape closed; wrap separately; pack standing up; mark container "Fragile" and "This end up."

• Tools—Dismantle power tools; pack parts separately.

• Antennas, swing sets, recreational equipment—Mover charges for dismantling; consider taking them apart yourself.

• Items needed immediately upon arrival—Mark the boxes clearly so they can be picked out of the crowd.

• Prohibited items—Movers won't carry pets, food, plants, or things likely to cause spills or fires (paint, turpentine). For your own sake, don't pack money, good jewelry, important papers, or other valuable personal items.

Documents

When you decide on a mover, he'll give you an *order for service* that includes his name, address, and phone number; the number of the actual delivering agent; the location of the weighing scale; phone numbers for where you can be reached during shipment and at destination; a list of all the special services you've ordered; the estimated charges; the maximum amount that would have to be paid before unloading can begin; a note as to whether you want to know the exact charge in advance; and the shipment and delivery dates. When the shipment is picked up, you get a *bill of lading,* which is a receipt for the goods. Be sure it includes the proper weight of the van prior to loading; the correct place of delivery; and the place where you or a friend can be reached during delivery if there are any delays. During the loading you get an *inventory* of the exact goods shipped, including a note about their condition. Have these documents with you on the road in case you have to trace the shipment, and keep them afterward for reference if you have to file a claim.

Shipment and Delivery

Certain dates will be specified, but they're not always kept. If the mover can't get there when he says he will, he'll give you a new date. Always make contingency plans in case both pickup and delivery are late. Movers cannot by law deliver ahead of the scheduled date. But *you* must be on the spot, with money, when the goods arrive. Some companies will wait up to three hours (ask about this), but if you don't show, the goods go into storage. If there's going to be a delay before you move in, movers generally offer *in-transit storage* for up to 180 days. During that time they retain responsibility for your goods, including liability for damage. Past that date, however, responsibility passes to the warehouse.

Loading and Unloading

When the moving crew first arrives, someone will be there to make an inventory of everything loaded. He'll also note what condition it's in. You should be right there with him, checking the list to see if it's right. If a coffee table that's only scratched is marked "gouged" and in fact emerges gouged from the van, you'll have trouble making a claim. When you sign the inventory, note on the sheet any disagreements you have about the condition of various items of furniture.

When you unload, check each item off your inventory sheet as it comes from the van. It's more important to do this than to be in the house directing where the furniture is to go. If anything is missing or damaged, point it out and mark it on your copy of the inventory. Don't sign the driver's inventory or the delivery receipt unless it contains the same notations. Telling the driver isn't enough; the damage must be written down.

Some people sign the sheet right away, then "protect themselves" by adding the words "subject to unpacking," or "to future inspection." This doesn't help much if you find something broken and have to file a claim. Once you've signed a clean inventory sheet, the legal burden of proof shifts away from the mover and on to you, which makes it more difficult to recover damages. Also, don't sign for the delivery until everything is in fact in your house.

Checking the goods as they come off the truck is the most important moment of your move. Claims noted on the inventory sheet will probably be paid; later claims may run into heavy weather. If you do discover damage after the driver has left, leave the item in its packing carton and call the mover immediately. You have up to nine months to file a claim, but the longer it takes you to report damage, the less likely you'll be paid.

Liability

The price of the move includes liability for the mover of 60 cents per pound per article. That's no bargain. If the crew breaks a four-pound lamp, for example, you could recover only $2.40. And you wouldn't even get that if the loss were due to an "act of God." Unless your employer picks up the bill for losses in transit, or your homeowner's policy covers moving losses, pay the extra it costs to be more fully protected.

To be paid full value for lost or damaged items, you must declare a lump sum value for the shipment and pay a commensurate fee. The standard valuation is $1.25 per pound—so if your shipment weighs four thousand pounds, it will be valued at $5,000. If you want more coverage, just enter the amount on the bill of lading. The charge is 50 cents per $100 of valuation; that's $25 for a $5,000 load.

The mover will then be responsible for either the value of the damaged item (figured at present retail cost less depreciation) or its repair, whichever is less, up to the total amount of valuation declared. For your own protection, list valuable items with the mover. You'll want him to know which chairs or lamps are antiques, and that a particular box contains an important stamp collection. This encourages him to take especially good care of them and also proves that they were loaded on the truck. If the stamp collection is lost, the mover might claim it was never loaded—but if it is listed on the bill of lading, he has to pay up.

There are still some limitations on the mover's liability. If he breaks one of a set of chairs and it can't be repaired or replaced, he has to pay you only for that chair, not for the cost of a new set. Nor does he have to pay for the mechanical failure of appliances, unless you can prove external damage or show that the failure was due to the negligence of the mover *or* the serviceman the mover sent to prepare them for shipment.

Keep whatever sales slips you have, in case it becomes necessary to prove the cost of a particular item. It wouldn't hurt to have appraisals made of anything valuable that you think might get lost in the van. Don't let the mover leave until you've checked the truck yourself, to make sure everything was unloaded.

Filing a Claim

After you note the damage on the inventory sheet, call the mover and ask for a claim form. Someone will be sent out to inspect the damage. Be extremely detailed in filling in the form; the chief reason for delays in payment is that the mover doesn't have enough information. If you have to get an appraisal, you (not the mover) generally must shoulder the cost (appraisals are usually unnecessary, however, if the mover handles repairs). The mover may want you to send in the original transportation bill and bill of lading, in which case you should keep copies for yourself. To put a value on damaged items, find out what it would cost to replace them today and reduce that sum according to the item's age and condition.

The ICC requires movers to acknowledge a claim within 30 days and handle it within 120 days. If that's not possible, you must be notified every 30 days as to what's holding matters up. The ICC can help get a claim expedited but has no authority to argue about the amount offered; for that you have to go to court. To get the name of the agent on whom to serve papers, write to the Bureau of Operations, Interstate Commerce Commission, Washington, D.C. 20423.

Storage

If your goods will temporarily go into storage, ask about rates both in the city you're moving from and the place you're moving to. Charges are usually higher in large metropolitan areas; so depending on the direction of the move, it might be cheaper to store either at the beginning or end of the process. Storage charges are due when you take the goods out. Compare the *total* storage charges of the movers who bid on your job, including all service charges, handling, and delivery fees.

With longer-term storage, compare rates at several warehouses; the charges can vary dramatically. Also, there are some rotten eggs in the business who will quote you a low monthly fee, then hit you with exorbitant "extras" when you come for the furniture. Here are some of the things to ask about: (1) a minimum fee, often equivalent to three months' storage; (2) a fee equal to one month's storage for moving goods in and out; (3) an access charge of $15 to $25 each time you want to check your furniture or take something out; (4) a platform fee equal to two months' storage if you have another firm call for the items; (5) fees for camphorizing, sanitizing, and fumigating.

Ask about liability protection, since the warehouseman's insurance is generally minimal. If stored furniture isn't covered by your home-owner's policy, you'll probably want to arrange for additional protection.

The Company Transfer

Large companies often have special deals for transferred employees, so take every advantage of them. Here are some things to ask for:

• The company may help you get a mortgage on the most favorable terms available in the new area.

• If your new mortgage rate is significantly higher than the old one, some companies will make up the difference. Some pay the "points" on the new mortgage.

• They may buy your house at a fair appraised price, or pay you the difference if you have to sell below that price.

• If your old house doesn't sell by the time you have to buy a new one, the company may lend you the down payment.

• Many companies provide a "settling-in" allowance, to cover new drapes, rugs, installing utilities, and so on.

• You'll probably be reimbursed for house-hunting, moving, and travel expenses.

• The company may pay part or all of any income tax liability you incur by accepting a moving allowance.

• In lieu of a higher moving allowance you may, if you ask, get a first-year bonus at your new location.

In the past these favors were offered mainly to high-paid employees, but they're increasingly available to middle-level people as well. They may also be extended to new employees, so ask about them before you accept a job that requires you to move.

Chapter Nineteen

A SECOND HOME

Every state of society is as luxurious as it can be. Men
always take the best they can get.

SAM JOHNSON

The house you live in is probably the best investment you ever made,
so why not put that magic to work again? A *well-chosen* vacation home
can be just as profitable, and give just as much pleasure, as your permanent home. I stress the words *well-chosen* because some second homes
are white elephants on the market. A poorly constructed or maintained
cottage, in an unattractive or inconvenient location, will be just as hard
to make money on as a principal home with those drawbacks. And even
if you have a prince of homes in a glorious spot, it may not sell quickly
in a recession. Real estate generally can't be disposed of as easily as
stocks. If there's a chance you'll need the money fast, don't tie your
capital up in land.

But all this treats a second home purely as an investment. There's an
even more important value, and that's the pleasure it gives you and
your family. If you choose the place well, get a lot of enjoyment out of
it, and have the income to carry the place (or can rent it out to help with
the payments), a second home is worth every nickel you put into it.
When and if you finally decide to sell, you should get a respectable
return on your money. *The key is to buy a convenient, attractive house
that makes you happy. If you're glad to go there, it should be equally
attractive to potential buyers when the time comes to sell.*

347

Buying and Closing

All the rules, cautions, and suggestions that apply to buying a principal home (see Chapter 13, "Buying a House [or Condominium]") are pertinent as well to vacation homes or condominiums. You may not always be able to get long-term financing; banks sometimes limit their mortgages on beach homes, for example, to ten or fifteen years. Ask the real estate agent, or an agent selling prefab vacation homes, what kind of financing is available in the area. You'll probably have to use a local bank or savings and loan association—lenders rarely finance properties far from their home area. Also, use a local lawyer rather than your lawyer back home. Because he knows the people and the local real estate customs, he can generally get things done more easily. Lawyers are also an excellent source of information as to which lender has the best terms and lowest closing costs. To find a lawyer, ask the real estate agent for recommendations.

Charming Old Houses in the Country

City mice, touched by the rural beauty of a tumbledown farmhouse, may pay the country mice a pretty penny, then move into what turns out to be a rural slum. Meanwhile, the country mice are living it up in Florida. Real estate brokers are chock full of stories like these about the naiveté of city buyers, their inability to understand the problems of country living, and the snap judgments they make about real estate.

If you're in the market for a country house, have it inspected just as thoroughly as you would your principal home (see page 246), with these additional precautions:

1. Have the utilities thoroughly checked by a qualified inspector. Old houses rarely have the electrical power needed for today's appliances; many are insufficiently heated; and the water supply may not be enough for a dishwasher, washing machine, and a second bathroom. You might make the sales contract contingent on getting a well drilled and finding enough water. If you have to add to the power line or heating system, find out in advance how much it will cost. Also, ask if the house is likely to need rewiring.

2. Check the sewage system. Many old houses have a cesspool; new environmental laws may require you to put a septic system in. If there is a septic tank, when was it last pumped?

3. Is there a survey? Some old properties have not been surveyed in modern times and their farmer owners may be loath to do so. They may even resent the suggestion that a survey is necessary, as if you're somehow doubting their word (or their personal map) as to where their boundaries are. But get a survey, nevertheless, even if you have to pay for it yourself. With acreage as valuable as it is today, it's important to know how much you're buying.

4. Is there zoning in the area? Small towns are increasingly adopting zoning regulations to preserve the character of their neighborhoods and farms. But a significant number of places are still without. If there's no zoning or land-use regulation, you should think twice about buying; otherwise, you may wind up with a chicken farm or used-car dump next door.

5. With lake property find out if the lake is used as the water source. This is the case with many older homes, and a danger if the lake has become polluted. You may need to install a water purification system. Also, find out what land-use laws affect the lake properties—is there good zoning, sewage regulation, road maintenance, a lakefront owners' association? Does your deed guarantee you access to the lake?

6. If you're buying a big piece of land in hopes of selling a few lots and keeping the rest, ask a local real estate lawyer about subdivision laws; the town engineer about whether all the lots can be built on; and a contractor about what it would cost to survey the property, put roads in, and otherwise prepare the land for sale.

7. Find out when the property taxes last went up. In small towns long-time residents often pay low taxes, but outsiders who move in are socked. Visit the tax assessor *in person,* tell him how much you look forward to becoming part of his fine community, and get an estimate of what your tax bill will be.

8. Are there screens and storm windows on the house? If not, they'll cost a lot to install.

9. If the house will be empty much of the week or during an entire season, you risk vandalism or theft—and may not be able to insure against it. What security arrangements can be made? What will it cost?

10. One smart move is buy just after the season ends—after Labor Day for summer houses and in the spring for ski homes. Prices drop as sellers begin to fear that they'll be stuck with the houses for another year.

Country Land

It's perilous to purchase land in an unzoned area—a cement plant may go up next door. Don't buy property at auction without inspecting it first; you may wind up with bottom land infested with rattlesnakes. And even if you spot a good piece coming up at auction, check with local real estate brokers regarding its value. It's easy to get enthusiastic at an auction and pay too much. You'll also want to get a handle on your building problems before you buy—is the land rocky or too wet? If there are no electrical poles nearby, it might cost a fortune to bring in power, so get an estimate from the electrical company before going ahead with the purchase. Also find out what it will cost to drill for water and bring in telephone lines. Some small towns lack good carpenters, so any house they build may be drafty and out of plumb. (If that's the situation, consider a prefab house—see "Building a House," page 272.)

If You Want to Rent Your House

Renting the house when you're not there is a splendid way of reducing its cost. Over time, you may even be able to get enough in rentals to cover most of the out-of-pocket expenses. Some suggestions:

1. If you're building and furnishing a cottage—perhaps one of the excellent prefab vacation homes—get the best you can afford. The same is true when you choose a piece of land or buy a condominium. The more desirable the location and comfortable the house, the more renters you'll attract. The cost is higher up front, but the extra rental income should repay the investment. During the height of the season all cottages in the area—both good and shabby—will probably be full, but the difference comes in the off-season. When business is slow, rental agents fill their best houses first in order to encourage the renters to come back another year. It's those off-season rentals that give you a shot at having the house pay for itself.

2. Rentals are easier to get if you locate in a rental community rather than in solitary splendor out in the woods. You have to be in a spot that attracts a lot of business. The house itself need not be on Main Street —in fact, that would hurt the rentals. But the town must be one that attracts a growing number of seasonal visitors every year.

3. Work with an aggressive rental agent. You yourself may be able to keep the house or apartment rented for at least part of the season. But it takes time, and if you aren't on the spot, your customers don't have anyone to turn to when a screen is broken or the toilet won't flush. A rental agent may charge 20 or 30 percent of the rent, but he'll more than pay for himself in the extra business he brings in. He's also right there to arrange for the house to be cleaned after each visitor leaves, make quick repairs, and answer any questions the renters may have about the area. If there's a choice of rental agents, don't necessarily pick the one with the lowest commission. You want someone who can keep your house filled. Look for an agent who handles rentals full time, advertises widely, and has been in the business for some time. He should be well located on the main street, accessible to casual traffic. What keeps your house full in the off-season is people driving into town and asking the nearest rental agent if there's a house available. Before you decide on an agent, ask other owners in the area who handles their cottages, and why.

4. If you can't afford the place unless you make a certain amount in rentals, buy with great caution. The salesman may assure you that "rentals are no problem," but don't take his word for it. Talk to the other people who own similar houses or condominiums in the area, and ask how much business they do. Lay it all out: how much for mortgages, taxes, utilities, insurance, and maintenance; how much income from rentals (after agent's commissions). Can you afford it? Will you be able to carry the cottage even if rentals are 50 percent less than expected?

If you can't afford a house right now, consider this: Buy a piece of land, and try to pay for it within three or four years. If it's well chosen, the land should appreciate in value. The next step is to build a house. Apply for a mortgage based on the combined value of the land and proposed house, which should give you enough cash to put up a house and furnish it as well. A steady stream of rentals would help defray the monthly mortgage payments.

5. Renters do a certain amount of damage. But if the house is nicely enough furnished to command respect, and the rental agent is prosperous enough to screen his customers, you'll probably find your losses surprisingly small. Keep track of any replacements you buy; they're tax-deductible (see below). And by all means keep the place looking fresh and inviting. If you let it go, the renters will let it go, too.

6. If you rent the house regularly, insurance costs more. Also, you may not be able to get coverage for theft and vandalism. But if you insure with the company that has your present homeowner's or renter's policy, you'll get a discount. Be extra-cautious about keeping the house and grounds free of hazards; you don't want any lawsuits. And be sure the liability section of your policy is high. Anyone in a susceptible flood area should get federally subsidized flood insurance if it's available.

7. *Taxes.* When you rent your house during the time you aren't using it yourself, the following rules apply:

• If the property is rented for less than fifteen days, both the income and business expenses relating to the rental are ignored for tax purposes (although mortgage interest, property taxes, and casualty losses are deductible as usual).

• If personal use (see below) does not exceed fourteen days or 10 percent of the days the property is actually rented (whichever is larger), you may consider the property a business and tax-deduct the expenses allocable to rental use—including depreciation, maintenance, repairs, utilities, rental commissions, the cost of travel to open the house and close it, and so on. This is in addition to taxes, interest, and casualty losses, which would be deductible anyway. There's one hitch: You have to be able to prove that you are indeed running a business, which generally means showing a profit in two years out of five. If you fail this test, the Internal Revenue Service will probably rule your home a "hobby" and disallow certain deductions.

• If personal use is more than fourteen days or more than 10 percent of the days it's rented (whichever is larger), your business tax deductions may not exceed the total amount of rental income. Interest, taxes, and casualty losses are deductible in any event, but in figuring the business deduction, you must first consider the amount of these expenses allocable to rental use. If that amount is less than gross rentals, you can throw in a few other expenses until the level of rental income has been reached. The upshot: You break even. There's no reportable income from rents and no business deductions to tax-shelter regular income.

• If you don't expect your house to make a profit in two years out of five, you might be better off using it more than 10 percent of the rental days. This happens for reasons only an accountant could love, or calculate. Ask for an expert evaluation of your situation before making any tax-related decisions on how the property will be used.

• *Personal use* means use of the home by you and your family; use by friends and relatives at less than a fair rent; and a swap, whereby you give someone the use of your cottage in exchange for the use of his.

Time Sharing

A cheaper way of owning a vacation condominium is to buy it with others under an arrangement called time sharing. You buy a fractional interest in the property and get the right to occupy it for a specified period each year. For example, there might be twelve owners, each with a right to twenty-eight continuous days of occupancy, with the days in between given over to cleaning and maintenance. The manager of the condominium, who put the deal together, may provide maid service, rent it out during weeks that an owner can't come, and take a fee for his pains. If the condominium is ever sold, you get one twelfth of the profits, if any (but there may not *be* profits, since a condominium sold fractionally costs more than if you had bought as a single owner). It's possible to sell your fractional interest if you can find a buyer.

There are risks to time sharing. If the legal agreement makes all owners *tenants in common,* any owner can petition the court to have the condominium sold. You'd get your pro rata share of the proceeds but would lose the property. Furthermore, you'd probably lose money, since the sale would very likely not cover the high cost you paid for the right to buy fractionally. A waiver might be written into the agreement whereby buyers agree to forgo the right of partition, but the law on this point is undeveloped in many states.

Another possible form of ownership is *interval ownership,* which avoids the pitfalls of tenancy in common. Under this agreement you own an undivided interest in the property for a specified period each year. This prevents someone who "owns" another period (or his creditors) from interfering in any way with your ownership interest. If you decide to buy into a time-sharing arrangement, look for this type of setup. *Always* ask a lawyer to look at the documents before you buy, to alert you to any other risks.

There's yet another problem, and that's your relationship with your fellow owners. Does the deed allow you all to make changes to the property during your time of ownership, or does it require you to leave things untouched? Either way, you may not like the apartment that results. What if one owner leaves the condominium a mess or doesn't pay his cleaning bills? What if one is negligent about his portion of the maintenance fee? And what if you want to change your vacation time but no one will switch with you? There are so many problems attendant on multiple ownership that you should think carefully before taking it on. If you want out but can't sell, your expenses will go on running, like it or not.

Home Exchanges

Hundreds of people "borrow" second homes by exchanging with someone else. Your apartment in San Francisco for theirs in London; your
home in New York for theirs in Hawaii. The Vacation Exchange Club,
350 Broadway, New York, N.Y. 10013, publishes an annual directory of
homes in the United States and abroad that are available for exchange.
You pay a modest annual fee for the directory, plus a little extra for the
listing. The VEC leaves it up to you to work out any exchange arrangements.

Buying Land in a Vacation Subdivision

You can buy and live happily with your purchase ever after. Or you can
buy, grow disillusioned, be unable to sell, and settle into bitterness
about the whole land game. Which way it happens to you depends on
the care and attention you gave to the transaction. You're liable to wind
up unhappy if you

• Buy the land without seeing it.
• Take a "free" trip to visit a subdivision and let a salesman talk you
into signing a contract before you leave.
• Stop casually by a subdivision to look at property and buy that same
day.
• Buy without testing the land for rocks or water to see if it can be
built on.
• Buy the land without having a lawyer read the contract, the land
covenants, and the bylaws of the property association, all of which you'll
be bound by.
• Buy without reading the property report, which must by law be
given to you before you sign the contract.
• Ignore the fact that there's not yet any water or electricity available
to your lot (land like this may never be buildable and impossible to
resell).
• Believe that *all* real estate investments are good ones.

Thousands upon thousands of people have bought pieces of land in
the desert or mountains that have no access roads, no water supply, no
nearby electric poles. The developer assures the buyers that these facili-

ties will go in by a certain date. But if he goes broke or turns his attention elsewhere, people are left holding an uninhabitable piece of sand *and* a debt that must nevertheless be paid. Some developers promise to exchange uninhabitable lots for lots in the built-up area if a buyer wants to build before the utility lines have been extended to his property. But when the time comes, the developer may refuse the exchange or set too high a price on the new lot. Or there simply may not *be* a built-up area. An assistant attorney general of New Mexico once said that half of the $1 billion worth of land sold in his state between 1966 and 1976 was misrepresented.

Some lots are underwater, badly drained, or otherwise unbuildable. Unscrupulous developers generally foist them off on mail-order buyers, since it's hard to sell them to a person who insists on looking at the land and digging test holes before he buys.

Some developments are sold on the promise of golf courses and swimming pools that never materialize. Some are so far from hospitals and other medical services that they don't make sense for the retirees who buy them. Many are appallingly overpriced; similarly situated land just outside the development will likely go for much less.

Over time, new problems arise. Assuming that the lot is buildable, you might have to use a contractor "approved" by the developer, paying an extra 5 or 10 percent for his services. An architectural committee will have to approve your building plans. At some point the developer will stop subsidizing the property owners' association, which means that the annual fee you pay will jump sharply. The cost of maintaining the swimming pool, clubhouse, and other common areas will also go up. The sales literature appears to limit possible cost increases, but in practice there's little you can do about rising fees. A wide range of legal remedies can be taken against you if you refuse to pay. If you want to sell, you probably won't be able to put up a for-sale sign, and the developer may keep outside brokers off the property.

If all of this makes you afraid to buy into a subdivision, then I've done my job. Not that you shouldn't—you may find a great lot, put a lovely house on it, and years later sell at a nice profit. But at the start your proper attitude is *skepticism*—of the desirability of the lot, of the salesman's assurances, of the likelihood that the land will increase in value, and of the fairness of the contract. A suspicious buyer will double-check every detail before he puts down his money; a trusting one won't and may get burned.

The salesman is the real problem. Some are honest, but land developments have become notorious for their hustling, high-pressure sales tactics. Without a blush the salesman may assure you that the land is a good investment and will inevitably increase in value; that if you don't buy right now, he has another customer who will take the lot away from you; that roads and utilities will be installed long before you want to build; that you can exchange your undeveloped lot for a developed one; that it's a no-risk purchase; that the developer can easily resell the land for you at a profit if you ever want to get out; that the developer will repurchase the land himself; that the developer is in the black and not likely to go broke. *All of these things may be false.* Yet the salesman may be so friendly and enthusiastic that you can't help but believe him. It is very hard for an honest person to imagine that he is being deliberately taken in, and it's on that trusting attitude that the salesman plays.

To avoid being trapped by your own good nature, *never* buy on the same day that you look around. Take all the documents away with you, including the all-important property report (see below), and show them to a lawyer. If you can't get all the documents, *DO NOT BUY.* Ask yourself whether the land will give you pleasure even if you can't resell it. Once you understand all the risks and figure you can live with them, go ahead and buy.

Resale Value

Salesmen always assure land buyers that the property will increase in value. But that isn't always true, especially if you paid an inflated price to start with. Real estate runs in cycles. When everyone is hot to buy, land values are run up; when times get tighter and there are more lots for sale than people to buy them, values decline. Many a person has had to dump land for less than he paid for it, and some lots aren't salable at all. If there are no utilities and no hope of getting any, you won't be able to *give* the property away. Even in a developed community, perfectly good lots may not be salable—not because there's anything wrong with them, but because there's more land for sale than there are potential buyers. Real estate is simply not a sure thing.

If you're buying property strictly for your own use and the land meets your requirements, buy and enjoy. But if you're buying for investment purposes, you're generally better off avoiding big subdivisions. First, the land is probably overpriced. Second, there are high carrying costs. You not only have to pay interest and taxes, but also have the burden of mandatory dues and assessments levied by the property owners' association. And third, when you put your property up for resale, it will be hard to find a buyer. You probably won't be able to put a for-sale sign on it, and any customers who come looking will be diverted by the developer to his own lots rather than yours. All of this is not to say that it's impossible to make a profit on land in a subdivision. Only that it's generally harder there than on land in other attractive locations.

The Office of Interstate Land Sales Registration

OILSR is a federal agency devoted to helping customers get *full information* about subdivision property before they buy. Land developers selling fifty or more lots, using interstate commerce or the mails, are required to file reports with OILSR, giving all material facts about the land. Before you buy, you should be given a copy of that same report. *Warning:* OILSR does not double-check the report to see if the developer told the truth. Any representations that OILSR has "okayed" the property are false. But by filing that report, the developer attests to its truth. If it turns out that you were misled, the falsity of the report is grounds for suit.

You are supposed to receive the property report before you sign the contract, and you must acknowledge the receipt in writing. *Another warning:* Some developers ask you to sign for the report before they actually give it to you. Then, a week or so after the sale, you'll get the report in the mail. Don't sign if you don't yet have the report. If it turns out that the land was misrepresented and you didn't get the property report before the sale, you could get out of the whole transaction. But if you signed a paper saying that you'd received the report, even though it wasn't true, you'll be hard put to make your case.

ALWAYS ask for the property report during the decision-making stage, not on the day you're ready to sign the contract. Get copies of the land covenants which spell out any limits on your ownership, and the bylaws of any property owners' association you have to join. If the salesman won't give them to you (because "we don't want our good ideas to get around"), it means there's something there he'd rather you didn't know about. Walk away from the deal. And don't let him talk you into signing something in return for the documents. You're entitled to see them free and clear. Read them yourself then give them to a lawyer to check for you. A real estate lawyer is essential to this transaction. You may not understand the implications of some of the disclosures on the property report, and it's a mistake to rely on the salesman to explain them to you.

The Property Report

An amazing number of things are disclosed in the property report. It's the perfect antidote to the salesman's charm. A smart developer puts in every one of the faults and flaws because then it's hard for you to sue him on grounds of misrepresentation. Here are some of the things to look for:

• *Does the developer have a "blanket mortgage" on the entire piece of land?* If he does, and defaults, the bank that granted the mortgage can foreclose on everything, including the piece of land you've been paying for. You'd lose the property, with no recourse but to sue the bankrupt developer for restitution (chances are slim he could ever pay). A few states require that your money be put into escrow so you could get it back, but most don't. However, the bank that holds the blanket mortgage may release individual pieces of land if the buyer promptly pays a certain sum.

• *Is the sales contract recordable?* This is important. When you buy land on a sales contract, you normally don't get the deed, or title to the property, until the land is fully paid for. So unless you can "record" the sales contract with the town authorities, there's nothing to show that you have any interest in the property. Should the developer default on a blanket mortgage, all people with recorded interests in the land will be notified of the foreclosure in time for them to try to negotiate settlements on their individual lots. If your sales contract isn't recorded, there's no way for the mortgage holder even to know who you are. He'll foreclose on the property as a whole and your land will be lost. If your sales contract is not recordable, there's nothing you can do but hope for the best; if it is recordable, it's up to you to get that document to the town office and stake your claim. When you finally get the deed, make sure that's recorded, too.

• *How large is the development?* If you want a little cottage in the woods but the development plan calls for turning the woods into a city of five thousand souls, you'd best look somewhere else. But even the size stated in the property report is not the last word. The developer may own land adjacent to your subdivision that is not included in the present offering but will be turned into lots as soon as this group is sold out. Because of the voting control he holds over the property owners' association (spelled out in the bylaws), he'll probably be able to enlarge the development without the property owners' consent.

• *What happens if you get into financial trouble, can't make the payments, and can't sell the land?* Normally, you'll lose the property and all the money you've paid so far. But sometimes the developer can also sue you for the rest of the money owed.

• *What special assessments will you have to pay?* Vacation subdivisions usually are governed by a property owners' association (with the developer either holding a majority of votes or retaining veto power). Membership is mandatory, as are the annual dues and special assessments. The association is responsible for maintaining the facilities (such as swimming pools and tennis courts), plowing the roads, providing for security, hiring any necessary staff, and eventually buying the common lands and facilities from the developer. The expected annual dues will be set forth in the property report—but that figure may be low. The developer often keeps costs down in the beginning, so as to attract buyers. As soon as the lots are largely sold, he'll announce that he can't subsidize the property owners' association any longer and dues will go up. In some associations the developer can single-handedly levy an assessment on all property owners. If you don't pay your dues and assessments, the developer may be able to move against your property.

• *Will the down payment or installment payments be put in escrow* so you can get your money back in the event that the builder goes bankrupt? In most states there are no escrow provisions.

• *Are there safety hazards, noise, or pollution problems* that would affect the subdivision?

• *What recreational facilities are currently available, plus any costs or assessments?* Determine whether title to the facilities will eventually pass to the property owners' association or whether you'll simply lease them from the developer. In the latter case the developer will likely raise the rent every year, and under the conditions of your contract you'll have no choice but to pay. On the other hand, when the facilities pass to the property owners' association, you'll be responsible for your share of the upkeep, which is bound to increase in future years. There may be special assessments for additions or major repairs. In other words, your financial commitment to the community is open ended.

If all the amenities have not been built, the developer will list what's proposed along with an estimated date of completion. This is generally not binding on him (unless he has put up a completion bond). If he doesn't get around to finishing the golf course, there may be nothing you can do.

• *Does the subdivision have electricity, gas, water, sewage disposal, roads, and telephone service—and if not, what will it cost to get them?* These are vital questions to explore, since some subdivisions have none of these things. Salesmen will assure you that by the time you want to build, the utilities will probably have reached your lot, and if not, you can exchange for a lot that has already been supplied. But at building time the developer may renege. If it doesn't say in your contract that you have the right to exchange at a specified price, you may be out of luck. In the Southwest you must find out whether the developer has permission to tap the local water supply. If the property report says that he hasn't yet applied for permission, stay away from the land. Permission may not be granted.

In subdivisions where utilities are already available, the property report will tell you the price of having them hooked up to your house. If you'll need a septic tank, that cost should also be estimated. But on a problem lot the septic system may be far more expensive than predicted. In fact, some lots will be totally unable to support a septic field, so before you buy, ask the town health officer whether he'll issue you a septic permit. If he won't, the land is useless for a home site.

When you evaluate raw land, it is prudent to assume that nothing more will be added to the development than what is already there. If you would be happy with your lot as is, then buy. If it requires an additional large investment on the developer's part, or by the local water and sewage authorities, to make it livable, think twice. It's safest to buy in a development where the utilities and amenities already exist.

• *How far is the property from population centers?* Those so careless as to buy by mail may be disconcerted to find when they visit their land that it's one hundred miles away from the nearest doctor and thirty miles from the nearest shopping center. Reading the property report will at least tell you whether health, school, and shopping facilities are nearby.

• *Is there water on some of the lots, and will fill be needed?* The property report may not identify exactly which lots have this trouble, but it will alert you to check for the problem on any lot you might want to buy.

• *How many homes are occupied?* Some reports may say that there are five hundred homes in the "area" but none on the subdivision. That's often a sign that the subdivision is not yet habitable.

• *What roads are on the property?* If there's no access to your lot, there's no assurance there ever will be unless the property report says that the developer has put funds in trust for road building. Even when roads have been built, the developer may not commit himself to maintenance, which means that unless the property owners pay to keep up the roads, they will eventually become unusable.

• *Have the developer's financial statements been certified?* If not, the figures may not be trustworthy; if so, see whether the accountant took any exceptions in the letter accompanying the financial report. For example, he might have written that the developer's ability to fulfill his promises depends entirely on whether more lots can be sold, which is a shaky foundation for a fledgling town. Also look to see if there's a deficit or operating loss. When the builder is in financial trouble, it's possible that he won't be able to finish the roads or complete the amenities. If he goes bankrupt, the bank would foreclose on his mortgage, which might cost you your investment (see page 358). Any serious deficit in the accounts of the property owners' association should also be disclosed, as it's a sign that your dues and assessment will go up.

• *Can you choose your own builder, or must you use someone approved by the developer?* The "approved" builders usually kick back part of the price to the developer, which may raise the cost of building by 10 percent or more. There will typically be a developer-dominated architectural review board, which must approve your building plans.

• *What restrictions are there on resales?* Typically, you won't be able to put a for-sale sign on your property and may not be able to use any agent but the developer. Under these conditions it can be practically impossible to sell (see the following section).

• *Are there any lawsuits against the developer,* and if so, what are the charges?

When You Want to Sell

It can be enormously difficult to sell a lot you own in a subdivision. Naturally, a piece of sand with no water supply won't sell (although somehow the salesman managed to sell it to you). But perfectly buildable lots in attractive and functioning subdivisions may also be unsalable, for these reasons:

1. The price is too high. The developer probably paid a few hundred dollars an acre, added a clubhouse and some electric poles, and started selling for a few thousand dollars an acre. You paid his inflated price because you weren't familiar with land values in the area and were under the influence of a persuasive salesman. Other people may not think the lot is worth the asking price. To sell, you may have to take a loss.

2. You may have to use the developer as real estate broker, and his salesman often won't show the land. Typically, when a customer walks in the door, the developer tries to sell him the lots he himself still owns. Resales will be shown only if the buyer shows no interest in the developer's lots. The casual visitor to the subdivision won't know your lot is for sale because bylaws prevent you from putting up a sign. Even if you're allowed to use an outside broker, he may be reluctant to poach on the developer's territory or may think the land there is overpriced.

3. The competition is stiff. When there are many subdivisions around and not enough customers for everyone, it's unlikely that even good lots will sell. When the economy gets soft, vacation land is a drug on the market.

A whole racket has grown up around unhappy land investors desperate to sell out. It's called *advance fee listing.* A con man will get the names and addresses of everyone in a particular subdivision and send them letters, offering to list their properties in a booklet for an advance fee of $350 or so. The letter implies that this booklet gets wide circulation among people looking for just the type of land you have for sale. You send in your $350 and get back a copy of the booklet, but it's unlikely to have a much wider circulation. You won't sell your property and will be out the fee.

If your subdivision lot is buildable and the developer has not tried very hard to sell it for you, all you can do is advertise it yourself and lower the price. You might offer the salesman a double commission as an incentive. But if real estate demand is poor, even a good lot may be on your hands for years.

Despite these hazards, some people are indeed lucky enough to resell their subdivision lots at a profit. The most likely resales are (1) buildable lots in (2) fully developed communities, in (3) an attractive vacation area, where (4) there aren't many developer's lots competing with yours for customers, and where (5) there has been a history of *steady* and *growing* demand for land.

Your Right to Change Your Mind

If you can prove that the developer did not give you the property report before buying, you can cancel the contract and get your money back. If you received the property report less than forty-eight hours before signing up, you can revoke the contract by notice to the seller up until midnight of the third business day following the transaction. When you revoke the deal, either put it in writing or have a witness to your oral statement, followed up by notice in writing. If you buy by mail, the contract may allow you to cancel if you visit the property within a certain length of time and decide you don't like it. When none of these remedies are available, read the property report carefully and compare it both with what you were told and what the contract says. Also have an attorney read it. If the land was misrepresented, either the Office of Interstate Land Sales Registration or the attorney may be able to get you out of it.

Where to Complain

If you think you have been misled or badly treated, write to the Office of Interstate Land Sales Registration, U.S. Department of Housing and Urban Development, Washington, D.C. 20410. The office doesn't fully investigate every complaint, but does write to the developer to seek an informal resolution. If you didn't get the property report before buying (and didn't sign a form that said you did), you may be able to get your money back. If the land was misrepresented, OILSR won't sue for you individually (you have to do that on your own), but if enough people complain about the same developer, the government may bring suit. A state agency in a state where the land laws are strong may also be able to help.

But fundamentally, OILSR is a disclosure agency, not a policeman. It requires builders to set forth in a property report all the material facts that might affect your decision to buy. After that, it's your responsibility to read and decide. You can sue if the property report misrepresents the land. But if, for example, the report discloses that there are no roads and none will be built for ten years, the developer has met the government's disclosure requirements. If you buy that land and suddenly realize that without roads you can't build a house, there is nothing OILSR can do for you. In other words, *read and understand* the report. For the land laws to help you, you have to make an effort to protect yourself.

Chapter Twenty

LIFE INSURANCE

The seventeenth Rule of Friendship: A friend will refrain from telling you he picked up the same amount of life insurance coverage you did for half the price and his is noncancelable.

ESQUIRE MAGAZINE

We spend more money on life insurance, and know less about it, than almost any other consumer purchase. The business seems so difficult and complex that most of us are content to get all our information from the agent doing the selling. And in fact, agents often present themselves not as salesmen but as "advisors," who will evaluate your financial situation and suggest improvements.

Any salesman is an "advisor" to the extent that he knows his product and can make suggestions on how to use it. But his advice is colored by self-interest. Just as it is rare for a stockbroker to advise a client to get out of the market and put his money into bank term accounts, it is rare for an insurance salesman to suggest that a client may not need life insurance. Most agents are quicker to recommend expensive policies than inexpensive ones. Some are very good at finding the right kind of life insurance to meet your personal goals, but others operate on the erroneous principle that any insurance they sell you leaves you better off than you were before.

Most of us are ill equipped to question a life insurance salesman or evaluate the accuracy of his statements. The appearance of complexity works in the salesman's favor, since it forces us to rely on his judgment rather than our own. But in truth, insurance isn't as difficult as it sometimes appears. The basic concepts underlying life insurance are simple

—something anyone can understand. After reading the fundamentals in this chapter you should be equipped to make good decisions about the kind and amount of life insurance that would best suit your needs. The job of an agent, then, is not to make your decisions for you but to find the coverage you need at the best price.

INSURANCE AT THE LOWEST COST

The most inexpensive insurance is generally not sold individually by insurance agents. It's sold to members of special groups and, in some states, by special carriers, such as savings banks. The following list shows some places to turn for life insurance coverage before calling an insurance agent.

Employee Coverage

Many companies and unions provide group term life insurance coverage for employees. Sometimes the employer pays the full cost, sometimes the employee contributes. Often the employer finances a base amount, with the employee having the option of buying additional amounts himself. Since the rates are almost always better than you could get with individual coverage, especially for older people, it's smart to load up with all the employee insurance you can get.

What if you leave your job? Employee insurance is generally convertible into individual straight-life coverage, without a medical exam, within thirty days, but the cost is quite high. You're rarely allowed to convert to an inexpensive term policy. If you're otherwise uninsurable or insurable only at high-risk rates, it's essential that you convert. Otherwise, shop for cheaper coverage elsewhere. Generally speaking, it's a good move to have some insurance besides your employee group life —perhaps a policy with another group or an individual term policy. If you left your job, you could then be sure of continuing coverage with your other policies no matter what your health, and you wouldn't be forced to convert to expensive straight-life.

Teachers Insurance and Annuity Association

People employed by colleges, universities, independent schools, and certain other nonprofit educational and scientific organizations, and their spouses, can buy individual life insurance from the TIAA. The price on both term and straight-life coverage is much lower than at most life insurance companies. Many institutions also offer inexpensive TIAA group term. The address is 730 Third Ave., New York, N.Y. 10017.

Veterans' Insurance

Veterans of World Wars I and II and the Korean War were given the opportunity to convert their serviceman's coverage into $10,000 worth of term or straight-life at low, government-subsidized rates. If you have any of this insurance, *hang on to it*. Since then, servicemen and women have been allowed to buy up to $15,000 worth of inexpensive term coverage. But, on leaving the service, they have to drop the policy or convert it to straight-life with a commercial company at standard rates. Conversion to inexpensive term policies is not allowed. Since most young people who need insurance need term insurance, modern-day veteran's policies should probably be dropped in favor of individual term coverage with a good company. With this exception: If you're otherwise uninsurable, by all means convert your serviceman's coverage to regular straight-life. Several hundred insurers have agreed to accept conversions of GI policies.

Other Group Coverage

One of the fastest-growing segments of the life insurance industry is group term coverage offered by various associations to its members. Professional, fraternal, and alumni associations are particularly active in this business, offering policies at bargain rates. Sometimes you don't even have to take a medical exam—a great break if you're otherwise uninsurable. But in most cases the insurance carrier reserves the right to ask you to pass a physical. In general, group term coverage continues until age sixty-five or seventy, with the rate going up a little each year. At later ages the amount of coverage may decline.

When you need insurance, take a look at the various groups you're eligible to join to see if they have group plans. Compare the rates with low-cost individual policies, because not all group coverage is a bargain. But in most cases, group term *is* cheaper than individual coverage, even counting the cost of your annual membership fee to the organization. *Two warnings:*

1. Brand-new groups may be unstable, rates may rise, and the plan may even go broke, leaving members with the right to buy only a small amount of coverage without a medical exam. It's still worth buying insurance from a new group, if the rates are low, but don't count on it for the bulk of your coverage. Older groups, however, with large memberships and a history of stable insurance prices, can usually be relied on.

2. The organization or the insurance company can, if it wants to, terminate the insurance. This isn't likely to happen with a large and successful group, but it's another reason not to use the insurance plan of a single association for all your coverage. Hedge your bets by having some coverage somewhere else.

Non-Dividend-Paying Term Insurance

Nondividend term (see page 398), sold by life insurance companies, often has lower premiums than any of the "special" insurance sources on this list. Compare it with the cost of group plans before buying into the group. It almost always costs less than the dividend-paying insurance sold by savings banks in some states.

Savings Bank Life Insurance

If you live or work in New York, Massachusetts, or Connecticut, you can buy dividend-paying term or straight-life insurance cheaply from savings banks. In Connecticut the insurance industry has kept the maximum per person at a low $5,000, so although it's worth getting, it won't make a significant difference to your total insurance bill. But in New York the limit per person is $30,000 and in Massachusetts, $41,000. That ceiling can be increased in special circumstances—for example, savings banks in New York can sell up to $40,000 worth of decreasing term to cover your mortgage in addition to the regular $30,000. To qualify for coverage, you must have a legal residence in the state or you must hold a job there. Summer residents aren't eligible, but college students are. If you later move out of the state, you can keep the insurance. (*Note*: Nondividend term insurance, sold by insurance companies, costs even less out-of-pocket than savings-bank policies.)

Wisconsin's State Life Insurance Fund

Residents of Wisconsin can buy up to $10,000 worth of low-cost insurance from the state. You can get straight-life, ten-year nonrenewable term, or term to sixty-five. For information write to the State Life Insurance Fund, Commissioner of Insurance, 123 W. Washington Ave., Madison, Wis. 53702.

Credit Unions

Credit unions often offer a small amount of free life insurance to members who have savings accounts there (on the order of $4,000 in insurance for a $2,000 account). It's not much, but it's the cheapest insurance anyone can get! Survivors often don't realize that they're due a payment from credit union insurance, so be sure you leave a note to this effect in your insurance file. If you borrow money from a credit union, there may be an additional amount of free life insurance to pay off this debt.

Incidental Sources

Membership in an organization may entitle you to a small amount of free coverage. Holding a travel credit card may give a little free accident insurance. Be alert to any free or low-cost insurance plans associated with a membership organization, make a note of any you're entitled to, and *slip the note into your insurance file.* A lot of survivors lose incidental insurance payouts because they didn't know the coverage existed.

Small Business Owners

You can get group coverage for yourself even if your business has a "group" of only one. The corporation can pay the premiums up to a certain amount and tax-deduct them. Talk to an insurance agent about the tax benefits of having a company buy your coverage.

TERM INSURANCE

Term insurance is *pure* insurance. You buy it to provide your family with a death benefit if you die prematurely, and for no other purpose. It does not, like straight-life insurance (see page 376), include a savings element, so you can't cash a term policy in and get some money back. This form of life insurance is like the coverage you buy for your house or car—its sole purpose is to provide funds in case a disaster happens.

Term is also the cheapest form of insurance coverage. With it, you can leave your family a large sum of money at modest cost if you die prematurely. The following table gives you an idea of how much cheaper term coverage can be than straight-life insurance (I've shown a range of costs for each policy because of the wide price spread among insurance companies):

ANNUAL PREMIUM COST OF TERM VERSUS STRAIGHT-LIFE INSURANCE[a]

	$10,000 coverage		$50,000 coverage		$100,000 coverage	
Age[b]	Term[c]	Straight life	Term	Straight life	Term	Straight life
25	$ 19–40	$128–167	$ 87–198	$ 640–833	$ 195–396	$1,280–1,666
30	19–41	148–192	87–203	740–960	195–406	1,480–1,921
35	24–46	175–226	122–232	870–1,130	245–465	1,740–2,260
40	36–60	210–267	182–304	1,050–1,349	365–608	2,100–2,699
45	55–84	259–327	277–420	1,295–1,633	555–840	2,590–3,267
50	86–122	328–401	432–604	1,640–2,005	865–1,219	3,280–4,010
55	135–180	399–499	675–904	1,995–2,496	1,350–1,809	3,990–4,993
60	211–273	532–631	1,055–1,363	2,662–3,155	2,110–2,726	5,324–6,310

[a]Based on the cost per $1,000 of coverage for sample higher- and lower-priced policies.
[b]Cost shown for males.
[c]Five-year renewable, convertible term.

The price (or *premium*) for term insurance increases every year (or every five years, if you buy a renewable five-year policy), at a rate guaranteed in advance. However, the cost starts out so low that you usually can afford the increase. Furthermore, as you get older, your earnings usually rise, which makes the increase in term premiums relatively easy to handle.

Once you're past age forty-five, the price of term insurance starts going up much more rapidly than in the earlier years. By age fifty or fifty-five, you may want to save money by reducing the amount of term you carry. It's often reasonable to do this, since by that age the major expenses of raising and educating your children are usually behind you, so you don't need the large amounts of insurance you carried when you were younger. Most term insurance policies are not renewable after age sixty-five or seventy (although some will carry you to age one hundred).

Term Insurance vs. Straight-Life

Generally speaking, a young family on a limited budget should load up on term insurance and skip straight-life insurance entirely. As a young couple starting out, you usually don't have much money to spend on insurance. If you could afford only $300 a year at age 25 and spent it on a straight-life policy, you'd be covered for only around $25,000. By contrast, if you put that same sum toward term insurance, your family would have $100,000 worth of protection. If you died prematurely, a $25,000 policy might be gone in three years, whereas $100,000 might last them fifteen years or more.

Many a breadwinner is tempted by the $25,000 straight-life policy because if he lives and cashes it in at retirement, he'll get a sum of money back. In other words, he's thinking of his own future and gambling that he'll live. But if he loses his bet and dies prematurely, it's his wife and children who will pay the price. By deliberately buying a small straight-life policy when he could have afforded scads of term, he leaves his family with insufficient funds, forcing his wife to support the children after his death at a much reduced standard of living. If you're wealthy enough to afford all the coverage you need at expensive straight-life rates, you might consider it—it has some tax advantages for the rich (see page 378). But otherwise, think first about how to finance all the *protection* your family needs. Personal retirement savings can come later.

Many insurance agents offer young families combination coverage— a small straight-life policy packaged with a larger amount of five-year or decreasing term. The sales pitch is that although you need a lot of term for family protection, it's never too early to plan for your own future by buying "permanent" coverage. (Sometimes, these package policies require you to convert your term to straight-life insurance at specified times.)

But ask yourself: A small straight-life policy builds only a small amount of cash value, takes many years to do so, and the value of those savings is deeply eroded every year by inflation. Is it more important to start that coverage now, or to spend the money on a larger amount of term insurance to protect the family? Furthermore, maybe you'd rather plan for your future by building a savings or investment account than by saving via a straight-life policy (see page 379). A better plan is to buy all the term you need, with no strings attached. You can convert it to straight-life if and when you want.

Life insurance agents argue that it's important to start straight-life coverage when you're young because it costs less. If you buy at a later age, the premiums are higher. However, when you start younger, you pay premiums longer, so the lifetime cost is much higher than you imagine. And besides, what's more important to you: having your family fully protected in case of your death, or starting early on a straight-life policy? If you can do both, and you've determined that saving money via a straight-life policy meets your goals (see page 378), by all means do so. But if buying straight-life means sacrificing some of the protection your family needs, don't do it.

It is important to remember that insurance companies make more money from straight-life than they do from term. Consequently, they arrange commission scales so that insurance agents make more money selling it. An agent may earn 55 percent of the first-year premium on a straight-life policy, plus 5 percent of the next nine years' premiums. By contrast, on a level term policy he'll make only around 40 percent of the first year's premium and nothing thereafter. When an insurance agent advises you that a combination of term and straight-life would be better for your needs than pure term, you should always be aware that such a sale would be better for *his* needs.

Level Term

This means that the coverage remains the same, or "level," for a specified number of years. A five-year $10,000 policy is level because if you died anytime during the five years, your family would receive a death benefit of $10,000. The policy also carries a level premium, which means you pay the same amount every year. Level term policies are for people who don't expect their insurance needs to fall during the period the coverage is in force. The most common term policy sold is five-year level term, renewable at the end of each period for another five years. You can also get level term for periods of one year, ten years, fifteen years, twenty years, and higher.

The cheapest way to buy level term insurance is often through one-year renewable term. You pay for only one year's worth of coverage at a time, and the price goes up a little every year. In your twenties and early thirties the annual increase might be on the order to 2 to 5 cents per $1,000 of coverage; when you reach your forties, it will be going up 30 to 40 cents a year. Five-year term may cost a little less than one-year term for people in their twenties, but once you get into your thirties and forties, you might save $1 or $2 per $1,000 of coverage by buying one-year term. Ask your life insurance agent to make the comparison for you. Large policies, in particular, are cheaper this way (in fact, many companies won't sell small one-year policies). Term policies for long periods like ten or fifteen years are more expensive than five-year term and are generally avoided.

Make It Renewable

It's important to have a policy that you can renew every time the term runs out without having to pass another physical exam. Then, if your health goes bad, you will still be assured of coverage as long as you want it. Some policies are renewable only up to age sixty-five, which is pretty young; better to look for a company that will keep you on until age seventy or seventy-five, in case you need it. The price of term insurance goes up each time the policy is renewed—a few cents per $1,000 of coverage in the early years and a few dollars per $1,000 as you pass middle age. The future premiums are stated in the contract, and the company cannot exceed those amounts. Guaranteed renewable policies are a little more expensive than the nonrenewable kind, but well worth the extra cost. It's an assurance that you'll have coverage at standard rates no matter what happens to your health.

Make It Convertible

Besides renewability, you want insurance that can be converted into a different type of policy if you ever wanted to make the switch. Term insurance should be 100 percent convertible into straight-life without another physical exam and at standard, guaranteed rates, no matter what happens to your health. (Many insurance companies require you to convert at some point before your term insurance comes to an end.

On a ten-year policy, for example, you might have to convert before the eighth year—a definite disadvantage. Avoid a company that requires conversion as early as age sixty or sixty-two; also, avoid a company that limits the amount of insurance you can convert. Since you have no idea what your insurance needs will be in the future, you want a contract that gives you as many options as possible.)

Decreasing Term Insurance

This is the cheapest possible way to buy term coverage. It can be used two ways:

1. You buy a contract to provide your beneficiary with a certain monthly income over a specified number of years. For example, in December 1979 you might buy a contract that, at your death, would pay your family $300 a month until December 1989. If you die right after buying the policy, they'll get $300 a month for ten years. If you die four years after buying the policy, they'll get $300 a month for the remaining six years of the contract.

Alternatively, they can accept a lump sum settlement at your death. In that case, the policy will pay them the *current value* of the total remaining income due, which is less than the face value. But if that lump sum settlement is put in the bank to earn interest, and drawn on for $300 every month, it will last at least as long as the insurance contract would have lasted, and longer if the interest rate is higher. Many people, in fact, take lump sum settlements because they can get better interest rates somewhere else (even after taxes). Be sure that your contract allows you either option.

2. Another use of decreasing term insurance is to pay off a big decreasing debt, such as a mobile home loan or a mortgage. For example, assume that you cover your $35,000 mortgage with decreasing term. If you die today, the contract will pay $35,000. If you die ten years from now, when the amount owed on the mortgage is only $27,000, the insurance will pay $27,000.

It makes a lot of sense to carry mortgage insurance, so that if you die, your family will have the house free and clear. Your life insurance agent should be able to arrange a term schedule that coincides with the rate at which your mortgage is decreasing. (If the policy decreases faster than the mortgage does, you'll need a little extra term coverage at the start to cover the obligation completely.)

With decreasing term, the annual premium remains the same

throughout the life of the policy. It's called "decreasing" term because the total amount of money your survivors will get from the insurance company decreases over time. (For example, if you buy a ten-year policy for $300 a month and die immediately, your family will be insured for a total of $36,000. But if you die after four years, the proceeds from the remaining six years on the contract will come to $21,600.)

Some decreasing term policies limit the amount of coverage that can be converted to straight-life without taking a new physical exam. For example, you might be allowed only 75 percent of the coverage then in effect. If you become uninsurable, you're faced with an awful dilemma: If you don't convert, your insurance will run out on the specified date, but if you do, you'll immediately suffer a 25-percent reduction in coverage. When you buy decreasing term, look for a policy that can be 100 percent converted into straight-life.

One drawback to using decreasing term for your principal coverage is that it's less flexible than other approaches. The insured amount declines according to a set pattern. If you unexpectedly have another child or take on more financial obligations, you'll want more coverage and for a longer period than originally anticipated. There's no problem getting another policy as long as you're insurable, but if not, you're stuck with declining coverage and an increased insurance need. At that point all you can do to ensure continuing coverage is to convert the remainder of your decreasing term policy to straight-life (few companies permit conversion to renewable term). With *level* term, on the other hand, you can reduce the amount or hold it level, according to your needs. You might, for example, find that increases in your standard of living make it necessary to hold the coverage level for ten or fifteen years before you can start to cut back.

The advantage to decreasing term is that it's so inexpensive you can use it for cheap coverage while building up savings and investments. The more assets you have, the less you need insurance at all.

Deposit Term

This is a relatively new type of coverage, not sold by many companies, which muddies the waters of pure term coverage. It provides ten-year renewable level-term coverage at a lower cost than for other ten-year term policies and even many five-year policies. But one-year renewable term, for people buying larger amounts of coverage, is usually cheaper than deposit term.

The first-year premium for deposit term is a large one (paying the salesman a larger commission than the usual term policy does). It includes a deposit that is your pledge to keep the insurance in force for the full ten years. If you keep that promise, the deposit is returned to you, plus interest paid at a high rate (9 or 10 percent), compounded annually, and treated as a tax-free refund. If you die before the term is up, the deposit plus the face amount of the policy is paid to your beneficiary. But if you drop the policy before the end of the term, the deposit is forfeit. Some deposit term policies allow for conversion into decreasing term to age one hundred, a useful benefit since most term coverage stops at age sixty-five or seventy (avoid deposit term plans that permit conversion only to straight-life).

Credit Life Insurance

When you borrow money for a car, furniture, or major appliances, you're often offered a decreasing term life insurance policy to pay off the debt if you die or become totally disabled. This policy is not necessary if you have enough regular insurance to meet all your obligations. However, if you're underinsured and the loan is large, you might want to consider the extra coverage. In general, it's cheaper to buy regular term insurance from an insurance agent than to sign up for credit life (see page 103).

Converting Term to Straight-Life

If you decide at some point in the future that you'd like to convert some of your term insurance to straight-life, when is the best time to do it? The younger you are, the lower the straight-life premium (because when you're young, the insurer expects to collect premiums for a longer period of time). However, rates go up only 50 cents or so per $1,000 of coverage in your younger years—easy to pay on a rising income. As long as you're on a limited budget and need large amounts of insurance to provide for raising and educating your children, it's best to stick with inexpensive term. You do your family no favors by reducing their protection (or standard of living) just to carry straight-life. Convert to straight-life only if you like the savings element (see page 376) and can afford the higher premium.

Once the children start leaving home and supporting themselves, your financial obligations often decrease. At that point you might want to reduce the total amount of coverage you carry. You can cancel some of your term insurance, or, if you like the forced-savings element of straight-life, convert some of the term to a smaller amount of straight-life. The break point for straight-life rates is around age forty-five for men, forty-eight for women. Up to that year, insurance premiums increase at about the same rate every year, picking up modestly from the late thirties into the early forties. But after age forty-five, premiums for new straight-life policies begin to increase far more sharply every year. If you plan to convert, it's wise to do so before that age.

STRAIGHT-LIFE INSURANCE

Straight-life (or *whole-life,* or *ordinary-life*) insurance is two things in one: (1) life insurance coverage and (2) a savings (or investment) element. Every premium you pay is used partly to cover the cost of the insurance and partly to build up a savings element in the policy.

The Insurance Coverage

This is the face value of the policy. If you die, it's the amount that's paid to the beneficiary. The price you pay is based on your age and health when you take the policy out and remains the same as long as you keep the coverage in force.

The Savings Element

In the first few years that a straight-life policy is in force very little of each payment goes into savings. In later years relatively more is set aside. Any time you wish to cancel the policy, whatever savings have built up will be returned to you in cash. Or you can leave the insurance in force and borrow the cash value, at 5 to 8 percent (see page 383).

The Price

Straight-life is far more expensive than term (see table, page 369) because money must be provided for the savings element as well as for insurance coverage. Due to the expense, young families with straight-life coverage often can't afford all the insurance they need to protect their families in case of death.

The amount you pay for a policy is called the *premium,* and every company prices its policies differently. Because of the wide spread in price, by all means compare several policies before you buy.

Why the Premium Remains Level

Straight-life often seems more attractive than term insurance because, although the annual premium starts out much higher, it remains the same throughout the life of the policy, whereas term insurance grows more expensive as you get older. *But in fact, the same is true of straight-life insurance: The cost of true protection goes UP as you grow older.* You simply aren't aware of the cost increase because of the way the policy is packaged. Here's what I mean:

At death, whatever savings have built up in the policy are put toward paying off the death claim. The insurance company itself pays only the *difference* between the cash value and the actual face value of the policy. If the policy is fairly new, there's only a small cash value, which means that the insurance company has to pay the bulk of the claim. But if you've had the policy for a long time, the cash value might be quite large, leaving relatively little for the insurance company to pay. As the years go by and the cash value builds up, the insurance company's liability declines. So you're paying the *same premium* for *less and less insurance.* Put another way, it means that as you grow older, the coverage is getting more and more expensive, just as it does with term insurance.

The following table shows how that works. It assumes that a twenty-five-year-old man bought a $10,000 straight-life policy, paying a premium of $167 a year. As the cash value in the policy increases, the death protection provided by the insurance company goes down. If you divide the premium by the number of $1,000 units of insurance-company protection the policy actually provides, you can see how the cost per $1,000 of coverage *increases sharply as he gets older.*

HOW THE COST OF STRAIGHT-LIFE INSURANCE PROTECTION INCREASES EVEN THOUGH THE PREMIUM REMAINS THE SAME

Age	Annual premium[a]	Total death payment	Cash value	Insurance company liability[b]	Actual cost per $1,000 of protection
25	$167	$10,000	0	$10,000	$16.70
30	167	10,000	$ 490	9,510	17.58
35	167	10,000	1,270	8,730	19.13
40	167	10,000	2,000	8,000	20.87
45	167	10,000	2,790	7,210	23.19[c]

[a]From age 25, when the policy starts.
[b]Death payment minus the cash value.
[c]The actual cost per $1,000 will increase even more sharply at later ages.

Conceptually, straight-life insurance is the same as decreasing term insurance (page 373) plus a savings account. The insured amount declines as you get older and your financial responsibilities abate, and the savings build up to provide you with the cash you need at retirement. You can cover these needs separately by buying inexpensive term insurance and starting a savings account on the side. Or you can buy a straight-life policy that provides for both. Unfortunately, people with straight-life policies often wind up with half a loaf—doing a poor job with both their savings and insurance.

Is the Savings Buildup Worth It?

There's no way to tell what interest is being paid on the savings that accumulate in a straight-life insurance policy. The insurance coverage and cash value are priced as a package, and you simply don't know how much is being charged for each. Studies of particular policies have suggested that the interest rate is probably what you'd get on passbook savings, or perhaps less. At this writing, that would put the average interest rate on the savings element of a life insurance policy at 4 to 5 percent over the long term (lower in the early years, higher in the later years).

Although the return is low, it can be attractive to people with high incomes (in the 45 percent tax bracket and up). With insurance policies,

SAVING IN A STRAIGHT-LIFE POLICY
VERSUS SAVING ELSEWHERE[a]
Based on a $100,000 insurance policy

	Starting at age 25			*Starting at age 35*		
Age	Cash value in straight-life policy[b]	Savings at 8%[c]	Savings at 10%[c]	Cash value in straight-life policy[b]	Savings at 8%[c]	Savings at 10%[c]
30	$ 5,370	$ 7,540	$ 7,982	$	$	
35	15,210	18,618	20,862			
40	28,320[d]	34,572	41,264	7,770	10,892	11,545
45	46,090[d]	57,257	73,341	21,490	26,132	29,338
50	69,900[d]	89,369	123,726	39,420	47,315	56,726
55	101,600[d]	134,577	202,814	63,230	76,469	98,766
60	143,390[d]	197,881	326,974	94,500	116,223	163,235
65	196,970[d]	286,094	521,886	134,590	168,098	262,736

[a]With thanks to William Ardito and Scott Beckley, William G. Ardito Associates.
[b]Projected cash values, using dividends to buy additional paid-up insurance.
[c]Net return after taxes, no matter what the bracket.
[d]These numbers are all overstated, because they're before-tax returns. At this point, the cash value is higher than the premiums paid. The policyholder would subtract the premiums from the cash value and pay income taxes on the difference.

Note: The above chart shows the savings buildup in a straight-life policy compared with buying term insurance and investing the difference. A *low-cost* straight-life policy was used for the illustration; higher-cost policies would show up more poorly.

An important point: If one of the men illustrated above had bought straight-life insurance and died, his family would have only the face value of his policy, whereas if he had bought term and put the difference into a high-interest investment, like a money-market mutual fund, his survivors would have his life insurance *plus* all the savings — a significant increase in cash.

that part of the annual increase in cash value attributable to interest earned on your premium is not taxed every year, as it would be if your savings were in a bank. Instead, the annual interest buildup is tax-deferred.

If you ever turn the policy in for cash, part of the proceeds may be taxed—but then again, it may not. You're allowed to subtract from cash value all the premiums paid for insurance coverage. If total premiums add up to more than the cash value, no income taxes are due; if the cash value is higher, you declare as income only the amount that exceeds the premiums paid. That kind of tax break is not available with bank savings, where you have to pay taxes on the interest every year and aren't allowed to deduct the cost of insurance coverage.

Consequently, for people in high tax brackets life insurance can be a good tax shelter. (And such people are in a financial position to buy enough straight-life insurance to protect their families in case they die prematurely.) Alternative forms of tax shelter include municipal bonds, Individual Retirement Accounts, Keogh plans, and U.S. savings bonds. A wealthy person might choose one of these methods of deferring or avoiding taxes, or spread his savings among two or three of them, depending on convenience and the relative attractiveness of the interest rate offered.

People in the middle and lower tax brackets can do better by saving outside a life insurance policy. In the 25 percent bracket, all you need is a 6 percent bank term account or credit union passbook account to get the same return, after federal taxes, as a $4\frac{1}{4}$ percent insurance policy (to cover state income taxes, the bank interest rate would have to be a little higher). In the 35 percent bracket, you can do as well with a 7 percent term account. A $7\frac{1}{4}$ percent account or corporate bond would outperform the insurance policy by a comfortable margin. If, at retirement, your tax bracket is low, you'd get more out of a tax-deferred Series E savings program (see page 544) than out of an untaxed $4\frac{1}{4}$ or 5 percent in an insurance policy. A long-term investment in the stock market would probably be even more productive for a family saving up for retirement twenty-five or more years away (see page 567).

The table on page 379 gives an example of how a combination of term insurance and savings can outperform a straight-life policy. It takes three men at age twenty-five and three men at age thirty-five. The first in each group puts his money into a good $100,000 straight-life policy sold by a major insurance company. The cost for the twenty-five-year-old is $1,385 a year, and for the thirty-five-year-old, $1,964 a year. The second and third each buy five-year renewable term insurance and put the difference between the cost of straight-life and the cost of term into high-interest savings. The second man invests his savings at 8 percent after taxes (which can be done through a fixed-income vehicle, such as bonds or bank term accounts). The third man gets 10 percent, after capital gains taxes, from long-term stock investments, real estate, or even a money-market mutual fund. The table shows the amount of savings they each wind up with at age sixty-five.

As you can see, the people who save elsewhere can do better than the people who save in straight-life policies. Insurance agents will tell you to buy more insurance when you're younger because the premium is lower, but the tables clearly show how much smarter you'd be to put that money to work in other investments. If you use your money to buy straight-life, its long-term earning power benefits the insurance company rather than you.

Another common sales tactic is to tell you that by buying straight-life insurance you have coverage all your life and at retirement get back the same amount you paid in, so you have insurance "free" all those years. That bland assertion completely ignores all the money you lose by keeping your cash tied up in low-interest insurance rather than putting it to work for you somewhere else.

That's the story, in black and white. The insurance agent is bragging about giving you your money back when you cancel the policy. But if you put your savings somewhere else, you would get your money back *plus* many thousands of dollars extra, depending on the return you got on your savings after taxes. Furthermore, you could use your savings, if you had to, without reducing your insurance, whereas an unpaid loan against the cash value of the straight-life policy is subtracted from the policy proceeds at death.

Different life insurance policies would produce different results when compared with alternative forms of saving. Lower-cost policies than the one used in our example would compare more favorably, higher-cost policies, less favorably. But the principle always remains the same.

Putting Cash Values into Perspective

When Mary comes back from the cemetery after burying her husband, John, and the neighbors cluster around her to console her, no one will ask her how large the cash value portion of the life insurance policy was. What matters is how large the death benefit is. Savings in a life insurance policy should come only after a sufficient provision has been made for money in case of death.

Two final points about cash values: (1) They build up very slowly in the early years. If you need insurance for a relatively short period of time—say, ten or fifteen years or less—these policies give you very little in return for your large cash outlay. By and large, cash-value insurance shouldn't even be considered unless you expect to keep it for fifteen or twenty years or more. (2) *The purchasing power of cash is eroded every year. A $50,000 cash value may be worth only $25,000 in purchasing power just eight years from now.*

The Forced-Savings Aspect: Is It Worth It?

A straight-life policy gives people a powerful incentive to save money. If they don't send in their premium on time (a small part of which goes into savings), they'll lose their insurance coverage. An insurance agent's most powerful argument is to suggest to people that if they were left on their own, they might not save, whereas a straight-life policy makes savings automatic.

Most people are in fact able to save money on their own, especially as they get older and their children are grown. However, if you can't save money any other way, it's better to save in a life insurance policy than not at all. Start with a small straight-life policy and a lot of term (to be sure your family is adequately protected) and gradually convert the term policies to straight-life as you can afford it.

But there are other forced-savings methods that can be just as effective. Many companies have payroll savings plans, where you can have a certain amount taken out of each paycheck and put in a savings account, savings bonds, or company stock. Some people do well with Christmas Clubs, taking the money accumulated at the end of every year and putting it into a savings account. Banks will automatically move money from checking to savings accounts every month. For a fuller discussion of automated savings methods, see "Automate Your Savings," page 45. The point is that any reasonably determined person can build regular savings without paying an insurance agent a commission.

In truth, the ability to save money is as much a question of timing as it is of perseverance. A young family with high nest-building and child-rearing expenses can't save much. That makes them vulnerable to the argument that if they don't buy straight-life, they won't have any money at all for their old age. But as their salaries rise and their children grow older, they usually find it easier to put money aside. If they become homeowners, each mortgage payment is a form of saving, since it builds equity ownership in a home. They may also acquire a right to a significant pension. After the children leave home, considerable amounts of money can often be set aside for the parents' retirement. So just because you aren't saving money when you're young doesn't mean that life will always be that way. There's no need to be stampeded into buying a straight-life policy if it means scrimping on the vital insurance protection you need now.

Return-of-Cash-Value Benefit

If you live to an old age and cash the policy in, you'll get the cash value that you saved at such great expense. However, if you die, the cash value becomes part of the death benefit, reducing the amount the insurance company has to pay. If you want your survivors to receive both the face amount *and* the cash value, you can buy a return-of-cash-value benefit, which is simply a term policy that increases over the years at about the same rate that cash value builds up. Sometimes it's cast as a return-of-premium benefit, with the implication that you'll "get all your premiums back." Agents can make it sound like a lovely free gift provided by the company. But in fact, it's just extra insurance that you're buying at regular rates. This coverage typically lasts for only twenty years, so if you live longer and then die, there's no extra payment.

Loans Against Cash Value

Whenever you want, you can borrow the cash value in a straight-life policy (insurers are allowed to delay the loan for up to six months, but rarely do so). Depending on how old the policy is and which state you bought it in, the interest rate runs from around 5 to 8 percent. You can pay off the loan on whatever schedule you want, sending payments whenever it's convenient.

There's no need to repay this loan. In fact, the insurance company will never even send you a bill. As a result, many borrowers leave the loan outstanding year after year, compounding annual interest charges. But if you die with the loan outstanding, the total amount of the loan plus interest will be deducted from the proceeds of the policy, leaving your beneficiary with less money. (*Note:* If you own a dividend-paying policy, you can use the dividends to buy annual term insurance to cover the loan. In case of death, your family would then receive the policy's full face value. If you need the coverage, this is a wise option to choose, even though it means raising the cost of your insurance.)

Borrowing the cash value and not repaying the loan *increases the cost of your remaining insurance* by the amount of interest you owe every year. If you don't expect to repay the loan for some time (or not at all), you're still young, and the amount of cash value in the policy is small, it might make sense to cancel the policy, repay the loan, and buy term insurance. On the other hand, if you've owned the policy for ten or fifteen years, it makes more sense to hang onto it. At that point, cash values start to build rapidly—so you're getting a higher return on your money than would probably be available if you canceled the contract and invested elsewhere. Older people, borrowing from cash values to pay the premiums, might do better to switch to *extended term* coverage (see page 394).

One thing many people don't realize is the extent to which interest compounding can work against you in an insurance policy loan. If you don't pay the interest out of pocket every year, as many borrowers don't, costs mount the longer you keep the loan. Say, for example, that you take an insurance company loan at 6 percent. If you don't pay the interest, that amount is added to the loan's outstanding balance; next year, then, 6 percent will be levied against that increased amount. If you pay nothing back for ten years, the average cost over the period will be 8.5 percent a year. After fifteen years, the average annual cost rises to 9.4 percent. You can avoid this by repaying the interest every year, even if you don't repay any of the loan principal.

Interest on policy loans is tax-deductible when paid. If you pay it out of pocket each year, it's deductible on your current tax return. If you let the interest debt accumulate in the policy, it's deductible when the policy is terminated (either by death, cancellation, or cashing it in), and the unpaid interest is subtracted from the policy proceeds.

Automatic Premium Loans

When you sign up for a policy, one common option permits automatic loans against cash value to pay the premiums. If you neglect to pay a premium by the end of the grace period (usually thirty-one days after the due date), the company will take that amount of money out of your cash value and charge it up as a loan. With most companies, this can continue as long as the cash value covers premium costs plus unpaid loan interest (although some companies allow only two or three auto-matic payments). When the cash value is exhausted, the insurance will terminate unless you resume paying for it on your own. It's worth electing the automatic premium loan provision, as protection against having your coverage lapse accidentally. On the other hand, if you often use your cash value to pay premiums, you're raising the cost of the insurance (by 5 to 8 percent, depending on the policy loan rate) and depleting your long-term savings.

Limited-Payment Life

A regular straight-life policy is priced to cover you up to age one hundred, if you live so long, with premiums payable every year. (At one hundred, the cash value would finally equal the face value; the policy would then be terminated, and you'd receive the cash in a lump sum.) A limited-payment policy also covers you to age one hundred, but the premiums are payable over a shorter time. The idea is to "get the premiums out of the way" before you retire. So you pay a higher annual premium than you do for ordinary straight-life and stop paying it somewhere short of age one hundred. For ex-ample, you might buy a policy that is paid up in twenty years, or thirty years, or at age sixty-five.

However, just because a policy is "paid up" doesn't mean there aren't any expenses! The insurance company extracts the continuing cost of coverage from the interest it pays on your cash value. Hence, a limited-payment policy has a rapid cash buildup in the early years, while you're paying into the policy, and an extremely slow buildup in the later years, when the insurance company takes a portion of each year's interest as the price of continuing to carry the policy.

Insurance expert Joseph M. Belth says there's some evidence that many, if not most, insurance companies charge more per $1,000 of protection for limited-payment life policies than for straight-life poli-cies.

Aside from the cost, the concept of limited-payment life is question-able. The insurance is expensive, so it reduces your income during your earning years. Yet you're paying all that money to be sure of having insurance after age sixty-five—which is a time many people don't need coverage. The policy might make sense if you foresee a need for a certain amount of life insurance in old age (for example, because you married late and have young children), don't expect to be able to pay straight-life premiums after age sixty-five, and can afford the high premiums on limited-payment life. It also makes sense if you want to save through an insurance policy and as rapidly as possible. Otherwise, it doesn't.

What to Do with a Paid-up Policy

Although you pay no more premiums on a paid-up policy, the insurance company extracts a charge in the form of lower interest payments (see preceding section). Many people don't mind paying this charge, since it isn't costing them anything out of pocket. But if you cashed the policy in and put the proceeds in the bank, you'd earn more on your cash values. The insurance company might be giving you only 2 or 3 percent on your money, whereas the bank might pay 7 percent (at which rate money doubles every ten years).

If the paid-up policy is substantial and you still have financial obligations to survivors, consider keeping the insurance. Or turn it in, put the cash value in the bank, and use the interest it earns to finance another, smaller insurance policy. The value of a combination of savings account *plus* a smaller insurance policy financed by the savings-account interest might be larger than that of the original insurance.

If you have small paid-up policies of $2,000 or $3,000, perhaps bought by your parents or grandparents, by all means consider cashing them in. They're too small to make much of a difference to anyone's living standards, but if put in a bank, the cash value might eventually grow into a respectable sum. Many families who have kept small, paid-up policies for thirty or forty years are disappointed when they see how little they're finally worth.

Endowment Policies

The purpose of an endowment is to guarantee a specified sum of money at a certain age, with insurance coverage in the meantime. The cash value builds up rapidly and equals the face value on the endowment date. At that point you receive the cash in a lump sum and the insurance terminates. For example, if you buy a $25,000 endowment to age sixty and die anytime between now and age sixty, your beneficiary will get $25,000; if you live to age sixty, you'll get $25,000 in cash and the insurance will be canceled. The drawback is that it's an extremely expensive way to insure yourself—even more expensive than limited-payment life. And your savings build up more slowly than they would in savings accounts. (Some parents buy endowments on their children to help pay for their college, generally not a good idea. For more on this, see page 412.)

Retirement Income Policies

Generally, these are the costliest policies of all. They're designed to provide not only a death benefit if you die prematurely but a specified amount of income in your old age. Often the income is $10 per month for each $1,000 of face value, so if you bought a $25,000 retirement-at-sixty-five policy, you'd be buying insurance until age sixty-five, followed by a monthly income of $250 for life.

With these policies the cash value builds up rapidly; by around age fifty-five the cash value equals the face value of the insurance. At that point, the insurance company no longer has any of its own funds on the line. If you die, the entire payment you receive (the cash value) is money you yourself have saved. So all the payments you make after age fifty-five are not for insurance (since you no longer have any). You're simply depositing savings with the insurance company, which accumulate at a low interest rate. When you reach age sixty-five, the cash value is converted into a lifetime annuity or taken in a lump sum, whichever you prefer. You'll have a larger amount of retirement savings if you accumulate money in a high-interest bank account rather than in a retirement income policy. If you want an annuity, you can use your savings to buy one at age sixty-five or seventy.

Some Comparative Premiums
on $25,000 Policies

To give you an idea of how much these various types of straight-life policies would cost per year, compared with term policies, have a look at the following table:

SAMPLE ANNUAL COSTS OF
VARIOUS $25,000 POLICIES*

Term Policies	Age 35	Age 40	Age 45
Decreasing term to age 65	$ 98.00	$121.50	$153.75
Five-year renewable and convertible term	77.25	106.25	165.50
Level term to age 65	244.00	294.50	354.00
Decreasing term to age 100	213.75	272.50	355.25
Level term to age 75	325.00	402.25	500.00
Straight-life policies			
Straight-life	$ 438.75	$ 539.25	$ 661.00
20-payment life	637.50	743.75	870.00
20-year endowment	1,050.00	1,080.00	1,125.00
Retirement income at age 65 ($250 a month)	905.00	1,193.50	1,637.50

*With thanks to insurance agent J. Tracy Oehlbeck, author of *The Consumer's Guide to Life Insurance* (Pyramid paperback, 1975).

Family Policies

These normally combine cash value life insurance and a unit of term insurance on the husband, a small amount of term or straight-life insurance on the wife, and another small amount of term insurance on each child, convertible into a larger amount of straight-life when he or she reaches age twenty-one to twenty-five. The amounts for each family member are fixed and depend on the size of the term insurance unit bought by the husband. But why would you want to insure the family this way? To begin with, children don't normally need insurance. If the wife doesn't work outside the home, she probably doesn't need insurance either (see page 410). If a wife works outside the home, she normally has some life insurance with her employer. If her employer has no such plan and the family depends on her income, she'll need far more coverage than a family policy provides.

If a wife or child needs a small amount of coverage, it is usually inexpensive to add it to the husband's policy as a rider, but the amount of the rider should be your selection, not a predetermined amount set by the insurance company. Most companies will add a wife insurance rider only to straight-life policies, but some will do it with term policies, too.

Family Income Plans

These combine a segment of straight-life insurance, which lasts until you die or cash it in, with a segment of decreasing term insurance that will pay your family a certain income per month until a specified date. Typically, the decreasing term portion is meant to cover the family while the children are still home, and the straight-life to cover a dependent spouse after that date. If you buy this plan, check to see that the decreasing term can be converted to level term or straight-life without a medical exam if you want to continue that coverage past the expiration date. Also be sure that the income can be paid out in a lump sum at death in case your survivors prefer to take the money that way. It might be better to buy two separate policies specifically tailored to your needs rather than accept the predetermined amount specified by a family income plan. For more on the specific uses of decreasing term insurance, see page 373.

Modified Life

This is straight-life insurance designed for sale to the person who can't afford the premiums right now. For the first three or five years, the premium is lower than you'd normally pay; after that time, the premium jumps to a level higher than you'd have paid with a regular policy. That higher premium lasts the rest of your life. In general, if you can't afford to spend a lot of money on insurance and need the coverage, you should consider term insurance, not modified straight-life. If you sign up for a costlier policy than you can afford, you might have to drop it when the premium increases. You then would have wasted the large sum you paid for acquisition costs.

Minimum-Deposit Plans

These are large, straight-life policies sold to the well-to-do under a payment plan that's a tax ploy. To minimize the large, annual premium cost, the cash value is borrowed out of the policy every year to help pay the premium. As long as the policyholder pays four of the first seven premiums out of pocket, the interest on all the policy loans will be tax-deductible. Interest on the loan is paid currently, so it can be deducted from each year's tax return. In practice, it means an outlay of several thousand dollars in the early years (often borrowed); after that, the annual outlay for many years is no more than the interest on the policy loan, which at the start is quite low. Eventually the loan becomes quite costly, but it's rationalized away as being tax-deductible.

As the loan grows larger, the value of the straight-life policy grows smaller, since loans are deducted from the policy's proceeds at death. So to keep the insurance coverage level, the policyholder buys enough term insurance every year to cover the loan. If he dies, the loan amount will be subtracted from the proceeds of the straight-life policy, but the payoff on the term insurance makes up for that loss. At the start of this plan, the dividend paid on the policy every year is more than enough to pay for the term insurance and is automatically applied to its cost. This gives the illusion that you're not paying anything extra for the term coverage, but of course you are. If you weren't buying term insurance with the dividend, you'd have that money available every year for other purposes.

Since the cash value in the policy is constantly used for paying premiums, the effect of all this fancy footwork is to turn a straight-life policy into term coverage. If you cash the policy in, you'll get very little money back, since the policy loan approximately equals the cash value. Many insurance agents argue that for high-bracket people minimum-deposit is less expensive than term coverage because of the tax-deductible interest. But that ain't necessarily so. If you bought a low-cost term policy, put the difference between the cost of the term and the cost of minimum-deposit into tax-free municipal bonds or tax-deferred annuities, and reduced your term coverage as your savings grew, you would find that minimum-deposit is probably more expensive. It appears less expensive only when you don't count the value of the interest your money could be earning were you to hang onto it rather than spend it on unnecessary finance charges. People are too easily mesmerized by the word *tax-deductible*. Even after deductions interest paid is a *cost*, whereas even after income taxes interest earned is a *profit*, and well-to-do people can arrange to receive their interest tax-free.

More important, if you're in a high enough tax bracket to make minimum-deposit look good, why would you want to keep borrowing the cash value? Wealthy people are the only ones for whom the tax-sheltered aspect of insurance savings might make sense (see page 378). If you want term coverage, buy regular term and put the rest of your money into other investments rather than messing with minimum-deposit. If you want insurance savings, buy straight-life and let the cash values accumulate in peace.

One of the attractions of straight-life as opposed to term is that coverage can be continued into old age. But if you're wealthy enough to make minimum-deposit look attractive, you're unlikely to need insurance after age sixty-five, particularly the large amounts in which the insurance is usually sold. Furthermore, minimum-deposit gets less and less attractive as the years wear on.

When you're considering the policy, the insurance agent will show you figures for the first twenty years in order to prove how well everything works out. By the fifteenth year the annual out-of-pocket cost is getting pretty large, but he reassures you by reminding you that it's all tax-deductible interest. Around the twenty-first year, however, your annual payment will start to outstrip the deductible interest cost. By the twenty-fifth year the cost of annual term insurance plus interest is so large that the company is usually no longer willing to insure so large a package, and the death benefit begins to fall. Most minimum-deposit holders will probably cancel their insurance before this point (I say "probably" because the concept is so new that there's little real-life twenty-year experience). If personal reasons compel you to continue it, the more burdensome the out-of-pocket costs will become and the less the policy will pay in case of death.

Another point: When all your attention is on the wonderful tax breaks you're going to get, it may not occur to you to question the cost of the policy as a whole. Insurance analyst Joseph M. Belth warns that minimum-deposit plans may be used to divert attention from the fact that the basic insurance policy is high-priced. The premiums are particularly high because of the need to build up cash value in a hurry. If you wonder why the agent is trying to divert you, Belth gives this good reason: The first-year commission on $50,000 worth of five-year renewable term insurance sold to a thirty-five-year-old is in the area of $100 to $125. But if the agent sells you term coverage through a minimum-deposit plan, he'll make $500 to $600 in the first year.

The only time that a minimum-deposit approach might make sense is if you're around age sixty and suddenly find that you need more insurance. Renewable term is extremely expensive at that age, if you can get it at all. It's cheaper to buy a straight-life policy and immediately borrow the cash values to help pay the premiums. In this case, you'd start borrowing right away, without bothering to pay four of the first seven premiums out of pocket. This means that the interest on the policy loans would not be tax-deductible, but presumably you're looking for the most inexpensive coverage possible, not a tax gimmick.

Other Financed Policies

An insurance agent may persuade you to use the cash values of Policy A to pay for Straight-life Policy B. Considering the fact that the interest is tax-deductible, it may seem as if the coverage is practically free. But you've paid for it, all right—or, rather, your beneficiaries have—since the policy loan is deductible from the proceeds of the insurance. If you're "lucky" enough to die right away, your doubling-up would pay off. But if you live, you have to take over paying for both policies (and repaying the loans) out of your earnings, or else see the cash value in one policy totally depleted. Since you presumably chose expensive straight-life insurance for the tax-sheltered savings element, there's no point in depleting the savings. If you'll settle for an insurance policy with no savings, why not make your second policy term insurance— which you can probably pay for without borrowing money? Or switch from straight-life to term, put the cash value in the bank (at a higher interest rate than the insurance company pays), and use the interest to buy a second smaller insurance policy?

Another approach is to borrow money from a bank or finance company, use it to buy insurance, then pay off the loan with the insurance policy's cash value—thus transferring the loan from the bank to the insurance policy. But again, all this does is deplete your cash values. If you don't care about cash values, you shouldn't be buying straight-life insurance in the first place. Buy term instead. You'll probably be able to pay for it without borrowing, so you'll save yourself the interest costs.

Other Specialty Policies

Insurance companies have a wide variety of insurance policies, fit together in different ways and skewed to appeal to different needs. For example, there are variations on the modified life policy that have especially low premiums in the first few years and much higher premiums later. (These are designed for people who might otherwise be tempted to buy term.) There are low-cost straight-life policies that reduce the death payment after age sixty-five or seventy (and have lower cash values than ordinary straight-life). There are combinations of endowments and decreasing term; of retirement income policies and level term; of limited-payment life and a whole range of options.

But at bottom, everything is either straight-life or term, separately or in combination. The more complicated a policy, the harder it is to compare its cost with simpler policies that achieve the same ends. Complications frequently mask high prices. You can meet all of your insurance needs with straight-life or term, and you'd be wise to stick to them.

Variable Life

The idea here is to provide an insurance policy competitive with mutual funds. The death benefit generally isn't allowed to fall below face value but may increase if the insurance company's portfolio of investments rises significantly. Cash value may also increase, but if the stock market does poorly, it will go down.

It's a wise idea for a young person to have a good part of his savings in the stock market for long-term appreciation. Over long periods the stock market has always outperformed savings accounts, usually by large margins. But rather than leaving it to the insurance company to do your investing for you and pay the agent's commission, you may prefer to buy no-load mutual funds. Consider dividing your protection money among term life insurance, fixed-interest savings (such as bank term accounts or savings bonds), and long-term stock investments. It achieves the same result as variable life insurance, and at smaller cost. Furthermore, if you die, your family will have the advantage of both your insurance policy and your investments; with variable life they would get insurance proceeds and nothing else.

Split Life

Here, the basic elements of a straight-life policy are split into two separate contracts. For protection you get one-year renewable term insurance, often renewable to advanced ages, such as ninety-five; for savings you get a retirement annuity payable at age sixty-five. They're joined in a single plan, so the amount of life insurance depends on the size of your annuity payment, and you can't renew the insurance unless you keep up the annuity. The insurance element of split life is often quite low-priced when compared with regular one-year term contracts. But the insurance company balances that advantage with a big disadvantage: The retirement annuity segment is a poor savings plan. If you're going to buy term and save the difference, consider saving it somewhere else, where the interest rates are better.

Industrial Insurance

These are small policies, usually for less than $1,000, bought by low-income people as burial insurance. The premiums are collected weekly or monthly, often by people who call directly on the policyholders. The price of this coverage is high because of the expensive method used to collect the premiums. It's yet another case of "the poor pay more."

Switching Your Plan

Anytime you want, the insurance company will make certain adjustments to your insurance plan. You can

1. Use the cash value to buy "paid-up" insurance to last the rest of your life. The amount will be considerably less than your present policy's face value, but you'll have no more premiums to pay.
2. Use the cash value to buy *single-payment extended term insurance.* Here, the face value remains the same, but the policy lasts only as long as you have the cash value to pay for it. Again, you'll have no more premiums to pay.
3. Change a high-premium endowment or limited-payment life policy to straight-life, based on the issue date of the original policy. Straight-life has a lower cash value than the other two policies, so the insurance company pays you the difference. But since reducing the cash in your policy entails an increase in the amount of insurance protection the company has to provide, you'll generally be asked to produce evidence of insurability.
4. Change a straight-life policy to a higher-premium plan, such as limited-payment life or an endowment, based on the issue date of the

original policy. Since the latter plans have higher cash values than straight-life, you'll have to make a payment (plus interest) to bring those values up to par.

Who Should Have Straight-Life?

1. Upper-income taxpayers, for whom tax-deferred or tax-exempt savings, at a little below bank passbook interest rates, are attractive when compared with other tax-deferred or tax-exempt vehicles available.

2. People with a big estate tax, when the estate doesn't have enough liquid assets, such as savings or marketable securities, to cover the tax payment. Term insurance won't do because it typically runs out at age sixty-five or seventy (although there are a few term policies that continue to age one hundred, at a very high price). All straight-life policies continue their coverage into advanced ages. However, there's no need for young people to buy straight-life insurance just in case they might need it for estate taxes when they die. To begin with, most estates are not illiquid; they have enough cash or securities to meet the tax payments. In the second place, if you're wealthy enough to have an estate tax problem (starting in 1981, estate taxes won't even begin unless the taxable estate is larger than $175,625), you'll probably be able to afford the insurance when you're older.

3. People of any tax bracket who have tried other forced-savings plans, such as payroll checkoff or monthly savings bond purchase plans, and find that they can't stick with it, and who don't expect to be able to save a large amount of money after the children leave home. However, straight-life should be combined with enough term insurance to provide all the protection the family needs.

4. People who want to leave the money to charity. You designate a charity as your beneficiary, and get an income tax deduction for the premiums paid during your lifetime. Term insurance can be used the same way, but because it gets so expensive to keep in advanced ages (and may not be renewable after age sixty-five or seventy), straight-life is preferred.

5. Older men who marry young women and have children. Their life insurance needs continue past age sixty-five or seventy because they may still have children to put through college. If the wife doesn't work, she will most certainly need income as a widow. The bulk of the family protection should be in term insurance, but that amount of protection

needed past age sixty-five would have to be straight-life. (Generally speaking, a young woman who marries an older man should expect to have to support herself at some point later in life.)

RIDERS FOR TERM OR STRAIGHT-LIFE

The Disability Waiver

This rider is well worth the small amount it costs. It provides that if you're totally disabled past a certain amount of time—typically six months—the insurance company itself will pay the premiums on your life insurance policy until you recover. Furthermore, the six months worth of premiums you paid after becoming disabled will be refunded. If the disability proves to be permanent, the premiums will be paid for life on a straight-life policy, or until the contract finally expires for renewable term, usually between age sixty-five to seventy-five.

Companies vary in their definition of "disabled." The better policies state that you're disabled if you're unable to perform the usual duties of your occupation or any other occupation for which you are reasonably suited in terms of education, training, and experience. A less favorable definition would refuse to consider you disabled as long as you can perform any job at all.

Most policies require that in order for you to be covered the disability must occur before you reach a certain age (generally, somewhere between fifty-five and sixty-five). The higher the age, the better, as far as you're concerned. Some policies put limits on the period of time benefits will be paid for a disability occurring between age sixty or sixty-five —it's better to find a company that pays benefits for life. If the waiver of premium has been built right into the policy cost so that you don't pay it separately, the price of your coverage should go down a little after the age when the rider expires.

If you're buying a term policy, there are three important points to check about the disability waiver, all of them related to what happens if you want to convert your term coverage to straight-life.

1. Will the company allow you to continue the waiver after conversion without your passing a physical exam? Can this be done at any age?

2. Will the waiver apply if your disability arose from an accident or illness suffered before you converted your policy from term to straight-life?

3. Can you convert to straight-life even if you're disabled, and have the insurance company pay the premiums right away, without having to wait until you reach a certain age?

If all these questions can't be answered in the affirmative, you'd be wise to consider another insurance company. It is most important that you be able to convert whenever you want and regardless of health, without risking the loss of that important disability waiver.

Guaranteed Insurability

For a small extra payment you can be guaranteed the right to buy stated amounts of insurance at specified future times, regardless of health. You'll pay the full premium for the age at which you buy, but you'll be charged standard rates even if you've had a heart attack or some other serious illness in the meantime. And no matter how ill you are, you can't be refused the amount of insurance you contracted to buy. The guaranteed insurability rider is usually available up to age forty.

The rider will specify the various ages at which you can buy the insurance and the maximum amounts of coverage available. If you skip a purchase, it's gone forever; you can't make it up at a later time. For a young family person forced by budget limitations to buy less insurance than he really needs, the rider is probably a good investment. It insures that you'll be able to get more coverage in the future no matter what happens. One point: Find out if the waiver of premium for disability (see the previous section) applies to all future insurance bought under the guarantee, without the need for a physical examination. If you became disabled and took advantage of the guaranteed insurability to buy added insurance, it would be of little value unless the insurance company paid the premiums as long as you couldn't.

Accidental Death

Most insurance companies run a crap game called "double indemnity" or "accidental death rider." It provides that if you die in an accident, the insurance policy will pay twice (or three times) its face value. An accidental death rider costs less than a separate accident policy, so if you want such coverage, this is the best way to get it. But do you really want the coverage?

Young people like it because they figure that if they die, it will likely be in an accident rather than from disease. But the low cost of accidental death riders is a tip-off that few people die in accidents. Even young people are more likely to die of natural causes than in an auto accident or plane crash. To count on this rider to provide your family with sufficient funds after your death is a gamble you're most likely to lose. Anyone with financial responsibilities should be sure that his basic life insurance coverage is sufficient. Once that's done, there's no need to pay for an accidental death rider, airline trip insurance, or any other limited-use policy.

DIVIDENDS OR NOT?

Both term and straight-life policies come in two varieties—those that pay dividends and those that don't. Actually, the word *dividend* is a misnomer, implying, as it does, an earned return on an investment. In fact, an insurance dividend is nothing more than a return of part of the premium you paid, and it's for this reason that insurance dividends are not taxable.

The premium on a dividend-paying policy runs about 30 percent higher than on an equivalent policy without dividends. The company that pays dividends overcharges for the basic insurance coverage, then pays you back whatever money is not needed to cover claims and meet expenses. By contrast, a company that does not pay dividends charges less for the policy but keeps any excess over claims and expenses.

Which type of coverage is more expensive is the subject of hot debate in the industry. Over the long term, holders of dividend policies may seem at first glance to pay less for their coverage, because after fifteen or twenty years their dividends may get quite large. However, if you bought a less expensive, nondividend policy and were steadfast enough to put the difference in cost between that and a dividend policy into the bank every year, it is possible that your long-term cost of coverage might be less.

Another argument often given for dividend policies is that, since these companies are owned by their policyholders, all the surplus is distributed as dividends. Nondividend companies, by contrast, are owned by stockholders, who expect the company to show profits and pay them a return on their investment. It "stands to reason," the argument goes, that a company worried about profits will have to charge more than a company owned by policyholders, but unfortunately that's not so. It can be argued with equal force that a company with stockholders looking over its shoulder has to keep expenses down, and so can afford to charge less. You simply can't make easy assumptions about which type of company is better motivated to serve the public.

If the annual out-of-pocket cost is the key to how much insurance you can buy (which it is for most of us), consider a lower-priced, nondividend policy. The possibility of winding up with a lower net cost after twenty years in a dividend policy doesn't mean much if it reduces the amount of family protection you can buy now. If you plan to keep your insurance for no more than ten or fifteen years, nondividend policies are definitely a better bet because dividends are quite small in the early years. On the other hand, if the size of the annual premium doesn't matter and you plan to keep the policy for a long time, you might prefer the likely long-term advantage of dividend policies.

Dividends Not Guaranteed

When an insurance agent shows you the projected cost of your insurance policy, he includes dividend payments for twenty years in the future. But that projection is strictly guesswork because dividends aren't guaranteed. Up to now long-term dividend payments have generally been higher than originally projected because we've been living in an era of rising interest rates. But if, in the future, interest rates enter a declining trend, dividends will be lower than projected. Insurance companies often reduce dividends because of a bad year or a downward dip in interest rates. But they rarely tell their customers about it. To find out whether the dividend was lower or higher this year, you'll have to compare the annual year-end statements that most companies send their policyholders.

Dividend Changes to Favor
Certain Classes of Customers

Some insurance companies have begun to pay higher dividends to people who bought their policies in more recent years, and less to older customers. They justify it by saying that premiums paid by newer customers have been invested at higher interest rates, so the newer customers deserve a break. (It's worth noting that using a higher dividend structure for newer customers lets a company make the cost of its policies, when projected for twenty years, look lower than the policies of companies that pay everyone the same dividend.) It's fairer to pay everyone the same, since older policyholders were never told that they ran a risk of having their income needs given second place. The method of allocating dividends so that newer policyholders get more is called the "investment year" method. Ask your insurance agent if his company uses it, or anything like it. Unfortunately, if it does, there's not much you can do about it, since it's far more expensive for older policyholders to switch than to stay.

Dividend Options

If you have a dividend-paying policy, there are a number of things you can do with the money you get back. You can

1. Take the money in cash.
2. Apply it toward the annual premium. You'll then be billed for the difference between the premium and the dividend paid that year.
3. Leave the dividends with the company to accumulate at interest. The interest payment, however, is generally lower than you'd get at a bank, which makes this a poor choice. The interest on dividends is taxable, just as bank interest would be.
4. Use the money to buy paid-up straight-life additions to your policy. In effect, the dividends increase the amount of your insurance by a small amount every year. This can be a wise choice for a person who

is otherwise uninsurable, since no health exam is necessary. But for others, it's questionable. Assuming that you live a reasonable number of years, those small dividend payments may do you more good in a bank than as paid-up insurance.

5. Use the dividend (a few companies allow you to do this) to buy one year's worth of term insurance, the amount depending on your age and the size of the dividend. Often the term rate is quite low compared with the price of other term policies available, so a small dividend might purchase quite a sizable annual policy. If you need more insurance, this can be an inexpensive way to increase coverage.

SOME SPECIAL RULES

The following general principles apply to most insurance policies. But ask the insurance agent to go over the fine print with you so you will know exactly what your insurance policy has to say on the subject.

The Grace Period

The majority of insurance policies cover you for a period of thirty-one days after the policy expires. If you fail to renew a term policy on time, or pay a regular premium when it's due, you have thirty-one extra days to take action. Should you die during the grace period, the policy still pays off. (Not all policies give you this extra time, so ask the agent about it before you buy.)

Reinstatement

If you don't pay the premium by the end of the grace period (and if there's no provision to pay the premium out of the policy's cash values), the coverage will lapse. You can generally have it reinstated within a specified period of time, often five years, as long as you haven't withdrawn the cash values and can show that you're still insurable. You'll also have to pay all the back premiums, plus interest. But once you are reinstated, your policy continues to cost the same amount as it did when you first bought it, and will build up cash values more rapidly than if you started out with a new policy. The reinstatement requirements for your particular policy are spelled out in the contract.

Incontestability

If you inadvertently mislead the company on an insurance policy application, and die shortly after receiving coverage, the company may refuse to pay. But when two years have passed since the application date (or one, depending on the policy), the company can no longer contest the claim. By and large, the courts have required that proceeds be paid after two years even if it appears that the misstatement was deliberate.

Wrong Age

If it's found that a person put the wrong age on his insurance application, the proceeds are adjusted to what his premiums would have bought for the right age. (Some insurers use this clause only when it works in their favor—that is, when the insured was older than he said —and not when it works against them.) Problems can arise if for some reason the age given on the death certificate is incorrect; your beneficiary may not easily be able to prove your correct age. A way around this is to file proof of age with the insurance company while you're still alive, get an acknowledgment, and keep it with the policy.

Ownership

The person who owns an insurance policy has specific rights: To cash in the policy or borrow against it; to name the beneficiary; to receive any dividends paid by the company, and to give these ownership rights to someone else. If you apply for a policy in your own name, you become the owner. If you want someone else to own the policy on your life, that person should sign the application. If you already own an insurance policy and want to give it away, ask your insurance agent for an *assignment form.* Most employee and group insurance can also be assigned; ask your employee benefits officer about it, or the agent who handles your group coverage.

The primary reason for not owning your insurance policy is estate taxes. If you own the policy, the proceeds are taxable in your estate, whereas if someone else owns it, they're not (for more on this, see Chapter 27, "Wills and Estate Planning"). Ownership might also be transferred as part of a divorce settlement. Once a policy is given away, all of the ownership rights just enumerated go to the new owner, who can cash the policy in, change the beneficiary, or do whatever he wants with it. If you want to change ownership, discuss it with a lawyer to be sure you understand all the tax angles.

Suicide

Insurance companies normally pay off even if the insured commits suicide. However, a clause will generally state that if the suicide takes place within two years (or one year, depending on the policy), the company will simply return the premiums rather than pay the face amount of the policy.

Interest Paid After Death

Between the date of death and the date that insurance proceeds are paid, the insurance company is holding money belonging to the beneficiary. Some companies pay interest during this period, others don't. If paid, the interest can amount to a considerable sum—for example, 5 percent on $30,000 comes to $125 a month. In general, the better companies will pay interest, so ask your insurance agent about it before you buy. (And ask to see where the contract guarantees it, since the verbal assurance of an agent is nothing unless it's also written down and signed by a company official.) The better companies also refund the unearned portion of a premium after death; for example, if you died six months after paying an annual premium, the unused half of the premium would be refunded along with the insurance proceeds.

Joint and Contingent Life

Some insurance companies will write *joint* coverage on two lives. The policy pays off when the first of the two dies, and costs less than writing two separate policies for the same amount. There should be a "guaranteed insurable" clause that lets the survivor take out a new policy, if it's needed, after the death of the first owner (he'll pay the appropriate rate for his age at the time). In case of divorce, however, jointly owned policies can complicate the division of property. *Contingent* coverage is similar to joint life, but can be written on two or more lives. Each person covered on a contingent-life contract owns his or her piece of the policy separately, so there's no difficulty in dividing ownership in case of divorce.

Preferred Versus Substandard Risks

People in good health get the best rate available from insurance companies. Some policies are even written exclusively for people in tip-top shape, which allows the company to sell them at particularly low premiums. On the other hand, people with a health condition that the company regards as suspicious, or who have a hazardous occupation, get a *rated* policy, which means the premium is higher. You can later appeal for a regular rate if you change jobs or the health condition doesn't recur. Some companies mislead people as to the nature of their policies; for example, a policy called Standard B might in fact be one for substandard risks. So be sure to ask the insurance agent whether you've been "rated" or not.

For a person offered a rated policy, there's no substitute for a really good insurance agent. He'll know which companies are more liberal in their approach to substandard risks and may well be able to find you a policy somewhere at a standard rate. In some cases he might even find coverage for a person whose application has been turned down by several insurers.

SHOULD YOU REPLACE YOUR POLICY?

Suppose you decide that you have the wrong sort of insurance—straight-life, say, when you'd be better off with term. Should you drop your present policies and replace them with something else? Or should you switch from your present insurance company to one that you've found to be cheaper?

The trouble with switching policies to another company is that you have to pay the insurance agent's commission all over again, which is a significant cost. A lot of business has been done, to the consumer's detriment, by persuading him to give up a policy that has started to accumulate a significant cash value and switch to a policy where the accumulation has to begin all over again. Because of this, many states have passed laws requiring life insurance agents to make a full comparison between the costs of the old and new policies at the time they suggest the change. (When you switch, the suicide and incontestability periods begin again, but that's not very important to most people.)

However, there are times when a new policy is entirely justified. For example:

• *If you have a straight-life policy, need more coverage, but can't afford the additional premiums.* It then makes sense to switch to term insurance in order to get more coverage from the premium you now pay. Whatever cash value has accumulated could be used to finance premiums, or could be withdrawn and put in the bank.

• *If you have a substantial cash value and want to use it to finance a larger total amount of protection for your family.* You could cancel the straight-life policy, put the cash in the bank, and use the interest it earns to finance a new policy (generally, a term policy, but you could also buy a smaller amount of straight-life). Your family's protection would then be made up of the face value of the new policy *plus* the savings in the bank, which together would probably be larger than the value of the old policy alone. In addition, the money you had been spending for the old policy could be earmarked for a new one, preferably term.

• *If you have a term policy and find that the coverage offered by another company is cheaper as you advance in age.* (Compare interest-adjusted costs, as explained on page 441, not simply the premiums and dividends.)

It generally does not make sense to switch from one straight-life policy to another, even if you've found a company whose premiums are cheaper than yours. Insurers generally pay small dividends in the early years of a life insurance policy and larger dividends in the later years; also, cash value buildup is better in the later years. If you've held a policy for several years, you're just coming into the time when dividend payments and cash value buildup are relatively good. You could easily lose money if you canceled the policy and began again, even with a company whose premiums were a little lower. (However, if there's a big difference in premium costs between the two companies, the switch might still make sense.)

Also, it generally makes no sense to drop a straight-life policy that you've held for several years and replace it with term insurance *if* you're adequately insured and aren't having any trouble meeting the premiums. At this point, the high acquisition costs and period of slow dividends is behind you; you're finally approaching the time of higher dividends and faster cash value buildup. Having paid the price, you should stay around for your reward.

If you do decide to switch policies, don't drop your old coverage until your new insurance is in force. It's important that you always be covered in case something happens.

Whenever an insurance agent proposes that you switch policies, have him present all the data showing why, then go over it with your present agent. If there's anything wrong with the figures, you can be sure that your present agent will find it. He may even be able to offer you a better deal in order to keep your business. (But be warned that he'll do his best to talk you out of the alternate plan, even if its merits are superior.)

WHO NEEDS INSURANCE, AND WHAT KIND?

• *If you're young, single, and with no dependents,* you generally don't need life insurance. The money you'd spend on premiums would be better in the bank or in long-term investments.

Some life insurance agents argue that you should buy insurance now just in case you need it in the future. They give two reasons for this: (1) The premiums are lower when you're younger, and (2) in the future you might contract a disease that would make you uninsurable. It's true that the premiums are lower, but that's because you'll be paying them for a longer time. If you put the money in the bank, instead of into insurance premiums, the interest buildup would give you more than enough money to cover the slightly higher premiums charged a few years later. Looked at this way, life insurance costs about the same whether you buy it now or buy it later, so you might as well wait and see if you really need it.

As for insurability, you'll probably be able to qualify for insurance in the future if it turns out that you need a policy. The percentage of people refused coverage on grounds of health, especially in their late twenties or early thirties, is mighty small. However, if there's a history of illness in your family and it tends to strike young, you might want to hedge your bets by getting a small amount of inexpensive term coverage now and paying for the right to buy additional insurance in the future, no matter what your health then (see page 397).

• *If you're older and single, with no dependents,* perhaps a widow whose children have left home, you need no life insurance. In fact, if you have a straight-life policy, consider cashing it in and investing the savings for a higher income.

• *If you're single with dependents,* whether you need life insurance depends on what would happen to those dependents after your death. A divorced parent with children might expect them to go to the ex-spouse. Assuming that the ex-spouse has enough money to support them comfortably, you don't need life insurance. If you want to provide the children with a nest egg and the property you own is of little value, a small amount of life insurance would do the trick.

A single parent, or divorced parent whose ex-spouse doesn't want the children, might plan on having them go to his or her parents, or perhaps a brother or sister. In that case you'd want to leave enough insurance so the children didn't become a burden. If you're supporting elderly parents, and there's no one to take over after your death, you'll need insurance to cover your contribution to their expenses.

When your parents die, or your children begin to support themselves, you'll no longer need life insurance. At that point, you can cancel your policies and use the premium money for personal savings and investments, which can benefit you as well as your heirs. The best way to provide for temporary needs of this sort is to buy inexpensive group or term insurance.

• *If you're married without children,* and you both work and are able to support yourselves, you don't need life insurance. Use your extra money for savings and investments. However, if the wife, say, earns too little to support herself, or doesn't work at all, then the husband should carry life insurance.

A young, dependent wife doesn't need insurance protection to last her a lifetime; she needs just enough to tide her over until she can start supporting herself. A policy to cover funeral expenses and give her a couple of years' income should do the job. If the husband has group insurance with his employer, that's probably all he needs. Alternatively, he could get a small term policy. The rest of a young couple's money should go into savings, investments, and nest building for them both to enjoy. One point: If you expect to have children in the future and have doubts about your health, you might want to buy a small policy with a guaranteed insurability rider, giving you the right to buy additional insurance at standard rates (see page 397). Most companies offer these riders only with straight-life policies, but a few offer them with term.

If the wife is middle-aged and has never worked, or if she earns only small amounts, a year's worth of "tide-her-over" insurance won't do. Since you've both agreed that she should stay home rather than have a career, the husband is obliged to provide her with a lifetime income in case of his death. This can be done inexpensively with group or term insurance until middle age. Since you have no children, it should not be difficult to build up enough savings so that after middle age, life insurance can be gradually reduced, and finally eliminated when you reach retirement. However, if you want to do some saving in an insurance policy rather than a bank or the stock market, you should gradually convert the term coverage to straight-life, as you can afford it.

• *If you're married with children,* life insurance is essential. The younger the children, the more coverage you need, because you have so many more years to provide for their support. If only the husband works, he needs enough insurance to protect his wife as well as his children. If both parents work, each of them should be insured for the minimum amount of family income each must provide. For example, say the husband's salary can cover 60 percent of the household budget after the death of his wife, income from savings can cover 5 percent, and payments from her Social Security account, 15 percent. She then needs enough insurance on her life to pay the remaining 20 percent of expenses. And vice versa. To work this out for your personal circumstances, see the Insurance Planning Worksheet, starting on page 422.

Most young families *can* afford to buy the large amount of insurance necessary to cover the expenses of raising and educating a family—as long as they buy inexpensive group or term insurance. If you put your money into straight-life, or a combination of straight-life and term, you will almost inevitably wind up with less coverage than you really need simply because your budget won't stretch that far. The rule for families on buying insurance should be *protection first and savings later,* when you can afford it.

As the children grow older and your financial responsibilities to them decrease, reconsider the amount of insurance you're carrying. Some policies can be canceled. If you decide to save money through an insurance policy, begin converting some term coverage to straight-life. If you want to put your savings somewhere else, cut back on term coverage as the premiums get more expensive and start building savings in bank accounts, real estate, or the stock market.

• *If you're an older man who married a young woman and has had children,* you need as much insurance as any family breadwinner. But because of your age, it's more expensive to maintain a large amount of coverage until your children grow up. Term insurance is still your best bet, even though the premiums begin to increase more quickly as you reach your late forties and early fifties. If you already have a straight-life policy, you might be able to use the cash values to finance added term insurance (this often works well while you're in your forties and early fifties, but may be too expensive in your sixties). Nondividend term costs the least out-of-pocket. Term generally can't be renewed after age sixty-five to seventy, so consider buying some straight-life, the amount depending on what your financial responsibilities will be after age sixty-five. On a limited budget, the best you may be able to do is keep enough straight-life to get the children through college in case you die before that time. Unless you're wealthy, your young widow will probably have to help support herself after your death and should make career plans accordingly. If you're uninsurable or can get coverage only at higher-than-normal rates, you'd do well to buy credit life insurance with every major purchase, since it requires no medical exam. Then, if you die, those possessions will at least be paid for. If you're divorcing and naming your first wife or children beneficiaries of your policies, try to have that arrangement end when the children grow up, your ex-wife remarries, or after a specified period of time. Finally, an older person should turn over every stone to find groups he can join that have low-cost insurance.

• *If you're a wife who doesn't work,* life insurance is generally a waste of money. A lot of attention has been paid recently to the economic value of a housewife's services, with the implication that she should be insured for that amount. Insurance agents, making their own use of feminist attitudes, may suggest that you have a "right" to equal insurance, in order to prove your worth. But a wife's worth isn't measured by the size of her insurance policy. To say that you're entitled to your fair share of the coverage is no more than emotional flag-waving in order to part you from your money. Insurance isn't a "right," it's just another one of those unavoidable expenses that comes with having a family, and one you shouldn't undertake if it's not necessary. Women who don't support anyone out of their own earnings don't need life insurance, since the purpose of insurance is to replace lost income. Better to take the money that would be spent on premiums and put it into a bank account in your own name.

A more pragmatic argument is that a wife should carry life insurance to protect her husband against the cost of having to hire a baby-sitter to look after young children if she should die. That's a perfectly accept-able goal, as long as HE carries all the insurance needed to protect the wife and children as long as necessary. Unfortunately, most husbands are grievously underinsured. If they die young, their wives and children have a hard time of it. A housewife looking out for her own interests would urge that all available money for insurance premiums first be spent on her husband, so that if he died, she and the children would have the largest sum of money possible. If, after that, some wife insur-ance is wanted, the cheapest way to get it is through a term insurance rider to the husband's policy. As soon as the children are old enough to look after themselves, the rider can be canceled.

Insurance agents sometimes argue that a wife should have her own straight-life policy as divorce insurance. If her husband leaves her, she can cash the policy in and will have some savings of her own. But the inference from this argument is that a wife needs *savings,* not insur-ance. Instead of spending money on high-cost premiums, only a small part of which goes into the insurance policy's savings element, that same annual sum should go into a savings account in the wife's name. If they divorce, she'll have far more savings than she'd get by cashing in a straight-life policy and at no extra cost to the husband. If they don't divorce, the couple has more joint money for retirement than they'd have if they wasted money on unneeded wife insurance.

• *If you're at retirement age,* you probably have no further need for life insurance. The combination of Social Security, pension (if you have one), and savings (including the cash value built up in a straight-life policy) should, if you've planned well, provide enough income for you and your survivor to live on. Any term policies should be canceled, as being too expensive; any straight-life policies should be cashed in and the proceeds invested for income.

However, if a man's wife is still partly dependent on whatever earnings he brings in, or on his portion of the Social Security payment, not all the insurance should be canceled. He should keep enough to bridge the gap between what her income would be from Social Security, pension, and savings after his death, and her expenses. Normally, the amount needed will be quite small. Wealthy people with illiquid estates may also need insurance, to help with estate taxes.

• *If you have children, should they be insured?* The answer is pretty generally *no.* Child insurance is an easy sale for life insurance agents because it's so cheap. But who are you buying it for? Child insurance doesn't protect the child; the payoff goes to you if the child dies. So it's something you're doing for yourself, not for him. Some parents do want a policy to pay for the child's funeral, just in case, but for this purpose, a $1,000 term policy is plenty (you may be able to get it cheaply as a rider to your own insurance). And you don't even need that if you have enough savings in the bank.

As a gift for a child an insurance policy is worth far less in cash than if you took the same amount of money and put it into a savings account for him every year. Grandparents are often tempted to buy their grandchildren a small policy—say, $1,000—because it appears that they can make a $1,000 gift at a very small price (the cost of the premium). But that "gift" isn't really for the grandchild. It's a gift to his beneficiary if he dies prematurely—for his parents, or for his future spouse. Grandparents might do better by giving the child a savings bond every year.

To protect the child, you need adequate insurance on the family breadwinner. It's his death that would affect the child's standard of living or his chance to go to college. If you're going to spend a few more dollars on insurance, use it for an extra $5,000 term policy on the working mother or father rather than needlessly buying insurance on the child. If the breadwinner dies and is underinsured, any small policy you had on the child would probably be allowed to lapse because you could no longer afford the payments.

Life insurance agents argue that child insurance does protect the child, by giving him a policy with low payments that he can take over as an adult, and by guaranteeing him some coverage in case he becomes uninsurable before he grows up. The chances of his being so ill he can't get insurance as a young adult are pretty small—hardly worth spending your money on (unless, of course, there's a chronic, debilitating disease in your family); and even if it happened, the small policy you bought him as a child is not going to "protect" him as an adult. It's true that the premiums would be lower if he started younger (but not very much lower—there's not much difference in the premiums at age twelve and age twenty-two). Furthermore, since you pay the premiums longer (and lose the interest that that money would otherwise be earning in a bank), the overall cost is about the same. You would be doing more for the child if you took the money you were spending on premiums every year and put it into a bank account for him.

• *If your child will go to college, should you buy him an endowment policy?* Some parents are persuaded that endowment policies (see page 387) are the best way to put away money for college. The policy starts when the child is, say, three years old, and matures when he's eighteen. A fifteen-year $4,000 endowment policy would insure the child for that amount in case he dies and produce perhaps $4,580 (including dividends) when he's eighteen and ready to matriculate.

For that wonderful bunch of benefits, you'll pay around $250 a year (less for smaller endowments). But the portion you spend on insurance is really wasted, since the child doesn't need the coverage. There isn't even the excuse of "preserving his insurability," since this policy will terminate when he reaches eighteen, takes the cash, and goes to college.

If you really want to save for your child's college education in an insurance policy, a better way would be to buy an endowment policy on the breadwinner that would mature when the child reaches eighteen. If the father, for example, is twenty-six years old, $4,000 worth of fifteen-year endowment coverage would cost around $251 a year—only a dollar or so more than the cost of child insurance. You'd have the same amount of cash when your child reaches eighteen and goes to school, with the added benefit that if the father dies, that $4,000 college fund would be paid in the form of life insurance. (*Note:* Different companies charge different rates for endowments, but the principle remains the same.) Considered purely as savings, however, any life insurance policy is inferior to a bank or S&L account. If you put $250 a year into the bank at 5½ percent compounded daily, you'd have $5,890 for your child's college in fifteen years—$1,310 more than the endowment policy pays. If you gradually moved your savings into one-, two-, and four-year term accounts, as the amounts grew, you might accumulate as much as $6,500 (because term accounts pay higher interest).

If you want a combination of savings and life insurance, consider buying a low-cost term policy on yourself (assuming you are the bread-winner) to protect against the possibility of your dying prematurely; then start a savings account on the side. For the same amount of money as it would cost to buy an endowment policy, you could be covered for *more* insurance (with a term policy) and at the same time accumulate *more* savings (if you put the difference between the cost of the term coverage and the cost of the endowment policy into the bank). Using the example just mentioned, a twenty-six-year-old husband could buy $5,000 worth of nondividend term insurance from a low-cost company for around $25 a year at the start and $30 a year fifteen years later. If he put the difference between that and endowment insurance into a bank at 5½ percent, he would wind up with savings worth $5,250. So whether the breadwinner died or lived, the child would have at least $5,000 toward a college fund and maybe more, as compared with a maximum of $4,000 in an endowment at the same price.

• *If you're a college student,* you or your parents may be solicited for life insurance. Parents generally get letters from companies selling term coverage, the pitch being that as a parent you have a heavy financial investment in the child; if he died, you'd want your money back. The cost of $10,000 worth of college term coverage is $20 to $40 a year. But do you really think that the child owes you the cost of his education back? If so, why not insure him when he's thirty and forty, as well as when he's twenty? The fact that most parents don't insure older offspring indicates that most of them really don't expect to "get their investment back" in dollars and cents. They are only vulnerable to that sales pitch during the years that they're scrimping to pay tuition.

But there are some situations where it might make sense to cover the cost of past tuition if the child dies—for example, if you cosigned a tuition loan and would have to repay if the student couldn't; or if the student were obligated to repay the parent so a younger brother or sister could go to school. Term insurance would ensure that these obli-gations are met. Some parents also like to have term coverage for burial insurance, in which case $2,000 would be plenty. Otherwise, student life insurance generally isn't necessary.

These term policies generally must be converted into straight-life after the student graduates or around age twenty-five. The conversion cost per $1,000 of coverage is around the median for all policies, which means the young person can get the same amount of insurance from many other companies for less. Most college policies are not continuable as term insurance, which is a pity, since term is generally what young people need most.

The college student himself may be approached on campus by an insurance agent trying to sell him a straight-life policy at around $200 to $300 a year for $16,000 of coverage. If a student doesn't need term insurance because he has no dependents, he needs this high-cost straight-life policy even less. If he can't afford it, the agent offers to lend him the first year's premium (at 8 percent) just to get his signature on the line. Five years later the policy pays an "endowment" that's large enough to eliminate the loan. To the student the endowment money seems like a gift. What he doesn't realize is that he's been overcharged for the policy in order to build up enough cash to pay off the loan.

Most students simply don't need life insurance. For those few who do, $10,000 worth of term at around $20 is a good buy; for anything else he can get coverage at a lower cost by avoiding "college" policies and buying in the regular market.

SOCIAL SECURITY

The cornerstone of most people's insurance plan is Social Security (or its equivalent in government employee insurance, Railroad Retirement, etc.). You might think of Social Security only as a pension system for the retired. But, in fact, it offers significant benefits to the families of workers who die or become disabled (provided that the worker contributed to Social Security for a specified amount of time—generally not very long).

If a man dies, his widow is entitled to a monthly payment until the children reach eighteen. There's also a payment for each child under eighteen (up to a specified maximum family benefit). After that the widow's payments stop, but each child who is an unmarried full-time student remains entitled to a monthly benefit until he is twenty-two, the amount of the payment depending on your earnings and how long you worked (the total could run to $4,000, $5,000, or more a year). If the widow works, her benefit is reduced or eliminated, but the children are entitled to their benefits no matter how much she earns. If a wife worked in Social Security–covered employment, her surviving husband and children are entitled to payments on her account. If the worker supported his elderly parents, they too would be eligible for support checks from Social Security.

A widow or widower gets no payment from Social Security between the time the last child is eighteen and the time she or he retires, as early as age sixty. At retirement, you're entitled to your own Social Security pension (if you worked and were covered) or the pension due you as a spouse on your husband's or wife's account, whichever is larger. For more on Social Security, see Chapter 28.

Before you start insurance planning, it's essential to know how much Social Security income your family would get after your death. The first step is to find out what your total earnings have been for Social Security purposes. Ask your local Social Security office to send you the Statement of Earnings postcard, Form OAR-7004. Fill it in with your name, address, birthday, and Social Security number and send it to the Social Security Administration, P.O. Box 57, Baltimore, Md. 21203. You'll get back a statement of the amount of income on which you've paid Social Security taxes since you first started working. If both parents work, they should each get this information.

With that statement in hand, write the following letter to your Social Security office:

Dear Social Security,

In order to determine how much life insurance I need, I'd like to find out the size of the Social Security benefits due my survivors if I were to die immediately, or become disabled. I was born on [give date], and my statement of earnings is stapled to this letter. Will you kindly answer the following questions [use only the questions appropriate to your current situation]:

1. I have [number] children [give ages]. What survivor's benefit will they each receive up to age eighteen, and between age eighteen and twenty-two if unmarried and a full-time student? _____

2. What survivor's benefit would be paid to my nonworking widow [or widower] [and/or my divorced widow (or widower)], with my children under eighteen in her [his] care? _____

3. What is my total family limit? _____ [No matter how many children you have, monthly payments will not exceed this amount.]

4. What survivor's benefit would be paid to my widow [or widower] at age sixty? _____ At age sixty-two? _____

5. I pay more than half the support of a parent sixty-two or older. What benefit would he or she get [subject to the family maximum]? _____

6. What size check do I get if I become totally disabled? _____

7. If I become totally disabled, what size check will my children get? _____ My spouse with children under eighteen in her [his] care? _____ My spouse at age sixty-two? _____ At age sixty-five? _____

Thank you for your help.

Sincerely yours,

Don't ask any extraneous questions, stick with what you need to know. Some Social Security offices are reluctant to bother; they think they're there just to deal with actual beneficiaries, not to provide hypothetical information. But without these facts you can't plan your insurance intelligently, and Social Security has no reason to withhold them from you. If you run into resistance, stay courteous; visit the office and ask to see the manager (or talk to him on the telephone), and explain that this information is essential to your insurance and estate planning. They'll eventually come through. (*One warning:* The Social Security officer may misunderstand and think you're asking for pension benefits. If you're young, he'll tell you, correctly, that it's too early to get that information. Explain that you want *survivor's and disability benefits*— what your family would get right now in case of your death or disability. Those numbers can be calculated accurately at any time.)

If you and your spouse both work and both need life insurance, the above Social Security facts should be gathered for each of you. Remember: If your spouse works, his or her Social Security benefit may be reduced or eliminated by earnings (see page 737).

It may take several letters and phone calls to get all this information. It's more efficient to pay a personal visit to the Social Security office (look it up in your phone book under the U.S. government listings).

HOW MUCH LIFE INSURANCE SHOULD YOU HAVE?

The fundamental purpose of life insurance is to replace your paycheck if you die prematurely. The people now supported by your earnings— your spouse, your children, your elderly parents—would have to be supported instead by the proceeds of the insurance policy on your life.

In most cases insurance proceeds are not their only source of support. They might get checks from Social Security—a cornerstone of family income after the death of the wage earner that many people don't even realize they're entitled to. There also might be a lump sum settlement from your pension plan, rent from property you own, interest from bonds or savings, dividends from stocks, the earnings of the surviving spouse.

In deciding how much insurance to carry, add up all the income your family would have if you died tomorrow. Compare that with what it would cost them to live (they'd probably need around 75 to 80 percent of your present household budget). The gap between their living expenses and their projected income should be filled with insurance.

Insurance agents have "rules of thumb" that say you should be insured for three times, or four times, or six times your annual income. But those rules are mainly designed to make insurance easier to sell. They have no relevance at all to individual situations. A family earning $20,000, with two children, both spouses working, and substantial savings, needs less insurance than another family, also earning $20,000, with five children, no savings, and the wife at home.

Insurance agents may also have preprinted brochures from their companies, purporting to give you a simple method for figuring how much insurance you need. These are more sophisticated than "rules of thumb" but may be of no more value. Often, they leave out essential facts and figures; I've even seen some that make entirely meaningless calculations. The upshot is that they prove you need a lot of insurance (which may be true), but whether you need the amount that the sheet suggests is highly questionable.

In buying insurance your objective should be to get as much as is needed to protect your family *and no more.* Any less could leave them in a pickle; any more would be taking money you could more profitably use somewhere else. To find that exact amount there's no way around the method I just mentioned—calculating your family's probable income and expenses after your death and providing enough insurance to fill the gap. You doubtlessly have some insurance already, from your employer, from some other group policy, or from an individual policy bought previously. The question is, do you need any more?

The following pages provide an orderly, step-by-step Insurance Planning Worksheet to help you determine how much insurance to carry. It begins by estimating your expenses at death and subtracting them from the cash you'll have immediately on hand (from savings, insurance proceeds, and so on). The remaining amount is the nest egg you've left for your family. For planning purposes, assume that that nest egg is invested conservatively—say, in 7- or 8-percent bonds paying 5 percent after taxes—and figure that annual 5 percent return as part of the family's income.

You then add in the rest of the expected income. One key element is spouse's earnings. If the husband dies and the wife isn't working, is it your preference that she continue to stay home? If so, you'll need more insurance than if you decide that she would probably get a job and contribute to the family income.

Another important number you need for this calculation is the size of the Social Security payment your family would get if you died. It can amount to $4,000 or $5,000 a year, perhaps less, perhaps more, depending on the size of the family and your past earnings record. For information on how to find out the size of your family's Social Security payment if you should die, see page 415.

In estimating family expenses after your death, follow the budget form on page 24, but leave out any expenses pertaining to you, such as life insurance premiums, travel, lunches, hobby expenses. Also leave out education expenses; they're accounted for in a later calculation. If you're spending every nickel you earn, the family will need at least 75 to 80 percent of your take-home pay. If you're making regular contributions to savings and investments, they'll need, at minimum, 75 to 80 percent of the money you actually spend on living expenses, plus whatever extra you'd like to provide for a continuing savings program.

If you're a homeowner, a big chunk of your monthly expense is the mortgage payment. An easy and inexpensive way to eliminate that is to buy decreasing term insurance to pay off the mortgage at your death (see page 373). That leaves the family the house free and clear. You can then look to other life insurance to cover the remaining expenses. If your spouse works and earns a substantial income, it may be that the combination of decreasing term to pay off the mortgage and group insurance you have with your employer is all the coverage you need.

When both spouses work, the Insurance Planning Worksheet calculation has to be done for each of you. If a working wife dies, the children are entitled to Social Security payments based on her earnings, just as they would be if the husband died. She may also have a lump sum pension payment due or group insurance from her employer. Estimate what the family's income would be after her death and insure her for the difference between income and expenses; then do the same for the husband. If either of them dies, the other should be left with enough insurance money to plug the gap left in the family income.

A single person with family responsibilities should give careful thought to what would happen to the dependents if he or she died. If you're a divorced woman with children and at your death the children would go to your ex-husband, and he has enough money to support them adequately, you don't necessarily need life insurance. If you want to leave them with a larger inheritance, life insurance would do it—but there's no need to go through the Insurance Planning Worksheet. Just figure out how much your property is worth, how much more you'd like to leave the children—if anything—and insure yourself for the difference.

If your ex-husband doesn't want the children, or you're a widow, the children might go to your parents or a brother or sister after your death. In that case, you'd want to provide money for their support so they wouldn't be a burden. Consider the market value of what you own already (a house, group insurance, etc.), and if that's not enough to support them and pay for college, you'd want additional life insurance. Term insurance would be sufficient, since the need for coverage would end as soon as the children were on their own.

If you're supporting elderly parents, and there's no one else to take on that responsibility after your death, include in your annual expenses the sum needed for their care. The Life Expectancy Table on page 760 suggests the number of years you might have to provide that income. This need, too, should be covered with term insurance, cancelable at the parents' death.

There's a separate calculation for figuring how much insurance you need for college expenses. If those costs won't come up for some time, you need less coverage than you might think. Any lump sum received today for future college expenses could be put in a bank term account to accumulate at high interest. So a lesser amount of money today would provide a much larger sum at some point in the future. (For example, money invested at 7 percent will double in ten years.) The Insurance Planning Worksheet gives instructions on how to figure the amount of insurance needed today for future purposes. In estimating college expenses, don't forget that some amount of financial aid would probably be available.

The calculation for ordinary living expenses carries you up to the point where the youngest child leaves home or finishes his education. After that, the surviving spouse could make other living arrangements, and expenses would fall. So a separate household budget and a separate insurance calculation are needed for this period. If the survivor is a wife who doesn't work or whose earnings are low, your insurance protection will have to be large enough to support her during her middle years, although not as large as it was when she had to support the children. She might want to sell the house, so assume that the proceeds are invested conservatively, giving her additional income. If she rents an apartment, she'll be spared the expense of taxes, homeowner's insurance, and maintenance.

When a family simply can't afford all the coverage it needs, even by buying inexpensive term insurance, protection for the widow during her middle years is usually the first to go. It's essential to get the children raised and educated and to provide for the widow in retirement when she can't provide for herself. But it may be necessary for her to go to work after the children leave home and before she qualifies for Social Security at age sixty.

If the wife works and earns a good salary, the husband may be able to reduce or even eliminate his coverage in middle age. If the survivor is a husband, he can probably support himself, so the wife's insurance would have to last only until the last child left home. Or she could simply carry mortgage insurance to leave him the house free and clear. A single parent might want to drop his or her coverage entirely after the children are gone.

The final part of the calculation deals with the amount of insurance needed to provide for a widow in retirement. Again, the method is the same: What are her expenses, what is her income, and how much insurance (if any) is needed to fill the gap? If she was already provided with a nest egg that paid her some income during her middle years, when she had no Social Security benefits, then she has enough for her retirement. No additional insurance is needed. On the other hand, if your plan calls for her to support herself during her middle years and her assets are not large, your insurance should provide a lump sum to be put in the bank at a high interest rate and not touched until she retires. The Insurance Planning Worksheet helps you calculate how much insurance you need now to provide for that future need.

One important thing about insurance planning is that it should be done more than once—you have to go back and back to it as the years go by and your circumstances change. A young family doing insurance planning cannot look ahead with any certainty to the needs of a widow in retirement. Too many things can happen in the intervening years. If you're young, you should be absolutely sure that the needs of the surviving spouse and children can be met until the children graduate from college or leave home. If you can also afford a sum for middle age and retirement, so much the better; if you can't, let that part of the plan slide for the time being. As more children are born, increase your insurance. You might also want more coverage if your standard of living goes up.

When the older children reach high school age, you'll have a better idea of what the widow will need after they're gone and can adjust your insurance accordingly.

Once the children start graduating from college, your entire insurance program should be reevaluated. The coverage you kept to ensure their college tuition can be dropped. The coverage earmarked for family living expenses should be reconsidered in terms of the widow's real needs. If the husband died, would she be able to work and support herself? If so, he might cancel most of his life insurance and concentrate on amassing retirement savings. (If the wife has insurance on her life, she, too, should probably cancel it, on the assumption that the husband could support himself in case of her death.) If the wife couldn't support herself, enough insurance would be needed to fill the gap between her income and her expenses until she qualified for Social Security. And an additional lump sum would be needed to provide her with some extra income in retirement.

When you approach retirement, your objective should be to leave enough so that your survivor can live comfortably. Assuming that you have Social Security and savings, and perhaps a private pension with survivor's benefits, no life insurance should be necessary. If you have a straight-life policy, turn it in and invest the cash for retirement income. However, if your savings would be insufficient for your survivor to live on, and you can get along without cashing the policy in, by all means keep the insurance in force as long as necessary. If you have term insurance and still need coverage (unlikely, but it can happen), you'll generally find that a minimum-deposit policy is less costly (see if you can convert your term to that kind of plan). If your spouse dies, cancel the insurance. As long as your children are healthy, you're under no obligation to live in straitened circumstances just to leave them some insurance proceeds.

(One note: People with retarded or disabled children still in their care need a lifetime insurance and savings plan combined with trusts. See "Estate Planning for Retarded Children," page 725.)

Inflation, of course, is the joker in the deck. You can carefully provide for the amount of income needed, only to see your calculations knocked apart by a sudden spurt of rising prices. The Insurance Planning Worksheet provides an inflation adjustment for distant needs, such as college expenses, but at best this kind of thing is a wild guess. At least remember this: A fair amount of inflation protection is built into the economic system. Social Security goes up with the cost of living, and if your spouse works, his or her earnings will also rise. In times of inflation interest rates go up, which promises a higher income from certain investments. So although insurance policies pay a fixed amount, it doesn't mean that your family will be locked into a fixed income after your death.

The Insurance Planning Worksheet begins below. Make the assumption that the breadwinner will die tomorrow, and see how much income he would leave behind. In working the calculation through, you'll probably be appalled at how much insurance a young family needs. You may find yourself short $100,000 or more. But if you look around for group term coverage (page 366) or buy level or decreasing term, that insurance gap can usually be filled at a reasonable cost.

Insurance Planning Worksheet

STEP 1

Figure the family's cash assets and lump sum expenses at your death.

There will be funeral expenses; lawyer's fees for handling the estate, perhaps amounting to several thousand dollars; estate taxes if you're wealthy (see Chapter 27, "Wills and Estate Planning"); various short-term debts that must be paid immediately.

You may want to include your mortgage as a debt to be paid at death and provide decreasing term insurance to cover it. Otherwise, mortgage payments will be included under living expenses in Step 2.

Cash assets:

Savings	$_____
Proceeds from current insurance (including employee group insurance)*	_____
Lump sum pension payout	_____
Cash on hand	_____
Total	$_____

Final expenses:

Final illness	$_____
Funeral	_____
Lawyer	_____
Taxes	_____
Debts	_____
Other	_____
Total	_____
Subtract expenses from cash assets	$_____
Total cash assets remaining for family*	$_____

*Note that all the insurance you now have is accounted for here. The calculation shows your *additional* insurance needs.

STEP 2

Figure the family living expenses until the children leave home.

Use the budget form given on page 24, but leave out college funds (which are dealt with later) and all expenses pertaining to you (this is a budget for your survivors, after your death). Generally speaking, your family will need 75 or 80 percent of the money now spent on your household budget.*

Monthly amount needed $\underline{\quad}$

Multiply total by 12 $\underline{\quad} \times 12$

Annual amount needed $\underline{\quad}$

Enter the number of years remaining until the last child leaves home or finishes college. That's the number of years that this annual income will be necessary.

Number of years this annual amount is needed $\underline{\quad}$

How will the family meet these expenses?

Add up the amount of after-tax income they'd have from all sources if you died tomorrow—from spouse's earnings, Social Security, dividends on investments, etc. Follow the form on page 16. For information on how to estimate Social Security payments, see page 414.

Monthly after-tax income from present sources $\underline{\quad}$

Multiply total by 12 $\underline{\quad} \times 12$

In making this calculation, assume that the remaining cash assets that you estimated in Step 1 are invested conservatively in bonds and bank term accounts; include the earned interest in the family's annual income. For example, you might figure that this money will throw off income at an annual rate of 5 percent after taxes.

Annual after-tax income from present sources $\underline{\quad}$

*Inflation estimates can be built into this calculation, but it makes everything a lot more difficult. For practical purposes, it's best to assume that family income—from earnings, Social Security, rents, etc.—will increase approximately in line with inflation. Income from a conservative investment may lag behind inflation, but when you are making long-term plans, you can't factor in everything.

Compare annual expenses (figured above) with income.

If there's more than enough, enter the excess income. No more insurance is needed. If there isn't enough, enter the income gap.

Excess income $ _____

or

Income gap $ _____

How will that income gap be filled? Generally, with insurance proceeds. There are three ways to figure the amount of insurance needed:

1. Total amount of insurance needed to plug the annual income gap (assuming a stated interest rate) $ _____

1. You can provide a large cash stake, which, if invested, will throw off the income needed to plug the gap. For example, if the family is $5,000 a year short, they'll need insurance proceeds of $100,-000, invested at 5 percent after taxes, to produce the money needed. The advantage of this approach is that it provides a continual annual income for the early and middle years (even after the children leave home), plus a lump sum that can be converted to an annuity at retirement. The drawback is that it costs more than the other approaches.

To allow for inflation, the widow might want to put half the insurance proceeds in the bank and invest the rest in mutual funds for long-term appreciation. In that case you would have to provide a larger stake, since growth investments usually don't pay big dividends. Or you could figure that inflation would be covered by increases in Social Security and the widow's earnings.

2. You can assume that the family will steadily dip into principal, so that by the time the last child leaves home, all the insurance money will be gone. This requires less insurance than Option 1. How-

2. Number of years income will be needed (until the youngest child leaves home)   _____

ever, it reduces the amount of money available for the wife to live on in middle age.

Using the *Future Income Table* on page 436, find out how much money you have to invest today (at a chosen interest rate) to provide the monthly sum needed to plug the income gap for the necessary number of years. Follow the instructions given for current payments and consider using the inflation adjustment.

3. You can buy decreasing term insurance (see page 373) to provide your family with a fixed monthly income for a specified number of years. *This is the most inexpensive method available for guaranteeing income many years into the future.* It provides a lot of protection for families who otherwise couldn't afford it. Affluent families often buy it, too, because its low cost leaves them with more money to save and invest. Like Option 2, it leaves no insurance proceeds for the widow once the children are grown.

Before deciding among these three options, read the sections on term and straight-life insurance.

Using the Future Income Table:

Total amount of insurance needed to plug the income gap for the given number of years, assuming that the family dips into capital $_____

3. Monthly income to be provided by decreasing term insurance $_____

Multiply by the total number of months until the youngest child leaves home $_____   ×

Total amount of decreasing term insurance needed $_____

STEP 3

If your children will go to college, plan on an education fund.

Costs are now running at about $3,000 a year for state colleges and $5,000 for private colleges. Two-year community colleges cost less. Each unmarried child will have a benefit from Social Security, which can be applied to the cost of his education. You'll have to provide the rest. But unless

Amount each child will receive from Social Security in the event of your death $_____

your child is starting college immediately, or is in college already, you don't have to provide for the full cost in your insurance program. Insurance proceeds invested for many years will earn quite a bit of money, so you can cover future college expenses by providing a smaller lump sum now.

	Remaining amount needed	Number of years until needed*
Child A	$ ___	___
Child B	___	___
Child C	___	___
Child D	___	___

To plan this, use the *Lump Sum Table* on page 439. That tells you how much has to be invested today, at various interest rates, to produce a certain sum in several years. For example, to have $10,000 in fifteen years, you'd have to invest $4,800 at 5 percent over that entire period.

To allow for a rise in college costs, deduct an estimated inflation figure from the amount of interest you think the money will earn. For example, if you think inflation will average 3 percent over fifteen years and you can earn 6 percent on your money, the fund will make effective annual gains of only 3 percent. Using the 3-percent lump sum column on page 439, you'll see that in order to have the *purchasing power* of $10,000 in fifteen years, you'll have to invest $6,400 today.

Using the Lump Sum Table:

Amount needed today to invest for college in the future

Child A	$ _____
Child B	_____
Child C	_____
Child D	_____
Total Needed	$ _____

Savings already allocated for college $ _____

Remaining amount needed $ _____

STEP 4

How will your widow live after the children leave home?

Generally, a widow's income from Social Security stops once there are no more children at home under eighteen (income for full-time students stops when they reach age twenty-two). The widow will not again become eligible for benefits until age sixty or sixty-two (see Chapter 28, "Social Security").

Widow's annual expected income $ _____

Widow's annual expenses $ _____

*Number of years until child enters college.

Hence, her only income will be from investments, rents, the proceeds of your insurance, or her own earnings. A young family generally can't afford to provide insurance for the growing family *plus* enough to support the widow during her middle years. The widow may have to plan on supporting herself. For a family whose children are older, however, income for a nonworking widow might be a principle objective of the insurance program.

To estimate what's needed, add up the likely expenses for a widow living alone (probably in a smaller house or apartment than she had when the children were with her). Then estimate her likely income from savings, investments, etc. The gap will have to be filled with either insurance proceeds or her own earnings.

If you want to support her with insurance, use the *Future Income Table* on page 436, following the instructions given for delayed payments. From this you can estimate how much insurance money is needed today to provide your spouse with a specified monthly income starting a specified number of years from now. The instructions also tell you how to factor in inflation.*

Income surplus $_____

or

Income gap $_____

Number of years the income gap will have to be filled (from the time the children leave home to the year the widow qualifies for Social Security) _____

Using the Future Income Table:

The amount of insurance proceeds needed today to assure the above annual income for the necessary number of years $_____

STEP 5

Establish a widow's retirement fund.

When a widow reaches age sixty, she can retire on partial Social Security payments.

---

*If you're young and you covered Step 2 by choosing a large cash stake (Option 1), that stake will likely throw off enough income to carry the widow through these middle years and right into old age. If you're older, the group insurance you have with your employer might be enough to meet her needs.

If she waits until age sixty-two, she can
have the full amount. Social Security, however, provides only a subsistence income.
Additional funds will have to come from
pension, insurance, or investments.

The procedure here is the same as for all
the other parts of your insurance planning. Estimate the widow's probable expenses (which you did in Step 4), remembering that at age sixty-five she's eligible
for Medicare. Then estimate her probable
income from Social Security, pensions,
savings, investments, annuities, and the
proceeds of the life insurance policies you
already have. If there's a gap between income and expenses, you'll have to plug it
or depend on your children to help support their mother.

Retired widow's
annual expenses $_____

Retired widow's
annual income $_____

Income surplus $_____
                      _or_
Income gap $_____

A widow's retirement fund is too far ahead
for a young family to look. Much could
happen in the life of a young widow, including remarriage. If you're middle-
aged, however, funds for an older widow
should be very much on your mind. Some
people do the bulk of their saving through
straight-life insurance; others cover themselves with individual or group term policies (see page 366) and try to build a pool
of retirement savings in the bank or with
investments.

How much insurance should you provide
to plug the gap between your widow's expenses in retirement and her income from
Social Security, savings, and other
sources? At today's interest rates, a sum
equal to around eleven times the _annual
amount needed_ will provide her with a
lifetime annuity starting at age sixty-five,
(see "Annuities," page 786). For example,

Multiply income
gap by eleven
years   × 11

assume that the widow needs an extra $3,-000 a year for life. If you died leaving insurance proceeds of around $33,000, that sum would finance a lifetime annuity from an insurance company, paying around $3,-000 a year. So that's the sum to shoot for —a sum worth about eleven times the amount of extra income needed.

If your present age is sixty-five (or close to it), you'd want to be covered for the full $33,000. But if you're younger, you could make do with a smaller amount. For example, if you died at age forty-five and left a retirement income nest egg of $15,180, and your widow put it in the bank at 4 percent after taxes, it would be worth around $33,000 in twenty years—enough to buy her the retirement annuity you planned on. To find out how much insurance you need today to provide a certain sum of money in the future, use the *Lump Sum Table* on page 439.

Total income gap $ _____

Number of years before retirement income will be needed _____

Using the Lump Sum Table:

Amount of capital needed to fill this gap $ _____

STEP 6

Get it all together.

You now add up the amount of insurance needed to provide your family with financial security for each separate phase of their lives. You figured these separate insurance amounts in the foregoing calculation.

1. Is more insurance needed just to cover final expenses? If so, enter the amount.

Insurance proceeds needed for final expenses $ _____

2. Is more insurance needed to support the family while the children are growing up? If so, enter the amount. The size of this segment of your policy will depend on the method you chose for providing the funds—providing a permanent cash stake (Option 1); assuming that the family will gradually use up the capital (Option 2); or buying a decreasing term policy (Option 3).

3. Is more insurance needed to provide a college fund? If so, enter the amount.

4. Do you plan to have a fund to tide your wife over until she'll be eligible for Social Security? If you chose a permanent cash stake as your option in Step 2, no additional insurance will probably be necessary. Otherwise, you'll have to arrange for an extra sum.

5. If there are sufficient savings to provide an elderly widow with the income she needs (for example, from the permanent cash stake that once supported the younger family), no additional insurance is needed. If there's an income gap, enter the amount of insurance required.

6. Add it all up.

Insurance proceeds needed for Option 1 $ _____

or

Insurance proceeds needed for Option 2 $ _____

or

Amount of decreasing term needed for Option 3 $ _____

Insurance proceeds needed for college $ _____

Insurance proceeds needed to support widow in middle age $ _____

Insurance proceeds needed for widow's retirement fund $ _____

Total additional insurance proceeds needed in a lump sum $ _____

Total needed from decreasing term (if you chose Option 3 in Step 2) $ _____

STEP 7

Figure out how to pay for it.

The amounts of insurance needed for total security are generally enormous—more than most people can afford. So what you do is take it in stages.

First, find out how much group insurance you can get by joining various membership organizations (see page 365). Also check how much is available from employee coverage, savings bank life, and other low-cost sources. Then ask two or three life insurance agents to give you prices on the options shown in the right-hand column, from several low-cost insurance companies.

Amount of group insurance available $ _____

Price of group insurance $ _____

Amount of insurance from other low-cost sources $ _____

Price $ _____

The young family should concentrate on the amount needed to get the children raised and through school—in other words, the amount of insurance specified in Step 1, Step 2, and Step 3. Usually, that means loading up on inexpensive term insurance—either decreasing term, convertible, renewable term, or group term. You'll rarely be able to afford straight-life in the amounts needed; in fact, it's debatable whether you should even want it. If you buy expensive straight-life in *smaller* amounts than the full sum needed, you'll shortchange your family if you die prematurely.

Remaining amount of insurance needed to cover the total lump sum $ _____

Price of renewable term insurance for the remaining sum $ _____

Price of decreasing term insurance $ _____

Price of straight-life insurance $ _____

When it's close to the time for the children to leave home, you can look ahead to what would happen to your widow alone if you were to die prematurely. By now the big expenses of raising children are largely behind you, and you may have been able to build some assets. Many people no longer need the large amounts of insurance they had when they were younger.

Some of the term could be canceled. If it meets your savings objectives, you may want to convert part of your term coverage to straight-life (see discussion on page 375). If you chose decreasing term and it's about to run out, you may or may not need additional insurance. If you used the previous years (and the advantage of cheap coverage) to build savings, your employee group insurance may be enough. On the other hand, if you've arrived at middle age with hardly any savings at all, you'll want to buy or keep enough insurance to provide your widow with immediate income in case of your death, as well as a retirement fund (Steps 4 and 5). At this point, the cheapest insurance available is generally group term (see page 366).

At retirement, if you're both still living, you'll want to reevaluate your entire insurance program. Given good luck and forethought, you may not need any insurance at all. The combination of Social Security, pension, investments, and savings (including the cash-value portion of any straight-life policies you may have purchased) may well be enough to support the widow for life. In that case, you'd cancel your insurance and invest all your savings in mutual funds, bonds, bank accounts, or annuities (see Chapter 29, "Retirement Planning"). If you have insufficient savings and pension for your

For the amount of insurance needed, how much would it cost to convert some of your term coverage to straight-life, keep some term, and cancel the rest? $ _____

How much to convert everything to straight-life? $ _____

How much to continue part of your term coverage and cancel the rest? $ _____

How much to continue all the term? $ _____

How much to continue, or purchase, group coverage? $ _____

How much to buy new term? $ _____

How much to buy new straight-life? $ _____

How much would it cost to continue straight-life coverage? $ _____

How much to continue term coverage? $ _____

widow to live on should you die prematurely, the only kind of life insurance that it's usually practical to carry into old age is a straight-life policy, because term policies become too expensive. (In some cases, a type of policy called minimum-deposit may be the cheapest way to insure yourself in old age—see page 390).

How much to have a minimum-deposit plan? $_____

STEP 8

Adjust the formula to fit your personal circumstances.

The fundamental assumptions in Steps 1 through 7 are that the man is the principal breadwinner, the wife makes little or no money, and there are children. That is still the most common set of family circumstances in the United States today. But the same underlying concepts can help you arrive at the right amount of insurance for other family situations.

When both parents work: If the incomes of both are necessary to maintain the household, both should carry life insurance. For example, assume the husband's income can pay 70 percent of the essential bills. The wife should insure herself for enough to provide 30 percent of the household income until the last child leaves home. If the wife's income can cover 40 percent of the household bills, the husband should cover himself for 60 percent of the expenses until the last child leaves home.

Follow Steps 1, 2, and 3, first figuring what the family income would be if the wife died and then if the husband died. Insure him for enough to pay the bills his wife can't meet; insure her for enough to pay the bills her husband can't meet.

If the wife's income is insufficient for her to support herself, he should carry additional insurance to help cover her middle years and vice versa.

Follow Step 4. The husband should insure himself for the expenses his wife can't pay herself. And vice versa.

A one-parent household: What would happen to the children if you died? And would they need money for their support? If so, your savings and insurance should cover it. But there's no need to be insured after the last child graduates from college or leaves home.

In these circumstances, life insurance planning generally stops after Step 3.

An older parent with young children: He or she will have to carry large amounts of insurance at later ages, which is expensive.

See page 405 for a discussion of the alternatives.

Working parents with no children: If each can support himself, life insurance may not be needed. If the wife depends in part on the husband's income, he should carry enough life insurance to meet that need for as many years as necessary. And vice versa.

See Steps 1, 2, 4, and 5.

If you never thought seriously about life insurance until reaching middle age: Your dependents were darn lucky nothing happened. Insurance costs more at later ages, but just because you got away without much insurance in your youth doesn't mean your luck will continue to run. See a life insurance agent and do your best to meet your remaining financial responsibilities.

See page 409 for a discussion of the alternatives.

If you help support an elderly parent: Unless there's someone else to take over his or her support if you die, your insurance should provide a sum for the parent's maintenance.

Multiply the annual income you give your parent by the number of years he or she is likely to live (see Life Expectancy Table on page 760). Provide for that amount of term insurance coverage.

Future Income Table

What the following table shows: If you wanted to provide someone with $1,000 a year for fifteen years, and you kept the money in a mattress, you'd need a full $15,000. But if you put your money in a bank, in bonds, or other investments, where it could earn interest, you'd need *less* than $15,000 to provide the same income for fifteen years. That is the principle of this table: *It shows how much money you need now to provide a certain annual income for a specified number of years.* The line across the top shows the interest rate you expect to get; the column at left shows the number of years you want to provide the income. Directions on how to use this table are below.

Current Payments

Assume that you want to figure how large an insurance policy you need now to provide your widow with $300 a month for fifteen years where the proceeds could be invested at 5 percent after taxes. You run down the left-hand column to the fifteen-year mark, then follow across to the column under 5 percent. Multiply that factor by your monthly income objective of $300. You get $37,800, which is the amount of money invested at 5 percent that will produce the income needed. Use the same principle to calculate any other income requirements.

Decreasing Payments

Suppose you want to provide an income of $300 a month for the first ten years followed by $200 a month for the next twenty years. In effect, it's $200 a month for the full thirty-year period plus an extra $100 a month for the first ten years. Using the directions for current payments, calculate the $200 payment for thirty years and the $100 payment for ten years, at the appropriate interest rate, and add the amounts together. That total would provide the income desired.

Increasing Payments

What if you wanted to provide a widow with $300 a month for the first eight years followed by $400 a month for the next fifteen years? This can be viewed as $400 a month for the full twenty-three-year period, minus $100 a month for the first eight years. Using the directions for current payments, calculate the $400 segment and the $100

(*directions continued on page 436*)

segment separately, then subtract the total needed for the $100 segment from the total needed for $400 a month. The result is the amount of money needed to produce the required income. Any other income mix would be calculated the same way.

Delayed Payments

Suppose you want to provide your widow with an extra $300 in income each month when she retires, but retirement doesn't start until thirteen years from now? And at that point, you'd want her

(directions continued on page 437)

FUTURE INCOME TABLE
Investment result after taxes

Years the income is needed	1%	2%	3%	3½%	4%	4½%	5%	5½%	6%
1	12	12	12	12	12	12	12	12	12
2	24	24	23	23	23	23	23	23	23
3	35	35	34	34	34	34	33	33	33
4	47	46	45	45	44	44	43	43	43
5	59	57	56	55	54	54	53	52	52
6	70	68	66	65	64	63	62	61	60
7	81	78	76	74	73	72	71	70	68
8	92	89	85	84	82	80	79	78	76
9	103	99	95	93	91	89	87	85	83
10	114	109	104	101	99	96	94	92	90
11	125	118	112	109	107	104	101	99	96
12	136	128	121	117	114	111	108	105	102
13	147	137	129	125	121	118	115	111	108
14	157	146	137	133	128	124	121	117	113
15	167	155	145	140	135	131	126	122	119
16	177	164	152	147	142	137	132	128	123
17	188	173	160	154	148	142	137	132	128
18	198	181	167	160	154	148	142	137	132
19	208	190	174	166	160	153	147	141	136
20	217	198	180	172	165	158	152	145	140
21	227	206	187	178	170	163	156	149	143
22	237	213	193	184	175	167	160	153	146
23	246	221	199	189	180	172	164	156	150
24	256	229	205	195	185	176	168	160	152
25	265	236	211	200	189	180	171	163	155
26	274	243	216	205	194	184	174	166	158
27	284	250	222	209	198	187	178	169	160
28	293	257	227	214	202	191	181	171	163
29	302	264	232	218	206	194	184	174	165
30	311	271	237	223	209	197	186	176	167

retirement income to last twelve years. How much money do you need right now, invested at 5 percent after taxes, to pay $300 a month for twelve years, starting thirteen years from now? This is a three-step calculation. First you find out how much you'd need to provide $300 a month for the full span, or twenty-five years. Run down the left-hand column to the twenty-five-year mark, across to 5 percent, and multiply that factor by $300, which gives you $51,300. Then you calculate how much of that sum covers the years when she doesn't need the money—in this example, the first thirteen years. Take the 5-percent column again but this time at the thirteen-year mark; multiply the factor there by $300, which gives you $34,500. Then subtract $34,500 from $51,300, and you get $16,800. That's the amount of money needed now, invested at 5 percent, to provide $300 a month for twelve years, with payments not starting until thirteen years from now.

Inflation Adjustment

Suppose you want to provide $300 a month starting in thirteen years, with the income running for twelve years, but you know that by that time the dollar will be worth much less than it is today. You need an inflation adjustment in order to estimate the actual number of dollars that will be needed then to provide the equivalent of $300 a month in today's purchasing power. To make this calculation you have to estimate what inflation is likely to average over thirteen years (it's impossible to know, so just make a guess). Say you settled on 3 percent. Subtract that inflation estimate from the amount of interest you expect your investment to earn—say 5 percent. That leaves 2 percent. So you do all your figuring in the 2-percent column. If you want to provide $3,000 a year starting in thirteen years, follow the calculations for delayed payments. A larger amount of insurance will be necessary than if you made no inflation adjustment, but it gives your beneficiary some protection against the unknown future.

Lump Sum Table

What the table on page 439 shows: Using these numbers, you can calculate how much money is needed now, invested at a certain interest rate, to provide a specific sum of money a certain number of years from now. This table is *not* for money to be paid out in monthly income (for income, see the Future Income Table). This is for a specified sum to be used all at once, as for college tuition or buying an annuity. The line across the top shows the interest rate you expect to get; the column at the left shows the number of years before the money will be needed. The following section explains how to use the table. The end result of this calculation is to show how much savings or insurance you need now to fulfill your purposes.

Using the Table

Look for the number of years before the income will be needed, at left, and run your finger across to the column below the interest rate that you expect your investments to earn. Multiply that number by the total sum that will be needed. The result is the amount of money needed now to provide that sum on the date the family will want it. For example, assume that you'll need $12,000 for college ten years from now and expect that insurance money invested now will earn 5 percent after taxes. Looking for ten years on the left, and running over to the 5-percent column, you find the number .61. Multiplying .61 by $12,000 gives you $7,320, which is the amount of insurance needed now, invested at 5 percent, to provide $12,000 in ten years. Follow that form for any other calculation.

Inflation Adjustment

See directions under the instructions for the Future Income Table.

HOW TO FIND A LOW-COST POLICY

It is not true that all life insurance costs about the same, no matter who you buy it from. Some companies are much more expensive than others (and in this business, "more expensive" doesn't mean "better"). The difference arises from a number of factors, including the range of risks the company accepts, how well its investment portfolio has done, and how efficiently the company is run. The most expensive company may charge 100 percent more for the same coverage than the least expensive company.

Unfortunately, there's no single "least expensive" company for all

LUMP SUM TABLE

Investment result after taxes

Years before income is needed	1%	2%	3%	3½%	4%	4½%	5%	5½%	6%
1	.99	.98	.97	.97	.96	.96	.95	.95	.94
2	.98	.96	.94	.93	.92	.92	.91	.90	.89
3	.97	.94	.92	.90	.89	.88	.86	.85	.84
4	.96	.92	.89	.87	.85	.84	.82	.81	.79
5	.95	.91	.86	.84	.82	.80	.78	.77	.75
6	.94	.89	.84	.81	.79	.77	.75	.73	.70
7	.93	.87	.81	.79	.76	.73	.71	.69	.67
8	.92	.85	.79	.76	.73	.70	.68	.65	.63
9	.91	.84	.77	.73	.70	.67	.64	.62	.59
10	.91	.82	.74	.71	.68	.64	.61	.59	.56
11	.90	.80	.72	.68	.65	.62	.58	.55	.53
12	.89	.79	.70	.66	.62	.59	.56	.53	.50
13	.88	.77	.68	.64	.60	.56	.53	.50	.47
14	.87	.76	.66	.62	.58	.54	.51	.47	.44
15	.86	.74	.64	.60	.56	.52	.48	.45	.42
16	.85	.73	.62	.58	.53	.49	.46	.42	.39
17	.84	.71	.61	.56	.51	.47	.44	.40	.37
18	.83	.70	.59	.54	.49	.45	.42	.38	.35
19	.83	.69	.57	.52	.47	.43	.40	.36	.33
20	.82	.67	.55	.50	.46	.41	.38	.34	.31
21	.81	.66	.54	.49	.44	.40	.36	.32	.29
22	.80	.65	.52	.47	.42	.38	.34	.31	.28
23	.80	.63	.51	.45	.41	.36	.33	.29	.26
24	.79	.62	.49	.44	.39	.35	.31	.28	.25
25	.78	.61	.48	.42	.38	.33	.30	.26	.23
26	.77	.60	.46	.41	.36	.32	.28	.25	.22
27	.76	.59	.45	.40	.35	.30	.27	.24	.21
28	.76	.57	.44	.38	.33	.29	.26	.22	.20
29	.75	.56	.42	.37	.32	.28	.24	.21	.18
30	.74	.55	.41	.36	.31	.27	.23	.20	.17
31	.73	.54	.40	.34	.30	.26	.22	.19	.16
32	.73	.53	.39	.33	.29	.24	.21	.18	.15
33	.72	.52	.38	.32	.27	.23	.20	.17	.15
34	.71	.51	.37	.31	.26	.22	.19	.16	.14
35	.71	.50	.36	.30	.25	.21	.18	.15	.13
36	.70	.49	.35	.29	.24	.21	.17	.15	.12
37	.69	.48	.33	.28	.23	.20	.16	.14	.12
38	.69	.47	.33	.27	.23	.19	.16	.13	.11
39	.68	.46	.32	.26	.22	.18	.15	.12	.10
40	.67	.45	.31	.25	.21	.17	.14	.12	.10

Years before income is needed	1%	2%	3%	3½%	4%	4½%	5%	5½%	6%
41	.67	.44	.30	.24	.20	.16	.14	.11	.09
42	.66	.44	.29	.24	.19	.16	.13	.11	.09
43	.65	.43	.28	.23	.19	.15	.12	.10	.08
44	.65	.42	.27	.22	.18	.14	.12	.09	.08
45	.64	.41	.26	.21	.17	.14	.11	.09	.07

kinds of coverage. Some companies give particularly good prices to younger people; others specialize in discounts on large policies; still others save their best prices for nonsmokers, or give better prices on term insurance than on straight-life. A company might have an excellent policy for young nonsmokers, while its policy for smokers of the same age could be among the more expensive in the business. From all this, draw two conclusions:

1. Never buy from the first insurance agent who comes along, without first comparing his price with that of several other companies.
2. Once you've found a low-cost company, don't assume that it will always offer the best buy. Compare prices every time you add to your insurance.

Another problem with finding an inexpensive company is that it's very hard to compare prices accurately. Insurance agents usually use the *net cost* method of showing you what a policy costs. They'll add up all the premiums you pay over a specified time, subtract the cash value (and dividends, if any), and what's left, they say, is the price you pay for coverage. This works pretty well for term insurance. Generally speaking, the term policy with the lowest premium after dividends is the cheapest policy.

But when you apply the net cost method to straight-life insurance, everything goes haywire. When dividends and cash values are subtracted from the amount you pay in premiums over the long term, it often appears that you get back more than you pay in—as if you had insurance free all those years, plus a bonus for your patronage. (If you believe that—and there are insurance agents who'll tell you it's so—then I have a nice little bridge going over to Brooklyn that I'd like to sell you!) What the net cost method doesn't take into consideration is the fact that the insurance company is earning money by investing your premium payments over the years (conversely, you're losing money by buying insurance coverage rather than keeping the payments in your own bank account to earn interest). It's no great shakes to get your money back after twenty years once you realize that if it's put in a bank at 7 percent interest for twenty years, money increases 300 percent. Furthermore, the net cost method doesn't reveal subtle differences between policies that can make some of them far more expensive than they seem at first glance.

For example, consider two companies—A and B—that charge about the same for their insurance policies and give about the same money back in dividends and cash values. But Policy A is credited with cash values faster than Policy B. If you cancel your coverage after ten years, Policy A will return more money, hence cost less.

These differences between policies are accounted for in a cost comparison method called *interest adjusted,* which was developed by the life insurance industry. It's far from perfect, but it's a much fairer method than net cost for comparing straight-life policies. The term *interest adjusted* means that the cost of the the policy is adjusted for the amount of interest you give up by buying insurance rather then keeping your money in a bank. It is also adjusted for the size of the dividend you get, and—with straight-life policies—the speed with which your money is returned in cash values.

Several states require that agents give you interest-adjusted costs; the National Association of Insurance Commissioners (NAIC) is working to make this universal in all states. A few insurance companies automatically disclose interest-adjusted costs in all states, whether required or not. The majority of companies are prepared to supply these costs to any insurance applicant, in any state, if you know enough to ask for them. So by all means ask!

The NAIC model rule on interest-adjusted costs shows the cost two ways, and you should ask for both. First is the *surrender cost index,* which shows what your policy will cost if you cash it in after ten or twenty years. This is the index to look at if you're planning to cash the policy in at retirement (assuming that you live that long). The second is the *net payment cost index,* which shows the cost if you die after ten or twenty years and your survivors get the death benefit rather than the cash value. The second cost is much higher than the first and is more important to consider, since a life insurance policy is presumably being bought as death protection. The index numbers will be shown as a price per $1,000 of life insurance coverage (some states require that it be shown as a cost per $10,000 of coverage). Look for a policy that gives you a low cost. In cases where costs are about the same, make your choice on other factors, such as the cooperativeness of the life insurance agent.

One of the problems with these cost indexes is that they include dividends (when the policy pays them), and dividends are not guaranteed. They may be more or less than projected, which affects your real cost of coverage. To offset this imprecision, the cost indexes include another number—the *equivalent level annual dividend*. This shows the amount by which the company has reduced the indexed cost to account for the likely dividend. If a company has a low cost index but a high dividend, you'll know it's depending on a big return on investments to reach its low-cost goal. If its investments don't do as well as expected, and dividends are lower, the ultimate cost will be higher than projected. In comparing dividend-paying policies, add the dividend number to the basic cost index; this eliminates differences in dividend projections. You want a company that still shows up as low cost.

Unfortunately, this index doesn't really make it possible to compare nondividend with dividend policies. For further information on this point, see "Dividends or Not?," page 398.

In most of the states requiring interest-adjusted costs, the life insurance agent doesn't have to disclose them until you actually receive the policy, provided that the company gives you ten days to change your mind. This is useless for comparing costs among several companies. Most agents, however, will give you interest-adjusted costs in advance if you ask for them. If yours won't, find another agent.

When you make cost comparisons, do so only for policies with essentially the same provisions; otherwise, the comparisons won't be reliable. Also, compare the indexes for your specific age and the specific amount of coverage you want to buy. Just because a company is low cost for people in their twenties, or for policies larger than $50,000, doesn't mean it's also giving good buys to people in their forties who need smaller amounts of coverage. One more point: The majority of interest-adjusted indexes use 5 percent as the interest factor, but some may use 4 percent. When making comparisons, be sure the interest factor is the same.

A more complete method of comparing costs—one that takes into account such things as the probability of your living long enough to collect the twentieth year dividend, and the likelihood of your letting the policy lapse—is called the *company-retention method,* developed by Joseph M. Belth, professor of insurance at the Indiana University School of Business, and author of *Life Insurance, A Consumer's Handbook* (Indiana University Press, 1973). In essence, this method estimates how much of the money you pay in premiums the insurance company keeps as opposed to how much it pays out in claims.

In the meantime, where do you find an inexpensive insurance company? Hundreds of companies do business in your state; by the time you found out who they all were and compared interest-adjusted costs on all their various policies, you'd be ready for retirement pay. Here is a shortcut:

Call three different insurance agents who do business with several companies and tell each of them that you're looking for an inexpensive policy. (Don't let them talk you into a costlier company because it "gives good service"; plenty of inexpensive companies give good service, too.) Tell them that you want to compare the cost of the policies on an *interest-adjusted* basis.

Finding a Sound Company

A company's financial strength is of enormous importance to anyone buying a lifetime contract. Although state funds exist to bail out a failing insurance company, you don't want to be caught in that kind of uncertainty. Also, a weaker company may not give the same value for the life insurance dollar as a top company can.

The best-known insurance rating service is the Alfred M. Best Company, which publishes an annual volume called *Best's Life Insurance Reports.* Best's top rating for companies is A+ for excellent ranging down to C for fair. Ask your insurance agent or the reference librarian in your library to check the current Best's ratings for any company you're interested in. (It's important that you have the company's exact name; many insurers have similar-sounding names, and you want to be sure you're checking the right company.) There are other rating services, but they are less discriminating than Best's, sometimes giving top marks to companies that *Best's* downplays. If the insurance agent shows you a top rating from one of the other services, suspect that his *Best's* grade is not good enough to mention.

Choosing a Life Insurance Agent

Most of us buy from the first friendly—or persuasive—agent who comes through the door. And we buy from the company that he primarily represents, rather than shopping around for a better or cheaper policy. A smarter course is to research companies in accordance with the information given in this chapter, then call the company you're interested in and ask for the name of a local agent with a good sales record (successful salesmen often know more than salesmen with poorer records). Alternatively, get the name of a good agent (from a friend or business associate), and ask him to get policy costs from companies that you specify. If he can't because he doesn't do business with the low-cost companies you're interested in, get another agent.

Life insurance agents vary widely in competence. Some are excellent. Others are not well informed about insurance in general or even about the range of possibilities in the policies they sell. As a financial reporter, I have time and again been given incorrect information by life insurance agents I interviewed, simply because they didn't know their way around their own subclauses! The fact is that agents are primarily trained to sell, not to be technical experts in the product that they're selling. They know the emotional and persuasive answers but are not always competent to do a genuine job of analysis or answer well-informed questions with accuracy.

Most life insurance agents come equipped with financial analysis forms, provided by their companies, that purport to give you a total picture of your financial needs. The agent may even represent himself as a financial planner rather than an insurance salesman. In fact, these elegant forms are principally tools to help the agent sell insurance. A good agent may be extremely sophisticated about the various ways of using insurance to achieve your goals. But he won't necessarily tell you about alternative methods of reaching the same goals, as a genuine financial planner would. Or if he does, he may not present the alternatives fairly.

It is not easy to find a good life insurance agent. Company training emphasizes sales techniques rather than sound analysis. State licensing exams require only a minimum competence. Your best bet is an agent who has the letters CLU after his name. That means "Chartered Life Underwriter," and signifies that he's an experienced salesman who has passed a fairly demanding exam given by the American College of Life Underwriters. The CLU designation is no guarantee that he's fair, honest, or even smart. But it's a sign that he has put some extra effort into his business and may know more than the average agent.

The best insurance salesmen generally deal with people who are well off, because they have more money to spend on insurance. To find a good agent for yourself, ask your well-off friends or business associates whom they would recommend; ask the recommended agents to call on you, in order to see how you like them; request information about their professional background and education; discuss with them any general views you have on insurance, in order to see what they think; and ask if they are free to place business with companies other than the one they are principally affiliated with. This last is an important point, since what you want is an agent willing to survey a number of insurers in order to get you the best possible deal. If there's a particular company you're pretty sure you want to do business with, look in the phone book to see if it has an agency nearby, or call the company to ask for the name of a good agent. In general, it's best to buy life insurance from a *life* agent rather than an agent who puts more time into auto and home insurance.

One important point to remember: Most agents are biased toward the view that insurance is the cure for practically anything that ails you. A good agent can be extremely helpful in deploying your insurance money to the best advantage. But don't expect him to inform you about alternative ways of solving certain problems, or to be fair about the advantages of such competing financial instruments as bank accounts or investments.

And one more point: Avoid an agent who encourages you to misrepresent a health problem on the application form. If he'll lie to his company about you, he'll lie to you about the policy you're buying.

Mail-Order Life Insurance

A number of companies sell insurance by mail, thus cutting the agent out entirely. These may be a good buy or a terrible disaster, depending on the company, the policy, your knowledge of insurance, and the need you're trying to fill. Compare prices with policies sold by life insurance agents (mail-order policies have no special price advantage). Be dubious about plans that seem to offer marvelous benefits at a low price; those two things are usually mutually exclusive. For example, life insurance without a medical examination often has a lengthy waiting period before becoming effective. Many states have passed laws curbing misleading insurance advertising. If you do buy from a mail-order company, read the fine print carefully —every sentence of it—so you'll know just what you're getting. And buy from a company that's licensed to sell in your state (if the literature doesn't say whether it is or not, write to your state insurance department in the state capital and ask). Your transaction will then come under the protection of your state's laws.

BUYING AND HOLDING
AN INSURANCE POLICY

The Application

Part of an application for an insurance policy asks for such cut-and-dried information as your age, the kind of policy you want, and the options you're buying. The other part asks questions about your health, occupation, and manner of life, which the company takes into consideration in deciding whether to grant you a policy. If you're young or the policy is for a relatively small amount, no medical exam may be required. Older people, people with medical problems (past or present), or anyone applying for a large amount of insurance will probably have to be examined by a doctor before the application can be approved.

The Investigation

The insurance company may commission an investigative report to determine if you told the truth about your occupation and way of life. In many cases the investigator will double-check the information just by interviewing you and your family; he may also call your employer and one or two of your neighbors. Now that people are entitled to look at the investigative reports and challenge information, the amount of sensitive questioning (such as asking neighbors how much you drink) has been reduced. By and large, the questions asked are simple, straightforward, and routine.

As for health questions, the insurance company will run your name through the Medical Information Bureau, which stores data on millions of insurance applicants. The business of the bureau is to catch people who falsify insurance applications. If one company finds that you have a health impairment, it will report that fact to MIB. Should you approach another insurance company and fail to note the illness on your application, a routine check with MIB will turn the information up. If a subsequent physical exam shows that your medical problem has gone away, that fact, too, will be noted on your MIB record.

MIB used to record a fair amount of nonmedical information, such as whether a person was a homosexual. But under the impact of the privacy laws most of this has vanished. However, it does continue to carry such pertinent data as whether you have a reckless driving record, fly a plane, or engage in a hazardous occupation. Under the Fair Credit Reporting Act you are permitted access to your record to make sure it's right. MIB charges no fee for sending you (or your doctor) a copy of the data; write to the Medical Information Bureau, P.O. Box 105, Essex Station, Boston, Mass. 02112. If you're in good health or have never reported an ailment to an insurance company, you will probably have no MIB file at all (for more on MIB, see page 475).

The First Payment

It's smart to send in your first premium check right along with the completed application. That way, the insurance is considered to be in effect from the date the check was written. Even if you die the next day, or suddenly switch to a hazardous occupation, the insurance application must be evaluated on the basis of the information originally given. If it's acceptable, you're insured—no matter what has happened since. (If your application is turned down, you'll get your money back.) By contrast, if you wait until the application is approved before sending your money, and in the meantime die or take up sky-diving, the insurance company can change its mind about accepting you.

Method of Payment

Insurance premiums can be paid annually, semiannually, quarterly, even monthly, depending on your preference. But the cheapest way is to pay annually. The other methods are regarded as installment payments, and loaded with heavy carrying charges. Since these are exempt from truth-in-lending disclosures, you may not realize that the interest rate can run to 16 percent or more a year. If you find it difficult to come up with several hundred dollars once a year, do it this way: Put one twelfth of the payment into a bank every month (instead of making an installment payment to the insurance company). You'll earn interest on the deposit and have more than enough to meet the annual insurance bill when it comes due.

The Beneficiary

Most people name one or more individuals to receive the insurance proceeds, and leave it at that. But if there are young children involved, you might want to leave the insurance to your spouse, if living, or otherwise to a trustee to manage the money for the children's benefit (see "Ways to Leave Money to Young Children," page 692). A lawyer can best advise you how to proceed in accordance with your state laws.

It's possible to name a permanent beneficiary that can never be changed. But this is generally undesirable, since it prevents you from using the policy as a flexible instrument of financial planning. As family circumstances change, you'll want to review the beneficiary designation to be sure that your policy includes everyone you want to cover.

Where to Keep the Policy

Many people keep their insurance policies in a bank safe deposit box, but that's not always smart. Many states seal safe deposit boxes after death and won't let them be opened until a representative of the tax office can be present. This delays the filing of an insurance claim. Better to keep the policy at home where it can easily be found. But keep a list of your policy numbers and the name and address of the issuing insurance company in your safe deposit box, so that if the policy is lost or destroyed, you can quickly get a duplicate.

FILING A CLAIM

The survivor should simply get in touch with the insurance agent (whose name and phone number is, one hopes, attached to the policy). He will help you file the claim. Alternatively, you can write to the company yourself. It is not necessary to hire someone to help you make your claim or pay a fee to have the policy sent in. Nor is it necessary to decide immediately what to do with the proceeds. You can temporarily leave the money with the insurance company, drawing interest, while you make up your mind. Don't let the insurance agent push you into a fast decision about leaving the money with the insurer permanently. In the long run you may find it more profitable to withdraw the money from the insurance company and invest it elsewhere (see the following section, "Settlement Options").

In case of a dispute write to your state's insurance department and ask it to mediate the claim. Your insurance agent can usually give you the address of the insurance department; or call the information operator in your state's capital city and ask for the telephone number of the insurance commissioner or the state insurance department.

Settlement Options

Several things can be done with insurance proceeds. Which is best depends on individual circumstances. It's possible to specify one of these options in advance of death, but you can't know now what will best serve your family in the future. Your survivors (and your estate plan) have more flexibility if the decision can be made after the fact. If the proceeds will pass to someone unfamiliar with insurance and investments, discuss the possibilities in advance (maybe even write down your recommendations), but leave the final choice open.

Whatever happens, neither the insured nor the survivor should be pushed into a decision to leave the money with the insurance company after death. Insurance proceeds should usually go on "hold" until the survivors have a chance to take a good look at their financial situation. If you are due insurance proceeds, your options are these:

1. *Take the money immediately, in a lump sum.* This is appropriate for small policies, and for beneficiaries who already have an alternate investment in mind. Lump sum payouts occur automatically when insurance proceeds are payable into a trust.

2. *Leave the proceeds with the insurance company at interest.* This is a good temporary choice while you decide what to do with the money. It preserves all your options, including insurance company options.

3. *Receive the funds in fixed installment payments.* Here interest is paid on the money held; a fixed amount of principal and interest is distributed at stated intervals until the money is used up. If you choose

this option, be sure you have the privilege of changing your mind and withdrawing the entire sum at a later date.

If the insurance company's interest rate is within nodding distance of a bank's term-account rates and you need regular payments, this can be a good choice. (The other method of assuring yourself fixed payments is to withdraw the entire sum, put part of it into passbook savings for immediate use, and the rest into term accounts and bonds scheduled to mature at various times, as you expect to need the money.)

4. *Have the money paid out over a fixed period of time.* If you die, payments will be made to your beneficiary until the time elapses.

5. Turn the proceeds into an annuity. With an *immediate-pay annuity,* the company agrees to pay you a certain monthly sum for life, the amount depending on the size of the insurance policy and your age. This can be a good choice for an older person worried about outliving his capital, but a poor choice for a younger person, because at earlier ages the monthly income is very small. Alternatively, the company could put the funds into a *deferred annuity,* to accumulate at a given rate of interest and be paid out some time in the future. If the tax-deferred interest rate is attractive (say, in the 7 percent range), this could be a good choice for a younger person who wants to build savings. For more on annuities, see page 786.

If you want an immediate income, the key to a smart annuity purchase is getting a *good rate,* which means the highest monthly income possible for every $1,000 you have to spend. Companies vary enormously in their rates. So before selecting an immediate-pay annuity under a settlement option, get the answers to two questions:

First, would I get a better rate if, instead of using the settlement-option plan written into the policy, I bought the annuity as if I were an outsider? Since interest rates are so much higher than they used to be, the current single-purchase annuity rate is often considerably better than the guaranteed rate offered through the insurance plan. The company should automatically give you the better of the two rates. But some saddle you with the less favorable rate unless you know enough to ask.

Second, could I get a better annuity rate from another company? For the same amount of money, Company A might give you a monthly income that's larger than that offered by Company B. So don't sign with the company that paid the death claim without first asking an insurance agent to check the annuity purchase rates of several companies, to see where you can get the best deal. (*Note:* If you want to switch companies, be sure the funds are transferred directly to the new company, without passing through your hands. Otherwise, there will be tax consequences.)

Life Insurance and Taxes

• The proceeds of life insurance are not taxed as income to the beneficiary. Neither are any other death benefits paid under accident or health insurance contracts, or workers' compensation.

• If you leave insurance proceeds with an insurance company to earn interest, that interest is taxable as income.

• If you take the insurance proceeds in installment payments, they're taxed this way: The portion of each annuity or installment payment attributable to the basic death benefit is tax-free, but the portion attributable to interest earned on the proceeds is taxable. *Exception:* A surviving spouse can receive the first $1,000 of income attributable to interest earnings tax-free.

• Life insurance proceeds may be taxable in the estate of the person who died, if he owned the policy. If you have enough assets to owe estate taxes at death (see page 707), you may want to arrange to get your insurance policy out of your estate (see page 709).

• If you cash in a straight-life insurance policy, you owe income taxes only on that amount of cash value which exceeds the premiums you paid (minus dividends actually received, policy loans, and a few minor odds and ends). GI policies from World Wars I and II are exempt from this tax. If the cash value is less than the premium paid, there's no tax —but also no deductible loss.

• You can avoid income taxes on the excess cash value by leaving the money with the company and designating a beneficiary, provided that you give up the right to withdraw the funds.

• If you convert your straight-life policy to an annuity, and do so within sixty days of surrender or maturity, taxes on the excess cash value are stretched out over the life of the annuity payments. The same is true if you elect an installment option within sixty days. But if you delay past that date, the tax on the excess cash value will all be due in the current year.

• Dividends paid on insurance policies are not taxable, since they're merely a refund of overpaid premiums (see page 398). But if you leave the dividends with the company to earn interest, that interest is taxable when it's credited to your account.

• Income from a disability policy you bought yourself is not taxable.

• Use of insurance as a business fringe benefit has a number of tax consequences. When you arrange personal insurance in a business context, get the advice of a tax lawyer or accountant.

• Ask a tax lawyer or accountant about tax consequences before you make decisions on sizable insurance policies. Insurance agents may not know enough about taxes to advise you properly.

OTHER CONSIDERATIONS

If You're Rated a High Risk

People whose health or habits pose higher than usual risks are generally charged higher than usual rates for life insurance. This includes not only people in poor health but also those who have hazardous occupations, engage in hazardous sports, or who have a history of drug use or heavy drinking. (Some companies, believe it or not, charge higher rates to those they consider "moral risks," such as unmarried people living together.)

Some people, on learning they have to pay extra for life insurance, get mad and refuse to buy. This is the worst thing you could do. A person with a health or occupational risk needs coverage more than anyone else, since he's more likely than others to die and leave his family on its own. If you find yourself in a high-risk category, there are several places to turn:

1. See what's offered by your regular insurance policy. A wise buyer who knows he's likely to need more insurance in the future than he can afford right now usually gets the "guaranteed insurability" option, which reserves his right to buy additional insurance in the future *at standard rates* (see page 397). If you have that option, the company must sell you whatever amount of insurance the policy provides for, no matter what your state of health. It even has to sell if you're on your deathbed.

2. See if you're eligible to join any membership association that sells group insurance. Many of these group policies don't require medical exams (although one may be necessary for older people). And even if they do require a doctor's report, their standards for writing insurance at group rates may be more relaxed than the standards applied to individual policies. The top coverage is sometimes no more than $10,-000 or $15,000, but if you belong to several groups, you could amass quite a bit of insurance. Organizations that offer group coverage include trade and professional associations, alumni clubs, fraternal orders, credit unions, and many others. Also check your employee plan. Your company or union may allow you to buy additional coverage at your own expense, and without a medical exam. If you leave the company, you can usually convert the policy to individual coverage at standard rates, no matter what your health.

3. The next place to turn is a good life insurance agent. Some companies are more willing than others to accept high risks, and a good agent should know which they are. Companies even specialize—one being more willing to cover people with heart problems, another being more receptive to diabetics. The rates offered to higher-risk people vary enormously from company to company, so be particularly careful to shop widely before you buy a policy. Straight-life coverage is generally a little easier to get than term insurance, but term is also available to the careful shopper. Among the companies that specialize in higher-risk applicants are Manufacturers Life of Canada (in Toronto, but the company underwrites a lot of insurance in the United States); Beneficial National Life (in New York City and licensed in all fifty states); and Fidelity Bankers Life, Richmond, Virginia (licensed in all states but New York). Metropolitan Life, New York City, also writes a fair number of policies on people with medical problems.

4. If you can't find coverage anywhere else, look to the *guaranteed issue* policies sold by several companies. These are available without a medical exam; you can get insurance even if your health problem is so severe, or your occupation so hazardous, that no one else will cover you. There's a hitch, of course. If you die within two or three years of taking out the policy, your survivors will get little more than your premium back plus interest. You have to stay alive past the probationary period for the policy to pay full value. Some companies, such as Colonial Penn of Philadelphia, offer guaranteed issue coverage in severely limited amounts (such as $10,000 or less) and only to people aged fifty or over. However, if you got several of these policies from various companies, you could acquire quite a bit of coverage. A few other companies—such as Federal Kemper Life of Long Grove, Illinois, and Globe Life Insurance, Chicago, Illinois—sell larger amounts of guaranteed-issue coverage and place no limit on age. As with any other life insurance policy, the cost of guaranteed issue varies widely according to company, so compare all your options before buying.

5. Just because you're a rated risk today doesn't mean you will be next year. Right after a heart attack the rate at which you can get life

insurance would be quite high, but as time passes and attacks don't recur, your premium costs will drop. Some people who once had medical problems will eventually be insurable at regular rates. So check with your insurance agent from time to time to see if he can get you a lower premium. Your premium will also drop if you give up a hazardous sport or occupation.

In some cases, a person might have to decide between a regular policy at high-risk rates, and a lower-cost guaranteed-issue policy with a two-year waiting period. If your health problem could abate, the regular policy might be the better bet, in hopes that sometime in the future the rate would drop back to normal. But if your problem is permanent, you might have a better lifetime cost by buying guaranteed issue. It all depends on the cost of the two policies and your state of health.

6. It's even possible to get some insurance for the terminally ill. Guaranteed issue won't help, because you have to live two or three years for the policy to pay off. But you may be able to buy coverage through your employee group plan or a membership organization that requires no medical exam. Another possibility is to buy some of the expensive items that your family might need, such as a car or a mobile home, borrow the money to pay for them, and take out credit life insurance with the lender (see page 103). When you die, those things will then be paid for by the insurance policy. A person who has been told that there's a definite limit on his life might also consider converting his straight-life policy to extended term (which uses the cash value to pay for term coverage as long as the cash value lasts). That saves you the cost of annual premiums; the premium money can instead be put into a bank account for your family.

The Need for Review

A life insurance program is not graven in stone. Every five years or so review your plan, recalculate your income and savings, and see if you need more or less coverage than you have now. If something happens that increases your financial responsibilities—such as the birth of a child or the dependency of a parent—add to your insurance coverage immediately. Other events decrease your need for insurance, such as coming into an inheritance or having a child leave home and start supporting himself. Always try to keep your insurance coverage in line with your current needs.

Where to Complain

First try to settle the problem with the insurance company, keeping copies of all the letters you send and receive. If you get no satisfaction, call the information operator in your state capital and ask for the phone number and address of the state insurance department or insurance commission. Call or write the state commission about your problem, sending copies of all the correspondence with the insurance company. (Do *not* write to any of the consumer agencies in Washington, D.C.; the insurance industry is regulated by the separate states, not by the federal government.) Some states are more vigorous than others in dealing with consumer complaints, but they all should be able to help. Depending on the nature of the problem, you might also get help through the industry trade association, the American Council of Life Insurance, 1850 K St. N.W., Washington, D.C. 20006.

Chapter Twenty-One

HEALTH INSURANCE

Do you, dear reader, feel infirm?
You probably contain a germ.
OGDEN NASH

Going without health insurance is like gambling everything you have on the turn of a card. Your savings, your earnings, your assets could be wiped out by one serious accident or a prolonged and expensive illness. Most people are covered by one form or another of group insurance, but some 31 million of us still have to buy our own, individual health policies. Even some people with group plans need individual coverage because their group benefits are insufficient.

People with group plans may lose their benefits and, practically overnight, have to find a substitute individual or family health plan. *Some of the circumstances that could suddenly cut you out of the group are* (1) losing your job, and not finding a new one right away; (2) leaving your job to try a business of your own; (3) taking early retirement, which means you have to wait several years for Medicare; (4) working for a small company that decides to cancel its group coverage; (5) getting a divorce or legal separation (if you're a woman formerly covered under your husband's plan, you'll probably have to find insurance of your own); (6) growing up (past age nineteen, sometimes twenty-one or twenty-three, a young person can no longer be covered under his parents' plan unless he's mentally or physically incapable of earning a living and remains in that condition).

Here, then, are the main things you need to know about health insurance:

Types of Coverage

Basic Hospital Expense

This covers the basic cost of your treatment and care in a ward or semiprivate room. It should include routine nursing services, hospital supplies, drugs, and surgical procedures. Often, the policy contains a list of specific dollar benefits paid for various types of operations, but some plans pay the surgeon's "reasonable" charge in full. If you have to go to a nursing home after the hospital for a short stay, some of these costs may be covered, too. Depending on the policy, you may be insured for all or a percentage of your basic costs, perhaps after paying a deductible amount.

Some policies also include doctor bills for lesser services. Employee group plans, for example, might pay part of the bill for minor office visits. But if you're buying an individual policy and money is tight, this kind of odds-and-ends coverage is generally more expensive than it's worth. Better to spend insurance money on protection against the big illnesses and pay the smaller bills yourself.

Major Medical

Basic hospital policies pay benefits that by today's standards are only modest. For example, the annual limit might be only $5,000. If you were badly injured, or came down with a debilitating disease, your bills would run much higher than that. So what you need is major medical coverage, which picks up where basic coverage leaves off.

Major medical is something that every family needs in its health insurance plan because high-cost illnesses are the very ones that threaten your financial security. If you can't afford to spend much on health insurance, it would be smart to skip the basic protection and buy a major medical plan instead, with perhaps a $500 or $1,000 deductible. You'd have to pay medical bills up to the deductible amount, but from there on the insurance company would pick up most of the cost. If your employee plan doesn't include major medical, then buy it yourself from a private insurer. Try to arrange for a policy that picks up exactly where your group coverage leaves off.

Excess Major Medical

This policy picks up where major medical leaves off and should be considered by anyone with a low lifetime limit on group or individual coverage. Some major medical plans, for example, have lifetime limits

of only $10,000 or $20,000, which really isn't enough to protect against
the high cost of a severe accident or prolonged illness. (Coverage up to
$50,000 is generally enough for most families, although upper-income
people may want protection for $100,000 or more.) Excess major medi-
cal plans are designed to piggyback on your present coverage, taking
over only when the old limit has been exhausted. Because such expensive illnesses are rare, this type of insurance doesn't cost very much. At
this writing, only four companies write separate, individual excess
major medical policies—Lumberman's Mutual (with the Kemper
Group, Long Grove, Illinois); Mutual of Omaha; Lincoln National (Fort
Wayne, Indiana); and Madison Life (New York City). Terms, deductibles, and prices vary, so compare them all.

Comprehensive Coverage

Many group and individual policies wrap all or most of the above benefits into a single, comprehensive plan. For individuals they can be
expensive, running from $1,000 to $2,000 a year for a family of four. But
most of your health risks will be covered.

A Note About Duplicate Benefits

Some people supplement employee plans with private coverage, typically for major medical (or excess major medical) expenses. Or you may
own several individual health insurance policies from different companies, originally bought to cover various types of losses. These plans may
well result in duplicate coverage for certain bills. But that doesn't necessarily mean you can collect twice. Some individual policies allow it,
but others deduct the sum paid by another individual or group policy.
If you're under more than one group policy, you may be able to collect
from both insurers, but their combined payment will not exceed the
face amount of the bill. Because of the high price of medical insurance
it's best to keep duplicate coverage to a minimum.

Pregnancy

Typically, insurance policies pay only small amounts for pregnancy, for
the following reasons:

1. Pregnancy (for most people) flies in the face of the basic insurance
concept, which is protection against hazards unforeseen.
2. When pregnancy is covered to the same extent as any other
medical problem, the overall cost of health insurance goes up. People
not of child-bearing age, or who don't intend to have children, are
forced to subsidize the people who do have children.

3. It leads to insurance gamesmanship. For example, a young couple could buy a comprehensive insurance policy for $800, ten months later collect childbearing expenses of $1,500, then cancel the policy and buy something cheaper. The cost would fall on all the other policyholders.

In a few states legislatures have decided that despite the cost it's a greater good to cover pregnancy like any other illness, sharing the cost among all the policyholders. If you plan to have children and live in one of those states, your pregnancy coverage is a bargain. But in most states insurers are allowed to make individual pregnancy benefits optional and limit them to a small amount. Normal medical benefits may be paid, however, for unforeseen complications of pregnancy and for cesarean delivery.

Group policies are another matter. Under a new law, employee health plans must cover the pregnancy expenses of female employees to the same extent that they cover any other medical condition.

Many individual policies pay pregnancy benefits only to married women, but this is gradually changing. If you're a single woman and of childbearing age, or have unmarried teen-age daughters, you might want an insurer that pays pregnancy benefits for *any* of the women covered under the policy. Many policies also cover abortions.

Flat Cash Payments While You're Sick

These are called *indemnity* policies. Most of them pay a certain amount of money per day only if you're in the hospital, but a few will also pay for surgery done when you're an outpatient, for emergency-room treatment, or for home health care. These benefits can generally be received even if you're also covered by another health insurance policy, which is one of their chief attractions. The amount paid by indemnity policies is generally so small that they're no good for basic health protection, but they can serve in some instances as supplements to other health plans. If you buy an indemnity policy, read the fine print carefully to see exactly what you're covered for (see "Mail-Order Insurance," page 476).

Disability Insurance

This important coverage, sold by life and health insurance agents, provides an income if you become disabled and can't work. Yet despite its value, it's a much-neglected form of coverage. For details on disability insurance, see page 480.

Dread Disease Insurance

Here you're covered only if you contract the one or two illnesses specified in the policy, such as cancer or spinal meningitis. It's cheap because the chance of your coming down with a disease you'd "planned for" are pretty small. Better to skip dread disease coverage and put your money toward general protection, which pays off no matter what the illness.

Medicare Gap Insurance

At age sixty-five, most people qualify for Medicare, which covers hospitalization and doctor bills. Private insurance will not pay any costs that could be covered by Medicare, even if you haven't bothered signing up for the program. Many private policies lapse when you reach age sixty-five, others convert to limited coverage for the bills that Medicare doesn't meet.

The discussion of Medicare on page 483 gives you a general idea of how much is paid by the government and what you'll have to pay yourself. Generally speaking, the amount you'll have to pay out-of-pocket is small. Some people want insurance coverage even for the small gaps in Medicare—ask the insurance agent to make a specific line-by-line comparison between the insurance policy and Medicare, so you'll know exactly how the two fit together.

If you're in poor health and can't get regular coverage, it's possible to supplement Medicare with an indemnity policy (see page 459) that takes all comers. But you may have to wait two years or more before being eligible for payments arising from your current health condition. Check this part of the policy carefully before you buy.

Warning: Unscrupulous agents prey on the fears of the elderly by selling them several overlapping Medicare-gap policies. This is a form of theft, pure and simple, since most insurance companies won't pay duplicate benefits (see page 458). If you have an elderly parent, ask if he or she has bought more than one of these policies and, if so, cancel the excess coverage.

Short-term Health Plans

If you're between jobs or laid off, you may not have health coverage, which exposes you and your family to considerable risk. Your former employer's group policy may cover you for a week or more, but after that you're on your own. Several companies have recently begun offering short-term health policies for periods of 60 to 180 days. Two companies—Time Insurance Co. of Milwaukee and Allstate Insurance in North Brook, Illinois—will renew their plans once; other plans are nonrenewable. You can choose among a variety of policies and payment levels. Most short-term plans are only for basic hospitalization; however, Washington National Insurance in Evanston, Illinois, writes a short-term major medical plan.

Group Plans

Many employers buy group coverage for their entire work force and pay all the premiums. Others require employees to pay something. Don't skip any of the benefits—such as disability or major medical—just because they cost a few extra dollars a month. This is the lowest-cost coverage you can get, and having it may save you thousands of dollars if a serious illness strikes. Another advantage of group plans is that they often don't require evidence of insurability, so you can get coverage even if you're in poor health.

Typically, an employee plan establishes a certain deductible for each family member. Once you've paid that amount out of pocket, the medical insurance takes over all or most of the bills. There may also be a family deductible, which is less than the sum of all the individual deductibles (see page 467).

Some company plans are comprehensive—offering coverage for psychiatric consultations, dental bills, and the pregnancies of unmarried women, as well as the more common doctor and hospital bills. Other plans are sparse. By and large, it's not possible to cover gaps in a company plan with private insurance (although you can certainly talk to your employer about getting the group plan improved). However, if you don't have group coverage for expensive illnesses, by all means buy a major medical policy from a private insurer.

If you quit your job to take another one, your old employee coverage should continue for a short period of time (often, to the end of the month in which you quit), by which time you should be included in the company plan of your new employer. If there's a hiatus between jobs, however, you risk being without coverage for a while. People who are fired or laid off may go for some period of time without health coverage —a dangerous situation, particularly if someone in the family is in poor health.

If you've left your job and aren't yet covered under a new group plan, there are three solutions:

1. Do nothing and hope for the best—a course often chosen by young, healthy people but risky even for them.

2. Buy private health coverage. Some companies offer short-term policies for people between jobs (see page 460). At Blue Cross–Blue Shield you can generally pay on a monthly basis, then drop the coverage when you find another job and get back into a group plan. This is important for the older family, or any family that includes someone in poor health.

3. Convert your old group plan to individual coverage with the same insurer. The price is a lot higher and the benefits often poorer, but if you're in poor health, it may be your only choice. Anyone with a chronic illness or with a family member in poor health should take great care never to be without health insurance, since serious illness could strike at any time.

Other organizations, such as fraternal groups and professional societies, may offer low-cost group plans. If you're eligible by all means investigate them. But if the plan offers only incidental benefits, it's better to pay more and have broader coverage. With any group plan check to see if coverage can be continued for your family on an individual basis if you die or leave the group.

Your group plan should give you a booklet or contract spelling out your benefits in detail. Read it, then file it in a handy place so that when treatment is optional, you'll be able to check whether or not it's covered by insurance.

Blue Cross and Blue Shield

Blue Cross covers hospital bills and sometimes bills for outpatient and at-home care. Blue Shield covers surgery and other doctor bills. Each state or community plan is a little different and charges different rates. If you're shopping for individual coverage, always start with the Blues (even though they may not be as efficient in answering your inquiries as an insurance agent would be). The Blues offer broad coverage at a reasonable price. About half the plans, however, don't include major medical insurance, so you'd have to buy that segment of your coverage from an insurance company.

Because the Blues are nonprofit and have certain tax advantages, they pay better benefits per dollar of insurance premium than profit-making health insurers. Generally speaking, you should buy from other insurers only if you want more extensive coverage than is available through the Blues, or want a cheaper, limited-coverage policy. If your employee group plan buys from the Blues and you leave the company, you can convert to an individual policy on generous terms—an important thing to do if you aren't going directly into the group plan of another employer.

Blue Cross pays the hospital directly, so you never get involved in the transaction. This is often an advantage, since the hospital may charge Blue Cross customers a slightly lower rate. (But be sure you're using a hospital that's a member of Blue Cross. You may be allowed only a small daily amount toward the bill in a nonmember hospital, forcing you to pay most of the bill yourself.)

The advantage of individual Blue Cross plans over those of most private insurers is that they'll pay the entire hospital bill for the number of days stated in your policy (if you use a member hospital, which most major community hospitals are), whereas other insurers usually pay only part of the bill. Blue Shield generally pays the doctor a flat dollar benefit for his services; if his fee is higher (and it usually is), he'll bill you for the difference. Some doctors, however, will agree to accept the Blue Shield payment as their total fee, so always ask about this in advance.

Insurance Companies

Many major life insurance companies sell individual health plans; there are also companies that specialize in health insurance. When you're shopping for coverage, ask two or three insurance agents to present some policies for you to compare. Make it clear that you're shopping for the best coverage at the lowest price and that you expect the agents to look over the products of several competing companies for you (otherwise they may just offer the plan of their principal company, which may be high-priced). The cost of private health insurance varies tremendously, depending on the company you choose and the coverage you want. It's important to compare in great detail the costs and benefits of competing companies if you hope to get the best value for your dollar.

Health Maintenance Organizations

These are membership groups, generally organized by doctors and hospitals, that provide all or most of your family's medical needs for a flat annual fee. The cost is usually higher than the premium payment for a Blue Cross–Blue Shield policy, but the benefits are more extensive. For example, they include coverage for routine physical exams, diagnostic screening, immunization, and other preventive care. You don't always have your own doctor at an HMO; it may be necessary to go to whoever is on duty that day. (Some HMOs, however, do provide for personal physicians.) A wide variety of competent services are usually available under the same roof.

When considering an HMO, get its brochure to see exactly what medical services are included in the fee. Then add up everything you spent last year, both out-of-pocket expenses and the cost of health insurance premiums. You may find that comprehensive coverage under an HMO is cheaper, despite its apparent higher fee. Check, too, to see what variety of services are offered. If the HMO will cover more types of illnesses, whether at the hospital or at home, it's a better buy for the money.

You generally have to pass a health exam to become an HMO member. But the law requires that there be an open enrollment period every year when anyone can join, regardless of health.

Other Health Plans

Special plans may be sponsored by various community or medical groups, usually requiring the use of a particular hospital or clinic or a specific pool of doctors. If the price is right, the services good, and the doctors convenient to your home, these may be good buys. However, the benefits are often more limited than those offered by insurance companies or the Blues. Check the coverage carefully, and if it's sparse, see if you can afford something better.

Free Community Services

Depending on where you live, a large number of free or low-cost services may be provided by the community or local groups. These are generally thought of as serving only low-income people, but in fact many of the programs are open to anyone who walks in the door. For example, there may be free consultation on problems of aging, alcoholism, family planning, aid to the handicapped, psychiatric services, and so on, as well as low-cost homemaker services, care for the chronically ill, hot meals for older people, etc., etc. You might as well use these services, because it's your tax money that supports them. Ask the department of health in your city or county exactly what's available and at what price.

Blood Banks

This is a form of insurance that many people overlook. If you or someone in your family should ever need a blood transfusion, the cost could run as high as $50 per pint for commonly available blood and much more if your blood type is rare. Even if you find your own donor, there may be a $20 or $25 processing fee. Health insurance may or may not cover the full cost of blood transfusions. But you can protect yourself by contributing blood periodically to a nonprofit blood bank or the Red Cross. Some blood banks let you (or a family member) withdraw only as much blood as you've donated; others give you an open line to as much blood as you need, at low or no cost.

You can only give blood if you're in good health. Those with jaundice, anemia, high blood pressure, and other conditions are turned away. One risk to buying commercial "blood insurance" is that the blood often comes from paid donors who need the money and hence may have concealed certain illnesses. You want to draw on the blood of unpaid, voluntary donors, who gave through community, employee, hospital, or nonprofit, group-sponsored blood banks.

What to Ask About Health Insurance Policies

Don't ever assume that "everything is covered," in either a group or individual plan. Many things are not covered. With any group plan it's important to take a close look at what's included and consider buying additional private insurance if something important (like major medical) is missing. With individual coverage, take great care in deciding which benefits to buy and which to forego. Inexpensive policies don't cover very much, no matter what the advertisement may lead you to believe. Here are the items to check:

How Much of the Bill Is Covered?

Insurance plans may cover (1) 100 percent of the hospital bill, after a small deductible that you pay yourself; (2) a smaller percentage of the bill (such as 80 or 75 percent), also after a small deductible; or (3) a flat dollar amount, such as $100 or $150 a day for hospital room and board. The more coverage you buy, the more it costs you—for example, a policy paying 100 percent of the bill costs more than one paying only 80 percent. A policy paying a flat dollar amount costs less than either. The advantage of a policy that pays a stated percentage of the bill, no matter what its size, is that your coverage increases automatically as hospital charges go up. But with a flat-payment policy all the increases in hospital charges come entirely out of your pocket. If you buy a flat-amount policy, at least try to start out with coverage that comes close to the room-and-board charge at your local hospital. And consider supplementing the policy from time to time to keep your coverage within nodding distance of actual hospital costs.

Surgeon's bills are covered the same way. The policy may pay all or a stated percentage of the charge, or else pay a flat dollar amount toward various types of operations. If it's a flat-amount policy, a list of the maximums paid toward various surgical charges will be included in the contract. The surgeon's bill is usually larger than the amount the policy grants (unless he has agreed in advance to accept no more than the insurance payment), which means that the balance of the bill comes out of your pocket.

Some policies that cover a stated percentage of the bill make no further limitation on payment. Most, however, will pay only "reasonable" doctor's bills, and the insurer decides what "reasonable" means. When you submit a bill that you thought would be 80 percent paid, you might find that the insurer has deducted $100 as being "unreasonable" and paid 80 percent of the remainder. With optional surgery it's smart to ask your insurer in advance how much it will pay toward the doctor's bill you expect. If the insurer considers the fee unreasonable, ask the doctor if he'll do it for less. As far as hospital charges are concerned, insurance payments are based on the rate for a semiprivate room. If you take a private room, the extra charge is all yours.

Lifetime Maximums

Most policies put a top limit on what they'll insure you for over a lifetime. Sometimes the limit is a single amount for all illnesses; other times there's a maximum per illness. Generally speaking, you have more flexibility if there's a single maximum for all illnesses, as long as the maximum is high enough to cover more than one or two major problems.

The lifetime maximum for some policies is $250,000 or higher, which you're unlikely to need. A $50,000 maximum costs less and is generally enough protection (unless your family is large and there's a history of expensive illnesses). One point: Insurers may require high-income people to take a high maximum, on the ground that they're more likely to go to expensive doctors and get top-drawer treatment. They can also afford the higher premiums that high maximums require.

Deductibles

These are the amounts you must pay yourself before health insurance takes over. Group-plan deductibles are usually quite low. But if you're buying individual coverage, you might want to set the deductible higher in order to save money. The general rule in health insurance is that the more medical bills you're willing to shoulder yourself, the less the insurance costs. Estimate how much you think you can afford to pay toward the cost of any illness and insure yourself for the rest.

Be sure you know exactly how the deductible works. Does it apply to each illness ("per cause"), or is it an annual amount ("all cause")? A $750 deductible once a year might be affordable, but not a $500 deductible for each illness. Policies generally apply the deductible to an "accumulation period," and here's what that means: With a three-month accumulation period and a $200 deductible, you must accumulate $200 in medical bills within three months after your illness starts. Only then will the policy take over and start paying the bills. The effect is that if your illness costs you just a little bit here and there, you might have trouble accumulating enough expenses to trigger the policy coverage. That's highly unlikely, but it's something to be aware of in case you're ever hit with a larger deductible than you expected.

Find out if the deductible applies to each family member. A plan might pick up 80 percent of all doctor bills over $50 a year for each person in the family; a five-person family, therefore, would have a $250 deductible. Many policies, however, also apply a *family deductible*, which takes effect even though all the individual deductibles haven't been met. For example, the plan might have a deductible of $50 per person, but once the family's total medical bills reached $100 or $150, the insurance would begin to pay off, even though the person who is ill has not met his or her individual deductible.

If you don't bother keeping track of the small bills you pay, and file with the insurance company only when you have a major claim, the deductible will be taken out of that first claim. So you'll be paying more of your annual medical bill than necessary. Check with the insurance agent or your company's employee benefits officer as to how the deductible should be handled. Generally, the best course is to file all your bills with the insurer as they come in, even if they're below the deductible. As soon as the limit is passed, you'll start getting reimbursed.

In deciding how large a deductible to take on an individual or family plan, look at what else the policy calls on you to pay. If you're responsible for 25 percent of each bill, you might want a smaller deductible than if you're responsible for only 20 percent. *A good thing to look for in a policy that requires you to pay part of each bill is a cutoff point.* For example, the policy might pay 80 percent of all bills up to $2,500 (after a $100 deductible), but after that it would pay 100 percent. In that case your maximum liability would be $100 plus 20 percent of $2,500, or $600 in all. If you could afford to pay more, you might move the deductible up to $500 (if you have a choice), and save some money on policy premiums. On the other hand, if your policy pays a flat dollar amount, and it's considerably below the room-and-board charges in your hospital, you're already committed to paying a lot out of pocket if you get sick. So it makes more sense to have a small deductible.

If your major medical plan is coordinated with a basic hospitalization policy, you may be responsible for a larger deductible than you realize. The major medical deductible may be $500. But it might kick in only after the requirements of the basic plan have been satisfied, and there the deductible might be $100. So your total deductible would be $600. A concept gaining acceptance is the *variable deductible,* which coordinates an individual policy with group coverage. Whatever amount the group plan pays toward each medical bill is considered the deductible, so the bill won't be paid twice.

Ask your insurance agent how all these deductibles coordinate. In fact, an important question to ask about any health insurance policy is "How much money does this policy require me to pay from my own pocket?"

What Conditions Are Covered?

Each health insurance plan covers a slightly different list of ailments and pays different amounts. State insurance departments get a tremendous number of complaints about health insurance policies, mainly because consumers find out too late what is and isn't covered. If your family has a history of a particular ailment, by all means ask the insurance agent to what extent it's covered in the policy. Also, read all the policies you're considering and compare them paragraph by paragraph to see what's included and what's omitted.

In general, you should at least have coverage for hospital room and board, routine nursing care, minor medical supplies, the services of the hospital's staff doctors, lab tests, X rays, use of the operating room, anesthesiology, drugs and medications, surgical dressings, ambulance service, maternity care (if you're of childbearing age), illness and accident, convalescent nursing-home care after a hospital stay, and a long list of surgical procedures, whether done in the hospital or at the doctor's office. Some policies also cover physical therapy, private nurses, psychiatric care, certain dental bills, treatments for alcoholism, heart pacemakers, artificial limbs, assorted medical supplies, rental of medical equipment for home use, iron lungs, and prescription drugs. One useful thing to look for is whether the policy covers at-home care. If your illness can be treated at home rather than in a hospital, the total medical bill will be much lower. This is particularly important if you're paying a percentage of the bill out of your own pocket.

Exclusions

As important as checking what the policy covers is to see what it does *not* cover. The longer the list of exclusions, the less attractive the insurance. Among expenses that are normally excluded are those arising from war injuries or suicide attempts and those eligible for coverage under Medicare or workers' compensation.

Preexisting Conditions

Most individual insurers impose a waiting period on illnesses you had prior to taking out the policy. No benefits will be paid on those illnesses until or unless you've recovered and/or a certain period of time has passed. With good policies, the waiting period is fairly short—perhaps three months or less. But some make you wait more than a year, which is something to avoid if possible. Always ask what a "preexisting condition" means. To some companies it's simply an illness you had within three or six months of taking out the policy, or an illness you have at the time the policy is actually applied for. To others it means practically any illness you've had since birth.

Many mail-order policies have played havoc with the preexisting conditions clause, refusing claims on the ground that the illness must have been present (even though not diagnosed) before you took the policy out. With reputable insurers, a preexisting condition is one which occurred shortly before the policy was applied for; was diagnosed and treated; or was an obvious condition which you should have had treated, even though you didn't go to a doctor. If you don't report a recent ailment on your policy application and become sick with it again, the insurer will treat it as a preexisting condition and perhaps decline payment.

The trend is toward limiting the preexisting-conditions clause. In fact some insurers have eliminated it entirely. Instead, they charge people with past or present health problems more for their policies. Also, fewer and fewer ailments are being specifically excluded from coverage. If you have group coverage, you will find that in most cases preexisting conditions are fully covered.

Poor Health

You'll be given a medical questionnaire before you get your health insurance policy. If it raises questions, you'll have to take a physical exam. Should the company find a chronic condition, they may attach a rider excluding that condition from coverage, which is something to avoid. Look, instead, for a company that will cover the condition, even though it means paying more for your health insurance.

If you have a health problem, there's no substitute for a good life-and-health insurance broker who will try several insurers to find you the best possible coverage at the lowest possible cost. Group policies often cover preexisting conditions and health problems that individual policies exclude. *Note:* It is illegal for an employer to refuse you a job just because you have a medical problem that might make his group insurance more expensive. If this happens and you're angry enough to sue, you have a good case. You can be refused, however, if your state of health could lead to absenteeism and poor performance.

It's foolhardy to falsify medical information on your application for individual health insurance. In the first place, the companies computer-check to see whether you've told the truth (see "Your Medical History," page 475). In the second place, if they find out later that you gave false information, they will deny any medical claim related to that falsehood. If the insurance agent fills in the form for you, read it over carefully to make sure it's right.

If You're Uninsurable

A small percentage of people can't get insurance at any cost because of their health. But many states have "open enrollment" periods, when Blue Cross–Blue Shield must accept all comers. Health maintenance organizations also have periodic open enrollments. Ask your insurance agent about this. If he doesn't know for sure, call your state insurance department (ask the information operator in your state capital for the phone number).

If a breadwinner can't get health insurance, it could go badly with his family. Normally, dependents are included in the breadwinner's policy. A housewife who doesn't work outside the home and has no financial resources of her own generally can't get individual coverage for herself and the children. Nor can a child usually get his own coverage. This loophole doesn't affect many people, but those whom it does are at considerable risk. You're lucky if your state's Blue Cross–Blue Shield has open enrollments. A housewife in this position who decided to take a job should choose an employer with a group health policy.

Length of Coverage

The average hospital stay for people under sixty-five is eight days. Individual policies may cover each illness for as little as thirty days (well over the average, but not allowing much margin for error), or as much as a year or more (probably more coverage than you really need). A second hospital stay, hard upon the first, is generally considered the same confinement, unless it's for a totally different illness. The fewer the covered hospital days, the lower the policy premiums. But check what the coverage would be if you developed a chronic illness that put you in and out of hospitals and nursing homes for years. *Warning:* Some mail-order insurance policies that pay daily cash benefits while you're in the hospital may impose a waiting period of several days before payments begin. Since most hospital stays are quite short, that sort of restriction all but nullifies the policy's value.

Waiver of Premium

Many insurers offer a "waiver of premium benefit" that allows you to quit making premium payments on individual health insurance during the time you're sick or disabled. This doesn't cost very much, and if it's available, it's is a smart thing to buy.

Premium Payments

Group insurance usually costs you a fixed amount each year (unless, of course, your employer buys it for you). Individual and family policies, however, generally increase in cost every year as you get older. (*Note:* Sometimes group premiums increase, too.) Some insurance companies require that you pay by the month. But if you can pay quarterly or annually, the premium is usually a little smaller.

Duration

Some individual health insurance policies can be renewed for a lifetime; after you have reached age sixty-five, however, they convert to limited coverage that simply fills the gaps not paid by Medicare. If you're in poor health and expect to need a policy for the Medicare gaps, it's smart to start out with a company that offers this continuous coverage. Otherwise, it's sufficient to have a policy that's renewable to age sixty-five (which costs a little less than those renewable for a lifetime). After sixty-five you switch to Medicare plus—if you want it and can pass the health exam—a Medicare gap policy from a private insurer.

Guaranteed Renewable

It's important to have a policy that the insurance company can't cancel as long as you pay the premiums. Also, you need a policy whose scheduled premiums can't be raised if your health gets poor. The company should be allowed to cancel coverage only if all holders of that health insurance policy are similarly affected. And even in that case, you should be offered an alternative policy without having to pass a health exam. This protection is essential! Make sure that these provisions are spelled out in any policy you buy. You'll pay less for a policy that the company can cancel any time they decide they no longer want you as a policyholder, but it's a mistake to buy it. You might be dropped as soon as you have a run of medical bills, and you could have a hard time finding alternative coverage.

Another thing: Be sure the policy will carry you for current illnesses even if the policy is canceled. For example, you might be in the hospital when that entire line of policies is withdrawn by the insurance company, or when your coverage under a spouse's policy runs out because of divorce. Look for a clause that will cover that illness for up to a year after the policy runs out.

Children

Get a policy that covers them from the first day they're born. If coverage doesn't begin until after the first fourteen days, you're not insured for the period when expensive infant illnesses are most likely to strike. Individual policies usually require that for your coverage to be continued, you must notify the company about the new child (and pay any additional premium) within thirty days of birth, so don't neglect to do so. (In some cases a claim might be paid even if you don't tell the company and pay the extra premium, but it's foolish to risk it.) Adopted children are generally covered from the time the adoption petition is filed. Stepchildren are included, even if they're not living with you, as long as you're responsible for their support. Foster children are similarly covered. Typically, a policy will cover your children until they're nineteen, and perhaps until age twenty-three (or even older) if they're dependent, unmarried, full-time students. Find out when the cutoff date comes so the child can get his own coverage immediately.

Some states require insurers to cover your child for life if he's handicapped or retarded. In that case the insurer must be notified of the condition within thirty days of the time the child's insurance would otherwise expire. If you're in this situation, by all means check exactly what your group or individual coverage requires.

Wives

This section actually pertains to spouses, but in almost all cases it affects women rather than men. If you're covered under your husband's *group plan,* your insurance (and that of your children) will probably run out within thirty days of his death. Not many widows think of searching for new health insurance immediately after they've buried their husbands, but that's exactly what should be done. Otherwise, you and your family may be without coverage.

If you have individual coverage, the policy will probably automatically cover you and the children after your husband's death (check this point when you buy). Notify the company of the death right away. Your premium will be lowered because one less person is being insured. Some widows don't realize that the death of a spouse means they don't have to pay as much for health insurance. But if you just go on paying the old amount, you may be overpaying your insurance premium by $500 or more a year. (If that has happened to you, notify the insurer and ask for a refund of your past overpayment of premiums.)

If you're unofficially separated from your husband, you're still included under his medical plan. You're out, however, as soon as you're legally separated or divorced (although the children's bills can still be paid). If you had group coverage under your husband's plan, you'll normally have to apply afresh for your own individual policy. If you were covered under a family policy, however, the insurance company may let you buy individual coverage without your passing a health exam —an important point if your health is poor.

Grace Period

You generally have thirty-one days after the due date of the premium to make the payment. If anyone in your family falls ill during this period, the illness will still be covered under the policy. But double-check to be sure that this grace period exists.

Young Adults

If the family policy stops covering your child at age eighteen and the next year he's struck by an expensive illness, you'll doubtlessly wind up paying for it yourself. So by all means see that your child gets his own health insurance as soon as his protection under your policy runs out.

Injuries

Be sure that your hospitalization policy is for illness *and* accident, not just one or the other. You should also be covered for medical bills arising from any injury, no matter what the source. Some policies won't cover injuries if they were in some way related to a medical condition, which is a serious limitation.

Loss Ratio

A way to tell which insurance company is giving you the most for the dollar is to know its loss ratio. That measures the percentage of premiums that the company pays back to its policyholders in benefits. If a high percentage of the premiums are being paid out, it means that the money is being used efficiently on the policyholders' behalf; only a small amount is being kept for expenses and profits. On the other hand, if the loss ratio is low, the policyholders are getting a smaller return for the premiums they pay; the insurance company is keeping a much higher amount for its own use.

Some state insurance departments publish the loss ratios of selected health insurance companies. Many insurance departments will tell you the loss ratio of specific companies if you call and ask. Sometimes the insurance salesman knows what his company's loss ratio is. Blue Cross and Blue Shield typically have loss ratios in the 90-percent area. Good individual insurers have loss ratios of 60 percent and up.

Your Medical History

Few people have ever heard of the Medical Information Bureau. But if you've applied for individual life or health insurance, the company probably checked your name with MIB before it wrote a policy.

MIB is the place where most insurance companies in the United States and Canada exchange information on prospective policyholders. Its basic purpose is to help companies catch people who falsify insurance applications. If one company discovers that you have a health impairment, for example, it will report that fact to MIB. Should you then approach another company and fail to note the illness on your application, a routine check with MIB will turn the problem up. MIB itself does not do insurance investigations. It just files data sent to it, and releases reports to companies entitled to have them.

Files are kept on eleven million people. If you're in good health, the odds are that you don't have a MIB file.

Insurance companies are not supposed to use MIB data directly when they decide whether or not to insure. A report serves merely as a red flag, alerting insurers that one of their brethren once found a risk condition in the applicant. The particular condition is identified by code. Once alerted, the company should do its own investigation. If the problem still exists, they'll report it to MIB; if everything is now all right, they'll report that, too. The record then contains both entries. Each bit of data accumulated in a record is carried for seven years and then wiped out.

Besides scores of specific medical conditions, MIB reports pertinent X rays and lab tests; suicide attempts; occupational poisoning; overweight or underweight; a family history of cancer, diabetes, sickle-cell anemia, or similar diseases; psychiatric disorders (a controversial area, since labels are so imprecise); and drug addiction or alcoholism, if confirmed by the applicant or a medical source. The codes also can note how many attacks of a particular illness you've had, when the condition last manifested itself, whether you're currently under treatment, and whether the illness is slight, moderate, or severe. It's not a full history, but it does cover essential facts.

In the past, MIB has taken some lumps because of certain nonmedical information in its files. For example, it used to identify homosexuals and people considered "socially maladjusted." But no more. Furthermore, it no longer accepts data from the investigative reports that insurers do routinely to make sure you've given honest information on your personal life. If any derogatory information shows up on such a report (whether medical or nonmedical), MIB will note merely that the report exists, without giving the nature of the information. Each insurer then has to ferret the problem out itself. MIB does report on whether you have a reckless driving record, fly a plane, or engage in a hazardous sport (such as scuba diving, snowmobiling, or mountain climbing). Their "nonmedical" category includes whether or not you work in a hazardous occupation or are unlikely to pay your bills. But there's no record of whether any insurance company ever rejected your application.

Under the Fair Credit Reporting Act, you are permitted access to this information to make sure it's right. MIB charges no fee for the service. Write to MIB at P.O. Box 105, Essex Station, Boston, Mass. 02112, and it will send you an authorization form. All nonmedical information in the file will be sent to you directly. Medical information goes to any doctor you designate, who can then discuss it with you. If it's wrong, MIB will correct the record. If you dispute the accuracy of certain information, but the person who gave it stands fast, you can have your side of the story put into the record. (For a medical dispute, have a doctor help you draft the rebuttal.) All insurance applications used by MIB members now contain the warning that MIB exists and that any information the company gets on you may be reported. It also tells you how to gain access to the file.

Mail-Order Insurance

A large number of insurance policies are sold through the mails or by means of newspaper ads. They often require no health exam and appear to offer significant values for a small amount of money. They pay a flat, daily cash benefit while you're in the hospital (or, with some policies, sick at home), and they'll pay it even though you're covered by other insurance. There is nothing intrinsically wrong with this type of policy —in fact, it can be very useful as supplemental insurance. Some companies, however, mislead you into thinking you'll get better benefits than the policy actually pays. Some things to watch out for:

• The big type in the advertisements may say "collect up to $800 (or $1,000 or $1,500) a month while you're in the hospital." That sounds like a lot. But it breaks down to only $26 (or $33 or $50) a day, which compared with the average hospital bill of some $200 a day is a drop in the bucket. The ads also imply that the daily cash benefit will ease your mind about all the ongoing home expenses while you're laid up. But again, when you break the payment down into daily amounts, you can see that a benefit that small won't ease your mind very much. Don't let these policies give you a false sense of security. Know exactly how much they pay a day and how that compares with the magnitude of your likely daily expenses.

• The average hospital stay for people under sixty-five is only eight days. For people over sixty-five, it's fourteen days. If your policy pays "up to $1,000 a month" (or $33 a day), the average benefit paid will be $264 for younger people and $562 for the elderly (as against average hospital bills of $1,200 and $2,400 respectively). Whether or not that kind of benefit is worth the price only you can say. It might do as a supplement to Medicare or other health coverage, but it's too small to serve as your total health insurance.

• With some policies there's a waiting period of three, five, or even eight days before the cash payment starts. So you could be in and out of the hospital without ever qualifying for benefits. This kind of limitation makes a policy virtually worthless.

• If you got the policy without taking a medical exam, there's a waiting period of some time before illnesses will be covered. Check this carefully. Some ads say "no waiting period" in big type but in smaller type add "except under the following circumstances. . . ." Often, this rules out payment for illnesses that wind up costing you a pretty penny. Accidents should be covered from the first day, with no waiting period.

• The policy typically won't cover illnesses you already had when you took out the policy, and this may extend to illnesses that you don't yet realize you have. When you make a claim, the company might refuse to pay it on the ground that that particular illness must have begun before the policy was taken out. And how would you disprove it? Don't buy any insurance unless it agrees to pay benefits for any illness that is contracted or *first becomes apparent* after the date the insurance went into effect (see "Preexisting Conditions," page 469).

• If you buy from a mail-order company that's not licensed to do business in your state and it unfairly rejects a claim, you generally will not be protected by your state's insurance laws. So buy your coverage only from a licensed company. To find out if it's licensed, call or write the state insurance department in your state capital (the information operator can give you the phone number).

These policies are no substitute for regular health insurance. They often appeal to low-income people because they seem to offer a lot for a small price. But that's an illusion. Compared with the high cost of hospital care, mail-order insurance benefits are generally very small. These policies can, however, be used to supplement other insurance, such as Medicare or a poor group plan, provided that you buy honest coverage with no weasel clauses.

There has been some movement to improve the hospital cash payment policy. A few insurers have begun offering hospital benefits as high as $200 per day, as well as some coverage for out-of-hospital services. So keep an eye on the ads. If these policies do start offering meaningful benefits, they could be a convenient way to buy insurance. As of this writing, however, you should approach these policies with a great deal of skepticism. Apply the same stern tests to mail-order insurance as you would to any other health insurance policy.

Ways to Save Money on Prescription Drugs

1. Have your doctor write prescriptions under the drug's generic name rather than the brand name of a particular company. Then you can shop for the company that offers the best price.

2. Take the time to compare prices at the various pharmacies in your town. The one you usually deal with may be charging 50 percent more for the drugs you need than a discount store a few blocks away. This may not matter for the occasional drug purchase, but if you have a chronic illness and use a lot of drugs, the savings can be large.

3. Buy the cheapest brand of aspirin. They're all the same.

4. Ask your doctor if he has any free drug samples he can give you.

5. If you're over age fifty-five, join the American Association of Retired Persons (1909 K St. N.W., Washington, D.C. 20049). It has a mail-order pharmacy service that sells drugs at low prices.

Ways to Save Money on Hospital Bills

Many people don't bother with this, since the insurance company pays the bill. But it's that kind of thinking that puts your health insurance premiums up. Also, many of you are obligated to pay part of the hospital bill yourselves, which should increase your incentive to lower the overall price. Here are some ways to save:

1. Ask your doctor which of the hospitals in the region charges least (assuming that you have a choice). For hospitalization "more expensive" doesn't necessarily mean "better."

2. Choose an insurance policy that has benefits for at-home care. You'll then have the option of leaving the hospital a little early and being reimbursed for the cost of recuperative care at home, which is much cheaper. Things to look for in your insurance policy include payment for visiting nurses, prescription drugs, physical therapy, and renting hospital-type equipment for use at home.

3. Ask a doctor how long your hospital stay is likely to be. If you'll need a long time to recuperate, see if there's a less expensive place you could go, such as a good nursing home. This kind of postoperative planning often doesn't occur to doctors (especially if the hospital has plenty of beds that it wants filled). But if you're footing part of the bill, it should occur to you. Most insurance policies cover some of the cost of nursing-home care while you're recovering from an operation. (If yours doesn't, however, it might be cheaper to stay in the hospital.)

4. Don't enter the hospital on a Friday if you can avoid it. Little is usually done over the weekend, so all you're doing is running up a larger bill.

5. Hospitals always perform a series of medical tests on people due for surgery. See if you can have these tests done the day before you enter so you won't have to spend an extra night there.

6. Take a semiprivate room rather than a private room.

7. Get a second opinion before you accept surgery. It may turn out that a proposed operation isn't really necessary.

8. Learn to take care of your illness yourself, and follow your doctor's directions exactly. Studies have shown that a large percentage of the people readmitted to the hospital soon after being discharged are there because they didn't follow their doctor's orders.

9. Practice preventive medicine. If someone in your family died of a particular disease, you may also be susceptible. Regular checkups might catch it in its early stages.

If You Can't Pay for Medical Care

Hospital emergency rooms will generally accept anyone who has had a bad accident. You can also pretty much count on being admitted if you're dangerously ill. But if you walk in with a less critical complaint and can't show the receptionist proof of medical insurance, you might be sent away. Although some hospitals are still generous with free emergency-room treatment, many others are refusing to take care of anyone they can refer to a doctor. Some are just plain declining to accept anyone who looks like a bad debt (unless it's a real emergency).

Medicaid provides some medical insurance for low-income people (generally dispensed through the welfare office). Doctors sometimes cut their fees if they know you're unemployed or make so little that you can't afford full-scale medical insurance. Hospitals may also settle for less if you go into the office, explain your financial condition, and offer to make regular payments on a reduced bill.

Disability Insurance

If you were seriously injured or became too ill to work, what would your family do for money? You can get private insurance that would pay a regular income during the months or years of a disability. But before you consider this, check out the various sources of disability income that you may not even realize you have. For example:

• *Sick leave.* When a disability strikes, the first source of income is typically whatever sick leave or wage continuation plan (if any) is provided by your company or union. Depending on the plan, you'll get full or partial salary for a certain number of weeks before you go off the payroll.

• *State funds.* Several states run disability insurance funds for qualified workers. The Rhode Island fund, for example, pays up to 50 percent of lost income plus a small dependents' benefit for a maximum of twenty-six weeks. This insurance pool is financed entirely by a small tax on paychecks. California, New Jersey, New York, and Hawaii are other states that use the fund concept.

• *Workers' compensation.* If the disability resulted from a job-related injury or sickness, qualified workers can receive benefits from the state workers' compensation fund. The amount and duration of payments varies widely according to state law (maximums run from about 60 to 80 percent of your predisability earnings); the general trend is to extend coverage to more and more workers, increase payment levels, and lengthen the period of time you can receive income.

• *Group insurance.* If your company or union offers an insurance plan for employees, it may include long-term disability coverage, which would take over when the sick-leave benefits stop. This would provide payments amounting to perhaps 50 percent of your income (up to a ceiling amount) for a specified number of years. Generally, where this insurance is offered, employees must contribute something toward the cost. It's a few dollars every month well spent. One wrinkle in most plans is that they deduct your other sources of disability income from the company benefit. If you get workers' compensation or Social Security, for example, the insurance payment may be cut by a like amount.

• *Social Security.* Long-term disability (including mental illness) is covered under Social Security, provided that you've met the work requirement. To collect, you have to have been laid up for at least five months and the disability must be expected to last at least a year (or to result in death). Also, you must be unable to do any substantial work. The disability payments are the same as those you would get at age sixty-five, and your spouse and children may get payments, too. Social Security can be paid along with workers' compensation up to a ceiling of 80 percent of your previous earnings.

• *Veterans insurance.* If your disability was service-related and happened during active duty, you're eligible for some level of monthly payment, depending on the degree of disability. Low-income veterans may also get payments even if the disability wasn't service-related.

To check the adequacy of your disability coverage, compare your household budget with the income your family would have if you couldn't work. The money would come from spouse's earnings, savings, investments, and the various sources of disability income just listed. Since most disability payments are tax-free, you're reasonably well protected if you can cover something in the area of 60 to 70 percent of your present income. People making less than $15,000 to $18,000, with good company plans and Social Security protection, usually have all the disability coverage they need.

But people with a poor company plan, or who have higher incomes to protect, generally need some private *disability coverage.* These policies guarantee you a specified income for whatever time you choose—from a few years to age sixty-five or life—and are available through life and health insurance agents. As with everything else in the insurance business, prices and benefits vary widely. Here are some of the policy features to shop for:

Guaranteed Noncancelable and Renewable

This means that you're guaranteed the right to renew the policy every year *at the rate you're now paying.* An increasing number of companies guarantee renewability but reserve the right to raise the price—something you don't want. So shop around.

Rates

They vary widely from company to company, so have your insurance agent check around before you make a decision (to be sure that he does indeed check around, you might have a second insurance agent looking, too). Rates for women are typically 50 to 60 percent higher than those for men because, historically, women have made more claims.

Waiting Period

You can buy a policy that starts making payments after you've been out of work only seven days, or you can choose a waiting period of ninety days or longer. The longer the wait, the less costly the policy. If you have some savings and a sick leave plan with your employer that will pay your salary for two or three months, you can afford to take a longer waiting period.

Definition of Disability

For the initial claim total disability should be defined as being unable to perform the regular duties *of your own occupation.* After about two to five years of receiving benefits (depending on the policy; the longer the better), you can generally continue to receive benefits only if you are unable to perform any occupation for which you are reasonably suited by experience, education, and training. In other words, a doctor is disabled as long as he can't practice medicine. The insurance company can't withhold disability payments by arguing that he's fit for a telephone sales job. Under an older definition of disability, not much used anymore but to be avoided if you see it, you were considered totally disabled only if you couldn't perform any meaningful work at all.

You can get a rider for partial disability, generally defined as being unable to perform one or more major duties of your occupation. However, you can't get coverage for preexisting conditions.

Rehabilitation

A few insurance companies will pay for the cost of a rehabilitation program. A larger number of insurers will continue paying disability benefits while you see if you can handle a job—a clause to look for. You don't want a policy that cuts off your payments as soon as you return to work in case it turns out that you can't work full time.

Wife Insurance

A few disability policies will cover the cost of household help if the wife becomes ill or disabled.

Gimmicks

Some companies have "return of premium" policies, which cost quite a bit more but will pay some of your premium back if you don't file a claim for a certain number of years. As a general principle, it's rarely wise to deliberately overpay an insurance policy. You need your money more than the insurance company does.

File Promptly

Don't let medical bills linger in a desk drawer. Insurers require prompt filing for payment. If you delay too long (say, a year or more) the bill may be refused. The outside limit on payment will be spelled out in your insurance contract.

Complaints About Health and Disability Insurance

Notify your state insurance department to see if it can help you resolve the problem. To get the address and phone number, call the information operator in your state capital.

MEDICARE

Who's Eligible

Practically everyone can get Medicare benefits at age sixty-five. You don't have to be retired; nor does it matter how much money you earn. Even if you keep a private health insurance contract in force, it won't pay benefits that could be paid by Medicare, so after age sixty-five it's necessary for everyone to understand and deal with this government program.

Even if you haven't worked long enough to qualify for free hospitalization under Medicare, you can still join the program. In that case it would cost you a modest amount every month ($78 in 1980). By all means sign up for it; there's no better coverage available for the price.

The following people under age sixty-five are also eligible for Medicare: Disabled people who have been entitled to Social Security disability benefits or railroad disability annuities for at least two consecutive years; disabled widows who are getting mother's benefits (instead of disability benefits) because they take care of children but otherwise would have been entitled to disability coverage for at least two consecutive years; people insured under Social Security or Railroad Retirement who, because of permanent kidney failure, need dialysis treatments or a kidney transplant. The spouses and children of insured people are also eligible for kidney benefits.

The Two Medicare Plans

Hospital insurance, fully paid through Social Security taxes, is available to most people sixty-five or over at no cost. Only the few people who haven't met the work requirement of Medicare have to pay for this insurance. *Medical insurance,* which covers doctor bills, costs a small amount every month ($9.60 in 1980). You aren't required to buy this coverage, but everyone should do so. The price is low and the benefits very high. The odds are great that you'll get much more out of this coverage than you pay in.

How to Apply for Medicare Benefits

Register at the Social Security office three months before you reach age sixty-five. That should give them enough time to complete the paperwork so you'll be eligible for coverage from the first month you turn sixty-five. If you don't apply at age sixty-five and are later struck by an illness, there are two consequences:

1. Medicare will cover hospitalization bills retroactively to one year but no bills earlier than that date.
2. Doctor bills will not be covered.

You could lose a lost of money by not getting your Medicare application in on time.

If you're sixty-five or over and still working, you must specifically enroll in one or both parts of the Medicare plan and pay the premium for doctor-bill coverage. If you're sixty-five or over and receiving Social Security retirement benefits, you will generally (but not always) be enrolled automatically in both plans, with the premium for medical insurance deducted from your monthly retirement check. Double-check to be sure that enrollment has occurred.

If you don't apply for the medical insurance section of Medicare (which covers doctor bills) within three months of your sixty-fifth birthday, you can't sign up again until the next general enrollment period —January 1 through March 31 of each year. Your premium will be 10 percent higher for each twelve-month period when you could have been enrolled but weren't. Any doctor bills incurred during the period when you were without coverage will not be insured.

What the Hospital Plan Covers*

1. Hospital charges are paid in full for the first sixty days, after a deductible of $180. The next thirty days are fully paid except for $45 a day. This ninety-day cycle of care can occur more than once during a year, as long as there are at least sixty days between your discharge for one spell of illness and the start of the next one. If you're readmitted to the hospital within less than sixty days, it's counted as the same illness.

2. There's a lifetime "reserve" of another sixty hospital days that can be used if you ever need more than ninety hospital days for a particular period of illness. For these reserve days you pay the first $90 a day and Medicare covers the rest. Reserve days are not renewable; once used, that's it.

3. You get up to one hundred days of care in a skilled nursing facility for each spell of illness, provided that the care is related to treatment you just received in the hospital. The first twenty days are fully paid; the remaining eighty days are paid except for the first $22.50 a day. To qualify, you have to have been in the hospital at least three days before you transfer to the skilled nursing facility, the transfer must be within two weeks of your discharge from the hospital, and your doctor must certify that you need (and get) the care. Be sure that you meet *all* these requirements; otherwise, you'll have to pay the nursing facility bill yourself.

4. There are up to one hundred free home health visits from a home health agency for each period of illness (as defined under point 1). These visits can be spread over a twelve-month period after your latest discharge from a hospital or skilled nursing facility, provided that you meet *all* of the following conditions: You were in the hospital for at least three days; the home care is related to your hospital stay; the care includes part-time skilled nursing, physical therapy, or speech therapy; you're confined to your home; the home health agency participates in

*As of 1980; increases are announced annually.

the Medicare program; and your doctor sets up the home care program for you within fourteen days of your leaving the hospital or skilled nursing facility.

5. The hospital plan will *not* cover services unconnected with the diagnosis and treatment of an illness or injury; private duty nurses; doctor bills (although you can get coverage for this under Medicare's medical insurance plan); such convenience items as TV or a telephone in your hospital room; the first three pints of blood; custodial care in a nursing home; and homemaker services in your own home.

What the Medical Insurance Plan Covers

Medicare pays 80 percent of the "reasonable charge" for most of the following services listed, after a $60 annual deductible (exceptions to the 80-percent rule are noted):

1. Doctor bills, medical supplies, services of the office nurse, and drugs the doctor administers (but not prescription drugs that you buy).

2. A doctor's services in an emergency room or outpatient clinic.

3. Up to one hundred home health visits a year, provided that you need part-time skilled nursing care, physical therapy, or speech therapy; a doctor sets up this home care program for you; you're confined to your home; and the home health agency participates in the Medicare program. All these conditions must be met for Medicare to pick up the bill. These visits are in addition to the one hundred visits provided by Medicare's hospitalization program. After you meet the $60 deductible, home health services are paid for 100 percent.

4. Outpatient physical therapy and speech pathology services, received as part of your treatment in a doctor's office, hospital clinic, skilled nursing facility, or as administered by a home health agency. The services must be prescribed and reviewed by a doctor. They're 80 percent paid.

5. Other medical and health services prescribed by a doctor, including diagnostic services, X rays, surgical dressings, splints, artificial limbs, and rental or purchase of certain medical equipment, such as a wheelchair for use at home.

6. Certain ambulance services.

7. Limited services by chiropractors.

8. Home and office services by licensed and Medicare-certified physical therapists. Payment, however, is limited to a maximum of $80 a year.

9. Doctor's psychiatric services outside a hospital (limited to $250 a year).

10. Radiology and pathology. When you're in the hospital, Medicare will pay 100 percent of the doctors' bills for these services, even if you haven't met the deductible.

Medical insurance does *not* cover routine physical checkups, prescription drugs and patent medicines, glasses and eye exams, hearing aids and exams, dentures and routine dental care, homemaker services and meals, full-time nursing care at home, orthopedic shoes, personal comfort items, the first three pints of blood received in a calendar year, and services and supplies not needed for the diagnosis or treatment of an illness or injury.

Medicare pays "reasonable" charges, which may lag behind the actual increase in doctor's bills. If you submit a $100 bill, you may find that the computer is programmed to consider $90 a reasonable charge for that particular service. So instead of being reimbursed for 80 percent of $100, you'll only get 80 percent of $90 and have to pay the extra amount yourself. Some doctors accept as payment in full the "reasonable charge" as determined by Medicare, so don't fail to ask about it.

Be sure to keep copies of the medical bills you pay yourself. As soon as your bills total more than $60 each year, send them to the carrier that handles your medical insurance claims and ask for a Medicare payment form; after that, send in the bills as received. If you have a big bill and can't prove that you already paid your $60 deductible for that year, Medicare will subtract $60 from your first claim.

Questions and Complaints About Medicare

Get in touch with your Medicare carrier or your local Social Security office. Disputes about bills must be submitted in writing. If you're not satisfied with the decision, and the amount in dispute is $100 or more, you can request a hearing.

Perhaps the most help that children can give to their elderly parents is to see that the Medicare paperwork is done properly so the parents can receive all the insurance money they're entitled to.

Chapter Twenty-Two

PAYING FOR COLLEGE

> Wolfe asked me once why the devil I ever pretended to read a book, and I told him for cultural reasons, and he said that I might as well forgo the pains, that culture was like money, it comes easiest to those who need it least.
>
> REX STOUT

College costs rise every year, in step with the general inflation rate. When the costs of food, energy, and professors leap up, so does the cost of tuition, room, and board. Parents with children in college wonder every year, "How much more?" Parents with college still ahead worry about how they'll pay the bills.

One way you'll pay is with the help of grants and loans. The amount of financial aid available to students has been increasing faster than college costs. In 1978–79 the total pool of college aid (including subsidized student loans) rose 15 percent, on top of an 11 percent increase the year before. But more people are applying for aid, including adult students and those attending school part time, so there's not necessarily more money available per student.

Which Type of College?

State colleges and universities and community colleges offer the best value to parents on a tight budget, since they cost about 40 percent less than comparable private schools. You can see the difference in the table below, which shows the averages for the 1979–80 school year. The price

I've shown includes everything—room, board, tuition, transportation, books, supplies, and personal expenses. A separate column shows how much more the student will likely pay if he wants to live off campus in his own apartment rather than in the college dormitory. Remember that these are average costs, so some schools will cost less. Others cost much more.

For information on current costs at some twenty-nine hundred colleges and other postsecondary institutions, write for the excellent booklet *Student Expenses at Postsecondary Institutions.* At this writing, it costs $5, from The College Board, P.O. Box 20, 888 Seventh Ave., New York, N.Y. 10019.

Type of institution	Average annual cost for student living on campus	Average annual cost for student living off campus*
Public two-year	$2,760	$3,246
Public four-year	3,258	3,576
Private two-year	4,552	4,919
Private four-year	5,526	5,733

*In their own apartments, not with their parents. Source: The College Board, 1979–80 school year.

Should a Student Commute?

You can save money if your child lives at home and commutes to school, but not as much as you might think. He pays the same as everyone else for tuition, books, and supplies and may have higher transportation expenses. He saves the price of room and board, which is considerable, but will probably spend more money than the live-in students at the campus snack shop (unless he goes home for lunch or brings a lunch every day). And of course, he's not cost-free at home, since money is still needed for his food and clothing.

The following table shows what the colleges believed your child's commuting expenses would be, at various types of institutions, in 1979–80. Compared with the cost for live-in students, it appears to be only around $250 to $550 cheaper. You'll find that the colleges have exaggerated the case. Some, for example, include an estimate for the cost of housing him at home; since you would probably keep the same house whether he was home or not, that is not a cost that should be assigned to the price of his college year.

Nevertheless, it's important to realize that college isn't cheap, even for students who live at home. Some students look at a tuition of $700 or $1,000 and think they can handle it easily with just a small loan. But once into the school year, they're hit with a lot more expenses than they'd planned for. Student-aid officers at community colleges say that a high proportion of their dropouts simply underestimated the true cost.

Type of institution	Average annual expenses for a student who lives at home
Public two-year	$2,506
Public four-year	2,735
Private two-year	4,194
Private four-year	4,977

Five Ways to Save Money for College

1. *A steady savings program.* If you put away just $29 a month at 5¼ percent interest, starting from the time your child is three years old, you'd have $8,000 by the time he's eighteen years old and ready for college. *As soon as the account had at least $500 or $1,000 in it, you could earn much more money on your savings by switching to a term account that paid higher interest.* If a six-year term account expired, say, a year and a half before the child went to college, there's no need to keep it in passbook savings for that final period. Ask your bank to give you a term account for the number of days between now and the day you'll need the money for college. Many people don't realize that banks can tailor term accounts exactly to your needs, but they can and will.

If you didn't start saving until the child was eight years old, you'd have to put away $50 a month at 5¼ percent in order to have $8,000 when he's eighteen (again, you'd have even more money by using high-interest term accounts). If you waited until he was thirteen, you'd have to save $145 a month. To figure out how much to save to reach a certain goal, see the table on page 50 and read the directions for using it. It gives the numbers for three-, five-, ten-, fifteen-, twenty-, and twenty-five-year periods, but you can estimate for years in between.

One thing this table leaves out, however, is inflation. A sum of $10,-000 might be enough to pay for four years of state college right now, but it certainly won't be in the future. Assuming an annual average inflation rate of 4 percent a year, it will cost a total of $16,500 to send a child through state college ten years from now, and $20,128 in fifteen years. How are you going to raise those sums?

The thing to remember is that as inflation increases, so do most working people's wages and salaries. A total cost of $16,500 in ten years will pinch no more (and no less) than $10,000 does today. Start out your savings program based on today's college costs, and increase your monthly savings by the rate of inflation each year. You'll probably be able to finance those additional savings out of increased annual earnings, so they won't cut into your living style. By the time college looms, you should be within nodding distance of the actual cost.

One tip: There's a way you may be able to avoid paying taxes on the interest your college savings earn. Instead of keeping the savings in an account in your own name or in trust for the child, give the child the money each month via an account solely in his name. All the interest will then be taxed to him, and since he probably doesn't have enough income to owe taxes, the interest will escape tax-free. Even if he does have to pay taxes, it will be in a much lower bracket than yours. This simple step will give you a much larger sum for college than you otherwise might have had. Once you give the child the money, of course, you can't take it back. The account can't be raided to pay family bills. Even if the child eventually doesn't go to college, the money remains his to spend as he pleases (for more on giving money to children, see Chapter 27, "Wills and Estate Planning").

2. *A savings bond program.* Many employers will deduct money from your paycheck each week or month to buy a U.S. savings bond. Many banks will also buy you a bond each month with money deducted from your checking account. If you spend $50 on bonds every month starting from the time your child is four, you'll have nearly $13,572 when he's eighteen and ready for college.

Savings bonds pay 6½ to 7 percent compounded semiannually. If you accumulated the same $50 in the bank until you could buy a term account, and then put the money to work at 8 percent or more, you'd have an even larger sum when the child was eighteen. But many parents find the ease and regularity of the savings bond program more attractive. Also, savings accounts can be awfully tempting when there's something you want to buy, whereas you might be more reluctant to cash in savings bonds.

The table on page 549 gives you an idea of how many bonds you'll have to buy to reach your savings goal. If you start when the child is eight and want $16,000 when he reaches age eighteen, you'll come close by spending $100 on bonds each month. As inflation increases, add to your bond purchases so your savings will keep pace.

Like savings accounts, bond purchases for college should generally be put in the child's name in order to save income taxes. But there's a wrinkle with savings bonds. You're allowed to defer the taxes until the bonds are cashed in *or* report the taxes annually. If the child defers the tax, the amount of interest received the year the bonds are redeemed for college might be large enough to create a tax liability. It would be better, therefore, to report the interest income annually, which would doubtlessly let it pass tax-free every year. Here's how to do it: The first year the child owns the bond, file a tax return for him showing that no taxes are due. After that, no further tax returns will be needed for that particular bond (although you'll have to file one for each subsequent bond you buy). For details, see "Savings Bonds As a Tax Shelter," page 544.

3. An insurance program. Insurance companies sell *endowment policies* that guarantee a certain amount of money in a certain number of years. You might, for example, take out a policy on yourself that would pay $10,000 cash in twelve years (assuming that's the year when your child will be eighteen). If you died in the meantime, there would be a death benefit of $10,000, plus something extra from interest and dividends. So there would be money for college, whether you lived or died. This, of course, costs a lot more per month than a straight bank savings program, since you're paying for savings *and* insurance. Also, insurance companies generally pay a lower rate of interest than you can get in a bank term account.

The advantage is that if you die, there's a cash benefit to pay for college. The disadvantage is that you may not be able to afford the program. If you already carry enough life insurance to provide for the children's education in case of death, you don't need an endowment policy.

If you need more life insurance, there's a cheaper way to get it than by buying the endowment policy. You could buy $10,000 worth of term insurance (see page 371), to be canceled in a certain year (say, the year your child finishes college). If you die anytime between now and that year, there would be a cash benefit for college expenses. By combining term coverage with a regular monthly savings program (in a bank or via savings bonds), you'd have the same kind of coverage an endowment policy offers (savings plus insurance) at a lower monthly cost.

One thing an insurance benefit does not allow for is inflation. You get a flat dollar payout regardless of what happens to the consumer price index. So even if you decide to buy an endowment policy, you should make gradually increasing monthly deposits in a savings account in order to cover the amount that inflation adds to the cost of college.

Some parents buy an endowment policy on the life of the child rather than the life of the principal breadwinner. That's a mistake. If the child dies, you'd get the life insurance payoff, but you would no longer need it for that child's college expenses. And if the breadwinner died, money might be so tight that you couldn't afford to keep up the child's endowment policy. Instead, buy the policy on the principal breadwinner, so that if he dies, the child's college career will not be endangered. If you buy the policy on a father in his twenties, the price per $1,000 of insurance may be almost exactly the same as the price of the same policy for a child. If the father is older, the price will be higher—but in that case it's even more important to insure the breadwinner, since he's more likely to die.

A fair number of people buy straight-life insurance policies on their children, intending to use the cash value for college. Straight-life policies are cheaper than endowment policies, but the cash you'll have when the child is eighteen is much, much smaller. If the real objective is to have cash for college, you'll accumulate far more by putting the money in the bank each month than by using it for insurance.

4. *A crash savings program.* Many families do all their savings for college in the few years before college begins. This is not as impossible as it first sounds. A young family has many big expenses—a down payment on a house, furniture, maternity costs, and so on. During those years it's often hard to put anything away. But as the children get older, those major expenses are usually behind you. The money that once would have been spent furnishing the living room can now be set aside for furnishing your children's minds. A number of interest-paying tuition plans, combined with life and disability insurance, are offered through the Richard C. Knight Insurance Agency, 53 Beacon St., Boston, Mass. 02108.

5. *A short-term trust.* Parents with substantial earnings and assets can reduce taxes and build a college savings fund through a short-term trust. Assets are put in the child's name for a minimum of ten years; during that time the trust's earnings are taxed in the child's low bracket rather than in your high one, saving a substantial amount of money. The trust's earnings, plus the tax savings, can be applied to the cost of college. When the trust expires, the assets revert back to the parent. For details, see Chapter 27, "Wills and Estate Planning."

Getting Financial Aid

The cardinal rule is, *start early*. Some students lose out on aid because they start looking too late to get all the paperwork done, miss the deadlines, or aren't aggressive enough in pursuing all the leads. College aid officers say you should start thinking about sources of money during your child's junior year of high school. That's the time to research the various types of financial aid and send away for information booklets.

Your child's high school guidance counselor should know about the federal aid and state grants available. Find out if he's eligible, and, if so, about how much money to expect. The application forms are sometimes difficult, but don't let that put you off; the guidance counselor can help you fill them in. Another thing available in the guidance office is a book listing specialized scholarship programs, such as military, ethnic, or fraternal grants. Students should apply for any that seem appropriate to them (especially if their grades are good).

Not all guidance counselors are good at their jobs. If you feel you aren't getting all the help you need, try the financial aid officer of a nearby college where your child is likely to apply. Besides knowing all the outside sources of aid, the college has its own funds and campus jobs to parcel out. Aid officers are always happy to make suggestions to parents; just make an appointment and be ready to take notes.

A mistake many parents make is to take no part in the financial aid search until late in the game. Generally, the student is left on his own —and he may be too shy to pursue leads aggressively. A wise parent makes an appointment himself with the high school guidance counselor to ask about aid, and he also visits the college financial aid offices. It's your money that's going to be spent for college, so you might as well take a front-line position in the frantic hunt for college funds.

Apply for financial aid at the same time as you apply for admission to the college or university. Some students delay sending in the aid form because they're afraid it might hurt their chances of being accepted. But if you delay, you're often out of luck as far as money is concerned. Whatever funds the college has to allocate are passed out as part of the admissions procedure; late applicants usually won't find much money left. Admissions officers say that the need for financial aid does not affect their evaluation of applicants.

When you write for a college's admissions application, ask also for the financial aid form. Parents will have to fill it out, giving all manner of personal financial information. From this a college scholarship service estimates how much the parent should contribute toward his child's education each year, no matter where the child goes. In 1978 the College Scholarship Service began a new system whereby one form can be used to determine your eligibility for a wide number of aid programs, even the federal government's Basic Grants (see page 500). If you want to apply for a Basic Grant, there's a box to check on the front of the form. Basic Grants are critically important, the floor of all financial aid programs—so check the box, even if you think you're only marginally qualified. It doesn't cost you anything to apply. Depending on your state, this single form may also be used in applying for state grants. It's available from high school guidance counselors as well as college aid offices.

How Much Aid Should You Expect?

Middle-class parents almost always underestimate the amount of money they'll have to pay out of their own pockets. Already living on a tight budget, and perhaps with one or two other children to educate, they expect to get quite a bit of financial help. But college aid officers think that you ought to make sacrifices in your standard of living to pay for the children's education. Generally speaking, you'll have to pay more than you might have thought. (By contrast, lower-income parents often have to pay less than they expected.)

If you simply send in the aid form and wait until spring to find out how much grant money has been made available, you may be in for an awful shock. Far better to make a ballpark estimate right now of how much you'll have to pay. Do this by getting a copy of *Meeting College Costs,* prepared by the College Scholarship Service, which is available free from your high school guidance counselor. This booklet takes you through your income, assets, and obligations the way a financial aid officer looks at them. The bottom line tells you how much you'll have to pay. *One warning*: In calculating how much a family can spend on college, it's assumed that the student himself will have something to contribute from summer jobs. If the student spent all his money, that's too bad—an expected contribution from him is cranked into the financial aid calculation all the same.

Low-income students, regardless of high school grades, can generally get a large amount of aid. Middle-income students with good marks may get some aid, but they will also have to look for subsidized student loans; those with average marks may have to depend much more on loans. Students from higher-income families generally can't expect any aid at all (unless their families have especially heavy expenses), except whatever they can earn from merit scholarships or other special programs (see below). Nevertheless, always apply for aid. It doesn't hurt your admission chances, and you may be surprised to learn that you do in fact qualify for a little help.

Sources of Financial Aid

The majority of education grants are reserved for the neediest students. Definitions of "needy" vary, but by and large you won't qualify unless family earnings are below the national average (or not far above) and the family has few assets. Some upper-middle-income students may be offered aid, especially if they're gifted and the family has heavy expenses; families in this position should always apply for financial help, just to see what happens. Those with higher incomes will generally not be eligible for any help, no matter how pinched the family feels.

There are, however, a few scholarships awarded entirely on the basis of merit, regardless of family wealth. Some money is also available to students following particular lines of work. Following is a list of the possibilities for students with above-average incomes. Needier students are eligible for all these awards plus the many stipends for the needy (see page 500).

For All Students Regardless of Income

COLLEGE MERIT SCHOLARSHIPS
An increasing number of colleges and universities offer annual grants to exceptionally bright students whose family income otherwise excludes them from aid. The intent of these grants is to attract the student to the school. The money usually isn't much, but every little bit helps. Apply for these grants through the college aid office. For a listing of schools that offer them, get *The As&Bs of Academic Scholarships* ($2) from Octameron Associates, P.O. Box 3437, Alexandria, Va. 22302.

TALENT SCHOLARSHIPS
These are awarded to gifted students in the arts. Many are specifically for music or art schools, but liberal arts colleges may have similar awards. Ask the head of the arts department what's available.

ATHLETIC SCHOLARSHIPS
A top athlete may get substantial aid without regard to family wealth. Only boys are eligible for the really big grants, although more athletic scholarships are being awarded to girls. Write to the college coach at the same time as you send in your financial aid application.

NATIONAL MERIT SCHOLARSHIPS
These are awarded largely on the basis of a competitive exam, given in October of a student's junior year. Winners need superior test scores, varied extracurricular activities, and a good recommendation from their high school principal. About one thousand students receive one-time $1,000 grants, regardless of need. Another three thousand get stipends ranging from $250 to $1,500 and more a year, with the higher grants going to the needier students. For a few awards, need may be a prerequisite. Ask your high school guidance officer when and where the exams will be given.

STATE MERIT SCHOLARSHIPS
Some states have ability awards based on exam scores. A minimum scholarship is granted regardless of need, but more money goes to lower-income students. Your high school guidance office should have information on these programs.

MILITARY OFFICER-TRAINING PROGRAMS
If a student is willing to serve four years in the military after graduation, he can apply for a Reserve Officers' Training Corps scholarship. These pay full tuition, books, and college fees, plus $100 a month. To qualify, a student needs Scholastic Aptitude Test scores totaling 1,200 or more, varied extracurricular activities, and leadership ability. ROTC scholarships (and nonscholarship programs) are also available to students already in college. For details, consult an Army, Navy, Air Force, or Marine recruiting office, or your college ROTC office. The Navy leans toward engineering students, but the other services spread a wider net.

MILITARY IN-SERVICE PROGRAMS
People enlisted in the armed services are eligible for a wide range of tuition-assistance programs. They can take part-time courses (usually at night), with the service paying 75 percent of tuition. If they want to study something that the service has particular need of, it may even pay all their expenses. The biggest money scholarships are in the medical and nursing fields and can include full scholarships to medical school. But there are also scholarships in other fields. Tuition assistance plans cover studies in technical and vocational schools as well as colleges. Ask any recruiting officer for information.

VETERANS BENEFITS
Anyone who entered the armed forces before January 1, 1977, is eligible for the GI bill, which pays a monthly stipend for forty-five months while he's in an approved school. But those benefits expire in 1989, even for veterans who are in school at the time. Those who want to get

a full four- or five-year education out of the GI bill must start college no later than the fall of 1983 or 1984.

Men and women who have entered the service since January 1, 1977, are eligible for a different program, called Veterans Education Assistance. While they're in the service, they can elect to have a certain amount of money deducted from their pay each month and credited toward an education account. When they get out of service and enroll in an approved school, the government will put up $2 for each $1 they saved. They're entitled to a check for each month they're in school, up to a maximum of thirty-six months. One important point: They must start the program from the day they enter service, or else their education benefit will be reduced. A GI who doesn't want schooling and then changes his mind in the last year of his hitch can't make up the payments he missed in the earlier years. It's well worth his while to sign up for Veterans Education Assistance, even if he doesn't now expect to go to school when he gets out. If he changes his mind, he'll get the full government contribution; if he doesn't go to school, he'll get all his savings back in a lump sum.

VETERANS' DEPENDENTS BENEFITS

The child or the spouse of a veteran who died or became totally disabled because of military service may be entitled to a monthly education benefit. To find out if you or your child is eligible, write to the nearest office of the Veterans Administration. It will be listed in the phone book under "U.S. Government" in your city or the nearest large city.

There are other programs of loans and grants to military dependents. For a list, write for the excellent booklet *Need a Lift?*, $1 from the American Legion, National Emblem Sales, P.O. Box 1055, Indianapolis, Ind. 46206.

COMPANY, UNION, OR FOUNDATION SCHOLARSHIPS

Unions have funds for children of members, often granted on merit. Many companies and foundations also give merit awards—sometimes big ones—to students entering particular fields. Ask about these at your high school guidance office, union, or company-benefits office.

SPECIAL SCHOLARSHIPS AND PROGRAMS

High school guidance officers have books listing special scholarships for people in particular situations or interested in particular careers. These grants are made by churches, ethnic and fraternal associations, some sororities and fraternities, clubs such as the 4-H Clubs and National Honor Society, civic groups, and trade associations. These grants are generally small.

SOCIAL SECURITY
The child of a parent covered by Social Security and now retired, dead, or disabled, may get a monthly education benefit. He qualifies if he's unmarried, aged eighteen through twenty-one, and a full-time student. For information, write to the nearest Social Security office.

SELF-SUPPORTING STUDENT
If a student supports himself, he may be entitled to financial aid regardless of the wealth of his parents. For details, see page 501.

COMPUTERIZED SCHOLARSHIP SERVICES
A number of companies offer, for a fee, to check your qualifications against a computerized list of scholarships available in order to help you find sources of aid. The people who run these services may imply that millions of dollars in scholarship aid go unused every year just because people don't know where to look for it. Sadly, that's not so; very little grant money fails to be awarded. A computer service will check the various specialized scholarships against your general qualifications, which is more efficient than your plowing through all the books yourself. And it may indeed turn something up for which you can apply. But don't count on discovering a major new source of funds through a computer.

COOPERATIVE EDUCATION
A number of colleges help students earn their own tuition money by offering a program of study alternating with periods of work. You might, for example, spend the freshman year in residence, then complete your education by studying six months and working six months. Often the college even helps you find a job. (If a student has to support himself on his earnings, however, there may be little left to pay for college.) For a list of colleges offering cooperative programs, write to the National Commission for Cooperative Education, 360 Huntington Ave., Boston, Mass. 02115.

ADVANCED PLACEMENT
Students taking college-level courses in high school may be able to receive college credit for the work by passing a competency test. Two widely used programs are the Advanced Placement Program and the College Level Examination Program, both sponsored by The College Board. For details, ask your high school guidance office or write to CLEP, Box 2815, Princeton, N.J. 08541. If a student passes enough of these exams and also loads up on some extra courses, he may be able to save money by graduating six months or even a year earlier than his classmates.

COLLEGE WORK-STUDY

Jobs on and off campus are generally reserved for needy students and awarded as part of the college's total financial aid package. But in many cases, students who didn't qualify for direct aid may be able to secure one of these jobs. Apply for them through the financial aid office.

HANDICAPPED STUDENTS

Most of the states have special education programs for people with various handicaps. Ask your college financial aid office, or write to your state's Division of Vocational Rehabilitation in the state capital.

MORE INFORMATION

Three excellent guides to scholarships are the booklets *Don't Miss Out* ($2) and *The As&Bs of Academic Scholarships* ($2), from Octameron Associates, P.O. Box 3437, Alexandria, Va. 22302, and *Need a Lift?*, $1 from your local American Legion Post or from the American Legion, National Emblem Sales, P.O. Box 1055, Indianapolis, Ind. 46206. The American Legion booklet is especially helpful on state and military scholarship programs.

For Needy Students

BASIC EDUCATIONAL OPPORTUNITY GRANTS

These critically important grants are the cornerstone of the entire student aid program. They're given by the federal government for use at any accredited college, vocational school, technical institute, nursing school, or other eligible postsecondary institution. It's immaterial whether a student has good or bad grades. If he's admitted to any eligible institution and his family income meets the requirements, he gets a grant. *This year, BEOGs have been expanded to include the middle class.* Depending on your assets, expenses, and family size, you may qualify for aid even if your family income is in the $30,000 area. So it makes sense to mail in the application form, just to see if you're eligible. An easy way to apply is to check the "Basic Grants" box on the Parent's Confidential (financial) Statement of the College Scholarship Service, used by many colleges to evaluate need; the CSS will then make application for you. You can also get forms from your high school guidance office, or from Basic Grants, P.O. Box 84, Washington, D.C. 20044. The actual amount of money awarded depends on family income and the tuition of the school attended.

Basic Grant forms aren't available until January. By all means apply right away, so you'll get a prompt response. In the February, March, and April crush, it may take many weeks to get an answer. A college aid officer generally starts with the size of your BEOG in deciding how much aid you should get, so it's extremely helpful for him to have your BEOG in hand when the college's funds are being allocated.

SUPPLEMENTAL EDUCATIONAL OPPORTUNITY GRANTS

These federal grants are for especially needy students in colleges and vocational schools. The vast majority of SEOGs go to people whose family income is below $6,000. A SEOG grant is worth double its face amount, since the school has to match it with other aid funds. These are administered through the college financial aid office.

STATE STUDENT INCENTIVE GRANTS

This is a federal-state matching-grant program, administered through the states. Ask your high school guidance teacher how to apply.

GRANTS FROM THE COLLEGE'S OWN SCHOLARSHIP FUND

This pool of money is administered by the college financial aid office. The college will first gather as much outside aid (from state, federal, and private sources) as the student is eligible for, estimate how much (if any) the parents are expected to pay, then make a grant for all or part of the remainder from the school's own funds. If the total package of grants is not enough to pay for a year in school, the student may be encouraged to take a subsidized student loan for the difference (see page 502).

Self-Supporting Students

If your son or daughter is supporting himself, he can apply for financial aid based on his own income rather than on yours. Assuming that he doesn't make very much, it's quite likely that he'll qualify for an education grant based on need. By federal definition a self-supporting student is one who, in the year for which he is applying for aid and in the previous calendar year, (1) was not listed as a dependent on his parents' tax return; (2) received no more than $750 from them; and (3) lived at their home for no more than six consecutive weeks. If he meets these criteria, he can apply for a Basic Educational Opportunity Grant on the basis of his income alone; write to BEOG, P.O. Box 84, Washington, D.C. 20044.

College aid officers, however, are skeptical of young self-supporting students. Many are genuinely independent and need all the help they can get. But others have well-to-do parents who have simply declined to pay for college. Some may even be in collusion with their parents to make it appear that they're self-supporting.

Should all independent students be considered equally for financial aid? Different colleges answer this question differently. Some are cautious about claims of self-support, demanding tax returns to prove income and dependency claims, and querying parents. If they find that you lied to the government when you applied for a BEOG, your grant will be rescinded. Sometimes colleges require financial information from the parents of self-supporting students; if the parent is judged able to contribute to his child's education, the student is given less financial aid, even if the parent positively refuses to pay. Other colleges ask self-supporting students to prove that their parents can't afford to help. If the student declines, he goes to the bottom of the list of aid applicants.

But some colleges are more lenient. If the student qualified as self-supporting under the government's guidelines, no more questions are asked. A student might have to submit a financial statement and could be ruled ineligible if he keeps a car or has other assets. But short of this, he could receive a grant for his tuition and living expenses even if his parents were affluent.

In states where eighteen-year-olds are considered adults, students may come from out of state and work for a while to establish residence. After a year (and sometimes less) they can apply to a nearby university not only as a self-supporting student but as a state resident, which at state universities may qualify them for lower tuition.

College Loans

A growing proportion of the college bill is being shouldered by students themselves in the form of low-interest student loans. Sometimes a parent may tell the student to take a loan, promising to help him pay it back, but in some cases, the student winds up paying it himself. *A student should be extremely cautious in taking out a loan.* The amount may not seem like much when he signs up. But if he borrows $2,500 a year for four years, he'll graduate from college with a $10,000 debt. His starting salary may not be very much higher than that, which could make his loan payments quite burdensome. Added to all the other expenses of supporting himself—rent, a car, furniture, a family—those payments could be crippling. Expensive colleges often lure the bright, middle-income student with a package of grants and loans, and he may go there for the prestige. But after graduation the loans are on his back. In general, it's smarter for a student to go to a less expensive college and avoid assuming a large debt for his education.

Government-Guaranteed Student Loans

These are now open to anyone, regardless of income, who attends an eligible college, business school, vocational school, or other approved institution—even some schools abroad. Most states accept half-time students (although a few require them to go full time). The interest rate on a guaranteed student loan is only 7 percent. The government pays the interest as long as the student is in school; after that, he pays. No principal repayments are due until nine to twelve months after the student leaves school, and he has ten years to pay the loan off. Payments may be deferred for up to three years if he joins the Peace Corps or Vista or if he goes into the armed services. Deferrals are also available if he goes to graduate school or returns to other full-time study.

Guaranteed student loans are available through many commercial banks and some savings banks, savings and loan associations, credit unions, and colleges. It's a voluntary decision on the lender's part to join this program; if he does join, he can decide for himself who he'll lend to and how much. Your best bet is to have your child apply for a student loan at the institution where you have your checking or savings accounts or some other business relationship. Often, lenders provide student loan money to children of their own customers but not anyone else.

If your bank or S&L isn't part of the program, you'll have to shop around. Ask your bank for a referral, or call a number of banks to see if they make these loans. If you can't find any, ask the department of education in your state which local lenders participate (get the number from the information operator in your state capital). The department should refer you either to the state Student Loan Guarantee Agency, or a regional office of the U.S. Office of Education. It may be necessary to switch your bank account to another lender in order to be considered for funds. The government and the lenders set maximum annual limits on their loans. If money is a problem for you, be sure you know how large a student loan you can get before saying yes to an expensive college.

Government-guaranteed loans are granted to the student, not to his parents. If a student defaults, the lender can't force the parents to pay. (With this exception: If the student is a minor—under eighteen in most states—the parents may have to cosign, in which case they'd be responsible for payment.) The lender collects from the government on defaulted loans, and the government tries to collect from the students. Lawsuits usually aren't brought against student delinquents who are unemployed or who can't pay because of illness, marital problems, or unforeseen debt. But the government is making stepped-up efforts to collect from students who have coldbloodedly walked away from their obligations. In the past some students went bankrupt in order to evade their student loan debt, but a law passed in 1976 allows judges to exclude student loan debts from the bankruptcy process. So even after bankruptcy the loan would still have to be paid. In case of death or total disability, however, the loan is canceled.

College Loan Programs

Colleges have dreamed up a number of ways to help parents handle the ever-higher costs. Some make low-interest loans, with payments spread out over several years. Some accept payment for tuition, room, and board in twelve monthly installments, rather than all at once at the start of each semester. Some arrange with certain banks to help parents get loans. These loan programs aren't always publicized, so pay a visit to the financial aid office to see what you can arrange. Often, the interest charged on loans made by colleges is lower than you'd get on a personal loan from your own bank. Several hundred colleges offer extended repayment plans through the Richard C. Knight Insurance Agency, 53 Beacon St., Boston, Mass. 02108.

National Direct Student Loans

Needy students can borrow money for college, vocational, or technical training through this program, supported by the federal government and administered through the schools. Your child is eligible if he attends school at least half time. Interest is 3 percent and doesn't start accruing until he leaves school, so there's nothing to pay while he's actually studying. Repayment begins nine months after leaving school and can be stretched over ten years. There's a moratorium on payments of up to three years if he joins the armed forces, Vista, or the Peace Corps. If he serves in a combat zone, teaches in Head Start or certain poverty areas, or teaches the handicapped, part or all of his debt may be forgiven. National Direct Student Loans are available only to students in serious financial need, and it's up to the college aid officer to decide whether your child is in that category. If you think he might qualify, ask the financial aid office about it. These loans are often available to self-supporting students.

Government Agency Loans

The U.S. Department of Health, Education and Welfare makes 3 percent loans to needy students seeking a degree in nursing. The U.S. Department of Justice lends to students interested in criminal justice fields. Both programs are administered through schools and colleges; for details inquire at the school's financial aid office. The various states also have loan programs for students in special categories or those going into special fields. Ask about them at your high school guidance office or college financial aid office. In some cases outright grants may also be available.

Loans from Organizations

Your union, employer, professional or fraternal group, or other organizations may make student loans to the children of members. You should make inquiries to see what's available.

Loans from Private Lenders

If you're still short of money, you'll have to borrow from a commercial lender (see Chapter 7, "Where to Borrow Money"). As always, look for the best possible interest rate and try to repay the loan as rapidly as possible. You should think twice before you do something drastic, such as refinancing your home, in order to pay for a classy college; your child, after all, can get just as good an education from a top state university at half the price. Refinancing a home costs thousands of extra dollars in interest payments over the years.

If Your Child Isn't Accepted in the Schools He Applied To

There's a place in college for every qualified student in the United States. So if all your child's applications were turned down, he simply didn't apply to the right schools. Your high school guidance counselor should be able to tell you the names of several schools that normally have openings for late applicants. There's even a list of 1,841 colleges and universities that expect in January to have openings that spring ($2 from Chronicle Guidance Publications, Moravia, N.Y. 13118).

Write directly to the admissions officer of some possible colleges, telling about your child, his interests, his grades, his test scores, and his ambitions. Ask if there's any sense applying at this late date. If the school is interested, they'll let you know right away. Generally speaking, it's better for a child to go to a second-rate college than to stay out of school and apply again the following year. If he gets good grades, he'll be able to transfer to something better—perhaps even to one of the colleges that turned him down.

Some parents turn for help to private placement counselors, who charge anywhere from $30 to $150 to find a freshman opening. Many of these counselors are employed by specific schools (generally, by expensive liberal arts schools, some of them not as good as they should be for the price). You, however, are not aware of this fact. When you come to the counselor for help, he sends the child's profile to his client schools; if they're interested, he puts you in touch.

It really isn't necessary to pay a counselor to get your child into college. You should be able to find an opening yourself, and probably at a school that charges less than the ones the counselor works for.

Warning: There's very little financial aid available to late applicants, so if money is a problem, concentrate your applications at lower-priced schools.

Finding a Vocational School

There are many excellent vocational schools offering training in useful and well-paying lines of work. But mixed in with the good schools are others whose training is poor, equipment out of date, and reputation low. Some schools even train for jobs not in demand, or accept high school graduates for training in fields where the jobs go only to people with college degrees. Vocational training courses can cost as much a year as a private college, so you have a lot to lose by spending your money on a poor school.

How do you tell the good schools from the bad? One way is to watch their advertising. Reputable schools do not make extravagant promises about high salaries if you'll take their course, or guarantee that jobs will be available. The truth is that most vocational school graduates can expect only modest salaries at first, working up over several years. The better schools can be of help in finding you a job, but in general, an ad is misleading if it implies that graduates will easily find work. A good school advertises its programs without a flurry of promises and claims.

Another way to find a good school is to do a little research before signing up. A hopeful student all too often gets all his information from the school as to whether there's demand for the line of work he's interested in, or whether the training is up to date. Naturally, the school will speak well of itself. But before signing up, it's smart to double-check what it says. A student should (1) ask someone in the line of work he's interested in whether he thinks the school is any good; (2) ask the students now at the school what they think about the training; and (3) most importantly, ask an employer whether he'd hire someone with a training certificate from that particular school. The employer will probably not want to make a job commitment, but at least he can say whether he considers the certificate a sufficiently good qualification. The student should make an appointment with the personnel office to discuss how to qualify for the job he wants; if he can't get an appointment, he should write a letter asking whether the line of work he's interested in has qualifications beyond a vocational training certificate.

Paying for Vocational School

All government funds available for college can also be used at accredited vocational schools and training institutes. Apply through the school's financial aid office. Subsidized student loans may also be had for vocational training. On the other hand, many of the private sources of funds, such as the specialized scholarships, may be reserved for college and university students. A student should check the eligibility requirements of any of the special programs he thinks he may qualify for to see if they'll fund the kind of training he wants. *Warning:* A student should not use a loan to pay for a training course unless he's dead sure that it's good and that he'll follow through. If he drops out, there may be little or no refund and the loan still has to be repaid.

Correspondence Courses

These can be just as expensive as vocational training schools but are the least likely to lead to a job. Many of the courses offered through home study actually need classroom practice with particular machines or other equipment to make the student job-qualified; taking paper-and-pencil tests is not enough. Also, the quality of home study courses is often poor. The student may find the course interesting, or an introduction to an area that he may want to pursue further. But if his goal is employment, he'd be wiser to go to a vocational training school.

Chapter Twenty-Three

INCOME
TAXES

I'm a middle-bracket person with a middle-bracket spouse
And we live together gaily in a middle-bracket house.
We've a fair-to-middling family; we take the middle view;
So we're manna sent from heaven to Internal Revenue.

PHYLLIS MCGINLEY

Changes are made in the U.S. tax law every year. Sometimes they're sweeping adjustments, affecting the majority of taxpayers; other changes are narrow, arising from court decisions on small points of law. This constant ebb and flow of clauses and subclauses makes it impossible to get out last year's tax return, follow it line by line, and be confident that you're paying this year's taxes correctly. You'll always need an up-to-date tax guide to find out what's new.

The regularity of change makes it impossible to write a detailed chapter on tax strategies and deductions. Some of the ideas would be out of date before the book even went to press. This chapter, therefore, focuses on those parts of the federal tax system that have remained unchanged for many years and shows how you can use them to minimize your tax.

Where to Get Detailed Information
on Tax Deductions

Most taxpayers get their tax returns by mail, enclosed in an instruction booklet which is itself a mini–tax guide. You'll generally find

508

the year's major changes highlighted right on the booklet's first page. For more detailed information, write or call the Internal Revenue Service for the free guide *Your Federal Income Tax (for Individuals)*, known as Publication 17. For tips on tax savings, try the various tax guides available at bookstores. If you have a lot of money or your tax situation is complex, by all means get the advice of an accountant or tax lawyer.

Who Has to File Income Tax Returns

This unpleasant duty falls on anyone who makes a certain amount of money in earnings, dividends, or interest. The tax instruction booklet has a paragraph right in the front, saying what the minimum income requirement is every year. Low-income workers and young people with summer or part-time jobs generally don't make enough to file. Older people with only a small amount of money from taxable sources may also escape (for a list of what income is taxable see the following section).

Some people should file tax returns even though they don't owe any taxes. This applies, for example, to:

1. Young people who have taxes withheld from their paychecks, even though they make too little money for taxes to be due. The only way to get withheld payments back is to file for a refund.

2. Working people with low incomes who may be entitled to an "earned income credit," payable in cash if they don't owe any taxes. To claim the credit you have to file a tax return.

What Income Is Taxable

• All the earnings you receive from an employer, including your wages, bonuses, fees, commissions, severance pay, benefits paid to laid-off employees from a company-financed unemployment fund, and moving allowances. You may also owe taxes on certain items of noncash compensation, such as the value of rent-free living quarters.

• Cash dividends received from stock and mutual funds if the income is more than a certain amount. *Tax Tip:* You may not have to pay income taxes on the full sum! (1) Payments from a mutual fund may include your share of the fund's profits from stocks that have increased in value. These profits, called capital gains, are taxed at a lower rate than ordinary dividends and reported separately from your regular income. (2) Sometimes, part of the dividend check represents a return of the cash you originally invested, which is not taxable. This is most likely to happen with utility companies and mutual funds. Any nontaxable return is excluded from dividend income on your tax return. Always take a careful look at the statement that comes with your dividend check to see if it contains either of these special items. (*Note:* Sometimes you get dividends in the form of stock rather than cash. Stock dividends are not reported until the stock is sold.)

• Interest earned on savings accounts, bonds, mortgages, insurance proceeds left on deposit with an insurance company, tax refunds, and any loans you've made to other people. Interest earned on municipal bonds, however, is federal-tax exempt. (You'll owe state and local taxes if you buy the bonds of another city or state.)

• Income from pensions, profit-sharing plans, and annuities, to the extent that they were entirely financed by your employer. You also owe tax on income from tax-sheltered Individual Retirement Accounts and Keogh plans. However, if you contributed to a pension plan from your own, after-tax income (for example, by making a voluntary addition to your employee pension plan), the return of that contribution is not taxed. Whoever set up your pension plan can tell you what is, and what is not, reportable as income.

• Rental income, from houses, commercial buildings, land, or any other type of property. The expenses of renting the property can be deducted from income.

• Royalties from books, music, inventions, gas and oil wells, mines, and timberland. You can deduct whatever it cost you to produce the work or make the investment. (*Exception*: There's no deduction for the cost of your own labor.)

• Income from partnerships, corporations, and your own business.

• Income from estates and trusts. The inheritance itself is subject to estate tax, not income tax. But you pay an income tax on any income earned by the assets and paid to you. You'll get a statement from the trustee every year, explaining how much of the money that you got from the estate or trust was taxable income.

• Alimony (but not child support).

• Odds-and-ends income, such as director's fees, awards from contests you've entered, strike benefits, jury fees, and so on.

• The profit on any investments you sold (see "Capital Gains and Losses," page 521).

You do NOT pay taxes on the following income:

• Social Security or Railroad Retirement benefits.

• Any portion of an employee pension that represents your personal, *after-tax* contribution. The income earned by your contribution, however, is taxed.

  • Veteran's benefits.

  • Workers' compensation.

  • Benefits paid under an accident and health insurance policy.

• Damage payments for sickness or personal injury, received in a lawsuit or from no-fault insurance. Other damage awards, however, may be taxable.

• Benefits paid under a disability insurance policy that you purchased yourself.

• Up to $100 a week of sick pay if you're permanently and totally disabled and your gross income doesn't exceed $15,000. If your income is over that level, the sick-pay deduction is gradually reduced, phasing out entirely at $20,200.

  • Welfare payments.

• Unemployment compensation (but not benefits paid to laid-off employees from an employer-financed fund).

  • Gifts.

  • Cash awards recognizing past achievements.

  • Inheritances (subject to estate taxes but not income taxes).

• The proceeds of life insurance policies. (Although not normally taxed as income, insurance proceeds are subject to estate taxes *if* the policy was owned by the person who died. If someone else owned it, however, it usually isn't even subject to estate taxes—see page 709).

  • Interest on tax-exempt securities.

• Certain allowances paid to military personnel (your branch of service can give you a complete list of all the tax breaks).

• A certain amount of the profit on a house sold by a person fifty-five or over.

• A certain amount of any payment given by a company to the survivors of an employee who died.

• Scholarships and fellowships (unless the fellowship is in return for some hours of teaching or performing another campus job, in which case it's considered income).

  • Certain income earned in foreign countries.

• A limited amount of stock and mutual fund dividends (and, in 1981, a limited amount of interest).

  • Federal income tax refunds.

Your Filing Status

Here's where you have perhaps the greatest opportunity to save money on taxes. If you choose the wrong status—as many do—you may pay hundreds of dollars more than you really have to.

There are five possible filing statuses, each one taxed at a different rate. *Married people filing jointly* and *qualifying widows and widowers with a dependent child* pay the lowest rate of tax in all tax brackets. Next up the tax ladder come *unmarried heads of household*, and then *single people*. The last category, *married people filing separately*, pay the highest rate. Many single people overpay their taxes every year because they don't realize that they qualify for the head-of-household tax break. And many widows, widowers, and separated couples don't pick the filing status that will result in the lowest tax. Here's how to figure where you fit:

• *You're single if* you were unmarried or legally separated on the last day of the tax year, even if your divorce or separation decree came through the day before. (However, if your spouse died during the year, you're still considered married for tax-filing purposes.) Some single people are able to file as head of household or as a widow or widower with dependent child (see below). But if you don't meet all the qualifications of those categories, you'll have to pay taxes as a single.

• *You're married if* you were married on or before the last day of the tax year, even if the wedding took place the day before. You're also married for tax purposes if you're separated from your spouse, either informally or by signed separation agreement, but the separation isn't final according to judicial decree. Most married people file jointly (which you can do even if your spouse has no income) because it saves them taxes. You can even file a joint return if your spouse died during the tax year.

• *You can be married but file separately rather than jointly.* Normally this imposes a tax burden. But occasionally, if the deductions and income levels break right, separate returns may result in a lower federal tax. When in doubt, figure your returns both ways to see which is best. If your spouse is a *non*resident alien, you must pay taxes as a married person filing separately (unless you can qualify as head of household— see below). You'll also have to file separately if you live apart from your spouse and the spouse won't sign a joint return.

Warning: Several important tax breaks are not available to married people if they file separately. You're not allowed certain deductions, such as child-care expenses. Low-income people can't take the earned income credit. High-income people have to give up their right to the 50 percent tax ceiling on earned income. All told, the tax penalty of filing separately rather than jointly may be considerable.

• *Widows and widowers with a dependent child* are entitled to a generous tax break that is all too often overlooked. You can go on filing jointly (hence, paying the lowest possible tax) for the *two* tax years *after* the spouse's death, provided that *all* of the following conditions are met: You were entitled to file a joint return with your spouse in the year of the death (whether you did or not); your child or stepchild lives with you and qualifies as a dependent; your home is the child's principal residence for the entire year, except for temporary absences; and you furnish more than half the household's support. *Note:* To get this filing status, you must file the long form, 1040.

• *If you're unmarried and qualify as a head of household,* you'll save hundreds of dollars on your tax bill. This status generally applies to divorced or widowed people who have custody of a child, or single people supporting their parents or other relatives. You get this break if your home was the principal residence, for a full tax year, of a qualifying relative, and you paid more than half the cost of maintaining the household. A "qualifying relative" means (1) a mother, father, in-law, or other close relative whom you take as a tax dependent; or (2) your unmarried child, stepchild, foster child, or grandchild, whether dependent or not. (If you're divorced and you and your ex-spouse have joint custody of your child, neither of you qualifies as head of household, because neither of you makes a permanent home for the child for the entire tax year. You both have to file as singles.)

You're also head of household if you contribute more than half the cost of maintaining your *dependent mother and/or father* in their own home or in a nursing home. They don't have to live with you.

Tax Status of Separated Couples

• *When you're legally separated, with a final decree of separate maintenance,* you pay taxes in one of two categories: (1) If you have full custody of a child, you may file as *head of household*—provided that you meet all the other tests listed above. (2) If you have partial custody, or no child in your custody at all, you file as a *single* person.

• *If you're informally separated, or have a signed separation agreement but no judicial decree of separate maintenance,* you may file in one of the following four categories. Be sure to read each section carefully to determine exactly which one fits your circumstances.

1. As long as you don't have a judicial decree of separate maintenance, you can still file *jointly*. This is an advantage for couples whose earnings are approximately the same, since joint returns are taxed at the lowest rate. But if you have a lower income than your spouse, you may pay less tax by filing individually, in one of the remaining three categories. It also pays to file individually if you don't trust the other's accounting enough to sign the joint tax return.

2. You're an *unmarried head of household* if you meet *all* the following conditions: You've lived apart from your spouse all year; file a separate tax return; pay more than half the cost of maintaining the household; and your child or stepchild (whom you claim as a dependent) lived with you for the entire year except for temporary absences. A child is considered "temporarily absent" if he's on vacation, away at school, visiting the other parent, and so on. This filing status provides the lowest tax rate available on an individual return. *Special note to parents receiving alimony:* Alimony is considered your personal income. If you use it to help support the household, it's considered your contribution to costs, not a contribution from your spouse. Therefore, you can use alimony income in figuring whether you pay more than half the cost of maintaining the household.

3. You're *single* if you meet *all* of the following conditions: You've lived apart from your spouse all year; file a separate tax return; pay more than half the cost of maintaining the household; and your child or stepchild (whom you claim as a tax dependent) lived with you for more than six months (but less than a year) except for temporary absences. This filing status is for separated people with partial custody of a child. *But note:* If you and your spouse share custody at exactly six months each, neither of you can file as a single. You'll both have to use the unfavorable status, married person filing separately.

4. You're a *married person filing separately* if your child doesn't live with you or lives with you for six months or less, and your spouse won't sign a joint return. You're also stuck with this filing status if the child lives with you but you don't pay more than half the cost of supporting the household.

Itemized Deductions and the Zero Bracket Amount

All taxpayers get a flat deduction from income called the *zero bracket amount. Itemized deductions* are also available for various special categories of expenditure. If your itemized deductions add up to more than the zero bracket amount, you're entitled to subtract the *excess deductions* (that is, the amount by which itemized deductions exceed the zero bracket amount) from your adjusted gross income. When you have a lot of itemized deductions, always add them up to see if you can use them to reduce your tax.

Note: When married couples file separately, they have to use the same method, both itemizing or both taking only the zero bracket amount. People in certain specialized filing statuses must itemize—see the tax booklet for instructions.

Personal Exemptions

Everyone who files a tax return gets at least one personal exemption, which is a fixed sum deducted from your income. A second exemption goes to taxpayers who are blind, and a third to those who are sixty-five and over. You may claim the personal exemption even if you're listed on someone else's return as a tax dependent. For example, a student with part-time earnings gets a personal exemption even though he is claimed as a dependent on his father's tax return.

If you file jointly with your spouse, there's a spouse exemption (plus additional exemptions if the spouse is blind or sixty-five and over). On a separate return you may claim an exemption for a spouse only if he or she had no income and was not the dependent of another taxpayer.

Dependents

Each dependent you have is worth another exemption on your tax return. Dependents are generally your children and anyone else you support, with this exception: You can't include the man or woman you sleep with out of wedlock (the IRS forbids dependency exemptions for "illicit" relationships). But even for acceptable relationships the rules on exemptions are stricter than you may realize. It's easy for someone in your household to step over the line, which sends his exemption up in smoke.

Anyone you list on your tax return as a dependent must meet *all five* of the following tests:

1. *You have to furnish more than one half his support.* In making this calculation, add up the total spent on his support to see if your own personal contribution came to more than one half. To figure how much the dependent spent on his own support, take into account his income from all sources, including his earnings, any savings he spent, income from Social Security, welfare, and even money he borrowed on a student loan. *Note:* Two key sources of income that you don't have to count when you figure support are Medicare payments to an elderly dependent and scholarship money paid to a student in school. *Another note:* If the dependent puts part of his income into the bank rather than spending it on himself, that money doesn't count as having gone toward his support.

TAX TIP 1: If you're supporting an elderly parent, recalculate his income and expenses every time Social Security hands out a cost-of-living increase to be sure you're still paying more than half his support. To keep the dependency exemption, you may have to increase your contribution a little.

TAX TIP 2: If you're helping to support both parents, the money you give will normally be divided evenly between them. If the amount is not large, you may lose the dependency exemptions because you're paying less than 50 percent of what it costs to support each parent. The right way to handle this kind of situation is to specify that your entire contribution is for the support of one parent. That way, you'll get at least one exemption for your money.

TAX TIP 3: Don't let your child borrow so much on a student loan that, together with what he spends from his earnings, he winds up paying more than half of his own support. Unless you keep his contribution to less than half, you'll lose the exemption.

TAX TIP 4: It often happens that several people contribute to the support of one dependent (children, for example, supporting an elderly parent), with no one person paying more than half. Fortunately, the tax code makes special provision for cases like this so the dependency exemption won't be lost. You can all mutually agree which one gets the exemption, as long as the person chosen contributed at least 10 percent of the dependent's support (and no one contributed more than 50 percent). Next year, the exemption can be rotated to someone else. Technical note: The person claiming the exemption will have to file a "Multiple Support Agreement."

2. *The dependent (except for children) may not have a gross income of more than $1000.* But this isn't as harsh as it sounds. In applying the income test, the government doesn't count nontaxable income. In other words, if you're supporting a parent who has income from Social Security, which is not taxable, you don't have to count it for purposes of the gross income test. (But you do count it for purposes of the support test —see page 515. If the law sounds inconsistent on this point, well, that's why you're reading this tax chapter!)

A major exception to the income test is made for children. If your child is under nineteen or a full-time student, he can make any amount of money and still qualify as a tax dependent. *Warning:* To keep the dependency exemption you have to provide more than half the child's support. So if he makes a lot of money, be sure he isn't spending it all on himself. He can put his money in the bank or invest it without endangering your exemption.

3. *If the person you support is not a close relative, he qualifies as a dependent only if he lives with you for the entire year* (except for temporary absences). By contrast, a close relative can be taken as a dependent even if he doesn't live with you, provided that he meets all the other tests in this list.

4. *A dependent must be a U.S. citizen or U.S. resident for some part of the tax year in which you claim the dependency,* or a resident of Canada or Mexico.

5. *You're generally not allowed a dependency exemption if the dependent files a joint tax return.* In other words, if your son or daughter was married this year but still qualifies as a dependent, you'll lose the exemption if he or she files jointly with the new spouse. There is, however, an exception to this rule. If the couple wouldn't normally have to file a tax return but does so in order to claim a refund of taxes withheld, they may file jointly without endangering your exemption.

The child of divorced or separated parents is generally presumed to be the dependent of the parent who has custody. However, the other parent gets the exemption if he furnishes at least $600 for each child claimed and the separation agreement gives him the dependency exemption; *or* if he pays $1,200 for each child claimed and the custodial parent can't prove that she (or he) paid more than that amount.

Short Form or Long Form?

The short form is mercifully brief, and in 1977 it was made much simpler. It's called Form 1040A and is designed especially for people whose tax situation is uncomplicated. The long form (Form 1040), by contrast, is for people with special sources of income (see below), or who want to claim some of the tax code's luxuriant varieties of tax credits and deductions.

You may file the short form if you meet all (not some, but *all*) of the following conditions: You made less than $20,000 last year (or $40,000 if married and filing jointly); all your income was from wages, salaries, tips, and other employee compensation (but not pension income); you made no more than $400 in interest or $400 in dividends; and you do not itemize deductions.

You MUST use the long form if you have income from sources other than employee compensation—for example, from pensions, annuities, rents, capital gains, alimony, partnerships, or your own business. The long form is also necessary if you itemize deductions; if you contributed to an Individual Retirement Account or Keogh plan; if you made estimated tax payments; or if your income this year is so much higher than it was in past years that you can lower your taxes by income averaging (in effect, spreading your income over the past five years).

Warning: Even if you plan to use only the zero bracket amount and qualify for the short form, don't take it for granted that that's the right form to file. You may qualify for some lucrative tax credits or adjustments, available only if you file the long form. Don't be concerned that the long form will complicate your life. If your tax situation is basically simple, filing the long form won't be too difficult. In 1978 the special credits and adjustments available to taxpayers on the long form, but not on the short form, included (1) a credit given to working parents for money spent on child-care expenses; (2) a similar credit for the costs of taking care of a disabled spouse or other dependent; (3) a credit for the elderly who have low taxable incomes; (4) alimony payments; (5) a deduction for moving expenses, if you moved in order to take a new job; (6) any business expenses that weren't reimbursed by your employer. *Note:* These credits and adjustments are available on the long form in addition to your itemized deductions or your deduction for the zero bracket amount.

The tax instruction booklet that comes with the short form spells out clearly whether the short form or long form is better for you.

Joint or Separate Returns?

In most cases, it's better for married couples to file joint returns. The tax rate is lower than for married people filing separately, and there are special tax breaks that married people can get only with joint returns (see page 512). But there's a third advantage, which is just as important. Married people filing jointly are allowed to split income between them, which has the effect of lowering their tax even further. For example, if a man makes $20,000 and his wife doesn't work, they're taxed as if each made $10,000. What makes this an advantage is that higher incomes are taxed at a higher percentage rate. The tax on two $10,000 incomes is smaller than the tax on one $20,000 income—so by filing jointly and splitting the income between them, the couple has saved some money. Similarly, if a man makes $20,000 and his wife makes $10,000, they're taxed as if they each made $15,000. This eliminates the higher tax on the $20,000 income and, again, saves money. (*But note*: Because of quirks in the tax law, a working couple generally pays more in taxes after marriage than before.)

Nevertheless, there are a few special circumstances where filing separately may be better for working couples (or for couples in community property states, where a spouse may separately report half the income even if he or she doesn't work). For example, if one spouse has a large medical expense, the deduction would be more effective against a single income than against two incomes. If in doubt, figure the taxes both ways to see which is better.

Warning: If you're married and file a joint federal return, don't automatically do the same with your state income taxes (unless state law requires it). Unlike the federal government, most states don't allow married couples to split income between them. If you both have income and you file jointly, it may have the effect of pushing your combined tax into a higher bracket. As an experiment, figure your state taxes both ways to see which is best. You may well find that your best strategy is to file jointly on federal returns but separately on state returns, if state law allows it.

Adjusted Gross Income

This is your total personal income for the year. It includes not only earnings and other sources of income, but also certain "adjustments" that can reduce income, such as contributions to an Individual Retirement Account or business expenses that were not reimbursed by your employer. For current details, check the chapter on adjustments to income in the IRS's free booklet *Your Federal Income Tax (for Individuals)*, Publication 17. Adjustments to income are made only on the long form, 1040, not on the short form, 1040A. They're available to all taxpayers, whether or not you itemize. If you file the short form, your adjusted gross income is simply the total of employee compensation, dividends, and interest.

Tax Deductions

A tax deduction is an amount subtracted from adjusted gross income before you figure your tax. The extent of the saving depends on your tax bracket. If you have a $150 deduction and pay taxes in the 30 percent bracket, it will save you $45 in taxes (30 percent of $150). If you're taxed in the 40 percent bracket, that same deduction will save you $60 in taxes (40 percent of $150). The higher the tax bracket, the more each tax deduction is worth.

The tax books are filled with lists of itemized deductions that may or may not survive the next shake-up in the tax law. Among the more durable deductions have been those for (1) interest paid on loans and mortgages; (2) sales taxes; (3) state and local taxes; (4) medical and dental expenses over a certain percentage of your income; (5) casualty and theft losses over a certain minimum; (6) contributions to charity; (7) the cost of getting tax advice. To check the current situation, get a copy of the free IRS guide *Your Federal Income Tax (for Individuals)*, Publication 17, and go through the chapter on itemized deductions.

Tax Table Income

This is the income on which your tax is figured. To establish tax table income, start with your adjusted gross income (see page 519); then subtract exemptions and any excess itemized deductions. The remainder is the income subject to tax at the appropriate percentage rate.

Tax Credits

A credit against taxes is a dollar-for-dollar reduction in the amount of taxes due. For example, if you owe a tax of $3,000 and have a tax credit of $400, you subtract the full $400 to reach an actual tax due of only $2,600. Tax credits are given for various special purposes and are lumped on the tax return after the line where you figure the tax due. At this writing there are tax credits for the child-care (or dependent-adult-care) expenses of working parents, a credit for the elderly, an earned income credit for the working poor, improving your home so as to save energy, and several others. Before you decide to report your income on the short form, read the instructions carefully; it may be that an important tax credit you qualify for can be taken only if you file the long form.

Tax Bracket

This refers to the percentage rate at which the *top dollar* of your income is taxed. For example, in 1977 a single person with a taxable income of $23,200 owed tax of $5,230 on the first $22,200 plus 38 percent of the remainder. He is said, therefore, to be in the 38 percent bracket. You'll notice that 38 percent does not refer to the total percentage of his income that goes for taxes. In the above case, the total tax was $5,610, which is 24 percent of his income. Only the amount over $22,200 is taxed at 38 percent.

Capital Gains and Losses

If you sell stocks, bonds, real estate, or other investments for more than you paid for them, the profit is called a capital gain. Capital gains are divided into two types:

Short-term gains—where you've held the property for a year or less. These gains are taxed at the same rate as ordinary income.

Long-term gains—where you've held the property for more than a year. These gains are taxed at the low capital gains rate.

If you sell investments for less than you paid, you sustain a capital loss, which is deductible from your income. Short-term losses provide larger tax deductions than long-term losses. In either case, there is a sharp limit on the amount of money that can be deducted from ordinary income in a single year. If your loss exceeds that amount, it is carried over into future years and deducted then.

Decisions on when to buy or sell stocks should be made on the basis of investment results rather than tax consideration. But all things being equal, the following tax strategies may improve your investment returns:

• Try not to sell an improving investment until you've held it long enough to qualify for the favorable long-term capital gains treatment.

• Consider selling a bad investment fairly soon, while it still qualifies as a short-term loss, because your tax deduction will be larger.

• Take capital losses. When you sell stock that has gained in value, you'll have a tax to pay on the profit. But any losses you have on investments are deductible from the gains without limit. Consequently, if you sell some stocks that are down in value, those losses will offset the gains—perhaps eliminating your tax. If you still have faith that the losing stocks will come back, you can repurchase them after thirty days (if you repurchase any sooner, it eliminates your deductible capital loss that year).

A word about capital losses: Many people hold onto a losing stock because they can't stand to "take a loss." As long as they hold the stock, they imagine that the loss hasn't really happened. But if a stock is below what you paid for it, you've already lost money whether you sell that stock or not.

If you hold onto a loss, hoping it will go away, you lose the chance to make it count for something on your tax return. By selling a loser, you at least get a tax deduction, which shelters some of your other income from taxes. If you still have faith in that particular company, you can buy back the stock after thirty days.

Income Averaging

If you have an unusually high income one year, the law allows you to spread it over five years for tax purposes. This gives a fairer result to people whose incomes take erratic swings—a year of feast followed by a year of famine.

But if you choose income averaging, there are certain other tax computations you're not allowed to make, which could cancel out the advantages of averaging (check the instructions in your tax book). Also, you must have a sizable income swing before averaging makes sense.

Excess FICA

On Form 1040 (and in the Form 1040A instruction booklet) there's a mysterious line that reads "excess FICA or RRTA tax withheld." That refers to the contribution made to Social Security (FICA) and Railroad Retirement (RRTA). If you made your full payment for the year while you worked for one employer and then switched jobs, the second employer would start deducting Social Security or Railroad Retirement taxes all over again. The tax instruction booklet tells you the maximum contribution needed for the year; any excess should be entered on the tax return and claimed as a refund. (However, if only one employer inadvertently withheld too much, you have to get it back from him rather than claim it on your tax return.)

Self-employment Tax

If you have income from self-employment over a certain small amount, you owe a self-employment tax. It's the equivalent of a Social Security deduction and goes toward financing your Social Security and Medicare benefits. You owe this tax on self-employment income even if you also have income from an employer (unless your maximum Social Security contribution for the year is paid entirely through your employee contributions). Self-employment income includes earnings from operating a business or profession and acting as a consultant or independent contractor. It does *not* include income from rents, dividends, interest, and capital gains.

Tax Due Dates

Your return is due by midnight, April 15 (or the next Monday, if April 15 is on a weekend). However, you can get automatic two-month extensions by filing Form 4868 and paying the amount of tax you think is due. *Warning:* The extension is only for filing the tax return, not for paying the tax. There's a late charge on any tax paid after the due date. If the estimated payment you sent in with Form 4868 is less than 90 percent of the full tax due, you may be hit with an additional penalty.

Tax Tip for Young People

If you make less than a certain amount of money, you won't owe any taxes. In most cases the small amount you earn in a summer or from part-time jobs after school will be tax-free. Unless you do something about it, however, your employer may automatically withhold tax payments from your paycheck and send them in to the government. To get that money back, you'll have to file a tax return claiming a refund.

You can avoid this hassle by arranging for your employer *not* to deduct tax payments. Do this by having him report your earnings to the government on Form W-4 rather than the usual Form W-2 (employers who hire young people should have W-4 forms on hand; if not, they can get them from the IRS). You're entitled to use Form W-4 if you owed no taxes last year and don't expect to owe any this year, either. If no tax payments are withheld, you'll have a larger current paycheck and won't have to go to the trouble of filing a tax return.

But there will still be one deduction from your pay: a Social Security deduction, which qualifies you for the wide range of Social Security benefits.

Taxes and the College Student

Parents can continue to claim a student as a dependent as long as he goes to school full time and they provide more than half his support. This is true even if the student has substantial summer and after-school earnings of his own, which he owes taxes on. Any financial aid the student receives is not counted in figuring whether you paid more than half his support. However, if a student borrows money to help pay for college, that is considered a personal contribution to his own support. Be sure that the loan, when combined with the earnings he spends on his own needs, isn't so big that the student winds up paying more than half his support, thus wiping out your dependency exemption.

Financial aid is generally not considered income for the student. However, if the aid is granted in return for services, such as teaching assignments or a campus job, it is considered taxable income.

Tax Tips for the Elderly

A few years ago a Congressional committee concluded that as many as half of all older Americans probably overpay their federal taxes. They aren't sure which segments of their retirement income escape tax; they're unaware of many of the special tax breaks for older people; and they often don't know where to find inexpensive advice.

The IRS puts out a free booklet called *Tax Benefits for Older Americans,* Publication 554. Get it by calling your local IRS office (but call early in the tax-filing season because the office sometimes runs out of copies). Some points to watch for:

• To find out what income is not taxed, see page 511.

• If your income from taxable sources is small, you may not have to file a tax return. The tax instruction booklet tells how much income you have to earn before taxes are owed. In making this calculation, figure only taxable income—nontaxable income, such as Social Security, doesn't count.

• There are a number of special deductions and tax credits that affect older people. In 1978 these included a credit for the elderly; a special tax computation for older people who sell their houses at a profit; a credit for the cost of taking care of a disabled spouse so the other spouse can go to work; and an extra personal exemption for each spouse sixty-five or over.

• If you receive a lump sum from a pension plan, there are two ways to handle it for tax purposes. The computations are rather technical, but depending on your total financial picture, one method will probably be significantly more attractive than the other. Ask an accountant to figure the tax both ways to see which is best for you. His fee for this simple task should be small, and your potential tax savings are large.

Record Keeping

The IRS will generally not accept estimates on itemized deductions. You have to be able to prove every single expenditure. Canceled checks won't do; during an audit the agent may want to see copies of bills in order to be sure that the money was indeed paid for deductible items.

Keep a file of everything that might relate to your itemized deductions: medical bills; travel vouchers; sales slips on expensive items (to prove you're entitled to a big sales tax deduction); records of state and local tax payments; the date you bought and sold securities, and for what price; receipts from charities; records of interest paid on your various debts; and so on. For business expenses keep a detailed notebook. You can't deduct the cost of a lunch unless your notebook shows the date, the place, the person you lunched with, his business affiliation, and the business purpose of the lunch. If the bill was over a certain amount ($25 in 1978), you need a receipt. Your notebook should also show such things as taxi expenses, business miles logged in your car, and business gifts.

Employers are required to send you a W-2 form in January, showing the amount you earned, the amount withheld for taxes, and the money paid to Social Security. Attach a copy to your tax return when you send it in. In addition, you may get various 1099 forms, which are "information returns" about other sources of income. This income must also be reported, but the 1099s needn't be attached to your tax return; the U.S. Treasury has its own copies. Among the people who might send you a 1099 are the bank where you have your savings account (to report interest earned); companies whose stock you own (to report dividends paid); and employers for whom you did work as a free-lancer or independent contractor. If you're in a partnership, your share of the income or losses will be reported to you on an information return, Form 1065.

If you have a small business in your home, keep track of the bills for rent (or mortgage), heat, light, and upkeep, as well as all your daily business expenses—phones, supplies, travel, advertising, and so on. Ask an accountant to help with your books and advise you on the various tax advantages of being in business for yourself.

Estimated Taxes

Most people have income taxes withheld from their paychecks. But if you have income that's not subject to withholding, you may have to make "estimated" tax payments during the year. You have to file if (1) no withholding is taken from your earnings at all; or (2) you have mixed sources of income—some subject to withholding and some not—and your total income is over a certain amount (see the IRS tax guide for the income limits that would apply to you).

The procedure for estimating taxes is fairly simple. You make a reasonable guess as to what your probable tax will amount to next year (including the self-employment tax, if it applies) and make that payment in four equal installments during the year. If any one payment is less than 80 percent of the amount due at that time, you're subject to a penalty. *Note:* You can avoid penalties by estimating your tax at exactly the same amount you paid the previous year, or more. In that case no penalties will be due even if your final tax is far larger than estimated.

You have to file a declaration of estimated taxes by April 15, along with the first payment. You do so on Form 1040-ES, available at an IRS office. The remaining payments are made on the due date shown on the form.

Fixing Your Mistakes

If you find that you made a mistake on your tax return—for example, you filed as a single person when you could have taken the more favorable tax status, head of household—you can file an *amended return.* There are various ways to file, but the best is on Form 1040X. Refunds can normally be claimed any time within three years of the due date of the original return. But you're allowed seven years if you failed to take a bad debt deduction or a loss on worthless securities. The government pays interest on any extra tax you paid that was not refunded within forty-five days of the due date of the tax return.

Where to Get Help with Your Tax Returns

The right place to turn for help, if you need it, depends on your personal tax situation. Sampling done at various times by the government shows that of all the services that help prepare simple returns the IRS does the best job, with public accountants second, and commercial tax preparers third. On more complex returns certified public accountants and tax lawyers have the best records, better even than the IRS. The cost of having your tax return filled in is deductible if you itemize on your return. So is the cost of tax booklets and tax advice. Here are some specifics on your various alternatives:

1. *Help is free at the local office of the IRS.* Just appear with all your tax records in hand, and an employee will help you fill in the return. If you need only a couple of questions answered, use the toll-free telephone lines (check the tax instruction booklet for the number to use, or look up the IRS in the telephone book under "U.S. Government").

Warning: Some people weasel their taxes by not giving the IRS tax preparers all the facts, assuming that if the IRS fills in the return it will be accepted without question. But every single tax return goes through the same routine tax-screening process. If an error is found, you'll still have to pay the tax plus interest and penalties.

If you make less than a certain amount of money and your tax situation is simple, the IRS will figure your return by mail. Instructions on how to get this free service are included in the booklet that comes with your tax return. You simply fill in certain lines of the return, leaving the tax calculation unfinished. If more taxes are due than the amount withheld from your paycheck, the IRS will send you a bill; if you're owed a refund, you'll get a check.

2. *Public accountants* are people who have passed an accountancy exam that isn't as rigorous as that required of "certified" public accountants. But they can do good work for people with middle incomes who itemize returns. They generally charge more than tax preparers but less than certified public accountants. You can find them in the Yellow Pages under "Accountants—Public."

3. *Enrolled agents* are similar in competence to public accountants. They've either passed an IRS exam in tax preparation or are former IRS agents qualified to do tax returns. You can get a list of the enrolled agents in your area from the IRS district office.

4. *Commercial tax-preparation firms*—some of them large chains, others individual businesses—will do your taxes at modest cost. They put all their people through courses in tax preparation, but the competence of the individual employees varies widely. Generally speaking, tax preparers are best for people who take the standard deduction. If you itemize deductions, consider using an accountant. At the very least, try to do business with the senior tax preparer in the office.

Choose a firm that is open for business all year round, so that if a question comes up about your tax return, you can get help. The preparer should be willing to explain why he made the choices he did and even go with you to the IRS, at no extra cost. (But the law doesn't let tax preparers represent you in any formal argument you have with the IRS. You have to be represented by accountant, attorney, or enrolled agent).

During tax time a large number of storefront operators open for business, then close after April 15. Generally speaking, unless they're attorneys or accountants, it's risky to use their services. Some of them have had little or no training, and even if they've learned to do simple returns, they may be poor on itemized deductions. Also, they may not be around if your return is audited and you need help.

5. *Certified public accountants* are generally used by people with middle-to-higher incomes. They're experts in tax law and can give you tax-planning advice as well as help fill in your return. Large accounting firms generally don't do individual returns, unless it's for key employees of a major corporate client, and even then they'll charge a lot of money. But a small firm or individual practitioner is glad to have your business and charges reasonable fees. Look up "Accountants—Certified Public" in the Yellow Pages or ask a lawyer if he knows an individual practitioner he can recommend.

6. *Tax attorneys* are usually used by people with high incomes and fancy tax problems that the rest of us wouldn't mind having. They may expect to do your estate planning as well as help with your return and make income tax-planning suggestions.

What If the Tax Preparer Makes a Mistake?

A good accountant, attorney, or tax preparer will offer to pay any penalties and interest you're assessed because of a mistake he makes (ask about this in advance). However, if the error comes about because you gave incorrect information, you'll have to pay the charges yourself. If an IRS employee made a mistake in filling out your return, no penalty will be assessed, but you may have to pay interest on any additional taxes due. If you go to a storefront operator who isn't around when you have to go for an audit, or a firm that refuses to pay for its own mistakes, you'll be stuck with all the charges.

Can the IRS Catch Tax Mistakes?

In many cases, yes—which is a great break for the several million people every year who accidentally overpay their tax. The data from every single tax return are fed into a computer and scanned for mistakes. There's no way the computer can tell if you've reported all your income or if all your deductions are justified, although anything suspicious can be flagged for further examination. But simple errors are easily found. You'll get a notice that your tax return was corrected, followed by a refund check or a bill for additional taxes due. Among the errors that can be caught and corrected by computer are math errors; picking up your tax from the wrong tax table; forgetting to take the special low-income tax credit; and treating routine deductions incorrectly. But note: Don't automatically pay every bill you get from the IRS. The person running the computer sometimes makes mistakes, too. Check your tax return carefully; if you don't think you owe the money, call the agent at the number listed on the bill.

How the IRS Screens Your Tax Returns for Audit

A tax audit is a detailed review of your income tax return by an IRS agent. If you're in a low bracket and take the standard deduction, the chance that you'll ever be audited is minute. In the middle brackets, perhaps 2 to 3 percent of taxpayers hear from the IRS every year. The most attention goes to the upper brackets; some 10 percent of the people making more than $50,000 can expect to be called in. Not all audits turn up taxes due, in fact sometimes the taxpayer walks away with a refund. But if you've padded your deductions here and there, the agent is bound to find at least some of them.

In deciding which tax returns to check, the IRS takes the following five steps:

1. First your return is checked by computer for simple math errors.

2. Next, it goes through a computer screening system known as DIF, for "discriminate function." IRS agents are not generous with explanations of exactly how it works. But basically, it's a composite of average taxpayers, derived from past income tax returns. The computer model takes into account various income levels, number of dependents, even addresses—zip codes can tell something about income and living standards. Your return is compared against a computerized norm for people like you and "points," positive or negative, assigned to each of your deductions. It's not known how the point system works. You might have low interest deductions for a person in your circumstances and high sales tax deductions, but you can't tell whether those two will balance out. In the end, the points are totaled. If your number is high, you're ripe for an audit.

3. If you get past DIF, your return is examined for simple tax errors, such as taking a deduction for a spouse who filed a separate return. If you made a mistake, in your deductions or your arithmetic, but DIF didn't recommend an audit, you'll be mailed a notice of taxes due or, if you accidentally overpaid, a check for a refund.

4. Even if you've been flagged for audit, it may never happen. IRS agents go through all the returns picked by DIF, to see if they smell as fishy as the computer thinks. If you had unusually high medical expenses but attached a letter explaining why, the revenue agent may drop the matter. On the other hand, you could be audited even if you weren't nabbed by DIF. If something is wrong with a partnership return, for example, each partner's individual return will also be checked. Or the IRS might decide to audit a sampling of returns prepared by an unscrupulous tax preparer.

5. Once the truly suspicious returns are winnowed out, IRS agents begin the audit process, generally starting with those that look the worst.

What the Auditor Looks For

There's this to say for the IRS: They know where the bodies are buried, even if they don't find them. Long experience has taught them where people are most likely to err (or cheat) on their tax returns; in fact, they can even program a computer to spot suspicious cases. Here are some of the places where agents commonly look for errors:

• Some occupations and trades tend to be connected with unreported income. For example, whenever fees or commissions are involved—as with doctors, plumbers, electricians, and salesmen—work can be done for cash and never reported. Small businessmen are notorious cash-skimmers.

• Auditors find hidden income by showing that you've made more purchases, or added more to your net worth, than your reported income would permit. Generally, this works only with large sums of money. If unreported cash transactions are small in relation to your total reported income, it's often impossible to turn them up.

• If you have an income of any reasonable size and report no dividends or interest, it makes an IRS agent curious. He expects you to have a savings account somewhere, or a little stock.

• Undocumented cash contributions to charities are thorny. How much the agent allows will depend on how he feels about your tax return in general. Strictly speaking, he could disallow everything for which you have no receipt. But in practice he'll accept a reasonable amount for such things as the church collection plate and street corner donations to the Salvation Army. To get by, however, these contributions must be small.

• Travel and entertainment are favorite places for taxpayers to pad, if their business situation allows. Personal trips may be given a business cast. Entertainment diaries may show lots of business lunches for under $25 (which don't have to be substantiated with a receipt). Travel ex-

penses for business conventions come under especially close scrutiny.
So do deductions for expenses your employer might have paid. Small-
scale padding is tough to nail down, but that doesn't mean the IRS won't
bother looking for it.

• Transactions between family members, or among family-controlled
corporations, are looked at pretty closely. The IRS might decide that a
bad debt of a brother-in-law was really a taxable gift you made to him.
Stock transfers giving favorable tax results will very likely be questioned.

• The IRS is suspicious of "education expenses" purportedly needed
to improve your skills in your present job but for some reason incurred
at a foreign university. That looks very much like a vacation in disguise.
Large education deductions will likely be questioned wherever they
were incurred.

• An office-at-home deduction raises a flag if you're apparently employed outside the home and have no other income.

• Large medical and casualty deductions are often questioned, on the
ground that they may well have been covered by insurance. You can't
deduct expenses that an insurance company paid.

• If you take large interest deductions that seem more than your
income could reasonably support, the IRS will suspect you of deducting
principal payments as well as interest.

There are many other places an experienced agent looks for errors.
The more complicated the return, the harder the job, but the greater
the potential rewards.

Up the Audit Ladder

Getting called for an audit doesn't necessarily mean you'll be stuck with
a big tax payment. Sometimes it turns out that the taxpayer is due a
refund. In procedure, audits range from the routine to the exhaustive.

The first-level is the *correspondence audit.* The IRS wants more information to justify some of your deductions and is willing to accept it by
mail. Simply send in your explanation, along with copies of your supporting records (not the originals). If the IRS accepts your proof, it's all
over; if not, you'll be billed for taxes due—at which point you can begin
an appeals procedure.

*Warning: Don't neglect to respond immediately. If you delay, the IRS
may declare itself the winner by default.* If you're out of the country
and someone else is opening your mail, ask him to arrange for an
extension of the deadline.

An *office audit* is more formal. You'll be notified as to which particular items on your tax return are being questioned and asked to appear at the IRS office on a certain day with supporting documents in hand. If that day isn't convenient, you can arrange another time.

If the issue is merely a matter of proof, you may want to appear by yourself. If someone else filled in your return, he should be willing to accompany you (or, if he's an accountant, tax lawyer, or enrolled agent, go to the tax office in your place). If matters of law are in question, you should definitely be represented by an accountant or tax lawyer. *Warning*: When you go in for an office audit, bring only the particular proofs requested, not your whole tax file. You don't want to open another matter inadvertently.

A *field audit* is a far more extensive affair and often warns that the IRS thinks you may have something to hide. It's conducted at your home or business so the agent can get a feeling for how you live and whether it jibes with the income you reported. Rather than focusing on one or two questionable deductions, it usually involves your whole return. For a field audit you'd be wise to have an accountant or tax lawyer on hand.

Appealing the Decision

If you and the auditor can't come to terms about how much tax is due, you have the right to appeal. At each point in the process the IRS will advise you of your rights and exactly where to appeal next.

First, you go to the auditor's superiors—beginning with the *district office supervisor,* then to the *appellate conference.* It may well happen that during those discussions you reach a compromise at a lower figure than the auditor first proposed. On the other hand, you may find a whole new area suddenly opened up to question, which your original auditor let pass. You can't be sure of what will happen in these conferences. A lot depends on your relationship with the IRS agents and the plausibility of the case. It's in your own interest to be polite every step of the way.

If you still resist the findings and the amount in question is $1,500 or less, you can appeal to *small-claims tax court,* whose judges travel around the country hearing cases. Like any other small-claims court, the procedures are informal; you don't even need a lawyer, unless you want one. A judge settles many of the cases through negotiation. If you and the government can't reach agreement even with the aid of the judge, you present your arguments in an informal trial and will get the decision by mail. That decision cannot be appealed.

If the disputed tax is for more than $5,000, appeal to the regular *tax court*. You'll probably need a lawyer and may rack up a lot of expenses if the case is complicated. You don't have to pay the tax until, and unless, you lose (in which case, you'll owe interest for the entire period since the original due date). The vast majority of tax court cases are decided against the taxpayer, so be pretty sure of your case before you take on the expense of appealing.

You can skip tax court and bring your case in a *U.S. district court*, which is generally thought to be more lenient toward taxpayers. But these courts are usually used for complex cases involving a lot of money. You have to pay the tax in dispute, then sue for a refund.

If you lose in court, you can appeal all the way to the Supreme Court if you have the money and the stakes are worth it. One thing you may not know is that when you deal with the IRS, you are presumed wrong unless you can prove yourself right. The burden of proving the case is on you, not the IRS.

Tax Penalties

Be sure you file your tax return (or ask for an extension) by April 15, even if you don't have the money to pay your taxes. If you don't mail your return on time, you're assessed a penalty of 5 percent of the amount due every month, up to a maximum of 25 percent. There's also a penalty for not paying your tax on time, which is ½ of 1 percent a month, also up to a maximum of 25 percent. There are additional penalties for such crimes as paying your tax with a bad check; concealing property from the government; failing to file certain information on returns; willful failure to file a return or pay your tax (which is worse than "negligently" failing to pay); and willful attempts to evade or defeat taxes. *Note:* The 12 percent interest charged on a late tax payment is deductible on next year's tax return. But penalties are not deductible.

Who Pays the Penalties?

You are responsible for paying the proper tax on your own income. If you underpaid, you owe penalties. It makes no difference that the underpayment arose from someone else's advice; the liability is still yours. The person who advised you may voluntarily step in to pay (as will many accountants and tax preparers), but if they don't, you're stuck for the money.

If you sign a joint tax return, you're liable for the tax due on your spouse's income as well as your own. If your spouse underreported income or took false deductions, it's your problem as well as his. Even if you didn't know about it, you can be forced to pay the tax deficiencies (with one exception—see the following section). So it's smart to go over the tax return in detail before putting your name on it. If you're separated from your spouse and aren't sure his or her returns are honest, it may be better not to file jointly, even though it may result in a higher tax on your own income.

The Innocent Spouse Rule

This law was passed by Congress in 1971 to protect spouses (mostly wives) who innocently sign joint tax returns that omit income. In the past, if the husband stole some money, failed to report it as income, and skipped town, the IRS went after his wife for the taxes and penalties due. This was obviously unfair. Today, that trusting wife can no longer be prosecuted.

However, a fair number of wives know exactly what their husbands are up to but keep their mouths shut because they like having the extra money. So Congress wrote some limitations into the law. A spouse can invoke "innocent spouse" protection only if she proves that (1) when she signed the joint tax return, she didn't know that some income was unreported; (2) she had no reason to know it; and (3) she did not significantly benefit from the unreported money.

Unfortunately, this protection is granted only for relatively large sums of money. Even an innocent spouse has to pay taxes and penalties if the omitted income is 25 percent or less of the couple's gross income. Also, you can claim this protection only for omitted income. If your husband took false deductions and you innocently signed the return, the liability remains yours as well as his.

What to Remember If You Ever Get a Notice of Taxes Due

The IRS can and does make mistakes! Just because the notice states firmly that you owe the government more money doesn't mean it's really true. Always double-check the notice to be sure that you understand the issue and to determine whether the extra tax is in fact due. If you aren't clear about what the IRS has done or if you disagree with the arithmetic, call or write to the agent in charge at the address given on the notice.

The IRS typically sends four notices of taxes due, but only the first one explains why the tax is being assessed. If for some reason you didn't get the first notice, call the agent listed on the notice to find out what's happening. If you don't have a copy of your tax return, the IRS can arrange for you to receive one (at a cost of $1 a page). If you owe the taxes but are having financial troubles and can't pay, the IRS Service Center, which sends the bills, can arrange for a sixty-day payment delay, or even installment payments.

But whatever your financial position, don't delay in answering these notices! If you haven't replied within a short period after the fourth notice, your bill will be turned over to the Tax Collection Division, where you'll get rougher treatment than you would at the Service Center.

IRS Collections

Don't get involved with the collection office if you can possibly avoid it. The process can be awful. The government has the power to seize your whole paycheck (except for $50 a week) every week until the tax obligation is paid. It can seize all your bank accounts, your car, your securities, your home, and any other assets, without further warning. It even has the right to sell those assets for less than their actual value. If the IRS puts a lien on your house, which is a legal notice that it's being seized to satisfy a tax obligation, your other creditors may hear of it and start calling in their own loans. You may find it impossible to get new credit, now and for some time in the future.

If you can't pay the bill right away because of financial hardship, the IRS has the authority to make other arrangements with you. But whether they do or not depends on the agent handling the case. You can stack the deck slightly in your favor by calling the agent right away, explaining your situation (politely), and asking for help. If you're a first-time delinquent and the tax due isn't too large, he may be willing to arrange installment payments or put off collection for a short time until your situation improves. Get your settlement in writing, so there won't be any doubt about the arrangements. If you agree to installment payments, be sure you don't skip any, or else the IRS may call in the whole debt.

Chapter Twenty-Four

PROPERTY TAXES

Thrust ivrybody, but cut the' ca-ards.
FINLEY PETER DUNNE

A good many of you are paying higher property taxes than you have to. Local assessments often show a crazy-quilt pattern, with some home-owners paying too little and others paying too much. The middle classes, in particular, are likely to be overassessed—hence overtaxed—in relation to their fellow property owners in the upper-middle brackets. Wealthier people tend to know more about how the tax system works and can tell more easily if their own assessment is too high.

Another group of people apt to be overtaxed are those who buy newly built homes. These assessments may be based on current market values, whereas older homes in the neighborhood may not have had their assessments brought up to date for years. Assessors may argue that your rate is fair because it's based on accurate property values. But that's not the right way to look at it. *Equity requires that all houses be taxed proportionately alike.* If other homes are appraised at less than market value, yours should be, too.

Every county, city, or town has an appeals board made up of local people who listen to citizens who think they've been overassessed. If the board agrees, it can order your assessment cut. Only a small fraction of homeowners ever challenge their assessments. But of those who do, a fair number come out winners.

The appeals board generally meets once a year—often at night, so

538

you don't have to lose time from work. When you get a new assessment, the notice should state the date and time when appeals will next be heard. Or call the assessor's office and ask. No lawyer is necessary for most appeals. You simply go before a board of your fellow citizens and state your case. All boards are different; some have to be triple-convinced, others give token tax cuts to most of the people who come before them. But in general, board members are reasonable people and the process is fair.

Many of the cases heard by property tax appeals boards are brought by real estate investors. Buildings in many cities carry assessments dating from their palmier days; today those values may have declined. If you've invested in an older urban area that's ripe for rehabilitation, you may be able to save quite a bit of money by getting your assessment lowered to conform to the current low value of the neighborhood.

In many communities property appraisals are not done by local assessors but by outside firms. Appeals boards may put off complaints by saying that the appraisal is out of their hands. That's an answer you shouldn't accept. The local assessor is responsible for the fairness and accuracy of all the work done.

The key to winning a property tax case is good preparation. You ought to talk with the assessor about the town's procedures, know what the grounds for a lower assessment are, and be able to show that they apply to you. Here are six ways to get your tax lowered:

1. *Prove that the assessor made a mistake.* Mistakes are more common than people realize and can be an open-and-shut case for a lower assessment. Your record on file at the assessor's office might credit you with one bedroom or bathroom too many, assert that your house is faced with brick when it's not, or give dimensions that are too large. It always pays to check your property description, even if it hasn't occurred to you that the assessment might be too high. You might find that you've been taxed on the wrong basis for some time. Bring the actual facts about your house, with photographs, to the hearing.

2. *Prove that the assessor overestimated the market value of your home.* To be sure of this, it's important to know how houses are assessed in your city or county. Some areas base their assessment on *current* market values (the price that the house would sell for today); others use a *fraction* of market value, which is more confusing. As an example of fractional value, assume you have a $50,000 home and, unknown to you, your town assesses at 50 percent of market value. If you get an assessment of $30,000, you may think you've had a lucky break. But in fact, the valuation is too high; 50 percent of $50,000 would be only $25,000. Homeowners who don't know whether their local government assesses at full value or a percentage of value can't tell whether they're paying too much. Another point: Note whether the assessor considered all the bad points about your house when setting the value—for example, you may have a basement that leaks and a garage too small for many modern cars; a highway may be under construction nearby; there may be restrictions on your deed. If your home is overvalued, get a statement by one or two real estate brokers or a local appraiser to that effect.

3. *Prove that your house has declined in value.* Again, a statement by a real estate broker or appraiser may do the trick.

4. *Prove that a recent addition to your home was assessed on the basis of what you paid for it, which is wrong.* What matters is how much the addition increased your home's market value. It often happens that the addition adds less value to the house than its actual cost. To prove this, get the testimony of a real estate agent as to your home's current value.

5. *Prove that you're paying a higher tax in relation to the market value of your home than other homeowners are.* Do it by getting a list of houses sold recently that are similar to yours (a real estate agent can help). Then look up their assessments in the assessor's or treasurer's office; the records are public. Divide their *average* assessment by their *average* sales price, to see what percent of value assessments generally are. Then divide your own home's assessment by the current market price. If the percentage of value on which you're paying taxes is significantly higher than the average, you have a good argument for a cut.

6. *Prove that your neighbors, who live in houses similar to yours, are assessed for less.* Bring their assessments into the hearing to show that yours is out of line. This is less precise than figuring the ratio between assessment and sales, as in point 5, but can be just as effective. You might also want to check the assessments of people in other neighborhoods to see if your entire neighborhood is being overassessed.

When you go to the hearing, have the figures neatly prepared with copies for all the board members and photographs if they'll help. Be prepared to state what level of assessment you think is fair so the board knows what your thinking is. If you have an honest case, you should get relief.

Should the decision go against you, you can appeal further. If the case is strong and the potential tax savings large, you may want to hire a lawyer, either to appeal to the state or go to court, if necessary. Sometimes an entire neighborhood is overassessed in relation to similar neighborhoods, in which case the lawyer's fee could be split among a group of homeowners.

You should also ask the assessor's office whether you're entitled to any special tax breaks under the law. These are sometimes granted to veterans, older people, and low-income people. There may also be property-tax incentives for improving or maintaining your property.

Chapter Twenty-Five

SAVINGS BONDS

In general, the art of government consists in taking
as much money as possible from one class of citizens
to give to the other.

VOLTAIRE

As investments, U.S. savings bonds are underachievers. They pay 6½
percent compounded semiannually, if held for five years, which is well
below the rate available on insured five-year term accounts. They pay
11 percent if held a full eleven years. Nevertheless, there are some
interesting aspects to savings bonds:

1. You can earn 6½ percent on a very small investment. The lowest-
denomination bond costs $25. If you put that same $25 into a 5¼
percent savings account, compounded daily, you'd get an annual percentage rate of only 5.47. A five-year term account, compounded daily
at 7½, pays 7.9 percent a year, but the minimum investment is $500.
Only a credit union paying at least 6½ percent compounded quarterly,
or a Keogh or Individual Retirement Account, offers a higher rate, over
five years, on a deposit as small as $25.

2. Bonds are often available through automatic savings plans. Many
banks will buy you a bond a month, deducting the money from your
account. Some employers will subtract money from your paycheck for
the same purpose. At some companies you can put away as little as $1.25

Note: Since January 1980, the old Series E and H bonds have been replaced by Series EE
and HH.

from a weekly paycheck and $3.75 from a monthly one. The money is held in a non-interest-bearing account until it adds up to $25—enough to buy a bond.

This method of saving is practically painless. Since you never see the money, you never miss it. Many companies make alternatives available on the payroll savings plan, in which case you might find a credit union account more attractive than savings bonds. But where choices are not available, it's better to sign up for an automatic bond purchase than not to save at all. The following table shows how much you can expect to save over the years by making regular contributions toward savings bonds.

HOW SAVINGS BOND INVESTMENTS GROW

If you put this much toward a savings bond every week:	You will have this much at the end of*			
	1 year	3 years	5 years	15 years
$ 1.25	$ 67	$ 209	$ 366	$ 1,628
2.50	135	419	736	3,279
3.75	202	629	1,106	4,929
5.00	270	841	1,479	6,579
6.25	337	1,051	1,848	8,227
7.50	405	1,261	2,218	9,876
12.50	675	2,104	3,700	16,477
25.00	1,350	4,210	7,407	32,979

*Assuming an interest rate of 6½% compounded semiannually; 7% after 11 years.

If you put this much toward a savings bond every month:	1 year	3 years	5 years	15 years
$ 3.75	$ 46	$ 143	$ 251	$ 1,116
6.25	76	240	421	1,874
7.50	91	288	506	2,252
12.50	152	481	847	3,767
18.75	229	722	1,270	5,651
25.00	306	965	1,702	7,577
50.00	611	1,930	3,403	15,153
75.00	917	2,895	5,105	22,732
100.00	1,223	3,861	6,807	30,310

*Assuming an interest rate of 6½% compounded semiannually; 7% after 11 years.

3. Savings bonds pay less than 6½ percent if you cash them in before five years are up (see page 547). For some savers this provides an incentive to leave the savings untouched. And even after five years

many people are still reluctant to redeem their bonds. For whatever the reason, savings bonds often seem more permanent than savings accounts and hence are less likely to be raided for frivolous things.

4. Some people buy savings bonds for safety's sake. They trust the U.S. government to pay off, even if all else fails. (If safety is your primary motivation, however, federally insured savings accounts are just as sound and offer higher interest rates to long-term savers.)

5. The interest on savings bonds is not subject to state and local income or personal property taxes. So the net return to an investor is higher than it seems at first glance, expecially if you live in a heavily taxed jurisdiction. There are also ways to defer payment of federal income taxes (next paragraph).

Savings Bonds As a Tax Shelter

When you are deciding whether it's better to keep money in savings bonds or a savings account, taxes are a factor to consider. *Savings bonds are exempt from state and local income taxes,* whereas the interest earned on savings accounts is not.

If your tax bracket is relatively low and your state and local tax burden small, you will generally get more after taxes from a taxable corporate bond or term account than from a 6½ percent savings bond. But a top-bracket taxpayer living in a place that levies heavy income taxes will actually get more from the savings bond.

Savings bonds offer another tax advantage: With Series EE bonds you can put off paying federal income taxes for years. You don't have to declare the interest on the bond as income until you cash the bond in or give it away, or until it reaches final maturity. At that time, the interest is taxable in your current bracket. This is particularly valuable if you're saving for retirement. You pay no taxes of any kind during your earning years. Instead, the taxes fall due after retirement, when you presumably are in a much lower tax bracket.

When Not to Defer Taxes on Savings Bond Interest

If you expect to cash in your Series EE bonds before retirement, chances are you'll find yourself in a higher tax bracket than you're in today. So it would be better to pay income taxes currently. Simply report the increase in value of your bonds on your federal income tax return each year, even though you haven't actually received the income. (Interest on EE bonds isn't paid until you redeem the bond—see page 546.)

It would also be wiser to pay taxes currently if the bond is bought in the name of a child. Assuming he doesn't have much other income, he will owe no income taxes—so the interest he earns on the savings bond will escape tax-free. File a tax return for the child at the end of the first year, reporting the gain in the value of the savings bond plus any other income he has, and show that no tax is owed. After that, you don't even have to file a return for those particular bonds, as long as he continues to owe no taxes. Follow this system with any subsequent bond purchase.

If you want to change from deferred to current reporting of income, you can do so, but you must report all the income accrued to date. You cannot switch from current to deferred without getting special permission from the Internal Revenue Service.

If you deferred income taxes on bonds bought in your child's name, he'd be wise to cash them in before he's out earning a living for himself. As long as his earnings are only from summer jobs, he'll pay little or no taxes on the savings bond proceeds. But if he has a regular paycheck, he'll have to pay taxes in his bracket on his bond income.

Series EE Bonds—for Savers

If savings bonds make sense to you, buy them through a payroll savings plan; from your bank, savings and loan, or credit union; from a Federal Reserve bank (see addresses on page 833); or from the Bureau of the Public Debt, Securities Transaction Branch, Washington, D.C. 20226. There is never a fee for buying or redeeming savings bonds.

When you buy a Series EE bond, you pay less than its face value, and its value gradually increases. The difference between what you paid for it and what you get at redemption is your interest. If held for five years, the bond will have earned an average of 6½ percent a year, compounded semiannually. The denominations of Series EE bonds, their purchase prices, and their values at maturity are shown in the following table:

SERIES EE BONDS— BOUGHT AND HELD

Price of bond	Value of bond at maturity*
$ 25.00	$ 53.28
37.50	79.92
50.00	106.56
100.00	213.12
250.00	532.80
500.00	1,065.60
2,500.00	5,328.00
5,000.00	10,656.00

*Assuming continued payment at 6½% compounded semiannually, 7% after 11 years.

Interest is not paid on Series EE bonds until they are cashed in. You have to hold them for at least six months, but after that can redeem them anytime you want at most financial institutions that sell them. If you wish, you can redeem part of a bond. For example, a bond currently worth $1,000 can be turned in for an equivalent $500 bond plus $500 in cash. You sacrifice no interest on the segment you retain; if your $1,000 bond has been earning 6½ percent, so would its $500 replacement.

Bonds earn interest from the issue date, which is the first day of the month that payment is received. If you buy a bond on the last day of the month, it will be backdated to the first day. After the initial six-month holding period, interest is credited on the first of every month for the first two and a half years. After that, it is credited every six months from the issue date—for example, if the issue date is February 1, interest will be credited on August 1 (which is six months later) and again on the following February 1. You earn more by cashing your bond in just after an interest date rather than just before.

If You Have to Redeem an EE Bond Before Maturity

EE bonds can be redeemed any time after six months from the issue date. But if you cash them in in less than five years, you will earn at an annual rate of less than 6½ percent. The following table shows your annual return on a new EE bond cashed in early. As you can see, the penalty may be quite high.

THE LOW INTEREST RATE PAID ON EE BONDS CASHED IN BEFORE MATURITY

If you redeem an EE bond after:	Your annual yield will be:
6 months	4.00%
1 year	4.51
1½ years	4.68
2 years	4.75
2½ years	4.85
3 years	4.94
3½ years	5.02
4 years	5.32
4½ years	5.80
5 years	6.50

If you have several bonds and must cash some in, it's generally best to redeem the ones you bought the most recently rather than those that are close to either the five-year or eleven-year maturity. Bonds nearing maturity earn interest at higher and higher rates. In fact, during the six months before five-year maturity, interest is credited to your savings bond at the rate of 12.86 percent a year. During the six months before eleven-year maturity, interest is credited at 17.74 percent. The higher rates at the end of the period compensate for the lower rates paid earlier, so that over the entire period the interest paid will average 6½ or 7 percent.

If the question is whether to cash in a savings bond or liquidate another investment, the next table will help you decide. It shows at what rate your savings bond is earning interest, from the present until maturity. Cash in your EE bond only if it's earning at a lower rate than the alternative investment.

Don't let the table fool you; you earn only 6½ percent over five years. But because the first payment is so low (only 4 percent during the first six months), later payments must be at a rate higher than 6½ percent to make it come out right in the end. Once you've passed those low payment dates, it makes less and less sense to cash the bond in. The rate at which interest is paid during the last two and a half years is higher than you'll get in some long-term savings accounts. After five years, however, the bonds resume earning at an annual rate of 6½ percent —not very competitive with rates elsewhere.

THE HIGH RATES OF INTEREST
PAID ON EE BONDS
AS THEY GET CLOSE TO MATURITY

During this holding period:	Your investment earns at this annual rate:
From issue date to maturity*	7.00%
From 6 months after issue date to maturity	7.14
From 1 year after issue date to maturity	7.25
From 1½ years after issue date to maturity	7.37
From 2 years after issue date to maturity	7.50
From 2½ years after issue date to maturity	7.64
From 3 years after issue date to maturity	7.78
From 3½ years after issue date to maturity	7.93
From 4 years after issue date to maturity	7.97
From 4½ years after issue date to maturity	7.83
From 5 years after issue date to maturity	7.42
From 10 years after issue date to maturity	12.04
From 10½ years after issue date to maturity	17.74
From maturity on	7.00

*11 years.

Using EE Bonds for an Education Fund

You can get extra mileage from your bonds by earmarking the proceeds for your child. If you buy bonds in his name and report the interest income currently, he will get the 6½ or 7 percent return tax-free (see page 544). The following table shows how much the child will have at the time he enters college:

FORECASTING THE SIZE
OF YOUR EDUCATION FUND

If you start a bond investment program when your child is this age:	This is what your child will have at age 18 through monthly investments of:*			
	$25.00	$37.50	$50.00	$100.00
2	$8,421	$12,632	$16,842	$33,685
4	6,786	10,179	13,572	27,144
6	5,347	8,021	10,694	21,388
8	4,110	6,165	8,210	16,439
10	3,053	4,580	6,107	12,214
12	2,124	3,186	4,248	8,495

.*Assuming an interest rate of 6½% compounded semiannually; 7% after 11 years.

However, you would accumulate even more if you gave the same monthly sum to the child for investment in a higher-paying term savings account (for the best ways to give money to a child, see Chapter 27, "Wills and Estate Planning"). Assuming the child has little or no other income, interest from the savings account would also pass tax-free. The next table gives you an idea of how much better he would do by accumulating the college fund at a higher interest rate:

YOUR CHILD'S EDUCATION FUND:
IN EE BONDS OR IN A BANK?

	A matured $1,000 bond left to accumulate at 7% will be worth:	A matured $1,000 bond redeemed and reinvested in a bank term account will be worth:*
After 5 years	$1,402.55	$1,482.98
After 10 years	1,967.15	2,199.24
After 15 years	2,759.03	3,261.44

*Assuming 8% compounded daily, for an annual percentage rate of 8.2. Higher rates are also available.

If you buy a savings bond in a child's name, remember this: You have given him a gift. The bond is his to use as he chooses. You can't park funds in his name in order to avoid taxes, then take the money back. If you do so, the income from the bonds will be taxed to you. If you put the bond jointly into your name and the child's name, the income will also be taxed to you.

Series HH Bonds—for People Who Want Income

Series HH bonds give you current income. You pay the face amount at purchase and receive an interest check every six months. HH bonds come in the following denominations: $500, $1,000, $5,000, and $10,000, and they yield 6½ percent.

SERIES HH BONDS:
YOUR SEMIANNUAL INTEREST CHECK*

	Bond denominations			
	$500	$1,000	$5,000	$10,000
Each check	$16.25	$32.50	$162.50	$325.00

*Subject to federal income tax only.

The fact is, however, that you can get more income from bank term accounts than from HH bonds. The table at the top of page 551 shows you the difference.

You can buy HH bonds from Federal Reserve banks (addresses on page 833) or the Bureau of the Public Debt, Securities Transactions Branch, Washington, D.C. 20226. Banks, savings and loan associations, and credit unions will forward your application (although they do not sell HH bonds directly).

Bonds earn interest from the issue date, which is the first day of the month when payment is received. Checks are mailed every six months; if the issue date on your bond is November 1, you'll get a check on May 1, and again the following November 1. If you redeem a bond, it's best to do so just *after* the interest date so you'll get the last payment due

TERM ACCOUNTS:
YOUR SEMIANNUAL INTEREST CHECK[a]

	Bank accounts[b]			
	$500	$1,000	$5,000	$10,000
Your check, every 6 months	20.50	41.00	205.00	410.00

[a]Subject to federal, state, and local income taxes.
[b]At 8% compounded daily.

you. In fact, if a bond is presented for redemption anytime during the month before the semiannual interest check falls due, the government won't cash it until the interest is paid.

HH bonds pay regularly and are safe. But for people in need of income, they don't produce a lot. Corporate bonds and bank term accounts will generally give you better value for your money.

Should You Switch from E or EE Bonds to HH Bonds in a Tax-free Exchange?

If you've saved up money in E or EE bonds, you will probably at some point want to switch to an investment that yields current income. Assuming you've deferred payment of taxes on the E or EE bonds, the tax will fall due when you cash the bonds in. However, if you exchange them for HH bonds, you can continue the tax deferment. You'll owe federal taxes on all the HH bond interest that is paid currently. But the tax on the increase in value of your original E or EE bonds won't be payable until you finally cash the HH bonds in. If you never do, the tax is paid by your estate or your heirs.

The E or EE bonds you give in exchange must be worth at least $500, and the HH bonds must be bought in multiples of $500. If your E and EE bonds fall short, you can add cash to make up the difference.

The question you have to ask yourself is whether this tax-free exchange is really a good deal. Rather than switching to HH bonds, you might keep the E and EE bonds and cash in 6½ percent of them every year. You'd still have your 6½ percent income and only part of it would be taxable, since part of each redemption represents a return of your own, original capital. By contrast, with HH bonds, the full 6½ percent interest is taxable income. Another possibility is to cash in the E or EE bonds, pay your taxes, and put the money to work in a higher-yielding investment. What to do depends on your tax bracket, the amount of state and local taxes you have to pay, and the investment options open to you. Some people are better off in savings bonds, other people aren't.

People in the lower tax brackets are generally better off cashing in their E or EE bonds, paying the taxes, and putting the proceeds to work in high-grade corporate bonds or bond funds, in high-dividend stocks, or in a high-interest savings account. Either investment yields more income after taxes than they'd get from 6½ percent HH bonds. People in the middle brackets who live in heavily taxed states or cities may do better with savings bonds, while their counterparts in lightly taxed areas should look to other investments. People in the top tax brackets are generally better off making the tax-free exchange to HH bonds, or cashing in 6½ percent of their E or EE bonds every year.

When you're ready to make this decision, give your bank a list of your E or EE bonds, complete with issue dates and denominations. Ask (1) what are your bonds now worth; (2) how much interest have you earned; and (3) if you exchanged these bonds for HH bonds, how much income would you earn a year? With that information, fill in the following worksheet. This will show you which investment yields the greatest income:

Total value of the EE bonds   _____
Subtract: What I paid for them   _____
Total interest earned   _____

Total federal income tax due if bonds are cashed
   in (interest earned, times your tax bracket)   _____
Amount available for other investments (total value
   of bonds, less taxes due)   _____

Annual income possible from corporate bonds
   (amount available for investment, times the bond
   interest rate)*   _____
Annual income possible from savings accounts
   (amount available for investment, times the annual percentage rate of an attractive term account)*   _____
Annual income possible from any other invest-
   ment*   _____

---

*Don't forget that the income from these investments is subject to state and local income taxes, whereas savings bond income is not.

COMPARED WITH:
Annual income possible from HH bonds after a
   tax-free exchange _____

If You Have to Redeem an HH Bond Before Maturity

Bonds bought through an E or EE bond exchange yield 6½ percent no matter when you cash them in, but bonds bought for cash and redeemed before five years are up will earn less than 6½ percent. The following table shows your annual average return on a new HH bond, bought for cash and redeemed early:

THE LOW INTEREST RATE PAID ON HH BONDS CASHED IN BEFORE MATURITY

If you redeem an HH bond after:	Your annual yield will be:
6 months	4.00%
1 year	4.51
1½ years	4.69
2 years	4.75
2½ years	4.85
3 years	4.94
3½ years	5.02
4 years	5.32
4½ years	5.80
5 years	6.50

If you have to cash some of your HH bonds in early, redeem the ones you bought for cash most recently. Bonds that are closer to maturity earn more than newer bonds.

In Whose Name Should a Bond Be Issued?

Single Owner

Bonds can be issued in the name of a single individual—in your name, or in the name of the person you've given the bond to. The owner alone decides when to cash it in; he alone owes the taxes on the interest. When he dies, the bond can either be cashed in or reissued to an heir. The proceeds pass according to the terms of the will.

Coowners

Bonds can also be issued in the name of two coowners (but no more than two). Either of the coowners can cash the bond in—so in effect, whoever holds it controls it. If one owner dies, the bond becomes the property of the other, who can continue to hold it as long as he pleases. The survivor can also name another coowner, or a beneficiary.

If one coowner wants the same bonds changed to his name alone, the other owner must agree. They must also agree if one of them is to be dropped in favor of a different coowner. Because a minor child may not be able to give legal consent, it is hard to change the registration on bonds coowned with minors.

The person whose money was used to pay for the bond is called the "principal coowner," and the income is taxed to him. If the coowners are married, the issuing agent may assume the funds are the husband's, so if a wife is buying the bond with her own money, she should make that clear. If both people contribute to buying the bond, there is no principal coowner. The income is taxed to them in the same proportion as their contribution to the bond's purchase price.

With E bonds, both coowners and the beneficiary must agree to a change in beneficiary. With EE bonds, however, the former beneficiary's consent is not needed.

If one coowner wants to exchange E or EE bonds for HH bonds, it may be done without the other's consent. On an exchange, the principal coowner may drop the other owner without the other's permission. However, if both coowners contributed to buying the bond, both names must go on the HH bond to preserve the tax deferral.

As you can see, coownership requires a friendly couple. If one owner refuses to go along with changes desired by the other, it could be a nuisance for both of you. For this reason, you might prefer to keep the bond in your own name. On the other hand, coownership assures easy access to funds if one of you becomes too ill to function.

Single Owner with a Named Beneficiary

You can register the bond in your name and add the name of a beneficiary who will receive it if you die. This avoids the drawbacks of coownership yet provides for the bond to pass automatically to a new owner at your death. You control the bond during your lifetime and can cash it in anytime you want. If you want to change the beneficiary on an E bond he has to agree to the change. If he doesn't, the only way around his recalcitrance is to cash the bond in and buy a new one or exchange it for HH bonds. If the beneficiary dies, you have to show proof of his death before you can name a new beneficiary. With an EE bond, however, you can change the beneficiary without the former beneficiary's consent.

Which Bond Transactions May Result in Taxes?

1. If you decide to give a savings bond away and have it reissued in the recipient's name, you will owe income taxes on any unreported interest that has built up. Once the gift is made, however, the new owner has responsibility for future taxes.

2. If you paid, or helped pay, for bonds bought with a coowner and have the bonds reissued solely in the coowner's name (or in the name of a new coowner), you owe income taxes on the accumulated interest, in proportion to the amount you paid when the bonds were bought.

3. In the two preceding transactions, you may also owe a gift tax if the value of the bonds is more than $3,000 (or more than $6,000 if the gift is made jointly with your spouse).

4. You might also owe gift taxes if you pay for the bonds but allow your coowner to cash them in or use all the interest. There are other and more complex circumstances where tax liabilities might arise. It's smart to ask the Internal Revenue Service about possible tax consequences before you give your bonds away.

Note: Savings bonds can be reissued only to certain people—your husband, wife, or other close relatives.

What If You Want to Change the Name on a Bond?

If a woman marries, she may change the name on her bonds if she likes, but she doesn't have to. If her name changes because of divorce, however, the bonds should also be changed. When one coowner dies, it's not necessary to reissue the bonds in the name of the surviving owner, although it's convenient to have the bonds solely in your own name in case you want to make any further changes in ownership. You may also want to change the name of the beneficiary. Whatever the reason, go to a place where bonds are sold and ask them to help you, or write for information to a Federal Reserve bank or to the Bureau of the Public Debt. There is no fee.

Limits on Bond Ownership

Right now, the Treasury allows you to spend no more than $15,000 on EE bonds a year (although coowners can spend up to $30,000). This ceiling changes from time to time. For HH bonds, the ceilings are $20,000 and $40,000 respectively. You cannot pledge bonds as security for a loan (because no one but you can cash them in). If you need collateral, you have to redeem the bonds and put the proceeds into an investment which the lender will accept as security. Neither can you give anyone your bonds in payment of a debt.

Old Bonds

If you find any bonds of series A, B, C, D, F, G, J, or K, by all means cash them in. They're no longer earning interest. The Freedom Shares sold in 1970 are still earning interest. So are *all* Series E and Series H bonds—the older issues having had their final maturities extended. Over the years bonds issued originally at low interest rates have had their rates gradually raised. Today, all outstanding bonds may earn 6½ percent, compounded semiannually. Savings bond rates may increase but are guaranteed not to go down during the original maturity period, or during any specified extension. All series E bonds issued since January 1951 will earn a bonus of ½ of 1 percent if held for 11 years from their first interest date in 1980.

Final Maturity

Final maturity dates have been announced for all Series E bonds. If you hold a bond beyond its maturity date, shown below, you'll earn no more interest on your investment. You may, however, exchange maturing E bonds for the new EE bonds, if you like this kind of savings vehicle.

Dates of issue	Dates of final maturity
May 1941–Apr. 1952	May 1981–Apr. 1992
May 1952–Jan. 1957	Jan. 1992–Sept. 1996
Feb. 1957–May 1959	Jan. 1996–Apr. 1998
June 1959–Nov. 1965	Mar. 1997–Aug. 2003
Dec. 1965–May 1969	Dec. 1992–May 1996
June 1969–Nov. 1973	Apr. 1995–Sept. 1999
Dec. 1973–June 1980	Dec. 1998–June 2005

What If There's an Error in the Way Your Bond Was Issued?

Don't make any changes at all on the face of the bond, or you may compromise your ability to cash it in. Return it to the place where you bought it and ask the clerk to make the correction. A common error to watch for is the issue date put on a bond bought on the last day of the month. By law the bond is supposed to be dated from the first of the month. But by late afternoon banks sometimes switch their date markers to the following day, so your bond would be dated the first of the following month. This cuts you out of one month's interest. Other errors to look for are an incorrect denomination or the wrong spelling of your name.

Cashing Bonds In

Any agent authorized to sell bonds can also cash them in. However, it's easiest to go to a place where you're known, such as your own bank. Otherwise, there may be a detailed identification procedure to make sure you're entitled to the bond's proceeds. If you redeem bonds at a Federal Reserve bank, you normally need a signature certification.

Series E or EE bonds issued in the name of a guardian, a trustee, or any sort of institution, and all Series H or HH bonds, must be redeemed by a Federal Reserve bank or the U.S. Treasury. Your bank will forward them for you, along with the necessary identification.

If You Lose a Bond

Keep a record of your bonds' denominations, serial numbers, and issue dates. If you lose a bond or it becomes badly torn, the government will replace it at no charge. Newer bonds carry your Social Security number, which helps the government verify the purchase when your own documentation is poor. (When you buy a bond for a child, he gets a Social Security number, too.) To replace a bond, write to the Bureau of the Public Debt, 200 Third St., Parkersburg, W. Va., 26101. Should you find a bond you've already had replaced, don't destroy it; send it to the bureau along with an explanation of what happened.

Pay Your Taxes

Until recently, the government kept no records of who redeemed E bonds in amounts smaller than $500. It has always been up to you to remember that income at tax time and report it. But beginning with E bonds issued in 1974, redemption records will be kept for interest payments of $10 or more. So if you redeem a bond purchased from 1974 on and forget to report the proceeds, the government's computers can pick it up. You don't report the entire value of the bond—just the difference between what you paid for it and what you got at redemption. The receipt you get from the bank tells you exactly what to declare on your tax return. If you received the bonds as the result of someone's death and owe taxes on the entire increase in value, you can deduct any estate tax paid on the interest accumulated at the time of death. (Note to recipients of H-bond income: The government has always kept records of your payments.)

Chapter Twenty-Six

INVESTMENTS

> When the market is doing well and your friends and
> neighbors are buying stock, sell and put your money
> in the bank. The market will go higher—maybe quite
> a bit higher. Ignore it. Eventually there will be a
> recession. When it gets so bad as to arouse the politi-
> cians to make speeches, take your money out of the
> bank and buy stocks. The market will go lower—
> maybe quite a bit lower. Ignore it. This investment
> advice always works, but the procedure is so difficult
> that almost no one can do it.
>
> FRED SCHWED, JR.

"A customer," mused Fred Schwed, Jr., in his classic send-up of Wall
Street, *Where Are the Customers' Yachts?*, "may be loosely defined as
anyone who is willing to put up some money." For the right investment,
that's the best money you'll ever spend. But if the choice is a bad one,
you may come to hate yourself, or your stockbroker, for getting involved. Some people get so mad about the money they lose that they
turn off investments entirely. That's a shame, because putting *capital*
(which means *savings*) into growth situations is the chief way for aver-
age-income people to increase their wealth. The purpose of this chapter
is to help you choose good investments by sorting out which ones are
the most appropriate for your circumstances and most likely to fulfill
your hopes.

Before You Invest

The first dollar of savings should *not* go into investments, no matter
how eager you are to get started. If you're married and have children, your primary need is adequate life and health insurance; then
money in the bank to cover emergencies and provide your family

with a little comfort; then a home of your own, which may be the best investment you'll ever make; then secure, long-term savings for clear and present needs, such as college tuition. Only then are you ready to think about stocks, bonds, mutual funds, real estate, gold coins, and other investments.

The situation is a little different if you're young and single, or married but with no children and both spouses working. In that case, you may need little or no life insurance and may not even be ready for a home of your own. As soon as you've put aside some money in the bank, you're free to begin an investment program.

The approach is this: Money goes first to pay bills, build a bank account, and meet your financial obligations to those who depend on you. Only then are you ready to invest for your own future.

Risk

Investment risk can be considered two ways. The first and most common way is *risk of losing your money*. By this definition, some investments have relatively low risk—for example, the bonds of good companies where there's little doubt that the interest will be paid and the bonds redeemed on time. Other investments are so risky that it's like betting on the turn of a card. These might include the stocks of small, new companies or put and call options.

High-risk investments, if they work out, can produce a big payoff; if they don't work out, you may lose a lot of money. Lower-risk investments, by contrast, generally produce smaller profits but also carry smaller chance of loss.

There's another way to define risk—namely, *risk of losing the purchasing power of your capital*. Viewed this way, so-called "low-risk" investments aren't always so attractive. You're perfectly secure with the bonds of a good company, if your goal is simply to collect interest and cash in the bonds at maturity. But if the interest payment is 5 percent and inflation rises to 8 percent, you're losing purchasing power. Even if your interest payment keeps up with inflation, there's often nothing left over for profit—and profit is the reason for making investments.

Which type of risk weighs heavier in your investment decisions depends on your investment judgment and skill. If you do badly with stocks, then by all means choose bonds. It's better to lose a little money to inflation than a lot of money to a bad stock market. On the other hand, if you can make annual gains in stocks, real estate, or other investments that may exceed inflation, then it's "safer" to go in that direction.

If you're looking for absolute safety of principal, and other goals are secondary, you may want to consider only guaranteed investments— insured savings accounts, U.S. savings bonds, and Treasury and federal agency securities.

Risk and Income

People who need income from their capital generally turn to the classic "income investments"—high-dividend corporate and utility stocks, bonds, income mutual funds, and income-producing real estate. This is the proper course for anyone with little time for investing and no more than average knowledge of market trends. But if you have a superior investment record, you might want to put a good part of your capital into growth stocks even if they pay low or no dividends. For income, you would sell off a certain amount of your portfolio every year, on the assumption that, over the long run, it would increase enough in value to maintain your principal or even increase it. "Income," in other words, can derive from *either* dividends and interest *or* capital gains. Which type of income you aim for depends principally on your investment skills.

Up the Ladder of Risk

Defining risk as "the chance of losing your original capital," the most risk-free investments are the securities of the U.S. government. Next up the ladder come bonds of high and middling quality which you intend to hold until maturity—corporate and utility bonds for taxable income, municipal bonds for people who want some of their income tax-free. Then come blue-chip stocks, which are of two types: (1) leading corporations and utilities that show regular, though moderate, growth and have a long history of paying good dividends; and (2) established "growth" companies that show high annual earnings gains, even in poor economic years. Growth companies pay low or no dividends, because management thinks it can reinvest profits in the business to produce a higher-than-average rate of return on its investment (which could be realized in the market as substantial capital gains).

After the blue chips come major corporations whose dividends and growth record, while good, may be sharply reduced in years when the economy slows down (called *cyclical* stocks). From that point on, investment risks increase in approximately the following order: Newer growth companies; medium-sized companies; small companies—even those with a history of excellent earnings growth and dividend payments (because they have fewer products, thinner management, less geographical distribution, less financial strength, and the higher vulnerability in economic downturns), and "fad" investments, which everyone piles into at once. Bonds bought as short-term price speculations are also among the higher risks. Most speculative of all are the exotica of the investment world—brand-new companies, options (except those used strictly to limit risk—see page 638), warrants, oil drilling and real estate tax shelters, commodities, and so on. All these investments will be explained in detail later in the chapter.

The relative riskiness of a mutual fund depends on the types of investments it makes. An "income fund" that specializes in high-quality bonds and dividend-paying stocks carries moderate risks; a growth fund specializing in small companies is high risk. Real estate can be low, medium, or high risk, depending on its character (see page 669).

What Risks Can You Afford?

A cliché of the investment business is that "higher-income people can afford higher risks." That's how they often *lose* a good slice of their higher incomes. They take high risks, and the money goes down the drain.

Middle-income people, on the other hand, are urged to invest more conservatively, because they can't afford a big loss. But "conservative" sounds unadventurous, as well as unprofitable. Legend has it that you won't get rich unless you take risks, and who wants to be left behind?

A look at the net worth statement of an upper-income person who didn't inherit wealth might tell you quite another story about risk. His gains, in recent years, may well have come from (1) money added from his high earnings to savings, and (2) the increase in value of his home. Investments in the "high risk" category were probably a net drain. In fact, if he hadn't taken those risks, he'd likely be worth more today.

A look at the portfolio of someone who profits from his investments would tell you something else about risk. Income, and wealth, generally derive from traditional "conservative" investments—blue-chip stocks, utilities, growth companies, municipal and corporate bonds—well diversified, representing leading corporations and sound municipalities. Floating on top of this rich mix are the playthings—and that's what the wealthy investor is likely to talk about. His naked options, his over-the-counter speculations, the tip his stockbroker got last week from the secretary to the president of a company that might be bought by Xerox. Listening to his conversation, a tyro investor might think this the basis of his fortune. But in fact this is his fun, his lottery ticket—great if he wins, no disaster if he loses. The foundations of his fortune are the "old reliables."

Both the high- and middle-income investor, then, would do well to analyze investments in the same way: with an eye toward preserving capital as well as adding to it.

Risk and Tax Deferral

You can get a high average annual yield, at low risk, if it's possible to defer paying income taxes. In effect, you're then able to earn interest and dividends on the government's share of your salary, as well as your own. The most common tax-deferred savings-and-investment vehicles are pension and profit-sharing plans, corporate thrift plans, deferred compensation, restricted property, and deferred annuities. With these vehicles, you can invest conservatively in bonds or savings accounts and, through the power of untaxed interest compounding, secure long-term yields on an original investment of 15 to 20 percent a year and more.

Risk and Age

A young or middle-aged person can afford to keep relatively more of his money in stocks and less in bonds. That's because over long periods of time, such as twenty to twenty-five years, the stock market has always done extraordinarily well. If you invest in America's leading corporations and have the time to sit back and wait, you will gain for yourself a profitable share of America's long-term growth.

When a person reaches retirement age, he needs more income from his accumulated capital. So relatively more of his money should go into bonds. But even when you are age sixty-five, it's unwise to put everything into bonds; you may have another twenty-five years to live, during which time the stock market will advance considerably. For maximum income, combined with a shot at increasing the value of your capital, you might want to keep some money in good companies with a history of excellent dividends. By age seventy or seventy-five, however, the need for secure annual income may dictate a 100 percent switch to the classic "income investments."

Risk and Circumstances

If the money you have to invest comes from a one-time windfall, be particularly chary of high risks. This applies, for example, to the widow with low or no earnings who has just received an insurance payout; a divorcee with a lump-sum settlement; or a family of modest means that has just come into an inheritance. If you lose that money in the stock market, you probably can't replace it; your potential for financial security and independence goes down the drain. Low risks are also essential for people able to invest only modest sums out of their incomes. Any money lost on a flyer would take years to recover.

Another test of how much risk you can afford is how badly you need all your money. If you depend on it for income, education, or retirement, you don't want to chance a big loss. On the other hand, if a few thousand dollars one way or another won't make much difference to your style of life, you can take more risks, if that appeals to you.

Single people with no dependents can generally afford more risks than married people with children. People with retarded children need more conservative investments than those whose children can support themselves. If you aren't interested in investments, you should take fewer risks than people who follow the stock market closely. Whatever your decision on relative risk, it should mesh with your personal situation and not be swayed by the opinions of others in different circumstances.

A reminder: Even those who can "afford" high risks aren't necessarily advised to take them (see page 562).

Risk and Temperament

Some people are unhappy with high risks, even if they can "afford" them. They worry about the investments, don't sleep well, and are vastly relieved when they're sold. Similarly, many people are so distressed by losses that they won't sell a stock that's down, even if it has little or no hope of recovering anytime soon. If this describes you, stay away from high risks. Money should serve your peace of mind as well as your pocketbook. Steer a conservative investment course and don't let anyone talk you out of it.

If, however, you're drawn toward high risks, try to limit the damage you can do to yourself. Set aside a specific percentage of your investment money for taking big plunges and put the rest in stocks or bonds carrying low or moderate risks.

Balancing Risks

For some people investment is an all-or-nothing game. If they want growth, all their money goes for growth stocks or growth mutual funds; if they're conservative, they're 100 percent in bonds. But neither course is particularly prudent. The person tied to growth stocks is not protected from a market drop; when the price of stocks declines, all his investments will decline, too. The bond investor, on the other hand, hasn't protected himself against the possibility that the market will *rise;*

if the price of stocks goes up, he'll miss his chance to increase the value of his capital.

A thoughtful investor, whose general goal is capital growth over the years ahead, positions himself so his risks are balanced. The idea is to have something going for you no matter which way the market moves. For example, you might consider keeping 60 percent of your investment money in stocks and 40 percent in bonds (or in mutual funds specializing in each). If the stock market goes up, 60 percent of your portfolio could also go up, while the rest delivers a regular income from bond interest payments. If the stock market goes down, 60 percent of your portfolio may go down (unless you sell promptly), but income from your bonds will help cushion any losses. If interest rates rise while the stock market falls, which often happens, the bonds you hold will increase in market value (for details, see page 621), so the gain on your bonds will partly offset your losses in stocks. A 60-40 split may be too conservative for you; you might prefer as much as 80 percent in stocks. But whatever portfolio percentages you choose, they need not be fixed: When the stock market is in a broad uptrend, try increasing the portion devoted to stocks; then sell them during a declining trend before the profits slip away.

An extraordinarily lucky and well-informed investor may be able to buy stocks when the market is going up and sell them before the market falls, but the ability to do so is rare (some would say nonexistent). Your most intelligent approach is to assume that you'll miss the market's tops and bottoms. By spreading your investments among the various types of risks, you'll give yourself at least some protection no matter what happens.

Investment Goals

Tied in with your assessment of risk is the overall goal of your investment program. Are you investing primarily in order to increase your capital? To provide yourself with a current income? To have some fun? Many people wind up with the wrong investments simply because they didn't stop to figure out what they really wanted. A stock that's right for a neighbor who likes high-risk speculations is not right for you if your goal is income and preservation of capital. That's one reason why investment tips from friends can serve you so badly: the friend's goals and yours may not be the same.

Capital Growth

This is, quite properly, the fundamental goal of most investors. The benchmark of performance has long been considered a long-term average increase of around 9½ percent a year. (That's the average annual pretax gain in stock values on the New York Stock Exchange, after investment commissions, between 1929 and 1976, assuming that dividends were reinvested in the market.) Over twenty-five-year periods, 9 percent is the low, with increases ranging as high as 17 percent.

Starting with the 1929 market low stacks the deck, of course. Gains in each twenty-five-year period beginning from 1925 to 1929 range from 4.9 to 8.9 percent. There have been no similarly dreadful twenty-five-year periods since then, but nothing is guaranteed.

Cash returns for higher-income people, after all taxes and commissions, averaged about 8 percent a year between 1930 and 1976, according to a study by Lawrence Fisher and James H. Lorie of the University of Chicago, with returns in twenty-five-year periods ranging from 7.3 to 13.6 percent. Starting back in the years 1925–1929, however, returns were only about 4 to 6 percent.

Most people can't expect to do better than the stock market as a whole, so your own investment performance (assuming a diversified portfolio) will probably lie somewhere within these ranges. Some years you'll do well and others you won't. But over the long term, aim for a *minimum* of 9 percent a year. Skilled investors can exceed that amount.

An increase of 9 percent sounds good when bonds are paying an interest rate of only 5 percent. *But in recent years good-quality bonds have yielded 9 percent and more. That's the same minimum return as you can expect from a diversified stock portfolio over the long run, but at much less risk.* Faced with circumstances like these, many investors —even those with growth as a primary goal—have switched some money to bonds. *But note:* The sharply reduced capital gains tax, effective in 1979, improves the position of stocks vs. bonds, yielding a higher reward for the higher risk of stock investments.

Preserving Capital

In evaluating investments, people often look only at the potential for gain. But just as important as making money is the goal of *not losing* money. Think about it both ways. If you go for some high-risk opportunities, balance them with low-risk investments in order to keep your total exposure to risk at a moderate level.

Income

It may be more important to receive a steady income from capital than to invest it for appreciation. High-dividend stocks, bonds, government securities, income mutual funds, and income-producing real estate are all appropriate for this purpose. You may have begun your investment program with an eye on long-term growth only to have your circumstances change. If you need more income from capital than you're getting now, ask your broker to help you rearrange your portfolio. (A reminder: It's also possible to get a good income by investing primarily for big capital gains, and cashing some of the portfolio in each year. But this should be tried only by an experienced investor, with a proven record.)

Liquidity

"Liquidity" means the ease with which an investment can be sold at your asking price. Real estate, for example, is generally not liquid because it can take many weeks or months to find a buyer. The stocks and bonds of leading corporations, on the other hand, are highly liquid because they can be sold immediately through any broker. Try not to have all your money tied up in illiquid investments, such as real estate, small companies, or your own business. It's important to be able to raise cash quickly if you should ever need it.

What Are the Odds That Stocks Will Rise in Value?

The case for investing in common stocks is compelling, despite the poor investment results of the late 1960s and 1970s. Over medium-term and long-term holding periods the average returns from common stocks (including dividends) are much higher than you'd get from traditional savings accounts. For most periods (but not all) stocks have also tremendously outperformed bonds and treasury bills.

The following is a summary of results for various holding periods, starting with 1930, as determined by professors Lawrence Fisher and James H. Lorie. (The twenty-five-year periods begin with 1930–1955, 1931–1956, 1932–1957, and go all the way to 1951–1976. Ten-year periods start with 1930–1940, 1931–1941, and so on.) The results, adjusted for brokerage commissions, assume buying and holding an equal number of shares of all the stocks on the New York Stock Exchange, with dividends reinvested. Here are the average annual investment yields:

• *For all twenty-five-year holding periods:* The most recent showed an average annual return of 10.9 percent a year. Overall annual returns ranged from 9 to 17 percent.

• *For all twenty-year holding periods:* The most recent was 9.6 percent, close to the low for the entire period. The high was 19.6 percent.

• *For all fifteen-year holding periods:* With only one exception, annual returns ranged from 8 to 22 percent, mostly clustered in the 11-to-16-percent area. The most recent was 8.4 percent.

• *For all ten-year holding periods:* The most recent showed an average annual return of 8.4 percent, but the two before that were poor (4.3 and 3.0 percent). Prior to the period ending in 1973, returns ranged from 8 to 19 percent a year, with most in the 11-to-15-percent area.

• *Five-year holding periods are more erratic.* Returns in the most recent periods ranged from plus to minus 6 percent a year. In the Great Depression years they were as high as 35.6 percent and as low as minus 9 percent. For periods between 1940 and 1966 the annual range was 10 to 17 percent.

Long-term stock yields, in other words, have been excellent, and even short-term yields are good much more often than they're bad. An investor with a diversified portfolio of good stocks, and time to wait, should get good results.

There are a couple of flies in this ointment. For holding periods starting in 1925 to 1929, both short- and long-term results are pretty bad. Even after twenty years, some average annual returns were as low as 3 percent. In other words, if you buy stocks at one of the market's historic speculative peaks, you'll have cause to regret it. The years leading up to 1929 were definitely such a peak; it took stocks fifteen years to exceed the 1929 highs. The years encompassing 1966 and 1968 were another peak, but not as severe for investors—stocks returned to those levels in 1973 and again in 1976. Nevertheless, for shorter-term holding periods investors recently would have done better with their money in the bank. *This suggests that high-interest bank or savings and loan term accounts are generally the best bet for people who can't risk any losses over five or ten years*—for example, if they're putting money away for college tuition. At current compound interest rates, average annual returns can be very high (see page 761).

What Are the Odds That Bonds Will Rise in Value?

Since World War II, bonds have been a terrible investment. As inflation and interest rates rose—slowly at first, then more rapidly—bonds lost value. If you had to sell your bond before its maturity date, you generally lost money, even counting the interest earned over the years. If you held all your bonds to maturity, you wouldn't have lost capital, but the yield would generally have been quite low. And you'd have lost a lot in purchasing power.

There are two exceptions to this dreary past. Bonds bought during 1925–1929 and held for ten or fifteen years generally produced more handsome investment results than you'd have gotten from stocks.If the present investment climate turns out to resemble 1925–1929 rather than all the years since, bonds could, for now, be a better investment than stocks.

Measuring Your Investment Performance

Most people haven't the faintest idea how well their stocks have done over the long term. Maybe they'd rather not know. It's nicer to comfort yourself by remembering investments that did well than to add up your losses in stocks that died. But if you can get a good overall look at what's actually happening to your money, you might make different decisions. Over the ten-year period 1965–1975, for example, the best bank-managed pension funds had increases of only 2 percent a year, and most others showed losses. If you saw that your own investments were doing no better than that, you might have switched to government securities or even savings accounts.

Here's how to create a rough index of your monthly investment performance so that you can compare how well you do with the published stock market averages:

Add up the current market value of the various stocks you own, then divide by 100. This gives you a number from which your index will start. For example, if you own $12,000 worth of stock, your starting index number will be 120.

Now assume that by the end of the month your stocks have risen in value to $14,000. You divide again by 100 (the divisor) to get a current index number of 140. So your stocks have gone from the starting number of 120 to 140—a 17 percent increase. (If the market value of the portfolio had fallen, you would divide the new value by 100 to chart your loss in the same way.)

If your stocks rise to $14,000 and you invest an additional $7,000, you will increase your investment by 50 percent. So you also increase the divisor by 50 percent, bringing it to 150 from 100. From then on, you divide the total value of your securities by 150 each month, to keep the performance index consistent. When you take money out of the market, you reverse the process. Reduce the divisor by the same *percentage* that you reduce your investment in equities.

By jotting down an index number every month, you'll get a rough comparison between your own investment performance and that of the mutual funds. The comparison isn't exact because mutual funds include dividends in their performance calculations, which is too complex an exercise for the average individual. (Do, however, jot the dividends down in a separate column so that you won't lose sight of how much you earned.) If your own performance is fairly close to that of the good funds, you're doing well. But if the funds do considerably better, it might make more sense for you to buy one rather than to continue managing your money yourself.

Another advantage to charting your own performance is this: You'll pay more attention to which stocks are doing well and which aren't. If one stock is going nowhere while a couple of others are heading up, you might want to switch your money to the better performers.

Finding a Stockbroker

Most investors are advised by stockbrokers, who are agents licensed to buy and sell stocks, bonds, government securities, and other investments. His advice is generally free, but you pay a commission if he does any business for you. If you don't know a broker, ask friends for recommendations or look up "Stockbrokers" in the Yellow Pages of your phone book. By and large, it's best to use a firm that's affiliated with the New York Stock Exchange. If there are no brokers in your town, you can do business by phone or mail with a firm in the nearest large city. The New York Stock Exchange publishes a free directory of member firms, making special mention of those who work with small investors; write to Directory, New York Stock Exchange, Publications Section, 11 Wall St., New York, N.Y. 10005. But before trying this hit-or-miss method, ask your friends or business colleagues if they have brokers, and if so, whether they'd recommend them to you.

If you don't know much about investments or have only a small amount of money, it's best to do business with one of the large national or regional brokerage houses. (If the names of the firms aren't familiar to you, ask how many offices they have around the country or region; only the major firms have a sizable number.) The big firms generally have competent research departments that provide investment reports on many companies. They may also have special services for small investors, such as cut-rate commissions on certain small orders, or monthly investment plans that let you accumulate stocks by setting aside a certain sum of money every month. Ask what services are available before you open an account.

Wealthier investors generally deal with one of the profession's stars, the brokers known in their firms as "big producers." These are the smartest brokers, quick and aggressive, often knowledgeable about taxes as well as investments, and ready to provide extensive services. Because they have good investment ideas of their own, it may not matter whether their firm has a big research department; they'll serve you just as well from a smaller firm. You find these brokers by asking around among people in a financial position to use their services. They'll take less monied people, too, if they think you're likely to have more money at some point in the future.

As with any other professionals, stockbrokers—even big producers— have varying levels of talent. Some have good ideas of their own, others follow what everyone else is saying. Some have a good sense of when the market is in trouble, others insist that all's fine even when stocks are falling apart. Some give you good advice on when to sell a stock as well as buy, others forget about the stock once they've sold it to you. It takes some working with a broker to get an idea of how well he'll actually serve you and whether his investment ideas are in line with your personal goals. Many people like to work with more than one broker, at least at first, in order to get a variety of suggestions and opinions.

One thing: Don't expect your broker to be always right! Like everyone else, he'll make mistakes about the market, a lot of mistakes. He's a genius if he's right only half the time. Gerald Loeb, author of *The Battle for Investment Survival*, believes that if a person is right only three or four times out of ten, and cuts his losses, it is possible for him to make a fortune. What you want from a broker is candor, a willingness to acknowledge that the market sometimes goes down, good service, an understanding of your investment goals, and a reasonable amount of good judgment.

Questions to Ask a Stockbroker

An amazing number of people will put their savings at risk on the say-so of a person whose abilities they've investigated only in a most cursory way. Either they don't know the questions to ask, or they are nervous about asking them. So I asked a successful stockbroker what *he* would want to know about another broker before opening an account. Here are his questions:

1. Has the broker been in the business long enough to have perspective? It's better to deal with someone who has been through at least three or four market downturns than a person whose experience is limited to a single victory or knockdown. Do you want young brokers to learn their lessons on your money? Or would you prefer the approach of someone who's been through the wars?

2. How successful are the broker's own investments? If he's made a lot of money for himself, he should be able to do the same for his clients. The stock exchange requires brokers to keep detailed records of their own transactions; if you ask to see these sheets, a confident broker should be willing to show you. You may find from the record that he's a genius in rising markets but loses badly when stocks fall—a tip to steer clear of his advice in bad times. Watch also for the stocks he likes. If he prefers speculative flyers to blue chips, he'll probably recommend the same to you. Go with him only if his portfolio is something you wouldn't mind having yourself. If he doesn't invest at all, pass him by; he may have had so shattering an experience that he doesn't trust himself.

3. Will he let you inspect his customers' records (with the names blocked out, of course)? You especially should look at some of his *discretionary accounts* (if the firm allows him to have any), where he manages money without having to clear every move with the customer. These accounts are a good measure of what he can do for you. Study the type of stocks he has bought and how long the securities were held. Also, look to see how often he buys and sells. A lot of activity with little net gain suggests that he's *churning* the portfolio, just to create some commissions for himself.

4. How highly does he value preservation of principal? Between 1966 and this writing (1978) there has been one cyclical disaster after another in the stock market. Yet there are still brokers who will tell you gladly that the best way to "preserve" capital is to double it, which means making risky investments. The truth is that an annual 10-to-12 percent gain is an ambitious goal; an annual 50 percent gain, illusion. Unless you're a sophisticated investor, you want a broker who will approach your nest egg with caution, starting you out with conservative stocks

and suggesting that you also consider bonds and cash savings. You can find out how much your broker values capital by checking his records for what he did with other new accounts, especially in poor markets. Was he wise enough to sell out before the market fell too far?

5. What's his personal life like? If your broker fights with his spouse, drinks too much at lunch, or is in the middle of a messy divorce, your financial affairs may suffer along with his. Direct personal questions are difficult to ask and may elicit less-than-truthful answers. But you might be able to find out something in casual conversation or by asking his other customers. If you open an account with him and later find out that he has serious problems, watch his decisions carefully. At the first sign of neglect take your business somewhere else.

6. Does he question you closely about your own financial needs and goals? A good broker tailors his investment suggestions to your personal circumstances, so the more he knows about you, the better. To get top service you should be perfectly candid with the broker about how much you make, what your assets are, and what you expect of the future.

Once you've opened an account, watch the broker's performance in light of the following questions:

1. How hard does the broker sell? When he wants you to buy, does he push for "now-or-never" decisions? Are all his deals "the chance of a lifetime"? Does he intimidate you with machine-gun shots of information without giving you time to think about them? These are all signs of a broker determined to raise his commission income rather than find you a good stock. He'll also "oversell"—that is, advise you to buy 1,000 shares when he knows you have only a 100-share bankroll. Flattered, you might up your order to 150 shares.

When he wants you to sell a stock, does he scare you with hints that the company is in trouble, that professional investors are dumping, that the stock will collapse? When he plays on your fears this way, he knows you'll be highly vulnerable to his suggestions. There may well be situations when a good broker will call to advise a quick sell, but if it happens regularly, you should start to wonder. You want a broker who calmly lays out the case for buying or selling stocks or bonds, sends you supporting data, gives you time to make a decision, and avoids crude pressure techniques.

2. Is the broker willing to tell you when the news is bad? Many brokers can't face their customers in bad markets. They'd rather let you lose more money than go through the agony of calling you when a stock they recommended is down. A broker who keeps in touch on the downside is a professional to be treasured. That, after all, is when you need him the most. Lacking such help, you have to be strong enough to cut your losses yourself—never an easy thing to do. A broker who's willing to advise you not to buy because the market looks poor is a rare bird indeed. In general, you're likely to get more candid opinions of bad markets from a wealthy broker, who can afford to miss a few commissions, than from a broker who's struggling to make a living.

3. Is he well read? The best brokers have an insatiable desire for information, since anything at all may tell them something important about the market. It's mainly from newspapers, magazines, and journals —as well as his own company's research reports—that a broker is able to distill significant trends. A broker too lazy to stay informed is unlikely to do well by you. Good brokerage firms are also well organized— keeping their accounts well serviced, dividends accounted for, annual reports mailed out, and stock certificates delivered on time.

4. Is he honest? Does he present facts accurately, without exaggeration, laying out the positives and negatives with equal force? You should save his letters and take notes on what he tells you, then compare his sales pitch with the facts as presented in the company's annual report. If he misleads you, confront him with it. If his response is to dodge and feint, get another broker.

5. Can he develop his own concepts about stocks and the market, and do they work? Or does he simply parrot the successive recommendations of his firm's research department? Brokers able to marshal separate strands of information into an investment theory are thinking the right way, even if the stocks they pick don't always go up. You want an advisor who has the mental equipment to spot the trends that move markets and stocks as soon as they come along.

6. Does he explain the risks of every investment—especially those that are new to you, such as puts and calls—or does he emphasize only the potential rewards?

As with any other profession, there are many good and honorable stockbrokers. This list of questions is intended to help you find them and to avoid those who will take advantage of you.

Brokerage Commissions

A commission is the amount you pay the broker to execute your order for stock. Part of it is retained by the broker, part goes to the brokerage firm. The commission structure varies from firm to firm; in general rates are higher on small orders than on large ones. *Odd lots,* which are stock orders of less than one hundred shares, often (but not always) carry a higher transaction price than *round lots* (even multiples of one hundred shares).

The largest brokerage firms that deal with the public—Merrill Lynch and Paine, Webber are good examples—have various special discounts for small investors. For instance, they may not charge extra for an odd lot, or they might reduce the commission if you bring the broker the stock in advance of the sale and agree to accept tomorrow morning's price. Ask the broker if any such discounts are available. Smaller brokerage houses, on the other hand, rarely give any cost breaks to small investors.

Discount Brokers

If you don't need investment ideas and advice, you should probably be dealing with a discount broker. This is strictly a no-frills service—no flossy investment booklets, no network of salesmen, no fancy offices or hand-holding brokers, no long discussions of investment alternatives, few (if any) research services. A discount broker is mainly an order taker: You tell him what you've decided to buy or sell, he does it for you. On small trades his commission runs 20 to 25 percent lower than that of regular brokers; on large trades the savings may be as high as 80 percent.

Most discounters will accept small accounts, even those good for only one or two trades a year. But there's generally a minimum fee of $20 or $30. If your purchase is in the area of $600 to $800 or less, you'll probably do as well on commission rates with a regular broker (and better, if it's a large brokerage house with a discount service for small investors). But on larger orders you're likely to save money—perhaps a lot of money—by dealing with a discounter. Here are three common situations where using a discount service makes good sense:

1. When you actively manage your own investments and don't normally expect advice from a broker.
2. When you get your market advice from a paid advisor.
3. When you have a single large order to buy or sell—for example, if you have to sell shares to pay estate taxes. The larger the order, the greater the discount.

At this writing, there are some fifty discount firms in the United States, and the number is growing rapidly. To find a discounter watch the ads in financial publications or on the financial pages of your newspaper. If there's no such firm in your city, it's easy to deal long-distance:

Discounters are glad to accept orders over the phone. They'll either have a toll-free (800) telephone number or permit customers to call collect. A few discounters discourage small orders by levying annual service charges of $100 or more (Source Securities in New York City is one of these), but most will be glad for your business. To become a customer, simply write or call for an application. The firm runs a credit check, just as any other broker would. Discounters all belong to the Security Investors Protection Corporation, which insures individual accounts for up to $100,000.

Here are some of the discount brokers:

Boston—Brown & Co.; C. W. Clayton & Co.; and StockCross.
Charlotte, North Carolina—Conner Redwine.
Chicago—Rose & Co.
Cincinnati—John Finn.
Cleveland—Baker & Co.; and Daley, Coolidge.
Denver—Columbine Securities.
Houston—Letterman Transaction Services.
Indianapolis—Springer Investment & Securities.
Memphis—Kahn & Co.
Minneapolis—Burke, Christensen & Lewis Securities; and Thrift Trading.
Newport Beach, California—Letterman Transaction Services.
New York City—Marquette de Bary; W. T. Cabe & Co.; Odd Lots Securities; Quick & Reilly; Source Securities; and Maxwell Ule.
San Francisco—Charles Schwab.
Springfield, Virginia—Kulak, Voss.
Westbury, New York.—Robinson & Co.
Westwood, New Jersey—Darby Securities.

Disputes with Brokers

If you're having a dispute with your stockbroker, there are several possible ways of handling it. Going to court is the last and most drastic solution, suitable only for cases involving large losses. The vast majority of problems are settled through a series of less formal methods and procedures. Here are the steps to take:

1. Write a letter of complaint to the head of the brokerage office. Customer complaints can lead to all kinds of problems for the brokerage firm, so managers usually answer them pretty fast. Often complaints arise from misunderstandings. Dividend checks may get fouled up; errors occur in transferring an account from one firm to another; novice investors may not realize that it takes a week to get the stock they bought. Problems like this can usually be cleared up just by calling the broker. But some customers are suspicious of what their brokers tell them and want independent verification.

Other complaints are more serious. For example, you might charge that a broker advised you to invest in risky securities, even though he knew you were retired or a widow living on a fixed income. This kind of problem is rarely settled with letters or phone calls.

2. The stock exchanges have strict rules as to how member firms should conduct themselves. They require that brokers make suitable recommendations for their customers and that brokerage officers supervise the conduct of their employees. If you have a complaint that can't be resolved locally and the broker is a member of the New York Stock Exchange, write to NYSE Investor-Broker Liaison, 55 Water St., New York, N.Y. 10041; for the American Stock Exchange, the ASE Rulings and Inquiries Department, 86 Trinity Place, New York, N.Y. 10006; for over-the-counter brokers, one of the fourteen district offices of the National Association of Securities Dealers (check your phone book) or the NASD Surveillance Dept., 1735 K St. N.W., Washington, D. C. 20016. Every complaint is acknowledged and investigated. If wrongdoing is found, the broker may be disciplined. These surveillance bodies cannot order you to be repaid, but their investigations may prove helpful to your case.

3. To press for recovery of market losses, see a lawyer. He may think you should sue in federal court under the securities laws. If the suit involves no more than broker negligence, a suit in state court or arbitration proceedings may be called for. Even if you go to arbitration, you'll need a lawyer, since the procedure is carried out under state law with a full panoply of witnesses, documentation, and cross-examination.

4. When you open a margin account, the agreement you sign generally calls for binding arbitration of disputes (except those involving violations of federal securities laws, which can always be taken to court). If you have no such agreement, you can choose arbitration *or* a lawsuit. The advantage of arbitration is that the procedure is fairly quick, simple, and much less expensive than going to court. You may have a decision in a few months, whereas in a state with a crowded court calendar it may take three or four years.

An arbitration proceeding is like an informal court. There's a panel of one or more arbitrators, agreed to by both sides; typically, they're lawyers, businessmen, or people familiar with the securities industry. Each side states its case, puts on witnesses, and cross-examines the other's witnesses. The arbitrators then render a decision that is binding on both sides. You may choose the arbitration services offered by the New York or American Stock Exchanges, the National Association of Securities Dealers, or the independent American Arbitration Association (140 W. 51st St., New York, N.Y. 10020). Investors sometimes think that stock exchange procedures may be biased in favor of brokerage firms, but the exchanges say that, if anything, their panels bend over backward to understand the customer's problem. Arbitration panels travel to various cities hearing cases, and their fees are small. A simplified small-claims procedure has just been developed by the stock exchanges, requiring no lawyer and handling claims of less than $2,500.

Suing a Broker

If you have lost a good part of your life savings through the actions of a stupid or greedy broker, you don't have to suffer it in silence. You may well have grounds for a lawsuit that will make good your losses. You can't sue a broker just because you lost money on his recommendations; if you buy stocks, you accept that risk. But some risks are considered excessive, particularly for unsophisticated investors. If you have a grievance against a stockbroker, only a lawyer can tell you whether there are grounds for suit. But here are three general areas of liability for you to consider:

1. *Unsuitable recommendations.* Brokers are supposed to know their customer's age, resources, desires, and financial needs and recommend investments to suit. If a broker sells an elderly person's small portfolio of conservative stocks and bonds and plunges into high-risk investments that go down in value, that person may have a lawsuit, even if he gave permission for all the trades. Ditto for a widow or a working person of modest means. Unsophisticated investors are not necessarily held responsible for saying okay to a reckless broker. However, if the investor is presumed to be sophisticated—for example, if he's a retired businessman—he may not be able to recover.

2. *Misrepresentation.* You may be able to sue if the broker gives you false information about a stock, withholds bad information that would affect your investment decision, says that a company is sound when just a little research would show that it's not, or works from information that is out of date. Sometimes there's just your word against the broker's. But there may be circumstantial evidence that supports your case—for example, he may have given the same information to other customers. If the company goes bankrupt while the broker is recommending it, you should have a very good case indeed.

3. *Churning.* That means the broker has been getting you to buy and sell stocks at a rapid clip, solely to earn brokerage commissions for himself. If you never traded that rapidly before and the broker talked you into it, you may be able to sue even if you gave him permission (provided that you are an unsophisticated investor). It's easier to bring a churning case, however, if you gave the broker full authority to handle the account and he took advantage of your trust.

Opening an Account

You can't just stop by a brokerage office and place an order to buy or sell. Under the rules of his firm and the stock exchange, the broker has to know something more about you. It's like opening a charge account at a store, you'll have to reveal something about your financial position and credit history. There are three main reasons for this:

1. If you have shares to sell, the broker wants to be reasonably sure that the shares are yours—or that he knows where to find you if they aren't.
2. If you place an order to buy, the broker executes it for you, then sends you a bill. He wants to be sure that the bill will be paid.
3. A broker is supposed to make investment recommendations appropriate to someone in your financial position, so he has to know what that position is.

You can have stocks registered in your name and mailed to you personally, or you can have them registered in the name of the brokerage house (called a *street name*) and kept in the broker's vault. If you buy and sell only occasionally, it's generally best to keep the stocks or bonds in your own safe deposit box so that you don't lose track of them. But if you're an active trader, it makes more sense to leave the securities with your broker. All your business can then be efficiently transacted by telephone, with statements mailed monthly or quarterly. The broker can either mail your dividend checks or deposit them in your brokerage account. If Wall Street ever gets into financial trouble, however, it makes sense to have street name stocks reregistered in your name and mailed to you for safekeeping. In past panics investors whose brokers went bankrupt had their stocks tied up for a long time.

If you sell a stock registered in your name, you have to endorse it just the way you would a check and get it to your broker before the *settlement date*—five business days after the sale. Either deliver the stock by hand or send it by registered mail. On settlement date the proceeds of the sale will be credited to your brokerage account or mailed to you by check. If you buy, payment must be received by the broker within five business days after the purchase. The broker always sends you a *confirmation* of your transaction; check it for accuracy, then file it away for income tax and inheritance tax purposes.

A *cash account* is for stocks you buy and sell in the normal way. A *margin account* is for people who want to put down only part of the price of the stocks or bonds, borrowing the rest from their brokers (see margin buying, page 600). The financial requirements are higher for opening a margin account, and you have to make a cash deposit. Stocks bought on margin are always held in street names.

Once you've opened a brokerage account, you can do all further business by phone or mail. Husbands and wives can open joint accounts, but before you do so, consider whether you really want to have the stocks in joint names (see page 713).

Finding an Investment Manager

Wealthier investors often turn their money over to an advisor who manages it for them in a *discretionary account*. That means that the manager has the right to buy and sell for your account without getting your specific permission. The manager typically charges a fee for his investment advice; in addition, you pay brokerage commissions to whatever firm handles the buy and sell orders.

Most investment advisors won't take a client unless he has $100,000 to invest, and some of the top people won't talk to you for less than $1 million. But there are a few firms that accept smaller amounts, such as $25,000 or even $10,000. You find them by word of mouth, or through the advertisements they occasionally place in such investment publications as *Barron's*. Some brokerage firms keep lists of managers they consider competent. Three investment managers that take smaller accounts are Danforth Associates, Wellesley Hills, Massachusetts; T. J. Holt, New York City; and Bayrock Advisors, also in New York City. Management fees generally run in the area of 1 to 2 percent.

One tip on dealing with managers: They generally have about the same stocks in all their clients' accounts. This sometimes makes them hesitant to sell a weak stock because the very act of dumping so much of it on the market might depress the price even further. But if you personally order the manager to sell that stock, he must do so, which would get you out ahead of all the other clients. *Another tip:* When you interview a prospective manager, ask him how much he keeps in cash.

A manager who is always fully invested is exposed to more risk during market declines and lacks the cash to take advantage of good opportunities that suddenly arise. A good manager will sell some of your stocks every year, in order to keep a cash reserve.

Get several recommendations on a manager before you entrust him with your money. Consider giving him a relatively small amount at first, to see how he does. If his record is good, give him more of your funds; if it's bad, quit and try someone else.

Mutual Funds as Investment Managers

The cheapest way for a smaller investor to get professional, diversified management of his money is to buy a mutual fund (see page 643). Consider a "family of funds," which is a number of mutual funds, all under the same roof, each investing for different objectives—capital growth, income, tax-free income, and so on. These fund groups will generally consult with you at no charge about how to split your investment among their various funds in order to spread your risk and achieve your objectives. Also, they'll advise you on how to alter your strategy if you believe market conditions are changing. The large fund groups have toll-free (800) telephone numbers. Call them and say that you're looking for advice.

Bank Trust Departments as Investment Managers

Many good banks have services for smaller investors as well as for the wealthy. Their programs, however, are not much advertised, so you'll have to inquire about them yourself. Bank services are usually favored by (1) those who feel unqualified to choose a mutual fund or individual investment advisor; (2) those who are more comfortable with bank management (although banks aren't necessarily safer; many bank funds show poorer performance than a good mutual fund); (3) older people who want their money in reliable hands in case they themselves should become incapacitated; (4) those who are leaving money to be managed for heirs, and want to avoid probate. For more on living trusts, see page 721. Here's what's available:

POOLED TRUST FUNDS

Banks combine the funds of smaller investors into pooled or "commingled" funds, which are similar to mutual funds. Some have only one fund, geared toward investors needing income. Others may give you a choice of two or more funds, specializing in income or capital growth. Banks usually have standardized trust documents for smaller accounts; income is generally paid quarterly. In some cases you may receive a report of the account's current value only once a year. The minimum investment varies; some banks will take as little as $2,000, others start at $25,000 or even $100,000. Fees vary, too; 1 percent of assets per year is a common charge, with a minimum fee in the area of $100 to $250.

Always ask to see records of the fund's past performance before you sign up. If you don't know how to evaluate whether it's good or bad, ask someone who does. A lawyer who specializes in estates and trusts will know which banks have the better investment departments. You'll need a lawyer, in any event, to go over the trust documents.

INDIVIDUAL MANAGEMENT

Normally you need in the area of $100,000 or $200,000 to have money managed individually by a trust department. But a few banks offer individual services to smaller investors. Trusts of this type offer more investment flexibility than if you used pooled funds. Also, they can be set up to suit various types of tax and estate-planning situations.

ADVISORY SERVICES

A few banks give investment advice to investors who want to manage their own money and not put it in trust.

INVESTING IN STOCKS

Common Stocks

Also called *shares* or *equity securities, stocks* are segments of ownership in a corporation. If a given company has been divided into one million shares and you have one hundred of them, you own one ten-thousandth of that company and are entitled to receive one ten-thousandth of any earnings that are distributed to the owners. The reason companies sell shares to the public is to raise money. For example, assume that a company needs $5 million to build a new plant. It could get it by selling five hundred thousand shares to the public at $10 each. That initial sale is generally the only time a company makes money from its stock. If you buy some of those shares and resell them to another investor at a higher price, the profit is all yours. Almost all stock trading is between investors for their own profit (or loss) rather than between investors and the company.

For every share of stock you own, you get one vote in the company's affairs. That vote can be exercised in person at the company's *annual meeting* of the shareholders; alternatively, you can sign a *proxy*, authorizing one of the company's officers to vote for you. The main thing you vote on is the composition of the company's board of directors. In theory, the shareholders can fire the board and install a new one, but in practice that almost never happens. As a small shareholder, your only recourse if you aren't happy with the way things are going is to sell the stock.

When you buy stock, you receive a *certificate of ownership,* which is normally registered in your name. The certificate may show a face value, or *par value,* of $1 to $10, but ignore that figure. Once upon a time par value may have indicated what the company's physical plant was worth, but over the years it has become meaningless. In fact companies now tend to issue shares without a par value so as not to confuse investors. All that really matters is the stock's *market value,* which is the price you could get if you sold it.

Dividends paid on *common stock* will change from time to time, whereas dividends on *preferred stock* (see page 584) are generally fixed.

Dividends

When a company makes money, it keeps part of the profits to plow back into the business and distributes the rest to shareholders. The money that's kept is called *retained earnings.* The amount paid out is called the *dividend.* If the dividend is $1.20 a share and you own one hundred shares, you'll get a check for $120. Dividends are normally paid *quarterly,* which means once every three months.

Companies trying to grow rapidly generally retain most or all of their earnings and put that money toward business expansion. This attracts investors who don't need regular dividend income but very much want a rapidly growing company whose stock increases sharply in value. (There's no guarantee that the stock price will indeed shoot up, but that's what management aims for.) Other companies plan to grow more slowly and distribute a large portion of their earnings in dividends. This latter situation is good for investors who want regular income.

The dividends paid on common stock rise and fall according to the fortunes of the company (although great effort is generally made to avoid cutting a dividend). The exact amount of the dividend is determined each quarter by the board of directors.

A number of companies allow you to reinvest your dividends in company stock without paying brokerage commissions on the purchase. Write to your company's stockholder services department to see if it has such a program.

Sometimes dividends are paid in stock rather than cash. The company issues a fractional share of free stock to every shareholder—for example, you might get one eighth of a share for each share you already own. If you sell the free shares, you'll realize a profit; if you hold them, they'll earn you future dividends and perhaps capital gains.

Preferred Stock

Preferred stock carries a high dividend payment, quoted as a percentage of your original investment. For example, the stock might pay 7 percent, which on an investment of $1,000 is $70 a year. Normally, that dividend doesn't fluctuate with earnings. Preferred stockholders must receive their full dividend before the common stockholders get a nickel. Preferred shares are generally *cumulative;* if earnings ever dropped so far that a preferred dividend was skipped, that dividend would have to be made up in future years before anything could be paid to the holders of common stock. If the company ever went bankrupt and money was left over after its assets were sold and debts paid, preferred shareholders would receive payments ahead of common shareholders (although in actual fact, there's rarely any money for either).

A disadvantage to preferred shares is that the holders usually don't share fully in the company's good fortunes. If earnings increase, larger dividend payments go only to the common stockholders; preferred dividends remain fixed. A few companies have *participating preferreds,* which do allow dividend increases; but that's the exception, not the rule. Because dividends on preferred shares don't fluctuate, the preferred-stock price won't rise or fall as fast as the price of common stock.

During a rising trend in the stock market, a popular type of stock is the *convertible preferred* (see page 586).

Most preferreds carry a *call provision,* which allows the company to redeem, or "call in," your stock at a stated price, whether or not you want to sell. Stock is called if the company thinks it can sell a new issue of preferred at a lower dividend, thus saving itself some money. This is likely to happen if interest rates fall; the high-income preferred, which you thought would be yours for life, could be snatched away.

Preferred stocks are bought by people who want two things from the same investment: (1) a predictable quarterly income that's higher than current common-stock dividends and is reasonably sure of being paid; and (2) the possibility of capital gains if the stock increases in value. The reverse side of this coin is that the income is not as high as you'd get from the same company's bonds, and the preferred stock will not gain in value as much as the common. Another way of meeting your twin goals may be to forget the preferred and divide your investment between high-quality bonds and common stock. One point for preferred stock over bond investments: You can buy with only a small amount of money. For a good price on bonds you generally have to put up at least $5,000 to $10,000.

Rights

When a company decides to raise more money by selling more stock, the old shareholders usually have first chance to buy. For each share you own, you'll be given the *right* to a fractional part of a new share, at a *discount* from market price. For example, assume you own one hundred shares of a $17 stock. This might entitle you to half a share of new stock for every share you already own, with the new stock priced at a $2 discount. That means you can buy fifty shares at $15 each. If the market price of the stock doesn't fall, you'll have a built-in profit.

Rights are guaranteed on a special certificate that comes in the mail. If you don't want the new shares, you can sell that certificate in the marketplace—in this case for about $1 a share, or $50. But call your broker immediately if you want to sell. Rights expire within a short time, such as a couple of weeks, after which they are worthless. All the stock that's not bought by the old shareholders (or by other investors who bought their rights) is then offered to the general public at full market price.

Investors often overlook a rights offering by not opening and reading all the mail they get from the companies whose shares they own. The money they could earn from those rights then goes right down the drain.

Warrants

Warrants are generally issued by companies in a package deal with certain stocks and bonds. They give you the right to buy more shares at a specified price within a certain period of time (often one to five years). For example, you might buy a $15 stock accompanied by a warrant entitling you to buy one more share at $20 within twelve months. If the market price rises to $25, you can exercise the warrant and make an instant $5 gain.

The purpose of warrants is to make the accompanying stock or bond more attractive to investors. Sometimes they're issued by blue-chip companies to ensure that a new stock issue sells out even though times are tight. More often they're issued by higher-risk companies that need something extra to get their stocks or bonds sold at all. Some warrants are "free" if you buy the stock (although a value for the warrant will be included in the stock's price); other warrants carry a specific price. Some are bound to the stock or bond they came with; others can be detached and traded separately in the marketplace. Speculators may buy only the warrant—if the stock goes up, they'll win big; if it doesn't, the warrant will expire worthless. *Warning:* It's hard to evaluate whether you're paying a fair price for a combined stock and warrant, or even a warrant alone. As a rule, these should be bought only by sophisticated investors.

Convertibles

Convertibles are bonds or preferred stocks that can be exchanged for a fixed number of shares of the company's common stock, within a specified period of time. Basically, they're a double hedge—when the market falls, well-chosen convertibles don't fall as far as the common stock. Also, they generally pay a higher dividend. There are two drawbacks: Although they rise in a good market, they usually don't do as well as the common stock; also, they pay less interest than you'd get from bonds.

The worst time to buy convertibles is when interest rates are rising and stocks falling. But when stocks rise and interest rates decline, convertibles can do very well. The strategy is to decide whether you think a particular stock is going up, then consider whether to hedge your bet with a convertible.

Convertibles are judged by two measures—their *conversion value* and their *investment value.*

Conversion value is what the security would be worth if converted intó common stock at current market prices. For example, take a bond convertible into twenty shares of stock at $50 a share. If the stock is currently selling for only $25 a share, the bond's conversion value is just $500. Because of the interest rate, however, the bond might sell for $700, which is $200 (or 40 percent) over its conversion value. It is said, then, to have a *conversion premium* of 40 percent, which is high. If the stock were selling much closer to its conversion price (say, $45 where the conversion price is $50), the premium would be low.

When the conversion price is close to the stock price, a convertible rises and falls pretty much in tandem with the common stock. If the market rises, you'll get good capital gains plus higher income than the stock would yield. There's also more risk if the market falls.

When the conversion price is well below the stock price, the convertible rises and falls more slowly. On the downside, it theoretically won't fall any lower than the price where it's similar in yield to other bonds of comparable quality and maturity. That's called its *investment value.* At that level, you're basically buying an income investment with an equity kicker.

If you're playing convertibles mainly for their appreciation in a bull market, you'd buy those with low conversion premiums. If you want a hedge against investment risk, you'd look for convertibles with higher yields, selling further from the conversion price of the underlying stock. These won't rise as fast in bull markets, but produce higher income and more protection against loss.

By and large, individuals should stick with the convertibles of good companies, rather than speculating in "junk" issues. Four good investment criteria are:

1. You must like the company as a stock investment.
2. The convertible should sell at a modest premium over conversion value, say 15 to 20 percent.
3. It should yield more than the common stock.
4. It should be easy to resell (some of the speculative convertibles don't readily find takers).

If you want to spread your risk, consider investing in one of the various convertible mutual funds—some specializing in higher income, others taking more market risk.

Stock Splits

A stock split doesn't make you any richer. If you own one hundred shares selling for $90 each, a 2-for-1 split leaves you with two hundred shares at $45 each. A 3-for-1 split gives three hundred shares at $30 each. In every case, the total market value of the shares is $9,000.

The corporate purpose of a split is to adjust the price of the stock downward, so as to attract more investors. It's a psychological gimmick: People who think a stock "too expensive" at $90 may be glad to buy three shares at $30 each.

Why do investors get so excited about stock splits? For one thing, they're sometimes accompanied by good news from the company, such as a dividend increase. For another, if the lower price in fact attracts more investors, their buying interest may push the price up. But news of a split is not, by itself, a good reason to buy. If the company's earnings or dividends do not improve, any price increase that accompanied the stock split will probably vanish.

The Stock Exchanges

The *stock exchanges* are places where the major stocks are bought and sold. When you give a buy order to a stockbroker, he sends it to the *floor* of an exchange; there, your stock is bought from another broker, whose customer has decided to sell. The exchanges themselves don't own stock; they merely provide a place where buyers and sellers can come together. The exchanges also try to keep markets honest and orderly by (1) requiring that prices be publicly posted (no secret trades); (2) keeping good records so that suspicious price moves can be traced; (3) decreeing rules of fair play between broker and customer; and (4) requiring certain financial standards of the companies whose stocks are allowed to trade there. A company is said to be *listed* if its stock trades on a public exchange.

The *New York Stock Exchange,* also called the Big Board, deals in the stocks of the largest and most financially secure companies. The *American Stock Exchange* lists medium-sized companies, as well as government securities and put-and-call options. *Regional exchanges* in several cities list local companies not found on the two major exchanges, as well as many large companies that also sell on the Amex or Big Board. The prices on all these exchanges were recently consolidated into a single reporting system, making it possible for your stockbroker to execute your order easily on whichever exchange offers the best price.

Specialists

On any given day, the number of people wanting to sell a stock will not exactly match the number of people wanting to buy, yet normally everyone will complete a transaction without sharp changes in the stock's price. What makes this possible is the service of *specialists*— private brokerage firms that do business only on the floor of stock exchanges and deal only in a few stocks. If you want to sell at a moment when no one else wants to buy, the specialist will buy your stock himself. If you want to buy when there are no sellers around, the specialist will sell to you out of his own inventory. This assures that you'll be able to trade whenever you want to.

The activities of specialists also prevent prices from swinging wildly up and down in a single day. If you wanted to sell at a time when there was no buying interest, and no specialist stood ready to accept your order, you might have to slash your price to find a buyer. Conversely, if you wanted to buy a popular stock, you might have to offer a price considerably above the market level to induce someone to sell. The specialist's middle-man activities normally prevent such sharp price changes. If there's a surplus of sellers, he soaks up the extra stock while gradually moving the stock price down—normally in eighth- or quarter-point drops. If there's a surplus of buyers, he feeds his own stock into the marketplace while gradually moving the price up. It's the job of the specialist to keep markets liquid and orderly.

In a panic situation, however, the system breaks down. When everyone wants to sell, the specialist can't possibly accept all their stock. Instead, the exchange *halts trading*—which means that no one can buy or sell—while the company's situation is examined and publicized. Trading may be stopped for a few hours, a few days, or many weeks, depending on the severity of the situation.

Specialists and Limit Orders

Sometimes investors place orders to sell a stock only if the price moves up to a specified amount, or buy only if the price moves down. These are called *limit orders* and are noted in the specialist's book. Say, for example, that a stock is selling at $15 and you place an order to buy "at the market." By the time your order arrives, however, there's no more $15 stock around and, in fact, no sellers at all. The specialist will then consult his book. If he finds a limit order from an investor to sell at 15¼, he'll fill your order at that price. Specialists are required to fill orders out of their books before buying or selling from their own inventory, as long as that method assures an orderly market. In the example above, if the only sale order in his book were for $16, he'd sell from his own inventory at 15¼, then 15½, then 15¾, if necessary. Only then would he fill the next order from his book at $16.

Over-the-Counter Markets

Thousands of stocks don't trade on the major or regional exchanges. These are handled *over the counter,* which means they're bought and sold through certain dealers who *make a market* in the stock. When you want to buy an over-the-counter (OTC) stock, your broker checks the various dealers offering it for sale to see who has the best price. You buy directly from a dealer rather than through a stock exchange; when you sell, you sell directly to a dealer. Prices are based on the amount of stock the dealer has on hand, what he paid for it, the level of demand, and the price quoted by competing dealers (if any). Most stocks traded over the counter are those of small companies, but the market also includes the stock of many large banks and insurance companies, bonds, government securities, and American Depository Receipts (which represent shares in foreign companies).

Small companies don't have many shares outstanding (the investing world calls this a *thin float*). If investors suddenly get interested in a small company, the price will shoot up, but it can fall rapidly when enthusiasm drops off. There may be no market at all for the stock because no one wants to buy, even though the company shows good growth and earnings. Investors may be stuck with an OTC stock for years with no hope of selling out. By contrast, there's almost always a market for stocks listed on the major exchanges.

The best way of speculating in the OTC market is to stick to the largest companies, whose stocks trade often and whose buying and selling prices are shown on *NASDAQ*, the automatic quotation system of the National Association of Securities Dealers (NASD is the organization that oversees the over-the-counter markets). All dealers making a market in a particular stock enter their prices daily on the NASDAQ computer. Your broker can check the prices on his own desk-top terminal and place your order where the price is best. As long as your stock is on NASDAQ, you'll probably be able to sell. It's the less active stocks not listed on NASDAQ, or that used to be on NASDAQ but dropped out, that are the most likely to give you trouble.

Stock Market Averages

The *Dow-Jones Industrial Average* is the most widely reported measure of stock market prices. When you hear on the evening news that "the market" rose two points today, it means that the Dow rose by that amount. But the Dow is of limited usefulness in judging the broad range of market activity, since it represents only thirty leading manufacturing companies on the New York Stock Exchange. Professional money managers tend to judge general market activity by the *Standard & Poor's Average,* which covers five hundred stocks and represents most of the activity on the New York Stock Exchange. The NYSE itself publishes an index of the daily changes in all of its fifteen-hundred-plus stocks, with the larger companies weighted more heavily in the average. All of these indexes generally move up and down at the same time, but the Dow Jones industrials may move faster or slower than the market in general.

What Sets the Price of Stocks?

Listed stocks are sold in an auction market. Buyers and sellers come together (through their representatives, the brokers) to reach a mutually agreeable price. That price reflects all the information that investors in general currently possess about the company and about the economy as a whole. If investors come to believe that the outlook will brighten, they'll bid more aggressively for the stock and the price will rise. If they grow pessimistic, the stock's owners will accept lower and lower prices in order to sell. Stripped to its essentials, the market mechanism is this: When more people want to buy the stock than sell it, the price moves up. When there are more sellers than buyers, the price moves down.

Stock prices sometimes plunge while the company's earnings are making new highs, or jump while they're registering new lows. This seems perverse to many investors, but in fact it makes perfect sense. Stock prices generally reflect what is likely to happen, not what has happened already. When prices fall on rising earnings, it suggests that the company's profits will probably be lower six months from now; when they rise on lower earnings, it means that the outlook has improved.

These "predictions" may be right—but they may also be wrong, in which case the stock price will turn around. That's what makes stock picking so slippery. You're dealing not only with what the company and the economy actually do but also with what other investors in the market think they'll do.

Stock Prices and Fads

Fad investments are like contagious diseases. One investor catches it from another, and before you know it, the stock's price is riding high. People make big money while the fever persists, but sooner or later the company reports lower earnings than investors had hoped for, and the price collapses. Nursing homes, conglomerates, bowling alleys, and discount furniture stores are some of the more recent fad investments that came to a bad end. Whenever you buy a *hot stock* that everyone is talking about, watch it like a hawk. If it drops 10 percent, sell out and never look back.

Stock Prices and Book Value

A company has *assets,* which is everything it owns, and *liabilities,* which is everything it owes. *Book value* is the money that remains if the assets were sold and the debts paid off. If the company went into bankruptcy, that money would be distributed to the shareholders. Dividing book value by the number of shares outstanding gives you a number called *book value per share.*

Some market advisors call a company a "safe buy" if its shares are selling below book value; you're said to be buying the company's assets "cheap." But in fact, the stock market is far more interested in growth, profit margins, and dividends than it is in the underlying value of the company's plant. Some companies consistently sell below or just above book value. A low price relative to book value is not in itself a good reason to make an investment.

Stock Prices and the Price-Earnings Ratio

A company's total earnings over the past twelve months divided by the number of shares outstanding is its *earnings per share.* Dividing earnings per share into the current stock market price gives its *price-earnings ratio,* or *P/E.* A company that earned $3 a share over the past year and sells for $33 has a price-earnings ratio of 11. Put another way, it is selling for 11 times earnings. Investors are willing to pay $11 for each

$1 of current earnings because they think future earnings will be higher. In making their recommendations, brokers often base their P/E ratios on *estimated* earnings, on the ground that it gives you a better idea of current performance. (This will be true only if the estimate is right.)

Companies that have grown fast and are expected to continue in that track sell at relatively high price-earnings ratios—perhaps 20 to 25 times earnings, and sometimes 40, 60, or even 80. Companies with lower growth rates or whose earnings rise and fall along with economic conditions (the *cyclical stocks*) sell at lower price-earnings ratios. Ratios of all stocks generally rise as the market improves and fall as the market drops.

Studying price-earnings ratios can sometimes be helpful to investors. If a growth company is selling at the low end of its historic P/E range and there's no reason to believe it's in serious trouble, it may be a good time to buy its stock. If it carries its highest P/E ever, there's a lot more risk that the stock will drop. If the ratios for all but one of the major companies in an industry have moved up and the outlook continues good, the lagging company may soon catch up with the rest. If a stock has ballooned to 80 or 100 times earnings, it's in the grip of speculative fever and is riding for a fall. The P/E ratios of cyclical companies are a little harder to evaluate; often they're high in periods of low earnings, expecting a recovery, and low in periods of high earnings, expecting a decline. Judge the P/E ratio of a company in relation to its *own* past performance as well as to the market as a whole. Your stockbroker can lay hands on the historic price-earnings ratios of any stock that interests you.

Warning: There's no rule that a stock's price-earnings ratio will advance to its previous high. What's considered "high" or "low" depends very much on current market conditions. When investors can get only 5 percent interest from top-quality bonds, they may cheerfully pay 25 or 30 times earnings for growth stocks. But when the same bonds yield 8 or 9 percent, the stock market isn't as attractive, so growth stocks may be fully priced at only 15 times earnings. P/E ratios are useful but shouldn't be the sole basis for an investment decision. You cannot say that a stock is "cheap" just because its P/E ratio is low.

Stock Prices and Profit Margins

It's not enough to look at a company's annual report, spot a rising earnings trend, and conclude that the company is doing well. Investors are interested in *profits,* which is the amount left over after *operating costs* are paid. If operating costs are rising faster than earnings, *profit margins* are being squeezed. When that happens, a stock's price generally levels off and starts to fall. *When you make an investment, look for companies whose earnings are rising faster than costs, which means profit margins are widening.* Your broker can help you get this information from annual reports. As soon as profit margins start to level off (which you can see from the company's quarterly reports), consider selling the stock. This is not an infallible guide to stock prices (what is?), but it's a useful tool much ignored by individual investors.

Warning: Not all profits deserve the same consideration. Professional investors look at the *quality of earnings* to see if accounting manipulations have made profits appear better than they really are. For more on this, see page 616.

Stock Prices and the General Market

When the stock market is moving up, most individual stocks move with it. The same is true when the market is moving down. It's uncommon to find a stock that bucks the general market trend for very long. In a falling market, therefore, you're wise to sell even the stocks of good companies and put the money in a bank until the market looks better.

Stock Prices and News

Every day the financial pages of newspapers explain that stocks rose or fell "because" of this or that event. That's rarely so. Stockbrokers give out that explanation because it's the easiest thing to say; the true causes of each day's move are too complex to unravel. Stock prices do respond to major news events, for example the assassination of a President. But those moves, down or up, are usually temporary in nature. Once the meaning of the event is absorbed, stock prices usually resume their former trend. Generally speaking, investors should ride with broad economic trends and not be deflected by daily news events.

Stock Prices and Inflation

In general, stock prices rise when it appears likely that the *rate* of inflation is going to decline. Prices fall when the rate of inflation prepares to rise.

Conspiracy Theories

You hear it over and over, especially from investors who have lost their shirts: "The market is rigged. . . . They're stealing our money. . . . Insiders get rich while the little guy takes it on the chin." In the vast majority of cases this isn't so; you lose your money all by yourself, not because someone steals it from you. If the professionals do better than you in the market (and they do), it's that they study it full time and don't expect to make a killing on just five minutes reading of a research report.

The stock exchanges are closely watched and heavily regulated in order to keep prices fair. When abuses occur, they generally involve small, over-the-counter companies, whose prices are artificially pumped up.

For example, in a speculative market a group of dealers may conspire to trade a certain OTC stock through the accounts of their customers, increasing the price each time. As the price rises, it attracts the attention of outsiders, greedy for a hot stock. The insiders sell to the outsiders at a high price, then withdraw from the market. When the outsiders try to sell, there are no more buyers, so the price collapses. This is illegal but hard to catch in a heady market where a lot of small dealers are toying with dozens of companies. Best advice: Stay away from fast-moving, small companies unless this kind of gamble appeals to you.

Issues of small new companies can also be heartbreakers for unsophisticated investors. The Securities and Exchange Commission requires new companies to disclose their financial position in a lengthy *prospectus,* but many investors don't read the material or don't understand it when they do. A great many of these outfits have little going for them but hope, yet in speculative markets they can sell to the public at twenty or thirty times earnings. For the first few days the *underwriters* (who manage the sale of new stock to the public) and other dealers in the selling group may be able to support the price. But after that the stock is more apt to fall than to rise.

Once a wave of speculation has passed, even honest companies may suffer a price drop and not recover for many years. The stock of *cats and dogs*—marginal businesses that never should have been sold to the public at all—will become entirely worthless. The promoters often know the companies won't make it, but as long as you're crazy enough to buy, they're greedy enough to sell.

A favorite villain of many investors is the stock exchange specialist (see page 589). He can tell from his books how many people are waiting to buy or sell a stock at lower or higher prices. Since he also buys and sells the same stock from his own inventory, he's in a position to profit from that information. But the specialists are closely watched by the stock exchanges. If individual orders were being held up while the specialist bought and sold for his own account, it would soon be discovered and stopped. If stock prices move up and down too quickly, or seem to run counter to investor demand, the exchange investigates immediately. Sometimes it happens—no doubt about it—but it's not a common abuse. When it does occur, illegal specialist actions affect prices only briefly and in small amounts; it doesn't result in major market collapses.

Nowadays it's easier to manipulate prices in markets other than stock, such as commodities, put and call options, and municipal bonds. As long as you trade in companies listed on the stock exchanges, you're not likely to be mousetrapped in a price conspiracy.

A Market Cycle Theory

The rise and fall of stock prices is related to the amount of money available for investment, which in turn is influenced by the relative level of interest rates. When interest rates are high, money is attracted out of the stock market and into bonds and government securities because the income is good and the risks are small. When interest rates fall, fixed-income investments become less attractive and money flows back into stocks. Wesley McCain, a pension fund manager and author of the newsletter *Financial Markets Review,* relates interest-rate and stock-price movements this way:

Phase One

The recession is on. Business is poor and unemployment high. Because businesses don't need loans for increased production, demand for money is slack and short-term interest rates fall (short rates may be measured by the interest paid on Treasury bills). Around this time, when everyone's wringing his hands about how bad things are, the stock market makes a bottom and turns up. No one knows, however, that the bottom has been reached; in fact, most Wall Street seers are predicting that stocks will fall much further.

Phase Two

The business decline comes to an end and the recovery begins. This is signaled by a modest pickup in business and consumer demand for loans; short-term interest rates cease their decline and even rise a little. Nevertheless, the relative level of interest rates remains low, as does the relative demand for money. Hence, tremendous funds are available to the financial system, which find their way into stock and bond investments. As these funds pour into the market, stock prices rise on a broad front—the classic "easy money" rally. But because it takes place in an atmosphere of pessimism (business, though recovering, is still weak and unemployment is still high), the average investor is suspicious. Typically, he stands on the sidelines, watching stock prices go up but afraid to risk an investment of his own.

Phase Three

The recession is now clearly over and business is recovering well. Business and consumer demand for loans increases strongly. Interest rates go up some more, but not yet enough to pull money out of stocks. The market continues to rise, and individuals begin to reinvest. However, not all companies share in the good fortune, as happened in Phase Two. The money flows principally to companies with strong, expanding profit margins, whereas the stocks of other companies flatten out. Phase Three typically lasts longer than Phase Two but produces smaller percentage increases in overall stock prices.

Phase Four

Interest rates get high enough to attract money out of stocks, so stock prices start to fall. Economic activity may continue to increase a while longer, deceiving investors, who assume that booming business means that stock prices should go up. But eventually, the tremendous demand for money pushes interest rates high enough to slow down business loans, consumer loans, and mortgages, and choke off economic activity. The economy and the stock market then fall in tandem, bringing the cycle back to Phase One.

You can't predict how long each of these phases will last or how high they will carry interest rates and the stock market averages. Phase Two typically shows the largest gains. Each upward phase is typically followed by a decline before prices rise to greater heights.

Tips on Buying Stock

1. If you're a beginner, keep three-quarters of your money in savings accounts or government securities and invest with the other quarter until you learn your way around. If you keep on losing, maybe the stock market isn't for you.

2. Concentrate on the stocks of leading companies. A lot of information is available on these companies, and you can always be sure of a buyer when you want to sell.

3. Buy only when you can state a clear, simple, and sensible reason for the stock to go up. For example, "This auto insurance company got

a big rate increase, so its earnings will move out of the red." Or, "Mortgage interest rates are going down, which means good business for this leading housing company." Or, "My neighbors and I love the new products of this soap or cosmetics company, and other people will, too." If you don't have a definite reason to invest, wait until you do. As soon as that reason passes, consider selling out. Incidentally, it's not enough to say that XYZ "is a good company." You need a specific reason for current earnings to *improve*.

4. Don't buy just because you have the money. Keep it in the bank until you find a good reason to like a stock. If you can, keep extra cash on hand in order to take advantage of new opportunities as they arise.

5. In thinking about which stocks to buy, begin by choosing a promising industry. Is this a good time for auto companies? Housing? Airlines? Once you have a good business reason for liking an industry, then zero in on one of the leading companies whose future looks good.

6. Try to own stocks in several different industries so that all your eggs aren't in one basket. But don't overdiversify on a small amount of money. You can keep track of five stocks more easily than you can fifteen stocks. The more expert you become at investing, the more you can risk putting large amounts of money into one promising stock.

7. One good strategy is to invest by degrees. Put some money into a stock that interests you, and if it goes up, increase your investment. That way, you're not putting all your money at risk at once. If the stock disappoints you and goes down, you can sell without a big loss. Similarly, if you own a stock that has gone up in price but seems to be falling off, you could protect the profits by selling part of your holdings. If the stock goes back up, you still have some participation; if it falls further, you can sell the rest.

8. The best time to buy stocks is when business is terrible and everyone expects it to get worse. Stock prices will be low, with the potential for enormous gains as soon as business improves. Unfortunately, investors find it hard to commit money in that kind of climate. By the time they're convinced that business is getting better, the stock market may be up 60 or 70 percent.

The same reasoning works on the high side. An old saw is that if you ask, "How's business?" and get the reply "It couldn't be better," it's time to sell stocks, because the market goes up only on expectations of *improving* profits. The major selling opportunities come when stocks are hot, prices are high, and everyone's buying. But because everyone around you is so optimistic, the normal reaction is to buy rather than sell. Too late, you find that you bought into a market top.

Successful investing often calls for going against your basic instincts. Because of this, a step-by-step system can be very helpful. At a time of great enthusiasm, when the market seems high, try selling 10 percent of your holdings. If prices rise further, sell another 20 percent. You're still participating in the market rise if it continues, but you have limited your risk. Should the market start to decline, you'll be psychologically prepared to sell the rest of your stock fairly quickly. In times of pessimism try moving 10 percent of your investment funds into stocks. If the market continues to decline, you have only a small amount at risk, so it's not too hard to take the loss and wait for stocks to go even lower. Then test the waters again with another 10 percent investment. When the market finally starts to move up, continue to add funds to your best-performing stocks.

9. If you own a stock that's going down, your broker may advise you to *dollar-cost-average* by buying more at a lower price. This reduces your average cost; for example, if you buy one hundred shares of a stock at $30, then another one hundred at $26, you'll own two hundred shares at an average cost of $28 each. When (and if) the stock improves, you'll have a better profit. That's fine as long as you have a strong reason to believe that the stock will rise fairly soon. But maybe it dropped because it was ill chosen—in which case you'd be throwing good money after bad. You'd probably do better in the long run by cutting your losses and selling out rather than buying more at a lower price.

There's another form of dollar cost averaging that's particularly popular with mutual funds. You buy the fund on a regular basis—investing, say, $50 a month, no matter what the stock market is doing. During those periods when prices are low, your purchases lower the average cost of your shares. Also, when stock prices are low, your fixed-dollar investment will buy more shares than when prices are high, which brings the average cost of your holdings even lower. Over a long period of time this is believed to give superior investment results.

Unfortunately, you can't beat the market with a fixed system no matter how persuasive it may sound. According to a study done by *Barron's,* the investment magazine, dollar cost averaging works only while the market is in a strongly rising trend. A regular fixed investment in the market every three months produced ten-year returns averaging 10 percent a year on programs begun from the mid-1940s to the mid-1950s. After that, average ten-year returns dropped to around 5 percent a year, and in the decades ending in the mid-1970s, you'd have gotten only 1 percent a year. Many investors believed that the up-and-down markets of 1966–1978 were an ideal chance to profit via dollar cost averaging, but the *Barron's* study showed otherwise. In the long run it's the market, not the method, that counts.

10. Investors often fear to buy a stock that has already risen in price, believing that they've "missed their chance." But a stock that's going up may be the very best candidate for continued gains. By contrast, a stock that has gone nowhere in a general market rise might be a singularly poor investment. Clearly, there are times when a rising stock is "overvalued" and a low stock "undervalued," but in judging stocks it's always important to consider trend.

11. A *market order* is an order to your broker to buy or sell a stock at the going price. Usually the price won't have changed by more than a quarter- or half-point (25 or 50 cents) by the time your order is filled.

You can also place a *limit order* for a specific price. For example, if a stock sells at $30, you might place a limit order to buy at $29. If the market dips to that price, you'll get the stock at a $1 saving per share. But if it goes up, your order won't be executed; the next day you might have to pay $31 for the same stock. You can also place limit orders to sell at a specific price, again running the risk that your order won't be executed. Limit orders don't make sense for individual investors who definitely want to buy or sell. To have any chance of succeeding they must be at prices quite close to the market, and that half- or quarter-point won't make much difference to the average purchase. Better to place a market order and get the transaction over and done with. Another point: If you place a limit order to sell at, say, 35¼, and the price moves directly from 35½ to 35, your order won't be executed. It also won't be executed if there are so many orders ahead of yours that the price changes before your stock comes up. With a market order, on the other hand, you know that the stock will definitely be bought or sold that day.

12. A *stop order* is an order to sell your stock if the market reaches or passes a certain price. If you buy a stock at $30, for example, you might at the same time enter a stop order to sell if it drops to $26. That ensures that you'll keep your potential losses to a reasonable amount, without being tempted to ride the stock any further down. If you invest for quick profits, you might also give a stop order for a stock to be sold if it swings up to a certain price. Generally speaking, an order that "stops" your profits isn't a good idea. But an order that automatically sells you out when losses are still small can be a great help (see page 606).

13. When buying stocks, you don't necessarily have to pay the full purchase price. You can buy on *margin,* which means you put up part of the price and borrow the rest from your broker, paying a specified rate of interest. This gives you a shot at a greater percentage return on investment, which the investment world calls *leverage.* For example, say you have $1,000 to invest in a stock priced at $10 per share. If you buy the stock outright, you'll get one hundred shares. Should the price go to $12, you'll have made $200, or 20 percent. Now let's say that you

buy the same stock on margin. The amount you can borrow changes from time to time, but at this writing it's 50 percent of the purchase price. With your own $1,000 plus $1,000 borrowed from your broker, you can buy two hundred shares. If the price goes to $12, you've made $400, which is 40 percent on your $1,000 investment (less, of course, interest charges on the brokerage loan).

Leverage works both ways. If the stock price declines, you'll lose a larger amount than if you hadn't bought on margin. If the stock price drops far enough, you'll get a *margin call,* which means the broker wants more cash (or other securities) in order to maintain your loan. If you can't pay, the broker will sell the stock at a loss, recover his loan, and give you what's left. Buying on margin is riskier than buying out-right, but it returns a bigger profit if you guess right.

Any stock bought on margin must be left with your broker, registered in the name of the brokerage house (the *street name*). The broker may pledge *(hypothecate)* that stock as collateral for a bank loan in order to raise cash for more margin loans. But the stock is still yours, and you get all the dividends.

The Federal Reserve Board in Washington sets minimum margin requirements. When stocks are high and speculation rampant, the board raises margin requirements to perhaps 70 or 80 percent. This forces margin buyers to pay more for each stock purchase, hence cuts the amount they can buy and reduces upward price pressure on the most speculative stocks. When the market is falling or stock prices are sluggish, the Federal Reserve may lower margin requirements to 50 percent or less. *Note:* The stock exchanges may impose margins even higher than the Federal Reserve's on certain high-flying stocks—sometimes forbidding margin purchases entirely. Brokerage houses also have their own margin rules. For example, they may not accept margin purchases on low-priced stocks.

14. Stocks are often bought on the basis of *earnings projections* (predictions) by *security analysts* (professionals who research stocks). They may forecast a growing earnings trend for several years in the future, on the basis of which a high current stock price seems fully justified. But when it comes to predicting the future, analysts are just as right or wrong as the next guy. The farther ahead they look, the more likely they are to err. In general, the best earnings forecasts come from the company's own management, but even they are apt to be off the mark.

15. The most common investment strategy of the small investor is *buy and hold.* When he purchases stocks or mutual funds, he locks them up in a safe deposit box and expects them to be worth much more at some point in the future. If you buy a good mutual fund or the stock of a leading company, this usually works, as long as you have fifteen years or so to wait. But over shorter periods, such as five or ten years, the record is mixed: Sometimes stocks do well, sometimes they don't (see page 567). Middle-aged people investing for retirement in fifteen or twenty years may be successful with a strategy of buy and hold. Young parents investing for college tuition ten years hence may or may not achieve the gains they need. In general, a better strategy is to sell stocks when they start to fall (see page 604) rather than holding on in hopes they will rise again.

16. To *trade* a stock has come to mean buying and selling quickly, in hopes of a fast profit on the small price changes that flash through the market every day, week, and month. A *day trader* buys in the morning and sells in the afternoon, glad for profits of less than $1 a share. *Trading the tape* means to buy and sell according to daily price movements, with no reference at all to how well the company is doing. You can make money as a trader only if you're a good stock picker and have a lot of time to watch the market. The average investor is better off investing in longer-term market trends.

17. Typical investor errors are to sell a good stock as soon as it shows a small profit (so you won't lose it) and to hang on to a losing stock (in hopes it will come back). The art of taking losses is discussed in the next paragraph. On the profit side, try to *let profits run* by sticking with a stock as long as it's in a rising trend. What troubles investors is that a rising stock often falls a point or two before resuming its advance. At that point, you might panic and sell. But to make money in the stock market, you have to be willing to risk small, early profits in hopes of getting something better.

A useful way to deal with this problem is to set *guideposts* for yourself. If a $30 stock rises five points to $35, you might decide to sell only if it falls back to $32. Should it drop to $34 and $33, your resolve might weaken, but try to hang on. In the following days it might turn around and rise to $40. Then set a new guidepost: You'll sell if it falls to $36. You're now locking in $6 of profit (less commissions and taxes) but risking the other $4 of profit in hopes of getting something better. As long as the stock doesn't take a big drop, that approach will keep you in the game. If the price ever declines past one of your guideposts, don't hesitate to sell out.

18. A lot of stock is bought and sold on rumors and tips. Sometimes they're true, often they're not. If you buy this way, you'll probably lose more money than you make. By the time a tip gets down to the level of the average investor, it's usually too late to profit.

19. Beginners may start out investing on paper—plunging into growth stocks, cutting losses, and generally doing all the right things. But it's a lot harder to invest in real life, when your personal money is involved and your stomach aches every time the market drops. The best education is to read a few books, find yourself a stockbroker, then put a little money in the market. Start with one stock or mutual fund to find out how it feels, then add another. Put half your money in a safe place like a savings account and gradually feed the other half into the various investments you want to try. You'll have some losses, but as long as you invest gradually—keeping the dollar value small at first and playing only with money that can be replaced—you'll be all right. Only trial and error will make you a better investor.

20. *Fundamental analysis* includes all those stock evaluation methods based on judgments about the economy and the future of corporate profits. *Technical analysis* evaluates stocks entirely in terms of historical market prices, which the technicians follow on *charts*. It's their theory that all fundamental knowledge about the company is contained in past price performance, so there's no need to examine company reports. There's a lot of disagreement as to how well technical analysis works. The average investor is better off with fundamental analysis, which is much easier to understand and apply.

21. A *bull market* is one where stock prices are going up. In a *bear market* they're going down. Market commentators speak of *primary* bull and bear markets to indicate what they believe to be a major trend. You can have a temporary rise in a primary bear market, or a temporary fall in a primary bull market. If these changes of direction last only a few days, they're often called market *corrections*.

22. Shares bought and sold in multiples of 100 are called *round lots.* Amounts of less than 100 are *odd lots.* If you sell 259 shares, the 200 are treated as a round lot and the 59 as an odd lot. When you trade an odd lot, you generally pay a slightly higher commission, although a few of the big brokerage houses execute both odd lot and round lot orders for the same charge.

23. *Growth stocks* are companies whose earnings grow by a high or increasing percentage every year, holding up well even in bad times.

Glamor stocks are the best and most consistent of the growth stocks. Investors buy these companies at high price-earnings ratios, but if earnings growth unexpectedly slows down, the stocks will tumble. Growth and glamor stocks generally pay low or no dividends.

Blue chips are long-time leaders in an industry. These companies grow more slowly, but they generally pay good dividends. Investors may be tempted to hold blue chips even during years of stagnation, just because of their good name and reliable dividend income. When earnings slow, the stocks generally don't drop as fast as growth stocks.

Cyclical stocks are companies whose earnings and dividends shoot up during economic upturns and collapse during recessions. Typically, these are basic-industry and housing stocks. Broadly speaking, the higher the dividends in a good year, the higher the market risk.

Defensive stocks are those recommended during bad stock markets because they fall less in price than other stocks. Pharmaceuticals are a good example. But in bad markets it makes more sense to sell out entirely rather than switch to defensive stocks.

Income stocks are those that reliably pay a good dividend and don't fluctuate much in price. Utilities are the prime safety-and-income group.

The *Nifty Fifty* are the top fifty stocks held by institutional investors. If a stock has been on the list a long time, its potential for rapid price increases may be exhausted. But a stock newly added to the Nifty Fifty may be a good prospect; it has already attracted the attention of several leading money managers and many more may soon become interested. A list of these stocks is published regularly in *Barron's,* the investment magazine.

A *special situation* is a buy not because the company's history is so good, but because of a new development that will likely cause the price to rise. It might be an internal development, such as a marvelous new product, or an outside change, like the passage of a law that means more business for the company. During the period that investors expect improving profits the stock moves up nicely, but at the first sign that things aren't working out, the price could collapse. Brokerage houses often put out lists of special situations, but by the time you hear of them, they may not be as special as they were a few months earlier. These can be very profitable investments, but only a few work out as well as hoped.

24. Whenever you buy or sell a stock, your broker will send you a *confirmation* of the order, showing the commission and the price. Check the confirmation to see that the order was filled properly; then file it for tax purposes.

When to Sell a Losing Stock

The answer is *almost immediately,* but that's easier said than done. There are six problems associated with selling a loser:

• *The judgment problem.* When you buy a stock, you have various reasons for expecting it to rise. If it falls, that won't immediately affect your reasons: You're still sure the stock will soon fulfill its rich potential —and you may turn out to be right. But if the stock continues to fall, you've probably made a mistake. The trouble is that you're now committed to the stock, you may have talked it up to your friends, they may even have bought it on your advice. It's easier to hang on and hope it comes back than admit your judgment was wrong and sell out.

• *The optimism problem.* Investors tend to believe that any stock will come back if you hold it long enough. That's not true; some stocks vanish entirely. Others take so long to "come back" that they're terrible investments. If you buy a stock at $20, watch it drop to $10, then return to $20 in five years, you've made no money at all. In fact you've lost the opportunity to make 7 percent a year in a savings bank, or more from another stock. If the stock eventually rises to $28 in five years more, you've averaged only 4 percent a year over the ten years. Some highly speculative stocks may not rise to their old highs for ten or fifteen years, or even more. So even if it "comes back," it's a bad stock to have held.

• *The inertia problem.* Selling stocks is an effort. Not only do you have to reach the sell decision, but you're then immediately presented with new problems. Should you put the proceeds in the bank? In bonds? In another stock? It's far easier simply to keep what you have, even if it's going down.

• *The emotional problem.* If you were playing poker and had bad luck on a draw, you'd simply throw the hand in. You're not emotionally committed to sticking with that hand at the risk of higher loss. But many investors find it hard to adopt a similar, dispassionate attitude toward stocks. They tend to stick with a bad stock, even as losses mount. To some people, stocks are as hard to give up as a family pet. Yet hanging on to two or three losers can wipe out years of profit from your more fortunate selections.

• *The fear of loss.* Many investors hold on because they "can't afford" to sell. As long as they still own the stock, it's just a *paper loss,* unreal, something that will go away when the stock "comes back." But if your stock drops, it's a *real* loss, whether you sell out or not. Your net worth has declined. Anyone reluctant to take small losses will sooner or later wind up with large ones, which he can ill afford. If you're absolutely unable to accept losses, your best course is to stay away from stocks entirely.

• *False expectations.* Individual investors tend to expect good performance from every stock they pick, which is why it's so hard for them to let go. But professionals know that if you're right just half the time, you're a genius. If you can accept the fact that every one of your investment choices has at least a 50 percent chance of being wrong, it may be easier for you to concede a mistake and look for something better.

The ability to take losses while they're still small is what separates successful investors from the unsuccessful. A smart approach is to swear to yourself that you'll sell any stock or mutual fund if it drops 10 percent, no matter how strongly you believe in it. Sometimes that's a mistake; the stock may turn around and rise again. But in most cases, that rule will save you from a much larger loss. If you stop all losses at 10 percent and let all profits run (see page 602), you're on the road to being a smart investor.

What if your loss is already much larger than 10 percent? If you've held through a long decline and believe that the market is ready to start up again, you might as well hang in there a little longer to see if your stock benefits from the rise. But if you aren't that optimistic about the stock, sell some. If it keeps on declining, sell the rest and chalk it up to experience. When the market moves back, you can rebuy it if you still have hopes. Holding a loser not only runs the risk of further declines but deprives you of money for alternate investments.

You can have your losses cut automatically by entering a *stop order* with your broker when you buy (see page 600). That ends the agony of watching the papers every day and wondering whether to hold on just a little longer. It also prevents the loss from getting so big that you "can't afford" to sell.

When to Sell a Profitable Stock

Consider selling (1) anytime the stock falls 10 percent or so; (2) if the stock has been doing well for two or three years but its gains are slowing; (3) if you foresee a recession ahead (perhaps because interest rates are rising); (4) if the stock is not doing as well as others in your portfolio—indicating that it might be better to sell the weak one and add the proceeds to the stronger stocks; (5) if the company's profit margins stop widening; (6) when you find a stock you like better; (7) when the reason you had for buying the company is no longer operative, and there's no new reason in sight.

Selling Short

There's a way to make money when stock prices fall, if you make quick decisions and have the temperament to take the risk. It's called *selling short*. You borrow stock from your broker, putting up as collateral a certain percentage of the stock's price. This stock is then sold in the open market. At some later date, you buy the same stock in the open market (called *covering your position*) and use it to replace the stock you borrowed. If the stock price declined, as you hoped it would, you profit from the difference between the high selling price and the lower buying price. For example, if you sold a stock short at $15 and covered when the price declined to $8, your profit would be $7 a share, less brokerage charges and taxes. But if that stock went up instead of down and you had to cover at $20, you'd lose $5 a share. Always limit your losses by placing a *stop order to buy* the stock if its price rises by a certain amount, say 10 percent.

The amount of money you have to put up on a short sale is governed by the current margin requirements (see page 601). Short sales have to exceed some minimum dollar amount and may not be accepted on certain stocks if no shares are around to lend. If the stock price goes up and you hang on to your short position, you may get a margin call from your broker for additional cash to maintain the position; otherwise, that transaction will be closed out at its current level of loss. If the company pays a dividend during the period the stock is on loan to you, you'll owe that payment to the lender.

Shorting stocks is risky; investors generally have more losses than gains. The best shorts are generally on stocks that are declining already, not speculative stocks making new highs. It's true that those high flyers will eventually fall, but before they do, they may rise so much that they wipe your short position out.

New Issues

A *new issue* is new stock or bonds sold by a company in order to raise money. It may be an established company or a new one that's just starting to sell shares to the public (called *going public*).

The Securities and Exchange Commission requires *full disclosure* of all the pertinent facts—good and bad—about a company whenever a new issue is sold. This comes in a booklet called a *prospectus,* which every investor should read. The SEC checks the prospectus for general accuracy but does not "okay" any stock. A perfectly dreadful company is free to sell you worthless stock as long as the prospectus reveals how dreadful it really is. If you don't read the prospectus, that's your lookout, not the SEC's. Small companies selling limited amounts of stock don't have to go through a full SEC filing. Instead, they're allowed a shorter form of disclosure under *Regulation A.* Be warned that when you buy a "Reg A" issue, you're not getting all the facts. Many dubious enterprises deliberately go public via a Reg A in order to avoid telling all the bad news to prospective investors.

Investment Clubs

Many people get together to invest jointly through an investment club. You all put up a certain amount of money every month and meet to decide which stocks and bonds to buy and sell. Some legal work is needed in order to establish a way of apportioning profits and losses and providing a way for members to quit; for advice, write to the National Association of Investment Clubs, 1515 E. Eleven Mile Rd., Royal Oak, Mich. 48068. Investment clubs can be a pleasant and interesting social experience. But they aren't much help if you're all amateurs. Successful clubs include experienced brokers or investors, who can give market guidance.

Monthly Investment Plans

At some banks or brokerage houses you can invest a certain dollar amount every month in the stocks of specified companies. This encourages thrift but is no guarantee of good investment results. If the market is in a rising trend, regular investments will be profitable. But during a period when the market rises and falls with no overall advance, you generally won't make money. You'd do better to put a fixed amount of money into the bank every month and buy stocks only when the time seems favorable. When you start a monthly investment plan, you generally sign a "contract" to contribute a certain amount per month, but it's not obligatory and you can quit at any time.

Employee Stock Purchase Plans

Many large companies make it possible for employees to buy their own stock through regular payroll deductions. There's no brokerage commission, and sometimes you're sold the stock at a discount from market price. This is a splendid opportunity during periods when your company is in an upswing. If you start buying when company profits decline and the stock price is relatively low, your investment should increase considerably in value when conditions improve. But if you buy at a time of peak profits, the stock may soon start to decline. Don't abandon your market judgment just because it's your own company. Look for a favorable time to buy and cancel the stock purchase program when the stock price gets too high for your taste. The stock of your own company should be sold just as freely as the stock of any other company if it drops 10 percent or so.

Because of the ease and attractiveness of stock purchase plans, many employees invest mainly in their own company's stock. You'd be wiser, however, to *diversify*. Sell some of your company stock and use the proceeds to invest in other industries, or a mutual fund.

Some companies have tax-deferred employee savings programs, where employees put up a certain amount per month and it's matched by the company. These sums are put in an investment pool managed by a stock market professional. The pool may contain a good chunk of company stock but also includes the stock of many other companies and industries. This is generally an excellent way to invest—not to be missed if such a plan is available.

Where to Get Information on Stocks and Investing

1. *Your stockbroker.* His firm's research department publishes reports on many companies; he may also have some general pamphlets on investment techniques. In addition, he can get current information on any particular stock that interests you.

2. *The company itself.* Ask for the most recent annual report, a year's worth of quarterly reports, and, if a new issue of stock or bonds was sold recently, a copy of the prospectus. Your broker or the public library can get you the company's address.

3. *Books.* There are a great many good and interesting books on investment techniques available in libraries and bookstores.

4. *Investment courses*—given by big brokerage houses or through your community's adult education program.

5. *The New York Stock Exchange's Investor Information Kit,* five useful pamphlets available for $2.50. Write to the exchange at 11 Wall St., New York, N.Y. 10005.

6. *Business and investor publications,* such as *Forbes, Barron's,* and *The Wall Street Journal.*

7. *Stock market letters.*

A special word is needed about stock market letters. These are often expensive ($100 and up), but if they provide sound analysis and good stock picks, they're well worth the money. The writers of these letters may advertise in such investor publications as *Barron's;* look for one that has been around for a while, which indicates some measure of success. Market letters publish on a regular schedule and therefore must have something to say every time, not all of it of equal value. The best way to use a market letter is wait until the writer has a really strong opinion about the market or a particular stock, and pay attention to that. Give special weight to the stocks he mentions over and over with enthusiasm: Those are his best ideas.

Some letters concentrate on *market timing* (forecasting when the general stock market averages are likely to move up and down); others combine timing advice with specific stock selections. Unfortunately, writers of market letters often neglect to tell you when to sell a stock for fear of offending whatever contacts they have developed with the company's management. If a stock suddenly isn't mentioned for several issues, you should wonder why. Give the writer a call; he may tell you over the phone what he's reluctant to say in print. If you find you don't trust the letter or aren't making money on its suggestions, cancel it; either the letter is poor or you haven't the knowledge to use it well. Cancel a letter whose writer refuses to acknowledge a mistake or keeps insisting that sooner or later the market will see things his way.

You have to give some study to the stock market if you expect to profit. You're kidding yourself if you think you can put some money into stocks without knowing what you're doing, and wind up ahead. The stock market can be very profitable, but its profits are yielded to those who work at it, not to those who expect something for nothing.

Help from the Stock Exchanges

Investors with questions about their stocks, their brokers, or the technical side of investing can turn for help to the New York and American Stock Exchanges. As a general rule, you're better off getting a question answered at your brokerage house because you can sit down and talk the matter over until you're satisfied. But if your broker can't help, the exchanges will do their best to please. Here are the kinds of questions you can ask them:

• *Problems with a listed corporation.* Perhaps you didn't get your dividend on time; or the company merged and you haven't heard from the successor corporation; or you're no longer getting annual reports. Depending on the nature of the problem, the exchange will either tell you where to write or perhaps write to the corporation on your behalf.

• *Problems with brokers who are members of the exchange.* Maybe you haven't received securities you believe you own; you think your broker has behaved unethically; or the brokerage house hasn't sent you all the interest and dividends you think you're entitled to. The first step is to try to solve the matter with the head of the brokerage office, but if that doesn't work, write to the exchange his firm belongs to. These letters are generally turned over to the compliance division, which looks into the merits of the complaint. If you have a money claim against your broker, send copies of your confirmation slips and other documents that support your story. The exchanges provide arbitration for disputes between customers and members. The argument need not be over listed stocks. If you're having problems with an options trade, bonds, or unlisted stocks, the compliance division will help as long as the broker is a member of the exchange.

• *Old securities.* The New York Stock Exchange will send you an instruction letter on how to find out if old stocks and bonds have any value. If the search becomes too complex for you, the letter refers you to stock-tracing services that will do the job for a small fee.

• *Recently delisted securities.* If a company falls below the financial minimums required by the exchange or is bought by another company, its stock will be removed from the exchange, or *delisted.* If you missed the event but suddenly can't find your stock in its accustomed place, the exchange can give you the company's current address.

• *Bankruptcies.* If you're holding the securities of a bankrupt corporation, the exchange can often send you the names of the trustees in bankruptcy who can answer your questions. Similarly, they can put you in touch with a failed or inactive brokerage house if you have some unfinished business. Write to the exchange that once listed the stock or to which the broker once belonged.

• *Information on industry practices.* The exchanges will answer questions on such matters as the specialist system, odd-lot practices, and trading procedures. However, they do not give advice on the kind of investments to make or when to buy and sell stocks.

• *Where to place an order.* The New York Stock Exchange's Investors Service Bureau publishes a free directory of the member firms that accept small orders. It also includes the names of brokers abroad who are NYSE members.

• *Technical questions.* The exchanges can give you information on such things as how to transfer stocks into a different name. Questions on the trading of a particular stock are referred to the pertinent trading unit. Tax problems are referred to the Internal Revenue Service.

The New York Stock Exchange will send you a free bibliography of investment books and a flyer on NYSE publications; write to the NYSE Investors Service Bureau, 11 Wall St., New York, N.Y. 10005. At the American Stock Exchange, write to the Inquiries Department, 86 Trinity Place, New York, N.Y. 10006. For problems with over-the-counter brokers affiliated with the National Association of Securities Dealers, write to the NASD Enforcement Department, 1735 K St. N.W., Washington, D.C. 20006.

Reading the Stock Quotes

Stocks traded on both the New York and American Stock Exchanges are quoted the same way in the newspapers. An example is shown on the next page, from *The Wall Street Journal.* They're called *composite quotes,* because they include prices from other exchanges around the country.

To read the quotes, you first have to know how your stock is ab-

52 Weeks High	Low	Stock	Div.	Yld %	P-E Ratio	Sales 100s	High	Low	Close	Net Chg.
31	22¾	GnSignl	.80	2.5	12	187	u31¾	30⅝	31¾	+ ⅞
7⅞	5¾	GnSteel	.05e	.6	8	41	7⅞	7⅝	7¾	− ⅛
33½	28⅛	GTE	2.24	7.7	7	1046	29⅜	29⅛	29⅛	− ⅛
35⅜	30⅝	GTE	pf 2.50	7.8	—	2	31⅞	31⅝	31⅞	+ ¾
29⅝	26⅛	GTE	pf 2.48	9.5	—	17	26¼	26⅛	26⅛	− ⅜
29⅞	21¾	GTire	1.30	4.8	5	255	27⅛	26¾	27⅛	+ ¼
8⅛	3⅜	Genesco	—	—	—	142	7	6⅝	7	+ ¼
26	21⅝	Genstr	1.48	5.6	5	11	u26½	25⅞	26½	+ ⅞
38⅝	29⅝	GenuPt	1.10	2.8	16	136	u38⅞	38½	38⅝	—
32⅜	23½	GaPac	1	3.7	10	993	27⅜	26¾	27⅛	+ ⅜
29⅛	26	GaPw	pf2.52	9.6	—	46	26¼	d25¾	26¼	—
30¾	27½	GaPw	pf2.75	9.8	—	3	28⅛	27⅞	28	+ ⅛
89¾	78	GaPw	pf7.72	9.9	—	z100	78	78	78	−1
25⅜	20	Geosrc	.51e	2.1	8	56	24¼	23⅞	24	—
36¾	25⅞	Gerber	1.50	4.7	11	141	32¼	31¾	32	—
206¼	146	Getty	4.80	2.9	11	54	168½	167	168¼	+ ½
42⅜	40¾	Getty	wi	—	—	1	u42½	42½	42½	+ ⅛
19	18	Getty	pf1.20	6.7	—	1	18	18	18	—
9	7⅛	GiantPC	.60	6.6	304	22	u 9⅛	8⅞	9⅛	+ ¼
17¾	8¾	GibrFn	.60	3.6	5	2111	17⅝	16¾	16⅞	− ⅜
16¼	9⅛	GidLew	.70	4.5	6	201	15¾	15⅜	15⅝	+ ¼
18½	13¼	GiffdHill	.90	5.0	7	48	18⅛	17⅞	18⅛	+ ½
30	23¼	Gillette	1.50	5.2	11	1849	29	28⅜	29	+ ⅜

breviated. For example, the first line above is for "GnSignl," which is General Signal. Most company abbreviations are easy to figure out—if in doubt, ask your broker. Here's an explanation of the other headings, reading from left to right:

52 Weeks High/Low—Tells you how high and how low the stock price has been for the past year.

Div.—The annual rate of dividends per share, based on the last quarterly or semiannual dividend. For GnSignl, it was 80 cents a share. There are often small letters after the dividend amount; these indicate special circumstances—for example, that the dividend was paid partly in cash and partly in stock, or that a quarterly dividend was omitted at the last dividend meeting. "Pf" indicates the dividend on preferred stock. Explanations for all the letters are given in footnotes, at the end of the listings.

Yld %—The current percentage return on investment. For GnSignl, an 80-cent dividend on a share selling at $31.75 gives a 2.5 percent yield.

P-E Ratio—The current ratio of selling price to earnings over the past twelve months. This figure means nothing in itself but can be helpful if compared with the company's historic performance in various markets and with other companies in the industry (see page 592). GnSignl is selling for twelve times earnings.

Sales 100s—The number of shares bought and sold that day, *in thousands.* For GnSignl, the volume was "187," or 187,000 shares. A small "z" before the number means sales *in full;* for example, "GaPw," Georgia Power, traded "z100," which means only 100 shares changed hands all day. Rising volume tends to push a stock farther along its present price path. A rising price on rising volume is often a good sign; a falling price on rising volume, a bad one. Declining volume, on the other hand, may precede a change in direction. You can also use volume numbers to see how popular the stock is. Generally speaking, you're safer with a stock that does a large business every day, because its price will usually move up and down in orderly fashion. A *thinly traded* issue, where only a few shares change hands, can move up or down more sharply on the actions of just a few shareholders.

High/Low—These record a stock's high and low prices for a day. A "u" indicates a new high for the year, and a "d" a new low.

Close—The price of the stock at the end of the trading day. GnSignl closed at 31¾, which is $31.75 a share.

Net Change—How the price changed from the previous day. For GnSignl, it's +⅞, which means up seven-eighths of a point, or 91 cents. Other stocks show minuses, which means they lost since the day before. A row of dots,..... (here a dash), indicates that the price was unchanged.

Over-the-counter stocks are quoted differently from those traded on the New York and American Stock Exchanges. On the exchanges there's one firm price for every stock; but over the counter there are only representative buy-and-sell prices, from the various dealers who make a market in the stock (see page 590). Reading left to right:

Stock	Div.	Sales 100s	Bid	Asked	Net Chg.
Charles Rv	.24	5	16¾	17¾	− ¼
Charmg Sh	.30	18	16¼	17	—
Chart Hous	.72	175	23⅛	23⅝	—
ChathamM	.80	6	11¾	12¼	—
Chef Pierre	In	20	16¼	16¾	—
ChemNuc	.05d	23	7½	8¼	—
ChemedC	1.20	100	25	26	+ ½
ChLeamn	.40b	25	14¾	15¾	—
Chemineer	.36	3	11½	12	—
Ch NW	Trans	88	9½	9⅞	+ ¼
ChrisSec	3.95b	26	115	118	− 3
ChubbCrp	1.60	271	34⅜	34⅞	− 1
CinciFclCo	.80	46	17¼	17¾	—
Circl Inc	1.27b	3	15½	16	− ⅛
CitizenFid	1.60	33	36¾	37¾	+ ¾
CitzSthnCp	.96	6	15	16	− ½
CitSoNBGa	.24	317	4⅝	5	—

Stock and *Div.*—The name of the company and its dividend, quoted the same way as on the major exchanges.

Sales in 100s—Sales in thousands. Charles Rv, for example, traded 5,000 shares. Notice the much smaller trading volume than on the major exchanges, which is one of the reasons the OTC markets are considered more speculative.

Bid—The approximate amount that market makers will pay for the stock—in other words, the price if you want to sell.

Asked—The approximate amount that market makers are asking for stock they own—in other words, your price if you want to buy. The asked price is always higher than the bid price.

Net Change—The stock's change in price from the day before.

Reading a Financial Report

In recent years the government has pressed for more and better disclosure in financial reports. Companies always put the best possible face on the facts, but the careful reader can at least get a glimmer of what's really going on. Before you make an investment, write to the company for the most recent annual report and any subsequent quarterly reports. Once you've bought the stock, always read the reports as they're mailed to you, as a clue to whether to continue holding the investment. Only experienced stock analysts can wring all the juice out of an annual report, but certain key facts are accessible to every investor who bothers to look.

1. *The president's letter.* This gives a general summary of why earnings performed as they did. The tone is always upbeat, but weaknesses will be mentioned as well as the strengths; for example, watch for sentences starting with phrases like "Except for," "Despite the," "Improvements are expected in." The president always expects better next year, but ask yourself whether you think the soft spots are capable of reacceleration or whether they're likely to go nowhere—perhaps because a better product has come on the market or because government funding for that line of activity has slowed down.

Two tips: If the president brags about his current expansion program and the country is in a general economic boom, the expansion may be ill timed. Business is characterized by ups and downs; on the next down cycle, that big expansion may become surplus capacity, putting a serious drag on earnings. Overoptimism gets a lot of companies—even big, seasoned companies—in trouble. A major expansion may signal an end to profit increases for a while, hence a time to sell.

Also think twice about companies that expand every year by buying other companies, rather than through internal growth. The new acquisitions put earnings up but may mask weaknesses in the management of the original company or slowed demand for its products. A lot of acquisitions may also weaken the company financially, by adding too much debt. A pattern of buying companies will usually give the stock a boost for a while, but if the basic businesses aren't also healthy, that stock is riding for a fall.

2. *The accountant's letter, at the end of the report.* If the company's accountants have no objection to the financial data, the letter will state simply that the results are in accord with "generally accepted accounting principles." This is the case with the vast majority of corporate reports. But if the accountants are worried about some of the company's evaluations, they'll certify the report "subject to" certain items working out the way the company expects. That's a bad sign; it means that the accountants don't trust the company's figures. Normally, a company and its accountants try to negotiate their differences. So if a "subject to" actually makes it into the annual report, it's usually pretty serious.

3. *The financial data.* These tables don't mean much to the average investor, but there are some points that are easy to check in deciding whether to buy, hold, or sell the stock. One thing: You generally can't make sense of financial data based on one report alone. You'll have to compare it with several back reports, available from the company or from your broker.

• *The balance sheet* shows the company's total financial position as of a particular day. On the left side are the company's *assets*—everything it owns; on the right side, the *liabilities*—everything it owes. *Current liabilities* are the debts due within a year, which will be paid out of current assets. Look for significant changes in any of these items, and footnotes to explain why. Assets include *accounts receivable,* which is money owed to the company. If this number increases sharply in a period of tight money, the company's customers are paying more slowly and the firm may have to borrow at high interest rates to tide itself over.

Watch what's happening to *inventories*—raw materials or finished products on hand. If inventories grow at a faster rate than sales (look for sales on the *income statement,* see below), the company is producing more than it's selling and may have to cut back. It's best to have a fairly constant ratio between the value of finished goods and sales. Regarding companies that stockpile a lot of raw materials, such as copper or soybeans: They may show big profits during an inflationary period, due to the inflated value of their inventories. But when raw materials prices start to fall, as they do when business slows, the pared inventory value will hurt profits.

The difference between current assets and current liabilities is the *net working capital,* an enormously important figure for stockholders to watch. If working capital shrinks, the company may not have the money it needs to reinvest for future growth. You want a company whose working capital is expanding steadily. *Tip:* Check the income statement to see if total capital is increasing because of earnings (good) or because of new financing—loans or bond issues. Raising money through debt is fine for new or expanding companies, but in mature companies it may be a sign of poor management or weak business.

• *Stockholder's equity,* the difference between total assets and liabilities, is the dollar value of what the stockholders own. To the extent that earnings grow and are retained in the business, this number should grow every year.

• *The income statement, or statement of profit and loss,* records the activities of the company over the past year. Basically, this shows where the money came from and where it went. Look first at *net sales:* Are they still rising nicely, or has the *rate of increase* slowed? It's not enough that sales have risen over the last reporting period; you want them to have risen at a faster rate than they did before. When sales increases start to slow, so may the increase in the stock price—suggesting that it may be time to sell. The other side of the coin is that when the rate of decline in sales starts to slow toward the end of a recession, it may indicate that the stock is a buy. Another thing to check is the *operating costs*—the money paid out in order to keep the business running.

If income from sales is rising faster than operating costs, profit margins are expanding—an excellent sign. However, if costs are rising faster, profit margins are being squeezed, which generally forecasts a falling stock price. Profit margins are a key factor for investors to watch from quarter to quarter. It's not shown on the income statement as such; you have to make the calculations yourself. But it's perhaps the most rewarding piece of analysis you can do.

It also works on the downside: When sales fall at a slower rate than operating costs, profit margins widen, an indication that the stock may be ready to rise.

The one number that investors most commonly check is *net profit,* or *net profit per share*; unfortunately, this can also be the most deceptive. For example, in a period of slowing sales, management may show a big profit increase by selling off a plant or other asset. But this is obviously something it can't do in every reporting period; sooner or later they have to let the bad news about slowing sales show through. Sometimes companies change accounting methods or engage in other fiddles to show profits; fortunately, these things are mentioned in the footnotes, so the close reader will know what he's up against. If you don't understand the footnotes, ask your stockbroker to explain. Whenever profit gains have come from one-shot sources rather than increases in sales, there's some doubt that the increases will be sustained for another quarter—hence there's a strong possibility that the stock price will fall.

Some companies are even more precise about their income, by including a *statement of sources and uses of funds.* This eliminates some of the accounting items normally found on the income statement (such as depreciation, which is a sum subtracted from earnings to account for wear and tear on the company's machinery but doesn't actually represent a loss of cash). Here, you'll see with great clarity what the company is doing with its money, and whether its cash position is improving or shrinking. Unfortunately, companies with financial weaknesses are not likely to include this statement in their financial report.

Ten Resolutions for Investors

The columnist Sam Schulsky once printed the following ten resolutions from John Magee, one of his favorite no-nonsense market observers:

1. I will not make a donkey of myself in the broker's board room, at the club, or at home by proclaiming where the market averages will stand by March 31, mid-year, or any other future time.

2. I will not alienate my friends and antagonize my family by reminding the world on every possible occasion how right I was about the upturn or downturn.

3. I will keep in mind that my broker is my agent. I will make use of any help he can give me, but I will make decisions myself and accept the responsibility for whatever may transpire.

4. When I buy a stock, I will not mobilize all the good news to make it look pretty. I will try to consider both the favorable and unfavorable angles.

5. I will not close out a stock position that is doing well for me for no other reason than that I have a profit. I will not cut short my gains in a good situation.

6. I will not hang on to a stock that is persistently going against me. I will limit my loss and close out any position that seems to have gone really bad before I am in danger of serious trouble.

7. I will not be swayed or panicked by news flashes, rumors, tips, or well-meant advice.

8. I will not put all my eggs in one basket; nor will I be swept off my feet to plunge into some unknown or low-priced stock on a purely emotional basis.

9. I will not attempt to tell the market what a stock ought to be worth. I will try to understand what the market has to tell me about what people are willing to pay for it.

10. I will never forget that I am not in the market primarily to prove (to my broker, my friends, my spouse, etc.) that I am smarter than everybody else; but to protect, and, if possible, to augment, my capital.

INVESTING IN BONDS

Bonds Defined

A bond is an IOU. When you "buy" a new bond from a company (or a government unit), you are actually lending it money. The bond is a promise to repay that money on a certain date. You get a specified rate of interest on your money, with payments usually made twice a year. For example, on a $1,000 bond paying 8 percent ($80) interest, you'd receive a $40 check every six months. *Intermediate-term* bonds mature in five to ten years; *long-term* bonds, in 20 to 30 years.

Bondholders are entitled to receive their interest payments before the company (or government) spends money on anything else, which is the reason they're considered safe. In the event of bankruptcy, bondholders must be paid in full before stockholders can expect any money at all.

Buying and Selling Bonds

What if you own a bond and want your money back before it matures? The company is not usually obliged to redeem it ahead of time. But you can generally sell the bond in the open market to another investor (ask any stockbroker to help). There's one risk: You won't necessarily get what you paid for it. Most bonds come in denominations of $1,000, but if you decide to sell before maturity, you may get more or less than $1,000, depending on conditions in the bond market (see page 620).

When you buy bonds, you can choose among any of the many issues currently available in the open market. Or you can buy bonds newly issued by the company. Which is better depends on your financial situation. Some pay more current income than others; some promise a big profit when you cash them in; some mature on the exact date you know you're going to want the money. From the following discussion you should be able to figure out which is the best for you.

When you buy a new bond, the issuing company pays the broker's fee; on older bonds you pay it. Generally speaking, the minimum bond investment is $5,000 to $10,000 (a $1,000 purchase is too small for most brokers to bother with, and generally not economic for a purchaser either). Buying and selling costs are higher on small transactions than on amounts of $100,000 and up. But in any case, the commission on bond transactions is lower than the commission on stocks.

One important thing for individuals to look for is liquidity—the ability to sell a bond quickly, if need be, without having to accept a big cut in price. Deal only in the bonds of leading issuers that have a large and ready resale market: major companies, the federal government, and municipalities whose bonds are considered desirable. Question your broker closely on the saleability of any bond he recommends to you. Small investors may find it advantageous to sell through a major, nationwide brokerage firm, which can generally find a buyer for your bond more readily than a smaller firm can.

Bond Prices, Interest Rates, and Yields

In understanding the bond market there are three main elements to consider: The *price* of the bond itself, the *interest rate* (or coupon rate) it pays; and your actual *return on investment* (yield).

A bond is issued at a specific face value, generally $1,000, and a specific interest rate. An 8 percent rate means that you're entitled to 8 percent of $1,000, or $80 a year. Traditionally, bonds carried a page of coupons, each one entitling the owner to an interest payment; when payment date arrived, you clipped the coupon and exchanged it for cash at a bank. Nowadays, companies will mail your interest checks automatically, but the term *coupon rate* still survives.

The general level of interest rates in the financial markets does not stay the same for the life of the bond. When business picks up, demand for credit rises, and the inflation rate increases, bond interest rates also increase. When business slows, credit-demand eases, and inflation falls, bond rates decrease. In one year's business climate, a company may be able to attract investors by offering bonds at 8 percent, but the next year the going rate may be 8½ percent, or 7½ percent. Changes in interest rates affect the market value of the bonds you already own.

Assume, for example, that you own a $1,000 bond at 8 percent, which means an interest payment of $80 a year. If long-term interest rates move up, the next bonds the company sells may come out at a coupon rate of 8½ percent, or $85 a year. What does this do to the older bond?

Its value will fall, from the $1,000 you paid for it to perhaps $960 on a thirty-year bond. The interest payment is still $80 a year, but $80 on a $960 investment gives a return of close to 8½ percent, which is the going market rate. The interest payment, as a percentage of the bond's current value, is called the *current yield.*

If you sold your $1,000 bond for $960, you'd take a $40 loss. The person who bought it for $960, held it until maturity, and turned it in for $1,000 would have a $40 gain. The value of that gain is figured into the bond's market price. The *total return* to an investor—counting interest rate and gain (or loss) in price—is called the *yield to maturity.*

The rule, then, is that when interest rates rise, bond prices fall. But this is relevant only if you have to sell the bond before maturity. As long as you hold it to maturity, you'll get your full investment back.

Assume, now, that you own a $1,000 bond paying 8 percent, or $80, and that long-term interest rates fall. The next bonds that the company sells come out at a coupon rate of 7½ percent, or $75 a year. What happens to the older bond? The value moves up—to around $1,035, because an $80 interest payment on $1,035 is close to 7½ percent, the current level of market rates.

If you sold your $1,000 bond for $1,035, you'd have a $35 gain. The person who bought it at that price and held it to maturity would get only $1,000 when the bond was redeemed, a $35 loss. That loss is figured into the market price in calculating a competitive yield to maturity.

The other part of the rule, then, is that when interest rates fall, bond prices rise. When a bond is selling at more than $1,000, it's said to be at a *premium.* When it's selling for less, it's at a *discount.* Anyone who holds his bond to maturity will be able to turn it in for face value. But if you sell before maturity, you may get more or less than you paid for the bond, depending on what has happened to interest rates since you first bought.

Bonds and Risk

Bonds are not necessarily a "safe" investment. There are two forms of risk: (1) If you have to sell before the bond matures, the price may be different from what you paid. You might make or lose money on the transaction, depending on market conditions at the time. (2) Inflation may erode the purchasing power of your fixed interest payment.

Risk and the Short-Term Investor

You may not realize that bond prices can fluctuate as rapidly as stocks. As measured by the Merrill Lynch Taxable Bond Index, the total return from bonds fell at an annual rate of 23.3 percent in the second quarter of 1974, then rose 32.7 percent in the fourth quarter. With wild price swings like that, you can't very well park your money in bonds for short periods of time and expect to get it all back when you sell. The only "safe" short-term investments would be savings accounts or short-term government securities (see page 628).

Risk and the Longer-Term Investor

What if you want steady income with a guarantee of your money back at maturity? Are bonds a good buy? Given the history of bond yields from 1945 to 1980, the answer would have to be "no." Bond prices generally declined, and increased inflation destroyed the value of interest payments. Bonds in the early 1960s were selling at fixed, thirty-year interest payments as low as 4½ to 5 percent. If an investor had to sell those bonds today, he might suffer a 35 to 40 percent loss. If the average rate of price inflation increases to even higher levels than we have today, bonds will remain a bad buy.

But every great inflation of the past has come to an end—not all at once, but gradually, reluctantly changing trend and starting down. Should that happen again, the outlook for long-term bond purchases will change dramatically. When inflation slows, long-term interest rates come down and bond prices gradually rise.

If you buy bonds, and it turns out that—in ten or fifteen years—inflation is lower than it is today, you'll profit two ways: (1) You'll have locked in several years of high-interest income that won't be available from newer bonds (see "Call Protection," page 623); and (2) your bonds will rise in price, so they can be sold for a profit.

One important point for the long-term investor: There's small, initial risk in buying bonds on a bet that long-term inflation will decline. Because of today's high interest payments, you can lose a little on the bond and still be ahead. If inflation eventually does decline, you'd profit handsomely—so the risk may be worth taking. But by all means buy bonds that can be sold easily, in case you're wrong and want to sell out fast.

How Long to Invest?

Long-term bonds, maturing in twenty to thirty years, generally have higher investment yields than intermediate-term bonds, maturing in five to ten years. That's because long-term holders run more risk. If the rate of inflation increases, the price of long-term bonds will fall more rapidly than the price of intermediates. Therefore, intermediates are a better hedge against the chance of renewed inflation. But if inflation moderates in the years ahead, long-term bonds will have a higher payoff.

Sinking Funds

Corporate and utility bonds have *sinking funds*—money set aside to redeem the bond issue on a predetermined schedule. Starting perhaps five or ten years from the date of issue, a certain percentage of the bonds outstanding will be redeemed every year. If bond prices have fallen, the company will try to retire its quota of bonds each year by buying them in the open market. But if bond prices are up, the corporation will redeem (or *call*) the bonds by lottery—drawing the numbers of certain bonds and requiring the holders to turn them in. You're paid face value for the bond, but you no longer have that nice, high-interest investment.

Refunding

If interest rates fall, a corporation may sell a new bond issue and use the proceeds to redeem certain older, high-interest bonds—a process called *refunding*. With long-term bonds, you generally get ten-year protection against this risk. But if the company can raise the money some way besides selling a new bond issue, it may be able to call in your high-interest bonds at any time. If a bond is called via refunding, you're generally paid the face value plus a small premium to compensate for the loss of your high-interest investment. But that's not as profitable as having a high-interest payment locked in for twenty years.

How to Give Yourself Call Protection

This is essential protection for the long-term bond investor. If inflation falls in the years ahead, and interest rates decline, corporations will call in their older, high-interest bonds and replace them with bonds paying lower interest. You would then lose that steady, lucrative payment you thought you had locked in for twenty or thirty years.

Bonds are generally sold with *call protection*, which means that the company won't call the bond in for a specified number of years. But most utilities offer only five-year protection, which isn't worth much to the investor wanting guaranteed high income for a long time. Industrial bonds tend to offer ten-year call protection, which is better. Neither type of bond, however, may be satisfactory to the investor who wants his payments guaranteed for an even longer time.

There are three ways to get truly long-term call protection:

1. Buy *deeply discounted* corporate bonds. These are bonds selling for sharply less than face value. Typically, they were issued many years ago at low interest rates—hence have lost value in the market. Your current income is lower with these bonds, but because of the low interest rate, they're not likely to be called away. When the bonds are redeemed at maturity, you'll get a large capital gain. Counting the capital gain, the average annual yield to maturity will be about as high as the current level of interest rates.

2. Buy *government bonds*—not Savings Bonds, but long-term twenty- and thirty-year bonds sold by the U.S. government through banks and brokers. Their interest rate is slightly less than that of corporate bonds, which is the reason so many investors prefer corporates. But most government bonds give call protection of twenty years or more. By investing in governments, you're accepting a slightly lower current yield in return for the right to hold the bonds for a long time. Fifteen years from now, your government bonds may still be paying you $7\frac{1}{2}$ percent, while people who bought corporates have had them replaced with issues paying much less. If inflation accelerates, government bonds can be sold quickly and easily, to limit your loss.

3. Among tax-exempt securities, *general obligation* bonds generally provide long periods of call protection, whereas revenue bonds may be callable in relatively short periods. For a full discussion of the various types of municipals, see page 630.

Bonds and Income

The highest current income is paid by bonds selling at a premium (more than $1,000). But if you have corporate bonds, there's a higher risk that these bonds will be called away by the company if interest rates fall. The next highest income is paid by newly issued bonds. The lowest current income is paid by discount bonds (selling at less than $1,000); but these bonds produce a capital gain when they're redeemed at maturity for face value. If interest rates fall, discount bonds are less likely to be called away, so investors can use them to lock in today's high yields.

Bond Quality

Two companies rate the safety and investment quality of bonds—Moody's and Standard & Poor's. Their ratings, down to the
Baa/BBB level, are shown in the box on the
right. Ratings continue below those levels,
but such bonds are not considered of investment quality. A common term for lower-
rated issues is *junk bonds*—of interest to
speculators, but generally not to serious
investors.

Moody's	S&P
Aaa	AAA
Aa	AA ($\pm$)
A1*	
A	A ($\pm$)
Baa1*	
Baa	BBB ($\pm$)
*Municipal bonds only	

Quality ratings translate directly into bond prices and yields. A top-
quality bond is a "safer" investment, hence it can be sold at a slightly
lower interest rate or yield than a bond of lesser quality. Companies or
municipalities that have only a Baa or A rating have to offer higher
interest rates to compensate investors for the increased risk. In poor
markets lower-quality bonds tend to fall faster in price than higher-
quality bonds.

Sometimes, bonds of higher and lower quality sell at about the same
yield because of special factors of supply and demand. In that case it's
always wise to buy the better quality, since the market is offering no
extra compensation for taking higher risks. But when lower-quality
bonds offer attractively higher yields, the choice is yours: Do you want
the security of a portfolio of Aaa/AAA bonds, or do you want the higher
income that comes from accepting slightly lower ratings? Maybe you
want a little of each.

In any event, it's important to realize that there are no free lunches
in the bond market. If a particular bond is selling at a much higher yield
than other issues, it's because investors consider the bond less secure.
If you accept the risk and the bond does indeed pay off in the end (as
most investment-quality bonds do), you'll have received a higher income from your investment than you would have by sticking with
top-rated issues. But the lower-rated bonds may have given you a few
bad moments along the road to redemption.

One important point about quality: When you're speaking about
investment-grade bonds—those rated from Aaa to Baa—"lower quality" does not mean unsafe. There are occasional, spectacular bankruptcies and defaults. But practically all the bonds in this range pay off. In
deciding between Aaa and A, you're balancing the difference in income
(which for small investors may not be much) against the security of

knowing that even if this country goes into a prolonged slowdown, your money is invested with the very best companies and cities, hence is probably safe. If you should ever want to sell your bonds—perhaps to cut losses during an inflationary upsurge—you'll take less of a loss with top-quality bonds than with those of lower quality.

Bottom-quality bonds—those rated from Ba/BB down to C—are speculations, with the risk increasing as the quality falls. You can get extremely high yields from bottom-of-the-barrel bonds, but those payments should be viewed as compensation for the pain and suffering of wondering whether the company will default on its debt or go bankrupt. You can even speculate in bonds that are already in default. This can be a profitable arena for sophisticated investors, guided by a knowledgeable broker. But for most of us, low-quality bonds aren't worth the worry.

Methods of Ownership

Bearer bonds are payable to the bearer, whoever he may be. If you have a bearer bond and lose it, the interest can be collected by anyone who finds it (unless you report the loss and the finder is caught). The interest on bearer bonds has to be collected by clipping coupons and mailing them to the company, since the company has no record of your ownership. Any bearer bonds you own should be kept in a safe deposit box, against loss or theft, or left with your broker for safekeeping. Most municipal and federal government bonds are in bearer form, and many older corporate bonds as well.

Registered bonds, on the other hand, are registered in the name of the owner. This gives you some protection against theft or loss and gives the issuer protection against forgery. Most newer corporate bonds are registered; a developing trend is for more government bonds to be registered, too. If a registered bond is lost or stolen, it can be replaced. Interest checks are sent automatically to the registered owner (although some registered bonds also have coupons that have to be clipped). When you buy a bond, the stockbroker should advise you on the pros and cons of having it registered, on what dates the interest is paid, and what (if anything) you have to do to collect that interest.

Types of Bonds

There are three major issuers of investment-quality bonds: Corporations, the U.S. government (including federal agencies), and states and municipalities.

Corporate Bonds

Thousands upon thousands of corporations sell their bonds to the public. If you have special knowledge about a small or lesser-known company and trust its bonds to pay interest until maturity, you might want to buy some. But it might be hard to sell those bonds in the open market if you ever wanted to raise some cash. Generally speaking, an individual investor should stick to leading companies whose bonds are listed on the New York and American Exchanges and can be sold easily.

The bonds of manufacturing companies are usually backed only by the company's promise to pay; such bonds are called *debentures,* and generally mature in twenty to thirty years. Other bonds are backed by tangible property; if the company couldn't meet the interest payments, that property could be sold to pay the bondholders off.

Mortgage bonds, generally issued in thirty-year maturities by electric utilities, are backed by the utilities' real property.

Equipment trust certificates, issued by railroads, are backed by locomotives and other rolling stock; in fact, the certificate holder owns a share in them. If the railroad defaults on its payments, the cars can easily be leased to another railroad. For this reason, ETCs have always been extremely safe. They're generally issued as a fifteen-year *serial—* that is, some portion of the issue matures every year for fifteen years. These certificates cannot be called in before maturity.

Guaranteed loan certificates are issued by airlines for the purchase of aircraft and work the same way as the equipment trust certificates. These bonds, however, have a single maturity date and can be called.

Convertible bonds are debentures with a "kicker": They can be exchanged for a certain number of shares of common stock, which could be profitable if the stock goes up considerably in price (see page 586).

Floating rate notes are occasionally issued by banks in various maturities. At specified times the interest rate can change, to reflect changes in the general level of market rates.

Optional maturity bonds offer the holder a chance to turn in his bond at face value at a specified time before maturity.

Corporate bonds usually pay a higher interest rate than federal government bonds or tax-free municipals of similar quality. Interest on the bonds is taxable. They can be good income producers for people in low tax brackets or for tax-deferred investment vehicles, such as individual pension plans.

U.S. Government Bonds

Savings bonds are discussed in Chapter 25. This section covers marketable securities—those that can be bought and sold in the open market.

TREASURY SECURITIES

Treasury bills are short-term investments; they mature anywhere between thirty days and one year. At present, the minimum denomination is $10,000. Treasury bills are sold at a *discount*—that is, you pay less than face value but receive full face value at maturity. The difference between what you paid and what you get back is your yield on the investment. A three-month bill, for example, might cost $9,750, redeemable at $10,000 for a $250 profit; if you invested your $10,000 in four such three-month bills over a year's time, you'd realize an annual yield of around 10 percent.

You can buy Treasuries through banks at minimum cost, or from stockbrokers at a slightly higher fee. There's no charge at all if you buy direct from a Federal Reserve bank or branch. Ask your own bank for the address of the nearest Federal Reserve, then write a letter asking for instructions on how to buy Treasuries by mail. Sales are held weekly for some maturity dates, monthly for others. Treasuries can be redeemed at no cost through the Federal Reserve.

Large investors use Treasury bills as a place to park cash that they'd rather not keep in the stock market. During times of rising short-term interest rates, the yield on Treasury bills also rises, so every time a bill matures, you can roll over the money into another, higher-paying bill. At past interest rate peaks, Treasury bills have sold for as much as 14 and 15 percent—an enormously high return on a security as safe as a U.S. Treasury issue.

When yields get that high, it becomes attractive for small investors to take money out of their savings accounts and put it in Treasury bills instead. However, if the Treasury bill rate is only 1 or 1½ percent above the rate available at a bank for comparable maturities, the transfer may not be worth it. On a $10,000 investment an extra 1 percent is an additional $100 per year. To get that $100, you have to take money out of your savings account, send it by registered mail to the Federal Reserve, receive the Treasury statement, put it in a safe deposit box for safekeeping, wait for a check for the proceeds, and redeposit it in your savings account or in another Treasury bill. Some people are glad to go to that trouble for an extra $100; others aren't. You can have a bank or a broker handle the transaction for you, but that might cost $40 or $50, which reduces your profit. When Treasuries are paying 2½ or 3 percent more than bank accounts, however, you're talking about an extra $250 or $300 on a $10,000 investment, which may well sound more interesting.

Treasury notes have maturity dates of one to ten years. Anything over ten years is called a *Treasury bond.* Notes and bonds are sold in minimum denominations of $1,000 or $5,000, and pay interest twice a year. The price of Treasuries fluctuates in the marketplace, as does the price of any other bond. Notes and bonds are for medium- to long-term investors who want income, maximum safety, and protection against having their bonds called away if interest rates decline (see page 620).

The interest on Treasuries is exempt from state and local income taxes (though not from federal income taxes). This makes them particularly attractive to higher-income people living in heavily taxed jurisdictions.

FEDERAL AGENCY NOTES

These securities are issued by various agencies of the U.S. government, some backed by the issuing agency, others backed by the government itself. They are just as safe as Treasury issues but generally carry a slightly higher interest rate, mainly because the market for these securities is smaller than the market for Treasuries. Most (but not all) are exempt from state and local income taxes, just like Treasury issues. They are not callable—a good feature when interest rates are declining. However, they're generally not as easy to sell as Treasuries if you need your money before maturity.

The major agencies of interest to individual investors are the Banks for Cooperatives (minimum investment: $5,000); Federal Intermediate Credit Banks ($5,000); Federal Land Banks ($1,000); and Federal Home Loan Banks ($10,000). The first three of these agencies make loans to farmers; the fourth is the reserve bank for savings and loan institutions and savings banks. All of these securities are exempt from state and local taxes. They're bought through stockbrokers and some commercial banks for a small fee. Maturities range from six months to ten years. If you're going to need your money on a particular date, you can generally find an agency note redeemable around that time.

There are several other federal agencies whose notes may be of interest. Ask your broker for the complete list and the pros and cons of each.

Municipal Bonds

These make up the largest segment of the bond market. They're issued by cities, counties, and states for various projects, or by authorities set up for a special purpose, such as building a bridge or a mass transit system.

Interest paid on municipal bonds is exempt from federal income tax. If you buy the bonds of your own state or city, they're exempt from state and city income taxes as well. But if you buy the bonds of another state, the interest earned is subject to your state or city income taxes, if any.

Municipal bonds pay lower interest than corporate or government securities. But because that interest is tax-free, the actual yield to a high-bracket investor is generally higher than he'd get from a taxable bond. Low-bracket investors, on the other hand, net more money from corporate and government bonds. The following table shows what a taxable bond has to pay in order to equal the yield from tax-free municipals, for investors in tax brackets high enough to make municipals attractive. As you can see, the higher your bracket, the better your return from municipal bonds.

If your income-tax bracket is:	A tax-free yield of:						
	4%	4½%	5%	5½%	6%	6½%	7%
	Is equivalent to a taxable yield of:						
32%	5.88	6.62	7.35	8.09	8.82	9.56	10.29
36	6.25	7.03	7.81	8.59	9.37	10.16	10.94
39	6.56	7.38	8.20	9.02	9.84	10.66	11.48
42	6.90	7.76	8.62	9.48	10.34	11.21	12.07
45	7.27	8.18	9.09	10.00	10.91	11.82	12.73
48	7.69	8.65	9.62	10.58	11.54	12.50	13.46
50	8.00	9.00	10.00	11.00	12.00	13.00	14.00
60	10.00	11.25	12.50	13.75	15.00	16.25	17.50
70	13.33	15.00	16.67	18.33	20.00	21.67	23.33

There are several kinds of municipal bonds. The largest group comprises *general obligation bonds,* which are backed by the taxing power of the issuing government. The municipality is obligated, by law, to levy whatever taxes are necessary to pay the bondholders on time. This generally makes general obligation bonds extremely secure. (*Note:* Some bonds limit the total tax that can be levied. These are called *limited-tax general obligation bonds,* and carry slightly higher yields.)

Revenue bonds are backed by revenues from a specific project—for example, tolls from a bridge, tunnel, or turnpike, or user fees from a water or sewer system. The security of these bonds depends on the economic soundness of the project. Because payments aren't guaranteed by taxes, revenue bonds generally carry higher yields than general obligation issues. Some revenue projects are entirely sound, some are high-risk. As with other bonds, the relative security of revenue bonds is indicated by their quality ratings.

Special tax bonds are backed by a tax levied especially to pay the bondholders—for example, school taxes to pay off school bonds. *Industrial revenue bonds* and *pollution control bonds* are issued by a municipality to build a plant or finance other facilities for a company it's trying to attract or keep in the area. The company leases the facilities from the municipality, which in turn uses that revenue to pay the bondholders. How sound these bonds are depends on the financial stability of the company. *Housing authority bonds* finance low-rent housing projects and are secured by a pledge of unlimited contributions from the Housing Assistance Administration, a U.S. government agency. Hence, these bonds are extremely secure. *Hospital bonds* are backed by hospital revenues. *Project notes* are short-term investments issued to finance urban renewal and housing. Their particular attraction is that they're guaranteed by the U.S. government. The most recent bond innovation is the so-called *moral obligation bond,* backed by revenues from a particular project, with a promise from the state (but not in writing) to bail out the bondholders if the project runs into financial trouble. This promise may not always be good, which is the reason that moral obligation bonds carry higher yields.

For safety, the general obligation bonds of municipalities are generally rated just below issues of the federal government and above corporate issues. They're so safe that many conservative investors are willing to choose slightly lower quality in return for a higher yield. Since the 1930s no general obligation bond rated Baa or better has gone into default (except for New York City in 1975, which was rated A at the time; a court eventually ordered the city to pay the interest owed). There have, however, been some defaults in revenue bonds when the projects failed to produce enough money to pay the bondholders. During the Great Depression some general obligation bonds went into default for several years—a situation that would probably recur among the lower-rated municipalities in the event of another depression.

Municipal bonds are generally issued in *serial maturities.* That means that a certain number of bonds mature every year starting in perhaps the first year and lasting for twenty years. The further away the maturity date, the higher the yield. This lets you choose a yield and redemption date most consistent with your financial needs.

One risk with municipals is that they're not very marketable if you want to sell before maturity. Because of the serial maturities the market for a single issue may be very small; to sell at all, you'll probably have to take a big cut in price. The most saleable municipals are those from rural areas that haven't yet felt urban financial strains, school districts that rarely offer bonds, and sound local authorities issuing revenue bonds; but even these are not always easy to sell at the apparent market price. If you think you'll want to sell your bonds before maturity, you're better off with a tax-free bond mutual fund (see page 637).

In the past, municipal bond dealers were almost entirely free from government regulation. But a number of scandals in the 1970s resulted in legislation to bring at least some standards to the municipal market. The Municipal Securities Rulemaking Board set up shop in 1976 and began preparing regulations. In the future it is likely that investors will receive more information about the financial position of communities than they do today. Your best protection in buying municipals is to buy from a well-known dealer and pay attention to bond quality ratings. Also, look for good call protection (see page 623). Some municipals aren't callable for the life of the bond.

If you borrow money in order to invest in municipal bonds, the interest on that loan is not tax-deductible. If you own any municipals at all, this rule sometimes leads to trouble with interest deductions on loans taken for other purposes. For example, an executive who owns municipals, then borrows money to take advantage of stock options, may find the interest deduction disallowed (on the ground that if he didn't own the municipals, he wouldn't have had to borrow the money —hence the loan helped him maintain his municipal position). An accountant can advise you as to which loans are likely to lead to difficulties.

Your municipal investments should generally be timed to mature at retirement, assuming that you expect to be in a lower tax bracket. Your broker can help you find tax-free bonds with appropriate maturity dates.

Bonds on Margin

If you're buying bonds merely to speculate on a price increase, consider buying on margin. Under this arrangement, you put up only part of the price of the bonds and borrow the rest from your broker. Margin requirements are much lower than for stocks, which means that just a little money can finance a tremendous number of bonds. On government bonds, the speculator's favorite vehicle, margin can be as little as 5 percent. Of course margin buying carries greater risks: If bond prices fall instead of rise, you stand to lose more money than if you had bought outright.

Reading the Bond Quotes

Bonds	Cur Yld	Vol	High	Low	Close	Net Chg.
EasAir 10s02	cv	10	98½	98	98	—
ElPas 6s93A	cv	10	94	94	94	−1
Eltra 8½s01	8.5	10	100¼	100¼	100¼	−2¾
Englh 5¼97	cv	4	96¼	96¼	96¼	+ ¼
Ens 9¾s95	9.2	10	106¾	105½	105½	−1¼
Estrl 6¼95	cv	5	72	72	72	+1
Evans 6¼94	cv	10	103⅜	103⅜	103⅜	—
Exxon 6s97	7.3	7	83	82	82	—
Exxon 6½98	7.6	16	86⅜	86	86	− ¼
ExxnP 9s04	8.4	20	106⅞	106½	106⅞	− ⅛
ExxnP 8.05s80	7.9	61	101⅜	101	101⅜	− ¼
ExxnP 8¼01	8.1	3	101¼	101¼	101¼	—
FMC 4¼92	cv	9	74½	74½	74½	− ½
FairFd 9s96	cv	43	104	103	103	− ⅜
Famly 4¾90	8.5	5	55⅝	55⅝	55⅝	—
Farah 5s94	cv	7	44	44	44	− ¼
Feddr 5s96	cv	52	47⅞	47	47	− ⅛
FedN 4⅜s96	cv	20	77¼	77¼	77¼	+ ⅞
Ferro 5⅞92	6.8	5	86¾	86¾	86¾	− ¼
Fiber 6¾s98	cv	1	74½	74½	74½	− ½
FstChi 6¼78	6.3	20	99 1–32	99 1–32	99 1–32	—
FstChi 6¾80	6.9	20	98	97⅜	98	− ⅛
FstMd 9¾83	9.3	2	104¾	104¾	104¾	−1¼
FstNBAtl 9s84	8.8	5	102¼	102¼	102¼	+ ¾
FsNBo 7.6s81	7.6	45	100	99½	99½	− ¾
FsNBos 8s82	8.0	30	100⅛	100	100	− ⅜
FsPenn 7s93	cv	40	61⅜	60½	61⅜	−2⅜
FstSec 7½99	7.3	5	102½	102½	102½	+ ⅜
FlaPL 10¾81	10.	8	104¾	104¾	104¾	− ¼
Ford 6½79	6.6	10	98½	98½	98½	—
Ford 7.40s80	7.4	6	100⅛	100⅛	100⅛	+ ¼
Ford 7.85s94	7.9	3	100	100	100	—
Ford 9¼94	8.7	18	106⅞	106	106	− ⅜
FrdC 8⅞90A	8.6	13	103	103	103	−2

The leading bonds are traded on the New York or American exchanges; governments are generally traded over the counter. On the exchanges, bond quotes look like the illustration above. Run down the list to the first issue of Exxon, the "6s97." That means the issue of bonds carrying a coupon interest rate of 6 percent and maturing in 1997. The next column, *Current Yield,* shows the relationship of the interest rate to the current market price of the bond. This particular Exxon issue, which came out at a 6 percent coupon, now yields 7.3 percent. Why has the yield gone up? Because the price has fallen from $1,000 on the day it was issued to a *High* today of 83 ($830), a *Low* of 82 ($820), and a *Close,* or closing price of the day, of 82. (With bond quotes you always add a zero to the number to get the actual price.) *Net Change* shows the change of price since yesterday; the dash after this Exxon bond shows there was no change. Other bonds on the list have gone up or down in the amounts shown. The notation "−1" means down $10. The fractions all indicate a fractional part of $10. For example, "−½" indicates a loss of one half of $10, or $5; "+⅛" means a gain of $1.25. The column headed *Vol* means volume, the amount of trading done in the bond that day. Exactly seven Exxon 6s97's changed hands.

Under the *Current Yield* column you'll note a number of bonds merely marked "cv." That indicates that they're convertible bonds, whose yield is of less importance than their relationship to the current stock price. Other abbreviations are explained in the footnotes printed in the newspaper. The bond's yields to maturity (see page 621) are not shown, but any stockbroker can tell you what they are.

Sample listings of government securities are shown next. The issues are described according to *Rate,* which means coupon rate; and *Mat. Date,* or maturity date. The small "n" indicates a Treasury note rather than a bond. The *Bid* column shows the price the dealers are willing to pay—if you're selling, the bid price is the selling price. The first note on the list can be sold for 100, which means $1,000, or face value. The *Asked* column shows the price that dealers are asking—if you're buying, that's the price you'll pay. In Treasury quotes, one decimal place is ⅟₃₂d of 100, or $3.12½. Hence, an asked price of 100.2 means $1,000 plus ²⁄₃₂ds, or $1,006.25. *Bid Change* shows how much the price has changed from yesterday. The top bond has not changed at all, but others have risen by one or two thirty-seconds. *Yield* is the annual yield up to the date the bond can be called in, which for notes is the maturity date and for bonds, five years before maturity. (The maturity date of bonds, not shown on the table, is generally written like this: 1978–83, meaning that the bond matures in 1983 but can be called in 1978.)

The Uses of Bonds

Each type of bond is appropriate to a different financial situation. To get the best value from a bond investment, check the following paragraphs; these guidelines should at least point you in the right direction.

GOVERNMENT, AGENCY AND MISCELLANEOUS SECURITIES

Treasury Bonds and Notes

Rate	Mat.	Date	Bid	Asked	Bid Chg.	Yld.
7½s.	1977	Oct n.	100	100.2	—	1.69
7¾s.	1977	Nov n.	100.1	100.3	—	5.73
6⅝s.	1977	Nov n.	99.31	100.1	—	6.12
7¼s.	1977	Dec n.	100.1	100.3	—	6.56
6⅜s.	1978	Jan n.	99.29	99.31	—	6.40
6¼s.	1978	Feb n.	99.27	99.29	—	6.48
8s.	1978	Feb n.	100.13	100.17	—	6.34
6¾s.	1978	Mar n.	99.31	100.1	+ .1	6.64
6½s.	1978	Apr n.	99.26	99.30	+ .1	6.63
7⅛s.	1978	May n.	100.4	100.8	+ .1	6.66
7⅞s.	1978	May n.	100.16	100.20	—	6.70
7⅛s.	1978	May n.	100.3	100.7	—	6.74
6⅞s.	1978	Jun n.	99.30	100.2	+ .1	6.78
6⅞s.	1978	Jul n.	99.30	100.2	—	6.79
7⅝s.	1978	Aug n.	100.15	100.19	+ .1	6.85
8¾s.	1978	Aug n.	101.10	101.14	—	6.88
6⅝s.	1978	Aug n.	99.23	99.27	+ .1	6.82
6¼s.	1978	Sep n.	99.11	99.15	+ .1	6.85
5⅞s.	1978	Oct n.	98.29	99.1	+ .1	6.88
6s.	1978	Nov n.	99.1	99.5	+ .1	6.84
5¾s.	1978	Nov n.	98.22	98.26	+ .2	6.90
5¼s.	1978	Dec n.	98	98.4	+ .2	6.93
8⅛s.	1978	Dec n.	101.6	101.10	+ .1	6.94
5⅞s.	1979	Jan n.	98.17	98.21	+ .1	7.01
7s.	1979	Feb n.	99.29	100.1	+ .1	6.97
5⅞s.	1979	Feb n.	98.14	98.18	+ .2	7.01
6s.	1979	Mar n.	98.17	98.21	+ .2	7.01
5⅞s.	1979	Apr n.	98.8	98.12	+ .1	7.03
6⅛s.	1979	May n.	98.16	98.18	+ .1	7.09
7⅞s.	1979	May n.	101.2	101.6	+ .1	7.05
6⅛s.	1979	Jun n.	98.14	98.16	+ .1	7.09
7¾s.	1979	Jun n.	100.30	101.2	—	7.07
6¼s.	1979	Jul n.	98.18	98.20	+ .1	7.09
6¼s.	1979	Aug n.	98.16	98.20	+ .1	7.08
6⅝s.	1979	Aug n.	99.2	99.4	—	7.14
6⅞s.	1979	Aug n.	99.17	99.21	+ .1	7.08

• *If you're retired on a modest income:* Long-term government bonds provide perfect safety as well as income protection if interest rates fall. With governments you have call protection of twenty years or more (see page 623). If interest rates decline, high-yield corporate bonds will be called away and replaced with bonds that pay less interest, whereas high-yield government bonds will remain in your hands, paying a relatively high income for many, many years. Government bonds yield a little less than corporates, so a retired person may incline to corporates, instead. But because of the call protection, governments may offer you today's rate of interest for a much longer time—an important point for a younger retiree.

If the extra income from corporate bonds is important, you might split your investment between governments and high-quality corporates (or corporate bond mutual funds, called "income funds"). Consider buying corporates with staggered maturity dates, so some will be maturing every couple of years. When they come due, you can either spend the money or reinvest it, depending on your circumstances. This protects you from having to sell bonds before maturity, perhaps at a loss. Consider the call provisions of your corporate investments; utilities bonds generally offer the most protection. Your stockbroker can give you guidance here.

Younger retirees should also keep a portion of their money in the stocks of leading companies that pay high dividends. At age sixty-five, a person may have twenty years or more to live, during which time he'll need the protection of investments that can rise in value over the long term.

• *If you're investing in a tax-deferred retirement plan:* That part of your funds which you want in bonds should be in corporate bonds for their yield and government bonds for their call protection, the proportions depending on your age and expectations about inflation.

• *If you're worried about a severe business slowdown:* Government bonds will pay off, even in depression situations where some corporations may fail and municipalities default.

• *If you have substantial income:* High-quality, tax-free municipal bonds can net you more money than taxable fixed-income investments. For long-term call protection, general obligation bonds are better than revenue bonds. You also get good call protection from long-term federal government bonds. The interest paid on governments is subject to federal income tax but is exempt from state and local income tax.

• *If you're a younger person, living in part on a fixed pool of money —a widow, a divorcee, a family with a modest inheritance:* A good part of that money should be invested in leading companies and utilities paying high dividends so that you'll get the advantage of long-term stock market gains. The remainder could be partly in bank term accounts, partly in government bonds (for the security and call protection), and partly in high-quality corporate bonds or bond funds.

• *If you want a place to park money temporarily:* Say you've just sold some stock, or received a check from an insurance company, or redeemed a bond. What should you do with the proceeds while you're making up your mind about other investments? You could put the money in the bank. If short-term Treasury bills are paying more than passbook savings, you could buy bills (or buy a money market mutual fund that invests in Treasury bills and similar instruments—see page 659).

• *If you want a capital gain:* There are two ways to do it. (1) The sure way is to buy a bond that's selling at less than face value, called a *discount bond.* For example, you might pay $900 for a $1,000 bond. On redeeming that bond at maturity, you'll get the full $1,000; the $100 gain will be taxed at the favorable capital gains rate. The current interest paid on discount bonds is less than you'd get from a bond selling at around $1,000. But if you have high earnings, it's often preferable to skimp on taxable interest and go for the capital gain instead. Discount bonds can be chosen to mature on the date you'll want the money—for example, you might buy bonds that mature just when your children are ready for college. (2) A speculator's game is to guess the direction of interest rates and bond prices. Buy bonds when you think interest rates will fall; if you're right, bond prices will move up and you'll be able to sell at a profit. (If interest rates rise, instead, bond prices will fall and you'll have a capital loss.) A good vehicle for speculators is government bonds, since they can be bought on margin for as little as 5 percent of face value. You can also speculate in no-load (no sales charge) corporate or municipal bond funds.

Bond Funds

It costs a good deal of money to buy individual bonds at a favorable price. Anything under one hundred bonds—$100,000 worth—is an odd lot, hence more expensive to buy and sell than large numbers of bonds traded by financial institutions. A handful of bonds from a small company or municipality may not be saleable at all. By and large, individual investors are better served by mutual funds specializing in bonds (see page 656). You spread your risk by buying into a large portfolio of bonds, and if you ever want to sell, you can do so quickly, at the market price.

OPTIONS

Don't get involved with options unless you really understand the stock market. Played one way, options can be extremely conservative. But if you don't know exactly what's happening, you may inadvertently accept an option recommendation that's far more speculative than you'd intended, exposing you to large losses.

The key to success with options is a stock broker or investment advisor who makes options his specialty. The average broker may sell you a potentially good option position, probably recommended by his firm's option department. But he may not understand the nuances of the position well enough to make quick decisions when the market changes. In fact, he may pay only cursory attention to the options market because most of his time is taken up with the ebb and flow of stocks. If a broker doesn't notice until the end of that day that your stock fell $1, it may not matter. But with options that $1 might mean a 50 percent loss, with no hope of recovery. So search out a broker who spends a good part of every day exclusively on options. Generally speaking, this means someone whose customers include a lot of wealthy people.

Options trade on the Chicago Board Options Exchange, the American Stock Exchange, and several regional exchanges, and fluctuate with the price of the stock they represent. The two basic types of option investments are *calls* and *puts*.

Calls

A *call* on a stock is an option to buy one hundred shares at a particular price (called the *striking price*) within a specified period of time. If the stock price rises so should the option price, giving you a profit. If it doesn't, the option price will fall—leaving you with a loss.

Assume that the stock of RCA sells at $29. You might pay $2 a share for the right to buy (call) one hundred shares at $30 each within the next nine months. If the stock goes to $33 within the specified period, the gain for the stockholder is $4, or 14 percent. The option, on the other hand, might go from $2 to $4.50—a 125 percent gain. You can see from this why options are so attractive to high rollers.

If you had bought this call on RCA, you could theoretically buy the stock at $30 through your broker (paying normal brokerage commissions) and resell immediately at $33. But you'd more likely sell the profitable option in the open market to someone who hoped it would go higher yet. Commissions on option trades are lower than commissions on stocks.

If the stock doesn't rise, your option will expire in nine months, absolutely worthless. If you hold to the bitter end, you'll have a 100 percent loss. But more likely you'd start to lose faith in the stock after just a few months and sell the option before expiration—getting away with a loss of perhaps only 50 percent.

When Would You Buy a Call Option?

You'd buy a call when you believe strongly that a stock will increase substantially in price over a short period of time. If it behaves as you expect, you'll get a much larger gain on your money by buying the option than you would have by buying the stock. But you run the risk of a big loss if the stock doesn't perform. Buying call options is a highly speculative activity.

What Is a Conservative Use of Calls?

Assume that you own a substantial portfolio of stocks. You can increase your investment yield considerably by *selling* calls against your portfolio. For example, assume you own some RCA, now priced at $29. A speculator is willing to pay you $2 a share for an option to buy one hundred shares at $30 within nine months, so you sell him that option. If the stock doesn't rise, you've made $200 (taxed as a capital gain) and still own your RCA. If the stock rises to $33, it will be called away from you at $30. But you've still made $3 a share—$2 from the option and $1 in the price increase from $29 to $30. If the RCA stock falls in price, it can go down by as much as $2 a share (the price you got for the call) and you're still breaking even. If the stock falls even further, you can sell out. Using options this way sharply limits your investment risk.

A stock market that's basically flat is the best possible climate for selling calls on stock. You make money on the calls, yet get to keep the stock and collect the dividends.

Puts

A *put* is an option to sell a stock at a specific price (the striking price) within a specified period of time. If the stock price falls, you'll make a profit.

Assume that the stock of Honeywell is selling at $51. You might pay $2 a share for the right to sell (put) one hundred shares at $50 within the next six months. If the stock falls to $47, you could theoretically buy Honeywell at that price and resell it through your broker at $50 (paying the normal brokerage commission). But in fact, you would simply sell your option at a profit to someone who hoped the option price would improve even more.

When Would You Buy a Put?

You'd buy a put when you believe strongly that a stock will fall substantially in price within a short period of time. It's a cheap and potentially more profitable way of selling a stock short. But you run the risk of a big percentage loss if the stock doesn't fall as expected.

What Is a Conservative Use of Puts?

Puts can limit your risk in a stock. For example, assume you bought Honeywell at $40 a share, saw it rise to $54, then begin to fall again. You're not quite ready to sell out, because you think it may turn around and go back up. So you buy puts at $50 in order to limit the risk of losing your profits. If the price falls to $47, the put gives you the right to sell at $50; the put cost you $2, so you get an effective price of $48. If the stock goes up, however, you still own it. (*Note:* Rather than paying $2 a share to limit your risk, you might simply apply the 10 percent rule: Sell Honeywell when it drops 10 percent, to $48½. If it goes back up and you still like it, buy it back.)

There are many combinations of put and call options, some far more complex than anyone needs. Before you buy such a combination, have your broker lay it out very clearly: What do you have to gain or lose if the stock goes up? goes down? goes nowhere? Is there a simpler way of achieving the same investment effect?

Some Tips on Options for
People Buying for Speculation

• Before you buy an option, decide exactly what you expect of the stock. For example, you might decide that RCA will go from $29 to $33 in six months, with the first $2 of the rise occurring during the first three months. If that first $2 of rise doesn't happen, decide ahead of time that you'll sell out. Most big losses in options occur because the stock doesn't behave as expected but the option holder hangs on, hoping for a change in the market at the last minute. The only way to fight this impulse is to decide in advance exactly where you're going to abandon the position and cut your loss.

• Set targets of profit as well as loss. If RCA reaches the $33 you were looking for within four months, you might be tempted to hold onto the option in case the stock goes even higher. But things move fast in the option market; if RCA drops $1, it could cut your profit by 50 percent. A good rule is to take profits as soon as the stock does what you were looking for.

• Follow the price of the stock and the option every day. If something looks wrong, be ready to sell fast. The option market is no place for people whose tendency is to wait and see. Use a broker or advisor who follows option prices all day.

• Beginners in the option market should invest only a small amount of money until they get the feel of the game.

• Options to buy or sell stock expire on a certain day. If your option isn't living up to expectations, it's important to sell, even at a loss, well before expiration date. If you hold on until the last minute, waiting for a turnaround, you may not be able to sell at all.

• Options on a particular stock expire in a cycle, every three, six, and nine months. Consider buying only those options with the most distant expiration date—generally nine months. This gives the stock more time to move and gives you more time to sell if the position doesn't seem to be working out. (This is not, however, a hard rule; sometimes near-month options are better speculations.)

• Some options trade at the rate of three hundred or four hundred a day. With others only three or four a day may change hands. Stick to the ones with large volume because they're the easiest ones to sell.

• If a broker recommends an option position, ask him exactly what his objectives are—when he expects the stock to move, exactly what stock price he's looking for, how much he expects the option to move, and at what point he'd concede that it wasn't working out and advise you to sell. If he doesn't have all these numbers down cold, he's not the right broker for your options business.

• It is vital in the options game that you not hang on to losses too long. If you find it hard to take a loss, don't buy puts and calls. Option buyers have more losers than winners; they stay in the game only because when they win, they win big.

• In a complex business like options, it's easy for you and your broker to misunderstand each other. So double-check every buy and sell order, to be sure it's right.

Reading the Options Tables:

CHICAGO BOARD

		— Jan —		— Apr —		— Jul —		N.Y.
Option & Price		Vol.	Last	Vol.	Last	Vol.	Last	Close
Alcoa	40	44	5¾	60	6	a	a	45⅝
Alcoa	45	92	1 9-16	94	2 13-16	3	3¾	45⅝
Alcoa	50	27	1-16	173	1	b	b	45⅝
Am Exp	35	5	2⅜	2	3¼	a	a	37
Am Exp	40	89	¼	32	1	a	a	37
Am Tel	.60	73	1	37	1⅝	51	2¼	60½
Am Tel	.65	41	1-16	61	¼	9	½	60½
Atl R	50	100	2 13-16	90	3⅞	54	4¾	51⅞
Atl R	60	a	a	130	9-16	32	1	51⅞
Avon	40	64	8¼	51	8½	a	a	48⅛
Avon p	40	a	a	a	a	5	⅝	48⅛
Avon	45	197	3⅜	106	4¼	27	4¾	48⅛
Avon p	45	111	3-16	93	1¼	59	1¾	48⅛
Avon	50	314	½	465	1 7-16	125	2⅛	48⅛
Avon p	50	51	2⅛	67	3½	10	4⅛	48⅛
BankAm	20	2	3¼	1	3¼	4	3¾	23⅛
BankAm	25	145	⅛	175	⅝	37	1 1-16	23⅛
Beth S	15	6	6	a	a	a	a	20⅞
Beth S	20	63	1½	54	2⅝	41	3⅛	20⅞
Beth S	25	37	1-16	95	⅝	b	b	20⅞
Beth S	30	a	a	6	⅛	b	b	20⅞
Beth S	35	3	1-16	a	a	b	b	20⅞
Bruns	10	50	5⅛	a	a	50	5⅜	15
Bruns	15	227	⅝	230	1½	42	1 13-16	15

Here's how the options listings look in the financial journals. There's a small "p" after puts, the others are calls. Third from the top is an Alcoa 50, a call on the Aluminum Co. of America at $50 a share. On the far right, under the heading *N.Y.*, you'll find the day's closing price on the

New York Stock Exchange—in this case, 45⅝. This table is from late December, 1977; at that time, Alcoa 50s could be bought on the Chicago Board Options Exchange with expiration dates in January, April, or July. Under each of those months in the heading, you'll discover how many option contracts traded that day *(Vol)*, and the day's closing price *(Last)*. For example, investors bought 173 of the April 50s which closed at $1 a share. The small "b" under the July column means that no option was open for trading for that date.

Now look down to the put on Avon at $40. The stock was selling at 48⅛, and investors clearly had little hope it would drop below $40 before their options expired. Hence, most of the January and April options show an "a," which means that no one was buying. The various other abbreviations used on option tables will be explained in the table's footnotes right in the newspaper.

MUTUAL FUNDS

Mutual funds are the very best investment vehicle for the average person. This includes people with relatively large sums of money to invest as well as those with only modest savings. You can probably get better returns, with less risk, by putting your money into mutual funds than by trying to select individual stocks and bonds yourself.

Mutual Funds Defined

In a mutual fund, thousands, sometimes millions, of people pool their investment money. Professional managers invest that money according to the mutual fund's stated investment goals. As new people come into the fund, new investments are bought.

When you buy a share of a mutual fund, you pay *net asset value*, which, roughly speaking, is the value of all the investments owned by the fund, minus any debt, divided by the number of shares outstanding. Net asset value is figured daily, in order to take the day's changes in stock and bond prices into account. The fund stands ready to pay you the value of your shares at any time, so you're assured of a ready market when you want to sell. If you sell the fund for more than you paid, you get a capital gain; if for less, you get a capital loss.

Dividends and interest received by the fund are distributed to shareholders, usually on a quarterly basis. When a fund sells some of its investments, the net gain is also distributed to investors (net losses will more likely be retained by the fund).

A lot of people soured on mutual funds in the 1970s because the records of so many funds were poor. But the problem was the stock market, not the fund concept itself. A mutual fund is simply a *method* of investment, offering significant advantages to nonprofessional investors. There are mutual funds for all manner of investments—stocks, bonds, gold, puts and calls, and so on—some of which have done exceedingly well in recent years. It's up to you to choose which type of investment is appropriate for the time and for your financial needs. Once you have chosen, you may find that the best method of making the investment is through a mutual fund.

The foregoing defines the traditional *open-end* mutual fund, which is what most investors buy. There are also *closed-end* funds, which sell a certain number of shares to investors and then quit. The only way you can buy into these funds is to buy a share from another investor. Closed-end funds are bought and sold like stocks, with the price set by supply and demand rather than the value of the shares in the portfolio. Sometimes closed-end funds trade above net asset value (at a *premium*), but more often they're below it (at a *discount*). It may seem attractive to buy a portfolio of stocks at a discount from what they're actually worth, but because so few investors are interested in closed-end funds, your shares may continue selling at a discount for years. You may even find it difficult to sell. Closed-end funds are bought and sold through stockbrokers, who charge a normal brokerage commission. Open-end funds may or may not charge a sales commission (see page 648).

Advantages of Mutual Funds

1. You spread your risk. If you own just a few stocks and bonds, one of which is a real stinker, the losses in that one may wipe out the profits in all your other investments. Mutual funds, however, own such a large and varied portfolio of stocks that one poor performer can't drag down all the rest. Buying shares in a mutual fund allows you to participate in a much broader range of stocks and bonds than you could afford on your own.

2. Your money is managed by professionals, who know a lot more about the market than you do. It's fashionable to snort at professionals because so many mutual funds didn't advance in the 1970s. But the stock market didn't advance, either, and in fact, large numbers of funds did better than the market. If you had been managing your own money during that period and kept it in stocks, your results probably wouldn't have equaled those of the mutual funds. Professional money managers, who study the investment markets all day every day, know more than you do about what's going on. As an investor your job is to decide whether now is the time to invest in stocks, bonds, Treasury bills, or whatever; once that decision is made, you'll generally do better by turning your money over to professional management, via an appropriate mutual fund, than by doing it yourself.

3. You reduce the amount of information you have to have about the market in order to make a good investment. Mutual funds usually rise and fall with the market as a whole; your only decision is when to buy and when to sell in order to catch the trend. By contrast, if you buy individual stocks, you not only have to make a buy-sell decision, but must also analyze particular industries and particular companies to see which ones will do well. In the case of bonds, you'd want to know whether the issuing company was in danger of having its rating lowered, and how could you really tell? If you buy a mutual fund, you leave those specific decisions to people equipped to make them.

4. You can sell quickly and easily. Open-end mutual funds stand ready to redeem your shares at any time, paying the current market price. This is particularly valuable to bond investors, since small numbers of bonds are extremely difficult to sell except at a discount from market price. A "small number" of bonds can be anything up to $100,000 worth; so even people with large amounts of money are often better off with mutual funds than investing individually.

5. You have less paperwork than if you managed your own investments. Instead of a large number of stock certificates, you have a single share certificate from each fund you own. At the end of the year the fund will send you a statement of your income and capital gains for tax purposes.

6. You can more easily diversify your investments. On a relatively small amount of money you can own one fund that invests in aggressive growth stocks, one in blue-chip stocks, and one in bonds—hence positioning your money to take advantage of several different markets.

Investment Objectives

Different mutual funds have different investment objectives. The most common reason for an investor to be disappointed with his purchase is that he bought a fund whose objectives were different from his own.

The fund's objectives will be set out right on the first page of the *prospectus,* which is the full description of the fund required by the Securities and Exchange Commission. One prospectus might say, "The primary objective is income through the purchase of stocks and bonds that pay high dividends and interest, with capital appreciation a secondary objective." That's a fund for a conservative person, looking for a high return on his investment. Another prospectus will announce, "The principal objective is long-term capital appreciation, primarily through investments in common stocks." That's for a person who's willing to give up interest income in hopes of higher capital gains. Some funds warn that they'll take an "aggressive" stance. That means higher risk. These statements of investment objective are always spelled out at greater length inside the prospectus, as well as in the sales brochure. Following are some of the many types of funds:

Growth Funds

These specialize in the common stocks of companies expected to show higher-than-average growth, in both earnings and the price of the stock. Typically, dividend payments are low; in fact, the prospectus will note that "income is secondary." These are good funds to buy when the stock market is rising, and good funds for younger, long-term investors. Growth funds break down into various categories of risk:

• *Aggressive growth funds*—specializing in smaller companies. These funds generally rise rapidly when the stock market is going up and collapse on the downside. They are good for capable, high-risk investors who are quick to sell out when the market drops 10 percent. The prospectus may describe these funds as aiming for "capital appreciation" or "maximum appreciation."

• *Industry funds*—specializing in a particular type of stock, such as energy or gold-mining companies. These are also high-risk because of their lack of diversification. They're top performers when their industry is doing well, but again, are only for investors ready to sell quickly when the string runs out.

• *Quality-stock funds*—emphasizing leading growth companies, with a long history of excellent performance. The tipoff words in the prospectus are likely to be "long-term capital growth." Like any other equity fund, these are best sold when the stock market drops, but they rarely fall as far as the mutual funds that invest in smaller, lesser-known companies. If America prospers, these quality stocks will prosper, too. They're good for young and middle-aged investors aiming at appreciation of capital over fifteen or twenty years.

Growth-and-income funds

These combine stock and bond investments in an attempt to return a reasonable income to investors while at the same time participating in the stock market's long-term growth. The stocks selected are generally of leading companies, often those paying high dividends. These are good for investors who need a certain amount of income from their capital yet also want to share in the long-term growth of stocks over fifteen or twenty years.

But even among growth-and-income funds objectives vary. Some (called *balanced funds*) emphasize income, which means more bonds; others emphasize stocks. Again, read the prospectuses and decide exactly which approach you prefer.

Income Funds

These invest almost entirely in corporate bonds or government-insured mortgages; any stocks they own are likely to be preferreds. They're good for investors seeking safety of principal and maximum income from their capital (for more on bond funds, see page 656) without concern for capital growth. Ironically, the income funds outperformed "growth" funds in the mid-1970s because the value of bonds was rising faster than the value of stocks.

AGGRESSIVE INCOME FUNDS
These are bond funds that buy lower-quality issues, in order to get a higher yield. The price rises and falls more sharply than with other income funds. Good for speculators betting that bond prices will rise.

MUNICIPAL BOND FUNDS
For investors who want tax-exempt income.

MONEY MARKET FUNDS
These combine safety of principal with an attractive interest rate, at times when the general level of short-term interest rates is high (for more on money market funds, see page 659). They're good for savers who can get a higher interest rate here than in a savings account; for

people who need a temporary parking place for money; for investors who sold stocks in order to wait out a market decline; for small businessmen who can use money market funds as interest-bearing checking accounts.

Specialized Funds

These serve a wide number of special markets. There are *hedge funds* —high-risk funds that borrow against their own portfolio to buy more stocks and often sell stocks short; *convertible stock and bond funds; venture capital funds*—extremely high risk investments in new businesses; *dual-purpose funds*—which allocate all their capital gains to one class of shareholder and all their income to another (these have not yet demonstrated that they'll do better for the capital-oriented or income-oriented shareholder than a straight investment in an income or growth fund); and *option funds*—some of which write options against their stock portfolios, others of which buy options. Every time a new investment idea becomes popular, there's soon a mutual fund to serve it.

Load or No Load?

A *load* is a sales charge. Funds that are sold by stockbrokers add a load of about 8½ percent to the sales price. That means that your mutual fund has to go up in value 8½ percent just for you to break even. *No-load* funds, on the other hand, have no sales charge; all the money you put up goes directly into investments. No-load funds are bought directly from the fund management. There's no difference in performance between load and no-load funds, both do equally well (or equally badly).

If you are able to pick a mutual fund by yourself, it makes no sense to pay a broker to complete the sale. You can get a free directory of no-load mutual funds from the No-Load Mutual Fund Association, Valley Forge, Pa. 19481. This directory not only lists funds that are members of the association (all reputable funds) but also gives investment details—their size, investment objectives, minimum purchase requirements, and fund services. A careful reading of the investment objectives will winnow down the number of possibilities; you can then apply the other selection tests discussed in this chapter and send for the prospectuses of the funds that seem most attractive. The last step is to compare performance and make your choice. Another list of no-load funds can be had from the Investment Company Institute, 1775 K St. N.W., Washington D.C. 20006. If, however, you don't feel able to apply this chapter and choose your own fund, ask a broker for help and pay the 8½ percent commission. The commission rate drops for large investments; for example, on purchases of $10,000 to $25,000, the rate may be 7½ percent.

One thing to watch for in no-load funds: Some aggressive growth funds are often used as temporary investments when the market is going up. People buy the fund for just a few months, then sell out when they've made a profit. Funds don't like this because large sums entering and leaving the fund can unbalance their investment portfolios. So, to discourage in-and-out trading, they impose a charge on investors who sell within a specified length of time after buying. Watch for these exit fees; they could cut into your profits on the fund. The vast majority of no-load funds, however, do not charge exit fees.

Other Fees

Mutual funds, both load and no-load, charge an annual management fee —usually ½ of 1 percent a year, but sometimes higher. Funds may also levy other, incidental fees. The prospectus specifies all the costs; generally speaking, avoid a fund whose charges are higher than normal.

Mutual Funds and Taxes

When it comes to income taxes, it's often best to let sleeping dogs lie. But those of you who own mutual-fund shares should at least be warned that you may be making mistakes on your tax returns. Specifically, you may be misreporting whatever income you earn from the fund each year.

It's not your fault. Even the Internal Revenue Service concedes that the general tax-instruction booklets are pretty deficient on the subject of mutual funds. The IRS does have a special publication—number 564 —which explains how to handle mutual-fund income. Ask the local IRS for a copy, or order one from the nearest IRS distribution center (the address is in the tax package, which comes in the mail with your tax return).

Mutual funds send year-end statements to their shareholders, informing them of all the income they received during the year and what kind of income it was. You should read this report very carefully. In brief, here's how to report the various types of mutual-fund distributions:

(1) *Dividends.* Report the amount on the dividend-income line of your tax return. If the dividends derive from stock owned by the mutual fund, you may exclude up to the first $100 from income taxes, and up to $200 on a joint return. (The exclusion goes to $200 and $400 in 1981.) If the dividends derive from interest payments on short-term securities, as with a money-market mutual fund, no exclusion applies until the taxable year 1981.

(2) *Tax-exempt interest from municipal bonds.* No federal tax is due, so the income isn't reported on your federal return. But you may owe state and local taxes on municipal bonds from other states.

(3) *Tax-free return of capital.* Sometimes, part of a mutual-fund distribution is a return of some of the money you originally paid in. No tax is due on that amount. The sum is simply not reported on your tax return. But when you sell fund shares, this tax-free distribution raises the amount of capital gain you must report. For example, if you buy for $5,000 and sell for $7,000, you might think you have a $2,000 capital gain. But if you also received $1,000 in tax-free returns of capital, your capital gain is actually $3,000.

(4) *Distributed capital gains.* If the fund sells stock at a profit, it generally sends you your share of that profit in cash (or you instruct them to reinvest the profit in the fund). You declare the profit as a capital gain and pay a tax. Capital gains are normally reported on Schedule D. But if your only gain is from a mutual fund, you can report it directly on the tax return, with no Schedule D.

(5) *Undistributed capital gains.* Sometimes the fund sells stock at a profit but holds on to some of the gain. It reports that gain to the IRS and pays taxes on it. Your share of the undistributed gain, and of the tax paid, is reported to you on Form 2439. You declare that year's undistributed capital gain on your tax return as if you had actually received it, and claim a credit for the tax paid by the mutual fund on line 61, Form 1040. When you finally sell the fund, you reduce your reported profit by the difference between the undistributed gain and the income tax already paid.

Confusion also arises over how to declare a capital gain when you sell shares. Your gain is the difference between the adjusted price you paid (after brokerage commissions) and the price you got when you sold. But what if you bought shares over a period of time, at different prices?

If you can easily identify the various shares you bought, and when, the IRS always assumes that the first shares you sell are the first ones you bought. But if you've been reinvesting dividends and capital gains, so that it's not easy to tell exactly how much you paid for all the shares

you own, an averaging process applies. The tax publications do a poor
job of explaining averaging. You may need an accountant to help you
out.

In recent years mutual funds have kept their records on computer,
so you can generally get back copies if your own statements can't be
found. But older statements are generally not available. If you've lost
your old statements, you'll have to depend on your copies of past tax
returns in order to add up the capital gains distributions and determine
the proper tax.

Two tips on funds and taxes: (1) If the fund has a large capital loss
built up over several years, you won't get any capital gains distributions
even if, this year, the stock market goes up. All profits will first be used
to offset losses; only excess gains are distributed to investors. This is bad
for people who want income. But it's ideal for those who don't. An
investor can buy this fund, knowing that his initial capital gains will be
completely sheltered from tax because of losses already built up in the
fund (and taken by others). Interest and dividends, however, are distributed annually, regardless of fund losses.

(2) When funds have capital gains, the best time to buy is *after* the
annual capital gains distribution has been made to present shareholders. If you buy just before, you'll receive an immediate distribution on
which you'll owe a tax. In effect, you'll get part of your purchase price
back along with an unwanted tax liability.

Fund Services

Most mutual funds offer a number of services in order to make the fund
more useful to investors. Among them:

Dividend Reinvestment

You can automatically reinvest dividends and capital gains distributions, using the money to buy more shares in the fund. It's like a forced-
savings program: You aren't tempted to spend the dividends on other
things. If you bought the fund for income, however, you'd want all
dividends and capital gains distributed to you.

Withdrawal Plan

This arrangement is particularly attractive during a period when the
stock market is in a broad, upward swing. You make a mutual fund

investment, then arrange to be paid a certain, regular income, regardless of investment results. For example, you might invest $48,000 and ask to receive $400 a month. Without interest, that $48,000 would last ten years; in a savings account earning 5 percent, it would last 15 years. But if your mutual fund investment advanced at an average annual rate of 9 percent (which about matches the long-term increase of the stock market as a whole, with dividends reinvested), it could last twenty-seven years. A mutual fund withdrawal plan, then, lets you draw on your capital for regular income while you expose that capital to the possibility of growth.

In periods of flat or declining stock markets, a withdrawal plan with a common-stock mutual fund is less attractive; your investment may grow at lower rates than you'd get from a savings bank. You might, however, switch to the withdrawal plan of a corporate bond fund, which might be yielding 7 or 8 percent. At those rates of return, your $48,000 would last eighteen to twenty-one years.

Keogh Plans and Individual Retirement Accounts

These are individual pension plans, allowing tax-deferred investments for retirement (see page 778). You buy your plan directly from the mutual fund, but you can shift it later to another investment if you're not satisfied with the fund. There's an advantage to having a Keogh or IRA with a mutual fund group that offers several different types of funds under the same roof. The IRS puts technical restraints on the number of times you can shift retirement funds from one kind of investment to another. But with a mutual fund group, you may move your money from fund to fund within the group as often as you want, without violating IRS rules.

Corporate Pension Plans

Small businesses can use mutual funds as investments for their corporate pension or profit-sharing plans. The funds have the basic paperwork all done for you.

Automatic Investment

Some funds can arrange for a certain sum of money to be withdrawn from your checking account every month to buy additional fund shares. This is a useful automatic savings device for people who would otherwise spend all their money on incidentals.

Telephone Purchase and Withdrawals

Some funds let you transact your business by telephone, which speeds things up. On telephone withdrawals you can sometimes arrange to have the funds wired directly to your bank.

A Family of Funds

Some mutual fund managements offer several different types of fund. There may be a growth fund, a growth-and-income fund, a high-risk fund, an income fund, a municipal bond fund, and even a money market fund—all under the same roof. If you're buying a load fund (which charges a sales commission), be sure that the family of funds will let you switch from one fund to another at little or no additional charge. That way, when the stock market turns down, you can painlessly move your money over to a bond or money market fund while you wait for the stock market to improve.

Choosing a Mutual Fund

1. *Investment objectives.* Find a fund whose investment philosophy matches yours (see page 646). The objectives will be spelled outright in front of the prospectus.

2. *Size.* A well-established, medium-sized fund is a good bet, something in the $100-million range. Funds with assets of $500 million and up may have trouble adapting to rapidly changing market conditions (although this is not always the case). On the other hand, funds smaller than $50 million may lack the money to pay for good management and research. (An exception to this small-fund rule is one that belongs to a large family of funds.) However, if your investment objective is a quick profit in a rising market, small, aggressive no-load funds are your meat; they tend to rise (and fall) faster than larger funds.

3. *Growth.* Mutual funds tend to rise and fall along with the general market averages, but some do considerably better than the averages. An excellent place to check comparative fund performance is the annual mutual fund issue of *Forbes* magazine, which appears every August. *Forbes* rates the performance of all the leading funds in both up and down markets, so you can see at a glance how well they've done. If you don't subscribe to *Forbes*, you can probably find back copies in

your library. Give weight to a fund that performs well in declining markets; it shows that the manager pays attention to preservation of capital.

Your stockbroker or library may have Johnson's Charts or Wiesenberger's Charts, which show fund performance. Also compare performance as shown in the prospectuses of the various funds you're interested in. You'll find it in a table showing annual *net asset value per share.*

4. *Income.* The table in the prospectus showing fund performance contains a line called *dividends from net investment income.* That tells you what dividend was paid per share, every year. Mutual funds also make distributions from capital gains if they had any (and provided that they didn't use this year's gains to make up for big capital losses in earlier years). That would be listed as *distributions from realized capital gains.* The total of the two—dividends and distributions—tells how much income per share was paid every year. Dividing the total distribution by the net asset value each year gives you the annual percentage return for the fund. Thus, you can compare percentage returns to see which fund produced the higher yield.

One useful point: If you see a buildup of capital losses, it means a reduction in the amount of capital gains distributions you can expect from the fund. Any stocks sold at a profit will generally be used to offset those losses before any distributions are made to shareholders (see page 650).

5. *Services.* Check the prospectus for the services you want in a fund. Does it have withdrawal plans? Keogh plans? Telephone withdrawals? These may be conveniences you'll need in the future, if not now. If you're buying into a fund group, how much does it cost to switch from fund to fund?

6. *New money flow.* Popular funds, in a position to attract new investors, can generally give better investment results than funds shrinking in size. When new money is coming in, an investment manager generally improves performance by putting it into his best stocks in a rising market, or investing in Treasury bills and other safe securities when the market is going down. Keep your fund's quarterly reports and watch the change in its total assets. If the fund is shrinking in size, consider looking for another fund.

7. *Minimum investment.* Mutual funds have minimum initial investments, most of them quite low ($250 to $500). But some funds charge higher amounts—the prospectus will have this information.

8. *The prospectus.* Read the prospectus for whatever other information it can give you. How much you learn from the prospectus, in addition to the points explained in the foregoing, depends on your financial sophistication. One easy point to spot: If the fund has a lot of lawsuits against it, it means unhappy investors, something you probably won't want to get mixed up with.

Redemptions

Mutual funds have various redemption procedures, explained in the information that came with the prospectus. Some funds issue certificates, which you must sign in the presence of your banker or broker, then send in to be redeemed. Others have redemption letters. Still others will cash in your shares by telephone, wiring the money to your bank. If you can't find your redemption instructions, write or call the mutual fund to ask; most funds now have a toll-free (800) telephone number.

Record Keeping

Keep all your confirmations of mutual fund purchases, sales, or exchanges, and your annual statement of account. Also keep the annual and quarterly reports and past prospectuses so that you can keep track of any changes in the fund. The fund should routinely send you an up-to-date prospectus so that you'll know where you currently stand.

Spreading Your Risk

An investment strategy to consider is spreading your money among several types of mutual funds or mutual fund managements. If you're after growth, buy two or three leading growth funds rather than putting all your eggs in one basket. If one fund continually outperforms the others, switch your money to the better fund. For a more balanced strategy, put some money into growth funds, some into growth-and-income funds, and some into income funds, the proportions depending on your age, income, and objectives.

Bond Funds

There are two types of bond fund, the *managed bond fund* and the *unit trust.* Each serves a different purpose, and can perform better in certain types of markets.

The Managed Bond Fund

This works like any other mutual fund. You buy a share priced at net asset value; as new investors come in, the fund managers use that money to buy more bonds. Dividends are paid quarterly. Anytime you want to sell, the fund will redeem your shares at the current market price, which may be more or less than you originally paid.

If interest rates rise, bond prices—hence a bond fund's net asset value —will fall (see page 620). But higher bond rates tend to attract new investors. When new money comes into a fund during a period of rising interest rates, it can be invested in higher yielding bonds, which tends to raise the yield of the entire fund. So despite the fact that the fund's market value falls, the dividend payment you receive could rise a little.

Conversely, if interest rates fall, the value of the bonds in the fund will rise, providing a capital gain if you decide to sell. Should new investors come into the fund, their money will be put into lower-paying bonds, so the interest payment could fall a little.

Dividend payments, in other words, fluctuate with interest rates. If the fund's managers are exceptionally good—buying and selling the right bonds at the right time—the fund could perform better than the bond market in general. But it's more likely to run about the same. Yields on managed bond funds have so far tended to run a little below yields on newly issued unit trusts.

Managed bond funds come in both load and no-load varieties, special- izing in either corporate or municipal bonds. There's a management fee averaging around ¾ of 1 percent a year, plus incidental charges. These funds are generally sponsored by mutual-fund groups.

The Unit Trust

This is a portfolio of specific bonds, either corporate or municipal. A certain number of shares in the portfolio are sold; then subscriptions are closed. These bonds are not sold or changed during the life of the trust; as each one matures, the proceeds are distributed to the participants. If you like, those proceeds can be reinvested in other unit trusts. The trust is offered at a specific interest rate (current yield), which remains unchanged for the life of the investment. Unit trusts are normally sponsored and sold by big brokerage houses; at this writing, Merrill Lynch, the largest issuer of unit trusts, has a new trust about once a week.

There are *intermediate trusts,* whose bonds all mature in about ten years, and *long-term trusts,* which mature in about twenty years. Normally, intermediate trusts yield less than long-term trusts. Dividends may be paid monthly or quarterly. If you want to cash in your shares before maturity, the brokerage house will buy them and resell them to another investor. Resales give you the chance to buy a unit trust maturing in something less than ten or twenty years. Tell the broker what maturity date you want and see if there are shares available in trusts falling due around that time.

If you hold the trust until maturity, you can be pretty sure of getting all your money back. But if you sell before maturity, you'll have to accept whatever price is then current, which may be more or less than you paid.

There's a modest sales charge for the trusts, but no annual management fee. So if you hold for a long time, the actual cost of owning a trust may be less than you'd pay for a no-load mutual fund with a management fee.

Which Is the Better Investment for You— A Managed Bond Fund or a Bond Unit Trust?

The long-term investor, who wants fixed income and the assurance that he'll get all his money back at maturity, should consider the unit trust (see page 622 for the pros and cons of a long-term bond investment). The fees are lower over the life of the trust than if you paid the managed bond fund's management fee. The yield on unit trusts is fixed; interest payments won't decline if interest rates fall (or rise if interest rates rise). If you hold until maturity, you don't have to worry about having to sell the fund for less than you paid; you're assured of all your money back. At this writing, unit trusts are generally yielding more than managed funds. If interest rates fall over the long term, holders of unit trusts and bond funds will both have capital gains. But unit-trust holders will show higher incomes, because only trusts will have locked in today's high rates.

The short-term investor, who expects to hold bonds anywhere from a few months to two or three years, should use no-load bond funds. This saves him the sales commission, which eats into profits on short-term investments. Bond funds are also the proper place for people who want to speculate on bond price movements—buying in when they think interest rates are going to fall (and bond prices rise), then selling out for a capital gain.

If interest rates rise over the long term, holders of bond funds will have higher incomes from their investments than holders of unit trusts. But relative to inflation, both investments would be poor. *In a long-term inflationary environment, marked by rising interest rates, you'd be wise to sell both bond funds and trusts rather than hold them.*

One thing to remember is that bond funds and trusts, like bonds themselves, do not necessarily keep your capital safe. If you buy a good-quality unit trust and hold until maturity, you can be pretty sure of getting your capital back. But if you have to sell before maturity, you may get more or less than you originally paid, depending on whether interest rates have gone up or down. With bond funds there's no maturity date: Shares can be redeemed any time, at more or less than you paid, depending on current market conditions.

Bond Funds and Quality

Most bond funds and unit trusts put their money entirely into higher-grade issues—either Baa (or A) and up. But even among investment-grade bonds, quality varies enormously. New York City, for example, was an "A" community when it defaulted on its bond interest payment in 1975. An advantage of buying leading funds and trusts is that the managers double-check the Moody's and Standard & Poor's ratings to see if any bonds are weaker than they look. This kind of study also turns up sound bonds with too low a rating; by buying them, the manager can increase his fund's yield without adding to risk.

Aggressive bond funds deliberately put riskier bonds into their portfolios to raise the yield even higher. The quality of the investments is fully disclosed in the prospectus, so be sure to read it.

Bond Funds and Taxes

Funds produce two types of gains—dividends, taxed as ordinary income, and capital gains. Dividends, paid monthly or quarterly, are taxable in the current year; this is true even if you've arranged to have those dividends automatically reinvested in another fund. When you sell the shares, you owe a capital gains tax on any profits; if you get less than you paid, you take a capital loss. Managed bonds funds may sell bonds in their portfolios; when they do, any net capital gains (after deducting losses) are passed along to investors at year-end and reported on your current tax returns, just as with any other mutual fund (see page 650). With unit trusts, bonds are normally held until they're called or mature. When they're redeemed for what you paid, the proceeds are a nontaxable return of capital. If the price is a higher or lower, you have a capital gain or loss.

Read your year-end statement from funds and trusts carefully in order to see exactly what is taxable income and what is not.

Dividends from municipal bond funds are exempt from federal income taxes. But you'll owe state and local income tax on dividends attributable to out-of-state bonds in the portfolio. Some fund managers sell one-state unit trusts and funds in order to make the income entirely (or mostly) tax-exempt for residents of that state; whether this is a good idea depends on the creditworthiness of the state. A small part of your dividend from a tax-exempt managed bond fund may include interest from federally taxable securities, such as Treasury bills. Again, read the year-end statement to see exactly what's taxable.

Money Market Mutual Funds

These funds are not much known to individual investors, yet they can be splendid money-makers during a time when interest rates are high. They also offer special checking-account advantages to businesses and individuals.

The "money market" is a financial niche occupied by institutions that need to borrow large sums of money for short periods and by people who can afford to lend it to them. Loans may be for as brief a time as overnight or as long as eight or nine months. The federal government borrows via *Treasury bills* and *agency notes;* corporations, through *commercial paper;* and banks, through *letters of credit* and large *certificates of deposit.*

When interest rates are low, these loans yield less than savings accounts so would not be of interest to individual investors. But when short-term interest rates rise, money market investments become extremely attractive. Unfortunately, individual investors normally can't afford to participate. The minimum cost of a U.S. Treasury bill is, at this writing, $10,000. The minimum for commercial paper is about $25,000 and for certificates of deposit, $100,000 and up, but to get a truly competitive rate on these issues, you'd actually need $1 million.

Enter the money market mutual fund. By pooling your savings with that of many other investors, you can afford a piece of the action.

As investments, money funds are extremely safe. Commercial paper, certificates of deposit, and similar instruments are straight IOUs; the issuing institution promises to repay all the money, plus interest, within a specified number of days. By and large, the funds buy only the paper of leading banks, corporations, and the federal government—so the likelihood that any of their investments will default is minute. A company with a high credit rating is not going to go broke within thirty or sixty days.

As a practical matter, there are no capital gains and losses in money funds. Shares are generally redeemed for exactly what you paid: You put $1,000 in, you get $1,000 out. The interest rate you're paid on that money while it's in the fund rises and falls, in line with the general level of interest rates. In effect, money funds are like uninsured savings accounts, paying interest at varying rates from day of deposit to day of withdrawal.

When Would You Buy?

You'd buy a money fund when short-term interest rates are higher than you could get from a passbook savings account. Invest with money that you formerly kept in savings, or that you have temporarily withdrawn from the stock market or other investments. When the fund's yield falls below that of bank accounts, withdraw your money and put it back in the bank.

Money market funds are no-load, which means they charge no sales commissions. There's a variety of management fee structures, but they're not important: The thing to look for is the fund's investment policy and the return to the investor over a period of time. *Note*: One fund—Fidelity Daily Income Trust—has a $3 monthly service charge that reduces the return on small accounts.

Money funds advertise in financial publications. The minimum investment is generally $1,000, although some set higher amounts. There are usually dividend reinvestment and monthly withdrawal plans. Any time you want your money out, just tell the fund and it will wire your investment directly to your bank.

Money Funds As Interest-Paying Checking Accounts

Most funds allow you to write checks on your investment in the fund in amounts of $500 or more. This is an excellent money-making opportunity for individuals with large expenses and for businesses. Simply put the cash you'd normally keep in a checking account into a money market fund, and write checks against it. You receive interest on your cash right up until the day the check clears.

Several large money funds of interest to investors are The Reserve Fund, 810 Seventh Ave., New York, N.Y. 10019; Kemper Money Market Fund, 120 S. La Salle St., Chicago, Ill. 60603; Capital Preservation Fund, 755 Page Mill Rd., Palo Alto, Ca. 94304; Oppenheimer Monetary

Bridge, One New York Plaza, New York, N. Y. 10004; Money Market Management, 421 Seventh Ave., Pittsburgh, Pa. 15219; Scudder Managed Reserves, 175 Federal St., Boston, Mass. 02110; and Merrill Lynch Ready Assets, One Liberty Plaza, New York, N.Y. 10006.

Reading the Mutual Fund Tables

Mutual funds are listed in financial publications as you see on the right. The first column shows the fund's net asset value *(NAV)*. In the second, you'll find its current offering price *(Offer Price)*. With load funds, the price is the net asset value per share plus the sales commission; with no-load funds (marked *N.L.* in the tables), the offering price is the same as the net asset value. The third column *(NAV Chg.)* gives the day's increase or decrease in the fund's net asset value. For example, with the Aetna Fund, third from the top, the net asset value is $7.43, but because of the sales commission your actual price per share would be $8.12. On this day, the value of the fund increased 7 cents a share. By contrast, the Acorn Fund, at the top of the list, gained 15 cents a share. Because it's no-load (N.L.), its sales price is the same as its net asset value, $16.25 per share.

	NAV	Offer Price	NAV Chg.
Acorn Fnd	16.25	N.L.	+ .15
Adv Invest	9.74	N.L.	+ .08
Aetna Fnd	7.43	8.12	+ .07
Aetna InSh	12.86	14.05	+ .02
Afuture Fd	9.88	N.L.	+ .07
AGE Fund	5.92	6.04	+ .03
Allstate	8.75	N.L.	+ .07
Alpha Fnd	(z)	(z)	—
Am Birthrt	9.60	10.49	+ .02
Am Equity	4.91	5.37	+ .04
American Funds Group:			
Am Bal	7.97	8.71	+ .04
Amcap F	6.41	7.01	+ .02
Am Mutl	9.46	10.34	+ .07
Bnd FdA	14.61	15.97	—
Cap FdA	6.86	7.50	+ .05
Gth FdA	5.47	5.98	+ .03
IncF Am	15.83	17.30	+ .06
I C A	13.43	14.68	+ .11
Nw Prsp	15.57	17.02	+ .14
Wash Mt	6.43	7.03	+ .05
American General Group:			
A GnCBd	8.89	9.72	+ .01
A GC Gr	3.87	4.23	+ .02
A Gn Inc	6.44	7.04	+ .02
A GnVen	14.15	15.46	+ .18
Eqty Gth	6.60	7.21	+ .05
Fd Amer	6.36	6.95	+ .04
Prov Inc	3.83	4.13	+ .01
Am Grwth	5.83	6.29	+ .05
Am Ins Ind	4.74	5.18	+ .02
Am Invest	5.70	N.L.	+ .06
AmInv Inc	12.19	N.L.	+ .02
AmNat Gw	(z)	(z)	—
Anchor Group:			
Daily Inc	1.00	N.L.	—
Growth	6.36	6.86	+ .06
Income	7.16	7.72	+ .01
Spectm	4.36	4.70	+ .03

COMMODITIES

This game is only for wealthy investors who love high risks. You can buy and sell contracts for the world's basic commodities—foodstuffs, fibers, wood, metals, and a growing list of other raw materials, as well as foreign exchange and other monetary instruments. Most of the trading in these markets is done by manufacturers, farmers, bankers, and other businessmen, who take positions in contracts to hedge their business risks. Professional speculators play the game along with them, trying to make fast profits on developing trends. And a few nervy nonprofessionals occasionally place a bet. Generally, the nonprofessionals don't stay around very long. Speculating on price changes in commodities is fast, risky, and sooner or later will generate a large loss, which puts nonprofessionals out of the arena. Commodities prices move on rumor, worldwide weather changes, political developments, inflation, worldwide industrial demand, and many other factors, which the individual investor will likely be the last to know. If you think you know something about the future price of a particular crop or material and want to try your hand, do it with a broker who specializes in commodity trading. He watches the market more closely than an ordinary broker possibly can, and may be able to advise you of market changes in time to avoid a loss. I've said that this is no game for amateurs—I mean amateur brokers as well as amateur investors.

TAX SHELTERS

A number of sound investments include tax savings—among them, municipal bonds, well-chosen real estate, and deferred savings and compensation plans. But investments set up solely to take advantage of tax loopholes, real or imagined, often wind up costing investors (or their heirs) far more than they save. Thousands of people have lost—and are still losing, every day—large sums in shelters with big "tax loss" write-offs in the first year, but which fundamentally are terrible investments. In the long run, they'd have been better off paying their taxes and putting the remainder into high-interest-paying deferred annuities or tax-exempt municipals.

The Tax-Shelter Trap

Many investors don't realize that most shelters merely provide tax *deferral*, not permanent tax savings. Thanks to the write-offs, you can temporarily avoid a portion of your taxes, giving you extra money to invest for possible capital gains. But down the line, taxes will often be due. The government takes back your write-offs several ways. For example, just as a shelter produces "paper losses" to reduce your income, it eventually shows "paper profits" on which taxes must be paid. If the shelter isn't generating real profits, you'll have to cover those taxes from other income or buy another shelter. Depending on the nature of the shelter, those paper profits may be capital gains, ordinary income, or a combination of the two.

Taxes may also fall due when your shelter is finally disposed of—by sale, abandonment, foreclosure, or bequest to your heirs. There's no problem if the shelter has true economic value; you can sell the property and use the proceeds to cover the tax. But if there's little or no value, the taxes due can decimate your other assets.

When people buy shelters, they often look only at the tax savings in the first year—and it seems terrific. Don't buy, however, without asking an accountant to track the tax effects through several years, and explain what would happen to your estate if you died. The probability of a large tax on the other end is often enough to rule the shelter out.

What If You Die?

If you, a high-income man, die holding a fancy "tax loss" deal, it will fall to your estate—or your widow—to pay whatever tax is due. A widow may lose a good part of her assets unwinding ill-considered investments. What's too bad is that many men don't realize that this is going to happen—they blindly buy tax write-offs, then leave their widows to pay the piper. This problem can be avoided only if the shelter is a sound investment, saleable for enough money to cover the tax.

Many tax-shelter partnerships require a multi-year commitment of money. If you die before the commitment has been fulfilled, your widow is contractually obliged to keep on paying—even though she needs the money and derives no tax advantages from the investment.

Who Should Consider Tax Shelters?

Tax-shelter salesmen urge them on anyone in the 50 percent bracket. But because of the likelihood that, in the long run, income will return to you at rates higher than 50 percent, that bracket is marginal. If most of your money is from earnings, the tax effects of shelters may cost you far more than you save. You'd probably do better to choose the various forms of tax-deferred savings (see page 761), or buy tax-exempt municipal bonds. The higher your bracket over 50 percent, however, and the more unearned income you have, the more attractive shelters become.

What Are the Good Shelters?

Look for something with considerable investment merit *before* taxes. An example might be good apartment houses, in a prosperous city that's temporarily overbuilt; buildings can probably be had at a low price, with a potential for gain when construction slows and the apartment market tightens up. Good investment results *plus* tax advantages can generate splendid yields. Also, these shelters provide the investor with whatever money is needed to pay his taxes. So the tax trap discussed above does not affect him.

What Are the Bad Shelters?

Anything with no economic value: an investment you wouldn't cross the street for if it weren't for the tax write-offs. These typically offer high write-offs in the first year, making the shelter look like a free ride. But these are the very deals that hit you with serious tax problems on the back end. In general, the higher the first year write-off, the greater the risk that, in the long run, your shelter will hurt rather than help. Anything promising more than a 100 to 150 percent write-off in the first year should be treated with the greatest caution. Besides the long-term tax risk, there's also the risk that the Internal Revenue Service will challenge any tax shelter whose assets seem overvalued and whose write-offs are gimmicky.

Public or Private Partnerships?

The better investments tend to be private partnerships, where investors put up a minimum of $25,000 to $50,000. (But private partnerships also encompass the very worst deals, because they don't have to meet the exacting disclosure requirements set by the Securities and Exchange Commission.) Public partnerships—often sold in units of $5,000 or $10,000—find it harder to make money for investors because of the high offering and distribution costs.

In either case, it makes sense to buy through a brokerage house. They're required to examine the status and standing of the tax-shelter operator, to be sure he's experienced and not a crook. There's no guarantee you'll make money, but you should at least be steered away from the patent frauds. If it turns out that the operator is indeed a crook, you can sue the brokerage house.

Who Can Advise You on Tax Shelters?

The last place to get advice is from the tax-shelter salesman or the literature he gives out. Booklets tend to be crystal clear on the beautiful promise of shelters, but opaque in the paragraphs on risk. Many offering statements don't even cover such things as the tax risk to your estate at death. The "tax impact" study a salesman shows you typically covers only the first year, without covering what happens to you down the line.

Anyone considering a shelter should have the material reviewed by an accounting firm with a strong tax-shelter section, or a lawyer specializing in shelters and taxes. They won't know whether there's oil in the fields or coal in the seams, but they can tell whether the cost figures are reasonable and will assess the impact on your tax return many years in the future. A simple review might cost $500; more, if the deal is complex. If you're not willing to spend the money, don't get involved in anything as risky as shelters.

GOLD

The price of gold responds to changes in the *rate* of inflation. When inflation speeds up, the price of gold tends to rise; when the rate of price increase slows down, gold falls.

Some investors hold gold as an insurance policy against economic chaos—a role it has admirably fulfilled in the past. But as an inflation hedge it performs less well—history shows that the value of gold has consistently lagged during long-term inflationary upswings. Now that gold is no longer formally connected with the international monetary system, it may behave differently in the future—it soared well ahead of inflation in 1980, but then collapsed. If your object is to make money on gold, rather than hold it in case of catastrophe, you'll have to apply all the normal rules of investment—buying when the price seems likely to rise (i.e., when the inflation rate appears likely to increase) and selling when it drops 10 percent or so. Market timing is especially important, because the only way to make money is through capital gains; unlike other investments, gold pays no interest or dividends.

Bullion Coins

These coins, legal tender in the countries that issue them, are minted without limit—and for most investors are the best gold play. Bullion coins can be sold anywhere in the world without assay expenses, a big advantage over small gold bars. You don't need the numismatic knowledge required of rare-coin enthusiasts. There's no need to worry about floods, political upheavals, or gold-production costs, all of which influence gold-mining stocks. And coins have lasting value, as opposed to gold options or futures, which self-destruct after a short period of time.

Today's bullion-coin market is made up principally of the South African Krugerrand, the Canadian Maple Leaf, the Mexican 50-peso piece, and the Austrian 100-corona. Investors gravitate to whichever sells at the lowest mark-up *(premium)* over gold content. For fewer than fifty coins, a 5 percent mark-up is a good buy; larger amounts cost less. When you sell, the dealer will normally pay *you* a mark-up over gold content. Bullion coins can be had through coin dealers (to be found in the Yellow Pages), a few large brokerage houses, and a handful of banks. Some dealers charge more than others, so make comparisons before buying.

Rare Coins

These have value as collector's items far and above their gold content. But collecting rarities is not a pastime for tyros. Prices vary according to age and type of coin, as well as such arcane criteria as whether it's B.U. (Brilliant Uncirculated) or merely V.F. (Very Fine). Selecting a portfolio of rare coins and buying them at competitive prices takes time, knowledge, and love of coin collecting in and for itself. Percentage gains and losses in rare coins may be more, or less, than the changes in the gold price, depending on the market at the time.

Small Gold Bars

These generally range in size from a fraction of a troy ounce to one kilogram (32.15 troy ounces), and are sold by coin dealers, some brokerage houses, and a few banks. The cost of a bar, over its gold value, is usually competitive with that of gold coins. The trouble with bars is that they can be more easily counterfeited than coins, which adds rigidity to the market. If the dealer is unsure of you, mistrusts the bar's identification, or doesn't know the refiner, he may require an assay, which could run as high as $75 a bar. Investors are strongly advised to buy only the products of leading refiners, and deal with long-established firms that promise to buy back the bars if you want to sell. Even with good identification for the bar, however, you can't count on walking into any shop and selling a bar as easily as you can a coin.

Large Gold Bars

These are bought only by the serious hoarder. Bars sized at 100 or 400 ounces are available from gold dealers and refiners, a few large broker-age houses, and a few banks. The drawback is that large bars can't easily be broken down into small amounts if you want to sell just part of your holdings. Nor are they as portable as coins.

Note on Sales Taxes

Gold coins and bars are generally subject to sales taxes, which raise the price and lower the potential profit. Leading dealers, however, can usually arrange for delivery in a state where no sales taxes are levied.

A Note on Fineness

Gold bars are generally .995 percent fine gold. Some bars are especially produced so as to be .999 percent fine, and sell at a higher price, but they're no better an investment than the standard bars. Gold coins come in various weights and fineness, both reflected in their price.

Gold Stocks

Their advantage over gold coins is the dividend paid on investment. Mining stocks generally move in the same direction as gold prices (and counter to the rest of the stock market), but their swings are sharper and more erratic. If the gold price runs above a mine's cost of gold production, virtually all the excess is paid out in dividends, causing a sharp run-up in the stock. Conversely, if the gold price drops below production costs, profits, dividends, and the stock price may tumble. "Conservative" investments are older gold mines, with low gold-production costs, that pay dividends regularly. "Speculations" are newer, high-cost mines that give quick capital gains when the gold price rises (and quicker losses when it falls).

Gold Mutual Funds

Neither the income nor potential capital gain (or loss) is as high in mutual funds as it is if you hit it lucky with a good gold stock. But there's diversification among many types of gold-mining stocks, a spreading of risks, and a professionally selected portfolio—generally the best choice for the average gold-stock investor.

Other Gold Investments

Gold *futures* are a commodity investment (see page 662), with high risks for the average person. Even in a strongly rising price trend, gold may temporarily drop by enough to wipe an investor out. If you're lucky, futures give higher percentage returns than gold coins or stocks, but the game produces many more losers than winners. Another form of speculation is buying options on gold-mining stocks, or on gold bullion (see page 638).

COLLECTIBLES

Specialists can, and do, make a good deal of money in fine art, rare books, antique silver, and all the other items people love to collect. Postage stamps are especially popular, because they're small, easily carried, and sell in an international market. But as with any other market, prices rise and fall. It takes a lot of money and a true collector's knowledge to make good investments. One thing you may not realize: Because of buying-and-selling commissions, values on some items may have to double just for the collector to break even! Almost all of the new stamps printed, pictures painted, and books published go down in price, not up. Unless you invest in items of top quality, your chances even of making as much money as you'd get from a savings account are remote.

PHONE HUSTLES

The more exotic investments, such as tax shelters, diamonds, and so on, are often sold over the telephone by high-pressure bucket shops to credulous investors. A company will get your name, advise you of the marvels of its deal, send you information by mail, and—wonder of wonders—make the sale. Often you could have gotten the same commodity through a regular broker at a lower price. Often the deal is not what it seems. Often the quality of the investment is misrepresented. There are few ironclad rules in investing, but this should be one: *Never, never buy anything over the telephone from a salesman you don't know.* Here's another: *Don't invest in anything you're unfamiliar with.*

REAL ESTATE

The chapter on your second home, Chapter 19, covers one type of real estate investment—a summer cottage, ski condominium, or piece of land on which you plan to put a house some day. This section deals with real estate bought entirely as an investment, with no aspect of personal use.

Professional Help

When you enter the real estate market as an investor, you'll need a lot of help from first-rate professionals. They have essential knowledge that you lack; without them your fledgling enterprise could be buried right from the start.

To find and evaluate properties and negotiate with the owner, work with a *real estate broker* experienced in rental or commercial real estate. He knows what's on the market, and can draw on his experience in judging the potential of various lands and buildings. Sometimes a broker can help you get a property that wasn't previously for sale and open doors at a bank that might handle the financing. But be warned that in the price negotiation, the broker represents the seller, not you; so make your own careful evaluation of what it's prudent to pay.

Once you're seriously interested in a house or building, have it inspected by a professional *engineer* experienced in that kind of property. He'll report on everything from the state of the plumbing and wiring to the structural soundness of the building itself. If something looks awry—for example, the roof or heating system—have an expert tell you what it will cost to fix. Also get price estimates on any additions you plan for the building, such as a porch or a parking lot. You'll need all these figures to decide whether the building can be profitable.

Before you make an offer on the building, ask a *real estate appraiser* familiar with this type of property to estimate its value. It helps if the appraiser has the engineer's inspection report in hand.

Talk to a *lawyer* experienced in this kind of transaction, whether the property is residential, commercial, or raw land. He'll know where the hookers are in contracts and can prevent the seller or broker from taking advantage of you. Also, he'll ensure that you don't lose any of the money you put down if the deal doesn't go through.

Go over the estimates for expenses, depreciation, and other cost factors with an *accountant* who handles a lot of real estate transactions. He'll help you judge the reasonableness of the figures, and can perhaps spot whether any significant expense items have been left out. He'll also work out your cash position before and after taxes and estimate your return on investment.

In every case, I've emphasized that the professional you consult should be experienced in the particular type of real estate investment you're about to make. A commercial-property appraiser may err in judging a rental home; a residential real estate broker may not know the hazards of buying an apartment house; a corporate lawyer may leave out an important protective clause in a land contract. You need all the help you can get to make a good investment, and that means working with people who know exactly what they're doing.

The Tax Advantages of Real Estate

All the expenses of finding, maintaining, and selling properties are deductible from income. Interest on the mortgages is deductible. Rentals are taxed as ordinary income, but profits from the sale of properties are capital gains. (*Note:* You can't defer capital gains taxes the way you can when you sell your own house, because the property is not your principal residence. You can, however, exchange the property for another, tax free). The key real estate deduction, however, is *depreciation,* allowed only on business properties, not on your own home. Depreciation is an allowance for the steady reduction in a building's useful life. The deduction may be high enough to shelter most or all of your rental income from taxes, hence giving you steady cash income from the investment (called *cash flow*) but eliminating all or most of the taxes on that income. The depreciation deduction may also be used to shelter some of your other income from tax.

Three Rules on Real Estate Investment

The three most important things in real estate investing, says the old gag, are (1) location; (2) location; and (3) location. One block is growing, another declining; one town is more desirable than another; one piece of land is in the direct path of development and another not; one lot has a view, another is hemmed in by houses. The same piece of property in various locations would bring drastically different prices. The best real estate investments are made in areas you are thoroughly familiar with. You know the good neighborhoods and the bad, the attitudes of the people, and the history of the town's development, so you have a better feel than others for where the best locations are. If you invest in an unfamiliar area, on the recommendation of someone else, you're more apt to make a mistake.

Getting Started

Big profits in real estate are often made with a small initial investment. You might put a few hundred dollars down on a land contract, or refinance your house and use the money to buy a second house with low-down-payment FHA financing. If these properties appreciate in value, they can be sold in two or three years and the profits put into something better. Try to pay off your initial investment as rapidly as possible, as a way of building savings. If you buy income properties, such as two-family houses or small apartment buildings, the rentals can cover your costs and give you a profit. As the property appreciates in value, you sell or refinance, buy another building, and do it again. A whole string of apartment buildings can be pyramided from a single investment.

Buying and Reselling Houses

In areas where residential values are rising rapidly, you can do well by buying a house, holding it for a while, and reselling. One strategy is to buy a house that's well located but underpriced because it needs repairs. Some work may have to be done by a professional—a roofer, plumber, and so on. But you can probably do the painting, staining, and simpler carpentry yourself. By bringing the house up to the minimum standard of the neighborhood, you can often sell for a good profit fairly quickly. This can be a profitable venture even if you hire others to do most of the work. Another strategy is to buy a house in reasonably good shape and rent it out while you wait for it to appreciate. Some rules on buying and reselling houses:

1. Take great care to buy in a neighborhood where there's steady demand for homes and real estate values are rising rapidly.

2. Look for properties that are underpriced because the house needs work, not because the location is bad. You can fix the house but not the location.

3. Don't put too much money into a house you're fixing up for resale. Face-lifting and basic repairs can raise the value of the property considerably, but you won't get your full investment out of luxury additions. Bring the house up to minimum standard for the neighborhood and let the next owner add his own luxuries.

4. Put the minimum amount of money down.

5. Don't buy a property that carries a higher selling price or higher rental than is standard for the neighborhood. The one expensive house in an area of modest homes is *not* a good investment, because people who can afford it will be looking for a better neighborhood.

6. Make detailed estimates of your rental income from the property, if any, and all the costs—maintenance, repairs, mortgage, taxes, buying and selling expenses, insurance, the expense of finding tenants, and so on. Can you carry the monthly out-of-pocket expenses? If you're counting on tenants to help carry the costs, have you the resources to cover months when the house may be vacant? Can you afford the necessary repairs?

7. Estimate a conservative selling price for the property, then figure your return on investment. You're looking for a *minimum* of 15 percent a year before taxes, and preferably more than 18 percent. The holding period for this profit shouldn't be any more than five to seven years. If you don't think you can make that much money, look for another property. In areas where real estate values are soaring, an investor may buy a house and rent it out at a loss, expecting to recoup when the house is sold. This can work, but it's a riskier investment than having a property where the income covers the costs.

8. Check the tax assessment. If it's low for the neighborhood (as is common with older houses), the house may very well be reassessed when you buy it. Put an estimate for higher taxes into your cost figures.

9. If you rent out the property, ask your lawyer to get a standard lease form or rental agreement, and go over it for any changes you'd want to make. You may not want to give a year's lease (if it's not required by ordinance); a month-to-month tenancy makes it easier to raise the rent if costs go up, and easier to get rid of tenants who mistreat the property. The rental agreement should specify how much notice must be given, by landlord or tenant, before moving day; also, who pays for the utilities (generally the tenant), minor repairs, snow removal, etc.; to what extent, if any, the tenants can redecorate; and other house rules. Always take a security deposit of two months' rent before the tenant moves in; this deposit, less a sum for damage other than normal wear and tear, is normally returned to the tenant when he leaves. It's also the landlord's cushion against a tenant who fails to pay his rent.

10. Prohibit pets. They do a lot of damage.

11. Collect rents promptly. Once a tenant gets behind, he may never catch up, leaving you holding the bag. It also pays to inspect the property regularly in order to be sure it's being well kept. A tenant who does a lot of damage, skips his last month's rent, and then moves out unexpectedly can eliminate your profit.

12. Live close enough to the house to reach it promptly if the tenant reports a problem, but not close enough so that the tenant rings your doorbell every time a little thing goes wrong. If you're not prepared to shoulder the hassle of being a landlord, don't get into it in the first place.

13. You'll save a lot of money and tenant trouble if you're handy enough to make small repairs yourself.

14. As a rule of thumb, you should rent the house for 0.8 to 1 percent,

per month, of the price you paid. If you can't get that much rent, it's a poor deal.

15. Don't invest in a town that has just one or two major employers unless you feel pretty confident their business is in excellent health. If a factory closes down or a lot of workers are laid off, the value of your property could fall.

16. Have a cash reserve to support the house in case the tenants move out and you can't get replacements right away.

17. Medium-priced houses in good or improving neighborhoods are your best bet. There's more rental demand in that price range; wealthier people are more likely to be shopping for homes of their own. With high-cost houses it's also hard to get enough rent to make the investment pay.

Buying Apartment Houses

Apartments can make excellent investments, whether they're two-family houses or larger buildings. The income from rents should cover your costs and return a before-tax profit while the building appreciates in value. Eventually, you can sell (or exchange) the property at a gain and invest in something else; or else refinance the property and use the additional money as a down payment on another apartment building. When the second apartment appreciates, you can refinance and buy a third, building yourself an empire of profitable properties from a single investment.

A common way to start is to buy a two-family house or an apartment house with three or four units, live in one, and rent the others. You can get FHA-VA financing, with a low down payment, for up to four units. Some rules on buying rental properties:

1. Buy in a good or improving neighborhood, where property values should rise and there's growing demand from renters. This allows you to raise rents.

2. Avoid rent-controlled areas. You want to be sure you can raise rents to cover rising costs.

3. Buy a building with the largest number of rental units that you can afford. The overhead for a six-unit apartment isn't much more than for a four, but the former generally delivers higher profits.

4. The first few investors in a run-down urban neighborhood, who start the ball rolling on rehabilitation, may wait many years for their investments to pay off. The second and third wave of investors, on the other hand, may be able to turn a profit fairly quickly—though it may not be as large as that of the patient pioneers.

5. Demand is greater for medium-priced apartments than for those in the luxury range. Modest buildings also cost less, require less maintenance, and need fewer expensive amenities. An excellent investment is a sound but run-down building whose value can be increased by a few cosmetic improvements.

6. If you need a second mortgage to buy the property, try to avoid dealing with mortgage and finance companies, which charge high interest rates. Often you can get a second mortgage from the seller at the same interest rate as you're getting from the bank. Second mortgages from the seller work this way: Suppose you're buying a $100,000 building, borrowing $80,000 from a bank. But you have only $10,000 in cash. You give the seller $90,000 (from the first mortgage and your cash), plus an IOU for the remaining $10,000, using the building itself as security for the note. Why would a seller give a second mortgage? Because he wants to sell the property and because you're offering him a higher interest rate on the $10,000 you owe than he could get by demanding the money in cash and putting the money in the bank. Generally speaking, the less cash you put down the better, providing that rents from the building will cover your monthly payments.

7. Go over all the costs with an accountant before you buy. Overlooking just one key expense, or overestimating what you'll get in rents, may cause you to pay too much for the building, hence fail to profit on the investment. Among the expenses to consider are taxes, mortgage, insurance, heat, light, water, janitor, management fees, uncollected rents, advertising, maintenance, yard care, furnishings, snow removal, repairs, reserves for replacing appliances and other items, and—most important—emergency funds in case you overlooked something. If the building has a low assessment, assume that your taxes will increase and allow for it.

The seller will have a list of expenses and income for you, but his list may skip some major items. He may also have fudged expenses—for example, by having two suppliers deliver oil and showing you the bills for only one. (Ask the supplier himself how often he delivers and whether he's the sole source.) On the income side, the seller may have made his projections on the assumption that every apartment is rented, when in fact you'll have a certain number of vacancies. Look over his records to establish the actual vacancy rate.

8. Apartment buildings are often bought in multiples of the rent roll. If total rents come to $40,000 a year and buildings of that type are selling for three times rent roll, you might be expected to pay around $120,000. But this rule of thumb says nothing about the proper price for a particular property that might have higher or lower expenses than others. Study the financial characteristics of each building individually, to establish the maximum you're willing to pay.

9. Sometimes buildings carry *balloon mortgages*—mortgages with low monthly payments until the end of the term, at which point a large sum of money falls due. The apartment house may look profitable on an everyday basis, but how will you pay the balloon? If you can't get the seller to lower the price, you may not be able to make it.

10. You're looking for a minimum of 12 percent cash return on your investment before taxes, preferably more than 15 percent.

11. Ask your lawyer to check the zoning ordinances and building codes to be sure the building is in compliance. Also, see if there's a legal barrier to any plans you may have for the building's future.

12. The brokerage commission on large buildings is often quite high. But the broker may be willing to take his commission in installments, which lowers the amount of cash you need up front.

13. In negotiating price with the seller, check the deed on file at city hall. In most states, the tax stamps on the deed should tell you what he paid for the property—a great help in deciding what price to offer.

14. In deciding on price, take into consideration all the building's expenses and problems—the repairs, balloon mortgages, future tax increases, vacancies, and so on. It is traditional to bargain over real estate, the seller starting high and the buyer low. But there should be a price above which you will not go for the property—a price worked out with your accountant that you can't exceed without reducing the potential profit to unacceptable levels. If the seller holds to a higher price, walk away from the investment and look for something else.

15. It may take a long time to find the right investment, but persevere. Better to wait and get a building where the numbers are right than to pounce on something that's hard to make pay.

16. It may be difficult, even impossible, to get financing on an older building, so discuss the deal with a banker before you make a bid. Buildings are generally considered to have an economic life of fifty years—something to take into consideration when you're shopping around.

17. Generally speaking, it is more expensive to put up a new building than to buy an older one and renovate. New buildings also have a way of escalating in cost beyond the original estimate, even beyond the contract price. Good, older buildings also rent faster than new ones because the rents are usually lower.

18. Have a lawyer and accountant, both experienced in real estate, go over the figures and contracts before you make a move. If there are problems, they can often make suggestions that will help the deal go through. It is foolish to skimp on professional help. Their advice can save you many times the cost of their fees.

19. One reason apartments are good investments for the ordinary individual is that they're something you can easily understand. You know what amenities people need in order to live, what comforts they want, what annoys them, what's reasonable for them to expect. Understanding the needs of your tenants is as important as understanding a geographical area when it comes to making money in real estate.

20. Inspect your building regularly. Damage caught early is inexpensive to repair. If you have the property up for sale, make doubly sure that everything is shipshape. Just a few obvious problems, even though minor, can force you to cut the price.

Other Investments

Executives and professional people often choose to invest in professional or office buildings, especially if they're going to occupy one of the offices. These buildings generally cost more up front than apartment buildings, it's harder to replace a tenant who leaves, and there may be high renovation expenses for a new tenant. On the other hand, leases are generally longer and the return on investment higher. Also, the tenants usually don't give the landlord much trouble. Executives and professional people are generally qualified to understand the business needs of these tenants, which means they may have better judgment than other investors in choosing a building or piece of land for office use.

Another popular investment is a shopping center or mini-mall. Like professional buildings, these promise higher returns but cost more up front and face risk of serious loss if one tenant leaves and can't be immediately replaced. Older shopping centers are vulnerable to competition from newer ones being built nearby.

Many motel and restaurant chains seek local investors to buy a good piece of land and lease it to them for their enterprise. Write to their headquarters for information.

Land and stores in older cities may be inexpensive but are poor risks if the urban center is still declining. Better to put a store in a shopping center or an urban area undergoing rehabilitation.

Any of these investments should be undertaken only if you yourself know the business or are in partnership with someone who does. You want a partner who has invested successfully in this kind of enterprise before and will show you his records to prove it.

Investing in Raw Land

Undeveloped land produces no income to offset your land payments and taxes, so the investment is purely for capital gains. You ought to see good reason for the land to increase sharply in value, at annual rates of 15 percent or more a year, within five to seven years. Otherwise, it may not be worth having. Land that takes many, many years to increase in price could wind up giving you an average annual return no better than you'd get in a bank. Such land may even prove unsaleable for long periods of time (see the section on investing in vacation land, starting on page 354).

The price of land goes up when it lies in the path of balanced development. The spread of homes, apartments, businesses, and recreation should move inexorably in its direction. Land on the fringes of current development costs more than land some distance away, but the land close by is surer to appreciate in value.

Some investors believe that all land will increase in value because "they're not making any more of it." In fact, that's the real estate salesman's favorite line. But as many people have learned to their cost, land prices can go down as well as up—or go nowhere for many years. Classically, what makes the price of land go up is that someone wants to convert it from its present use (say, a field) to a more economically valuable use (say, a housing development). If the field stays a field and no one wants to do anything else with it, you can't expect much, if any, price appreciation. Don't try to develop land yourself unless you have expertise and a lot of money behind you. Costs can be staggering, and a lot of tyros go broke.

No-Growth Laws

Many communities are passing laws to limit development and preserve what open land they have left. If you hold undeveloped property in those communities, the price may fall. But if you own developed properties, the price should rise considerably. Assuming that demand continues, the current supply of homes, stores, and industrial sites will become more and more valuable. Investing in rental properties in a town expected to pass a no-growth law can be an excellent strategy.

Farmland and Timberland

In recent years prices for this type of land have soared. It's a specialized investment, however, demanding knowledge of the farming or timber business, familiarity with the various government subsidy programs that affect value, and connections with the farmers or businessmen who will lease your land. As with every other type of real estate investment, the best profits are made by people who have a feel for the business and a close understanding of the market. If you yourself aren't familiar with this type of land, it's best to stay out of it.

Why Is the Seller Selling?

That's a good question to ask about any real estate investment. It may be that he's made his profit and is ready to move on. It may be that he's in financial trouble. Or it may be that he knows something about the property that you don't. Investigate the third possibility as best you can. If the property is an apartment building, talk to the janitor, the tenants, and the suppliers to see if they know any useful gossip. You can get a good price from an owner in financial trouble, but you'll very definitely want to know whether the source of his trouble is the building you're thinking about buying.

Real Estate Syndications

Deals sold by stockbrokers, in small or large participation units, generally come under the heading "tax shelter," and can be very risky for the individual investor. You probably don't know anything about the area being developed, so everything rests on the syndicator's expertise. These deals often take a lot of expense money out of the partnership, making it hard to show a profit. And although tax-loss real estate can make your income tax return look good for the first few years, you may be building up large potential tax liabilities (see page 662). The serious real estate investor should stick with areas he knows, and stay away from syndications.

Second Mortgages or Deeds of Trust

These generally offer the investor high yields and high risks. You buy a second mortgage on a business or residential property and hope the owner will remain solvent as long as it takes to pay the loan off. Terms and interest rates vary all over the lot. Loans generally run somewhere between one and ten years, with yields well above the rates on first mortgages. Two key things to check before making the loan: Can the property owner afford to make second-mortgage payments along with all his other obligations? If he defaults, is the value of the property large enough to cover both the first and second mortgages? But be warned that documentation may be poor. Second mortgages are typically sold by real estate lawyers, brokers, lenders, and others in the real estate business.

If the property owner defaults on the second mortgage, you can move to have the property foreclosed. This would bring the first-mortgage holder into the act. Any proceeds from the foreclosure sale go first to repay the first mortgage in full; often, there's not enough left over to pay off the second mortgage. That happens if the property was over-appraised for second-mortgage purposes (not uncommon, especially with business properties), or if the foreclosure sale brings less than full market value (also not uncommon). A second-mortgage holder may decide to delay foreclosure, in hopes that the borrower can resume payments at a later date. Waiting for payment may be your only realistic hope of getting your investment out.

If the property owner defaults on the first mortgage, the lender will probably have no such qualms about putting the property into foreclosure. Faced with the possibility of losing his investment, the second-mortgage holder may decide to take over payments on the first mortgage temporarily, while the property owner gets back on his feet. It's in return for risks like this that second-mortgage yields are so high. As usual, the higher the interest rate you're promised on your money, the greater the chance you may lose your investment.

Chapter Twenty-Seven

WILLS AND ESTATE PLANNING

Glad did I live and gladly die,
And I laid me down with a will.
ROBERT LOUIS STEVENSON

You need a will. If you don't have one, put this book down right now and put a note on your telephone to call a lawyer. It is often not expensive to make a will—maybe $75 or $100 assuming that your situation is not complex. If the lawyer has done other business for you, he may charge nothing at all. Having a will can save your heirs endless problems after your death and ensure that your property goes to the people who ought to have it.

But once involved in will making, some people carry things too far. They arrange their estates in complicated ways just to save a little in taxes, name trustees for money people should manage themselves, put conditions in their wills to try to control people's lives from the grave. It's important to have a will, but try to keep it simple in order to leave your heirs free to live their own lives without bumping into your arrangements every time they turn around.

Reluctance to Make a Will

Some people won't even discuss it. But three facts are inescapable: (1) You own property. (2) You are going to die. (3) Someone is going to get that property.

So you might as well have it go where *you* want, not where the laws of your state decree. When you've spent a lifetime acquiring property and making decisions on its management, it's regrettable not to make the final decision as to where it's going to go.

Some people don't make wills because of certain misconceptions. You may be relieved to learn that making a will doesn't in any way limit what you can do with your property; you can sell it, give it away, or buy more property with no reference at all to your will's provisions. No one has to know what's in your will if you don't want to tell them; the witnesses to a will are there only to attest that they saw you sign it, not that they read it. The will can be changed any time you want; you're not locked into any of your bequests. Finally, your financial affairs don't have to be in perfect order for you to make a will, nor do you have to make an accounting of everything you own. The lawyer can simply write that you leave "all the property to Joan," or "half the property to John," without even knowing what the property is.

If You Die Without a Will

People often assume that if they die *intestate* (without a will), their property will go to the "logical person"—their spouse, children, or grandchildren—but that's not always so. Each state has strict laws as to what happens to an estate not disposed of by will. The wishes or financial needs of the survivors are *not* taken into consideration. State laws in this area vary tremendously; the following table, applicable to many states (but not all), gives you a general idea of what could happen to your property:

If you're:	And die without a will, your property may go:
Unmarried or widowed, no children, parents living,	To your parents, regardless of their need. Brothers or sisters may get nothing. The person you live with, or close friends, will get nothing.
Unmarried or widowed, no children, parents dead,	To your brothers and sisters; if you were an only child, to other next of kin. Any friends who were closer to you than your relatives would be left out; brothers or sisters (or other kin) with whom you did not get along would be included.

Unmarried or widowed, with children,	To your children (though not to stepchildren or a child you had raised or befriended who was not legally yours). The court appoints a guardian for a minor child and his funds.
Unmarried or widowed, no relatives,	To the state.
Married, with children,	Partly to the surviving spouse, partly to the children (but not stepchildren). The spouse may get only one third or one half of *your* property (but all of the joint or community property).
Married, without children,	Partly to the surviving spouse, partly to your parents. The spouse may get half of *your* property (but all of the joint or community property). Some states give all the property to the spouse; others divide it among spouse, parents, brothers, and sisters.

Dying without a will could work a real hardship on your survivors. For example:

1. If you have a wife and three grown children, you might want all your property to go to her, for her support the rest of her life. But if you have no will, she might get only one half or one third, with the rest going to the children. If your wife can't live on her share, the children would have to support her, which can be difficult for all concerned.

2. If you have a wife and three minor children, the children's half or two thirds would be put aside for them in their names. There are strict limitations on how the money can be invested. The wife might be named guardian, but she could use those funds only for the children's support, not her own. If she drew on the funds, she'd have to specify what the money was for and make an annual accounting. At best, this is an inconvenient way to live, and could inhibit the use of that money for the family's general welfare.

3. If there are no children, money meant for your wife to live on might go instead to your parents or even your brothers and sisters, who may feel no obligation to support her. If they gave their share to the wife, they might incur gift tax liabilities.

4. Money set aside for minor children will be given them when they come of age, which in many states is eighteen. At that age, children may not be wise enough to handle it properly and may blow money that (they realize too late) should have been spent on a college education.

5. Without a will, stepchildren inherit nothing.

6. For the young family making a will, the most serious concern is what would happen to the children if the parents die. Without a will the grandparents take over, if there are any, and a court fight might develop over which set of grandparents is best able to raise them. A court appoints someone to manage whatever property the children get, so if the grandparents need money for the children, they have to petition for payments. Records have to be kept of the money distributed, and an annual accounting made. With a will, however, you can provide for the care of both the children and their inheritance.

7. Where there's no will, the court appoints an administrator to straighten out the estate. The fees he collects may be greater than what it would cost to have a will go through probate.

The Trouble with Alternatives to Wills

It might appear that, in some cases, you can get away without a will. For example, if all you own is a house and a bank account (both in joint names with your spouse), an insurance policy, and a few personal effects, there may apparently be nothing to divide. The joint property automatically goes to the other owner (as does community property); the insurance proceeds to the named beneficiary; the personal effects probably to your spouse and children even without a will. But it doesn't always work out that neatly. In some states even small personal effects have to be passed by will or else divided according to the intestacy laws. You may have property you've forgotten—an automobile, a lump-sum payment from a pension plan, your last salary check, or an inheritance. If you die in an auto accident and the estate collects damages from the other driver, your will directs where the money should go. Some types of property, such as stocks and bonds, are easier handled if they're not in joint names (see page 715). In community property states you have to think of what property, if any, is outside the community, hence will not automatically pass to your spouse (see page 718). What if everything is in joint names and you both die without wills, perhaps in a common accident? State law, not your personal wishes, then controls where your property goes and who will be the guardian of your minor children and their funds. If your joint property arrangement does not specifically say there's a *right of survivorship,* the court might rule that it does not automatically pass to the other owner (see page 713). In that case the property will be divided according to state law.

Wives and Wills

Both husband *and* wife need a will. This is self-evident where the wife has property to dispose of, but wives with little or no property in their names may think a will isn't necessary. IT IS. To begin with, you have personal property to bequeath—perhaps some jewelry or antiques. As you think about it, you may have more property than you realize. Second, what if your husband dies leaving everything to you, and you die with him (or shortly after him, without having had time to make a will)? State law then decrees where your property goes and who becomes the guardian of your children. Wives in community property states may not think of themselves as owning much, because everything might be in the husband's name. But under the law one half of the marital property is theirs. When husband and wife make wills, they should be sure that their bequests mesh, so if they die together, his mother and her sister don't wind up as coowners of the family homestead.

Joint Wills

Some married couples have one document, leaving everything to each other or to specified beneficiaries if they die together. Generally speaking, this arrangement is not wise; joint wills have led to problems and unexpected litigation. These wills often neglect to specify what happens if one spouse dies before the other. Questions have arisen as to whether one of the joint testators can change the terms of the will without the consent of the other. In some cases joint wills may deprive the estate of the important marital deduction, which means a significant increase in tax. Husband and wife should each have a *separate, individual* will.

Handwritten Wills

Some people write on a piece of paper where they want their property to go, put it away in a drawer, and think they've written a will. In many states that would not be legal. The court would throw it out and divide the estate as if you had left no instructions at all. State laws on wills are extremely precise. A few states accept a handwritten, unwitnessed will, but most require one to three witnesses who actually saw you sign it and who also witnessed each other's signatures. Even if you follow the correct procedure as to witnesses, you might make a technical error that would invalidate the will.

Another risk is that what appears to be a simple sentence may have more than one possible interpretation, leading to wrangling among the relatives and perhaps a challenge to the will in court. One reason will language is so technical is to avoid the ambiguities of common speech. Some people take great pride in writing their own wills, but they wouldn't be so pleased with themselves if they saw what happened when their wills got to court. If your will is defective, your estate is handled as if you hadn't made a will at all and divided according to state law without reference to your wishes or your survivors' needs. It costs very little to have a lawyer supervise the drawing of your will, and revise it from time to time. His advice could save your heirs untold time, trouble, and money.

Oral Wills

Oral wills are generally not valid unless they're made in military combat; and even then the soldier has to reaffirm his wishes in writing if he makes it back alive. A few states recognize oral wills made during a final illness, as long as a specified number of witnesses heard the will made.

Seeing a Lawyer

Any competent lawyer can handle a simple will. If you don't know a lawyer yourself, ask friends for references. Well-to-do people with potential estate tax liabilities need an attorney specializing in wills and estates.

When you visit the lawyer, have in hand an estimate of the value of your estate. Also, decide approximately how you want the property divided. You don't have to list everything you own or name a beneficiary for each item. Except for special bequests, wills usually divide the property in a general way. It's common to specify percentage amounts —for example, 30 percent to each of three children, 5 percent to a sister, and 5 percent to a charity. A lawyer will make suggestions as to how you can best achieve your goals.

How Much Do You Have to Leave?

All the property in your possession at death is your *estate*. When you make a will, take an inventory of all your property and establish its value. Count everything: your car, home, personal property, furnishings, art, jewelry, furs, investments, collections, insurance proceeds, pension plan distributions, revocable trusts, savings, money owed to you, and so on. *All jointly owned property goes into your estate, except that portion of the property which was paid for by someone else.* (*Warning:* If your heirs can't prove that someone else paid for the property—for example, your spouse—it will *all* be credited to your estate. So if you own property jointly, keep good records as to who paid for what.)

After you add up the total value, subtract whatever money you owe —mortgages, loans, income taxes. The remainder is the gross value of your estate.

Then subtract estimated burial expenses, the cost of your last illness, fees for administering your estate (see page 690), and the cost of turning assets into cash (for example, if real estate is sold, there will be a 6 or 7 percent brokerage commission). For most people the remainder is what goes to heirs.

If you're wealthy enough to be in the estate-tax range, apply the deductions that reduce your taxable estate (see page 707). A tax lawyer can advise you on about how much tax is owed and what strategies, if any, you can use to reduce it.

When you add up the value of your estate, take a moment to think what would happen to your family if you died. Is this property, plus Social Security, enough for them to live on? If not, the cheapest way to leave your family a larger sum of money is to buy term life insurance (see page 369).

HOW LARGE IS YOUR ESTATE?

Assets	Estimated value	Ownership (husband, wife, joint)	In will or outside will?
Savings accounts	$		$
Checking accounts			
U.S. savings bonds			
Money owed to you			
Personal property			
Your home			
Other real estate			
Stocks			
Bonds			
Government securities			
Mutual funds			
Other investments			
Equity interest in your own business			
Individual life insurance			
Group life insurance			
Death benefits from pension or profit-sharing plans[a]			
Total	$		

Liabilities[b]

Current bills	$	
Mortgage		
Auto loans		
Personal loans		

[a]Not counting funds left in IRA and Keogh plans and left to heirs.
[b]Excluding loans covered by credit life insurance.

Liabilities

Installment loans	$ _____
Life insurance loans	_____
Income taxes	_____
Total	$ _____

Total value of your estate (assets minus liabilities)[a] $ _____

Deductions from your estate

Burial expenses	$ _____
Lawyer's fee	_____
Executor's fee	_____
Cost of liquidating assets	_____
Deduction for estate tax credit[b]	_____
Marital deduction	_____
Orphan's exclusion[c]	_____

Total Taxable Estate[d] (estate value minus deductions) $ _____

[a]Include property in your name and property in joint names to the extent that you paid for it. Exclude one half of joint property if given to a spouse and a gift-tax return filed.

[b]$161,563 in 1980; $175,625 in 1981 and thereafter.

[c]Of bequests made to children, up to $5,000 is estate-tax-free, per child, for each year the orphan child is under 21.

[d]For estate taxes, see page 707.

Property Passing Outside the Will

A good part of your property may pass outside the will. For example, all joint or community property automatically goes to the other joint owner; bank accounts in trust for another person go to that person; life insurance goes to the named beneficiary, as do U.S. savings bonds and certain employee benefits and retirement plans; trusts set up during your lifetime are distributed according to the trust document; business interests may be provided for by contract. It is important to get a fix on the value of properties passing outside the will so that you can use your will to remedy any inequities. The will covers everything you own whose distribution is not separately provided for.

Fees

Maximum fees for executors (see page 700) are set by law in each state. Banks and lawyers generally charge the maximum; friends and family members, little or nothing. In any case, the charges are tax-deductible. Executor's fees usually apply to the *probate estate,* which is the property passed by will. Property outside the will, such as joint property, is not counted. The following fees may not apply to your particular state, but they give you a ball-park idea of the costs.

Sample executor's fees

4% of the first $25,000
3½% of the next $125,000
3% of the next $150,000
2% of everything above $300,000

Lawyer's fees for guiding the will through probate are negotiable. An executor should ask two or three competent lawyers what they'd charge; by making it clear that he's price-shopping, he can generally get a lower-than-usual quote. Sometimes the court fixes fees. To give you an idea of where the maximum fee might lie, here are price guidelines published by the Westchester County (New York) Bar Association. They usually apply to the whole estate, less life insurance proceeds. Again, the fees are tax deductible.

Sample lawyer's fees

5% of the estate up to $50,000 (with a minimum fee for small estates)
4% of the amount between $50,000 and $100,000
3% of the amount between $100,000 and $500,000
2½% of the amount over $500,000

Naming a Guardian

Be sure that the person you name as guardian for your minor children is willing and able to take on the job. It's not a responsibility to be taken lightly. If the children are old enough to understand the question, ask them where they'd like to live in the event anything happened to both of you. After all, their wishes are important here. Don't be afraid of raising the issue. Research has shown that children are often better able to cope with thoughts of death and dying than adults.

Your first thought as to a guardian may be your own parents. But in many cases they're too old to do a good job. Also, because of their age, you're setting up your children to lose a second set of parents. If you're close to one of your brothers or sisters, that person may be a good choice, but don't confine your search for a guardian to family members. A close friend who shares your attitudes toward life and child rearing may be better for your children than a relative whose values and temperament are quite different from yours. Whoever you pick as guardian of the children will probably need money to help support them—something to consider in deciding how to leave property to a minor child (see page 719).

It often happens that the person named as guardian hasn't room in his house for your children. You can solve this problem by providing in your will that the guardian be given use of your house rent-free if it's big enough; if he doesn't want it, your house could be sold and part of the proceeds given or loaned to the guardian so he can buy a larger house.

If the guardian is not as well off financially as you are, you might want to let the trustee of your children's property distribute money for the benefit of the guardian's children as well as yours. It could upset the family if some of the children have cars and go to good colleges while others don't. Evenhanded treatment of everyone under the same roof is probably best for the children's emotional well-being.

How Much for the Children?

Most wills leave the property equally to all the children. But in special circumstances unequal shares are more equitable. For example, if you've put two children through college and still have a young one at home, you might want to provide something extra for that one's education. A child with a serious illness or disability might need extra money for a lifetime of medical bills. If one adult child is rich and one struggling, you might all agree that it's better to leave more to the one who really needs it. Should circumstances change, by all means change the will.

It's a good idea to tell your children about the will's provisions, especially if you've left them unequal shares. You want them to understand and accept your reasoning, both to avoid bitterness and to head off a possible challenge to the will. The amount of detail you cover will depend on their ages and interest. They may even have ideas and suggestions that you will find helpful.

Ways to Leave Money to Young Children

It's a tough decision. You want the money kept safe but not under so many restrictions that it's hard to use for the child's benefit. You need good management but may not be able to pay for professional investment advice. You want the children well looked-after but cannot predict their future circumstances and relative need for money.

Married couples with total assets of less than $175,000 typically leave everything to each other, assuming that each will take care of the children's interests. (When assets are more than $175,000, you may want to use a trust—see page 710.) But what if you both die together in an accident—who takes care of things then? What if you're a widow or divorcee with children? What if you're in a second marriage and want to be sure that the children of your first marriage get their fair share of the estate?

State laws vary on methods of leaving money to children, so talk to an attorney about the various choices. This is no arena for do-it-yourselfers. The financial security of children is too important to risk the mistakes of amateurs. Some possible approaches to discuss with your lawyer:

1. Name a legal guardian for the children's funds (who may or may not be the person who will actually take care of the children). State law determines to what extent the guardian can spend the money on the children's welfare and what investments are considered proper. Generally, the guardian has to make an annual accounting to the court. When the child comes of age—now eighteen in many states—he gets the money free and clear.

2. In a number of states, funds can be left via the Uniform Gifts to Minors Act, often a good choice for modest amounts of money—up to $10,000 or $20,000. The funds are left to an adult, who acts as custodian for the child. As with guardianships, the law determines how the money can be invested and spent. A custodian may have more flexibility in handling money than a guardian does—something to discuss with your lawyer. Again, the funds go to the child when he comes of age.

3. If you're leaving a larger sum of money, the best choice is generally a trust. Many people think that trusts are only for the wealthy, but in fact they can be set up for modest estates of perhaps $30,000 or $40,000. That's not a lot of money these days. If you own a home and an insurance policy, you may easily be worth twice that at death.

Trusts can be tremendously flexible arrangements. You might provide that the trustee pay out income and principal for the child's benefit and turn over what's left at whatever age you think the child can handle it. The trustee can have wide discretion in deciding what the child is to receive, or you can limit him to just a few choices. He can be directed to pay the child his money in installments to see how he handles the funds. A lawyer can explain the many possibilities. The provisions of the trust are set down in your will and go into effect when you die. A named trustee handles the funds for the children, paying them out according to your directions.

Perhaps even more important than the form of the bequest is the answer to this question: Who will manage the funds until the children are grown? An individual guardian, custodian, or trustee may charge little or nothing for doing the job. But you must have someone you trust, who is close to your family, and who has good judgment about money. Larger sums can be managed, for a fee, by bank trust departments (see page 695). Your lawyer should be able to tell you about the capabilities of banks in your area.

Leaving Money in Trust

Money is generally left in trust for one of three reasons: (1) The person receiving it is too young, or too inexperienced, to manage it well; (2) the person leaving the money wants to set limits on the beneficiary's freedom to dispose of it; and (3) in your particular situation, a trust offers tax advantages. *Testamentary trusts,* discussed here, are those provided for in your will and become effective at death. *Living trusts* (see page 721) are set up while you're still alive.

In principle, a testamentary trust works this way: Instead of money being given directly to a beneficiary, it is given to a third person, who manages it in the beneficiary's behalf. Money from the trust can be distributed to the beneficiary for various purposes, as provided in your will, with the property passing to the beneficiary when he reaches a certain age (or in several distributions at different ages). If the beneficiary dies before then, the trust may be terminated and the property given to whomever you named.

You can have a tremendous variety of trust arrangements, depending on your needs. The assets can be invested and income paid regularly or irregularly to one or more beneficiaries. Income can be accumulated in the trust and paid out all at once, when the trust dissolves. Principal can be paid out to meet certain purposes. You can give the trustee wide discretion in using the funds (usually the best approach) or sharply limit his actions. Various criteria can be set as to when the trust will dissolve and the assets paid to a beneficiary. Talk over your situation with a lawyer. He'll propose trust arrangements that, as much as possible, meet your needs. Some of the uses of trusts:

• *To hold money until a child grows up.* You can provide that the funds be given to him all at once, at a certain age; paid out in installments; or paid at the discretion of a trustee.

• *To provide management for funds left to a widow.* The trustee can be a bank, an investment advisor, or a relative experienced in handling money. Banks require large sums for individual trusts but will accept smaller sums to be pooled with the funds of others and managed as a unit (see page 696). At the widow's death the assets in the trust can be distributed to your children or anyone else you name.

• *To save estate taxes.* Typically, you would leave money in trust for your children, with the income from the trust going to your spouse for life. The trustee could be empowered to distribute principal to the widow if she needs it. That way, the spouse gets the use of the money, but it is not taxed in her estate when she dies. You can also leave up to $250,000 to each child and then to your grandchildren in trust, with the income from the property going to the child for life. This eliminates any tax on the money until your grandchildren die. (Amounts larger than $250,000 for each child will be taxed when the child dies and again when your grandchildren die.)

• *To provide for retarded children* (see page 725).

• *For people in second marriages, who want to ensure that the children of their first marriage will inherit from them.* If you simply leave everything to your second spouse, he or she may not make adequate provision for the children of the first marriage. But you can protect both them and your spouse by leaving them money in trust, with income and principal from the trust to be used for your spouse during his or her lifetime.

Three Warnings About Trusts

1. People with upper-middle and upper incomes are sometimes "over-trusted." They may choose complicated ways of disposing of their estates when simpler ways would be better and cheaper. There are, inevitably, some lawyers who encourage trusts, in hopes of getting continuing legal fees. The best rule on trusts is to consider first all the methods of doing without, then go to trusts if simpler solutions don't meet your personal and tax goals. 2. Some widows and adult children are subjected to trusts when they'd rather manage the money themselves. Try not to restrict any beneficiary's control of his money unless it's absolutely necessary (see page 704). 3. Some people are so bent on avoiding taxes that they make pretzels of their estates. Don't lose sight of your human objectives. It's better that your estate pay a little extra in taxes than to lock your heirs into a planner's prison.

Naming a Trustee

The trustee is responsible for seeing that the money and property in the trust are prudently managed in order to achieve your objectives. His powers will be outlined in your will. Some people put reins on their trustees, but generally speaking, it's best to give a trustee wide latitude to respond to changing conditions. You don't know what's going to happen to your family ten or twenty years hence. Your trustee, seeing things from what might have been your point of view, should be in a position to act as he thinks you might have wished.

Because of the broad powers generally granted a trustee—to approve investments and distribute money to beneficiaries—it's important that you name someone you can trust and who's competent to handle money. Family members are often trustees for money left to minor children, especially if the sums are not large. Other choices are close friends, business associates, or your lawyer. The risk of an individual as trustee is that he may not be as good at money management as you had thought. If he himself gets into financial trouble, he may be tempted to dip into the trust funds (which is illegal). If the family grows unhappy with his management, it may take a court proceeding to replace him, unless the will provides for a substitute.

Bank trust departments also present problems: They can be slow, impersonal, and inflexible; dedicated holders of bad stocks; and unable to deliver enough income to keep up with inflation. But even so, they may be better than an inept relative or friend. And some banks are the very best trust managers around. Some of the advantages of having a bank as trustee:

1. If your family doesn't get along with the trust officer assigned to them, they can easily have him replaced.

2. The bank will continue doing business in the same place, whereas an individual you name may move to another city.

3. Bank trust officers devote their full time to managing money. Their departments pay a good deal for professional investment research.

4. In case of embezzlement, the bank will make good the loss. Federal and state banking authorities periodically audit a bank's trust accounts; there's no similar oversight of individuals.

5. Bank retirement plans protect you from the senile trustee. If your trust officer dies, there's someone else there to take over the account. Also, you're not hung up if the trust officer has a long illness.

Large banks generally take individual trusts beginning at $100,000 to $200,000, although some may accept lesser amounts. Smaller banks may take individual trusts of $50,000, but you'll have to hunt carefully in order to find competent trust officers. Your best choice is either a big bank with a large trust department that pays its trust officers well and spends a lot of money on investment research; or a smaller bank that has a full-time staff of trust officers and buys its investment research from a major investment advisor. Feel free to consider a bank in another city; most trust business can easily be done by telephone. A lawyer experienced in estate planning is probably your best source of information on the relative competence of bank trust departments.

For investment purposes, most large banks group smaller trusts into several large *pooled funds,* which operate like mutual funds. Each fund invests for a different objective—fixed income, tax-exempt income, or income and growth; you choose the investment that best suits your needs. The annual reports of these funds tell how well each bank has performed. They're also clues as to how well the bank manages individual trusts. But remember: Even the best management can't overcome ill-considered investment limitations that you yourself put into the trust document.

It can be complicated, expensive, and sometimes impossible to change a trustee. So after you've done your homework on bank trust departments, consider sampling your favorite bank's investment management before you make a binding commitment. Do it by setting up a *revocable trust* during your lifetime (see page 721). There are no tax advantages, but you'll learn a lot about how the bank performs.

You may want to name your spouse or other family member cotrustee along with the bank. His vote is then required on all investment decisions (although if you choose a pooled trust fund, the vote can only be whether to stay in or get out). *Talk with your lawyer and bank about writing an escape clause in the trust document so that your family can replace a trustee they are unhappy with.* Some banks won't allow an escape clause unless the estate is large.

A trustee is generally required to furnish a *bond* (a sum of money that insures honest performance of his duties), but you can eliminate that necessity by so stating in your will. If you name an individual as trustee, name a successor in case he should be unable to serve. Or empower your spouse or a family member to name a successor.

Trustee's fees are tax-deductible. They're set by law and vary from state to state. Banks and lawyers serving as trustees usually charge the maximum; friends and family members, little or nothing. The following fees may not apply to your particular state but give you a general idea of the costs.

Sample trustee's fees

1 percent of the principal paid to beneficiaries out of the trust, plus the following annual management commissions:

$7.00 per $1,000 of the first $300,000
$3.75 per $1,000 of the next $500,000
$2.50 per $1,000 of the remainder

Disposing of Personal Property

The things you care most about are probably not even mentioned in your will. I mean those personal effects that may be lumped together and left to your spouse or divided equally among your children. Just as William Shakespeare left his wife his "second best bed," you may want to consider separately the things that mean the most to you. Some bequests are for purely sentimental reasons; others will save bickering among heirs; still others ensure that the true value of special possessions won't be overlooked. You might draw a list of all the personal effects that have value or mean something to you—from furs, jewelry, and heirlooms to sporting equipment, guns, collections, and toy soldiers—and decide where they're all to go.

There are three general ways to dispose of special items:

1. Give them away while you're still living.

2. List the special bequests in your will. This approach has some drawbacks: If you change your mind about who gets the porcelain platter, you'll have to change your will or write a codicil; a long list of bequests may complicate the probate proceeding; and the very fact that you mention something separately may lead the Internal Revenue Service to overestimate its monetary value for estate tax purposes.

3. Leave all your personal effects to one person, usually your spouse, and write a separate letter telling him where you'd like the various items to go. If you change your mind, you'll have to rewrite only the letter, not the whole will. In some states the letter is just as binding as the will, but even where it's not, your wishes are usually honored.

A word about some of the special items you may own:

Guns

They must be left to a person who can possess them lawfully. In a state where you need a license to own a hand gun, a widow left a set of pistols could get in trouble with the law. The executor might even be breaking the law if he carries them to a gun dealer to be sold. When you draw your will, tell the lawyer about any weapons you have (including antiques and wartime souvenirs) so that he can help you dispose of them.

Wealthy Pets

Courts are generally not sympathetic to animals endowed with money for their lifetime care. A few states allow trusts for animals, but in most others such a trust would be thrown out. You generally have to leave an animal to a willing recipient, along with a sum of money for its care, and hope for the best. Your lawyer will advise you on what your state allows.

Books

When you've spent a lifetime buying books, a number of them are apt to be valuable, even though you're not consciously a collector. If your library is simply turned over to a secondhand book dealer, your heirs will never know which were the special gems. So get an appraisal from an antiquarian book dealer. Look in the Yellow Pages under "Books, Rare," or write to the Antiquarian Booksellers Center, 630 Fifth Ave., New York, N.Y. 10020, for a list of dealers.

Paintings and Prints

Inexpensive oil paintings rarely acquire value, no matter what the dealer told you when you bought them, but the work of well-known artists could be worth quite a bit. Original prints (lithographs, woodcuts, etchings, and so on) by recognized artists, signed and numbered, may also bring a good price. To separate the wheat from the chaff, get an appraisal from a qualified art dealer.

Hobby Collections

A boyhood stamp album or coffee can full of silver quarters is unlikely to have much special value. But it should be checked by a dealer in case you lucked into a rare item.

Special Collections

If you've spent a lot of time and money on a particular interest—be it rare books, etchings, model railroads, rare coins, or *Batman* comic books—the collection may be quite valuable. But an executor unfamiliar with the field may unknowingly let it go for a fraction of its worth. To be sure your heirs get their due, keep records of the collection in good order and leave a letter advising the executor as to who would be qualified to handle the sale.

Naming an Executor

An executor is an important person to your heirs. He sees that the will is probated, all your debts and taxes paid, an accounting made of all the assets, and property distributed according to the will. The executor usually works with a lawyer, so you don't need an expert in estate law or high finance. But you will want someone who presses the lawyer to move quickly, who's reliable and responsible in money matters, and who's personally interested in the needs of the heirs. The executor is often one of the adult beneficiaries: a spouse or a child. If your estate is complicated—for example, involving the shares of a small business— you might want to name a business associate or lawyer. Lawyers also serve when there's no one in the family or no close friend to do the job. Wealthy people with large estates may name a trust company. But if you name someone outside the family, it's often wise to name a family member as coexecutor, to keep track of what's going on. But be sure to get permission from any individual you name; being an executor can be quite a job. If money is misspent or errors made, the executor can be held personally accountable.

A lawyer or trust company is generally paid for the job (see page 690). A friend or relative, on the other hand, usually waives the fee. In many states the executor may be required to post a bond equal to the assets of the estate, as a guarantee that he won't run away with the money. But this is often a hardship. By and large, it's best to include a proviso in your will, allowing the executor to serve *without bond*.

The executor generally needs the help of a lawyer to get the estate settled and the property legally transferred to its new owners. The lawyer charges a percentage of the estate's assets, perhaps 5 percent for a small estate, less for a large one (see page 690). But your executor can probably save the estate some money if he talks to two or three lawyers and tells them he's price-shopping. Handling the average estate is not complicated, and many lawyers are willing to cut their fees. If the estate is simple and the executor willing to wade through the technicalities, it's even possible to do without a lawyer. Go to the courthouse, see the probate court clerk, and ask what's involved. A few states have passed laws in recent years that make do-it-yourself probate fairly simple.

The General Order of a Will

Wills should always be drawn under the supervision of a lawyer to be sure they'll be valid under the laws of your state. This section gives general information about what's in a will, and why, but should not be used as a model for writing your own will:

1. State who you are and that this is your will so that there's no argument as to who wrote the document or its intent.

2. Date the will and revoke all previous wills made by you so that someone included in a previous will but left out of this one can't make a claim.

3. Make *specific* bequests (such as "the ruby ring to my daughter, Anne") and *general* bequests (such as "$1,000 to my brother, Peter," without specifying where the $1,000 is to come from).

4. Divide the *residuary,* which is the amount left after all specific bequests have been made. If you made so many specific bequests that there's nothing left for the residuary beneficiary, he's out of luck. For example, if you leave $10,000 to each of your grandchildren and the remainder to your children, and the estate is smaller than you expected, your children might be left with much less than you had intended. Your lawyer will make some suggestions to avoid this problem.

5. Provide for any trusts you want to make and name the trustee.

6. If it's pertinent for tax purposes, husband and wife should state which person should be presumed to have died first in case they die in a common accident.

7. Name guardians for your minor children.

8. Name an executor, and a substitute.

9. Sign the will in the presence of *all* your witnesses. If any small changes are made in the document at this point, initial the changes in the witnesses' presence and before signing. Then the witnesses sign in the presence of each other.

Witnesses

These needn't be special friends or relatives. Often, they're your lawyer and some people in his office who are rounded up for the occasion. Anyone who is named in the will should ordinarily *not* be a witness; if the will is challenged and he has to testify, the law may deprive him of his legacy. A good practice is to have one more witness than your state requires, in case one dies or can't be located when the will is probated.

Copies of the Will

There should be only one executed will. If there are more than one, the court may hold up probate until all copies are found. You may, however, make photocopies for easy reference.

Keep the Will Current

An out-of-date will divides your property in a way that seemed sensible when it was written but may now be entirely inappropriate. If you die without changing its provisions, it will be difficult, maybe impossible, for your family to put things right. Here are some of the circumstances that should cause you to review your will: an increase in your net worth; the birth or adoption of a child or grandchild; your own marriage, separation, divorce, or remarriage; a child's marriage; a child's graduation from college; the death of an heir; the illness of a child that may go on for life; a change of mind about heirs, guardians, or the executor named in your will; a move to a new state. When you make a new will, destroy the old one.

State Laws Vary

Laws vary regarding wills, trusts, and other aspects of estate planning. Whenever you move to another state, have a lawyer review the will to see if changes should be made. A will that's technically invalid in your present state (perhaps because you had too few witnesses) will generally be accepted for probate as long as it was valid in the state where it was drawn. But review the will anyway to update its provisions and take advantage of any useful wrinkles in the laws of your new state. *Special note:* Be sure you meet all the legal tests of domicile in your new state and have no remaining links with the old; otherwise, your heirs might have to pay inheritance taxes in both states.

When you own property in another state, consider owning it jointly, so it will pass automatically to the other owner without probate. If you own it individually, consult a lawyer in that state about drawing your will in accordance with state laws. Unless your will is valid in that state, the court may distribute the property—even if it's just a bank account —as if you had left no will at all.

State Inheritance Taxes

Many states levy inheritance taxes, which are *not* deductible from federal estate taxes. People with large estates, living in states that tax heavily, might consider establishing domicile in a low-tax state.

Disinheritance

In most states you can't disinherit a spouse (although it is possible—for example, if you're separated). State laws generally require that he or she get at least some of your property—typically, one third or one half. If you leave a spouse less, he or she may be able to collect whatever share of the estate would be due had you died without a will. It is possible, however, to disinherit children in most instances. You might have to state specifically that they had been disinherited; otherwise, the court might divide the money as if the child had been accidentally over-looked.

Changing Your Will

Don't write changes into the will by hand after you sign it, and don't try to take someone out of your will by crossing out his name. Unless the change was made, initialed, and witnessed in accordance with your state's legal procedures, the court will ignore the change and probate the will as originally written. It's even possible that the handwritten change might invalidate that provision or, if changes are extensive, the entire will. To make a change, have your lawyer prepare a *codicil*, which is a document formally amending the will, or have the will rewritten.

It's generally best to prepare separate letters to family members for bequests of jewelry and other personal items. The number and type of these bequests may change often, and it's expensive to revise your will each time. The letter may or may not be considered part of your will, depending on your state, but it at least serves as a clue to your wishes. Your family will most likely follow your instructions.

Where to Keep Your Will

Many lawyers think it's unwise for people to keep the original of their wills. They may be tempted to make informal, written changes in it, which may be ineffective; they may lose it; they may take such good care of it that survivors can't find it; or they may put it in their safe deposit box, which is sealed at death and in some states may require a court order to open. It's better to leave the original with your lawyer and keep a copy for yourself.

Sexism and Wills

Some men assume that only they know what's best for their families, or that their wives don't understand (or care) about future financial arrangements. Their lawyers may agree, preferring to deal only with the husband. As a result, the will may be written and property arranged without any real discussion of the wife's opinions, fears, and objectives. This happens even in community property states, where, by law, half the property accumulated during the marriage belongs to the wife. Many women accept this arrangement, especially older women. Yet after the death of their husband, these same women are likely to blossom as independent people, able, even eager, to make their own financial decisions.

Unfortunately, a plan drawn up in a wife's "best interests" may deprive her of effective control of her life. The husband and lawyer may both have believed that she was incapable of understanding finance or was not to be trusted with the management of assets, something she herself may even have agreed with at the time. But once on her own, she may find that she has strong opinions about these things, too late to do anything about it. The will may have put her under the effective jurisdiction of someone else—a male relative or bank trust department —with little freedom to act on her own. At that point, it's not unusual for a widow to become resentful about the dependent life she's forced to lead.

Not all women respond this way; some are glad to have the management of money taken out of their hands. But a wife should be part of that decision, with all the implications fully explained to her. *She* is likely to outlive her husband; *she* will have to live with the financial decisions embodied in the will; so *she* should be very much a part of drawing that will.

Since most estate planning lawyers are males, any retrograde attitudes they may have about women might affect not only the widow but all female members of the family. Sons, but not daughters, may receive stock in the family company; sons may receive their inheritance outright, while daughters receive it in trust; daughters may receive less property than sons; what should be the daughter's property may be left to sons-in-law instead. This kind of treatment can deeply hurt the women in the family, arousing resentments that can last a lifetime.

When Are Inheritances Paid?

When the will is probated (that is, declared valid), and the executor has been confirmed, he can begin immediately to distribute assets. How long probate takes depends on how many people have to be notified about the will, how speedy your lawyer is in handling the paperwork, and whether anyone decides to challenge the will. A fast-working lawyer can often have a will probated in a week or month. A fast-working executor may distribute some cash within a few weeks. Other property —real estate, for example—will take longer to transfer because of the paperwork or the need to sell at a reasonable price. The average estate may be fully distributed in six months to a year or two; the estate of a wealthy person may take several years. A surviving spouse is generally allowed to withdraw modest sums from the estate during the probate process in order to help meet living expenses.

Should You Avoid Probate?

Probate is the process by which your will is filed with the court and declared valid. Your property will be inventoried and its value determined. Normally, this process is handled by a lawyer in the name of the will's executor. The executor can do it himself, however, if he has the time and is familiar with all the requirements of probate. A few states have passed laws in recent years to make it easier for executors to settle small estates without the help of lawyers. Not until the will is probated can inheritances generally be paid.

What's Wrong with Probate?

In the hands of a slow lawyer it can take a long time—maybe a year or two—before heirs get their inheritance. Complicated estates can drag on much longer. Costs are often high. Lawyers may charge large fees, and there may be extra costs, such as fees for people who appraise the property (or sign their names to the appraisals gathered by your lawyer) or fees to guardians to represent the interests of your minor children during probate. But states vary in these matters; in some you can get prompt probate without a lot of extra fees, and lawyers' fees are generally negotiable.

How to Avoid Probate

Probate is for property left by will. There is no probate for property left outside the will, that passes automatically to another owner. This includes money and property owned jointly; U.S. savings bonds and insurance policies paid to a named beneficiary; assets in corporate and individual retirement plans paid to a named beneficiary; trusts set up during your lifetime and distributed according to the trust document; business interests provided for by contract. All these assets can be paid immediately to the beneficiary or joint owner.

Even if all your property is held in the forms just listed, you may still need a will for personal property. But the value of those items may be so negligible that the probate process isn't necessary: Where it is, the fee should be small. Commonly, people have both property that passes automatically to another owner, and individually owned property passing by will.

Drawbacks of Arranging Your Property in Order to Avoid Probate

For some people, various ownership forms that avoid probate are risky or inconvenient. For example, if you keep a large sum of money in joint names with your son and something goes wrong with his business, he might draw that money out, leaving you without funds you had counted on. Some property, such as real estate or stock, could be impossible to sell if it's in joint names and the other person refuses to go along with your wishes. If you put your estate into a living trust with a bank as trustee, the bank may not manage your money as well as you'd like. (You can, however, name yourself as trustee.) The method of using named beneficiaries for insurance and savings bonds, and joint ownership for real estate, may result in an unequal division of property. If you avoid probate by giving most of your property away to your children during your lifetime, you might wind up dependent on them in old age, something to be avoided if at all possible.

The rule is this: Use joint property, named beneficiaries, and other methods of passing property outside the will if that's the way you would normally handle your affairs. Explore with a lawyer the costs and other ramifications of putting all your property into a living trust, with yourself as trustee, to be distributed after your death in whichever way you specify. This approach can be a good one if the costs are held down. But don't adopt these methods if you're uncomfortable with them or find that they restrict your freedom to manage your own property.

In any case, draw your will under the guidance of a lawyer. Do-it-yourself methods of avoiding probate may turn out to be expensive for your heirs.

Other Ways of Reducing Lawyer's Fees

Lawyers in a given area are often price-competitive for legal work that any competent lawyer could do. An executor could save the estate quite a bit of money by calling two or three lawyers, describing the estate, explaining that he's looking for a good price, and asking what they'd charge. If a lawyer knows you're price-shopping and wants the business, he's very apt to reduce his quote. However, if the person who died named a specific lawyer as executor, the heirs are pretty much locked in. (That's one reason not to name your lawyer to that post unless he's the best person available.) Some lawyers behave as if the lawyer who drew the will is entitled to the estate, but that's not so. The choice is entirely up to the executor. Naturally, price isn't everything in choosing a lawyer; you want someone experienced in estates and taxes. But among equally competent lawyers you might as well have the one that does the job for the least amount of money.

Estate Taxes

These are the taxes due on your property at your death. In 1976 the law was revised to reduce the number of people who owe estate taxes; now they're payable only if you have a fairly large amount of money. The IRS applies a specific credit against estate taxes, which in 1980 had the effect of exempting estates worth less than $161,563 from taxes. In 1981 and thereafter, estates worth less than $175,625 will all be exempt from tax.

Gift Taxes

When you make a taxable gift, a gift tax return has to be filed and taxes paid. Gift and estate tax rates are the same, and the credit against estate taxes (see the preceding section) includes gifts. Say, for example, that you have a $200,000 estate and gave no gifts during your lifetime. In that case $175,625 would escape tax-free and the remainder would be taxed. Say, on the other hand, that you had given taxable gifts worth $50,000. That $50,000 is, in effect, subtracted from the $175,625, so that at death, everything over $125,625 is taxed. In other words, you're allowed to pass only a specified sum tax-free. Whether you do it during your lifetime or at death, it's counted the same way.

How Much Are Gift and Estate Taxes?

Here's the rate schedule, as of 1980, on *taxable* gifts and estates (which is the excess, after applying the tax credit) up to $1 million. The rates continue to rise thereafter, to a maximum of 70 percent on amounts over $5 million.

On taxable gifts and estates of this size*	This sum:	Plus this percentage:
Up to $ 10,000	—	18%
Over $ 10,000 to $20,000	$ 1,800	20% of everything over $10,000
Over $ 20,000 to $40,000	3,800	22% of everything over 20,000
Over $ 40,000 to $60,000	8,200	24% of everything over 40,000
Over $ 60,000 to $80,000	13,000	26% of everything over 60,000
Over $ 80,000 to $100,000	18,200	28% of everything over 80,000
Over $100,000 to $150,000	23,800	30% of everything over 100,000
Over $150,000 to $250,000	38,800	32% of everything over 150,000
Over $250,000 to $500,000	70,800	34% of everything over 250,000
Over $500,000 to $750,000	155,800	37% of everything over 500,000
Over $750,000 to $1 million	248,300	39% of everything over 750,000

*These are the amounts *over* the exemptions given above in "Estate Taxes."

Ways to Reduce Gift and Estate Taxes

Some property can be eliminated from your estate in order to reduce your tax liability. This should always be done under the guidance of an experienced estate planning lawyer to be sure that nothing goes wrong. Do-it-yourself tax planning can lead to tax traps that you and I have never heard of and wouldn't believe if we had! Some areas to examine:

1. *Get life insurance out of your estate.* If you own the policy, the proceeds will be taxed in your estate. But if someone else owns it, the proceeds will bypass your estate and escape taxation. This can be the easiest and fastest way for a person of moderate wealth to bring his estate below the tax line.

When you apply for insurance and sign your name to the application form, you become the policy's owner. If someone else (say, your spouse) signs the application, he or she is the owner. To transfer ownership of your policy to someone else, ask the company for an *assignment form.* Your life insurance agent can handle this for you (but check it with your lawyer to see that it's done right; insurance companies may err). You can also transfer ownership of the group policy you have with your employer.

One important point: The assignment forms of some companies say that the policy has been transferred to another owner "for value or consideration," which means payment. Instead of *giving* the policy to someone else, you have, in effect, *sold* it. Under those circumstances the person who receives ownership will have to pay income taxes on the proceeds of the policy when you die! This is a tax trap that many people fall into, simply because their insurance company distributes poor forms. The assignment form should have no reference to "consideration." If it does, don't sign it. Talk to your lawyer about getting the insurance company to send a better form.

When you assign ownership of a policy, you have given it away. The new owner may draw out the cash value (if any), assign it to another owner, or even cancel the policy without your consent. The new owner should pay the premiums. If a man gives a policy to his wife but pays the premiums himself, the IRS will include three years of premium payments in his estate at death. Solution when the wife lacks funds of her own: The man gives her enough money each year to cover the premiums, she puts it into her own bank account, and makes the payments.

Another point about transferring insurance: The will of the person who receives the policy should be so arranged that the insurance proceeds do not wind up back in the insured's estate. For example, if a man gives his policy to his wife, her will should leave it to, perhaps, their children. If she leaves everything she owns to her husband, he'll get the insurance back and may not have time to transfer it to another owner before he dies.

In community property states—Arizona, California, Idaho, Louisiana, Nevada, New Mexico, Texas, and Washington—you must specifically waive community property rights in order to get life insurance out of your estate. The waiver may be on the insurance company's assignment form; more likely, you'll have to do it by a separate document.

2. *Use the marital deduction.* You can leave your spouse, tax-free, up to one half of your estate or $250,000, whichever is larger.

3. *Use the marital deduction plus a trust.* People with small taxable estates tend to use the big $250,000 deduction and think their tax troubles are over, but in fact, they've only been deferred. When the surviving spouse dies, his or her estate will be taxed on everything over $175,625, which is the maximum sheltered by the estate tax credit starting in 1981.

Good estate planning can vastly increase the amount of money sheltered in your joint estate after the death of your spouse. The key is to make use of your credit against estate taxes *before* taking the marital deduction. Do it by putting the sum sheltered by the estate tax credit into trust for, perhaps, your children, with the income going to your spouse for life. Provide, too, that the trustee can give your spouse principal as well as interest, if he or she needs the money. That way, the spouse gets the benefit of the money left in trust. But when he or she dies, the money in the trust goes directly to the children without being subject to another estate tax. This method of arranging money greatly reduces taxes, leaving much more to be passed to your children.

The table on the following page shows graphically how the trust saves taxes on your combined estates, as compared with using only the marital deduction.

All the arrangements in the table eliminate taxes in the estate of the first spouse to die. But you can see what a tremendous difference they make to taxation of the other spouse's estate. If you're married, it's clearly not enough to think only of your own tax problems; you must consider the situation of your joint estate.

Each spouse ought to set up a trust, so that you get the tax savings no matter which of you dies first. This means that you each ought to have a substantial amount of money in your name. If the husband now holds most of the property, he can equalize ownership tax-free via the

ESTATE TAX RESULTS FOR VARIOUS WAYS OF LEAVING MONEY TO SPOUSE AND CHILDREN

	Left to spouse	Left to children in trust[a]	Tax-free due to marital deduction[b]	Tax-free due to estate tax credit[c]	Amount taxed in your estate	Amount taxed in spouse's estate[d]	Tax due on spouse's estate
Leaving $250,000	$250,000	0	$250,000	0	0	$ 74,375	$23,800
	175,000	$75,000	175,000	$175,000	0	0	0
Leaving $350,000[e]	350,000	0	250,000	100,000	0	174,375	$57,800
	250,000	100,000	250,000	100,000	0	74,375	$23,800
	175,000	175,000	175,000	175,000	0	0	0
Leaving $425,000[f]	425,000	0	250,000	175,000	0	249,375	$83,300
	250,000	175,000	250,000	175,000	0	74,375	$23,800

[a] Income and principal from the trust goes to spouse during his or her lifetime; at death, the trust may dissolve and the money go to the children.

[b] One-half the estate or $250,000, whichever is larger.

[c] Maximum amount exempted from estate taxes is $175,625, starting in 1981.

[d] After estate tax credit, in 1981.

[e] Maximum that can pass both estates untaxed.

[f] The maximum estate that can pass untaxed to the first spouse to die.

law on marital gifts: A spouse can receive $100,000 worth of property gift-tax-free plus annual gifts of $3,000 (see page 712).

Here's a tax trap that many people stumble into: *If you hold all property jointly, you cannot take advantage of the tax-saving trust outlined in the foregoing.* Joint property automatically passes to the other owner at death, so it's not possible to put part of it in trust for your children. Holding all property jointly is, in effect, a decision to forego this big tax advantage. Some people think of joint property itself as a tax advantage, because, since 1977, only 50 percent of the property held jointly by a married couple is taxed in the estate of the first owner to die (provided that a gift tax return was filed when the joint tenancy was created). But as you see from the foregoing, joint property can lead to a higher tax in your combined estates than if you hold property separately. If there are reasons for holding some property jointly (see page 713), consider doing so only if there's enough separate property in each of your names to take full advantage of the trust.

This tax-saving trust is equally available to residents of community property states, where married couples each own half the assets accumulated in the marriage. Each spouse is generally free to dispose of his or her half of the property however he likes, including setting up a trust for the children.

4. *Make marital gifts.* You may give your spouse up to $3,000 a year tax-free. In addition, there's a marital allowance for large gifts. The first $100,000 given to a spouse during your lifetime is gift-tax-free; the next $100,000 is taxed normally; anything over $200,000 is 50 percent tax-free. Be sure that your spouse's will doesn't leave everything to you! You don't want these gifts to land back in your estate if your spouse dies first. The spouse's will could put these gifts in trust for the children, following the tax-saving arrangement just suggested. (*Note:* The lifetime gift allowance applies collectively to *all* your spouses if you marry more than once.)

5. *Make annual gifts.* You can give up to $3,000 each to as many people as you like, tax-free, every year. If the gift is made jointly with your spouse, the sum can go to $6,000. Be sure to file a gift tax return! Over many years of making gifts you can remove a good deal of money from your estate. One thing many people don't realize: These gifts are valid even if made on your deathbed (as long as they're not made just to avoid taxes).

6. *Make gifts larger than the tax-free amounts noted above.* A gift tax will be due on the excess, but it's no different from the tax you'd pay if that money remained in your estate. (*But note:* Any gift larger than $3,000 will be taxed in your estate if given within three years of your death.) Large lifetime gifts have this advantage: Any increase in the value of the gift will be out of your estate. For example, say you owned $25,000 worth of stock, gave it to your daughter, and the value of the stock rose to $75,000 by the time of your death. You paid a gift tax on the $25,000 (less the $6,000 you and your spouse can give your daughter, tax-free, in a single year). If you had kept that stock, your estate would have owed a tax on $75,000.

Large lifetime gifts are especially valuable to people who start small businesses. When the company is young and struggling you can give your children shares at small cost. But if you retain full ownership and the company gets into the million-dollar range, it might have to be sold after your death to raise money for the estate taxes.

7. *Make charitable contributions.* There are tax advantages to large charitable gifts. For example, if you donate property that has gone up in value since you bought it, there will be no capital gains tax on the profit. There are also ways of donating property during your lifetime, getting a tax deduction, and also getting a lifetime income from the gift. Many charitable institutions have tax specialists who will explain the mechanisms to you. Or see your own tax lawyer or accountant.

8. *Funds in Keogh plans and Individual Retirement Accounts (see page 778) can be kept out of your estate.* It's done by arranging that the beneficiary receive payment of the funds over two years for a Keogh, and thirty-six months for an IRA. See that these possibilities are included in the Keogh or IRA documents, and that your executor and beneficiaries understand them.

For details on these and any other tax devices, consult a lawyer experienced in taxes and estate planning. One reminder: It isn't graven in stone that you're obliged to avoid estate taxes for the sake of your heirs. Your first consideration should be your own financial security. Don't give away so much property that you become dependent on others, even if they're your own children!

Bank Accounts "In Trust For"

You may want to give someone money by starting a bank account in your name "in trust for" him. This has no estate or income tax value, the interest earned is taxed to you and the account is included in your estate. Its advantages are two:

1. At your death, it passes automatically, without probate, to the person named on the account.
2. While you live, the funds are entirely under your control, you can cancel the account or change the beneficiary, and the person you name cannot withdraw any of the money.

Should You Hold Property Jointly?

There are three forms of joint ownership. If you hold any property, investments, bank accounts, and so on with another person, you'll want to be clear which type of ownership you have, to be sure it's exactly what you want.

Joint Tenancy with Right of Survivorship
This is the most common form used by married couples. It means that each of you has a full and undivided interest in the property. One spouse cannot sell his or her interest without the other's consent (al-

though in the case of joint bank accounts one spouse can often empty the account without authorization from the other). When one owner dies, the property passes automatically to the other, without delay and before the will is probated. In some states this form of ownership between husband and wife is called *tenancy by the entirety.*

People who are not married can also adopt joint tenancy with right of survivorship. It is commonly used as an easy way to transfer property at death.

For property to be jointly owned, both names have to appear on the ownership document. If only one person is given as owner, it is the sole property of that person, to be disposed of as he sees fit. (*Exception:* In community property states assets of the marriage are jointly owned no matter whose name is on the property.)

Tenancy in Common

This is a form of joint ownership without rights of survivorship; when one joint owner dies, the other does not automatically inherit. Each person separately owns half of the property, can sell his interest without the consent of the other, and can leave it to any beneficiary he likes. If you have no will, your half of any property owned as a tenant in common will be disposed of according to the intestacy laws of your state (see page 682). This form of ownership is appropriate for property jointly held by friends or relatives as a convenience but where the owners want to preserve their freedom to dispose of their half as they like.

Community Property

This is in effect in eight states—Arizona, California, Idaho, Louisiana, Nevada, New Mexico, Texas, and Washington—and declares that all assets acquired during the marriage are jointly owned by husband and wife, no matter whose name is on the deed (see page 718). But you have the right to leave your half of the property, by will, to anyone you like. If you die without a will, your half is disposed of according to your state's laws on intestacy. Generally, everything goes to the surviving spouse, but unlike joint ownership with right of survivorship, this transfer is not automatic. Community property may or may not have to go through probate, depending on the state.

Some property does not count as part of the community—for example, property you owned before marriage, inheritances, or, in most cases, property acquired in non-community-property states. You can hold this property separately or jointly, as you choose.

Advantages of Joint Property for Married Couples

1. It's tangible proof that marriage is a partnership; that the contribution of each person is equally valued. (An alternative way to achieve this goal is to put half the property in the separate name of each spouse.)

2. Joint property protects a wife who has no funds of her own, because neither owner can sell the property or borrow against it without permission from the other.

3. In the case of divorce, a spouse with an interest in the property is in a better bargaining position than a spouse without.

4. When one owner dies, the property automatically passes to the other, without having to wait for the will to be probated.

5. If you hold out-of-state property in joint names, it will automatically pass to the other owner without probate. On the other hand, if you hold it individually, your will has to be probated in that state—an extra complication and expense.

6. If one spouse owes money and can't pay, and the other spouse isn't responsible for the debt, creditors may not be able to seize jointly held property (although they can file a lien against it).

7. If you owe no estate taxes (see page 707), joint property is often a clean, simple, and fair way of handling marital property.

Disadvantages of Joint Property for Married Couples

1. If your house or other real estate is put in joint names and one spouse didn't contribute the money for half its purchase, there may be a gift tax liability. With jointly held bank accounts, savings bonds, stocks, or bonds, a gift tax liability is triggered when the spouse withdraws money or investments are sold. In most cases the amount of the gift is sheltered from tax by the $100,000 you can give your spouse tax-free during your lifetime or the $6,000 tax-free annual gifts, so it's nothing to worry about. But if you have already given many gifts to your spouse, consult a lawyer about the effects of putting the property into both names.

2. In the case of a marital dispute one joint owner of a bank account can often clear out the funds, leaving the other one on the financial ropes.

3. Jointly held investments may need the signatures of both parties before they can be sold. If one of you is ill, incompetent, or stubborn, it can prevent investments from being sold at a propitious time.

4. If your combined estates are worth more than $175,625, joint property can increase your estate tax (see page 710).

5. If you've married more than once, joint property can result in an unfair distribution of your estate. For example, suppose you have children from a first marriage, then put everything into joint names, with right of survivorship, with a second spouse. If you die first, the second spouse will get all the property, and he or she may not provide for the children from your first marriage as well as you would like.

6. If they have only a joint bank account, spouses lack good records of their own for separate financial transactions. It can make a difference to income taxes and estate taxes whose property is whose—and separate accounts make that easy to prove. When you own investments or real estate in your own name, payments and receipts should be handled through your own account so there can be no doubt that the property is yours. Your signature on a check drawn on a joint bank account is not the same thing, because you might be dispensing your spouse's funds. If a wife owns an insurance policy on her husband's life, the premium payments should go through her account (even if the husband has to give her the funds) to make perfectly clear to estate tax auditors that none of the policy premiums should be taxed in her husband's estate. A joint bank account is useful for household expenses, but separate accounts should also be created for managing separate property.

7. In case of separation or divorce it can take a long time to unwind joint property. Money and property in your own name, on the other hand, is yours immediately. It's particularly important for a nonworking wife to have some money in her own name so that her estranged husband can't force her to a separation agreement by withholding funds.

8. In some states when one spouse dies, joint bank accounts may be frozen for a while. Having money in your own name provides an emergency fund for the family to live on while you're waiting for the joint funds to be released.

9. All joint property may be taxed in the estate of the first joint owner to die. At the death of the second owner it could then be taxed again. There are two exceptions to this rule: Fifty percent of property held jointly by a married couple can be excluded from the estate *if* the spouse who actually paid for the property makes a formal gift of half to the other spouse and so indicates by filing a gift tax return. Also, any portion of the property paid for by the other owner can be excluded from the estate, providing that there's proof of payment. If you hold any property jointly, be sure to keep records as to who paid for what and get advice from a lawyer on whether a gift tax return should be filed.

Special note: If you decide to put real estate in the name of the wife, it may be an uphill battle. Banks and real estate brokers are accustomed to putting joint names or the husband's name on the deed. Documents may come through misnamed, but don't let them pass. Keep insisting that they be in the wife's name only and that all correspondence regarding the property be directed to her. Some banks encourage joint names on a deed even if you don't want it. But don't give in; they're talking from habit rather than law. As long as both your names are on the mortgage, the bank is fully protected. It doesn't matter that only one name is on the deed.

Advantages of Joint Property for Unmarried People

1. It allows the property to pass automatically to the other owner at death, without having to wait for the will to be probated.

2. It's a sign of good faith toward the other joint owner.

3. It can be convenient—for example, a mother and daughter living together can both draw on a joint bank account for household expenses.

Disadvantages of Joint Property for Unmarried People

1. If real estate is put into joint names and one owner didn't pay his full half-share, it triggers a gift tax liability.

2. Taxes may also be triggered when the noncontributing owner withdraws money from the bank account, or when jointly held investments are sold. You can make a tax-free gift of up to $3,000 a year, but anything over that is taxable.

3. Either owner can withdraw funds from a joint bank account, without getting approval from the other. This could result in your losing money you had expected to have.

4. You'll need both signatures to sell an investment or other property, which may not be possible if one owner is ill, or disapproving, or has left town. In other words, you're deprived of sole control of your property. With U.S. savings bonds, you need the consent of the other owner if you want to take the bonds out of joint names or add the name of someone else.

5. *All* the joint property will be taxed in the estate of the first joint owner to die, except for that part which the other owner paid for, and can prove it. The portion of the joint property paid for by the other owner is excluded from the estate.

Changing the Names on Property

If this discussion makes you think you should take some property out of, or put it into, joint names, please consult a lawyer experienced in tax planning. Changing the ownership of property might trigger gift taxes and other unwanted results—something to be aware of before you make any moves. If you don't know such a lawyer, call the local Bar Association, or call any lawyer of your acquaintance and ask for a recommendation.

Community Property

The eight community property states are Arizona, California, Idaho, Louisiana, Nevada, New Mexico, Texas, and Washington. There, all assets acquired during the marriage are jointly owned by husband and wife, no matter whose name is actually on the property. Some assets are not counted as part of the community: for example, property you owned before marriage, received by gift or inheritance, or, in most cases, acquired in a non-community-property state. Property outside the community can be owned individually or jointly, as you prefer.

If you have ever lived in a community property state, you remain affected by its rules. Even though you now live in a non-community-property state, assets acquired as community property remain so, no matter whose name the property carries. Be sure to tell your lawyer which assets were acquired in a community property state when you draw your estate plan. In case of divorce, any community property is 50 percent owned by the wife, even though it may carry the husband's name.

Record Keeping for Joint and Community Property

At death it can be extremely important to know not only whose name is on each piece of property but who paid for it. For example, if a mutual fund investment is jointly held by husband and wife but she paid for it, the entire amount may be taxed in the husband's estate *unless* she can prove that she put up all the funds. With community property it's necessary at death to know what is and what is not in the community. Whenever you buy property to be held in joint names, put a note on the purchase statement as to whose funds the money came from and file it away.

Ways to Give Money to a Minor Child

If you're putting away money for a child during your lifetime—say, for his college education—you might as well do it in a way that will save you income taxes (and estate taxes, if you're in that bracket). Assuming that you really mean for him to have the money, it makes sense to put it in his name. That way, any interest the money earns is his and will be taxed to him rather than to you. Since most children don't have any income to speak of, the interest his money earns will generally escape tax-free. So will small dividends, rents, or capital gains.

You can give a child up to $3,000 a year without paying gift taxes, and $6,000 if you do it jointly with your spouse. Taxes are due on larger amounts, but if you give appreciating property, its further increase in value will not be taxed in your estate.

There are better and worse ways of giving money and other property to a child. Here are some of your choices, with the pros and cons:

Outright Ownership

You can put the property directly into the child's name without any fuss or expense. But this leads to a lot of problems. If the gift is in the form of a savings account or bonds, the child can take the money whenever he wants and blow it however he likes. If you try to get around this problem by hiding the bank books, the IRS could argue that the gift was never really given. Outright gifts of stock or real estate present the opposite problem: The laws set up to protect children's property make it hard, even impossible, for your son or daughter to sell the property as long as they're underage. Property you had intended them to convert to cash for college tuition might be tied up until they graduate. (*Note:* A bank account in your name, in trust for a child, is not an outright gift. You still own the property and have to pay both income and estate taxes on it. It does, however, pass automatically to the child at your death, at which point he owns it outright.)

Joint Property

Putting property in joint names with a child is even worse than giving it outright. You can't sell without his consent, and if he's underage, he usually can't give consent without a court order. You still owe taxes on at least part of the income, and if you die, the entire property will be taxed in your estate. The only joint property you can liquidate easily is a joint bank account, but that doesn't count as a gift (or save you taxes) unless the child withdraws the money.

Uniform Gifts to Minors Act

This is perhaps the best way to put modest amounts of money into a child's name. You can give cash, stocks, bonds, and, in some states, insurance policies to an adult acting as custodian for the minor, but you generally can't give real estate. The custodian manages the property and can spend it on certain things, including college tuition. When the child reaches age eighteen or twenty-one, depending on state law, the property becomes his free and clear.

There's no legal rigamarole to making the gift. Your bank, stockbroker, or insurance agent can give you the papers and tell you where to sign. In fact, it's almost too easy; without legal advice, you may make a gift you'll regret. The person who makes the gift should not name himself custodian. If he does, and dies, the money will be taxed in his estate, just as if he hadn't given it away.

Trusts

If you expect to give a substantial sum of money to a child, ask a bank trust officer, or a lawyer experienced in estate planning, about trusts. Trusts can be drawn to meet any number of financial goals and can remain in effect past age twenty-one (see page 694). A "present interest" trust, for one, is more flexible than the Uniform Gifts to Minors Act with respect to how the child's money can be invested and spent, and who can be trustee.

Three Important Things to Remember
When You Put Money into a Child's Name

1. Unless it's protected by a trust, the money must be handed over to the child at age eighteen or twenty-one, regardless of whether you think he's fit to manage it.

2. You can't use income from the gift to support the child, because support is your legal obligation. It's unclear whether a college education would be considered a legal obligation for people in wealthy circumstances.

3. Don't irrevocably give away something you might need back. Some properties are impossible to reclaim; others can be taken back only by risking absurd tax consequences. Normally, whatever you give to your child is his to keep.

Living (Revocable) Trusts

You can put money in trust for someone during your lifetime. An *irrevocable trust* is a permanent gift; once done, you cannot change your mind. The property is not included in your estate, but gift taxes are owed (which will be credited against the estate tax due—see page 708). A *revocable trust* remains under your control. You can change the terms of a revocable trust, change the beneficiary, or cancel it entirely. Revocable trusts are included in your estate.

Talk to a lawyer or bank about trusts. You generally need $100,000 and up to have your money managed individually by a bank, but many banks have pooled funds for smaller amounts.

Why Would You Want to Set Up a Living Trust?

Here are some possibilities:

1. You're getting old and fear that someday you won't be able to manage your money competently. Putting it in trust, perhaps with a bank as trustee, assures that you'll have continuity of income and management, no matter what happens to your health.

2. You plan to leave money in trust for your spouse and children when you die and want to try out a particular institution's investment abilities before committing yourself to it irrevocably.

3. You've inherited some money but don't know how to manage it. Putting it in trust with a competent manager relieves you of that burden.

4. You want assets to pass to your heirs without going through probate.

5. You want to shift income to someone in a lower income tax bracket (see next section).

Short-Term Trusts

A special form of living trust is the short-term, or Clifford, trust—*an excellent way to provide college money for your children or support for elderly parents, with tax advantages to yourself.* A short-term trust must be set up for at least ten years, during which time you may not cancel it. While the trust is in force, all income from the principal is taxed to the trust itself or to the trust beneficiary. Assuming that the beneficiary is in a lower income tax bracket than you are, you'll save a lot of tax money. At the end of the term the trust dissolves and you get all the property back. In effect, you have shifted some of your income to a lower tax bracket without giving up any property.

For example, say you're supporting your parents who don't have enough income to owe taxes, and you have bonds worth $40,000, paying 7 percent. That's $2,800 a year, on which you're paying taxes. If you put those bonds in a short-term trust, with your parents as beneficiaries, that $2,800 would pass untaxed. The same would be true if you named a child as beneficiary with the income to be used for nonsupport items —perhaps college tuition. (If you use it for child support, which is your legal obligation, the income will all be taxed to you.) The value of the income is a gift, which may be subject to gift tax (unless it can pass untaxed under your annual exemption—ask your lawyer about it). If you die, the trust is taxed in your estate.

Estate Planning and Single People

For the never married, quasi-married, widowed, or divorced:

• Make a will! Even more than married people, you may have special commitments to friends, protégés, young relatives, or charitable causes, all of which would be completely cut off if you died intestate. If you die without a will, your money would be divided according to the laws of the state, going only to your children, parents, brothers and sisters, or other relatives.

• If you live with someone but aren't married, and have no will, your partner may not get any of your property, even if he or she helped buy it. Everything you own will be distributed to your relatives. In a few cases, quasi-spouses have fought for, and won, certain property rights (notably in California), but the court fight is expensive. A few states recognize rights in common-law marriages, but by and large this is small protection. If you want your property to go to your partner, make a will.

• If you hold property jointly with someone else, he or she will get that property at your death, even without a will. (For the pros and cons of joint property, see page 717.)

• Unmarried people cannot use the marital deduction to shelter large estates from taxes. The maximum amount you can pass tax-free is $175,-625.

Special Problems with Investment Real Estate

The house you live in is generally no problem in your estate. If it's jointly held, it passes to the other owner; even with no will, most states give your spouse (if any) use of the home until he or she dies. But investment real estate is another matter. Unless its disposition is carefully thought through, it can give your heirs a good deal of trouble. Some things to consider:

• Are your heirs capable of managing the properties? If not, leave a letter for your executor covering all pertinent details about the investments, what they should be worth, and who is most qualified to sell them at the best price. If your executor doesn't have this information, he may inadvertently sell the properties for too little.

• If estate taxes are owed, is there enough cash on hand to pay them? Generally speaking, executors shouldn't have to sell real estate to raise money for taxes. Property often can't be sold quickly, except at distress prices; a forced sale might well deprive your heirs of money you wanted them to have. Figure your probable estate tax liability and provide liquid assets to cover it—cash, stocks, life insurance.

• Is the property in another state? If so, your will might have to be probated there as well as in your home state. Holding out-of-state property in joint names may be advisable, since the land will then pass to the other owner without probate.

• Is the real estate to be left in trust? Great care is needed in choosing a trustee capable of managing the property. A bank trust department may be willing to accept real estate in a large trust, but its expertise may not be as good as you'd like. If there's no truly capable person around, it might be better for the executor to sell the properties.

• Do you have an interest in real estate tax shelters (such as subsidized housing), from which you receive little income but large tax losses? Disposing of that interest may generate large taxes for your heirs—something the salesman didn't tell you when the shelters were bought. All or much of the tax loss you've declared may, in some circumstances, have to be declared as ordinary income, and taxes paid! Go over this carefully with your accountant or tax lawyer; you may have to provide your heirs with extra cash from life insurance to cover this liability. Otherwise, they'll have much less money from your estate than they expected.

Special Problems with Business Interests

If much of your net worth is tied up in a closely held business, you'll need estate planning of considerable sophistication. You'll want buyout agreements with your partners, cash to cover estate taxes, agreements to cover your family's interests. The capital gains tax on inherited property imposed in 1976, if not repealed, may force the sale of large family-held businesses. Unfortunately, many businessmen neglect personal financial planning—meaning to do it when they're older, then dying in middle-age, leaving everything in a mess. Personal estate planning should be part of a business scheme right from the start. The tax-wisest time for arranging ownership shares is generally early in the game, when the value of the shares is small. But it's never too late to get tax-planning advice. Talk to a tax lawyer about your situation to see where the financial gaps are and what can be done to protect your family's interests.

Special Problems with Tax Shelters

If you die while holding a tax shelter, your estate may be in for trouble. Shelters that give big up-front write-offs but have small economic value generate huge tax liabilities when they're disposed of, with no corresponding income to pay the tax. Many men don't realize that their shelters are no more than tax time bombs: They cheerfully take their tax write-offs during life, then leave their widows to pay the piper after their deaths. Unwinding a tax shelter may devastate an otherwise valuable estate. This kind of damage isn't done by shelters that have significant economic value and can be disposed of at a handsome gain—but even here, you have tax complications that you may not realize. Anyone who owns a tax shelter should talk to an estate-planning lawyer or tax accountant to see what the eventual tax liabilities will be and what, if anything, can be done to minimize them (for more on tax shelters, see page 662).

Estate Planning for Retarded Children

It's not enough to accumulate a pool of savings to take care of a retarded child after your death. You also have to arrange those savings so they'll do the most good. When well planned, a modest estate can assure a retarded child a reasonably comfortable life; unplanned, these same savings will soon be used up, leaving the child dependent on welfare benefits well below the poverty level.

State and federal programs pay basic medical and residential expenses for retarded children and adults. But they get this aid only if they have little or no money of their own. State law varies as to how much they're allowed to have. But it's possible that owning as little as $760 in a savings account could disqualify a retarded person from state medical benefits. In other words, a person with a little money left him by his parents suffers more hardship than a person with no money at all.

If, when you die, you manage to leave a $50,000 life insurance policy for the care of a retarded child, it might be used up in two or three years. The child would then be thrown entirely on the paltry funds provided by welfare, plus whatever else family members could contribute. But if you left that same $50,000 in a well-drawn trust, he could still qualify for state aid. The key is to leave the money for his incidental expenses, not his general care. He could then get state aid for all his basics, with the money from the trust available for all those extras you'd want him to have—vacations, some clothes, a record player, spending money, supplemental expenses if he's living outside an institution, and so on. Some planning suggestions:

• Consider leaving the retarded child out of your will entirely. Give money for his care to your other children or set up a trust. Tell other relatives about your plans, so they won't leave the child a small sum in their own wills, which would bar him from state and federal benefits. But by all means make a will. If you die without one, part of the property will automatically go to the child, no matter how severe his retardation. The court would have to appoint someone to manage it, and until it's used up, the child would be ineligible for state aid.

• Don't make the child the beneficiary of a life insurance policy. Instead, have the proceeds of the policy paid into a trust or to a person who can be relied on to see that the child gets what he needs. See if it's possible to draw the trust so as to exempt the insurance proceeds from estate taxes. Because you'll need a lot of insurance to provide for the retarded person as well as for the rest of your family, consider inexpensive term insurance. When you can afford it, you may want to convert some of the term to straight-life, to carry on after you reach age sixty-five or seventy, when most term policies stop. It's not worth spending money to insure the life of a retarded person, unless his case is mild and he marries.

• The trust must be drawn by someone thoroughly familiar with your state's laws affecting the retarded, as well as the rules on trusts and estates. You want to give the trustee as much leeway as possible for dispensing funds, without disqualifying the person for state and federal aid. Your state or local Association for Retarded Citizens should be able to refer you to a lawyer. Some states will seize a trust fund if the retarded person receives state aid. In that case, it's best to leave money to other family members for the retarded person's support, or set up a trust in another state.

When naming a bank as trustee, include a concerned family member or friend as cotrustee to be sure the retarded person's needs are attended to. Small trusts are usually managed by a relative.

You can get a booklet called *How to Provide for Their Future* for 50 cents from the National Association for Retarded Citizens, 2709 Ave. E East, P.O. Box 6109, Arlington, Tex. 76011.

Last Warning

This chapter cannot be used as a do-it-yourself guide to estate planning. There are all kinds of tax and other complexities that simply cannot be covered in a general chapter such as this one. Furthermore, each state has different laws affecting the disposition of property, and between the time I write this and the time you read it, state and federal laws may change.

Amateur will drafting and estate planning could cost your heirs a tremendous amount of money. The information given here is intended to help you organize your thinking about your estate and introduce you to the vocabulary and concepts you'll be working with. But every simple will should be drawn by a lawyer, preferably one who specializes in this line of work. Estate plans should *always* be drawn by an experienced tax- and estate-planning attorney.

Chapter Twenty-Eight

SOCIAL SECURITY

> Mr. Justice Holmes was . . . under no illusions about
> the law. He knew very well that its aim was not to
> bring in the millennium, but simply to keep the
> peace.
>
> H. L. MENCKEN

It's a retirement pension. A disability income plan. An income for your
spouse and children if you die young. Health insurance for the elderly.
It's the new, improved Social Security system, relied on for its benefits,
resented for its cost. In recent years Social Security payments have risen
tremendously; from 1972 to 1977, the average retirement check rose
by 53 percent, outstripping the cost of living by 7 percentage points.
Yet over those years, payroll taxes rose only modestly. In 1977 Americans were finally handed the full bill for Social Security, in a Social
Security tax hike of massive proportions. There was revolt, and for the
first time people began talking about limiting benefits rather than en-
larging them.

Who Pays for Your Social Security?

Many Social Security recipients think they're getting back only what
they contributed to Social Security over the years, plus interest. Some
think they're getting less. Both are wrong. Monthly retirement checks
alone are two to three times more than you'd get if payments were
computed only from your own (and your employer's) contributions. If
you had to pay the full cost of your disability, survivor's, and Medicare

727

insurance, there might not be anything left for retirement payments at all!

If a person retired in January 1978, after paying the maximum into Social Security since it began in 1937, the *most* that could be in his account, plus interest, would be $28,000. At 1978's rate of retirement benefits, that sum would last a married couple receiving the maximum check just a little over three years! Yet Social Security guarantees them an income, plus cost-of-living increases, for life. Similarly, younger workers may receive a lifetime of disability payments even though they contributed very little to the system. All of the elderly receive Medicare, even though it was added to the system only ten years ago (which means that those now drawing benefits haven't paid much in Medicare taxes).

The fact is that each beneficiary's Social Security check is financed not out of his own contribution, but from other people's taxes. The benefit you get this month comes from the taxes two or three other Americans paid last month, each of whom expects to get the same service in his turn. A typical beneficiary gets out of the system far more than he pays in.

Will There Be Enough Money for Social Security in the Future?

Social Security's current money problems are mainly the result of raising benefits faster than we raised taxes to pay for them. In the future, we'll have another problem: The rate of increase in workers paying into Social Security will slow in relation to the increase in beneficiaries. Fewer people will be taxed to provide more checks. The effects of this will start being felt around 2010.

Both of these problems can and will be solved, probably in three steps over the next several years:

1. Social Security taxes will rise.

2. Part of the Social Security program will be financed with income taxes (which means that either income taxes will rise or the government will switch tax money over from other areas).

3. Social Security benefits will be reduced—for example, by setting the retirement age at sixty-eight rather than today's sixty-five.

But note this: People now receiving Social Security checks will not have their checks reduced. Any changes in the benefit structure will be made for future claimants, not for those now on the rolls. Future benefit reductions will be made gradually, so that those affected will have time to plan. It is, of course, possible to avoid benefit reductions by raising Social Security taxes even more. But the potential cost is apparently more than workers are willing to bear. The political system will have to fashion a compromise between what nonworkers think they're entitled to get and what workers are willing to pay.

Social Security and Income Taxes

Social Security payments are not subject to federal, state, or local income taxes. You receive these benefits entirely tax-free.

Who Is Eligible for Social Security?

Almost all jobs, including self-employment, are covered by Social Security. But to qualify for benefits, you have to earn a certain amount over a given period of time. The following table gives the minimum earnings needed for one *quarter* of coverage (a *quarter* is a three-month period).

The following tables show how many quarters of coverage you need in order to qualify for the various Social Security benefits. These quar-

Type of worker	Minimum amount for basic eligibility	Amount needed to earn one quarter of coverage in 1978[a,b]	Amount needed for a full year of coverage[b]
Employee in a Social Security–covered job	No minimum	$250[c]	$1,000[c]
Agricultural worker (including domestic worker in a farm home)	$150 in cash pay (not counting value of room and board) from one employer during a year *or* working 20 days or more for a single employer, for cash pay (regardless of amount) figured on a time basis (so much per hour, per day, etc.)	$250	$1,000

Type of worker	Minimum amount for basic eligibility	Amount needed to earn one quarter of coverage in 1978[a,b]	Amount needed for a full year of coverage[b]
Homeworkers	$100 from a single employer	$250	$1,000
Employees in tax-exempt organizations			
Work not in the course of the employer's trade or business—for example, working for a businessman as a gardener			
Child under twenty-one working in a parent's business; wife employed by husband and vice versa	Not covered		
Parent working in a child's business; spouse in a partnership with spouse or working in spouse's company	No minimum	$250[c]	$1,000[c]

[a]Earnings can occur at any time during year.
[b]These amounts increase every year, in line with increases in wage levels.
[c]Count cash wages, tips of $20 or more while working for one employer, and the cash value of wage substitutes, such as free meals and a room.

ters need not be worked consecutively; as long as you have the proper count, you're insured. As you can see, the number of quarters needed for retirement benefits and Medicare is gradually being increased, from twenty-four quarters (six years) in 1978 to forty (ten years) in 1994. Survivor's benefits (paid to certain dependents after your death) and disability benefits can be earned after shorter periods of work.

What If You Were Eligible for Coverage but Contributions Weren't Made?

If you are an employee eligible for Social Security, you and your employer are supposed to make matching payments each year. It's the responsibility of the employer to deduct your share from your paycheck and send in the total amount. If the employer fails to do this, he becomes responsible for 100 percent of the payment—yours *and* his—

ELIGIBILITY FOR RETIREMENT BENEFITS AND MEDICARE

Year you were born	Quarters of coverage needed for retirement benefits and Medicare
1913	24 (6 years)
1914	25
1915	26
1916	27
1917	28 (7 years)
1918	29
1919	30
1920	31
1921	32 (8 years)
1922	33
1923	34
1924	35
1925	36 (9 years)
1926	37
1927	38
1928	39
1929 or later	40 (10 years)

ELIGIBILITY FOR SURVIVOR'S BENEFITS

If you were born in 1929 or before	If you were born in 1930 or later	
You need the same number of quarters as for retirement and Medicare, shown in the previous table.	Age at death	Quarters of coverage needed
	28 or younger	6 (1½ years)
	29	7
	30	8 (2 years)
	31	9
	32	10 (2½ years)
	33	11
	34*	12 (3 years)
	38	16 (4 years)
	42	20 (5 years)
	46	24 (6 years)
	50	28 (7 years)
	54	32 (8 years)
	58	36 (9 years)
	62 or older	40 (10 years)

IMPORTANT NOTE: *Regardless of when you were born, survivor's benefits are payable if you worked under Social Security for at least six quarters (1½ years, but not necessarily continuously) in the three years before your death.*

*For each year you advance in age, one additional quarter is needed; from this point on, the table advances in 4-year jumps.

ELIGIBILITY FOR DISABILITY BENEFITS

Age when you become disabled	Quarters of coverage needed
Under 24	6 quarters (1 ½ years) out of the 3 years prior to the start of your disability
24	6
25	8 (2 years)
26	10
27	12 (3 years)
28	14
29	16 (4 years)
30	18
31 or older	Fully insured* *and* with 20 quarters of coverage (5 years) out of the 40 quarters (10 years) prior to the start of your disability
31 or older for the blind disabled only	Fully insured*

*You're fully insured if you have 1 quarter of coverage for each calendar year after 1950. *Exception:* If your 21st birthday fell after 1950, you need one quarter of coverage for each calendar year since you reached age 21.

plus penalties. If you can prove that you worked and should have received Social Security credit, your earnings record may be corrected for at least three years back, and perhaps more.

SPECIAL WARNING to people who employ domestics, gardeners, and other home workers: These workers may ask that Social Security payments not be made so that they can keep their full paychecks. Do not agree! First, it would be against the law. Second, at some later date that same employee can complain to Social Security that the payments weren't made, in which case you will be liable for the full amount due, plus penalties.

Extra Coverage for Military Service

If you served in the armed forces or are the survivor of someone who did, you may have extra Social Security credits due. Your check may be higher, and eligibility period shorter, than would otherwise be the case. Ask about this at the Social Security office. Take with you the discharge papers (or get copies from the Veterans Administration) as proof of when the service occurred.

What Earnings Are Covered for Social Security?

Social Security taxes are levied on a certain amount of earnings every year. If you make that amount or less, all your wages are taxed; if you make more, the excess isn't taxed. The amount of earnings counted for Social Security is called the *earnings base,* and it's scheduled to rise steeply in the years ahead. The table below shows the increase in both Social Security taxes and the earnings base, as required by current law. (*Note:* As this book went to press, Congress was talking about lowering these high tax levels.)

YOUR SOCIAL SECURITY TAX

Year	Earnings base	Tax for employee[a]	Tax for self-employed
1978	$17,700	6.05%	8.10%
1979	22,900	6.13	8.10
1980	25,900	6.13	8.10
1981	29,700	6.65	9.30
1982	31,800[b]	6.70	9.35
1983	33,900[b]	6.70	9.35
1984	36,000[b]	6.70	9.35
1985	38,100[b]	7.05	9.90
1986	40,200[b]	7.15	10.00
1987	42,600[b]	7.15	10.00

[a]Employer contributes an equal amount.
[b]Estimated. Starting in 1982 the earnings base will rise in line with the increase in general wage levels.

How Is Your Social Security Check Figured?

All checks are figured the same way. The Social Security Administration lists all the earnings on which you have paid Social Security taxes for each year since 1950; if you didn't work for one year, you get a zero. A certain number of low-earning years are then crossed off, the number depending on your age. The remaining years are *averaged,* and your checks based on that average. A worker with a high average gets more money than a worker with a low average. The big increase in the Social Security earnings base will, therefore, lead to higher benefits for wealthier people, because it has the effect of raising their average reported earnings.

The averaging system produces one major inequity, with respect to disability and survivor's benefits. If an older worker becomes disabled, he'll get a smaller check than a younger worker, even though he has paid more into the system over the years. That's because the earnings base many years ago was lower than it is now, and those years of low Social Security wages lower the older worker's average. The younger worker, on the other hand, has contributed only during the years when the earnings base was high. His average will therefore be higher, and also his Social Security benefit. A change in the law effective in 1979 reduces somewhat the unfair gap between the checks of older and younger workers, but younger people still get more.

The averaging method establishes a Social Security–covered worker's *primary insured amount.* If he retires early, his primary insured amount is reduced. If his spouse or children collect on his Social Security account, they will receive varying percentages of the primary (or reduced) insured amount, depending on circumstances.

Checking Your Social Security Earnings

Because the amount of your Social Security check is based on average reported earnings, it's essential that those earnings be reported correctly. Employees of small, struggling companies or people with erratic job histories should be particularly careful to check their earnings record every three years. If your employer didn't report your earnings or reported them incorrectly, you may lose coverage that you ought to have. Generally speaking, errors in your record can't be corrected after three years, three months, and fifteen days have passed. (*But note*: Corrections can be made in some cases for errors farther back in time, provided that you have the proper proof of wages paid.)

To check your earnings record, ask the Social Security office for the Statement of Earnings postcard, form OAR-7004. Fill it in and mail it to the Social Security Administration, P.O. Box 57, Baltimore, Md. 21203; up in the corner of the postcard, write, "Quarters, please." You'll receive a current statement of the total amount of earnings credited to your Social Security record, plus the number of quarters you've accumulated.

Don't be jolted by the apparently small amount of earnings credited to the record! Your Social Security account is made up only of the amount of earnings on which you paid Social Security taxes, not on your total paycheck. The following table shows the Social Security maximums for 1951–1977 (for 1978–1987, see page 733). If you made less than these maximums, your actual wage for that year is the amount credited to the record.

MAXIMUM SOCIAL SECURITY EARNINGS, 1951–1977

Year	Maximum taxable amount
1951–54	$ 3,600
1955–58	4,200
1959–65	4,800
1966–67	6,600
1968–71	7,800
1972	9,000
1973	10,800
1974	13,200
1975	14,100
1976	15,300
1977	16,500

Estimating Your Social Security Check

When you send in the Statement of Earnings postcard to get your Social Security record and quarters of coverage (see foregoing section), you can also write in the corner, "Benefit estimate, please." You'll get back an estimate of your retirement check, based on the earnings currently credited. There's no point in asking for a benefit estimate when you're far from retirement, because your current earnings record is low. But when you are around age fifty-six, it starts making more sense. Your local Social Security office can help you estimate the probable size of your retirement check based on anticipated earnings through age sixty-two or sixty-five. Alternatively, get the brochure called *Estimating Your Social Security Check,* which shows how to figure it yourself.

There are two estimates pertinent to younger people—*survivor's benefits,* which is what your family would get if you died, and *disability benefits,* in case you become totally disabled. Social Security offices sometimes take the position that they don't have to make these calculations, but they usually will if they are approached politely and the need for the information is explained to them. It's important to learn what you'll get from Social Security so that you'll know how much additional life and disability insurance you need to protect your family. To get these estimates, send in a Statement of Earnings postcard, as discussed, and ask for quarters of coverage. Then visit the local Social Security office and ask for help with the calculation. You can request this information by mail, but it's often more efficient to pay a personal visit. For a list of the survivor's and disability calculations you may need, see page 415.

Note: Don't look at a table of Social Security benefits and assume that, since you've always paid the maximum tax, you'll get the top dollar shown. Social Security tables show future, as well as present, benefits. Footnotes in the table will show what the maximum average currently is for retirement checks. In 1980 the highest possible average earnings for a worker, age sixty-five, retiring in January were $9,405, for a maximum individual retirement check of $572.00 a month.

YOUR SOCIAL SECURITY BENEFITS

Benefits payable on your account are determined by the average earnings on which you've paid Social Security taxes over the years. *These benefits are subject to two limitations: the family maximum and the earnings test.*

The Family Maximum

Total monthly benefits paid to an insured worker and his family are limited by law. In general, the payment can't exceed 150 percent of the worker's personal benefit, no matter how large the family. If you have children by a former marriage, they're also included in the count. Big families, in other words, get less help from Social Security, relative to their expenses, than small families do. Moral: The more dependents you have, the more important it is to have a large life insurance policy.

If the total of Social Security payments to you, your spouse, and your children exceeds the maximum, each person's check is reduced proportionately until the maximum is reached.

The Earnings Test

If you make more than a certain amount of money in a year, your Social Security check will be reduced or eliminated. The amount you can earn is higher for those age sixty-five or more than for younger people—an incentive not to retire early. Over the exempt amount, Social Security payments are reduced by $1 for each $2 of earnings.

How does Social Security reduce your check? Each year you estimate next year's earnings, and payments are set according to that estimate. If you make less, Social Security sends you a check to compensate for the unnecessary reduction in your benefit; if you make more, the over-payment from Social Security will be withheld from the following year's checks, either all at once or in increments over twelve months. (By and large, it's best to overestimate earnings so that you won't run the risk of having your next year's Social Security checks sharply reduced.)

ANNUAL EXEMPT EARNINGS

	1978	1979	1980	1981	1982
Age 65 and over	$4,000	$4,500	$5,000	$5,500	$6,000
Under age 65	3,240	Future amounts to be increased in line with the cost-of-living.			

Your Social Security check is reduced by $1 for each $2 of earnings over these amounts; at double these amounts, your check is eliminated entirely.

This table is applicable to retirement and survivor's checks only. Different rules apply to the disabled.

Note 1: In the first year you retire, eligibility for Social Security is determined according to how much you make *each month* (the monthly limits are roughly the amounts shown in the table divided by twelve). After the first year, what matters is *annual* earnings, regardless of the months in which they were earned.

Note 2: These reductions apply only to earnings. You can receive any amount of money from rents, interest, dividends, royalties, pension payments, or investments without its affecting the size of your Social Security check.

Note 3: If you have enough earnings to reduce your Social Security payment, checks are also reduced for your spouse and other dependents. But if you get benefits as a dependent, your earnings affect only your own check, not the checks of the insured worker or anyone else drawing benefits on his account. *Example:* If a married, retired man has earnings over the exempt amount, checks are reduced for both him and his wife. But if only his wife works, her check is reduced while his remains unchanged.

Note 4: After you reach age seventy-two (seventy, starting in 1982), you'll collect a full Social Security benefit, for yourself and your eligible dependents, no matter how much income you earn.

Note 5: The exempt earnings in the preceding table and the $1-for-$2 reductions apply only to retirement benefits, survivor's benefits, and benefits paid to various dependents. If the disabled earn more than a certain amount, they may lose their benefit entirely. The cutoff point in January 1980 was $280 a month for most of the disabled and $417 for the blind disabled (with the levels to be increased in the future).

Cost-of-Living Allowance

In any year when the consumer price index (CPI) for the first quarter increases by 3 percent or more over the same period the previous year, you get a cost-of-living raise from Social Security. The percentage increase is the same as the rise in the CPI and becomes effective that June.

Benefits for Your Family If You Die

Many people think of Social Security only as a retirement plan for the elderly. But it also provides a lot of protection for young workers. For example, if you're covered by Social Security and you die, your family gets the following benefits:

Mother's or Father's Benefits

Your spouse is entitled to a monthly check during the time she or he is caring for your unmarried children under eighteen. If one of your children is retarded or disabled, and the condition began before age twenty-two, the spouse may get checks as long as that child is in her or his care, regardless of age.

If the spouse has earnings, this check may be reduced or eliminated (see page 737). But that money may not be entirely lost to the family. Part or all of what's taken away from the spouse because of earnings may be added to the benefit paid the children, subject to the limitations of the family maximum.

If the spouse remarries, this benefit usually stops. It also stops when the last child reaches eighteen or marries, and if your disabled child enters an institution for care.

To qualify for coverage, the marriage generally has to have lasted at least nine months (unless you die in an accident, or, under certain conditions, in military service). The spouse receives 75 percent of what the worker's check would have been, subject to the family maximum.

Your divorced wife (at this writing, not divorced husbands) caring for your children may get benefits on the same basis as your current wife. Mother's benefits paid to a divorced wife count against your family maximum, which must be spread over both families. Court cases are pending to extend this benefit to eligible men, as well.

A separated spouse gets full mother's or father's benefits, even though not living with the worker at the time of his or her death.

Children's Benefits

Your unmarried children each get a benefit, as long as they're under eighteen, or eighteen through twenty-one and full-time students. Benefits stop when a child reaches the cutoff age, quits school, or gets married. An unmarried, disabled child can get benefits for life, as long as the disability began before age twenty-two and prevents him from doing any substantial gainful work; checks may stop, however, if he enters an institution. If a disabled child tries a job, then has to quit because of his disability, he may requalify for the child's benefit provided that no more than seven years have passed.

Each child gets 75 percent of the worker's benefit, subject to the family maximum. It's generally paid to the parent or guardian (although at eighteen, the child may receive it directly). Children of a previous marriage are covered even if they don't live with you. Your adopted child can collect on your account; also your illegitimate child, if the child lived with you *or* you paid at least one half of his support.

If both parents were covered by Social Security and are now dead, the child's benefits will be figured on the record of the higher-earning parent. The family maximums on each record may be combined if that would result in a higher payment.

Children can collect on a grandparent's record if the child's parents are dead or disabled and the child went to live with the grandparent before he reached age eighteen. Also, the grandparent has to have provided at least half his support.

Widow's or Widower's Benefits

A widow or widower can collect on a spouse's account as early as age sixty, but at that age payment amounts to only 71.5 percent of the late spouse's benefit. By waiting until age sixty-two to collect, the check will rise to 82.9 percent of the spouse's amount. You won't get 100 percent of the benefit unless you delay retirement until age sixty-five. If your late spouse retired early, on a reduced benefit, your check will be based on his or her reduced amount.

A totally disabled widow or widower can get checks starting as early as age fifty. A disabled divorced widow (at this writing, not widower) gets the same benefit provided that the marriage lasted at least ten years.

If you are a widow and remarry at age sixty or older, remarriage will not reduce your Social Security check. You're still allowed widow's payments on the account of your late husband. But if you remarry under age sixty (or if you're a widower and remarry at any age), you generally lose your eligibility on your late spouse's account (even if the new spouse has no Social Security coverage). What happens if the new marriage doesn't work out and you divorce? You may once again become eligible for widow's or widower's benefits on the record of your first spouse.

Note this gap in Social Security coverage: A widow (or widower) will normally not be eligible for benefits after the youngest child reaches age eighteen and before qualifying for benefits at age sixty. If your spouse dies young, there's not enough life insurance, and you don't remarry, you'll have to support yourself during those middle years.

If you're divorced and your ex-husband dies, you're entitled to a widow's benefit on his account—provided that the marriage lasted ten years or more, and you don't have enough earnings to cancel the benefit out. Both an ex-wife and a current wife can receive benefits. In this case, checks paid to an ex-wife do not reduce the family maximum, which is payable in full to the second family. (At this writing, divorced widowers are not eligible for this benefit.)

A separated spouse receives full widow's or widower's benefits, even though not living with the worker at the time of his or her death.

Parent's Benefits

If you pay more than half the support of a parent aged sixty-two or more and you die, the parent may draw Social Security checks on your account. One dependent parent is entitled to 82½ percent of the worker's benefit, subject to the family maximum; two dependent parents may get a maximum of 75 percent each. Adoptive parents and stepparents are also eligible for these benefits, provided that the relationship was established before you turned sixteen.

Lump Sum Death Benefit

If your insured spouse dies, and you're living with him or her at the time of death, you get a lump sum payment of $255 to help cover funeral expenses. If you aren't living with your spouse, that money goes to whoever pays for the funeral. Beneficiaries may arrange to have this money sent directly to the funeral home.

Benefits for You and Your Family If You Become Disabled

Disability is generally defined as the inability to engage in any substantial gainful activity, by reason of a physical or mental impairment. The disability must be expected to last at least a year or result in death; payments do not begin until you've been disabled for five months. (After you reach age fifty-five, this definition is modified a little if you're blind: You're entitled to payments if you can't engage in any substantial gainful activity requiring skills comparable to those used in your previous employment. The blind are also allowed to earn more in a month without having their disability checks reduced, testimony to the power of a good lobby!)

To prove disability, submit medical evidence to the Social Security office. That evidence is turned over to a state agency, to determine whether your degree of disability meets the requirements of the law. Some people get private or government payments for total disability yet are turned down by Social Security because its requirements are stiffer. If your application is rejected, you can appeal (see page 757).

The disabled may have to accept vocational training or risk the loss of their Social Security checks. If you recover from your disability and go back to work, there's a three-month adjustment allowance before the Social Security checks stop. If you become disabled again within five years, benefits can resume immediately; you don't have to wait another five months. *Note:* If you try to return to work despite a severe and continuing disability, payments may continue for up to nine months while you see if you can manage. Assuming that you keep the job, you then get the three-month adjustment period before checks are canceled. (*Exception*: Disabled widows and widowers collecting on their spouses' accounts are not eligible for the nine-month trial period.)

Your Disability Check

Provided that you've met the work requirement (see page 730), you'll get a monthly check equal to the amount due if you were retiring currently at sixty-five. The check is reduced, however, by whatever you get from workmen's compensation.

Your Spouse's Check

Your spouse may receive 50 percent of your check starting at age sixty-five, or a smaller benefit starting as early as age sixty-two. A younger spouse may receive benefits if caring for your unmarried child under eighteen, or your disabled child of any age (provided that the disability began before age twenty-two). A divorced spouse may receive payments only if she or he is sixty-two or more.

Your Children's Checks

Your unmarried children—of present and previous marriages—may receive benefits as long as they're under eighteen, eighteen through twenty-one and full-time students, or disabled before age twenty-two. Each child is entitled to 50 percent of your check, subject to the family maximum. Checks are generally payable to the parent or guardian, although at eighteen the child, if he wants, receives them directly. Also covered is your adopted child; your illegitimate child, if there's enough evidence that you're the parent; and your stepchild, if the child lives with you or you contribute at least one half of his support. Children can collect on a grandparent's record, if the child's parents are dead or disabled, the child went to live with the grandparent before he was eighteen, and the grandparent provides half his support. For the spouse and children of the current marriage to collect disability checks, the marriage generally has to have lasted at least a year.

Earnings and Disability

You can earn a small amount of money and still be considered totally disabled, your status depending on physical condition as well as earnings. But earnings of more than $280 a month (or $417 for the blind disabled) usually disqualify you for further disability aid from Social Security.

Benefits for Your Family When You Retire

The Social Security law permits retirement as early as age sixty-two, but built-in financial incentives make it more attractive to retire at sixty-five or later. *The disadvantages of early retirement:*

1. Your monthly retirement check is lower.

2. Cost-of-living increases are proportionately reduced, so as the years pass, your monthly check will fall farther and farther behind the checks of those who retired at sixty-five or later.

3. The amount of money you can earn without having your Social Security reduced is lower for those under sixty-five, with the gap widening every year.

4. If you die, your widow or widower gets a lower benefit.

5. In many cases you cannot apply for retroactive benefits in situations where you failed to file a Social Security claim.

Your Check

You may retire at age sixty-five on full retirement benefits plus annual cost-of-living. If your retire earlier, your check is reduced. A retiree at age sixty-two gets only 80 percent of his basic benefit, for life; if he retires at sixty-three, he gets 86⅔ percent; at sixty-four, it's 91⅓ percent. Once you've retired on a reduced benefit, it stays reduced for life (except for cost-of-living increases).

The longer you wait after your sixty-fifth birthday to retire, the higher your benefit will be. Social Security adds ¼ of 1 percent to your check for each additional month you work (1/12 of 1 percent if you were born before 1917).

What if you retire, then go back to work, then retire again? Social Security will refigure your check, taking into consideration the extra time you worked and the extra taxes paid. *Warning:* If you originally retired earlier than age sixty-five, the early-retirement reduction will still be applied, with adjustments for earnings.

If you're still working at age seventy-two, you can collect your Social Security retirement benefit, regardless of how much you earn. Starting in 1982, full benefits will be payable at age seventy.

If you're a woman in Social Security–covered employment, you're entitled to retirement benefits on your own account or spouse's retirement benefits on your husband's account (see next section), but not both. Social Security will automatically credit you with whichever is higher. You can retire on your own account while your husband is still working, then switch to spouse's benefits on his account when he retires if that's more advantageous. (This works in reverse for a man claiming benefits on his wife's account.) *Warning:* If you retire early on your own account and get a reduced benefit, you'll also get a reduced spouse's benefit—even though you don't take the spouse's benefit until you reach age sixty-five. This trips up a number of women. *The general rule is, once a reduced check, always a reduced check*—with this exception: You may receive a full widow's benefit starting at age sixty-five or later, even though you previously had a reduced retirement or spouse's benefit.

Your Spouse's Retirement Check

When you retire, your spouse is also entitled to a retirement benefit. It amounts to 50 percent of your check if the spouse retires at age sixty-five, or 37½ percent starting as early as age sixty-two.

Your Spouse's Mother's (or Father's) Check

When you retire, your spouse of any age is entitled to mother's (or father's) benefits if she (or he) is caring for your unmarried child under eighteen, or unmarried disabled child of any age (where the disability began before age twenty-two). This benefit amounts to 75 percent of your retirement check. A spouse eligible for this check will get it in place of the spouse's benefit, not in addition to it. The Social Security rule is: When entitled to two benefits, a beneficiary is paid only the higher of the two.

A Divorced Spouse's Check

Provided that the marriage lasted at least ten years, an ex-spouse can get retirement benefits on exactly the same basis as the current spouse. This payment—equal to 50 percent of the worker's check—is made despite the fact that a current spouse is receiving the same benefit. Retirement benefits paid to an ex-spouse do not count against the worker's family maximum, hence don't reduce his or her own retirement check. As with a current spouse, an ex-spouse can't receive a benefit on a worker's account until he or she retires, even though the ex-spouse herself or himself is sixty-five. *Note:* An ex-wife may not receive mother's retirement benefits (see previous section) on the account of an ex-husband; mother's benefits are payable only if the ex-husband dies. The same is true for father's benefits.

Your Children's Checks

If you still have unmarried children when you retire, they're eligible for a benefit as long as they're under eighteen, or eighteen through twenty-one and full-time students. Benefits are payable to an adopted child, as long as he was adopted before you retired; to a stepchild if the stepchild lives with you, the relationship has existed at least a year, and you provide at least one half of his support; and to an illegitimate child if there's proof of parentage. Your disabled child of any age may also receive benefits, as long as the disability began before he reached age twenty-two. Each child is entitled to 50 percent of the worker's benefit, subject to the family maximum.

For the spouse and children of the current marriage to collect retirement benefits, the marriage generally must have lasted at least a year.

Your Health Benefits

You are eligible for Medicare at age sixty-five even if you haven't retired, so by all means put in an application. Other health insurance policies generally don't insure you after that age for benefits also covered under Medicare. (For details on Medicare, see page 483.) If you apply late, hospitalization expenses may be paid retroactively for up to one year, but doctors' bills will not be covered until you are actually on the rolls.

Sample Social Security Checks

The payment made to new beneficiaries increases each year as the cost of living goes up. So the numbers given on page 746 are not firm guides as to how much you'll actually get. But they give you a general idea of what to expect.

SAMPLE MONTHLY SOCIAL SECURITY CHECKS AS OF JANUARY 1980

Average yearly earnings[a]	Retired worker at age 65	Retired worker at age 62	Spouse, age 65, of retired worker[b]	Spouse, age 62, of retired worker	Widow with children[c]	One surviving child[d]	Widow at 65[e]	Family maximum[f]
$ 923 or less	133.90	107.20	67.00	50.30	100.50	100.50[g]	114.30	200.90
1,200	172.30	137.90	86.20	64.70	129.30	129.30[g]	147.10	216.30
2,600	252.90	202.40	126.50	94.90	189.70	189.70	216.00	379.40
3,000	276.80	221.50	138.40	103.80	207.60	207.60	236.40	397.50
3,400	296.80	237.50	148.40	111.30	222.60	222.60	253.50	478.00
4,000	325.60	260.50	162.80	122.10	244.20	244.20	278.10	556.40
4,400	348.80	279.10	174.40	130.80	261.60	261.60	297.90	618.20
4,800	369.30	295.50	184.70	138.60	277.00	277.00	315.40	673.40
5,200	388.20	310.60	194.10	145.60	291.20	291.20	331.60	728.40
5,600	407.30	325.90	203.70	152.80	305.50	305.50	347.90	755.20
6,000	426.70	341.40	213.40	160.10	320.10	320.10	364.50	782.60
6,400	445.80	356.70	222.90	167.20	334.40	333.40	380.80	810.10

6,800	466.10	372.90	233.10	174.90	349.60	349.60	398.20	837.80
7,200	490.20	392.20	245.10	183.90	367.70	367.70	418.70	867.10
7,600	511.70	409.40	255.90	192.00	383.10	383.10	437.10	895.40
8,000	530.40	424.40	265.20	198.90	397.80	397.80	453.10	928.20
8,400	541.70	433.40	270.90	203.20	406.30	406.30	462.80	948.00
8,800	555.20	444.20	277.60	208.20	416.40	416.40	474.20	971.30
9,200	567.10	453.70	283.60	212.70	425.40	425.40	484.50	992.40
9,600h	576.60	461.30	288.30	216.30	432.50	432.50	492.50	1,008.90
10,000	587.70	470.20	293.90	220.50	440.80	440.80	502.00	1,028.40

aFigured as explained on page 733.
bOr eligible child of a retired worker.
cWidow of any age with eligible unmarried children in her care and only a small amount of personal earnings.
dUnmarried child under 18, 18 through 21 and a full-time student, or disabled before age 22.
eAmount may be reduced if spouse received reduced retirement benefits before death.
fThe most a retired or disabled worker and his family, or a covered worker's surviving family, could receive.
gIf no surviving parent is eligible for Social Security, this amount is raised to $133.90.
h$9,405 is the maximum possible *retirement* average in January 1980. But averages could be higher for survivor's or disability benefits.

Recap for Divorced Wives

If your ex-husband was fully insured under Social Security, and the marriage lasted ten years or more, you're entitled to the following benefits:

1. *Spouse's retirement benefits when your ex-husband retires.* You can get a reduced benefit starting as early as age sixty-two or a full benefit starting at sixty-five. This payment is yours even if your ex-husband has remarried and his second wife is also drawing benefits on his account.

2. *Free Medicare at age sixty-five,* as long as your ex-husband is also sixty-five or has died. He need not be retired for you to collect. (If you're not eligible for Medicare on your own or your husband's account, you can buy it at low cost.)

3. *Spouse's disability benefits,* if your ex-husband becomes totally disabled. You qualify for reduced benefits at age sixty-two or a full benefit at sixty-five.

4. *Personal disability benefits* starting as early as age fifty if your ex-husband dies and you become totally disabled. After receiving disability benefits for twenty-four consecutive months, you become eligible for Medicare.

If your ex-husband dies and the marriage lasted nine months or more, you get *mother's benefits,* provided that you have in your care his unmarried child under eighteen, or his unmarried disabled child of any age (where the disability began before age twenty-two). If the marriage lasted ten years or more, you're eligible for survivor's benefits starting at age sixty.

There are no mother's benefits for divorced wives when the ex-husband retires or becomes disabled. Those particular benefits go only to current wives. But you will become eligible for spouse's benefits at age sixty-two.

Your ex-husband's eligible children are entitled to their own benefits on his account—in case of death, retirement, or disability—even if you yourself are not eligible.

A divorced wife has to enroll herself in order to get benefits. Take a copy of your marriage certificate and divorce papers to the Social Security office, as well as any other proofs needed (see page 756).

Remarriage

If you remarry, you must file for benefits on the account of your second husband, not your first. If the new husband has no Social Security, you're out of luck. However, if you remarry at age sixty or later, you can draw on the account of either your second or first husband (provided that the first marriage lasted at least ten years), whichever is better.

If your second marriage ends in divorce and you were married to your first husband ten years or more, you become reeligible for benefits on your first husband's account. If your second marriage also lasted at least ten years, you can claim on either account, whichever is better.

Recap for Divorced Husbands

You are entitled to the same *retirement* and *disability* benefits as divorced wives. At this writing, you're not eligible for *survivor's* benefits on the account of your ex-wife who died, but pending court cases are challenging this discrimination. Check with Social Security to see if you're now eligible. Normally, a man's own Social Security check will be higher than the benefit he'd get on the account of his ex-wife (or the amount of his earnings would cancel the benefit out). But some men are eligible to collect.

If You're a Remarried Widow or Widower

Your checks will stop if you're under sixty (unless you marry a person receiving Social Security widow's or widower's benefits, mother's or father's benefits, or childhood disability benefits, in which case your check will remain the same). If you remarry at age sixty or over, you can keep your present widow's (or widower's) check or receive spouse's benefits on the account of your new spouse, whichever is higher.

If There Are Two Wage Earners in Your Family

You have several options:

1. You can each collect retirement benefits based on your own accounts.

2. You can collect as spouse on the account of the other if that would give you a higher Social Security check. For example, a low-earning wife might get a higher payment by filing for a spouse's benefit when her husband retires rather than taking her own retirement check.

3. You can collect disability or retirement benefits on your own account, even though your spouse is working and supporting you.

4. You can switch from one account to the other. For example, a wife might retire on her own account, then switch to spouse's benefits on her husband's account when he retires. (*Warning*: If the wife retired early on her own account, taking a reduced check, she'll also get reduced spouse's benefits, even though she doesn't file as a spouse until age sixty-five.) Another common switch is for a wife to take her own retirement benefit while her husband lives, then switch to widow's benefits on his account after his death.

5. If you die or become disabled, your young children can get checks on your account, even though they're being supported by the other parent.

6. If both parents die or become disabled, children receive checks on the record of the parent who earned more money. However, the family maximums on both records may be combined, if that would result in a higher payment.

If Your Spouse (or Ex-spouse) Hasn't Retired

You cannot collect spouse's benefits until your spouse has actually retired. A wife, in other words, can't get a Social Security check at age sixty-five as long as her husband goes on working. The same is true of a divorced wife seeking to collect on her ex-husband's account. The general rule is that the insured worker must be receiving benefits before any of his dependents can receive them.

If You're Sixty-five but Not Planning to Retire

You qualify for Medicare at sixty-five, whether retired or not, so be sure to file an application. Whatever other health insurance you have, perhaps even group health with your employer, may not cover you after age sixty-four, so without Medicare you might have nothing. Part A of Medicare (hospitalization) will generally pay benefits retroactively for one year if you sign up late. But with Part B (which covers doctors' bills), no back benefits are paid. You must sign up for Part B within three months of your sixty-fifth birthday; otherwise, you have to wait for the next application period, which is the first three months of every year. In the meantime, you'll pay all doctor bills yourself.

You receive an extra retirement benefit of $\frac{1}{4}$ of 1 percent for every month you work past your sixty-fifth birthday ($\frac{1}{12}$ of 1 percent if you were born before 1917). Benefits may also increase for your spouse and other eligible dependents. At age seventy-two, you're entitled to full benefits whether you've retired or not, and regardless of how much money you earn. Starting in 1981, full benefits will be paid at age seventy.

If a husband and wife both worked, one can retire and get a Social Security check on his or her account while the other still works. But a spouse, ex-spouse, or children cannot draw benefits on your account as long as you haven't retired.

If You Go Back to Work After Retirement

Assuming that your wages exceed the amount allowed a Social Security beneficiary (see page 737), your retirement checks will be reduced or stopped. The same is true for checks paid to your spouse and other dependents. But you'll be building credits for higher retirement checks, against the day you retire again.

If You're a Student

You may qualify for benefits if your Social Security–insured parent is dead, disabled, or retired. If both parents worked, you can collect on one parent's account even though the other is still working and supporting you. If both parents are dead or disabled, and you went to live with a grandparent before age eighteen, you can collect on the grandparent's account—provided that the grandparent supplies at least one half of your support. To be eligible for benefits, you must be unmarried, eighteen through twenty-one years old, and a full-time student.

You must attend a qualifying school: a government-supported high school, vocational, or trade school; a state-approved or accredited private school or college; a state college, community college, or university; or an unaccredited private school or college, provided that at least three accredited schools or colleges accept its credits, on transfer, on the same basis as credits transferred from an accredited school. Schools outside the United States may qualify under certain circumstances; ask Social Security about it.

You must be a full-time student—which means that the college or university considers you to be in full-time attendance, according to its standards. If you're in high school, trade school, or vocational school, you're a full-time student if you meet its standards for full-time attendance, your course of study lasts for at least thirteen weeks, *and* you're enrolled for at least twenty hours a week.

Vacations

Your checks can continue during a vacation period of not more than four months, if you were a full-time student before the vacation started and intend to return to full-time attendance when vacation ends. If checks stop because you leave school but you decide to return before the end of four months, you can get back payments.

Earnings

If you earn more than the exempt amount (see page 737), your Social Security check will be reduced by $1 for each $2 of excess earnings.

Continuity

Child's benefits normally stop when you reach age eighteen, unless you're a full-time student. A few months before your eighteenth birthday, you'll get a notice regarding the kind of proof needed to establish student status. Take that proof down to the Social Security office right away so that your checks will continue as usual. A child's Social Security checks are normally sent to his parent or guardian; after eighteen, checks can still be sent to your parent or, if you prefer, directly to you.

If you apply late, back payments can be made for up to twelve months.

If You Haven't Contributed Much to Social Security

As long as you've worked long enough to be covered (see page 730), there's a minimum benefit below which your checks cannot fall. People with lower incomes receive higher benefits, relative to Social Security taxes paid, than people with higher incomes.

If Your Check Is Smaller Than Your Neighbor's

Social Security checks are tremendously variable, depending on how long you contributed, when you retired, whether both husband and wife worked, and what your earnings were. Due to the way the benefit formula works, a working couple gets a lower joint check than an individual with the same income. If you have questions about how much you're getting, ask Social Security to explain.

If You're Planning to Retire Abroad

The United States won't send Social Security checks to some Communist countries. But United States citizens living everywhere else can get checks regularly without having to return periodically to the United States. The same is true for citizens of fifty specific countries (the list runs from Argentina to Zaire) who have earned benefits here; ask your Social Security office for details. But citizens of other countries may lose their checks after they've been out of the United States for six months, unless they lived in the United States for ten years and have ten years of work credits. There are special wrinkles affecting citizens of a few countries; always check with Social Security before you make a decision to retire abroad.

If You Employ a Regular Baby-sitter or Domestic

You owe Social Security taxes if you pay an employee more than $100 a year. Half the payment is deducted from the worker's wages, the other half comes from you. But it's your responsibility to mail the entire payment to the government once every three months. If you don't, and the employee complains to Social Security, you may be assessed the full amount due—your contribution and the employee's share—plus penalties. Payment is made through the Internal Revenue Service. Call IRS, ask for an employer identification number, and get Form 941, for reporting and paying Social Security taxes.

If You Get Income from a Limited Partnership

Starting in 1979 that income is excluded from coverage. No Social Security taxes are owed on it, and it won't be counted toward figuring your benefits. Nor is it counted as earnings to reduce your Social Security check. Any such income prior to 1979, however, was covered for Social Security purposes and will be included in your earnings record.

If You Get Income from Another Pension

Social Security was specifically designed to be paid in tandem with private pension plans. Consequently, you may collect your full Social Security benefit *and* income from a private employer pension, an individual retirement plan, and even another government pension plan. (Dependents of people with government pensions, however, are being phased out of the Social Security system.)

If You Filed Late for Benefits

Most Social Security benefits are payable retroactively for up to one year. There are some exceptions, however, so check with your local Social Security office. There is also no retroactivity for Medicare Part B (covering doctor bills).

Supplemental Security Income

This is payable to the blind, disabled, and people aged sixty-five or older who have very little income. (You can be disqualified, however, or paid a reduced benefit if you live in someone else's home and are supported by them. If you live with your parent, child, or spouse, the law assumes that you share in their income and resources.)

The Income Requirement

Your first $20 per month of *unearned income* is not counted for SSI purposes. Also not counted is your first $65 a month of *earned income* (or $85, if you have no unearned income); state or local welfare payments; earnings of an unmarried student under twenty-two of up to $1,620 a year; one third of your child support payments; and other odds and ends. You qualified for SSI in the summer of 1979 only if your income (excluding this exempt income) was below $208.20 a month for an individual, or $312.20 for a couple. Those threshhold amounts increase as the cost of living rises. Unearned income over $20 is deducted from your SSI benefit dollar for dollar. Earnings over $65 (or $85 where there's no unearned income) reduce your SSI check by $1 for every $2 you make. *Note:* Some states pay low-income supplements to people with incomes modestly above the federal SSI level.

Resources

An individual can have savings of up to $1,500, and a couple, $2,250. You can also have personal goods valued at $1,500, a car worth $1,200 at retail, and life insurance with a face value of no more than $1,500. The value of your home and adjoining land is not counted in determining eligibility.

Applying for a Social Security Card

Apply for a card when you get your first job. You'll have to show proof of age, through a birth or baptismal certificate, and two proofs of identity. It usually takes three or four weeks for the card to come through, so if you're a young person expecting a summer job, apply in the early spring. Employers generally won't hire you unless you have a Social Security number.

If you marry and change your name, be sure to notify Social Security so that there won't be any confusion about reporting earnings. If you lose your card and forget the number, Social Security can find you on its computer and issue a new card.

Applying for Social Security Benefits

The address of your Social Security office is shown in the phone book, under the U.S. government listings. You can write or call for information; if the problem is at all complicated, a personal visit is more effective. When you apply for Social Security, try to visit the office three months before benefits are due to start in order to get the paperwork out of the way.

When you apply for retirement benefits, bring (1) your Social Security number; (2) proof of age (a birth certificate or baptismal certificate from shortly after birth); (3) your marriage certificate if you are applying for benefits as a spouse (your marriage and divorce papers, if an ex-spouse); (4) birth certificates of your children if the application for benefits includes them; (5) proof of a child's disability if applicable; (6) your last year's W-2 form, or tax return (the reason for this is that Social Security is nine months behind in posting earnings on your record; to get an accurate fix on your check, it's necessary to know what you earned in the most recent tax year).

When you apply for survivor's benefits, bring (1) the Social Security number of the insured worker; (2) proof of your relationship (a marriage certificate, if a spouse; marriage and divorce papers if an ex-spouse; birth certificates, if a child); (3) proof of your age; (4) a copy of the insured worker's last W-2 form or tax return, and proof of your own earnings; (5) proof that the insured worker was paying at least half of your support if you are applying as his parent; (6) proof that you're in school full-time if you are applying as a student.

When you apply for disability benefits, bring (1) your Social Security number; (2) medical proof of your disability from the doctor or hospital that treated you; (3) your last W-2 form or income tax return; (4) birth certificates of your children if the application includes them (and proof that they're full-time students if applicable); (5) your marriage certificate if you are applying as a spouse (and divorce papers if you're an eligible ex-spouse).

When you apply for Supplementary Security Income, bring (1) your Social Security number; (2) proof of income (from Social Security, pension, savings, and other sources); (3) proof of assets (your bankbook, insurance policies, and so on); (4) your marriage certificate if you are applying as a couple.

Appealing a Social Security Decision

If Social Security decides that you're not eligible for a particular payment, such as disability or SSI, you can appeal. Personnel in the Social Security office will explain your rights and help you fill in the forms. Following are the steps up the appeals ladder; if you lose your case at any level, you have a choice of dropping it or appealing to the next higher authority.

1. *Reconsideration.* In SSI cases someone in the local Social Security office, but unconnected with your case, will review the documents plus whatever new evidence you're able to submit. In retirement, survivor's, or disability cases, your folder will be sent to a program center and reviewed there. You must ask for reconsideration within sixty days from the date you received notice of the decision.

2. *Hearing.* Apply for a hearing within sixty days of getting the reconsidered decision. You or your lawyer may present your case to the administrative law judge of the Bureau of Hearings and Appeals of the Social Security Administration. You don't necessarily have to be present; if you are, the judge will ask you questions about your situation. You're allowed to bring witnesses and present new evidence.

3. *Review.* A request for review by the Appeals Council must be filed within the time limit set by the hearing decision. But review isn't automatic; the council decides whether to take the case or not. If it does, you or your lawyer may appear to present arguments.

4. If the decision goes against you, and you think you have an important legal point to present, you can sue in federal court.

Do You Need a Lawyer?

You may argue your case yourself up through the appeals ladder. But you'll probably do better with a lawyer trained at presenting a case, questioning witnesses, and making points of law. Social Security determines a fair fee for the lawyer, based on the work he does.

Direct Deposit

You can arrange for Social Security checks to be sent directly to your bank for deposit in your account. This saves you the trouble of visiting the bank every month and avoids any risk that the checks might be stolen from your mailbox. The Social Security office will help you arrange direct deposit.

If You're Ill or Disabled

If you can't get out to visit a Social Security office, in many communities the office comes to you. A representative will visit your home to help you fill in the forms and handle any of your questions.

Chapter Twenty-Nine

RETIREMENT PLANNING

Life is short. Live it up.
NIKITA KHRUSHCHEV

For most people Social Security is not enough to live on in their old age. It has to be supplemented with other income from pensions, private savings, earnings, investments, and so on. In a typical savings cycle, you'll spend your twenties and thirties building equity in a house and your forties and fifties adding to your net worth via savings and investments. By age fifty-five you should have a pretty good idea of what standard of living you can expect in retirement.

Many people find themselves flat broke in their old age because they never took a hard look at how large their pensions would be or, indeed, whether they'd get a pension at all; also many women who expected to be supported by their husbands suddenly find themselves alone. By your mid-forties, retirement planning should be very much in the front of your mind. The key questions: How much money will you need? Where will it come from? What can you do now to secure it?

Life Expectancy

There's one clue to how long you're likely to live—namely, how long your mother and father lived. Other than that, you have to play the averages. The following table is based on 1976 data. Take the life expectancy for your age at retirement, add enough years to make you feel secure, and base your planning on that number. For example, a woman retiring at sixty-five can expect to live to age eighty-three, for a life expectancy of eighteen years. If she's from a long-lived family she might throw in another ten years as a safety margin, bringing her to age ninety-three. That's twenty-eight years for which she has to provide a retirement income.

LIFE EXPECTANCY

Your age at retirement	Average number of years remaining	
	Men	Women
50	24.1	30.1
51	23.3	29.2
52	22.5	28.3
53	21.8	27.5
54	21.0	26.6
55	20.3	25.8
56	19.5	25.0
57	18.8	24.2
58	18.1	23.4
59	17.4	22.6
60	16.8	21.8
61	16.1	21.0
62	15.5	20.2
63	14.9	19.5
64	14.3	18.7
65	13.7	18.0
66	13.1	17.3
67	12.5	16.5
68	12.0	15.8
69	11.4	15.1
70	10.9	14.4

Note: U.S. average. Blacks, on average, have slightly shorter life-spans; whites, slightly longer.

The Joy of Compound Interest

Many investors have been conditioned to believe that all profit comes from the stock market. One reason for that is the tax deferral available on gains until you sell the stock, and the favorable tax status given to realized capital gains. But if you can arrange to defer taxes on fixed-return savings, the effects of compound interest can—over the long term—yield acceptable returns. *Tax-deferred, fixed-income vehicles are particularly appropriate for retirement savings.* The possibilities include corporate savings plans (see page 47), deferred compensation arrangements (see page 774), corporate and individual pension plans (see pages 767 to 777), and certain tax-deferred annuities (see page 787).

The following table shows the multiplier effect of interest compounding, when savings are allowed to accumulate untaxed.

THE PROFIT IN COMPOUND INTEREST

Money invested at this interest rate*	*Yields this average annual return on original investment after:*				
	5 years	10 years	15 years	20 years	25 years
5%	5.8%	6.6%	7.6%	8.8%	10.2%
6	7.1	8.5	9.4	11.9	14.3
7	8.5	10.3	12.7	15.7	19.6
8	10.0	12.5	15.8	20.3	26.4
9	11.6	14.9	19.5	26.0	35.2
10	13.2	17.6	23.8	33.0	46.5
11	14.9	20.5	28.9	41.5	61.0
12	16.7	23.8	34.7	52.0	79.8

*Compounded daily. If compounded semiannually or annually, returns would be slightly lower. Source: The Bowery Savings Bank.

How Much Retirement Income Will You Need?

Some expenses increase in retirement, mainly those that are health-related. But many other expenses decline. You'll no longer have business-related costs, such as town clothes and commuting; in most cases your children will be out of school; you'll generally be able to cancel your life insurance; if you move from a cold to a warm climate, you'll save on clothes and fuel; and you may own your home outright, saving the monthly mortgage expense. You'll also save money on income taxes: Social Security is tax-exempt; there's a double deduction on federal income taxes for people sixty-five or over; many communities provide property tax breaks to retired people; and a person sixty-five or over pays a smaller capital gains tax if he sells his house and moves into something less expensive.

Make a realistic retirement budget, using the budget forms in Chapter 3, "Trying a Budget." Inflation will drive up prices, but in the years ahead your earnings—hence pension and Social Security—will also rise.

How Much Income Will You Have?

Add up what you have on hand for retirement income. Include Social Security (see page 727), the pension due from your employer (see page 767), any annuity payments you've already arranged for, rental from income properties, and any earnings that you (or your spouse) expect in retirement. Also include interest from long-term bonds and dividends from high-grade stocks, *if* you plan to retain those investments and use only the income they provide. (Do not, at this point, count any investments you plan to sell at retirement, cash savings, savings bonds, or the value of your home.) The total is the basic income you've provided yourself to date (see calculation on page 764).

Plugging the Retirement Income Gap

Compare probable expenses with probable income. There will, most likely, be a gap between what you have and what you'll need. That's where the remainder of your savings come in. Add up the value of the investments you plan to sell before retirement, and all your cash savings. If you expect to move to a smaller home, include the net proceeds, after taxes and moving expenses. This cash pool is the kitty that will make or break your retirement standard of living. (See calculation on page 764.)

If your kitty is large enough, you can invest it conservatively and use the earnings to plug the gap between your basic retirement income (from earnings, pension, and Social Security) and your living expenses. But that takes a lot of money. Most people have to dip into savings to finance retirement. That means you must have a cash pool large enough to finance regular withdrawals over a lifetime. Good retirement planning hinges on your ability to calculate the amount of cash you'll need and secure it while you're still at the peak of your earning power.

How Long Will Your Savings Last?

The following table shows how long capital will last if put into fixed-return investments, such as bank accounts and corporate bonds. The column on the left shows the *percentage of the original investment* that you plan to use every year. For example, if you have $50,000 in savings and withdraw $5,000 a year, you're withdrawing 10 percent. The remaining columns show various rates of interest that your investments could be earning. You might, for example, put your money into a combination of passbook and term bank accounts, earning an average of 8 percent a year. Or you might buy corporate bonds that earn 10 percent (arranged to mature serially, as you need the cash). To use the table, decide what percentage of your original capital you'll withdraw every year, then follow across that line to the column that shows your expected investment return. The number there shows how many years your capital will last. An asterisk means that at that rate of withdrawal, the money will never be exhausted.

HOW LONG WILL YOUR SAVINGS LAST?

Percentage of original capital withdrawn annually:	*If invested at this interest rate:*							
	5%	6%	7%	8%	9%	10%	11%	12%
2%	*	*	*	*	*	*	*	*
4	*	*	*	*	*	*	*	*
6	*	*	*	*	*	*	*	*
8	21	24	31	*	*	*	*	*
10	15	16	18	21	27	*	*	*
12	11	12	13	15	17	19	24	*
14	10	10	11	12	12	14	15	18
16	8	9	9	10	10	11	12	13
18	7	7	8	8	9	9	10	10
20	6	7	7	7	7	8	8	9

*At this combination of investment and withdrawal percentages, the money will never be exhausted.

Data prepared by Coopers & Lybrand

This table assumes stable interest rates and an equal amount of money withdrawn every year. If interest rates fall, or withdrawal rates rise, your capital won't last as long.

The Retirement Income Calculation

The following steps will help you calculate how much more you need, in savings and investments, to maintain your standard of living in retirement.

STEP 1

Determine how much you will need to live on in retirement, per year. * $＿＿＿＿＿

STEP 2

Calculate how much retirement income you have already (from pension, Social Security, annuities, earnings, rents, and long-term investments that you will keep in retirement). $＿＿＿＿＿

STEP 3

Subtract income from expenses. Income, at present, is probably insufficient, leaving a retirement income gap of this amount: $＿＿＿＿＿

STEP 4

Add up the value of current savings and investments that you intend to convert to cash at retirement (low-dividend stocks, savings accounts, cash in your life insurance policy, etc.). This is your cash pool. $＿＿＿＿＿

*Make this calculation without taking inflation into consideration. Use today's prices, wages, and Social Security benefits.

STEP 5

*Assume that you withdrew from your cash pool enough money to cover one year's retirement income gap. What percentage of your cash pool would be taken? (*Example: *If you have $50,000 and the income gap is $5,000, you'd withdraw 10%.)*   _____ %

STEP 6

What average rate of interest do you think you can earn on your cash pool at retirement?   _____ %

STEP 7

Using the table on page 763, how many years will your present cash pool last if withdrawn at the rate needed to cover the retirement income gap?   _____

STEP 8

Estimate your probable lifespan (or the lifespan of you and your spouse combined). Step 7 showed you how many years your present cash pool will cover. How many years are left over?   _____

Can you reduce expenses so as to make your present cash pool last longer? If not, you'll have to save more money.

STEP 9

*Multiply the number of years not covered by the amount of your present cash pool (Step 8) by the retirement income gap. (*Example: *If you need ten more years of $5,000 a year, multiply for a result of $50,000.)*

This is the additional amount of money you'll need for a comfortable retirement. When invested, it will actually provide more than the annual sum you need, but that gives you a cushion for inflation.
                     _____

    If the savings you now have on hand are enough to cover your retirement years, add an arbitrary amount to provide for inflation. There's no way of figuring exactly what you'll need, since the future rate of increase is unknown. Social Security benefits rise with inflation, as will any wages you earn. Another possible buffer against inflation is the equity in your house, and the value of the stocks and bonds that you've invested for long-term income (Step 2 in the foregoing table). Those could be liquidated, if necessary, to supplement other income.

The Social Security Ratio

Social Security payouts are stacked to favor lower earners. You can see this in the Social Security *replacement ratios,* which show the size of Social Security benefits in relation the amount of earnings on which people pay their payroll taxes. The following table shows replacement ratios as computed by the pension consulting firm William M. Mercer. As you can see, a person earning $10,000 may have 47 percent of his covered earnings "replaced" by Social Security, whereas a person making $25,000 receives 22 percent. In dollars, Social Security benefits are higher for the higher earners. But unless he has other sources of retirement income, a higher earner's standard of living will fall more sharply in retirement than that of a middle or lower earner. The higher on the income scale you go, the smaller a factor Social Security becomes and the more important it is to have other guaranteed sources of income.

Employee's final year's pay	Estimated average earnings for Social Security	Annual Social Security benefit	Percentage of final year's pay*
$ 5,000	$3,339	$3,012	60%
8,000	5,343	4,028	50
10,000	6,598	4,679	47
12,000	7,747	5,147	43
15,000	8,087	5,458	36
20,000	8,258	5,518	28
25,000	8,258	5,518	22
30,000	8,258	5,518	18
40,000	8,258	5,518	14
50,000	8,258	5,518	11

*This is the Social Security income replacement ratio, in 1980.

COMPANY PENSIONS

Pension Integration

Many private pensions are *integrated* with Social Security, which means that in setting the level of pension payments, the company takes your Social Security benefit into account. Companies may shoot for overall levels of retirement income that replace 60 to 70 percent of the earnings of lower-income workers, 50 to 60 percent for middle-income people, and 40 to 50 percent for upper-income executives. Checking the foregoing table as to what percentage of income is replaced by Social Security, you'll see that lower-income workers may meet this standard from Social Security alone. The middle-income worker needs a small supplement from a private pension, and the upper-income worker, a higher supplement. Here's what this means in real terms: At retirement, low-income workers may get little or nothing from their corporate pension plan, even though they were theoretically covered. Middle-income earners may receive a small pension, and high-earners, a high one. Most of a company's pension fund will, in effect, be paid out to middle and higher earners.

Many private pension plans are integrated into Social Security at the "wage base," which is the amount of earnings each year on which you (and your employer) pay Social Security taxes each year. There are many ways of effecting this integration. For example, the plan may pay nothing to workers below the wage base and 1 percent of earnings to those above; or it may pay 1 percent benefit to those below the wage base and 2 percent to those above.

In the past, the wage base was relatively small. But in 1978 we were taxed on the first $17,700 of earnings, and by 1981, the wage base may be more than $31,000. This raises Social Security payments to middle-income workers but reduces their benefits from many integrated pension plans!

The overall retirement benefit for lower- or middle-income workers will probably not be affected by these changes. But relatively more will be coming from Social Security, and relatively less from private pensions. Is that bad? Not as long as your overall benefit remains the same. In fact, it's better, because Social Security payments rise with the cost of living, whereas private pension benefits generally do not. Also, Social Security benefits are tax-free while private pension payments are not.

Note: Proposals now before Congress would change the pension integration rules, improving the pensions of some workers and lowering them for others. In your retirement planning don't make any assumptions about your pension; get a true dollar fix, from the employee benefits department, as to what the actual amount is likely to be.

Will You Get a Benefit from Your Company's Pension Plan?

If the company has a pension plan, many workers believe that they're automatically covered. But it ain't necessarily so. A law passed in 1974 made pensions more certain for some employees, but workers in several categories are still not protected by the act. Here are some of the people who may not be due any benefits:

• Have you worked less than ten years for any one employer? Some companies will pay you a pension if you've worked five years or even one year, but it's common to require ten years on the job. If you hop from company to company, you may *never* find yourself entitled to a pension.

• Do you make less than the Social Security wage base? The benefit formula of your pension plan may give you little or nothing, even though you are theoretically covered. You may depend for retirement income solely on Social Security.

• Does your ten years of work include years prior to age twenty-two or twenty-five? Many companies don't start the clock running on pension eligibility until you reach those ages, in which case you might have to work until age thirty-two or thirty-five in order to qualify, depending on the plan. If you went to work right after high school, the years put in prior to age twenty-two might not count toward computing your pension.

• Did you go to work for your present employer at a late age? You may not be covered, no matter how long you work.

• Is your plan not insured by the federal government? Check page 772 to see what is and is not insured. If your plan isn't covered and the company goes broke, the pension plan may go down with it.

• Did you leave work for a time and then come back? That's called a *break in service.* You may lose credit for all the years put in before the break. The 1974 Employee Retirement Income Security Act (pension reform law) sharply limits this practice, but if the break occurred before the law was passed, there's nothing you can do. *Note:* You may also have a break in service if you cut your working schedule back to fewer than five hundred hours in a given year.

• Are you in poor health? If you die before age fifty-five—from illness or accident—your spouse will probably receive no pension at all (life insurance should cover this contingency). If you die after age fifty-five but before retirement age, no benefits may be paid unless you specifically arranged for them (although some plans make benefits automatic —see page 771).

• Is your category of work covered by the plan? Part-time or seasonal workers may not be covered unless they work at least one thousand hours during the year (that's about twenty hours a week for fifty weeks, or forty hours a week for six months). Full-time workers who temporarily reduce their working schedule to less than one thousand hours may not be covered for that year, so keep an eye on this; you don't want to lose a year's credit just by skipping a few days work.

• Were you excluded from coverage under the old pension plan, before the 1974 pension reform law? Many plans rejected certain categories of workers who, thanks to the 1974 pension reform law, have now been brought into the fold. Years worked prior to 1974 must count in toward establishing your *eligibility* for a pension. But they need not be counted in establishing the *dollar amount.* You may find that your benefits have accrued only since 1974, which means a minuscule pension. Other years may also be excluded in determining the size of your pension—including working years before age twenty-five; before certain breaks in service; and before your first two years of continuous employment.

Warning: The foregoing refers to *defined benefit pension plans,* which promise a specific payout at retirement based in part on your salary and the number of years you've worked. Eligibility may be different if you belong to a *profit-sharing plan,* or a *defined-contribution plan* (where the employer puts in a specific amount of money every year and benefits are paid according to how much the fund is worth). Additional categories of workers may find themselves excluded from these kinds of plans.

How Good Is Your Pension Plan?

Under the pension reform law, companies with defined-benefit plans are required to tell you, in simple language, how your plan works. Once a year, you should to ask (in writing) whether you're eligible for a pension, and, if so, how much has been credited to you so far. *Warning:* Even the simplified explanations contain words that you may not understand or that may mislead you. For example:

Eligibility—means whether you're among the workers covered, or *potentially* covered, by the plan. It does not mean that you are actually guaranteed a pension at the present time. For example, if you have to work ten years and have been with the company only four, you're *eligible* for a pension *provided that* you remain another six years.

Vested—means that you're guaranteed benefits at retirement. Once your pension benefits vest (at five years, ten years, or whatever is called for in the plan), they're yours for good. If you leave to work for another company, you'll normally receive your vested pension benefits in a lump sum. (For how to roll these benefits into another tax-sheltered pension plan, see page 775).

Accrued benefit—means the amount of pension credited to you so far. You may not actually get this benefit; first, you'll have to work long enough for the pension to vest (see preceding paragraph). This only tells how much, so far, you're *potentially* entitled to receive.

When you get your pension plan booklet, here are the key things to look for (or to ask the company about, if the booklet isn't clear):

• How many more years must I work for my pension to vest in part? In full?

• How much has accrued for my pension account so far, and how large a monthly pension would it provide for me alone? For me and my spouse?

• What is the effect on my pension if I leave work for a short time and then return? If I'm laid off for a while?

• How old do I have to be in order to collect regular retirement benefits? Early retirement?

• If I leave the company, how do I protect my vested pension?

• How is the pension benefit figured?

• Are there any benefits besides the pension check—for example, life insurance, disability, health benefits, etc.?

• If I die, is there a benefit for my spouse? If so, how much?

• Is my pension insured by the federal Pension Benefit Guaranty Corporation? In part or in full?

• Must I be a union member at retirement in order to collect?

• Is this a "multiemployer" plan, where time worked for various employers counts toward the pension benefit? What employers and what jobs are included?

Don't wait until retirement to find out how much, or how little, you have coming from your company or union pension plan! Check this now and every few years in the future.

If You Die, Are There Pension Benefits for Your Spouse?

If you die before the pension plan's official "early retirement age," there are normally no pension benefits for the spouse, even if you worked for the company forty years. For income, your spouse will have to look to your life insurance policy.

At the official early retirement age, which may be fifty-five to sixty, you have a choice:

1. You may do nothing, in which case there may be no benefits for your spouse if you die.

2. If your plan doesn't offer this benefit automatically, you may provide that if you die between that time and retirement, your spouse will get a portion of the pension that would otherwise have been yours.

However, if you don't die, your pension at retirement will be reduced by perhaps 5 or 10 percent, depending on the plan. This option should definitely be considered by people in poor health. Those in good health might also want to elect it as a form of "life insurance," if their spouse would need the pension income. A few plans have limitations on paying a spouse if death occurs shortly after the benefit is elected, so ask about this.

At retirement you have another set of choices:

1. You may take your full pension (or reduced pension, if you signed up for spouse's benefits at the early retirement age). When you die, this pension stops and your spouse gets nothing.

2. You may choose to have your pension cover both yourself and your spouse to the end of your respective lives. In that case, your benefit is reduced. The younger the spouse, the greater the reduction in pension benefit (since the sum in the pension account has to be stretched over a greater period of years). At your death, the spouse may get as little as half of your reduced benefit.

Which option should you choose? If there's enough income to support your spouse adequately after your death, without your pension, take the full benefit. If your spouse will be hard-pressed after your death, take the reduced benefit with a pension payable to your surviving spouse.

Note: The plan will probably provide that you can't get a spouse's benefit if you're divorced. This may be true even if you divorce after retirement, and your ex-spouse had provided for joint-and-survivor coverage. A new spouse, taken in retirement, will also be ineligible for the spouse's benefit. To qualify for a spouse's pension, you generally have to be married for a full year before the worker retires and also for a full year before he or she dies.

Another note: Profit-sharing plans and other types of pensions not covered by the pension reform act may provide nothing for the spouse after the worker's death.

Is Your Pension Insured?

The 1974 pension reform law set up the Pension Benefit Guaranty Corporation to insure that you'll get your pension even if your company goes broke. But the PBGC doesn't cover everything. Here's what's *not* insured:

• You're not insured if your pension is from a profit-sharing plan; a stock option plan; a plan where the employer contributes a fixed amount every year and employees are paid according to the value of the fund; or a plan financed entirely out of union dues. You may not be insured if your plan covers the workers of many different companies.

• You're not insured for ancillary benefits. For example, PBGC won't pick up the cost of medical payments, cash supplements, life insurance, education benefits, and other fringes in a terminated plan.

• Nor are you insured for benefits your employer decides to eliminate. For example, a union could reduce medical benefits for pensioners, and the PBGC won't cover your loss. (*Note:* A retiree's regular monthly pension check generally cannot be cut. Enough money to fund your pension for life should have been deposited into a permanent annuity for you at retirement.)

• Your entire pension isn't necessarily insured. PBGC covers payments in full to lower- and middle-income workers, and even some of the upper-middles. But there's no insurance over a certain monthly amount.

• If you're collecting a pension under a thirty-years-and-out plan, the benefit is not fully insured, nor is any benefit insured that was added in the five years prior to the date the pension fund was terminated.

If your company goes bankrupt, you may still collect your full pension and all the ancillary benefits. Whatever assets there are in the pension plan will be used to meet obligations, and many plans, even of bankrupt companies, have a considerable amount of assets. The law determines in which order obligations to retirees and employees will be paid.

Should You Contribute Your Own Money to Your Corporate Pension Plan?

Some pension plans require employee contributions; you *must* pay in order to be covered. In that case, it's smart to pay. If you leave the company, you'll get your money back plus interest, so it's a form of forced savings (deducted automatically from your paycheck). If you stay, your contribution will be matched with an employer contribution in order to fatten your pension fund. Check the rules on withdrawing your funds, if you should need the money. Note that employee contributions to a company pension fund are not tax deductible, but earnings accumulate in the fund tax-deferred.

Other pension plans are employer-paid but allow the employee to contribute if he wants to. The advantages of contributing are two: (1) There is a forced savings element, with automatic payroll deductions; and (2) your money builds up in the pension fund tax-deferred. No tax is due on the earnings until you retire and begin receiving payments. The disadvantage is that the plan's investment results may not be as good as you could get from U.S. savings bonds, which are also tax-deferred. Check the past performance of your pension fund. If it's better than 7 percent a year, consider putting your retirement money there; if it's worse, consider putting it in savings bonds or other investments.

Should You Retire Early?

Give it a lot of hard thought before going ahead. Quitting work at age fifty-five or sixty is great if you can afford it, but in these inflationary times many people who retire early find that their incomes don't stretch as far as they'd hoped. Early retirement means a reduced pension, and it may be harder than you thought to start your own small business in retirement or find part-time employment.

Should You Defer Income Until Retirement?

Generally it's a good idea. The money accumulates tax-deferred, and when you retire, you'll probably be in a lower income tax bracket. A common way to defer income is to buy U.S. savings bonds and let the interest accumulate untaxed. Other ways are with tax-deferred annuities, corporate and individual pension plans, corporate savings plans, and deferred compensation arrangements.

Some advice on deferred compensation:

1. Have the money deferred to a specified future date, such as retirement, termination, or your fifty-fifth birthday (but include a clause that lets you withdraw it earlier in case of hardship).

2. Have it compounded at a specified rate, perhaps one percentage point over the prime interest rate or at a bank's saving rate. Each year you can choose how much compensation you want to defer. There's one risk: Unlike regular pension contributions, deferred compensation isn't put into a guaranteed account. It simply becomes a general obligation

of the company. A big company will likely be around to pay off at retirement. But deferred compensation from a smaller company may not be as safe. If the company goes bankrupt, you'd probably have to settle for only a fraction of the sum you were due.

Think About Pensions Before You Quit a Job

Some workers go from job to job, never working long enough to be vested by any one employer. As a result, they have no private pension to show for a lifetime of work. And because they were always eligible for coverage under a plan (though never staying long enough to nail down their pension rights), they couldn't start their own Individual Retirement Accounts. Here's where knowing your company's vesting schedule can mean money in the bank. If your company partially vests, say, after five years, it may be worth working an extra few months to get a small pension benefit. If you're close to the ten-year vesting mark, it might be better to stay a little longer before you move on. If a better opportunity comes up, it may not be possible to wait (nor should you, since your vested benefit will be small). But if you know how much you're losing in pension benefits by changing jobs, you may be able to use that knowledge to bump up your starting salary on the new job.

What If You Get a Lump Sum Payout from Your Pension Plan?

This may happen when you leave a company after having worked there long enough to be vested. The money accrued in your pension account is now yours to keep. The company could hang on to it, not paying you until retirement; more likely, you will get a check for the lump sum when you leave.

By doing the right thing with that lump sum payout, you could save yourself a large sum in taxes! But not many people know their choices, and few companies advise them. Here are the possibilities:

1. "Roll" that pension money into a Rollover Individual Retirement Account (available through banks, savings and loans, insurance companies, mutual funds, and U.S. government retirement bonds). For information on these various IRAs see page 780. The key point: You must start a Rollover IRA within sixty days of getting the pension check. Otherwise, the opportunity is lost.

The great advantage of a Rollover IRA is that it preserves the tax shelter on your pension funds. You owe no income taxes when the money is received; and taxes on interest and dividends earned by the IRA will be deferred until you draw on the funds at retirement. In effect, your retirement savings are allowed to grow intact—just as they would in a corporate pension fund.

A Rollover IRA is only for pension funds contributed by an employer. Any money that you, personally, contributed to the fund must be subtracted before you make your IRA deposit. You may deposit all or part of the employer's contribution. Stocks and other property from the employer plan may be sold and the proceeds put in the IRA. Funds deposited in an IRA cannot be withdrawn before you reach age fifty-nine and a half without incurring a 10 percent tax penalty (except in the case of death or total disability). So IRAs are an excellent forced-saving vehicle for retirement funds.

When you withdraw IRA funds at retirement, they're taxed as ordinary income. For the wealthy, that means, at this writing, in brackets up to 70 percent. So if you expect to be in a high bracket at retirement, it might make more sense to handle a lump sum payout another way.

2. Take the lump sum payout, skip the IRA, and pay income taxes in the year of receipt. The tax can be figured in one of two ways, so be sure to choose the method that costs the least. The portion of the fund attributable to contributions made before 1974 can be treated as a long-term capital gain, with the remainder considered ordinary income eligible for ten-year averaging. Or you can treat the entire payment as ordinary income with ten-year averaging. In deciding how to handle this, by all means consult an accountant. The wrong choice could cost you money.

3. If you're close to retirement and your pension plan allows it, consider taking the distribution in regular pension payments. These qualify for the 50 percent maximum tax on earned income, which could make a pension annuity more attractive to people in high brackets.

Should You Incorporate Your Small Business?

You can generally put more into a tax-sheltered corporate pension or profit-sharing plan than into a Keogh plan, even after paying corporate taxes. The older you are when the plan begins, the more you can set aside each year. However, you shouldn't split all the profits of the company between salary and pension—the Internal Revenue Service would likely challenge that arrangement. Because of the nuisance and expense of the new pension reporting laws, a corporate pension or profit-sharing plan may not be worth it unless you make a lot of money and can put aside significantly more than you'd get from a Keogh. Before plunging ahead, talk to an accountant about the pros and cons of pension arrangements at your salary level.

There are other personal advantages to doing business as a corporation:

1. You're shielded from personal liability if the company is ever sued.

2. A corporate medical plan lets you tax-deduct every dollar you spend on medical care, drugs, health insurance premiums, and so on, without regard to the limits that apply on individual tax returns.

3. You can get group life insurance even if the "group" consists of only one person. The cost is tax-deductible to the corporation, not taxed to the individual up to $50,000 of face value, and favorably taxed over that limit.

4. It may be appropriate for the corporation to own your car and lease it to you, or pick up telephone expenses.

5. You can leave a certain amount of profit in the corporation, which is helpful to high-bracket people. Regular gifts of corporate stock can pass these assets to your heirs with a minimum of tax.

6. You can save taxes by having the corporation invest money, rather than drawing a bigger salary and investing yourself. Corporations may exclude 85 percent of U.S. dividend income from tax, as opposed to the $100 exclusion allowed individuals. (There are limits, however, to the amount of investment income a corporation can have and still retain certain tax advantages.)

7. If the business will produce a loss in its early years, you can use a corporate form and still take the losses on your personal income tax returns. This lets you tax-shelter income from other sources. A Subchapter S corporation allows you to take losses annually; with a special type of stock (called 1244 stock) you tax deduct all the losses at once if the venture fails.

INDIVIDUAL PENSIONS
OUTSIDE THE COMPANY

These are of two basic types: An *Individual Retirement Account* (IRA) for employees not eligible for corporate plans, and *Keogh plans,* for the self-employed (or for corporate employees with a side income from self-employment). Money you put into the plan can be deducted from income and not reported on your income-tax return. Interest, dividends, and capital gains earned in the plan are not taxed currently; the entire amount is left to compound and recompound until retirement. *Warning:* Funds deposited into these plans should be money you don't plan to touch until retirement. There's a 10 percent tax penalty on funds withdrawn before age fifty-nine and a half (except in the case of death or total disability, in which case only the usual income taxes are due).

Who Can Set Up Individual Pensions?

Following are the situations that might qualify you for an Individual Retirement Account (IRA) or Keogh plan:

• Start an IRA if you work at a company, or for an employer who doesn't have a pension plan for the employees; or if the company plan doesn't cover your category of employment. A working wife can start her own IRA even though entitled to spouse benefits from her husband's company-paid pension plan. If husband and wife both work and neither has an employer plan, they can both start IRAs and take a combined deduction on their joint tax return.

• Start an IRA if you work for a company that has a pension plan but doesn't count you as eligible for coverage until you've met certain requirements. You can contribute to an IRA for any year you're not eligible, provided that it's a full calendar year. People who might not be eligible for a company pension are those under twenty-two or twenty-five, certain older workers, and certain seasonal or part-time workers. As soon as you become eligible for coverage, no more funds can be paid into your IRA, but the account continues to grow untaxed.

If, at some point in the future, you're again without coverage under a pension plan, you can contribute to the IRA again. *SPECIAL NOTE:* You cannot start an IRA for the years you are *eligible* for pension coverage but haven't yet worked long enough to be *vested*! For details, see page 770.

• Start an IRA if you work for a company that has a poor pension plan for people in your position (for example, workers 65 and over), and allows employees to choose not to be covered. But there must be a formal way of dropping out of the pension plan. If you unilaterally declare that you're not covered and start an IRA, you'll face heavy tax penalties on your contributions.

• Start a marital IRA if you're the nonworking spouse of a worker eligible for an IRA. You and your spouse can have separate IRAs, with half the annual contribution going to each of you. Your half of the funds belong exclusively to you, even if you separate or divorce.

• Start a Rollover IRA if you've just left a job and received a lump sum payment from the employers' pension plan (see page 775).

• Start a Keogh plan if you are self-employed. It allows higher annual contributions than an IRA. If you have employees, they *must* be included in the Keogh, too. Your incentive to cover employees is that your contribution to your own, personal account can then be higher. If you don't want to cover your employees, you'll have to start an IRA instead.

• Start a Keogh plan if you are employed, covered by an employer plan, but with income on the side from consulting, free-lance work, director's fees, and so on. The Keogh covers that side income.

• Include your spouse in your Keogh if you're self-employed and the spouse helps out. By making the spouse a salaried employee or partner, you can make Keogh contributions for both of you.

Keogh Plans

Keogh plans are also called H.R. 10s, after the number of the House of Representatives bill that set them up. The maximum contribution to a Keogh is 15 percent of your earnings from self-employment, up to a total annual contribution of $7,500. Employees with small side earnings —say, $2,000 in free-lance income—may think a Keogh isn't worth it for that small an amount. But there's a special tax break in the Keogh law for people with middle incomes. If your adjusted gross income is no more than $15,000 and your side earnings are $750 or more, you can contribute at least $750 to a Keogh, even though that sum represents more than 15 percent of self-employment income; if you make less than $750 from self-employment, you can contribute all of it.

When you have employees, you can't have a Keogh for yourself alone. The employees must be included, and you have to contribute for them at the same percentage rate as you do for yourself. There's an incentive for setting up employee Keoghs: You can deposit an extra 10 percent of your self-employment income into the Keogh, up to a maximum contribution of $2,500 a year, even though that brings your total contribution above the normal 15 percent limit. Your employees and partners can contribute something extra, too, subject to the same limits. This extra payment isn't deductible from income as normal Keogh payments are, but can be accumulated in the plan tax-deferred.

Keoghs have a tax break not granted to IRAs: If the funds in the plan are paid out in a lump sum, you can use a special ten-year income-averaging calculation to lower the income tax.

A Keogh plan must be set up by the end of the year in order to make contributions deductible on your income tax. But once the plan is in place, you can make deductible contributions anytime up to the date your income tax return is due (normally, April 15). It's smart to wait until tax time to make the final contribution so that you don't inadvertently pay too much. There are tax penalties for excess contributions.

Individual Retirement Accounts

You can contribute up to 15 percent of employee compensation to an IRA every year, up to a maximum annual contribution of $1,500. The 15 percent is figured only on earnings, not on rents, dividends, and other types of income. In order to be deductible on your current year's income tax, IRAs can be started and contributions made anytime up to the due date of your return (normally, April 15). It's smart to wait until the last moment to make your final IRA contribution to be sure that you don't exceed the amount allowed. There are tax penalties for excess contributions.

A *Rollover IRA*, for lump sum pension distributions, is entirely different from a regular IRA (see page 775). Keep rollover funds separate from any other IRAs you may have, in case you're ever able to roll them into the pension fund of another company.

A *marital IRA* is for a worker eligible for an IRA and his spouse, provided that the spouse has no earnings. There's a different contribution level from regular IRAs: The worker's contribution is still limited to 15 percent of employee compensation, but at this writing the maximum contribution is $1,750 a year, as opposed to $1,500 for the usual IRA. The annual contribution is normally split half and half into two IRAs, one owned by each spouse. If the at-home spouse takes a job and becomes covered by an employee plan, she or he can make no further contributions to the IRA, although the funds already in the plan can continue to build tax-deferred. If the at-home spouse takes a job without an employee pension plan, she or he can contribute to the IRA up to 15 percent of employee compensation, with the a maximum annual contribution of $1,500.

Where to Invest IRA or Keogh Funds

Retirement plans, complete with all the necessary documents, are sold by banks, savings and loan associations, mutual funds, some credit unions, and insurance companies. You can also put your money into U.S. Treasury retirement bonds. One year's IRA or Keogh contribution can be split among two or more plans (as long as the total amount doesn't exceed the allowable level); or you can choose one type of plan one year and another the next. Keogh funds can be moved from one plan to another as often as you like (as long as the transfer is made from trustee to trustee), but IRAs can normally be moved only once in three years (unless the IRS, in a private ruling, allows an earlier switch). Within a particular mutual fund group, however, it's possible to shift IRA money from fund to fund as often as you like.

Some types of plans are far more expensive than others, resulting in a smaller accumulation of long-term savings. When you invest retirement money, compare the alternatives rather than buying the first plan that comes along! Your choices:

Banks, Savings and Loan Associations, and Some Credit Unions

At this writing, the legal maximum interest rate on IRA and Keogh deposits is 8 percent compounded daily, for three-year savings certificates; higher for floating-rates, six-month and 30-month certificates. These rates are allowed even for small deposits. When the three-year term for each deposit runs out, that money can be reinvested at whatever interest rates are then available, or moved to another type of IRA. If you move funds out of a three-year certificate before maturity, you pay the normal interest penalty. The penalty need not apply, however, if the plan-holder dies, becomes disabled, or is older than fifty-nine and a half.

Savings institutions offer different interest rates, so by all means shop around. One S&L in town may be offering the top rate, while another is paying only 7¾ percent. Some institutions, but not others, may require a minimum deposit of $200 or $500 to get the top rate.

There's generally no fee for maintaining IRAs or Keoghs, although some institutions may charge $5 or $10 to start. In general, every dollar you contribute to an IRA or Keogh at a savings institution goes toward fattening your retirement account.

Government Bonds

Bonds specifically designed for IRAs and Keoghs now pay 6½ percent until retirement, compounded semiannually (bonds bought prior to 1980 pay 6 percent). Interest payments on U.S. retirement bonds are exempt from state and local income taxes when they're cashed in, which raises the effective yield for people living in heavily taxed areas. Retirement bonds, available in $50, $100, and $500 denominations, are bought from the Bureau of Public Debt, Securities Transaction Branch, Washington, D.C. 20225, or from the nearest Federal Reserve bank or branch (ask your own bank for the address).

Mutual Funds

Despite the stock market's poor record of the past ten or twelve years, the odds are that over twenty years or more, it will produce excellent returns (see page 567). Your best bet is a good, established, no-load mutual fund group (see page 643). In a fund group you can easily switch Keogh or IRA money from one type of fund to another as market conditions change. In good times you might want a growth fund; in bad times, an income or money market fund. *No-load* groups have no sales charges, which gives them an advantage over *load* groups, which charge up to 8½ or 9 percent. For a list of no-load funds and fund groups, send for the free No-Load Mutual Fund Directory, Valley Forge, Pa. 19481, or write to the Investment Company Institute, 1775 K St. N.W., Washington, D.C. 20006.

One important tax point: Capital gains are normally given favorable income tax treatment. But if the gains are taken in a tax-sheltered IRA or Keogh, you lose the chance to use the capital gains tax. All withdrawals from IRAs are taxed as ordinary income, while other rules apply to Keoghs. If you expect to be in a low tax bracket at retirement, this is immaterial. But if you'll be in a high bracket, discuss with an accountant whether IRAs or Keoghs are the best choice for that part of your retirement fund that you keep in stocks.

Insurance Companies

These offer two types of plans—deferred annuities and endowments.

With *deferred annuities,* you deposit savings at an insurance company rather than a bank or S&L. The interest rate tends to be a little lower than that offered by savings institutions. But even if the interest rate appears comparable, the rate of savings buildup is usually not as good. That's because the insurance salesman generally takes sales commissions out of your first few annual deposits, so the full amount doesn't go into the pension account. A few insurers offer no-load annuities, but there may be fees when money is withdrawn. (*Note:* Some no-load companies have no withdrawal fee or drop it after a certain number of years.)

Insurance companies claim two advantages over savings institutions: First, there's a minimum guaranteed interest rate (generally in the area of 3 percent), whereas banks and savings and loan associations have no minimum guarantees. However, it's most unlikely that interest rates on bank and S&L term accounts will ever fall below the insurers' low guaranteed rate, so this "advantage" doesn't mean much. Second, insurers offer a minimum guaranteed rate for purchasing a lifetime annuity income at retirement, whereas people who wait until retirement to contract for an annuity have to take whatever rate is going at the time. But again, the insurers' guaranteed rates are so low that they're unlikely to make any real difference. On balance, you're probably better off accumulating retirement funds in whatever vehicle promises the highest level of savings (either savings institutions or no-load mutual funds). If, at retirement, you want a lifetime annuity, you can take your accumulated savings and buy one then (see page 788).

A few insurers (but not many) have experimented with a disability waiver, which means that if you're disabled and can't make annual payments into the retirement plan, the insurer will make them for you. The waiver doesn't cost much because the odds of your using it are low. Whether having a disability waiver is worth a sacrifice in retirement income should you not become disabled is something only you can decide. Remember that if you can't work, you might have to withdraw and use your IRA or Keogh funds; in that case the waiver wouldn't do you any good.

Withdrawal from IRAs and Keoghs

Under normal circumstances you cannot begin withdrawing funds before you reach age fifty-nine and a half without paying a 10 percent tax penalty. But if you die or become totally disabled, no penalty on withdrawals will be assessed. By age seventy and a half you *must* begin making withdrawals or you'll be subject to penalties as high as 50 percent. Starting at age seventy and a half, withdrawals must be in annual amounts calculated to last either your lifetime or the lifetimes of you and your spouse.

Putting Your Plan on "Hold"

What if you have an IRA or Keogh and, because of a change in job, are no longer eligible to make contributions? The plans you have remain as they are. You can't add to them, but they'll go on compounding, tax-deferred, until you draw on them at retirement. You're also perfectly free to switch the fund to other investment vehicles. If you again become eligible to make contributions, you can add to the plans as before.

Individual Pensions and Estate Taxes

Any balance left in an IRA or Keogh plan may or may not be taxed in your estate, depending on how it's handled. If the entire sum is paid to a beneficiary right away, estate taxes may be due. But if payments are made over a specific period of time, there is no estate tax liability. In order for estate taxes to be avoided, the balance in Keogh plans must be paid over a minimum of twenty-four months; in IRAs, a minimum of thirty-six months. You don't have to decide on this in advance, but make sure that the phased payout option is included in the Keogh or IRA documents. If your estate is below the estate tax level (see page 707), the entire balance can be paid at once without any problem. Otherwise, your beneficiary should choose the stretched-out payments, so as not to pay any taxes unnecessarily.

IRAs and Deceptive Advertising

At this writing, the Federal Trade Commission is studying IRA advertising to determine what additional regulation may be needed. Problems include:

1. False statements that a given interest rate is the maximum allowable.

2. False comparisons between IRAs.

3. The state of the law on disclosure statements, which show the cost and cash buildup of an IRA. At present, the buyer doesn't have to receive the disclosure statement until the time of sale—provided that he has seven days to change his mind and get his money back. But by the time someone gets around to putting his money down, he's not likely to withdraw it after getting the disclosure statement. Disclosure should be made in advance. Always ask the salesman for the statement; if he won't give it to you, take your business somewhere else.

4. Saying that IRA contributions are tax-exempt when in fact they're only tax-deferred.

5. Saying that only an insurance company IRA will give you "income for life." It's true that only insurance companies sell annuities. But you can accumulate money in a bank or mutual fund IRA, then buy an annuity at retirement. Just because you may want an annuity when you're seventy is no reason to start with one when you're thirty-five.

Pensions for Housewives

Slowly, slowly steps are being taken to win pension rights for housewives. This is an important issue not only for women but also for their husbands and children, whose responsibility it is (or should be) that a woman at home has some financial protection in her old age. Housewives' rights so far:

• Corporate pension plans must provide benefits for a surviving spouse after the worker's death (see page 770). However, the worker can choose to reject these benefits, and there's nothing the spouse can do to prevent it. Also, the pension benefit is generally small.

• Workers eligible for Individual Retirement Accounts can start a marital IRA for a spouse with no earnings. At this writing, the maximum

contribution is 15 percent of earnings, up to a maximum annual contribution of $1,750. One half of the IRA contribution belongs to each
spouse. If there's a divorce, the wife takes her half with her.

• In some states divorced wives have won rights to a portion of their
husbands' pensions (see page 810). They may also secure rights, by
consent, in the separation agreement.

• Divorced wives are now entitled to draw Social Security retirement
benefits on their ex-husband's accounts if the marriage lasted ten years
or more.

ANNUITIES

There are two basic types. *Deferred annuities* are a savings vehicle,
paying interest on money you deposit. They're generally used by
younger people to save money for retirement. *Immediate-pay* annuities are for people of retirement age. You give the insurance company
a lump sum, in return for which it guarantees you a specified monthly
income for life. Money accumulated in a deferred annuity can be
turned into an immediate-pay annuity at retirement. Alternatively, you
can save money in a bank or through stock market investments, then
use those funds to buy yourself an immediate-pay annuity.

Both types of annuities can be bought as part of a corporate pension,
IRA, or Keogh plan, in which case the contributions are tax-deductible;
or they can be bought without reference to a pension plan, with after-
tax dollars. In individual pension plans, deferred annuities are generally
not competitive with other IRA and Keogh investments (see page 782),
but when bought outside a pension plan, they offer special advantages
to the long-term saver, as outlined in the next section. Immediate-pay
annuities, bought as part of a pension plan, provide a higher income
than when they're bought outside of a pension plan (mainly because of
differences in the way they're taxed).

Deferred Annuities, Outside a Pension Plan

These can be useful ways to accumulate retirement funds for people not eligible for Keoghs and IRAs, or for people who want to save more each year than their Keogh or IRA allows. The contribution isn't tax-deductible, but interest earned on the annuity is allowed to accumulate tax-deferred until it's withdrawn. *Tax deferral is a tremendous advantage to savers* (see page 761), giving them an opportunity to accumulate far more money than if they had had to pay taxes every year. The odds are that long-term tax deferral for buyers of deferred annuities will be retained.

Single-premium deferred annuities are the most popular. You pay in a lump sum—sometimes as little as $1,500 but generally starting at $5,000 or $10,000. There's no upper limit on how much you can invest.

In the old days deferred annuities had so low an interest rate, and so high a sales charge, that no savvy person would buy them. But the modern single-premium variety may carry first-year rates as high as 10 or 11 percent. Sales commissions, where they exist, are in the area of 4 percent, and a number of companies have no-load annuities (no sales commissions). With no-loads, you generally have to pay a surrender charge of 4 or 5 percent if you withdraw all your funds, although some companies drop the charge after you've held your investment for five or ten years (a few have no surrender charge at all). Always ask about fees and commissions before you buy, and what your withdrawal rights are. Some companies offer lower interest while the money is accumulating, and higher rates, paid retroactively, if you convert the funds to an immediate-pay annuity at retirement.

At present any money withdrawn from the deferred annuity contract, up to the amount of your original investment, can be treated as a simple return of investment and not taxed. What remains in the contract is considered ordinary income and taxed as received. Single-premium deferred annuities are sold by many stockbrokers as well as by insurance agents.

Flexible-payment deferred annuities are for people who can't afford the large, single-premium payment. You're allowed to pay in small amounts, like $100 a month. The interest rate is generally lower, however, perhaps in the area of 6 percent. There's a sales charge of 8 or 9 percent that cuts so deeply into your retirement savings that you have to ask yourself whether the program is really worth it. If you quit a flexible-payment annuity within a few years, you may not even get your investment back. *In short, whereas single-payment, high-interest de-*

ferred annuities are a good buy, flexible-payment annuities often aren't. You'd do better to put your monthly contribution in a bank.

Be wary of salespeople who stress the wonderful things an annuity will do for you, while implying that the sales charge is a mere nothing. Paying a sales charge reduces the amount that goes into savings, and reduces the amount of income you could get in your old age.

If you accumulate money in a deferred annuity, you don't necessarily have to buy an immediate-pay annuity at retirement. The proceeds can be taken in a lump sum or in several installments. (Remember: Taxes are due when the earnings are withdrawn.) If you want an immediate-pay annuity but your insurance company offers poorer rates than the competition (see page 790), you can switch to another company without triggering income taxes on the exchange.

You can use the annuity as collateral for a bank loan. If you die, the funds in a deferred annuity contract are generally payable to a beneficiary without going through probate. They are, however, included in your estate.

Immediate-Pay Annuities

At retirement, there are two things you can do with your savings: (1) Leave it in savings, investments, Keogh plans, and so on, withdrawing money as you need it; or (2) use part or all of your savings to buy an immediate-pay annuity, which guarantees you a specific lifetime income. The insurance company levies a small sales charge on the purchase, of perhaps 2 to 4 percent. There's no fear that you will outlive your capital; the company guarantees a fixed monthly payment as long as you live. There are several types of immediate-pay annuities:

An Individual Life Annuity

This covers your lifetime only. If you die just a few months or years after starting the contract, all your remaining savings revert to the insurance company. This type of annuity gives the highest monthly payment. It's appropriate for someone who needs income, has no dependents to worry about, and doesn't care about leaving an estate.

A Joint-and-Survivor Annuity

This is for the lifetime of you and your spouse. The monthly payment is generally lower than with an individual annuity because the savings normally have to stretch over a longer period. The annuity check can be level throughout both lifetimes, or higher while both are alive and lower after one dies. After the death of the couple any money remaining in the contract reverts to the insurance company.

A Guaranteed Minimum Annuity

This is for people who want to be assured of a minimum return from their investment even if they die shortly after starting the contract. A popular choice is "life and ten years certain"; this gives income to you for life *or,* if you die before ten years are up, income to a beneficiary for the remainder of the ten years. You can also get "five years certain," "fifteen years certain," and so on. There's a *cash refund annuity,* which pays a beneficiary the remaining amount of your original investment if you don't live long enough to collect it. The trouble with these guarantees is that they reduce the monthly payment you receive during your lifetime. If your primary need is income, you're better off with a life-only or joint-and-survivor annuity, without worrying about what happens to your money when you die. However, if you want to protect someone after your death, elect one of the guaranteed minimums.

Who Should Buy an Annuity?

Someone who's worried that his capital won't see him through his old age, who's in good health, and whose family is long-lived might consider buying an annuity. Having an annuity means that you'll never outlive your income. *On the other hand, annuity payments are fixed for life and don't rise with inflation, so your fixed income will buy less and less.* Generally speaking, it's smart not to put all your savings into an annuity. Hold some back and try to live on Social Security, pension, annuity, and other sources of income. As inflation rises, you can dip into your remaining savings to help pay the bills.

If your capital is sizable, it generally makes more sense to keep it in the bank and investments than to buy an annuity. You can vary the size of the withdrawals to suit your needs, and will have some money left over for your heirs.

If you buy a joint-and-survivor annuity, or have a certain number of years "certain," the value of the remaining payments bypasses probate but is included in your estate.

Shopping for an Annuity

Each insurance company prices its annuities differently. For example, one might give a sixty-five-year-old man $8 of monthly income for every $1,000 he puts up, whereas another offers $8.50. On a $50,000 investment, that would translate into annual incomes of $4,800 and $5,100 respectively—an important difference to a retired person on a limited budget. Always compare the annuity rates of several companies before you make a choice. Even though you've accumulated money with one insurance company, you can switch to another company at retirement if your original insurer isn't competitive. Some no-load companies impose a surrender charge, which may make you reluctant to switch. But at this point all that matters is the size of your monthly retirement check. If you can get a higher income by going somewhere else, pay the exit fee and leave.

If you accumulate money in a deferred annuity, the company guarantees a certain annuity purchase rate at retirement. But don't take that rate automatically! It's quite possible that a better rate is now available, and you should get it. Most companies give the better rate automatically, but always ask your agent about it just in case.

Annuities can be either *qualified,* which means they're sold as part of a tax-deductible Keogh plan, Individual Retirement Account, or company pension plan; or *nonqualified,* which are the annuities you buy with after-tax dollars. Qualified annuities generally cost less and provide higher accumulations and payouts.

Which Insurer Has the Best Rates?

Following are the 1977 annuity rates of sixty-one companies, as compiled by the A. M. Best Company. The figures are for immediate-pay annuities and show *monthly income for life for each $10,000 of savings paid in.* Annuity rates change regularly, but this gives you an idea of the range and the differences among companies.

Companies offering deferred annuities also have different guaranteed rates and accumulations, and different projections based on the interest they pay. Compare these as well before buying.

SPECIAL NOTE: Canadian companies selling annuities in the United States often offer substantially higher payments. Three of those companies are Empire Life, Industrial Life, and Sun Life of Canada. Check them out!

IMMEDIATE-PAY ANNUITIES NOT PART OF A TAX-QUALIFIED PENSION PLAN

	Lifetime only				Life—10 years certain			
	Male		Female		Male		Female	
	65	75	65	75	65	75	65	75
Aetna Var. Annuity*	84.68	116.08	74.07	98.85	78.03	92.93	71.30	86.91
Aid Assn. Lutherans**†	85.14	127.91	75.44	103.75	80.49	102.47	73.46	93.85
American General, Del.*	91.79	120.90	81.56	103.54	85.63	99.90	77.98	92.39
American United*	81.77	113.26	72.61	99.27	76.58	93.22	70.43	88.11
The Bankers Life**	81.30	112.90	72.80	98.70	75.90	91.10	70.40	86.00
Bankers National*	82.20	107.96	74.75	92.81	78.00	92.76	72.32	84.99
Beneficial Standard**	76.54	103.82	68.85	92.00	72.47	86.41	66.71	82.24
Capitol Life, Colo.*	85.70	115.80	76.40	102.00	80.30	94.70	74.80	91.00
Connecticut General*	84.71	118.45	74.81	95.97	78.54	96.54	72.32	88.08
Connecticut Mutual*	84.70	111.32	76.96	101.39	79.34	93.34	74.48	89.87
Continental Assur.*	86.25	114.19	77.97	98.15	79.85	§	74.03	86.82
Country Life**	85.85	116.32	77.51	104.41	80.19	95.88	74.83	91.81
Crown Life, Canada*	83.69	118.96	74.96	105.24	78.05	95.35	72.21	90.70
Equitable Life, N.Y.*	89.39	119.85	78.27	104.73	82.81	98.14	75.86	92.57
Farm Bureau, Iowa**	78.80	109.59	70.88	98.21	74.05	91.48	68.71	87.22
Federal Kemper**	85.00	121.10	76.60	103.20	74.60	90.30	69.90	85.20
Federal Life, Ill.*	81.89	117.01	73.73	99.60	76.22	92.73	70.55	86.07
Franklin Life*	80.39	105.04	73.16	94.35	75.93	89.79	71.08	85.54
General American*	83.16	114.74	74.75	103.16	78.11	94.94	72.47	90.88
Great-West Life*	86.33	115.88	77.82	103.92	80.41	94.46	75.08	90.72
Hartford Life, Mass.*	80.87	109.99	72.01	92.93	74.93	89.73	68.71	82.19
Home Life, N.Y.*	87.50	119.40	78.20	106.80	81.20	97.90	75.70	94.20
Horace Mann*	89.10	125.33	79.10	103.75	82.76	98.80	75.93	90.68
IDS Life, Minn.*	84.64	116.01	75.26	102.86	77.92	94.30	72.77	90.71
INA Life*	82.89	113.40	75.08	101.86	77.27	92.33	72.44	88.82
Jefferson National*	81.00	112.23	71.86	100.30	75.42	90.67	69.69	86.32
Jefferson Standard**	81.96	116.10	72.42	101.02	75.21	90.95	69.15	86.15

John Hancock*	86.15	116.82	76.62	102.62	80.39	96.07	74.04	90.42
Kansas City Life.	84.05	116.92	75.54	103.65	77.91	93.75	72.57	89.30
Life & Casualty*	91.79	120.90	81.56	103.54	85.63	99.90	77.98	92.39
Life of Virginia*	83.43	117.79	75.57	104.59	77.77	94.21	72.75	89.98
Lincoln National*	84.10	114.71	76.28	103.07	78.47	93.54	73.61	90.01
Manhattan Life*	85.12	114.84	76.83	103.23	79.45	94.66	74.19	90.81
Manufacturers, Can.*	88.95	118.50	77.42	99.19	83.04	98.01	75.16	90.13
Mass. Mutual*	85.16	117.20	77.20	105.92	80.34	97.27	74.33	93.07
Metropolitan Life*††	86.77	115.49	77.44	100.19	80.97	94.88	75.42	90.43
Minnesota Mutual*††	82.28	116.55	74.33	99.61	76.74	92.91	71.19	86.36
Mutual Benefit*	85.62	115.56	77.76	104.12	§	§	§	§
Mutual of New York*	82.64	110.12	75.40	99.69	77.89	93.66	73.01	89.43
Mutual Service**	85.43	114.69	77.24	102.81	79.73	94.55	74.56	90.33
National Life, Vt.*	83.88	114.11	73.81	98.67	78.44	94.33	71.59	88.44
Nationwide Life*	81.23	110.88	72.77	97.95	75.76	90.98	70.19	86.01
New England Life*	83.28	114.03	76.02	102.58	81.09	98.51	74.72	92.93
New York Life*††	82.14	111.38	74.87	99.85	76.01	90.91	71.57	87.45
Northwestern Mutual*	84.26	119.97	73.02	101.06	§	§	§	§
Northwestern National*	83.54	111.39	75.94	100.35	78.15	92.33	73.46	88.62
Ohio National**	86.28	111.23	78.03	99.70	79.92	90.85	75.05	87.27
Pacific Mutual*	84.65	115.34	75.54	100.98	79.30	95.34	73.16	89.40
Penn Mutual*	87.22	113.88	78.20	101.04	80.75	94.67	75.17	90.06
Phoenix Mutual*	83.17	116.93	74.80	104.38	76.89	94.52	71.21	90.34
Provident Life & Acc.*	87.82	120.90	80.63	108.74	82.03	98.13	77.67	94.40
Provident National*	84.88	120.63	75.59	105.96	78.70	95.85	72.60	90.85
Prudential*	84.93	113.90	77.06	103.19	80.55	94.54	74.07	88.79
Security Benefit**	80.50	113.90	71.50	100.20	73.60	88.80	67.50	84.00
Southwestern Life*	78.17	104.98	70.67	94.53	73.06	86.85	68.30	83.37
State Farm Life*†	84.69	114.58	77.11	103.49	79.61	95.23	74.82	91.55
State Mutual**	82.90	115.10	73.80	100.90	77.20	92.70	71.00	87.10
Union Central*	81.29	108.33	73.48	97.28	76.38	91.06	71.21	87.03
United Benefit*	78.87	111.26	69.62	96.84	73.52	90.48	67.15	85.25
Variable Annuity Life*	88.53	119.79	79.82	101.16	83.16	98.15	77.09	90.42
Western National*	95.52	131.94	82.20	111.06	87.03	101.64	79.04	95.09

IMMEDIATE-PAY ANNUITIES BOUGHT UNDER A TAX-QUALIFIED PENSION PLAN (KEOGH, IRA, COMPANY PLAN)

	Lifetime only				*Life—10 years certain*			
	Male		Female		Male		Female	
	65	70	65	70	65	70	65	70
Aetna Var. Annuity*	87.29	100.56	76.36	86.76	80.44	87.90	73.51	80.88
Aid Assn. Lutherans**†	89.50	104.35	79.70	90.49	84.65	94.74	77.72	86.23
American General, Del.*	93.67	105.66	83.23	93.67	87.38	94.28	79.58	87.38
American United*	84.52	96.71	75.54	85.47	79.42	87.07	73.36	81.02
The Bankers Life**	§	§	§	§	§	§	§	§
Bankers National*	82.20	92.81	74.75	82.20	78.00	84.99	72.32	78.00
Beneficial Standard**	76.54	§	68.85	§	72.47	§	66.71	§
Capitol Life, Colo.*	85.70	98.00	76.40	86.50	80.30	87.20	74.80	82.30
Connecticut General*	89.38	103.57	79.02	87.74	83.05	92.10	77.08	84.93
Connecticut Mutual*	89.37	100.89	81.33	91.46	83.81	90.86	78.74	86.09
Continental Assur.*	92.46	105.08	83.41	92.46	83.25	90.71	77.01	83.25
Country Life**	87.54	100.24	79.10	89.82	81.78	89.42	76.32	84.26
Crown Life, Canada*	89.06	103.68	80.15	92.58	82.98	91.63	77.13	85.95
Equitable Life, N.Y.*	94.19	107.69	82.47	93.94	87.26	95.20	79.94	88.20
Farm Bureau, Iowa**	§	§	§	§	§	§	§	§
Federal Kemper**	85.00	99.60	76.60	87.50	74.60	82.40	69.90	77.00
Federal Life, Ill.*	81.89	96.12	73.73	84.28	76.22	84.38	70.55	77.81
Franklin Life*	84.45	94.94	76.82	85.44	79.70	86.53	74.65	81.28
General American*	87.52	101.08	78.61	90.19	81.38	89.50	75.74	84.15
Great-West Life*	86.33	98.60	77.82	88.26	80.41	87.57	75.08	82.56
Hartford Life, Mass.*	85.11	97.83	75.78	85.11	78.89	86.52	72.29	78.89
Home Life, N.Y.*	90.13	103.93	80.55	92.39	83.64	92.19	77.97	87.04
Horace Mann*	§	§	§	§	§	§	§	§
IDS Life, Minn.*	86.80	99.92	77.18	88.41	79.91	88.03	74.63	83.03
INA Life*	§	§	§	§	§	§	§	§
Jefferson National*	81.00	§	71.86	§	75.42	§	69.69	§
Jefferson Standard**	85.48	99.80	75.78	87.59	78.41	86.37	72.31	80.63
John Hancock*	90.02	103.52	80.09	90.91	83.97	92.30	77.42	85.36
Kansas City Life.	84.84	98.41	76.33	87.71	78.71	86.53	73.26	81.18
Life & Casualty*	93.66	105.61	83.22	93.63	87.38	94.23	79.57	87.34

Life of Virginia*	88.98	102.59	81.06	92.38	82.93	90.64	78.02	85.71
Lincoln National*	90.01	102.12	82.10	92.20	83.91	90.87	79.14	86.29
Manhattan Life*	85.12	97.22	76.83	87.21	79.45	86.75	74.19	81.78
Manufacturers, Can.*	88.95	101.36	77.42	86.29	83.04	90.42	75.16	82.05
Mass. Mutual*	92.03	104.86	84.47	94.53	86.53	94.32	81.19	88.88
Metropolitan Life*‡‡	92.28	104.60	82.69	92.41	86.09	93.00	80.50	87.61
Minnesota Mutual*††	82.28	96.15	74.33	84.66	76.74	84.69	71.19	78.25
Mutual Benefit*	86.40	99.70	78.21	89.93	80.26	88.35	75.33	83.79
Mutual of New York*	85.95	98.15	78.42	88.92	81.01	88.83	75.93	83.78
Mutual Service**	§	§	§	§	§	§	§	§
National Life, Vt.*	88.50	101.59	77.87	88.29	82.76	90.85	75.53	83.59
Nationwide Life*	81.23	§	72.77	§	75.76	§	70.19	§
New England Life*	89.15	101.69	81.19	91.94	85.27	93.33	78.70	86.86
New York Life*††	§	§	§	§	82.61	90.44	77.80	85.58
Northwestern Mutual*	§	§	§	§	§	§	§	§
Northwestern National*	85.63	97.16	77.84	87.55	80.10	86.95	75.30	82.31
Ohio National**	93.14	104.27	84.39	93.54	86.38	92.24	81.21	87.37
Pacific Mutual*	86.33	99.20	77.12	87.62	80.88	88.90	74.65	82.47
Penn Mutual*	96.04	110.25	85.46	97.51	87.22	94.47	81.14	88.79
Phoenix Mutual*	85.26	100.00	76.59	89.64	78.78	87.75	73.01	82.27
Provident Life & Acc.*	87.82	101.12	80.63	91.87	82.03	89.80	77.67	85.41
Provident National*	89.22	104.41	79.58	92.46	82.69	91.52	76.46	85.46
Prudential*	94.07	107.85	84.28	94.07	87.34	94.01	81.14	87.34
Security Benefit**	88.12	102.71	75.37	86.65	80.95	88.60	72.28	79.44
Southwestern Life*	79.77	90.93	72.12	81.69	74.56	81.30	69.69	76.71
State Farm Life*†	87.05	99.03	79.51	89.62	81.88	89.17	77.11	84.49
State Mutual**	88.70	102.60	78.90	90.50	82.60	90.70	75.90	83.90
Union Central*	82.23	93.34	74.40	83.84	77.30	84.33	72.12	79.32
United Benefit*	§	§	§	§	§	§	§	§
Variable Annuity Life*	90.72	103.33	82.05	90.72	85.21	92.37	79.24	85.21
Western National*	95.52	111.09	82.20	93.91	87.03	94.56	79.04	86.73

*Figures exclude any consideration for state premium tax.

**Premiums apply in all states, regardless of state premium tax.

†Company issues dividend-paying annuities only. Current income dividends are included in the figures, but dividend payments are not guaranteed for the future.

††As the amount paid into the plan increases, monthly income per $10,000 becomes more favorable.

§Company does not issue this plan.

Investment Annuities

This is an annuity "shell," into which you put whatever investments you choose and manage them yourself. At this writing investment annuities aren't generally on the market, because the IRS challenged them in court. It lost its case, but is considering an appeal. Ask your stockbroker if investment annuities have since become available. They're good for experienced investors, because they let you manage your own funds rather than turn them over for management by an insurance company or mutual fund.

Variable Annuities

A few insurance companies accumulate your savings in an account whose value rises and falls according to investment performance. At retirement your payments will rise and fall, too, although they're not allowed to fall below a certain amount.

There's good reason to accumulate long-term funds in an investment exposed to stock market risk, since over twenty years or more the value will probably rise considerably. But it's questionable whether you'd want your monthly retirement checks to be exposed to similar risk. In a time of inflation, a reduction in retirement income could be a disaster —not something a retiree of limited means would want to chance. During the accumulation period, a good no-load mutual fund would probably do better than an insurance company because the insurer charges sales commissions.

Create Your Own Annuity

Consider holding on to your capital at retirement, rather than buying an immediate-pay annuity. You'll save yourself the sales charge and can generally get a higher rate of interest on your money than the insurance company pays. As you advance in age, you can increase the size of your withdrawals (it's safe to do that because, as your lifespan shortens, your need for capital declines). The calculation on page 764 shows how to create your own annuity by estimating your cash pool and determining the rate at which it can be withdrawn over your lifetime.

If your cash pool won't cover expenses, your options are these:

1. Reduce your standard of living.

2. Supplement your retirement income with a job.

3. Sell your house, move into something smaller, and use the extra cash to live on.

4. Liquidate other long-term investments, if you have them, and add them to your cash pool.

5. Use your cash pool to buy an immediate-pay annuity. You'd have to reduce your living standard, but at least you would know that the income is payable for your lifetime.

6. Live independently for a few years, then arrange to move in with one of your children.

None of these solutions may please you, but if you enter retirement with insufficient cash, your choices are limited.

Mutual Fund Withdrawal Plans

In a favorable investment climate a good way to give yourself a monthly income is through a mutual fund withdrawal plan. Invest your money in a good no-load fund and arrange to receive a check of a certain size every month. If the fund gains in value, your monthly payment will come out of capital gains; if it declines, you'll be dipping into principal. When the stock market is in an upward trend, this is a way of eating your cake and having it too.

For diversification, you might want to keep part of your money in bonds, part in the bank, and part in mutual funds with withdrawal plans to take advantage of stock market upturns. These plans are best for people with investment knowledge, who will quit the mutual fund when the stock market turns down.

OTHER RETIREMENT CONSIDERATIONS

The Cash in Your Insurance Policy at Retirement

Should you keep your cash value life insurance or turn it in? That depends on your situation. If you have no dependents, by all means cash it in and use the money. Cash it in if you're married and there's enough income to support your spouse after your death. Keep it if without that insurance your spouse would have a hard time after your death (but keep only as much as is really needed, and cash in the rest). Keep it if you still have young children to support.

Your Investments at Retirement

Unless you're an experienced investor with proven ability to make capital gains, don't keep growth stocks that have low or no dividends. It's generally better to have your assets invested so as to produce regular income. But neither should you drop out of stocks entirely (unless the investment climate is bad). At age sixty-five, you could live for another twenty years, and over twenty-year periods the stock market has always given good results. Consider, then, retaining high-quality companies that pay good dividends. After that, put part of your funds into top-grade bonds (if inflation subsides) or high-yielding short-term securities (if inflation stays high) and part in the bank or in money-market mutual funds. Take care to limit your losses! At this time of life, you have no time to wait for a stock to "come back." Sell all the investments in your portfolio that didn't work out; and sell any other investment if it drops 10 percent (see page 604).

Retirement is also no time to be saddled with a lot of illiquid investments. If you've made money buying land, now is the time to start selling it off—perhaps keeping those investments that bring in income but peddling pieces that are undeveloped.

Mortgages at Retirement

There's nothing like a paid-for home to lighten retirement expenses. In fact, one very good use for cash value in your life insurance policy is to retire whatever may be left of your mortgage. (A low-interest mortgage, however, is worth keeping, so as to leave you with more cash for high-interest investments.)

If you sell your home, the buyer might ask if you're willing to give a *second mortgage* to help finance the down payment. For example, say your house is worth $60,000, the buyer has $6,000, and he can borrow $48,000 from the bank. He might ask you to give a second mortgage for the remaining $6,000, at an attractive rate of interest. If there are plenty of takers for the house, you probably won't want to bother. But if the house has been on the market for a while, you might consider the proposition.

Some points to weigh:

1. An older person has no need for a long-term investment. If you give a second mortgage, try to keep it to five years.

2. Set an interest rate that's better than you could get in alternate investments.

3. Have a lawyer draw the second-mortgage agreement so that you'll be sure of having recourse if the buyer doesn't pay.

4. Don't give so large a second mortgage that the buyer has little or no money tied up in the property. That makes it easier for him to walk away from his obligations if he gets in a bind.

5. Don't give a second mortgage to someone who, for some reason, has not been able to secure a normal-sized mortgage from the bank. If the bank is giving 80 percent mortgages but your buyer can get only 70 percent, it probably means his finances are shaky.

6. Discuss frankly with the buyer whether he can afford the monthly payments, and what action you can take if he doesn't make them.

7. If he misses even one payment, move immediately to protect your interest.

Reverse Mortgages

This is a way of borrowing against the equity of your house in monthly installments in order to give yourself more cash for retirement. The trouble is that the loan will fall due in a few years, and you may not be able to pay it off. The mortgage might be extended for a while, but there's no guarantee. If you can't make the payment, you'll have to sell the house, repay the mortgage, and hope there's enough left over to finance alternative housing. At this writing, only one savings and loan offers a reverse mortgage, but the number is expected to grow.

Retirement is hardly the time to start playing housing roulette, counting on inflation to raise the value of your house by enough to repay a reverse mortgage. Some lenders are talking about the possibility of reverse *annuity* mortgages, giving you the right to stay in your house for life. If those ever come into being, they may be of interest. Until then, reverse mortgages should be regarded with a wary eye.

Sell Your House and Rent an Apartment?

This decision is personal as well as economic. Some people would be lost without their vegetable gardens; others are relieved to get the burden of home maintenance off their backs.

For the money side of the equation, estimate what price your house would bring, net of mortgage repayments. Then deduct capital gains taxes (including taxes deferred from the sale of previous homes, but not forgetting the tax break given sellers aged sixty-five or older), deduct moving expenses, and assume that the rest of the money is invested at a reasonable current return. This is the income you forego by continuing to live in your home.

If you don't move, your living costs include property taxes, mortgage payments, insurance, utilities, maintenance, other housing-related expenses, and the income you're losing by keeping equity in your home rather than investing it elsewhere. If you do move, your living costs include rent, utilities, and other apartment-related expenses. Comparing the two will tell you which, economically, is the better choice. Apartment rents will probably rise every year or so, but property taxes and home maintenance costs also go up. Often you'll find that renting is cheaper.

Your Health Insurance at Retirement

You're eligible for Medicare starting at age sixty-five (see page 483). If you no longer have an employee group plan, there may be no medical coverage for a younger, nonworking spouse—a dangerous gap in your finances. By all means try to secure your spouse some individual coverage until she or he is also eligible for Medicare.

Medicare, however, does not cover all your expenses. You may want to supplement it with a policy especially written to cover the gaps (see page 460).

If Your Retirement Income Is Low

You may be eligible for state-sponsored Medicaid to help with those bills Medicare doesn't cover. If you're a disabled veteran, you may get some veteran's benefits. See if you qualify for checks under Social Security's Supplemental Security Income program. Your community may also have special programs for nursing care, domestic help, and "meals on wheels."

Gifts to Children

Some parents like to give money and property to their children "while the children are young and need it most." That's fine as long as it leaves you enough in the bank. But it's not a good idea if it makes you dependent on your children for support. The money you've earned is yours! Don't give away in old age what you need to live on! Relationships between parent and child are generally better if the parent remains financially independent.

Should you use your money to buy your child a house and then move in with him? This may work out fine, but then again, it may not. What if the child gets a job in another state; do you really want to move away? What if he has financial difficulties and can't meet the mortgage payments? What if there's a divorce and your daughter-in-law gets the house? All in all, it's better to protect your residence from the ups and downs of your children's lives.

Should You Move to a New Town?

If you have that in mind, prepare the ground thoroughly before retirement. Spend several seasons visiting the place you propose to live; make some friends; establish ties at the bank, a club, a church. Sit on a park bench and talk to some retired residents about what life there is like. Nothing can be as lonely as facing retirement, new neighbors, and unexpected problems, all at the same time.

When you move, be sure to get your finances in order. Cut all legal ties with your old state and establish domicile in the new one (otherwise, both states might try to collect estate taxes). Talk to a lawyer about revisions in your will to conform with the new state's laws or take advantage of any special inheritance provisions. Find banks, brokers, and other professionals to do business with. Take out local credit cards and bank cards.

Moving into a Mobile Home

It can save money, but some mobile home parks can more easily raise rent, or evict tenants, than others. Check Chapter 15, "Mobile Homes."

Company Benefits

Discover what company resources and benefits, if any, are available to retirees. Many companies run preretirement counseling seminars to help employees plan intelligently for the future; if they're available, by all means sign up. Sessions typically cover budgeting, taxes, investments, wills and estate planning, Social Security, company benefits, leisure time, medical needs, housing, second careers, and psychological problems.

Inflation

Inflation is a grave risk to any retiree who gets part of his income from a fixed payment. Social Security rises with the cost of living, and good investments can also rise in value. But most private pensions are fixed, as are annuities and interest payments. The extent of your exposure to inflation depends on the percentage of your retirement income that doesn't rise in value and the size of your savings reserve.

There are plenty of tables that show how much income you'll need in five, ten, or twenty years if inflation rises annually at various assumed rates. But those tables are meaningless for specific planning because we simply don't know what the future will bring. All you can do is lay aside as much retirement income as possible, calculate your personal retirement needs according to the table on page 764, and try to keep expenses down.

Chapter Thirty

DIVORCE

Divorce, unlike marriage, lasts until death do you part.

THE BUSINESS WEEK LETTER

It's hard to appreciate the financial effects of divorce until after the split. Then two households try to live on an income that used to support one. A working couple with good jobs and no children can often make the adjustment fairly easily, but that describes only a small percentage of divorces. Where there are children, or where the wife has little or no income, money problems can be terrible.

In a bad marriage divorce may be inevitable, but before you press on, give some hard, honest thought to the money side. When the battle is over and all the troops have left the field, how will you live?

Effects of Divorce on the Wife

Generally, divorce means a drastic reduction in her standard of living. She may not get alimony, and child support isn't enough to maintain the household. Unless she has independent wealth, accommodating parents, or a generous settlement from a well-to-do husband, she will need a job to support herself and the children. If she has no skills, the job will likely be ill paid, perhaps with bad hours.

After a period of time, her husband may quit making support payments. There are some alimony drones who live idly on their ex-husband's money, but this is the exception, not the rule.

Besides loss of income, there's loss of general financial security. Unless the marriage lasted ten years or more, a divorced wife has no Social Security retirement benefits from her ex-spouse. In most cases she loses her right to share in his pension. If her ex-husband has medical insurance, it generally covers the children but not her. She'll have to buy her own insurance or find an employer with a group plan. If the marriage had any assets, such as savings or investments, she'll be lucky to get half. If there's a house, it's generally occupied by wife and children, although it may become her responsibility to pay half the mortgage.

Her ex-husband may carry no life insurance for her (unless specified in the separation agreement). If he dies, she could have nothing to substitute for her lost alimony or child-support checks. She's often dependent on those checks; if he skips a month, she may not be able to pay the rent or the dentist. If he stops paying, she usually has to hire a lawyer in order to collect. If he leaves the state, it may be impossible to get the money she's due.

On the bright side, she may meet a nice man and remarry. She may advance in her job and make a satisfying career. But before the happy ending, there are, more often than not, some hard, bitter years.

Effects of Divorce on the Husband

He, too, has a lower standard of living than before. A good part of his after-tax income—perhaps as much as half—may go to his ex-wife and children. He generally gives up all, or half, the equity in the house; up to half his savings and investments; most of the household goods; sometimes his life insurance. The husband generally pays the lawyer's bills, and may assume the debts of the marriage. Financially, it's like starting out all over again, but at an older age and with his income cut in half.

If he remarries, he may be hard pressed to support two households. In fact, the root cause of many nonsupport battles is the existence of two families, without enough money to go around. Generally, his second wife will have to work. That's fine if she wants to; but if she doesn't, it could mean another strained marriage down the road. When money is tight, a second wife may come to resent payments made to her predecessor, especially if the first wife doesn't work. In theory, the second wife knew about this in advance; in practice, it's hard to swallow.

The husband also provides his second wife with less financial security. If children are born, he may not be able to afford all the life insurance he needs to protect two families. If he dies or becomes disabled, his Social Security benefit is divided among the children of both families, which means less for everyone. In most cases the second wife gets the pension, but in a small number of instances she must share it with the first wife. When the second wife is younger, she almost certainly will be a widow, perhaps for many years, so had better be prepared to support herself. The husband, in fact, should make every effort to encourage her in work that will pay the bills after he's gone.

If the second wife is herself divorced and getting child support payments from her first husband, the second husband may count on them to help maintain the household. But support payments are chancy, especially after remarriage. Besides all the normal problems of support, he may be called on to help put his stepchildren through college.

On the bright side, he may advance in his work, build up new assets, and marry a lovely woman he's happy with. But at one time or another, divorce-related financial problems are bound to dog his heels and shadow his happiness.

Preliminaries

Each of you should talk to a lawyer—about divorce procedures in your state, what your rights are, what a possible financial settlement might look like, and what the divorce will cost. A look at the territory should help you decide which way to move. Sometimes, it may convince you not to move at all.

A woman with no income or savings of her own should try to remedy that lack before embarking on divorce. If a husband wants out, he may be generous with money, but if he's not, the wife may have to ask for a support order from family court. In some states and situations the lawyer may be free, but it's more likely that she'll have to pay. In the meantime, she may be on the ropes for cash. If the wife demands the split, the husband may feel justified in shutting off the bank account, and the wife may not be able to get a support order.

Finding a Lawyer
Lawyer's fees vary tremendously. A fancy firm in a big city may demand a $7,500 retainer, and even more if you go to court; a country lawyer might do exactly the same job for $1,000 or less. Many women's groups compile lists of lawyers who handle simple divorces at reasonable cost—a call to a group in your area might get you a good recom-

mendation. Also check the classified ads; some young lawyers advertise fees as low as $150 if you and your spouse are in agreement about the settlement (more if there's an argument). Don't hesitate to visit two or three lawyers, explain your situation, and ask about fees.

Many divorces are not very complicated. Where assets are limited, you don't need the subtlest, most expensive man in the field to devise a good agreement. Any competent lawyer, in an unpretentious office, may do just as good a job, at much lower cost.

Each of you needs a lawyer of your own, even though it raises the cost. One lawyer cannot properly represent the interests of both sides. Where state law allows, however, one lawyer may do if you're perfectly agreed as to the property split and just need someone to draw up the papers.

Be brief and businesslike with your lawyer. Don't conceal relevant facts or be unreasonable in your demands. If you take his time to complain about your spouse, remember that he may charge by the hour!

If you can't afford a lawyer, you may qualify for Legal Aid. But be warned that in some cities you may have to wait two or three years. Divorces are generally given low priority at Legal Aid; when funds are low, they may cut divorces out entirely. If Legal Aid can't help, ask a lawyer who's a friend if he'll help you at low cost (many will) or accept payment in small amounts over a long period of time. Husbands often, but not always, pay part or all of wives' legal fees, although this may depend on who started the action.

What puts up the price of divorce is arguments! The more you and your spouse quarrel about the property; the more you struggle over payments, custody, and visiting rights; the more you delay, fight, and punish each other—the more you'll pay. Going to court costs far more than settling things between yourselves. If you can tentatively draft a property settlement before even visiting a lawyer, you may be able to get the cost of your divorce down to just a few hundred dollars.

Beware of the "Bomber"

A bomber is a divorce lawyer who will do anything to win. He'll encourage perjury, bug apartments, file harassing motions, lure people into compromising situations, and try to starve or blackmail the opponent into submission. Some people deliberately seek out a bomber, assuming he'll do a better job for them than a lawyer who's less mean-spirited. Or they've grown so bitter over the years that the thought of hurting their spouse fills them with nasty pleasure. Other people stumble upon a bomber by accident and let him lead them down a far more punitive path than they might have chosen themselves.

Whatever your motives, hiring a bomber can hurt your cause more than help it. Judges know who the bombers are, so his tactics may boomerang. More important, the poison he spreads will blight your relationship with your children and ex-spouse for years to come.

How can you know if you're in the hands of a bomber?

• He'll lead you to believe he can get a bigger settlement than is reasonable by such statements as "we'll let her hang" or "we'll push him to the wall." You may then resent the final, and smaller, settlement when you have no call to do so.

• He'll advise a husband to offer his wife nothing, not even for the children. If she has no funds of her own, this tactic can force her onto welfare or starve her into submission. He'll advise a wife to run up bills and blackmail the husband by denying him access to the children. He may file a custody suit on behalf of the husband for the sole purpose of terrifying the wife. Tactics like these destroy any hope of an amicable relationship after the divorce.

• If a wife has no cash of her own, a bomber may deny her effective counsel. He does it by challenging the fee her lawyer asks (if the husband is to pay it), then filing a blizzard of motions that will cost the lawyer more than the fee he's allowed. This reduces his incentive to pursue the case. When the wife pays the fee, the bomber will stir up enough work to exhaust her money. She may then be forced to accept an unfair settlement.

• He encourages false testimony to prove the husband a bounder, the wife a tart, or either a monster to the children. It's simple to make these charges but expensive and complex to fight and disprove them in court.

• He won't permit a client to take a forgiving attitude. If you're inclined to be generous, he counsels against it. His desire is to whip up antagonisms, which tend to enlarge his fee. Many divorced people say they had a fairly good understanding with their spouses until the lawyer entered the picture.

If you find yourself in the hands of a bomber, the smartest thing is to change lawyers. The more bitter a divorce, the longer it takes to heal.

If you're confronted with these tactics from your spouse's lawyer, don't get a bomber of your own. These lawyers feed on each other, doing a *pas de deux* that raises their fees while leaving their clients wiped out, both emotionally and financially. But do be sure that your own lawyer is experienced with divorces. Bombers eat new lawyers, and real estate or corporation lawyers, for lunch. And see that your lawyer does thorough work. A careful and sympathetic lawyer can expose the bomber's tactics while leaving the door open for both you and your spouse to negotiate in good faith.

The Separation Agreement

Where state law allows it, it's generally cheaper to file directly for divorce than to go through the step of formal separation. But some states require separation first and then incorporate the separation agreement into the divorce decree. Whichever course you take, you have to negotiate a property settlement.

A separation agreement can say anything you want it to. Divorce lawyers know the general guidelines, as determined by court cases and local practice. But your personal agreement can have anything in it that the two of you want. *Warning:* The person most eager for the divorce —for example, the man who wants to shed one wife for another—is in a weak bargaining position. Anxious to be done with it and perhaps loaded with guilt, he may too readily sign his property and income away. When he realizes that he's given more than he can afford, it's too late—he's stuck. So try to take as much time with the negotiation as it needs in order to reach a settlement you can live with in the future.

Can a Separation Agreement Be Changed at a Later Date?

Normally, only by mutual agreement. It's a private contract, with which courts don't like to interfere. A court may, however, change a privately negotiated separation agreement if necessary to protect the children; also (in most states) if the financial circumstances of one of the parties changes radically. But normally, once you've signed a separation agreement, that's it. Some things to include:

Custody of the Children

Normally, young children go to the mother. The law, however, is increasingly considering the claims of the father if he can provide a more stable home. Older children may make their own choice about where to live. A few families have joint custody arrangements, with the children spending part of the year with each parent.

Alimony

Many wives who want alimony don't get it, simply because their husbands can't afford it. In general, alimony isn't even considered unless the man makes around $18,000 or more a year and the wife has no income of her own. When the money is there, a younger housewife can usually expect some alimony—but the trend is to award it only for a few years, during which time she's expected to learn a skill and get a job. Older housewives may still get alimony for life or until remarriage. But working wives almost never receive these payments. If the wife has wealth in her own right, that's usually considered in setting the level of payments. *Note:* In three fourths of the states, a wife might be required to pay her husband alimony in some circumstances—for example, if she has wealth or earnings and he's an invalid.

The separation agreement normally reads that alimony will be paid until the wife remarries. But an increasing number of women simply move in with boyfriends and continue to collect the alimony check. Consider providing that alimony will also stop if she lives with a man, or lives with him for a certain period of time.

Education for the Wife

An alternative to alimony is job training for the wife. The husband may agree to pay her maintenance for a few years, plus finance her tuition at college or a vocational training school. Once she's prepared for the work force, support stops.

Child Support

Separation agreements generally call for child support. If the father is well paid, there may be enough to cover the child's expenses, but often support is only token. The father may pay less than half of what it costs to house, clothe, and feed the children, with the rest coming from the wife. Child support normally is payable only until the child is eighteen or twenty-one, or leaves school.

College Education

Fathers often agree to pay for college if they can afford it and the child wants to go. Whether this agreement is honored, and how much is paid, ultimately depends on the father's financial condition and his relationship with his child. If the father pays room and board as well as tuition, it should be provided that support payments are decreased or even eliminated.

Property Division

All but nine states now have "equitable distribution" laws, which require that all property acquired during the marriage be figured into the divorce settlement. Some states even include property acquired before the marriage. It need not be split fifty-fifty, even in community property states. But where equitable distribution is required, husband (or wife) generally can't lay sole claim to property just because it was bought with his earnings, or is in his name. These laws may even cover a husband's business interests. For example, if he has a flourishing manufacturing company or medical practice, the wife may be "owed" a portion of the increase in value or "good will" that occurred during the marriage.

Note: Where the wife wins a bigger property settlement, she may have to accept less alimony, or none at all. In effect, she may be trading property for income. Even a woman in her fifties with no job skills may get only a year or two of alimony if her property settlement is a large one.

Warning: With the courts willing to give away so much more of the husband's property, men are making greater attempts to conceal assets. The biggest wrangle in a divorce case may now be over whether the husband has presented a fair list of what he owns.

Lump Sum Settlements

An increasing number of marriages end with a lump sum property settlement, and no further commerce between the parties. In some states, however, a wife who takes a lump sum settlement and spends all the money can then petition the court for alimony, on the ground that she's without support.

Escalator Clauses

Where there's alimony and child support, they may equal one third to one half of the husband's after-tax income. As the husband's earnings increase, that payment becomes less and less onerous. Inflation, on the other hand, reduces the value of these fixed payments to the wife. So some agreements contain escalators—increasing the payments as the husband's earnings rise, with a cutoff point at a certain level.

Pensions

If there are a lot of assets in a pension fund, the wife may get a share of it for herself. Or she may be given a payment from the husband's pension when he retires, provided that she hasn't remarried.

The House

Where there are children, the wife and children often remain in the house (unless it has to be sold to raise cash). If there are enough assets, the wife may get the house as part of the property division, although she must then be prepared to pay the mortgage. Where the house is virtually the only asset, the husband may keep the house and pay the mortgage, letting the wife and children live there rent-free. Or they might divide the house and split the mortgage; when the house is sold, each takes half of the proceeds. You might also provide that when the children leave home, the house must be sold so that the husband can get his money out. The size of the mortgage payment the husband makes is taken into consideration in setting levels of alimony and child support. If the house is coowned, or owned by the husband but occupied by the wife, you should agree on who will pay for which repairs; also, who pays the homeowner's insurance.

The Car

If there are two, each spouse usually takes one. If there's only one, the purchase of another might be part of the agreement.

Investments

In a long-time marriage, the wife should get a good share of the investments and savings. If the marriage has been of only short duration, however, she may get little. In determining the division of investments, as well as alimony payments, the personal wealth of husband and wife should also be taken into consideration. If the wife can expect a large inheritance or is the beneficiary of a trust fund, it's not fair for her to take half the assets from a husband who has only what he earns.

Life Insurance

The wife should be the beneficiary of life insurance so that if the husband dies, she'll have money to replace his alimony and child support checks. She can get insurance three ways:

1. The husband could give her one of his policies outright. The drawback is that he then loses all ownership rights, including the right to borrow against the cash value. Also, his ex-wife gets the money even if she remarries and has no further right to her alimony checks.

2. The wife could buy a policy on her husband's life, paying for it out of earnings or out of the money he sends her. The agreement should provide that the husband will take a physical exam if his ex-wife ever wants to buy more insurance on his life.

3. The husband could retain ownership of his policies but name his ex-wife as beneficiary as long as she remains unmarried. Or he could name the children beneficiaries as long as they're under eighteen or twenty-one. The advantage of this arrangement is that the policy reverts to the husband when there's no longer a support obligation (and he may need that policy to protect a second wife and family). *Note:* The separation agreement should name the particular policy that will be kept in force for the ex-wife and children and provide that she receive copies of all correspondence relating to it so that she'll know it's being kept in effect.

Health Insurance

If the husband is covered by group health insurance, it will include the children, even after divorce. But there's no more coverage for the ex-wife. If she works, she may have group coverage of her own. Otherwise, consider including husband-paid medical insurance in the separation agreement. And be sure it's activated before the divorce so that the wife won't be without coverage. If the husband has no group health insurance but the wife does, the children should be her medical responsibility. If neither has health coverage, the question of who should buy medical insurance for the children should be part of the negotiation.

Incidentals

Who pays for orthodontia? Summer camp? Vacations? Any other major expenses that may come up? Will the children of this marriage inherit property on an equal basis with children from a subsequent marriage? Are there any other special costs to consider?

Be Realistic

The foregoing list gives you a general idea as to what the separation agreement might cover. But if a husband doesn't make much money, a wife can't expect such luxuries as life and health insurance, alimony, pension, or a car. Nor can a husband with a good salary expect to get away with minimal child support just because his wife works. Your lawyers should advise you as to what is reasonable to expect.

If You Can't Agree

The case goes to court. Judges normally order the parties to get together with the lawyers and come up with some kind of settlement; if one party is unreasonable, he or she may get a stern lecture. But if negotiations have hopelessly broken down, the judge will indeed decide, and he's liable to make neither side happy. Generally the decision is purely monetary—so much in property, so much a month—without bothering with such niceties as orthodontia.

When you go to court, your fate very much depends on the attitudes of the judge you draw. Some continue to award alimony to employable women, some award a few years of maintenance, some give little or nothing. Some judges set high child support, some set it low. By and large, you're better off negotiating your own agreement than leaving it to the court. *Note:* If, in the future, the court settlement becomes oppressive, you can petition to change it. Court settlements are easier to reopen than privately negotiated separation agreements but not necessarily easier to change.

Do-It-Yourself Divorce

In many states, writers or lawyers have published books of forms and instructions for filing a divorce yourself. If you're able to understand the forms and fill them in properly, divorce might cost you $100 or less. But there are risks. By failing to talk to a lawyer, you may forgo some important right you didn't know you had. Lawyers say there's good business in undoing, or trying to undo, mistakes made by people who did their divorces themselves.

If you go this route, ask a lawyer to check your work to be sure you've understood the law and done things wisely. One or two consultations won't cost much, and his suggestions should be helpful.

Do-it-yourself divorces work best for intelligent working couples ending a marriage amicably, with no alimony obligations or children to worry about. If there are children to protect, by all means see a lawyer.

What If the Husband Doesn't Pay?

That's something a wife must be prepared for. Although many men (and second families) pay off like clockwork, never abandoning their obligations, others pay for a short time, then quit. The husbands more unlikely to pay are those who move around the country, going from job to job; those who get into a financial squeeze, perhaps because of the cost of a second wife and family; those who lose their jobs and have trouble finding new employment; those who feel strongly that the separation agreement was unfair; and those who nurture an abiding resentment toward their ex-wife. A wife's best shot at getting a separation agreement that lasts is to stay on the friendliest possible terms with her ex-husband, and reach a settlement that he, however grudgingly, concedes is acceptable.

When the Husband Won't Pay, the Wife May Be Stuck

On paper, good collection laws exist, but they're not always effective. In many parts of the country it can be costly and frustrating to try to use them, especially if the husband is determined to resist. In many states the district attorney or an official of the family court may represent an ex-wife in support actions at little or no cost. On the other hand, she may find that she has to hire and pay her own lawyer, which could amount to a lot of money. If she's owed $150 a month, it might be a year before the amount due is large enough to make it practical to file a complaint. In the meantime, she'll have to fill the money gap with her own savings and earnings.

In some states, if a large sum of money in back payments has built up, judges may cancel all or part of what's owed, on the ex-husband's promise that he'll pay in the future. So the wife loses that money entirely yet still has to pay her lawyer. If the husband again quits paying, she'll have to sue a second time. If the husband moves out of state, the collection procedure may become even more costly and complicated.

States are making an effort to simplify and speed up legal procedures connected with support. In some places they're also getting the courts more involved with collections, rather than leaving it entirely to the wife's initiative and expense. Where court personnel work out an agreement between the parties, there's often a high rate of compliance. One effective means of collecting from a persistent deadbeat is to have payments garnished from his wages, but courts in many states don't order this as often as they should. Wives often accept smaller monthly checks than the agreement calls for, because it's at least something. If they sued their ex-husbands for the full amount, the men might quit paying entirely until the court case was over. On the other hand, if the debt is sizable and the husband has assets that can be seized (a house, for example), a lawsuit may be worth it. Consult a lawyer on what to do. In some cases, husbands pay as soon as a formal complaint is filed, just to avoid the hassle. It depends entirely on his financial means and personal attitudes.

Sometimes the judge may require the husband to pay his ex-wife's legal fees. If she pays them herself and her lawsuit involved unpaid alimony, legal fees are deductible on her income tax.

Parent Locator Services

Thanks to the parent locator services recently set up by the federal government, runaway fathers are becoming easier to track down. The Office of Child Support Enforcement, Room 900, 6110 Executive Blvd., Rockville, Md. 20852, is empowered to search federal records for the missing parent's last known employer and address.

Everything from the Social Security Administration to the Veterans Administration to the Internal Revenue Service is being wired into this network. If the parent has any business at all with the federal government, his name should eventually turn up. When it does, his last known whereabouts is turned over to the state, whose job it is to track him down and force him to pay for the support of his children. The service also looks for missing mothers if they are in a position to support the children, but 99 percent of its business concerns men.

Some states run excellent parent locator services, getting their man over and over again; others are just getting started or aren't very efficient. So the service you get depends on where you live. Any mother is entitled to help, but some states give priority to welfare mothers. They will not, incidentally, track a man for back alimony payments. They're interested only in child support. The reason for this nationwide manhunt is to relieve taxpayers of the financial burden of paying, via welfare, for the support of other people's children.

Once a father is found, states may hire bill-collecting services to bring in the money. If the father refuses, other remedies are available, such as seizing his property or garnishing his wages, but whether they're used effectively depends on the state. In many cases fathers voluntarily make payments to avoid trouble with the law.

If you're owed child support by a father who has disappeared, apply at your city's office of social services, or welfare, for help from the parent locator service.

Changing Trend in Settlements

The trend is to award women less alimony, but more property. Some women resent this because of the loss of income. But if honestly apportioned, the substitution of property for alimony may be fairer, and better, for both spouses. Alimony and child support payments are notoriously unreliable; a wife, therefore, is better off with property that is hers to keep or sell than the promise of income that may stop at any time. If she remarries, the property is still hers, whereas alimony would stop. From the man's point of view, he's left with less property after divorce. But if there's little or no alimony, he's not being pecked to death in his monthly paycheck. He can better afford to remarry and start building his assets all over again.

No-Fault Divorce

All but three states now recognize some form of no-fault divorce. In effect, a divorce can be granted simply because the marriage has broken down or the partners have separated, without one party having to prove the other "guilty" of anything. Removing fault also removes the element of punishment from divorce, such as depriving a wife of property because she was "bad," or soaking a husband for alimony because *he* was. Instead, property settlements may be made on the grounds of fairness and need, without moral judgments.

There's only one problem with no-fault divorces in some states: They've become too easy to get! There's little time for reflection; in many states divorce can even be had without the other's consent. Removing the need for consent makes it impossible for one party maliciously to deprive the other of his or her freedom, or blackmail the other into an unfair settlement. But it also deprives the parties of an important bargaining chip in reaching a fair settlement. The weaker party, usually the wife, has to depend on the courts to provide her with sufficient support, and the courts may not be as helpful as they should.

Divorce and Social Security

A divorced wife who was married at least ten years has a right to certain Social Security benefits on her ex-husband's account. If her ex-husband dies, and the marriage lasted at least nine months, she may be entitled to mother's benefits (see page 739). Divorced husbands have similar rights.

Wills and Divorce

Change your will immediately so that your ex-spouse won't inherit property you don't want him or her to have. If you remarry, you and your new spouse should draw your wills carefully, and be clear about each other's intentions. If you leave everything to your new spouse and die, he or she may neglect to provide for the children of your first marriage. If there are enough assets, consider setting aside property for the children of the first marriage in a trust, with income to go to your present spouse for life.

Pensions and Divorce

Traditionally, ex-wives get no share of their husband's company pension. But an increasing number of separation agreements provide for the division of this income (as well as the division of funds from Keogh plans and Individual Retirement Accounts). In some states judges are even dividing company pensions in court. Forty-two states now allow a wife to sue for a pension division in court—something to ask your lawyer about.

Divorce and Taxes

Many lawyers who handle divorces are not tax experts. Their main job is to advise clients of their rights under the law and win the best property settlement possible. But it sometimes happens that clauses in a separation agreement have unpleasant, and costly, tax consequences. For this reason, always ask the divorce lawyers you interview whether they have tax expertise. If not, ask them to have the agreement checked by a tax expert before you sign. You might even want to take the agreement to an accountant or tax lawyer of your own choosing; a single consultation isn't expensive and could potentially save you a lot of money. The more property you have to divide, the more important tax advice becomes. And remember: Fees for tax advice are tax-deductible if you itemize on your tax return.

This chapter can't possibly cover the extraordinary range of tax consequences that could spring from an apparently simple separation agreement. But here are some of the key points to consider:

• Alimony is tax-deductible for the husband and taxable income for the wife. Child support, on the other hand, is neither. If the separation agreement doesn't specify what amount goes to child support, the entire payment is ordinarily treated as alimony. This could lead to unexpectedly heavy taxes for the wife, if she earns a good salary of her own.

• There are complex rules about what's considered alimony. If you fall afoul of those rules, the payment to a wife may be considered a lump-sum property settlement paid in installments, which is generally not tax-deductible. This could lead to unexpectedly heavy taxes for the husband.

• Difference in tax brackets between the two parties can sometimes be manipulated to provide more income for the wife, at no extra cost to the husband. For example, if the husband is in a high bracket and the wife in a low one, it makes sense to designate more of the payment as alimony, rather than child support. This gives the husband a higher tax deduction, hence more after-tax income that could be passed on to the wife. The agreement might provide that if the wife remarries, a larger portion will be designated child support so that the children will continue to receive reasonable payments.

• The parent who has custody of the child the greater part of the year generally claims the child as an exemption on his or her tax return. But the other parent gets the exemption if (1) he (or she) contributed at least $600 toward support and the separation agreement gives him (or her) the exemption in writing; or (2) he (or she) contributed at least $1,200 for each child claimed and the first parent can't prove that she (or he) contributed more. *Note:* Only the person who claims the child as an exemption can tax-deduct the child's medical bills, so where the bills are sizable, be sure that they're paid by the right person.

• A working mother may use the tax credit for child-care expenses even if she doesn't claim the children as tax dependents.

• As long as the wife has the children, she can file as head of household on her income tax, even though the husband takes the children as exemptions. (See page 512 for the tax status of divorced persons.)

• If the husband assigns the life insurance policy to the wife but continues to pay the premiums, the premiums are generally deductible to him, taxable to her.

• Some periodic payments are deductible as alimony (and taxable to the wife). These may include payments for the wife's medical bills, the wife's schooling, or her rent. Ask your lawyer or accountant about this.

• Legal fees for procuring alimony are deductible. The wife has to pay the fees herself and deduct them on her own tax return.

• Giving property to a spouse may trigger unexpected taxes. For example, if you transfer appreciated property, such as stocks or a house, you may have to pay a capital gains tax (even though the property wasn't sold). If you and your spouse jointly own a home and a vacation cottage, and each of you takes one, you may each owe capital gains taxes on the half of the property you gave up. Why the tax? The transfer is considered a sale in exchange for the surrender of the spouse's marital rights. If the transfer takes place *after* divorce, no capital gains taxes are due (but if one spouse then reneges on his or her promise to give up the property, there may be nothing the other can do).

If the wife gets the insurance policy, she may have to pay income tax on the proceeds when her ex-husband dies. Other property transfers also give rise to tax traps. There may be ways around these problems, so by all means check with a tax expert before you sign the separation agreement.

Prenuptial Agreements

These are becoming more common. They're attractive to (1) an older person, whether divorced or widowed, who wants to reserve his assets, after death, for the children and grandchildren of his first marriage; (2) people married before who were stuck with an expensive divorce settlement and don't want it to happen again; (3) anyone else who wants to set out the financial or economic terms of his or her marriage in advance.

In all but a few states, you're allowed to contractually waive your inheritance rights; you may also stipulate a property settlement in case of divorce. But traditionally, it's been considered against public policy to stipulate alimony payments in a prenuptial agreement. This rule is now being questioned. A few states have held that if the sum is fair at the time of the contract, the agreement will be upheld. But elsewhere, even if a wife signed such an agreement, she might be able to overturn it in court.

Each party should have a prenuptial examined by *his or her own lawyer,* who can explain its ramifications. In a premarital situation it's often difficult for the parties themselves to negotiate terms—but two helpful lawyers (not of the quarrelsome sort) can usually see that the rights of each party are protected, without causing either of you any anguish or loss of trust.

Chapter Thirty-One

FUNERALS

> The dead are always pop'lar. I knowed a society that wanst to vote a monyment to a man an' refuse to help his family, all in wan night.
>
> FINLEY PETER DUNNE

Some families like an expensive funeral and are able to pay for it. Others come away with the feeling that everything somehow got out of hand. Widows, for example, may impulsively spend all of a small insurance policy or union benefit on the burial, then find themselves hard pressed to meet immediate expenses.

No one would quarrel with the human need to give the dead "the best." But by defining "the best" entirely in monetary terms, the funeral industry has hiked the cost of burial far higher than necessary. Funerals, after all, are for the living, not the dead, and therefore should be chosen in light of what will be "the best" for the surviving family. This chapter examines some ways to control funeral costs.

Let a Friend Do It

The people most upset by the death are normally the last ones who should choose the coffin or deal with the mortician. In that emotional state they may agree to anything, just to get it done. Or, armed with a small insurance payment, they may blow it all on something fancy to show how much they cared.

820

If possible, send a level-headed friend or relative to examine coffins and discuss prices. The friend needs marching orders; for example, he might be told that you want "something nice, but not too expensive." He can then compare costs, find out what the package price includes, eliminate items you don't want, and report back. Culture, class, and social expectations have a lot to do with what kind of a funeral is chosen. But if money is tight—and for a surviving widow and children, it often is—it's no disrespect to get the least expensive "acceptable" funeral possible.

Which Funeral Home?

The home you choose is the major factor in determining what you'll pay. In a study of Washington, D.C. funeral homes done in 1973 the Federal Trade Commission found that the *lowest* price offered by the various homes ranged from $210 to $900; average prices ranged from $500 to $1,800. A cemetery plot, headstone, and other incidentals of burial raised the cost by an average of $700.

Unfortunately, there's not much time to shop around when someone dies, and funeral homes generally don't quote prices over the telephone. You might call one or two friends who have recently paid for funerals to see if they'd recommend the place they chose and get a line on the price. If there are a number of convenient funeral homes, try to visit two or three of them to look over the caskets and learn what they charge. Some funeral homes carry caskets in all price ranges, which is generally what you want. Others have just a few cheap ones (that look awful) to encourage you to buy their expensive stock, or they may carry only a high-priced selection.

Many funeral directors are perfectly straightforward about their services; if asked for a modest funeral, they'll provide one without argument. That's the kind of person you want to deal with, even if you're willing to pay a higher price. When a mortician obviously manipulates you toward the most expensive casket, deprecates the less costly caskets, and makes you feel guilty for wanting to save money, clear out.

In general, it's best to use a funeral home that charges separately for each item, such as casket, limousine, use of the viewing room, chapel, announcement cards, embalming, and so on. You can then choose and pay for only those services you really want. Less desirable are funerals with a package price, where you pay for everything whether you use it or not. Many funeral homes won't even give you an itemized bill (although in some states they're required to by law). Avoid a place that won't itemize if it's at all possible; by the same token, be alert to over-charges where services are separately bought.

Even in funeral homes that give package prices it's sometimes possible to get discounts for services not used. But the best time to negotiate is before the body is sent. Once the mortician is in possession, he has no reason to negotiate price.

Don't authorize a mortician to pick up the body from the hospital or nursing home until you've decided that he's the person you want to handle the funeral. Once the mortician has taken over, you may find it difficult or expensive to move the body somewhere else. A hospital or nursing home will generally keep the body for a day while you decide where you want it taken (although some do pressure you to move it fast).

Buying the Coffin

This is the most expensive part of any funeral (and usually where the funeral director makes his biggest profit). In package-price funerals, the auxiliary services may be about the same no matter how much you pay; only the elegance of the coffin accounts for differences in cost. Ask yourself: Is the coffin alone worth an extra $700 or $800? Funeral parlors may have low-cost caskets available that aren't on display, so ask about them. Don't be put off if the samples are badly displayed, chipped, or scratched. You'll have a new one and it will look fine.

Funeral directors also sell expensive burial vaults ($200 to $300) to enclose the coffin. They may even tell you the cemetery requires it. Some cemeteries do require a grave liner to keep the earth over the grave from collapsing, but a cement or metal one can be had for around $100. Another thing: It's pointless to pay extra for anything "guaranteed" to be airtight, watertight, and rot-resistant.

Some morticians encourage people to buy expensive caskets even for cremations. Sometimes they say it's required, by the crematory or by state law. Only Massachusetts requires coffins for cremations, and few crematoria do. Double-check with the crematorium before you agree to a coffin. Most require only a "container," by which they mean a rigid box. Fiberboard boxes are often available for around $25.

Embalming

No state requires embalming for a normal funeral. When burial or cremation is rapid, the body doesn't have to be shipped any distance, and there's to be no delayed ceremony with the body present, embalming is generally an expense you can skip. The funeral director may try to talk you into it, perhaps by saying it's required by your city's hygiene laws, or that an unembalmed body is a danger to funeral home personnel. In normal circumstances, neither is true. If you have any doubts, call the health department and ask. Many funeral directors automatically embalm any bodies that arrive, so if you don't want this done, make it clear before the body is picked up.

Ancillary Services

Sometimes funeral parlors charge exorbitant prices for some of their services. For example, there might be a fee for calling the newspaper with the obituary, which you could easily do yourself. Flowers supplied by the mortician may cost 25 percent more than the same flowers direct from a florist. In a package-price funeral you're charged for services you don't even use (see page 821). Request an itemized list of the funeral expenses, and go over each item separately to see if it makes sense. If you can't get an itemized list, deal with someone else. *Remember:* The best time to do this—the time when you have the most bargaining power—is before the funeral home has picked up the body.

Cremation

Cremation costs far less than burial. But again, if arrangements are made through a funeral parlor, price depends on the place you choose. In the FTC's 1973 study, *lowest* costs for immediate cremation ranged from $80 to $485, depending on the mortician, and for cremation after viewing the body, $350 to $890. In many states you can arrange to have the body delivered directly to the crematorium, cutting out the funeral director entirely; but in others the funeral industry has inspired laws requiring funeral homes as intermediaries.

If the funeral director tells you that the crematorium requires caskets and embalming, double-check it yourself. That is usually not true; in fact, some states prohibit it. If caskets are indeed required, there may be another crematorium in town that doesn't have such an unnecessary and costly rule.

Some cemeteries sell niches for funerary ashes. More commonly, families keep, scatter, or bury the ashes themselves. Some states have laws preventing the scattering of ashes (again, inspired by the funeral industry). But there's no hygiene problem, so what you do with the ashes ought to be your affair. You can provide your own container for ashes—no need to buy one from the crematorium. If the ashes are to be sent some distance, they can be carried in a bag or mailed parcel post.

Save Money with a Memorial Society

The best way to be sure that your family doesn't overspend on your funeral is to plan it yourself. That generally means joining a *memorial society*. There are around 150 nonprofit memorial societies in the United States, claiming three quarters of a million members and all dedicated to providing dignified, yet inexpensive, last rites.

A memorial society arranges with one or more funeral parlors in the area to provide its members with funeral services at prices well below the average. Some funerals can be had for as little as $200 to $400. Savings come principally from the simplicity of the arrangements. Funeral society members tend to want cremations or simple earth burials, with no open-coffin viewing and no elaborate services. But if you want a fancy funeral, many memorial societies can provide that, too, at reduced cost. Discounts may be in the area of 25 percent or more.

You usually have to join a memorial society in advance of death, although some are able to help if you call immediately after someone dies. Family memberships range from $5 to $20, plus an extra fee of $5 to $10 at the time of death. The money is used for printing, record keeping, and overhead; the societies are generally staffed by volunteers or run by a church.

Even when assisted by churches, memorial societies are open to members of all religions and often have links to funeral parlors that cater specifically to Catholics, Protestants, or Jews.

When you join, you decide on your own funeral arrangement at one of the participating homes and file it with the society. This relieves your survivors of the need to choose. They don't have to deal with the funeral director or feel guilty about asking for a cheaper model. At death, the funeral director is called and told which plan to proceed with. Memorial societies have nothing to do with arranging cemetery plots or gravestones. Nor do they handle funeral arrangements.

Some profit-making organizations use the term "memorial society" as a front for their own activities. If a "society" charges a large membership fee, tries to sell you any part of the funeral, or offers to prefinance the funeral, it's not the real thing.

To find out if there's a memorial society in your area, write for the free directory of the Continental Association of Funeral and Memorial Societies, 1828 L St. N.W., Suite 1100, Washington, D.C. 20036. This organization can also help if you want to start a society.

If the Body Has to Be Shipped

In most states, a body has to be embalmed before shipping; it can then travel either by train or by air. A funeral director will make the arrangements. Ask him to compare train and air fares and report back to you so that you can decide which to use. If the body is cremated, the ashes can be carried in a suitcase or sent through the mail with no special arrangements.

Donating Organs

You can provide for this in advance of death by filling in a donor card that makes your wishes known. These cards are available from doctors' offices and hospitals, memorial societies, and many medical and charitable institutions. But even without a card organs may be donated at the time of death, if your relatives agree and the medical personnel are alerted in time. If you want to leave your body to a medical school, ask the school in advance whether it wants it.

Cemeteries

In the absence of preference on the part of the person who dies, you'll want a place convenient for the family to visit and sufficiently well kept to make your visits comfortable. If more than one cemetery meets these requirements, compare prices; there's often a considerable difference.

Municipal cemeteries are generally cheaper than private ones. Non-profit cemeteries are often, but not always, cheaper than those operated for profit. New, more aggressively marketed cemeteries may charge more than older ones that have their major development costs out of the way. Because costs vary so much, your best rule is this: Don't believe what a salesman tells you about the competition without checking it out yourself.

Cemeteries often have a "good address," where plots cost more than in other areas. For the simple purpose of visiting a grave, an out-of-the-way lot is just as good as one by the fountain. If you're buying for future use, a lot in an undeveloped part of the cemetery should cost less than one ready now.

The average price paid for interment is in the area of $1,000—more in urban areas, less in rural ones. Double-decker graves for couples, where one is buried above the other, cost less than side-by-side plots. Burial above ground in a mausoleum is often more expensive than earth burial. A niche for cremated remains costs the least.

Many cemeteries require a grave liner, to prevent the soil from caving into the grave as time passes. Concrete burial vaults run $200 to $300, but you should be able to get a cement grave liner for around $100. If you buy a burial package that includes everything from plot to marker, ask whether it also covers the grave-digging fee. Often that costs around $150 extra.

Go over your contract with the cemetery carefully in order to understand the terms and conditions. Take it home, read it, then call the salesman with any questions you have. If you're buying on the installment plan, check the truth-in-lending agreement for the true annual interest rate. It will probably be cheaper to finance through a bank. Be sure to explore the question of perpetual care. A portion of the cost of every grave must be paid into a fund maintained for the general care of the cemetery—but in some places cemeteries offer separate contracts for special care of the grave you buy. Before spending several hundred dollars for special care, consider whether the general fund provides sufficient maintenance. Ask who the trustee is for the cemetery funds, and whether the funds are state-supervised in order to be sure they're properly spent.

Should You Buy a Cemetery Plot in Advance?

Lot prices have accelerated 20 to 40 percent in the past few years, so you could save money by buying ahead. But if you move, it can be a problem. Some cemeteries offer a lot exchange plan, but that won't help if you move to an area where no cemetery has joined the plan. In some states you can sell an unused lot back to the cemetery if they'll take it (they may not). In others, you'll have to sell it privately. Usually the cemetery salesman will handle the private sale, but, of course, you have to offer him an attractive fee. Alternatively, you could donate the plot to a church and take a tax deduction.

If you're along in age, and pretty sure that you're staying put for the rest of your life, a cemetery plot might be worth buying. But younger, mobile people might find themselves stuck with a piece of land they won't use.

Are We Running Out of Cemetery Space?

Not at all. The business is profitable enough to attract many new entrants, and growing interest in cremation has reduced the percentage of earth burials. A study done by the American Cemetery Association in 1972 concluded that if even no more cemeteries were built, there were enough lots and mausoleums to take care of the dead for the next 140 years.

Who Can Be Buried in a National Cemetery?

Any veteran can, as long as his discharge was not dishonorable; also his spouse and dependent children, if they are buried in the same grave. Burial is free, in whatever cemetery has space available (although there are strict limitations as to who can be buried in Arlington National Cemetery).

Normally the family pays to have the body shipped. But the Veterans Administration pays under the following conditions:

1. The veteran died in a VA hospital, or in transit to or from a VA hospital.
2. The veteran had a service-connected disability, whether or not he died from it.

Shipment is to the national cemetery with space available that is nearest to the veteran's home.

No matter where he's buried, an eligible veteran is entitled to an American flag, for draping over the casket. Apply at the nearest VA office.

What About a Grave Marker?

It's best to wait a while before you decide on a marker. Around the time of the funeral you may, in a rush of emotion, choose a far more expensive marker than you can really afford. A little later, when your life has settled back into place, you'll be more realistic about costs.

A veteran can get a free marker, of simple design, through the Veterans Administration. It's available whether he's buried in a national or a private cemetery. Grave markers for spouse and children are given only if they're buried in a national cemetery.

Prefinancing

Some funeral homes encourage you to pay for your funeral, in installments, in advance. But if you move or are buried elsewhere, it may be difficult for your heirs to get that money back. As prices rise, there will be more to pay when the funeral actually takes place, and the funeral director may be tempted to pad the final bill for your heirs. If the funeral home goes out of business, you generally have no recourse. By and large, it's better to put money for your funeral into the bank, building up an interest, than to pay it to a funeral director or funeral organization. If you do prefinance, be sure that your survivors know about it. And be sure that the money is in a trust or escrow account, where you can get it back if you change your plans.

At Death—A Financial Checklist

Here are some of the things to attend to:

• Notify the employer, and talk to the employee benefits office. Is there a last paycheck due? Company life insurance? A pension benefit? Money in deferred compensation? Profit sharing? Accident insurance?

• Find the will and talk to a lawyer about getting it through probate. The lawyer will also help the executor transfer the dead person's property, including the car, to its new owners; file estate taxes, if they're due; and (perhaps with the help of an accountant) fill in the final income tax form. If there's no will, the court will appoint someone to handle the property.

• Scrape up the important papers and documents. If they're not all in one spot, search closets, desk drawers, and safe deposit boxes for such things as insurance policies you didn't know existed; business agreements; loans the dead person may have made to others; membership cards that might be a lead to group life insurance payments; income tax forms; bank books; military records; and so forth. Don't throw away anything that looks official or that you don't understand; it may entitle you to a benefit you know nothing about. Give these papers to your lawyer to examine.

• Notify the life insurance agent, and file a claim.

• Ask for at least ten copies of the death certificate (the funeral director or lawyer can get them for you). You'll need them to file insurance and Social Security claims, probate the will, and so forth.

• Notify Social Security. If the person who died was covered by Social Security, and was living with his or her spouse at death, the spouse receives a funeral benefit of $255. Otherwise, the benefit goes to the person who paid for the funeral. A surviving spouse and children may be eligible for monthly survivor's benefits (see page 738).

• Notify the Veterans Administration if the person who died was a veteran whose discharge was not dishonorable. When the death is service-connected, the VA will pay up to $800 for the funeral. When the death is not service-connected, there's a $250 funeral allowance for (1) any wartime veteran; and (2) any peacetime veteran who was drawing disability compensation or was discharged from service because of a disability incurred or aggravated in line of duty. Those veterans are also entitled to a $150 burial allowance, if not buried in a national cemetery. You may collect both a VA and a Social Security benefit.

Surviving spouses and children of wartime veterans may be entitled to VA pensions if their income is very low.

• Accumulate debts for payment. Check with the lenders to see if any of them are covered by credit life insurance that will pay off the debt in full.

• Find the safe deposit box and see what's there.

• Get all joint accounts and joint property transferred into your name alone.

• Cancel credit cards or convert them to your name.

• If you need help and can't afford to pay for it, check the phone book for social service organizations, either in the Yellow Pages or under your city or county listings. Or else call Legal Aid. You should be able to find someone who'll show you how to file claims and collect benefits.

Making Decisions

A new widow (or, for that matter, widower) should make no important decisions soon after the death of a spouse! Still in a state of shock, she may do something she'll regret later. A good many people will offer advice—on where to move, what investments to buy or sell, what to do with the life insurance proceeds. Don't take any of it. Don't lend anyone money. Put the insurance proceeds in the bank (or in an interest-bearing account with the insurance company if the interest rate is as good as the bank's) and sit. As time passes and you adjust to your new life, things should gradually take shape. Only then will you be ready to make decisive changes in your living and financial arrangements.

Death Frauds

A number of criminals prey on bereaved families, finding their names through the obituary columns of the newspaper. The cons include:

1. Bibles sent to the family COD, as if the dead person had ordered them. A variety of other merchandise may also be sent for payment.

2. False notices of overdue premiums on a life insurance policy that you never heard of. This con works by appealing to your need for money. It appears that if you pay, even after death, the policy will be reactivated. There is, of course, no such policy.

3. Demands for repayments of loans the dead person is said to have taken out but never did.

4. Communications that appear to come from the Veterans Administration. These notices offer to sell you a variety of funeral services and may look like part of your VA benefits. In fact, they're overpriced cons. For a list of your actual VA benefits, see page 829.

If anything comes in the mail to be paid, turn it over to the executor of the will, or to your lawyer. Refuse all COD packages that you didn't know about in advance. If anyone comes to the door trying to collect some money, refuse him, even if he gets threatening. Tell him to send his bill to your lawyer. If he pleads, cajoles, or gives you a story designed to get the money immediately, he's probably a fraud.

Chapter Thirty-Two

CONSUMER COMPLAINT
AND
INFORMATION DIRECTORY

Advice, n., the smallest current coin.

AMBROSE BIERCE

This guide includes federal and private agencies and organizations able to help you solve many of your problems with products, with government, or with the law. The Washington offices of federal agencies are given and, in some cases, regional offices. If you write to Washington, the odds are that your letter will be forwarded to a regional office for action.

Many states have excellent consumer protection laws, which are often more helpful to a misled or defrauded consumer than similar federal laws. To learn what state agencies handle information and complaints, call the appropriate department (for example, the state Insurance Department) or the attorney general's office. Get telephone numbers from the information operator in your state capital.

Your city or county probably has a consumer frauds or consumer protection division, perhaps under the district attorney's office. Check

Note: These addresses and phone numbers were current when this book went to press. But organizations do move around a lot (we are, after all, a mobile society), so you may need help from the Information operator. If you're calling a government agency, the information operator may refer you to the federal government information system, which in turn will give you the number you need. That's three separate phone calls before you get the office you want. Government toll-free numbers may be understaffed, leaving you with busy signals, recorded announcements, or requests to call back. Have patience, and keep trying.

the listings in your phone book. If you can't find anything, call city hall. Somewhere, there's a staff charged with handling complains and enforcing the consumer laws.

Federal Government Agencies

Airline Services

Being bumped illegally from flights, ticket overcharges, failure to pay for lost baggage, failure to put you up overnight if you're diverted from your destination:

> Office of the Consumer Advocate
> Civil Aeronautics Board
> 1825 Connecticut Ave. N.W.
> Washington, D.C. 20428
> (202) 673-6047*

Automobile Complaints

Warranty problems, defective tires, recalls, safety inquiries:

> National Highway Traffic Safety Administration
> U.S. Department of Transportation
> 400 Seventh St. S.W.
> Washington, D.C. 20590
> Hot line: (800) 424-9393
> 　　　　　(202) 426-0123* (for Alaska and Hawaii)

Banking Problems

Bank, savings and loan association, or credit union violations of the Truth in Lending Act, complaints about discrimination in lending, questions about banking practices:

Regarding national banks (a bank with *national* in its name or the initials N.A., for "National Association," after its name):

---

*You pay for the first three minutes, but the department will call you back if your problem requires more time.

Office of Consumer Affairs
Comptroller of the Currency
490 L'Enfant Plaza S.W.
Washington, D.C. 20219

Regarding state-chartered banks that are members of the Federal Reserve System (most big banks are):

Division of Consumer Affairs
Federal Reserve System
21st St. and C St. N.W.
Washington, D.C. 20551

or to the Federal Reserve Branch nearest you:

400 Sansome St.
San Francisco, Calif. 94120

411 Locust St.
St. Louis, Mo. 63166

104 Marietta St. N.W.
Atlanta, Ga. 30303

33 Liberty St.
New York, N.Y. 10045

230 S. LaSalle St.
Chicago, Ill. 60690

1455 East Sixth St.
Cleveland, Ohio 44101

600 Atlantic Ave.
Boston, Mass. 02106

100 N. 6th St.
Philadelphia, Pa. 19105

250 Marquette Ave.
Minneapolis, Minn. 55480

400 S. Akard St.
Dallas, Tex. 75222

925 Grand Ave.
Kansas City, Mo. 64198

701 E. Byrd Ave.
Richmond, Va. 23261

Regarding a bank that is federally insured:

Office of Consumer Affairs
Federal Deposit Insurance Corporation
550 17th St. N.W.
Washington, D.C. 20429

Regarding a federally chartered savings and loan association (an S&L with *federal* in its name); also, a state-chartered S&L insured by the Federal Savings and Loan Insurance Corporation (in this case, complain to the appropriate state regulatory agency, with a carbon copy to the agency below):

> Office of the Secretary
> Federal Home Loan Bank Board
> 1790 G St. N.W.
> Washington, D.C. 20552

Also, to the Supervisory Agent of the Federal Home Loan Bank closest to you:

Maine, New Hampshire, Vermont, Massachusetts, Rhode Island, and Connecticut—One Federal St., Boston, Mass. 02106.

New York, New Jersey, Puerto Rico, and the Virgin Islands—One World Trade Center, New York, N.Y. 10048.

Pennsylvania, Delaware, and West Virginia—11 Stanwix St., Gateway Center, Pittsburgh, Pa. 15222.

District of Columbia, Maryland, Virginia, North Carolina, South Carolina, Georgia, Florida, and Alabama—Coastal States Building, 260 Peachtree St. N.W., Atlanta, Ga. 30303.

Ohio, Kentucky, and Tennessee—2500 DuBois Tower, Cincinnati, Ohio 45202.

Michigan and Indiana—2900 Indiana Tower, One Indiana Square, Indianapolis, Ind. 46204.

Wisconsin and Illinois—111 East Wacker Dr., Chicago, Ill. 60601.

Minnesota, Iowa, Missouri, North Dakota, and South Dakota—907 Walnut St., Des Moines, Iowa 50309.

Mississippi, Arkansas, Louisiana, Texas, and New Mexico—1400 Tower Building, Little Rock, Ark., 72201.

Nebraska, Kansas, Oklahoma, and Colorado—3 Townsite Plaza, 120 E. 6th St., Topeka, Kan. 66601.

Arizona, Nevada, and California—600 California St., P.O. Box 7948, San Francisco, Calif. 94120.

Montana, Wyoming, Idaho, Utah, Washington, Oregon, Alaska, Hawaii, and Guam—600 Stewart St., Seattle, Wash. 98101.

Regarding a federally chartered credit union:

> Office of the Administrator
> National Credit Union Administration
> 1776 G St. N.W.
> Washington, D.C. 20456

Child Support

To find a runaway parent who owes child support, apply to the following agency through your local welfare office:

> Office of Child Support Enforcement
> 6110 Executive Blvd.
> Rockville, Md. 20852

Consumer Frauds

Deceptive advertising, bill collectors, door-to-door salesmen, mail-order sales, retail violations of the Truth in Lending Act, credit bureaus, credit or sales contracts, any illegal practice by stores or salesmen:

> Bureau of Consumer Protection
> Federal Trade Commission
> Pennsylvania Ave. at Sixth St. N.W.
> Washington, D.C. 20580

Or to the regional office nearest you:

Federal Building
11000 Wilshire Blvd.
Los Angeles, Calif. 90024

450 Golden Gate Ave.
San Francisco, Calif. 94102

1405 Curtis St., Suite 2900
Denver, Colo. 80202

Gelman Building
2120 L St. N.W.
Washington, D.C. 20037

1718 Peachtree St. N.W.,
Rm. 1000
Atlanta, Ga. 30309

Melim Building, Rm. 6324
300 Ala Moana
Honolulu, Hawaii 96850

55 E. Monroe St., Suite 1437
Chicago, Ill. 60603

150 Causeway St.
Boston, Mass. 02114

Federal Building–2243–E3
26 Federal Plaza
New York, N.Y. 10007

Suite 500–Mall Bldg.
118th St. and Clair Ave.
Cleveland, Ohio 44114

2001 Bryan St., Suite 2665
Dallas, Tex. 75201

Federal Building
915 Second Ave.
Seattle, Wash. 98174

Consumer Complaints and Questions

> U.S. Office of Consumer Affairs
> Department of Health, Education, and Welfare
> 621 Reporters Bldg.
> Washington, D.C. 20201

This office also publishes a Guide to Federal Consumer Services, *which describes all the agencies that attend to your various questions and problems, and tells where you can write to them. Free copies are available from:*

> Consumer Information Center
> Pueblo, Colo. 81009

Information on the government's consumer publications can be had from:

> Consumer Information Center
> General Services Administration
> General Services Building
> Eighteenth and F Sts. N.W.
> Washington, D.C. 20405

Cosmetics, Drugs, Food

Complaints, hazards, additives, information on side effects, packaging, and labeling:

> Office of Consumer Inquiries
> Food and Drug Administration
> 5600 Fishers Lane
> Rockville, Md. 20857

or the regional office nearest you:

1521 W. Pico Blvd.
Los Angeles, Calif. 90015

50 U.N. Plaza, Rm. 524
San Francisco, Calif. 94102

500 U.S. Customhouse Building
19th & California Sts.
Denver, Colo. 80202

P.O. Box 118
Orlando, Fla. 32802

880 West Peachtree St. N.W.
Atlanta, Ga. 30309

175 W. Jackson Blvd.
Chicago, Ill. 60604

4298 Elysian Ave.
423 Canal St.
New Orleans, La. 70122

900 Madison Ave.
Baltimore, Md. 21201

585 Commercial St.
Boston, Mass. 02109

1560 E. Jefferson Ave.
Detroit, Mich. 48207

240 Hennepin Ave.
Minneapolis, Minn. 55401

1009 Cherry St.
Kansas City, Mo. 64106

20 Evergreen Pl.
East Orange, N.J. 07018

850 Third Ave.
Brooklyn, N.Y. 11232

599 Delaware Ave.
Buffalo, N.Y. 14202

1141 Central Parkway
Cincinnati, Ohio 45202

900 U.S. Customhouse Building
Second and Chestnut Sts.
Philadelphia, Pa. 19106

P.O. Box S 4427
Old San Juan Station
San Juan, P.R. 00905

297 Plus Park Blvd.
Nashville, Tenn. 37217

500 S. Ervay, Suite 470-B
Dallas, Tex. 75201

Federal Office Building
909 First Ave., Rm. 5003
Seattle, Wash. 98174

Education

Applications for federal student grants:

Basic Grants
P.O. Box 84
Washington, D.C. 20044
(800) 638-6700

Energy

Complaints about gasoline prices, heating oil, and other fuels:

Office of Consumer Affairs
Department of Energy
1000 Independence Ave. S.W., Rm. 8G-082
Washington, D.C. 20545

Food

Prices, quality, and availability:

Assistant Secretary for Food and Consumer Services
U.S. Department of Agriculture
Washington, D.C. 20250

Housing Problems
Difficulties with builders:

> Office for Consumer Affairs
> U.S. Department of Housing and Urban Development
> 451 Seventh St. S.W.
> Washington, D.C. 20410

If you've been discriminated against when applying for a mortgage or renting an apartment:

> Assistant Secretary for Fair Housing and Equal Opportunity
> U.S. Department of Housing and Urban Development
> 451 Seventh St. S.W.
> Washington, D.C. 20410
> Toll-free number: (800) 424-8590

Land Sales
Complaints about land swindles, requests for property reports on developments you plan to buy into:

> Office of Interstate Land Sales Registration
> U.S. Department of Housing and Urban Development
> 451 Seventh St. S.W.
> Washington, D.C. 20410

Mail-order Frauds
Complaints about paid-for goods not received, lost items, unordered merchandise you're billed for, lost mail, damaged packages:

> Your local postal inspector *or*

> Office of the Consumer Advocate
> U.S. Postal Service
> 475 L'Enfant Plaza West S.W.
> Washington, D.C. 20260

Moving
Complaints about late pickup or delivery, phony estimates, damaged goods not paid for:

Consumer Affairs Officer, Public Information Office
Interstate Commerce Commission
12th St. and Constitution Ave.
Washington, D.C. 20423
Hot line: (202) 275-7301*

Product Safety

Complaints about injuries, questions about which products have been found hazardous:

Bureau of Information and Education
Consumer Product Safety Commission
1111 18th St. N.W.
Washington, D.C. 20207
Toll-free number: (800) 638-8326

or write the regional office nearest you:

3660 Wilshire Blvd.
Los Angeles, Calif. 90010

100 Pine St.
San Francisco, Calif. 94111

Guaranty Bank Building
817 17th St., Suite 938
Denver, Colo. 80202

1330 West Peachtree St.
Atlanta, Ga. 30309

230 S. Dearborn St.
Chicago, Ill. 60604

International Trade Mart,
Suite 414
2 Canal St.
New Orleans, La. 70013

100 Summer St.
Boston, Mass. 02110

Metro Square
7th and Roberts
Twin Cities, Minn. 55101

Trader's National Bank Building
1125 Grand Ave.
Kansas City, Mo. 64106

6 World Trade Center
Vesey St.
New York, N.Y. 10048

Plaza 9 Building
55 Erieview Plaza
Cleveland, Ohio 44114

400 Market St.
Philadelphia, Pa. 19106

1100 Commerce St.
Dallas, Tex. 75242

3240 Federal Building
915 Second Ave.
Seattle, Wash. 98174

*You pay for the first three minutes, but the department will call you back if your problem requires more time.

Savings Bonds

Replacement of lost bonds, name changes:

> Your local bank
> *or*
> Bureau of the Public Debt
> 200 Third St.
> Parkersburg, West Va. 26101

Information on buying:

> Your local bank
> *or*
> Bureau of the Public Debt
> Securities Transaction Branch
> Washington, D.C. 20226

Securities

Unresolved problems with stockbrokers:

> Office of Consumer Affairs
> Securities and Exchange Commission
> 500 N. Capitol St. N.W.
> Washington, D.C. 20549

Trains and Buses

On-time problems, overcharging, lost baggage not paid for, and other complaints:

> Consumer Affairs Office, Public Information Office
> Interstate Commerce Commission
> Washington, D.C. 20423

Consumer Organizations

Some of these groups will handle questions or forward complaints, and some won't. But they're nevertheless a good place to write with a problem that needs redress. Your experience is part of the evidence they need to convince legislators and federal agencies that a specific wrong needs righting.

Center for the Study of Responsive Law, P.O. Box 19367, Washington, D.C. 20009. At the center of Ralph Nader's complex of consumer organizations.

Consumer Federation of America, 1012 14th St. N.W., Suite 901, Washington, D.C. 20005. A federation of consumer-oriented (but nongovernment) groups, heavily supported by the labor unions. Helps groups organize, serves as an information clearinghouse, lobbies Congress and federal agencies on consumer issues. Will often forward your letter to an industry group that can help solve your problem.

Industry and Other Private Groups

Every industry has a trade association to look after its interests. In recent years, these have become quite responsive to consumer complaints. Many will actively try to settle problems between the public and one of their members. Some even have formal boards where you can bring complaints. To find the trade group representing a particular business or a private nonprofit consumer group that polices the field, ask at your library for the *Encyclopedia of Associations,* which lists all the trade associations in the United States. Another source of information is your local Chamber of Commerce, which should have a copy of the national chamber's *Association Consumer Affairs Activities.* It lists a number of complaint-handling programs, covering such industries as dry cleaning, mobile homes, employment bureaus, shoes, apparel, real estate, finance companies, photo finishers, and others. Following is a list of some of the more commonly needed groups:

American Arbitration Association, 140 W. 51st St., New York, N.Y. 10020. A group that provides arbitration services for conflicts between consumer and business, employee and business, and any other groups that want to settle an issue without going to court.

Council of Better Business Bureaus, 1150 17th St. N.W., Washington, D.C. 20036. An association of all the BBBs in the country, and a splendid source of information on complaint-solving procedures run by business groups. Many local BBBs provide arbitration boards where businessmen and consumers can bring their problems (details on page 158).

Appliances

The major-appliance industry (refrigerators, stoves, washing machines, etc.) sponsors a consumer complaint panel to resolve disputes with manufacturers and stores:

> Major Appliance Consumer Action Panel
> 20 North Wacker Dr.
> Chicago, Ill. 60606
> Toll-free number: (800) 621-0477

Automobiles

The National Automobile Dealers Association sponsors more than thirty-five Automobile Consumer Action Programs—some in cities, some operating statewide—to handle disputes between car buyers and auto dealers. For information on where they are, or direct help in solving a problem with a dealer-member, write:

> Automobile Consumer Action Programs
> National Automobile Dealers Assn.
> 8400 Westpark Dr.
> McLean, Va. 22102

For warranty complaints, safety problems, or anything else you want to take up with the manufacturer, write first to the zone manager (at the address in your owner's manual). If that fails, try the manufacturers at the addresses below:

> American Motors
> Customer Relations
> 14250 Plymouth Rd.
> Detroit, Mich. 48232

For owners, there's a toll-free number; check your owner's manual.

Chrysler Corporation
Your Man in Detroit
P.O. Box 857
Detroit, Mich. 48288

Fiat Distributors
155 Chestnut Ridge Rd.
Montvale, N.J. 07645

Ford Parts and Service Division
3000 Schaefer Rd.
Dearborn, Mich. 48121
Toll-free number: (800) 337-8724

General Motors—write to
Customer Service at the
proper division headquarters:

Buick Zone Office
33117 Hamilton Ave.
Farmington, Mich. 48024

Cadillac Zone Office
25200 Telegraph
Southfield, Mich. 48034

Chevrolet Zone Office
25200 Telegraph
Southfield, Mich. 48034

Oldsmobile Division
25200 Telegraph
Southfield, Mich. 48034

Pontiac Motor Division
25200 Telegraph
Southfield, Mich. 48034

Toyota
Customer Relations
2055 W. 190th Street
Torrance, Calif. 90509

Volkswagen of America
Customer Assistance Department
Englewood Cliffs, N.J. 07632
(also for Porsche and Audi)

Volvo of America
Owner Relations Department
One Volvo Drive
Rockleigh, N.J. 07647

For information on car prices and options:

New-car and used-car price guides, $1.75 each from Davis Publications, 380 Lexington Ave., New York, N.Y. 10017

New-car, used-car, and foreign-car price guides, $2.50 each plus 50 cents postage, from Edmund Publications, 515 Hempstead Turnpike, Hempstead, N.Y. 11552

For computer pricing services and low-markup auto sales:

Car/Puter and United Auto Brokers, 1603 Bushwick Ave., Brooklyn, N.Y. 11207

Computerized Car Costs and Motor Club Auto Buying, Eleven Mile–Lahser Station, Southfield, Mich. 48037

Carpets and Rugs
For unresolved complaints about quality and dealer services:

Carpet and Rug Institute
P.O. Box 2048
Dalton, Ga. 30720

Charities
For information on the integrity of charitable institutions that solicit contributions from the public:

National Information Bureau
419 Park Ave. South
New York, N.Y. 10016

Philanthropic Advisory Service
Council of Better Business Bureaus

1150 17th St. N.W.
Washington, D.C. 20036

Contractors

For complaints against a member contractor who fouled up a building job or overcharged:

National Remodelers Assn.
Consumer Affairs Division
50 E. 42nd St.
New York, N.Y. 10017

Credit

Complaints about credit bureaus:

Associated Credit Bureaus
6767 Southwest Freeway
Houston, Tex. 77074

For the name of a nonprofit credit counseling agency in your area:

National Foundation for Consumer Credit
1819 H St. N.W.
Washington, D.C. 20006

Discrimination

For information on pressing housing discrimination suits:

National Committee Against Discrimination in Housing
Suite 410
1425 H St. N.W.
Washington, D.C. 20005

Door-to-Door Sales

For complaints about any salesman who high-pressures you in your home or misrepresents merchandise:

Direct Selling Assn.
1730 M St. N.W., Suite 610
Washington, D.C. 20036

Education:

For information on the cost of college:

Student Expenses at Post-Secondary Institutions ($5), published by
The College Board
888 Seventh Ave
New York, N.Y. 10019

For scholarship information:

The As&Bs of Academic Scholarships ($2); *Don't Miss Out* ($2)
Octameron Associates
P.O. Box 3437
Alexandria, Va. 22302

Need a Lift? ($1)
American Legion
National Emblem Sales
P.O. Box 1055
Indianapolis, Ind. 46206

Funerals

*For information on where you can join a memorial society, dedicated
to providing low-cost funerals:*

Continental Assn. of Funeral and Memorial Societies
1828 L St. N.W., Suite 1100
Washington, D.C. 20036

Insurance

For general questions about life insurance policies:

American Council of Life Insurance
1850 K St. N.W.
Washington, D.C. 20006

For general questions about health insurance:

Health Insurance Institute
1850 K St. N.W.
Washington, D.C. 20006

For general questions about accident and property insurance:

> Insurance Information Institute
> 110 William St.
> New York, N.Y. 10038

Investments

For complaints against stockbrokers and technical questions regarding the trading of specific stocks:

> American Stock Exchange
> Rulings and Inquiries Department
> 86 Trinity Place
> New York, N.Y. 10006
>
> National Assn. of Securities Dealers
> Surveillance Department
> 1735 K St. N.W.
> Washington, D.C. 20016
>
> New York Stock Exchange
> Investor-Broker Liaison
> 55 Water St.
> New York, N.Y. 10041

For general information on investing:

> New York Stock Exchange
> Investors Service Bureau
> 11 Wall St.
> New York, N.Y. 10005

For information on mutual funds:

> Investment Company Institute
> 1775 K St. N.W.
> Washington, D.C. 20006
>
> No-Load Mutual Fund Assn.
> Valley Forge, Pa. 19481

Mail Order

Complaints about nondelivery, unresolved problems with vendors, requests to be taken off or added to mailing lists:

Direct Mail/Marketing Assn.
6 E. 43rd St.
New York, N.Y. 10017

Mobile Homes

For information on whether your state or area has a mobile home owners' association:

American Mobilehome Assn.
P.O. Box 710
Golden, Colo. 80401

For complaints against dealers or manufacturers:

Consumer Action Bureau
Manufactured Housing Institute
1745 Jefferson Davis Hwy.
Arlington, Va. 22202

Retirement

For a variety of services of interest to retired people:

American Association of Retired Persons
1909 K St. N.W.
Washington, D.C. 20049

TV Sets

Stereos, hi-fi, and audio equipment:

Office of Consumer Affairs
Electronic Industries Assn.
2001 Eye St. N.W.
Washington, D.C. 20006

Toll-free Numbers

Many companies maintain toll-free (800) numbers that you can call to place an order or register a complaint. If there is such a number, it should be listed somewhere in the printed material that came with the product (a good reason to keep all those booklets filed away). Or call the local distributor and ask. Another source is the information operator (call [800] 555-1212, and ask if the company has a toll-free line for your area). Often these toll-free numbers cover only part of the country. But some companies will accept collect calls from other areas or are willing to call you back to discuss your problem in detail.

General Information

For the names and addresses of the presidents of the major companies selling consumer products; also, the names and addresses of state consumer agencies:

> *Complaint Directory for Consumers* ($2)
> *Everybody's Money*
> Box 431
> Madison, Wis. 53701

For a remarkable variety of excellent consumer information:

Help: The Useful Almanac (published annually, $8.95 plus $1 for postage and handling)
Consumer News
Washington, D.C. 20045

INDEX

851

Notes

Notes

Notes

Notes

Notes

Notes

Notes

Notes